FIELDING'S WORLDWIDE CRUISES 1995

Fielding Titles

Fielding's Amazon
Fielding's Australia
Fielding's Bahamas
Fielding's Belgium
Fielding's Bermuda
Fielding's Borneo
Fielding's Brazil
Fielding's Britain
Fielding's Budget Europe
Fielding's Caribbean
Fielding's Europe
Fielding's Far East
Fielding's France
Fielding's Guide to the World's Most Dangerous Places
Fielding's Guide to the World's Great Voyages
Fielding's Guide to Kenya's Best Hotels, Lodges & Homestays
Fielding's Guide to the World's Most Romantic Places
Fielding's Hawaii
Fielding's Holland
Fielding's Italy
Fielding's London Agenda
Fielding's Los Angeles Agenda
Fielding's Malaysia and Singapore
Fielding's Mexico
Fielding's New York Agenda
Fielding's New Zealand
Fielding's Paris Agenda
Fielding's Portugal
Fielding's Scandinavia
Fielding's Seychelles
Fielding's Southeast Asia
Fielding's Spain
Fielding's Vacation Places Rated
Fielding's Vietnam
Fielding's Worldwide Cruises

FIELDING'S WORLDWIDE CRUISES 1995

The Original and Most Trusted Guide to Selecting Worldwide Cruises

by

Anne Campbell

Fielding Worldwide, Inc.
308 South Catalina Avenue
Redondo Beach, California 90277 U.S.A.

Fielding's Worldwide Cruises

Published by Fielding Worldwide, Inc.

FIELDING WORLDWIDE INC.

PUBLISHER AND CEO **Robert Young Pelton**
PUBLISHING DIRECTOR **Paul T. Snapp**
ELECTRONIC PUBLISHING DIRECTOR **Larry E. Hart**
PROJECT DIRECTOR **Tony E. Hulette**
ADMINISTRATIVE COORDINATOR **Beverly Riess**
ACCOUNT SERVICES MANAGER **Christy Harp**

EDITORS

Linda Charlton **Kathy Knoles**

PRODUCTION

Tina Gentile **Gini Martin**
Chris Snyder **Craig South**

COVER DESIGNED BY **Digital Artists**
COVER PHOTOGRAPHERS — Front Cover **Courtesy of Crystal Cruises**
Background Photo, Front Cover **Robert Young Pelton/Westlight**
Back Cover **Courtesy of Renaissance Cruises**
INSIDE PHOTOS **Author's Photo, Sam Bleecker**

Inquiries should be addressed to: Fielding Worldwide, Inc., 308 South Catalina Ave., Redondo Beach, California 90277 U.S.A., ☎ *(310) 372-4474*, Facsimile *(310) 376-8064*, 8:30 a.m.–5:30 p.m. Pacific Standard Time.

ISBN 1-56952-030-5

Library of Congress Catalog Card Number

94-068356

Printed in the United States of America

Dedication

To

The men and women serving as staff and crew aboard the world's ships who work so diligently and conscientiously to ensure the safety and comfort of their passengers.

"For my part, I travel not to go anywhere, but to go. I travel for travel's sake. The great affair is to move."

—Robert Louis Stevenson

"...the single best source for unbiased cruise information."

-Everett Potter, Copley News Service

"Fielding's original five-star rating for ships has been widely imitated and sets the industry standard for vessel classification."

-Associated Press

"a standard for the water-bound vacationer."

-Los Angeles Times

"To be all things to all people is impossible, but this guide pretty well does it...a 'Best of' section foolproofs picking the perfect cruise...and the complete ship and itinerary descriptions magically evoke the romance of the sea."

-New York Daily News

"...offers descriptions of everything from finding the right ship to special interest cruises...sprinkled throughout with 'Author's Observations,' practical bits of advice based on inside knowledge of the cruise industry."

-Chicago Tribune

Letter from the Publisher

In 1946, Temple Fielding began the first of what would be a remarkable new series of well-written, highly personalized guide books for independent travelers. Temple's opinionated, witty, and oft-imitated books have now guided travelers for almost a half-century. More important to some was Fielding's humorous and direct method of steering travelers away from the dull and the insipid. Today, Fielding Travel Guides are still written by experienced travelers for experienced travelers. Our authors carry on Fielding's reputation for creating travel experiences that deliver insight with a sense of discovery and style.

Anne Campbell carries forward the unmatched standards set in the original Fielding's *Guide to Cruises*—historically the most provocative and influential guide to cruising. Campbell and Fielding knew that updating the world's preeminent guide to cruising wouldn't be an easy task. But rest assured, Anne tells it like it is, separating hype from fact and the generic from the superlative—whatever your price range and your choice of destinations and accommodations. *Bon voyage.*

In 1995, the concept of cruising has never been bigger. Our policy of *brutal honesty* and a highly personal point of view has never changed; it just seems the travel world has caught up with us.

Enjoy your cruising adventures with Campbell and Fielding.

RYP

Robert Young Pelton
Publisher and C.E.O.
Fielding Worldwide, Inc.

Fielding Rating Icons

The Fielding Rating Icons are highly personal and awarded to help the besieged traveler choose from among the dizzying array of activities, attractions, hotels, restaurants and sights. The awarding of an icon denotes unusual or exceptional qualities in the relevant category.

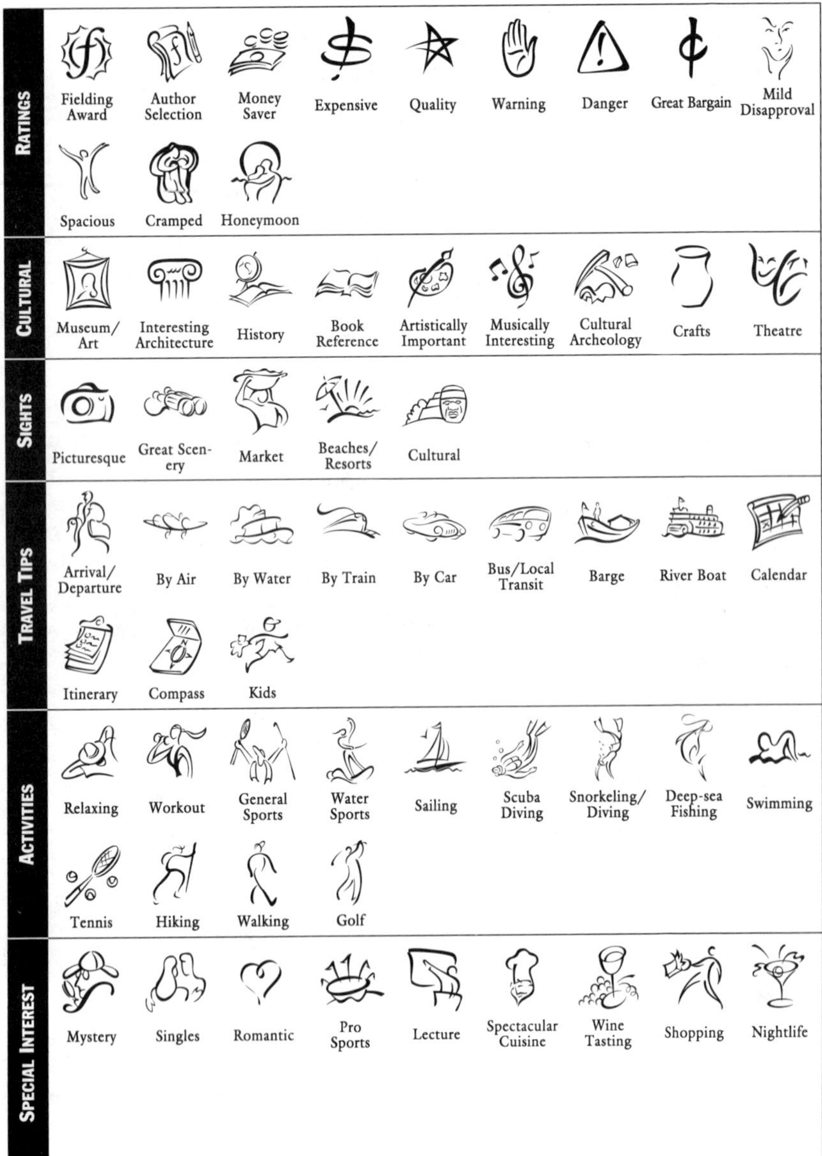

ABOUT THE AUTHOR

ANNE CAMPBELL

To the daunting task of rating more than 140 vessels worldwide and chronicling the ins and outs of the volatile cruise industry, Anne Campbell brings the experience of a true insider. Anne began her career at Cunard Line, worked with Cruise Lines International Association (CLIA) and has served as a travel consultant to the Brazilian Government Tourism Association while residing in Rio de Janeiro. Anne's numerous magazine articles have led to adventures such as a camel trek through Morocco's Sahara and exploring Argentina's pampas on horseback. A native of Corning, New York, she currently resides in New York City, where she pursues a second career as a jewelry designer.

FOREWORD

With my editor trying to grab the 1995 manuscript of Fielding's Worldwide Cruises from me and rush it to the printer ("I don't care about another goddam itinerary change!"), it's unsettling to try to capture the rapid-fire transformations that occur daily in the cruise industry. In the past six months alone, two ship lines (Royal Viking Line and American Family Cruises) have folded, dozens of vessels have emerged, disappeared, changed companies and been renamed, while new regions of the world are accessible by water-bourne conveyences. Today, you can take a riverboat to Siberia, a nuclear-powered ice-breaker to the Arctic circle and cruise ships to Beirut and Hanoi. The verbal mudslinging currently underway between Castro and Clinton could ultimately result in Cuba again becoming accessible to Americans—a dozen ships will beat the CIA to Havana! The dozen or so new vessels of all shapes and sizes emerging in 1995 plus the increased number of ships visiting regions of the world that were once unimaginable will affect always volatile fares. And, the cruise industry continues to grow with an estimated five million people taking a seagoing vacation this year.

In order to make sense of all these changes, we've instituted several new features in the 1995 edition of Fielding's Worldwide Cruises. New categories have been added to "Best of 1995" to enable you to narrow the selection process further. A year-long theme cruise calendar is but a sampling of some of the diverse special interests you may now pursue aboard ships. And, there are now two separate categories of vessel ratings—conventional cruise ships (awarded stars) and specialty vessels (receiving anchors). A travel agent reports that she uses *Fielding's Worldwide Cruises* because the book's star/anchor rating system reinforces the fact that not all ships are equal. While she grasps the significance of a rating system for ships, I hope she doesn't put too much importance in them when steering clients to one ship over another.

Keep in mind that ships are rated against each other, not measured by some absolute standard; the stars represent an objective critique of the maintenance, decor and flow of the physical ship, cabin size and amenities, and the all-important aspects of food and service. Moreover, one must always factor in price, length of cruise, passenger demographics and sailing region. For example, a miniscule cabin with bare essentials on a 3- and 4-day cruise is not the negative it would be on a voyage of seven days or more. In the former case, passengers tend to cram a lot of cruising into a few days, spending little time in a cabin other than to change clothes and flop at the end of day.

Since we rate ships against each other, some lose points when better vessels emerge, but that does not necessarily mean a ship has fallen off. Today you'll find fewer ships rated five-star and five-star plus. It costs tens of millions to maintain a ship at peak levels, and new vessels arriving on the scene in the mid-price range over the past few years have simply raised the overall standard. In other instances, the fierce price competition in today's marketplace sometimes results in cost-cutting measures. The easiest ways to save money are by decreasing the quality of food and service, the two most critical aspects of the on-board experience no matter what type of ship you choose.

My biggest concern is that readers and cruise counselors not make stars the sole determinant when selecting one vessel over another. Always remember, these are objective reviews, stacking vessels against each other in terms of quality. When you select a cruise, however, factors such as price, age of passengers, on-board ambience, facilities and services relative to your own personal interests and lifestyle are more critical. The vessel that is my own personal favorite does not have a five star/anchor plus rating. As the saying goes, "What's one man's trash is another man's treasure."

I learned this lesson firsthand when I landed a job at Cunard Line fresh out of college. I was determined that my father, newly widowed, must take a cruise; an avid outdoorsman and hunter, it was no small task getting him to even consider the idea. But arm-twisting prevailed and I nervously sent him off on the Cunard Adventurer (a

400-passenger ship that today would warrent three stars if one were overly generous). He returned beaming, eagerly sharing photos of new friends and proclaiming it one of the best times he ever had. I decided he was ready for the QE 2, at that time the "greatest ship in the world," and confidently saw him off. But this time at disembarkation the glow was missing—he was impressed by the ship, appreciated the QE 2's fine points, but didn't have fun. For him, the QE 2 was too large and formal and he missed the easy camaraderie of fellow passengers that one can only find on a small, informal ship.

When it comes to critiquing a vessel, my philosophy is to present my direct experience, relay the facts and let the reader decide. I certainly have no way of recommending one seagoing experience over another for a reader when my own tastes fluctuate: sometimes it's fun to get all dolled up in a sequined gown while on other occasions I'd rather be decked out in jeans, communing with nature.

Quite naturally, no individual could cover the 140 cruise ships plus a hundred or so specialty vessels. Senior writer Mary B. McDowell and I are the only individuals who award stars but anyone who can count knows there are just too many vessels for two individuals to cover. We have a very small cadre of experienced and knowledgeable professionals whose opinions we respect and trust. They travel aboard specialty ships and several vessels that have existing stars but should be revisited. The firsthand experience of several top-flight travel agents who sell these ships, gives us additional insight into what is really going on behind the scenes.

I wish you the gift of imagination in finding the perfect seagoing holiday, the joy of discovering new people and places, an escape from the stress and problems of everyday life, perfect weather and, of course, calm seas.

Bon Voyage!

Anne Campbell

ACKNOWLEDGEMENTS

This book would not be possible without the tireless work of senior writer Mary B. McDowell. With the energy of a team of Clydesdales, Mary has roamed the globe during this past year critiquing dozens of cruise ships plus sailboats, expedition vessels and riverboats. Mary's sharpened sense of what's great and only so-so is unparalleled and her reviews sparkle with wit and insightful glimpses of what goes on behind the scenes. While she travels for up to two months at a time and I miss her uncanny advice, Mary is always happiest when under sail.

My sincere thanks to so many others who have contributed to this effort. Boris Arnold, Arline and Sam Bleecker and Cathy Gehm provided invaluable critiques on a host of vessels. Veteran travel journalists Jim Glab, Jim Santo, Brian Major, Phil Sousa, Paul Lasley and Carla Hunt graciously supply wonderful feedback. I can't imagine even tackling the often perilous journey of writing this book without the continual support and guidance of Paul Snapp, Fielding's director of publishing; production assistant Beverly Reiss who always brought sunshine to the day—thank you both for always being there for me.

I thank the many readers who took the time to call or write about their own seagoing experiences, especially James B. Stricker, Jr., who passes along wonderful information and his own delightful reviews. Inside the cruise industry, there are too many wonderful professionals to list, but I give my gratitude for all their help and patience in covering their ships. There were many cruise specialists who generously lent their valuable time and insight, especially Dorothy Reminick of Jean Rose Travel in Jupiter, Florida, Cheryl Meyerson of The Cruise Director in Arvada, Colorado, and Carroll Paige of Carroll Paige Travel in Miami. And, others who have lent continual support include Stuart Grayson, Sharon Fisher, Barbara Anderson, Robert Fischel, Carol Frierson-Campbell, Robert Campbell and Marge Weinstein.

As always, I thank the late Antoinette DeLand, who started it all.

Anne Campbell

TABLE OF CONTENTS

LIST OF MAPS

CRUISING—THE MOST COMPLETE VACATION POSSIBLE

"All things considered, there are only two kinds of men in the world—those that stay at home and those who do not. The second are the most interesting."

Rudyard Kipling

In *The European Discovery of America*, Samuel Eliot Morison described what he considered the first pleasure cruise in American history. It took place around 1536 when a London leather merchant named Richard Hoare chartered two vessels to sail to Newfoundland for the double purpose of catching some codfish and enjoying the cruise. Sixty persons are said to have signed on (including thirty gentlemen), but the excursion was hardly a success. The first ship was lost soon after setting sail, and although the second did reach Newfoundland, the voyagers found nothing but misery there and had to eat each other to keep alive. When this ship eventually returned to England, there were few survivors and one could say the tourist trade was set back several centuries!

In fact, it was well over three hundred years before people went down to the sea for the sheer joy of sailing, and several more decades passed before life aboard was at all comfortable. One inveterate traveler and recorder was our beloved Mark Twain, who left us with *Life on the Mississippi* and *Innocents Abroad*. The latter described a yearlong, great Pleasure Excursion to Europe and the Holy Land in 1867, which he called a picnic on a gigantic scale.

The passage cost $1250, and five dollars per day in gold was recommended for shore excursions. Although his expectations that the excursionists would be filling the ship with shouts and laughter received some setbacks, he was grateful that at the end of the year he was still on speaking terms with many of his fellow passengers and had even made some friends. Above all, he recommended that people undertake such cruises regularly because his shore excursions had taught him that travel is fatal to prejudice, bigotry and narrow mindedness.

CIRCUMNAVIGATING THE GLOBE

This was also the time when Thomas Cook purported to organize the first world cruise, which involved rail travel in addition to four ships. Begun with a transatlantic crossing from Liverpool to New York in 1872, this tour had been abandoned by many of its participants by the time it reached Cairo 220 days later. Fifty years later, Cunard offered the first official world cruise, a four-month voyage on the *Laconia* from New York to New York. The 1922–23 itinerary included Honolulu, Shanghai, Hong Kong, Cairo, Naples and other ports of call still popular today.

Today's **global voyages** average more than 100 days, cover the world faster than ever before and offer passengers not only the old haunts of the 1920s but also a goodly number of ports never before visited. These modern circumnavigations are popular with the idle rich, of course, who book the best suites and have seen it all before, as well as less wealthy and more adventurous souls who stay as long as they can afford to and have a jolly good time of it. Companies still offering annual around-the-world cruises are Holland America Line (*Rotterdam*) and Cunard Line (*QE 2*, *Royal Viking Sun* and *Sagafjord*). In 1995, voyages are longer than ever before, and exotic lands one couldn't imagine ever visiting a few years ago, such as Vietnam, the Middle East and Russia's inland waterways, are readily accessible by seagoing vessel.

SEAGOING HERITAGE

Among the prestigious and historic ship lines still in existence, the Peninsular and Orient Steam Navigation Company (P & O) boasts more than a century of service worldwide. One of its most lucrative and popular passenger routes was between Britain and Egypt or India, long before the advent of the airplane. Sailing round-trip on this route precipitated the advent of a very special word in the English language *Posh* which, stamped on steamship tickets, indicated the passenger had bought Port Out and Starboard Home, the coolest and therefore most expensive cabins. Frankly, a reader or two has disputed this story but I stand by it. Doesn't it sound romantic?

According to company correspondence, P & O Line had such a fine reputation in the Victorian 19th century that even its shipwrecks were considered the best of any passenger fleet! In a letter dated 1863 from a Mrs. Dulcimer to her friend, Laura, the writer advises, "If you are ever shipwrecked, do contrive to get the catastrophe conducted by the Peninsular and Orient Company. I believe other companies drown you sometimes, and drowning is a very prosaic arrangement fit only for seafaring people and second-class passengers. I have just been shipwrecked under the auspices of P & O, and I assure you that it is the pleasantest thing imaginable. It has its little hardships, to be sure, but so has a picnic; and the wreck was one of the most agreeable picnics you can imagine." Didn't they have fun during the 19th century?

EARLY CRUISES

Cruises as we know them today began more or less in the 1920s, although on a grand scale and for a small segment of society. Transatlantic sailings and sea tours of the Mediterranean or South America were on three-class ships (four classes when there were immigrants). These cruises assumed the importance that a global voyage does today. Staterooms, as large as drawing rooms, sported heavy, hand-carved furniture. In first class especially, you traveled with trunks of evening clothes and dinner jewels, servants (who slept somewhere below deck) who cared for them and you, and pets who stayed above. Except that ladies and gentlemen often separated after the evening meal for their own pleasures, life aboard was usually not much different from today. Some rules were never broken. If a young woman alone wished the pleasure of a charming steward for the night, she would most likely not acknowledge his presence the next morning because, good heavens, they had not yet been properly introduced!

TRANSATLANTIC CROSSINGS

It is always so delightful to recapture the glamor of transatlantic crossings in their heyday. The old Fred Astaire movies become more wonderful each year, and Danielle Steele's *Crossings* captures the essence of the grand life that once was aboard the *Normandie*. True ship buffs can either read histories of the old liners by Frank Braynard and Bill Miller, or plan to spend some days at sea aboard such famous vessels as Swedish American Line's *Gripsholm* (now *Regent Sea*) or *Kungsholm* (now *Sea Princess*), even visit the *Queen Mary*, now an entertainment center in Long Beach (California), where those who once served aboard stop by from time to time to reminisce.

WEEKEND PARTY CRUISES

Weekend party cruises were popular in the 1920s from the East Coast to Havana, Bermuda, the Bahamas, and to Nowhere! Ships became floating speakeasies during Prohibition when liquor was legal (and very cheap) on the high seas. The low cost and steady flow of alcohol on cruises is still a lure, but most of us take to the sea for romance and adventure and for the temporary dream world that exists the minute we're aboard. The cruise vessel is a floating capsule of contentment as it transports us from one exotic port to another. And as we follow the progress of the ship on the navigation chart posted near the purser's office (and even place a dollar in the daily pool), the world looks so large and this voyage so small. Life at sea is such a fantasy of time and place that the glow lasts long after the cruise is over.

Weekend party cruises are still popular perhaps more than ever because the liquor is still cheap, the gambling very heady and there are facilities for the whole family. These include sailings that actually do stop at one or more ports from South Florida or southern California, as well as Cruises to Nowhere, which seem to fill in schedules that have a hole here and there. From New York, sailings out to Ambrose Lighthouse are always a sell-out, as they are the perfect way to get away from it all if only for 60 hours.

CRUISING TODAY

Sailing today is certainly safer and far more comfortable than it ever was before, despite the pint-sized staterooms and lack of ladies' maids and gentlemen's valets. Ships are better maintained and passengers have far more consideration than a few decades ago. We have stabilizers to cut down the roll, air conditioning to keep out the heat and plenty of ice in every bar. In addition to all passengers on board being equal (except on *QE2* where SuperClass has its own grill room), the run of the ship means more facilities, more food and drinks, more entertainment and generally more people than anyone can appreciate fully in just five, seven or 14 days. There is no doubt that today's travelers are offered more for their money aboard a ship than anywhere else on earth and 90 percent is paid for in advance. If the advantage of just one rate for everything and no hidden extras (except what you intend to spend for shopping, shore excursions, drinks and tipping) appeals to you, you may also enjoy the fact that all the many details of when, where and what time things happen each day have already been solved by the ship lines. You not only leave the driving to them, but the food and entertainment decisions as well. They have even eliminated any language problem. You just sit on deck and relax.

Perhaps you are nervous that a cruise is too slow a pace for you, that it doesn't allow enough time in ports, or that there is too much group activity. Cruising is not an individual experience and that is precisely why so many people enjoy it. If you are traveling alone, you can have instant companionship whenever you wish. Couples can be by themselves or seek others for conversation or cards. Children, no matter what age, make instant friends and become purveyors of all the news within this floating world. And if you're worried about being bored, there are so many different types of cruises available (see "Choosing the Right Cruise") that you can ship hop the rest of your life and never be satiated with the excitement of being at sea.

EXPLORING THE WORLD

If you demand a place in the sun, then the **Caribbean** is your natural habitat, with its potpourri of colors and people and splendid tropical climate (and should you ever tire, Hawaii or the South Seas might entice your senses). If you're looking for adventure and wildlife, you'll love the Galapagos and Antarctica, the Amazon or watching the whales off Baja. If majestic scenery fills your soul with wonder, then you should sail through the southern tip of South America, **Alaska's Inside Passage**, along the Saguenay River or in and out of Norway's saw-toothed fjords. Serious scuba divers will love the **Mexican Riviera** on sailings from either the West Coast or Florida, and our own eastern seaboard can be explored all the way from Ft. Myers, Florida to the rocky coastal islands of Maine. If you wish to stretch your mind, as well as your legs, in every port, the whole world is waiting for you. You will especially enjoy cruises to Greece and Turkey, Israel and Egypt, the northern capitals, the British Isles, around South America, through the Indonesian archipelago, and the Far East. And if it's river life you like, try the small boats on the waterways of Europe, the paddle-wheelers on the Mississippi and Ohio rivers, cruises along the historic Hudson, and the barges along the Nile. You can be as enriched and fulfilled as you desire, or pursue each day at a snail's pace. This is the perfection of a cruise.

THE BEST OF 1995

★★★★★ SHIPS THAT STAND OUT IN THEIR CLASS AND PRICE

Celebrity Cruises	*Horizon* *Meridian* *Zenith*
Clipper Cruise Line	*Nantucket Clipper* *Yorktown Clipper*
Crystal Cruises	*Crystal Harmony*
Cunard Line	*Queen Elizabeth 2* *Royal Viking Sun* *Sea Goddess I & II*
Delta Queen Steamship Co.	*Delta Queen* *Mississippi Queen*
Holland America Line	*Statendam* *Maasdam*
Norwegian Cruise Line	*Norway*
Special Expeditions	*Polaris*
Princess Cruises	*Crown Princess* *Regal Princess* *Star Princess*

★★★★★ SHIPS THAT STAND OUT IN THEIR CLASS AND PRICE

Royal Caribbean Cruise Line	*Nordic Empress*
Royal Cruise Line	*Queen Odyssey*
Seabourn Cruise Line	*Seabourn Pride* *Seabourn Spirit*
Seven Seas Cruise Line	*Hanseatic* *Song of Flower*
Star Clippers	*Star Flyer* *Star Clipper*
Windstar Cruises	*WindSong* *WindSpirit* *WindStar*

★★★★★ MOST IN-DEPTH DESTINATION EXPERIENCE

Abercrombie & Kent	*Explorer*
Alaska Sightseeing/Cruise West	*All ships*
American Canadian Caribbean Lines	*All ships*
Caledonia Travel	*Caledonian Star*
Clipper Cruise Line	*All ships*
EuroCruises	*All ships*
KD River Cruises of Europe	*All ships*
Marine Expeditions	*All ships*
P & O Spice Island Cruises	*All ships*
Pearl Cruises	*Pearl*
Quark Expeditions	*All ships*
Regal Cruises of China	*All ships*
Seven Seas Cruise Line	*Hanseatic*
Special Expeditions	*All ships*
Swan Hellenic Cruises	*Orpheus*
Victoria Cruises	*All ships*

★★★ BEST THREE- AND FOUR-DAY CRUISE SHIPS

CARIBBEAN	
Royal Caribbean Cruise Line	*Nordic Empress*
GREEK ISLANDS AND TURKEY	
Sun Line Cruises	*Stella Solaris* *Stella Maris* *Stella Oceanis*

★★★ BEST SHIPS FOR FAMILIES WITH CHILDREN

American Hawaii Cruises	*Constitution* *Independence*
Carnival Cruise Lines	*Sensation* *Fascination* *Fantasy* *Ecstasy*
Cunard Line	*Queen Elizabeth 2* *(Transatlantic)*
Le Boat	**Self-drive houseboats in Europe**
Royal Caribbean Cruise Line	*Majesty of the Seas* *Monarch of the Seas* *Nordic Empress*
Celebrity Cruises	*Horizon* *Meridian*
Premier Cruise Lines	*Star/Ship Atlantic* *Star/Ship Oceanic*

★★★ MOST EXTENSIVE HANDICAPPED FACILITIES

Holland America Line	*Maasdam* *Ryndam* *Statendam*
Norwegian Cruise Line	*Dreamward* *Windward*
Princess Cruises	*Crown Princess* *Regal Princess* *Star Princess*

★★★ BEST SHIPS FOR WATER SPORTS

Club Med Cruises	*Club Med I and II*
Cunard Line	*Sea Goddess I and II*
Princess Cruises	*Regal Princess* *Crown Princess*
Royal Caribbean Cruise Line	*Majesty of the Seas* *Nordic Empress*
Star Clippers	*Star Clipper/Star Flyer*
Windstar Cruises	*All ships*

★★★ BEST FITNESS FACILITIES AFLOAT

Carnival Cruise Lines	*Ecstasy* *Fascination* *Fantasy* *Sensation*
Crystal Cruises	*Crystal Harmony*
Cunard Line	*Queen Elizabeth 2*
Norwegian Cruise Line	*Norway*
Princess Cruises	*Crown Princess* *Regal Princess* *Star Princess*
Royal Caribbean Cruise Line	*Monarch of the Seas* *Majesty of the Seas* *Nordic Empress*

★★★ BEST ENTERTAINMENT AFLOAT

Crystal Cruises	*Crystal Harmony*
Cunard Line	*Queen Elizabeth 2 (transatlantic)*
Princess Cruises	*Crown Princess* *Regal Princess* *Star Princess*
Royal Caribbean Cruise Line	*Monarch of the Seas* *Majesty of the Seas* *Nordic Empress*

★★★ BEST SHIPS FOR GOLFERS

Princess Cruises	*Crown Princess* *Regal Princess* *Star Princess*
Royal Caribbean Cruise Line	*Monarch of the Seas* *Song of America* *(New York/Bermuda)*

★★★ MOST OUTSTANDING SPAS

Carnival Cruise Lines	*Ecstasy* *Fascination* *Fantasy* *Sensation*
Crystal Cruises	*Crystal Harmony*
Cunard Line	*Queen Elizabeth 2*
Norwegian Cruise Line	*Norway*

★★★ BEST FINE ARTS AND EDUCATIONAL ENRICHMENT PROGRAMS

Cunard Line	*Queen Elizabeth 2 (transatlantic)*
Paquet French Cruises	*Mermoz*
Swan Hellenic Cruises	*Orpheus*

★★★ BEST GUEST LECTURERS

Abercrombie & Kent	*Explorer*
Classical Cruises	*All ships*
Clipper Cruise Line	*All ships*
Cunard	*Queen Elizabeth 2 (transatlantic)*
Marine Expeditions	*All ships*
Quark Expeditions	*All ships*
Special Expeditions	*All ships*
Sun Line	*Stella Solaris*

★★★ BEST GUEST LECTURERS

Swan Hellenic Cruises	*All ships*

★★★ BEST SPECIAL INTEREST PROGRAMS

Music, Cuisine/Wine, Mysteries, Finance, Sports, Authors, History, etc.
(See "Theme Cruise Calendar")

American Hawaii Cruises	*Constitution* *Independence*
Cunard Line	*QE2* *Cunard Countess* *Cunard Princess*
Delta Queen Steamboat Company	*Delta Queen* *Mississippi Queen*
Norwegian Cruise Line	*Norway* *Dreamward* *Windward*
Royal Cruise Line	*All ships*

★★★ BEST PROGRAMS FOR NATURE LOVERS

Abercrombie & Kent	*Explorer*
Alaska Sightseeing/Cruise West	*All ships*
American Canadian Caribbean Line	*All ships*
Caledonia Travel	*Caledonian Star*
Clipper Cruise Line	*All ships*
Marine Expeditions	
P & O Spice Island Cruises	*All ships*
Quark Expeditions	*All ships*
Seven Seas Cruise Line	*Hanseatic*
Special Expeditions	*All ships*
World Explorer Cruises	*Universe*

★★★
1995 "QUIEN ES MAS MACHO" CRUISE AWARD

Winter "Icebreaking Weekend Adventure" in Finland. Those who wouldn't be caught dead on a wimpy weekend cruise in the Caribbean can escape to the Arctic Circle instead. Finnair flies you to Kemi, where a 20-mile snowmobile ride delivers you to the working icebreaker Sampo. *Survival suits are provided for those who care to swim among the bergs from the ship. Upon departing the* Sampo, *you'll be transported to a reindeer sleigh driving school (those who pass are awarded a driver's licence), then visit Santa Claus at Holiday Village, his home in the Arctic. The Wednesday-Monday package, available from Finnair January through April, 1995, is priced at $1399, including round-trip air, hotels, cruise and all the fun.*

THE MOST INTRIGUING ITINERARIES

CARIBBEAN

Star Flyer **Star Clippers**	*7-days from St. Maarten to st. Lucia, Dominica, St. Vincent, Grenada, Union Island/Tobago Cays (year-round)*
Regent Spirit **Regency Cruises**	*7-day "Land of the Maya" cruises from Cozumel to Honduras, Belize, Guatemala and Roatan Island with shore excursions to Tikal, Copan and other Maya sites (November–March)*
Nantucket Clipper **Clipper Cruise Line**	*"National Treasures of the Yachtsman's Caribbean," coastal Puerto Rico, The British & U.S. Virgin Islands (December–February)*
Silver Cloud **Silversea Cruises**	*14-day Ft. Lauderdale to Barbados voyage with port calls in Virgin Gorda; Sint. Maarten; St. Barthelemy; Montserrat; Antigua; Iles des Saintes; Guadeloupe; Martinique; St. Lucia; Ciudad Guyana, Venezuela and cruising the Orinoco River (April)*

MEXICO & PANAMA CANAL

Niagara Prince **American Canadian Caribbean Lines**	*12-day "Panama Canal/San Blas Islands/Pearl Islands/Darien Jungle" itinerary visiting Isla del Rey, Taboga, Isla Tigre with excursion to Choco Indian settlement (January–March)*

MEXICO & PANAMA CANAL

Sea Bird *Sea Lion* **Special Expeditions**	*10-day "Among The Great Whales" cruises through the Sea of Cortez (January–April)*

ALASKA & PACIFIC NORTHWEST

Spirit of '98 **Alaska Sightseeing/Cruise West**	*7 days from Juneau to Seattle visiting Tracy Arm Wilderness, Sitka, LeConte Glacier, Petersburg, Misty Fjords and Ketchikan (May–September)*
Yorktown Clipper **Clipper Cruise Line**	*11-day Seattle to Portland voyage visiting Matia, Sucia, Stuard Islands; Port Townsend; Astoria; the Columbia & Hood Rivers and Palouse River National Park (September)*
Sea Bird *Sea Lion* **Special Expeditions**	*8-day cruises between Juneau and Sitka, stopping in Tracy Arm, Le Conte Bay, Haines, Glacier Bay. Pt. Adolphus, Althorp Rock (June–August)*

ARCTIC CIRCLE

Kapitan Dranitsyn **Quark Expeditions**	*20-day voyage by ice breaker from Spitzbergen, Norway to Provideniya, Russia cruising the New Siberian Islands; Wrangel Islands; Big Diomede Islands; Bering Straight and Siberian Coast (July–August)*

WESTERN EUROPE/BALTIC SEA/ NORTH CAPE

Caledonia Star **Caledonian Travel**	*13-day "Britain & Ireland In Bloom" cruise with port calls in Aberdeen, Kirkwall, Fair Isle, Loch Ewe, Rhum; Duart Mull; Dublin, Waterford; Bantry Bay; Scilly Isles; Alderney; Sark, Cowes (July)*
Polaris **Special Expeditions**	*16-day voyage from London to St. Petersburg visiting Amsterdam, Kiel Canal, Lubeck, Rugen, Gdansk, Kaliningrad, Klaipeda, Riga, Latvia, Tallinn, Estonia, Kronstadt (May)*

WESTERN EUROPE/BALTIC SEA/ NORTH CAPE

Royal Viking Sun **Cunard Line**	*14-day London to Barcelona voyage with port calls in Amsterdam; Ghent, Belgium, Honfleur, Corsica, Villefranche, France; Vigo and Palma de Majorca, Spain; Lisbon; Gibraltar (September)*
Song of Flower **Seven Seas Cruise Line**	*13-day "British Isles and Great Wine Regions of Europe" cruise from London to Lisbon calling in Edinburgh, Kirkwall, Isle of Skye, Isle of Man, Waterford, Bordeaux and Oporto (August)*

NORTH ATLANTIC

Polaris **Special Expeditions**	*22-day Greenland to Halifax voyage exploring coast of Greenland, Davis Strait, Cumberland Peninsula, Baffin Island, Unfava Peninsula, Button Islands, Saglek Bay, Nulliak Islands, Harrison Bank, St. John's, Cape St. Mary's, St. Pierre and Louisbourg (August)*

EUROPEAN INLAND WATERWAYS

Actief **Abercrombie & Kent**	*3- or 6-night luxury hotel barge cruises on the Thames River between Windsor and Oxford, visiting Cliveden Park, Henley, Sonning, Reading, Pangbourne and Shillingford Bridge (May–October).*
Ursula III **KD River Cruises of Europe**	*8-day cruises along the Danube and the Rhine-Main-Danube Canal with stops in Nuremberg and Regensburg, Germany; Vienna and Linz Austria and Budapest, Czechosolvakia (May–September)*
Lady Ivy May **EuroCruises**	*7-day riverboat cruises on Portugal's River Douro round trip from Oporto through the wine county and the Spanish Sierra mountains (May–October)*

EUROPEAN INLAND WATERWAYS

Diana *Juno* *Wilhelm Tham* **EuroCruises**	*4- and 6-day Gota Canal cruises between Goteborg and Stockhold, Sweden, aboard historic paddle-wheel steamers (May–September)*
Sergi Kirov **EuroCruises**	*14-day Siberia Cruise on the Yenisey River from Dudinka (240 miles north of the Arctic Circle) to Krasnoyarsk in Southern Russia (June–September)*

MEDITERRANEAN

Royal Viking Sun **Cunard Line**	*15-day voyage from Istanbul to Barcelona calling in Odessa and Yalta, Ukraine Kusadasi, Turkey; Rhodes and Iraklion, Greece; Ashod and Haifa, Israel; Catania, Sicily (October)*
Seabourn Pride **Seabourn Cruise Line**	*14-day Venice to Nice voyage visiting Taormina, Sorrento, Capri, Civitavecchia (Rome), Sardinia, Elba, Corsica, Livorno (Florence) and Portofino*
Star Odyssey **Royal Cruise Line**	*12-day Athens-Istanbul cruise with port calls in Mykonos, Delos, Santorini, Rhodes, Marmaris, Ephesus, Pergamum, Skiathos, Thessaloniki, Mt. Athos (June, August & September)*
Stella Maris **Sun Line Cruises**	*14-day round-trip Monte Carlo cruise visiting Civitavecchia (Rome), Taormina, Capri, Portofino (Italy); Malta; Katakolon, Elaphonissos, Gythelon, Santorini, Paros, Piraeus, Mykonos, Volos, Itea (Greece); Elba and Kusadasi, Turkey*
Silver Cloud **Silversea Cruises**	*10-day Istanbul to Haifa, Israel voyage with port stops in Kusadasi and Antalya Turkey; Piraeus, Nafplion, Herklion and Rhodes, Greece; and Limassol Cyprus*
Orpheus **Swan Hellenic**	*14-day Cyprus, Egypt, Jordan, Israel & Greece cruise, with transit of Suez Canal, including port calls in Sharm el Sheikh & Aquaba, Jordan, beach stop on the Red Sea and day trips to Petra, Sea of Galilee, Luxor (Nov.)*

AUSTRALIA/NEW ZEALAND

Song of Flower **Seven Seas Cruise Line**	*12-day cruise from Sydney to Bali visiting Port Douglas and Cooktown on Great Barrier Reef; Cape York and Darwin in Northern Australia, Latantuka and Komodo in Indonesian Archipelago (January)*
Akademik Shokalski **Quark Expeditions**	*"Whale Shark Expedition:" diving and snorkeling on former Sovient research vessel off the coast of Exmouth in Western Australia with Ron and Valerie Taylor (April)*
Marco Polo **Orient Lines**	*21-day cruise/tour from Sydney, Australia to Auckland, New Zealand visiting Melbourne; Devenport and Hobart, Tasmania; Picton, Wellington, Napier, Rotorua and Bay of Islands, New Zealand (March)*

SOUTH PACIFIC

Caledonian Star **Caledonian Travel**	*29-day naturalists' excursion sailing round-trip from Singapore to the Spice Islands, New Guinea, Borneo, Banda Islands and the Moluccas (January)*
Rotterdam **Holland America Line**	*19-night cruise from Fiji to Los Angeles calling in Western & Eastern Samoa, Pago Pago, Christmas Island; Kona Hawaii, Lahaina Maui, Honolulu (November)*
Spice Islander *Island Explorer* **P & O Spice Island Cruises**	*8-day "Sandalwood and Dragons Expedition," between Bali and Kupang to remote Indonesian island where passengers join in local celebrations and ceremonies (year-round)*
Wind Song **Windstar Cruises**	*7-day round-trip cruises from Papeete, Tahiti to Huahine, Raiatea, Bora Bora and Moorea (year-round)*
Club Med 2 **Club Med Cruises**	*3-, 4- & 7-day cruises to New Caledonia and Vanuatu, visiting Noumea, Espirutu Santo, Les Banks, Mallkolo, Port Villa and Tana (Jan–March)*

FAR EAST

Pearl **Pearl Cruises**	*17-day "Vietnam" cruise/tours visiting Halong Bay, Haiphong, Da Nang, Nha Trang, Ho Chi Minh City (March and June)*
Sea Goddess II **Cunard Line**	*11-day Malaysia/Thailand cruises between Singapore and Bangkok with port calls in Kuala Lumpur, Putau Pangkor, Penang, Pulau Tioman, Kuantan, Malaysia and Ko Samui, Thailand (February)*
Seabourn Spirt **Seabourn Cruise Line**	*10-day China Cruise between Bejing and Hong Kong, calling in Xingang, Yantai, Nanjing, Shanghai and Xiamen, China with cruising on the Yangtze River (March)*

SOUTH AMERICA & ANTARCTICA

Hanseatic **Seven Seas Cruise Line**	*12- & 14-day Antarctica/Falkland Island cruises sailing round-trip from Ushuaia, Argentina (each January & February)*
Polaris **Special Expeditions**	*9-day "Venezuela: A Naturalist's Expedition" cruises between Ciudad Guayana and Trinidad, visiting Angel Falls, the Orinoco River, Gulf of Paris and Asa Wright Nature Centure (February)*
Sea Goddess **Cunard Line**	*10- and 11-day Amazon cruises between Barbados and Manaus, visiting Devil's Island, French Guiana; Santana, Alter do Chao, Parintins and the Anavilhanas Archipelago, Brazil (February)*

AFRICA/INDIAN OCEAN

Silver Wind **Silversea Cruises**	*14-day round-trip Mombassa cruises visiting Zanzibar, Mayotte, Diego Suarez, Mahe (Seychelles), La Digue, Nosy Be and Moroni (Jan.–March)*

AFRICA/INDIAN OCEAN

Seabourn Spirit **Seabourn Cruise Line**	*13-day Bombay to Asshdod, Israel cruise with port calls in Salalah, Oman; Aden, Yemen and Safaga, Egypt*

UNITED STATES

Caribbean Prince *Mayan Prince* *New Shoreham II* **American Canadian Caribbean Lines**	*12-day intracoastal cruises from Warren, Rhode Island, on the Saguenay and Hudson rivers, Erie Canal, Lake Ontario and St. Lawrence Seaway (June–October)*
Nantucket Clipper **Clipper Cruise Line**	*15-day "Colonial America/Battlefields of the Civil War" from Jacksonville, FL, to Savannah, Charleston, Intercostal Waterway, Wilmington, and Beaufort, NC, Norfolk and Richmond, VA, Baltimore, and Washington, DC (May)*
Spirit of Glacier Bay **Alaska Sightseeing/Cruise West**	*8-day "Spirit of Lewis and Clark" cruise from Portland, Oregon to the border of Idaho on the Columbia and Snake rivers (spring and fall)*

1995 WORLDWIDE CRUISING REGIONS

The chart below lists ships scheduled in regions of the world at the time of writing, although itineraries may change. If the ship operates multiple and/or seasonal schedules in the region, cruise length is indicated.

AFRICA - EAST COAST	
Caledonia Travel	*Caledonian Star*
Cunard Line	*Vistafjord*
Renaissance Cruises	*Renaissance IV*
Royal Cruise Line	*Star Odyssey*
Seven Seas Cruise Line	*Hanseatic*
Silversea Cruises	*Silver Wind*

ALASKA

(Season: May through September)

Alaska Sightseeing /Cruise West	*Spirit of '98 (14 days)*
Clipper Cruise Line	*Yorktown Clipper*
Crystal Cruises	*Crystal Symphony*
Cunard Line	*Sagafjord* *Crown Dynasty*
Holland America Line	*Statendam* *Rotterdam* *Noordam* *Nieuw Amsterdam* *Ryndam*
Norwegian Caribbean Line	*Windward*
Princess Cruises	*Crown Princess* *Regal Princess* *Sky Princess* *Star Princess* *Fair Princess* *Golden Princess*
Regency Cruises	*Regent Rainbow* *Regent Sea* *Regent Star*
Royal Caribbean Cruise Line	*Nordic Prince*
Royal Cruise Line	*Star Odyssey*
Special Expeditions	*Sea Bird* *Sea Lion*
World Explorer Cruises	*Universe*

ANTARCTICA

(Season: November through March)

Abercrombie & Kent	*Explorer*
Marine Expeditions	*Akademik Ioffe*
Seven Seas Cruise Line	*Hanseatic*
Special Expeditions	*Polaris*
Quark Expeditions	*Kapitan Dranitsyn* *Kapitan Khlebnikov* *Alla Tarasova* *Professor Khromov*

AUSTRALIA/NEW ZEALAND

Cunard Line	*Sagafjord* *Sea Goddess II*
Holland America Line	*Rotterdam*
Princess Cruises	*Island Princess* *Golden Princess*
Royal Cruise Line	*Royal Odyssey*

AUSTRALIA/NEW ZEALAND

Seabourn Cruise Line	*Seabourn Spirit*
Seven Seas Cruise Line	*Song of Flower*
Orient Lines	*Marco Polo*
Worldwide Travel & Cruise Assoc.	*Achilles* *Endeavour I and II* *Atlantic Clipper*

BALTIC SEA/SCANDINAVIA

(Season: May through October)

Bergen Line	*Multiple Ships*
Caledonian Travel	*Caledonian Star*
Crystal Cruises	*Crystal Harmony*
Cunard Line	*Vistafjord* *Queen Elizabeth 2*
EuroCruises	*Multiple Ships*
Holland America Line	*Maasdam (12 days)*
KD River Cruises of Europe	*Multiple Ships*
Royal Caribbean Cruise Line	*Sun Viking (12 days)*
Royal Cruise Line	*Crown Odyssey (12 days)*
Marine Expeditions	*Akademik Ioffe*
Odessa America Cruise Co.	*Kareliya*
Princess Cruises	*Royal Princess (13 days)*
Seabourn Cruise Line	*Seabourn Pride (7 and 14 days)*

BALTIC SEA/SCANDINAVIA

Seven Seas Cruise Line	*Song of Flower (12 days)*
Silversea Cruises	*Silver Cloud*
Special Expeditions	*Polaris*

BAHAMAS

Carnival Cruise Lines	*Carnivale (3 and 4 days)* *Ecstasy (3 and 4 days)*
Celebrity/Fantasy Cruises	*Britanis (2 days)*
Dolphin Cruise Line	*SeaBreeze (3 and 4 days)*
Majesty Cruise Line	*Royal Majesty (3 days)*
Norwegian Cruise Line	*Seaward (3 days)* *Westward (3 and 4 days)*
Royal Caribbean Cruise Line	*Nordic Empress (3 and 4 days)*

BERMUDA	
Celebrity Cruises	*Horizon and Meridian (both 7 days)*
Cunard Line	*Sagafjord* *Queen Elizabeth 2*
Norwegian Caribbean Cruise Line	*Song of America (7 days)*
Norwegian Cruise Line	*Dreamward (7 days)*

CANADA/NEW ENGLAND	
(Season: * June through October, other vessels visit region on fall foliage cruises)	
American Canadian Caribbean Line	*Niagara Prince* *Caribbean Prince* *Mayan Prince (all 12 days)* *
Clipper Cruise Line	*Nantucket Clipper*
Crystal Cruises	*Crystal Harmony*
Cunard Line	*Royal Viking Sun* *Sagafjord* *Queen Elizabeth 2*

CANADA/NEW ENGLAND	
Holland America Line	*Westerdam*
Princess Cruises	*Royal Princess*
Regency Cruises	*Regent Sun (7 days) **
Royal Cruise Line	*Royal Odyssey*
Seabourn Cruise Line	*Seabourn Pride*
Silversea Cruises	*Silver Cloud*
Special Expeditions	*Polaris*

CANARY ISLANDS	
Cunard Line	*Queen Elizabeth 2* *Cunard Princess (10 and 11 days)*
Odessa America Cruise Co.	*Azerbaydzhan*
Royal Cruise Line	*Crown Odyssey*
Seabourn Cruise Line	*Seabourn Pride*

CARIBBEAN	
American Canadian Caribbean Line	*Caribbean Prince(all 12 days)* *Mayan Prince* *Niagara Prince*
Carnival Cruise Lines	*Festival (7 days)* *Tropicale (7 days)* *Holiday (7 days)* *Celebration (7 days)* *Sensation (7 days)*
Celebrity Cruises	*Horizon (7 days)* *Zenith (7 days)* *Meridian (10 and 11 days)*
Clipper Cruise Line	*Nantucket Clipper* *Yorktown Clipper*
Club Med Cruises	*Club Med I (7 days)*
Commodore Cruise Line	*Enchanted Seas (7 days)*
Costa Cruises	*Costa Romantica* *Costa Classica* *Costa Allegra (all 7 days)*
Cunard Line	*Sagafjord* *Vistafjord* *Sea Goddess I (7 days)* *Queen Elizabeth 2* *Crown Dynasty (7 days)* *Crown Jewel (7 days)* *Cunard Countess (7 days)*
Radisson Diamond Cruises	*Radisson Diamond (3, 4, 7, 10 days)*
Dolphin Cruise Line	*SeaBreeze (7 nights)* *OceanBreeze (5 days)*

CARIBBEAN

Epirotiki Lines	*World Renaissance (12 day Caribbean/Amazon)*
Celebrity/Fantasy Cruises	*Amerikanis (7 days)* *Britanis (5 days)*
Holland America Line	*Westerdam (7 days)* *Noordam (7 days)* *Nieuw Amsterdam (7 days)* *Maasdam (10 days)*
Le Boat	*Crewed Yacht Charters*
Majesty Cruise Line	*Royal Majesty (4 days)*
The Moorings	*Bareboat & Crewed Yachts*
Norwegian Cruise Line	*Starward* *Dreamward* *Windward* *Norway (all 7 days)* *Seaward (4 and 7 days)*
Odessa America Cruise Co.	*Gruziya*
Princess Cruises	*Crown Princess and* *Regal Princess (both 7 days)* *Star Princess (10 days)*
Regency Cruises	*Regent Sea* *Regent Star* *Regent Spirit (all 7 days)* *Regent Sun (10 and 11 days)* *Regent Rainbow (3 and 4 days)*
Renaissance Cruises	*Renaissance III (7 days)*
Royal Caribbean Cruise Line	*Sovereign of the Seas* *Monarch of the Seas* *Majesty of the Seas (all 7 days)* *Sun Viking (10 and 11 days)* *Song of America (7, 10, 11 days)*
Royal Cruise Line	*Queen Odyssey*
Sacks Yacht Charters	*Bareboat & Crewed Sail and Motorboats*
Seabourn Cruise Line	*Seabourn Pride*
Seven Seas Cruise Line	*Hanseatic*

CARIBBEAN	
Silversea Cruises	*Silver Cloud*
Star Clippers	*Star Flyer and* *Star Clipper (both 7 days)*
Sun Line Cruises	*Stella Solaris (7 days)*
Seabourn Cruise Line	*Seabourn Pride (7 and 14 days)*
Special Expeditions	*Polaris* *Sea Cloud*
Tall Ship Adventures	*Sir Francis Drake (3, 4, and 7 days)*
Windstar Cruises	*Wind Star (7 days)*
Worldwide Travel & Cruise Assoc.	*Le Ponant*

FAR EAST	
(Season: November through April)	
Caledonia Travel	*Caledonian Star*
Crystal Cruises	*Crystal Harmony* *(13 and 14 days)*
Cunard Line	*Royal Viking Sun* *Sagafjord* *Sea Goddess II* *(7, 10, 11 and 14 days)*
Seabourn Cruise Line	*Seabourn Spirit*
Seven Seas Cruise Line	*Song of Flower (8,9,11,12 days)*
Pearl Cruises	*Ocean Pearl (13, 18, 20 and 23 days)*
Princess Cruises	*Island Princess*

FAR EAST

Renaissance Cruises	*Renaissance V (10 and 11 days)*
Royal Cruise Line	*Royal Odyssey*
Windstar Cruises	*Wind Spirit (7 days, year round)*
Orient Lines	*Marco Polo*

HAWAII

American Hawaii Cruises	*Constitution* *Independence (both 7 days)*
Holland America Line	*Rotterdam*
Royal Caribbean Cruise Line	*Legend of the Seas*
Royal Cruise Line	*Crown Odyssey*
Princess Cruises	*Golden Princess (9 and 10 days)*

INDIAN OCEAN

Caledonia Travel	*Caledonian Star*
Cunard Line	*Royal Viking Sun* *Sea Goddess II*

INDIAN OCEAN

Paquet French Cruises	*Mermoz*
Princess Cruises	*Island Princess*
Seabourn Cruise Line	*Seabourn Spirit*
Seven Seas Cruise Line	*Song of Flower*

MEDITERRANEAN/BLACK SEA

(Season: May through November)

Caledonia Travel	*Caledonian Star*
Club Med Cruises	*Club Med 1 (7 days)*
Crystal Cruises	*Crystal Harmony (10, 11, 12 days)*
Cunard Line	*Sagafjord* *Royal Viking Sun (7 and 14 days)* *Vistafjord (14 and 15 days)* *Cunard Princess (10 and 11 days)* *Sea Goddess I* *Queen Elizabeth 2*
Radisson Diamond Cruises	*Radisson Diamond (3, 4, 7 days)*
Epirotiki Lines	*Olympic* *Triton* *World Renaissance* *Neptune* *Jason* *(3, 4 and 7 days)*
Holland America Line	*Maasdam (12 days)*
Princess Cruises	*Island Princess* *Pacific Princess*
Le Boat	*Crewed Yacht Charters*

MEDITERRANEAN/BLACK SEA

Royal Caribbean Cruise Line	*Song of Norway (12 days)*
Royal Cruise Line	*Crown Odyssey* *Royal Odyssey* *Queen Odyssey*
Odessa America Cruise Co.	*Azerbaydzhan*
Paquet French Cruises	*Mermoz*
Sacks Yacht Charters	*Bareboat & Crewed Sail and Motor-boats*
Seabourn Cruise Line	*Seabourn Spirit* *Seabourn Pride (both 7 and 14 days)*
Seven Seas Cruise Line	*Song of Flower (8, 9, 11, 12 days)* *Hanseatic*
Silversea Cruises	*Silver Cloud*
Star Clippers	*Star Flyer (7 days)*
Swan Hellenic Cruises	*Odysseus*
Sun Line Cruises	*Stella Solaris* *Stella Maris* *Stella Oceanis (all 3, 4, 7 and 14 days)*
Windstar Cruises	*Wind Star (7 days)*
Worldwide Travel & Cruise Assoc.	*Le Ponant (all 7 days)*
Zeus Cruises	*Sailing Ships (7 days)*

MEXICO

Carnival Cruise Lines	*Jubilee (7 days)*
Clipper Cruise Line	*Yorktown Clipper*

MEXICO

Norwegian Cruise Line	*Southward (3 and 4 days)*
Princess Cruises	*Fair Princess (7 and 10 days)*
Royal Caribbean Cruise Line	*Viking Serenade (3 and 4 days)* *Nordic Prince (7 days)*
Royal Cruise Line	*Crown Odyssey* *Star Odyssey*
Seven Seas Cruise Line	*Hanseatic*
Special Expeditions	*Polaris* *Sea Bird* *Sea Lion*

SOUTH PACIFIC

(Season: November through April)

Abercrombie & Kent	*Explorer*
Caledonia Travel	*Caledonian Star*
Club Med Cruises	*Club Med 2 (7 days)*
Cunard Line	*Sea Goddess II* *Sagafjord*
Orient Lines	*Marco Polo*
P & O Spice Island Cruises	*Bali Sea Dancer (3 and 4 days)* *Spice Islander* *Island Explorer* *(7 and 8 days, year round)*
Princess Cruises	*Golden Princess* *Island Princess*
Regency Cruises	*Regent Calypso*

SOUTH PACIFIC

Renaissance Cruises	*Renaissance VI*
Seabourn Cruise Line	*Seabourn Spirit*
Seven Seas Cruise Line	*Song of Flower*
Special Expeditions	*Caledonian Star*
Windstar Cruises	*Wind Song* *(7 days, year round)*
Quark Expeditions	*Akademik Shokalski*

PANAMA CANAL

(Multiple and seasonal crossings listed below. The majority of vessels make a transit on positioning cruises.)

American Canadian Caribbean Lines	*Niagara Prince*
Carnival Cruise Lines	*Tropicale (10 and 11 days - partial transit)*
Crystal Cruises	*Crystal Harmony*
Cunard Line	*Crown Dynasty (10 and 11 days)*
Holland America Line	*Maasdam* *Noordam* *Rotterdam* *Ryndam* *Statendam*
Regency Cruises	*Regent Sea (14 days)* *Regent Star (7 days - partial transit)*
Royal Caribbean Cruise Line	*Legend of the Seas* *Song of Norway (10 and 11 days)*

PANAMA CANAL

Royal Cruise Line	*Royal Odyssey* *Crown Odyssey* *Star Odyssey* *(9, 10, 11, 12, and 15 days)*
Princess Cruises	*Sky Princess* *Royal Princess (both 10 and 11 days)*
Seabourn Cruise Line	*Seabourn Pride*
Special Expeditions	*Polaris*
Sun Line Cruises	*Stella Solaris (12 days)*

SOUTH AMERICA

(Season: November through April)

Celebrity/Fantasy Cruises	*Britanis (Circumnavigation)*
Clipper Cruise Line	*Yorktown Clipper*
Crystal Cruises	*Crystal Harmony*
Cunard Line	*Royal Viking Sun (Circumnavigation)* *Vistafjord*
Ivaran Lines	*Americana*
Princess Cruises	*Pacific Princess*
Regency Cruises	*Regent Sea (Circumnavigation)*
Seabourn Cruise Line	*Seabourn Pride*
Seven Seas Cruise Line	*Hanseatic*
Silversea Cruises	*Silver Cloud*
Special Expeditions	*Polaris*

SOUTH AMERICA

Sun Line Cruises	*Stella Solaris*
GALAPAGOS	
Galapagos Cruises	*All ships*
Galapagos Inc.	*All ships*
AMAZON RIVER	
Cunard Line	*Sea Goddess 1*
Princess Cruises	*Island Princess*
Royal Cruise Line	*Queen Odyssey*
Seabourn Cruise Line	*Seabourn Pride*
Special Expeditions	*Polaris*
Sun Line Cruises	*Stella Solaris*
ORINOCO RIVER	
American Canadian Caribbean Lines	*Niagara Prince*
Clipper Cruise Line	*Yorktown Clipper*
Seven Seas Cruise Line	*Hanseatic*
Special Expeditions	*Polaris*

U.S. & CANADIAN COASTAL

(Season April through October)

Alaska Sightseeing/ Cruise West	*Spirit of Discovery* *Spirit of Alaska* *Spirit of Glacier Bay* *Spirit of '98* *(all 7 days)*

U.S. & CANADIAN COASTAL

American Canadian Caribbean Lines	*New Shoreham II*
Clipper Cruise Line	*Nantucket Clipper* *Yorktown Clipper*
Royal Cruise Line	*Star Odyssey*
Seabourn Cruise Line	*Seabourn Pride*
Special Expeditions	*Sea Bird* *Sea Lion*

TRANSATLANTIC CROSSING

Cunard Line	*Queen Elizabeth 2* *Regularly scheduled crossings from April through November*

AUTHOR'S NOTE

Ships sailing in the Mediterranean, Black Sea and Baltic have transatlantic crossings as positioning cruises.

WORLD CRUISES

Cunard Line	*Royal Viking Sun* *Sagafjord* *Queen Elizabeth 2*
Holland America Line	*Statendam*

RIVER AND CANAL CRUISES

UNITED STATES

(Season: April through October)

Alaska Sightseeing/Cruise West	*Spirit of Glacier Bay*
American Canadian Caribbean Lines	*New Shoreham II* *Caribbean Prince* *Mayan Prince*
Clipper Cruise Line	*Yorktown Clipper* *Nantucket Clipper*
Delta Queen Steamboat Company	*Mississippi Queen* *Delta Queen*
Special Expeditions	*Sea Bird* *Sea Lion*

EUROPE/EASTERN EUROPE/RUSSIA

(Season: May through October)

Abercrombie & Kent

Cunard EuroAmerica Cruises

EuroCruises

French Country Waterways

RIVER AND CANAL CRUISES
French Cruise Line
KD River Cruises of Europe
Le Boat
Odessa America Cruise Co.
Premiere Selections
EGYPT/NILE
Abercrombie & Kent
Hilton International Nile Cruises
Sheraton Nile Cruises
Swan Hellenic Cruises

AUTHOR'S OBSERVATION

While Fielding's Cruises *is printed a mere few weeks from the time this list is finalized, there are constant changes in the cruise industry. Ships may change not only itinerary, but cruising regions as well.*

CHOOSING YOUR CRUISE

"Thelma, you get what you settle for."

From the movie *Thelma and Louise*

Carnival Cruise Lines' commercials—"The Fun Ships"—are brilliant advertising. After all, don't we all want to have fun on vacation? This works splendidly for Carnival, which reaches the one million passenger mark by the end of 1994—nearly one fifth of all cruise ship passengers worldwide. But what's your idea of fun? Indeed, it may be the frenetic Las Vegas-at-sea experience characteristic of Carnival's fleet, but perhaps it's exploring nature, being pampered in a sybaritic environment, studying antiquities with academics or a low-key, homey voyage along a river. In talking to countless passengers, I've found that those who seem less than enthusiastic about their cruise have landed on a ship that didn't match their own personal fantasy.

They often have no specific complaints about the ship; it just wasn't their cup of tea—although some unfortunately decided cruising is just not for them.

Finding the voyage of one's dreams requires imagination, research and restraint from jumping at price alone.

In 1995, you'll find some 140 cruise ships plus myriad expedition vessels, sail and river boats to choose from. The difference between each company's ships in terms of ambience, creature comforts and facilities is more distinct than ever, and it has never been more critical to study the specifics of ships in order to land on the one that suits your own needs. Remember, going on a cruise is not like booking a resort—which you can easily leave if you don't get what was promised, if the service is lousy, if you can't stand fellow guests or whatever.

Because the 90s offer cruises in a buyer's market, the brochure price should serve only as a general guideline to what a cruise will really cost today; many cruise companies inflate published rates because they know a majority of passengers will be sailing at a discount. In an effort to reverse the public's belief that last-minute bookers always get the best prices, most cruise lines have adopted early booking policies that offer substantial discounts so that those who plan early aren't penalized: there's nothing worse than boarding a ship and finding that fellow passengers are sailing at a fraction of what you paid for comparable (or even better) accommodations. Fortunately the traveling public has learned to explore these deals that can save up to 50 percent off published rates.

In the world of cruises today, there are so many choices of ships and destinations that the first-time passenger can be quite overwhelmed; even veteran passengers can be confused in searching out new cruise experiences.

The phrase "right cruise or right ship" means different things to different people. Shipboard life on the majority of vessels is so diverse today, the cruise industry is so segmented, that it's crucial to know just what you are buying before you make your deposit.

For example: two friends choose to sail aboard ships that are outstanding in all aspects (Crystal Cruises' *Crystal Harmony* and Celebrity Cruises' *Meridian*), but returned home somewhat disappointed —not with the ships, but rather their personal experience of the cruise. Both were traveling solo and wanted to meet other passengers. In the same way that you're more likely to know your neighbors in a small town than a city, on large ships like the *Crystal Harmony* and *Meridian*, (960 and 1106 passengers respectively) couples, friends and families tend to stick together; my friends didn't find the intermingling of fellow-cruisers they'd envisioned. However, aboard a ship half this size or smaller there is greater intermingling of passengers; on under 200-passenger specialty vessels and river boats the camaraderie is greatest.

AUTHOR'S OBSERVATION

The most important factors in choosing a cruise: your interests and lifestyle. These will help determine the right cruise experience, destination and price. Too many people look at price alone, not realizing that with a little research they will find a ship that's perfect in all aspects and within their price range.

For example, it used to be a relatively simple matter to select a Caribbean cruise when there were fewer vessels and the on-board experience was fairly standard. This winter there are around 70 ships in the region ranging from 2500-passenger megaships to tony yacht-like vessels, sailing and expedition ships. On some ships, Armani-clad passengers will sip Dom Perignon as they are serenaded by a string quartet; on others, Budweiser-drinking revelers in cut-offs will toast their favorite NFL stars; and on still others, L.L. Bean-attired nature lovers will hop aboard Zodiacs for a closer peek at local wildlife. Families with children will find some ships with nonstop activities for tots to teens, but won't feel especially welcome on others. Those traveling solo will meet lifelong friends on certain ships and feel like a third wheel on others.

AUTHOR'S OBSERVATION

A week can be a very long time if you're stuck on a ship with people you don't feel comfortable with, for whatever reason. And what sounded like a great bargain can be an enormous waste of money if you don't return home happy.

Even the wealthy have so many choices in cruise ships going to the most exotic destinations imaginable, that it's misleading to state that one or two are the best for anyone who can afford them. Those who can pay the $750+ per person, per day cost of a deluxe boutique vessel—small, very elegant, Ralph Lauren by day, high couture by night, might be happier on an expedition vessel bound for New Guinea or barging in Burgundy or sailing from Fiji. Such problems! The rest of us have hundreds of vessels to decipher and while it can seem terribly complicated at times, it's also fun to explore all the options. Always remember, the best ship is always that one *you* love.

AUTHOR'S OBSERVATION

Don't let the brochure be the sole determinant when selecting one ship over another. In general, the only information you can be certain is accurate in a brochure is itinerary.

Kathy Lee Gifford does not sail on *all* Carnival cruises and Gavin MacLeod ("Captain Stubing") is not the master of Princess Cruises Love Boats. Passengers rarely resemble models or dress like them (unless Cindy Crawford is a fellow passenger or the Ford Modeling Agency is aboard for a fashion shoot). Cabins in the photographs usually depict the highest category suites, and others are enlarged with a wide-angle lens; most deck plans don't indicate which lovely outside staterooms have views of a lifeboat or are located on a deck where joggers and fellow passengers like to peek in. And, for the most part, brochure prices are not what you'll end up paying. There are some exceptions: on vessels where one is paying a per person, per diem of $450-$750, the on-board experience usually is as good as it looks (sometimes better); ships that cater to nature lovers (e.g., Clipper Cruise Line, Special Expeditions, Alaska Sightseeing, American Canadian Caribbean Line, and P&O Spice Island Cruises) don't over inflate their atmosphere, cuisine, service or decor. True, some ships do offer a genuine gourmet dining experience, wonderful service, larger cabins and exquisite decor and are a delightful cruise experience. But don't be swayed by the lovely photos. Finding the right ship is a challenge.

PERSONAL CONSIDERATIONS

First examine your own lifestyle and special interests, keeping in mind that an honest appraisal will lead you to the right cruise vacation experience.

AUTHOR'S OBSERVATION

The process of choosing a cruise is similar to the mindset of buying a car. Your vehicle preference will be determined by your interests and lifestyle (sedan, station wagon to haul kids, four-wheel drive, something sporty) as well as your budget. You'll do research on the pros and cons of models and manufacturers in order to get the best quality in your price range—and no one pays sticker price. Furthermore, the type of car you select and the price you'll pay will change during the decades of your life.

I was amused when a friend commented that she didn't enjoy her vacation aboard a certain ship because there were too many of "those people" aboard. I didn't ask her to specify because we all fit the category of "those people" to someone. A few people are content in every situation and environment, among all varieties of mankind, but that's rare.

It's important to consider seriously your own lifestyle and preference before examining the myriad possibilities that exist. Here are a few aspects to ponder:

LIFESTYLE & PERSONALITY

Are you a "Type A" personality, couch-potato or somewhere in between? Do you enjoy meeting new people? If so, are you naturally outgoing or more reserved? Prefer to be by yourself? Do you like new experiences, or feel more comfortable with the familiar? Do you enjoy being with people who are different (age, income level, race/ethnic group) or seek a more homogeneous milieu? Are you happiest in a relatively calm, low-key environment or do you enjoy livelier surroundings? These are all personal characteristics that should be considered as they are critical to finding a seagoing vacation that suits you personally. Naturally, there are no right or wrong answers, and we frequently fluctuate in mind set depending on what is happening in our lives at the moment. For example, one's needs and criteria are different when single, on a honeymoon, or healing the wounds of divorce or other major life change. Moreover, it takes some imagination and sometimes a leap of faith in trying a vacation experience that is out of the ordinary, but it's frequently worth the risk. If you always take a traditional seven-day Caribbean cruise, why not try a week on a sailboat or chase whales in the Sea of Cortez aboard a hearty expedition ship? Conversely, it may be fun to just do nothing at all aboard a ship that offers the ultimate in pampering when you normally try to cram six islands into a one-week cruise.

INTERESTS

Interests are a lot easier to target, but many people are unaware of the degree to which they can follow their favorite pursuits on a cruise and should factor this into the choice. For example, if you are a fitness addict, today there are plenty of vessels that enable you to run miles around the deck, take aerobics classes and bench press till you drop. Other general interests and beloved activities you can easily satisfy when taking a cruise include:

- Sports: water sports (scuba, snorkeling, sailboating, water skiing); golf; tennis; professional sports.
- Nature: from viewing beautiful scenery to in-depth learning experiences.
- History/Archaeology/Anthropology.

- Music/Theater: festivals at sea showcase jazz, classical, big band, country & western, rock and roll as well as theater.
- Educational/Intellectual pursuits.
- Cuisine and wine.

You don't have to travel to exotic destinations to be able to pursue most of these interests; vessels in the Caribbean, Alaska, Panama Canal and Mexico abound with opportunities to indulge your hobbies and interests. See the "Theme Cruise Calendar" for a potpourri of 1995 special interest sailings plus an in-depth look at which vessels are best for savoring your passions.

TRENDS

SHIPS GET LARGER

With companies like Royal Caribbean Cruise Line (RCCL), Princess Cruises and Carnival Cruise Lines launching 1800- to 2400-passenger ships, it seems that every brochure touts vessels under a 1200 passenger capacity as being the alternative to the megaliner. RCCL built the first megaliner, *Sovereign Of the Seas*, based on passenger surveys that indicated that people wanted more on-board activities and the only way to justify adding them was to increase the size of the vessel. (On a typical Caribbean intinerary, when there is normally only one full day at sea, I personally don't need six things to do at once.) We're firmly entrenched in the era of these "resorts at sea," however—both Carnival and Princess have 100,000-ton ships under construction. Carnival's will carry an extraordinary 3300 passengers (nearly 1000 more than the largest sailing today). While cruise lines claim these giants are built to meet the needs of passengers who want more of everything, an executive of Finland's Kvaerner Masa-Yard shipyard (which builds many of the mega-liners) explained it's simple economics: they are less expensive on a per-cabin basis to build and operate. These behemoths may not be everyone's dream of a seagoing holiday, but Carnival, RCCL and Princess draw the lion's share of cruise passengers, so these vessels obviously fill a niche. And, one advantage no one should overlook is that they make cruising more affordable for everyone by keeping prices competitive in the industry. Their passengers include many first-time cruisers in the 20-45 age range and the more active experienced passengers who seek Las Vegas-style entertainment, water sports ashore, extensive fitness facilities and an active on-board atmosphere at an excellent price.

At the other end of the spectrum are the yacht-like boutique vessels carrying under 300 passengers, elegant and expensive (priced up to a grand per person, per day), usually formal and clubby. Each year a few more enter the market as cruise lines vie for the very wealthy who seek the decorous, country club-like on-board ambience, exotic destinations, most luxurious accommodations and highest ratio of staff to passengers. But in reality, the total number of beds of these famous yacht-like jewels combined don't add up to one mega-liner! In 1994, we saw the demise of Royal Viking Line, which operated two, small, five-star-plus ships. Much of the heavy discounting today is in the luxury end of the cruise industry.

A majority of vessels are somewhere in between. A die-hard ship romantic like myself is heartened by the refined craftsmanship and superb design that is increasingly evident in vessels launched in the past few years. In the 1980s, it seemed we were destined to a seagoing world of Formica and blandness. But a host of new ships in the mid-price range, including Celebrity Cruises *Meridian*, *Horizon*, and *Zenith*; and Princess Cruises' *Regal Princess*, *Crown Princess*, and *Star Princess* and Holland America's *Maasdam* and *Statendam* have genteel touches of brass, wood and marble, refined fabrics, works of art and attention to the flow of public rooms. Passenger cabins are generally spacious and well-equipped, bathrooms boast hair dryers and designer toiletries, twin beds convert to queen and private verandas are available in more categories.

AUTHOR'S OBSERVATION

Those who wish to avoid the mega-liners will find many vessels in the 800- to 1500-passenger capacity range large enough to provide extensive activities, ample lounges and deck space.

THE DESTINATION'S THE THING

Vietnam is in this year for those who want to beat McDonald's to this developing nation. Nearly every ship sailing in the Far East has port calls in Ho Chi Minh City today. In November, 1995, Royal Caribbean Cruise Line will deploy the 714-passenger *Sun Viking* on year-round Asia cruises promising to make this pricey destination more affordable for everyone. Formerly inaccessible areas of China and Russia are now plied by new European-style riverboats and exotic ports like Mombassa, Kenya and Mahe, Seychelles on the east coast of Africa can be visited aboard vessels of Silversea Cruises and Renaissance on multiple sailings. While Antarctica is nearly over-populated by expedition ships, one can cruise the Arctic from

Finland to Alaska aboard converted ice-breakers. Swan Hellenic adds Beirut and Libya as ports of call and a dozen or so ships stop in Yemen and Jordan on positioning voyages between Europe and the Far East. Even the Caribbean, traditionally a mass-market destination, has innovative itineraries in 1995 ranging from deserted tropical isles to the Maya ruins of Honduras, Belize and Guatemala for those who want to bypass ports where there are sometimes half a dozen or more ships and 10,000 people in port on the same day. What's next on the horizon? Miami-based cruise lines are poised and readly to beat a hasty return to Cuba the second we're allowed back in.

CRUISE/TOURS

Alaska-bound passengers aboard nearly every vessel sailing in the region find packages that combine a cruise with a land-based excursion. While this has been a staple in Alaska cruising for years, a growing number of companies now offer cruise/tours in other regions of the world. When traveling in a far-flung destination, there are advantages to selecting a cruise/tour that includes the voyage and a pre- or post-hotel stay of several days duration, often with organized sightseeing. While traveling on a standard air/sea package, you frequently miss the attractions of the city of embarkation or disembarkation or pay premium rates for additional nights' hotel stay. This can mean a hurried bus ride through wonderful places like Rome, Barcelona, Athens, Hong Kong or Singapore only to spend the first few days of the voyage in the twilight-land of jet lag. A cruise/tour, however, gives several days' sightseeing in the city at much better prices than you could do on your own.

For example, Renaissance Cruises' 1995 Mediterranean and Baltic itineraries are offered as cruise/tours. They include round-trip airfare, a four-night hotel stay before or after the voyage, transfers and a seven-day cruise at rates beginning at $3495 per person, double occupancy. Pearl Cruises' cruise/tours in the Far East and South Pacific include two-nights pre-cruise and one night post-cruise hotel with city sightseeing tour at per person, per diem rates starting around $160; the company also offers optional "Vacation Stretcher" programs for additional land tours of places like Angkor Wat in Cambodia and China's Xi'an. Sun Line's cruise/tours in the Greek Islands and Turkey are especially good deals: a 12-day package with round-trip air, three nights hotel stay in Athens with sightseeing, full-day excursion to Delphi and seven-day cruise on the Stella Solaris is priced from $2200 per person, double occupancy. Abercrombie & Kent and the new Silversea Cruises team up in Africa with very exotic fare: following a one-week cruise aboard the Silver Wind between Mahe, Seychelles and Mombasa, Kenya, one can choose from a five-day day safari to the Masai Mara National Reserve or a seven-day safari in Tanzania.

LENGTHIER CRUISES

Lengthier cruises are once again in favor, and even in the Caribbean, where a seven-night cruise is still the norm, you'll find more 10- and 11-day itineraries that provide added time to unwind and visit a greater number of islands. Moreover, while far-flung locales were once only possible on a lengthy sailing, many 10- to 12-day schedules now make it possible to visit an exotic region while escaping the office for only two weeks.

AUTHOR'S COMMENT

Consider a vessel you might not ordinarily choose if it's a place you've always wanted to visit and the choices are few. You'll be traveling with like-minded passengers who share your curiosity and enthusiasm for the appeal of the locale.

FIT AND TRIM AT SEA

A few years ago this was practically a contradiction in terms, but today nearly every cruise ship above a certain capacity has a jogging track, fitness equipment, exercise classes, personal instructors, sauna and massage. Some boast better health clubs than you'll find at home and spas that offer truly pampered experiences. Menu selections low in fat, cholesterol, sodium and calories, as well as vegetarian fare, are frequently available in all courses so if you can resist temptation, there is no reason to put on even a pound.

AUTHOR'S OBSERVATION

When leaning toward one vessel over another because of a "spa" or "fitness center," ask your travel agent to get specifics on what it offers. The facilities, on some vessels, may not live up to your expectations; in fact, sometimes the term is downright misleading.

IT'S A SMALL, SMALL WORLD

Perhaps the biggest growth area in cruising is family travel (Carnival alone carried 86,000 children last year), and kids can have more fun on a ship than practically anywhere else. Disney has entered the cruise industry and will launch its first vessel in 1998; today there are dozens of vessels with extensive on-board activities during the summer and holiday season. Best of all, parents can have a relaxing time and let the youngsters play with those their own age in supervised fun. (See "Traveling With Children")

I CAN GET IT FOR YOU WHOLESALE

Prices are better than ever, discounting is the norm and few passengers pay brochure price on conventional cruise ships. Nowadays, even the most expensive ships are discreetly discounted. This is great for the traveling public, but drives many cruise industry executives and travel agents crazy. The best news in the mid-1990s is the new wave of advance purchase discount plans offered by many lines, which guarantee the highest savings off brochure rates to those who book the farthest in advance of departure, and then offer gradual reductions in discount levels as the sailing date approaches. There's nothing worse than boarding a ship only to find passengers with comparable accommodations boasting about what a good deal they got when you've paid full price. (See "How Much Does It Cost?")

While last-minute discounting slowed a bit in 1994 when there was a brief lull in the launching of new ships, we'll see a steady stream of brand-new ships in the 1500- to 3300-passenger range enter the competitive fray during the next four years; last minute "fire sales" will undoubtedly resume, especially in the overcrowded Caribbean.

But even those with a modest vacation budget have myriad seagoing experiences to choose from. For example, if your vacation budget for a one-week vacation is $1000 per person (excluding airfare and extras), you have many options: a Caribbean cruise on a Carnival ship or numerous other low-cost lines; exploring Belize's barrier reef on a small expedition ship of American Canadian Caribbean Lines; a New England/Canada cruise aboard Regency Cruises' *Regent Sun* (with advance purchase discount); sail the Mississippi aboard Delta Queen's paddle-wheel steamboats; cast off from St. Thomas aboard the historic sailboat *Sir Francis Drake* or explore Greek Islands on the tiny sailboats of Zeus Cruises; rent one of Le Boat's self-drive canal boats for a cruise through any scenic region of France; meander the rivers of Europe and Russia aboard EuroCruises' and KD River Cruises of Europe's comfortable riverboats; sample a more luxurious cruise ship than you thought you could ever afford on a fall or spring positioning cruise by taking advantage of seasonal discounting and advance purchase plans.

TRAVEL AGENTS ARE BETTER THAN EVER

The proliferation of cruise-only sales counselors and agencies that focus only on travel by sea means you stand a better chance of landing on the right ship; they have personally inspected and cruised on many vessels (with a critical professional eye), receive feedback from other clients and colleagues, can often get you a better deal and a cabin upgrade and can iron out any problems that may arise before and after. Best of all, they are on your side and their time and their services don't cost you a cent. (The cruise line pays the commission.) (See "Finding A Travel Agent You'll Love.")

SINGLE TRAVELERS STILL GET A RAW DEAL

With the exception of a very few lines, the cruise industry virtually ignores those traveling solo, which is surprising when you consider the sheer number of single Americans and the large discretionary income they command. Some ships have no single cabins, and those that do charge 150-200 percent of the per person, double occupancy rate. But a few are more user-friendly in terms of facilities, prices and special activities. Those traveling alone can have a marvelous time, but not on every ship. (See "Traveling Solo.")

LENGTHS OF CRUISES

"When Cicero left Athens for Ephesus in 51 B.C. enroute to the southern part of Asia Minor, the ship set sail on 6 July and arrived on the 22nd—more than two weeks after departure. The distance covered over open sea was no more than 200 nautical miles."

Travel In The Ancient World

SHORT CRUISES

Time and money are primary considerations for those contemplating a cruise. As my cocktail napkin says, "It does not cost any more to travel First Class, you just can't stay so long!" Three- and four-day cruises are perfect for testing those sea legs, and a satisfying respite from the stress of everyday life. In the long, dark days of winter, a short flight to a warm-water port can deliver you to the carefree world of a pampered seagoing holiday that will lift your spirits and sooth frazzled nerves. The all-inclusive nature of a cruise coupled with the convenience and value of air/sea packages, usually makes it a better deal than a comparable number of days at a resort and you get an island or two thrown in for good measure, not to mention the sybaritic pleasure of being at sea. Short cruises, especially in the Caribbean and Mexico, were once the sole province of hard-partying young first-time cruisers and they'll still find plenty of vessels to choose from but today you'll find ships in all prices and atmosphere. For example, if money is no object and you wouldn't dream of traveling without a tux, the *Radisson Diamond* delivers a very tony four-night escape in the Caribbean. At a rate of around $500 per person, per day, and a **San Juan** to **St. Thomas**, **St. Kitts**, and **St. Maarten** itinerary, I think the price is exhorbitant. Royal Caribbean's *Nordic Empress* presents a very refined atmosphere at moderate cost on short escapes from Miami, which include a visit to a private island in the Bahamas. On a three or four-day cruise you can sail aboard an authentic clipper ship, Tall Ship Adventures *Sir Francis Drake*, built in 1917 and lovingly restored, or venture to the Arctic Circle on a EuroCruises vessel; wine enthusiasts can visit the **Napa Valley** and **San Francisco Bay** on Clipper Cruise Line's *Yorktown Clipper* in under a week in a casual but erudite milieu. Families love Premiere Cruise Lines short vacations aboard its Big Red Boats from Florida, with activities geared for all kids from tots to teens (Bugs Bunny frequently shows up at dinnertime) and shoreside fun at a private isle in the Bahamas.

Three and four nights are enough time to enjoy a taste of the Nile, the antiquities of Turkey and the Greek Islands, the Rhine and waterways of France, or develop the confidence to swim with a sea lion in the Galapagos Islands. But in the case of a transatlantic crossing, a short cruise should be considered as an extension to a longer vacation ashore whenever possible, even if it's a pre- or post-cruise hotel package. It can be wrenching to disembark in the early morning after you've had a wonderful time at sea (like taking down the Christmas tree).

You'll probably regret the experience wasn't longer, especially if it's necessary to suddenly shift gears once ashore: packing and unpacking each day, checking in and out of hotels, not to mention scrutinizing the right-hand column of menus.

AUTHOR'S OBSERVATION

On a 3- or 4-day cruise it usually doesn't pay to book a cabin above standard since so little time is usually spent there aside from changing clothes and flopping at the close of day.

ONE-WEEK CRUISES

One-week cruises are still the most prevalent these days, especially in the Caribbean, Alaska and Mexico, and they offer excellent value in time and money. A seven-day holiday at sea provides plenty of relaxation, diverse ports of call, and enough shopping opportunities to keep the credit card companies in business. One week is also long enough to make lasting friendships with others on board. Since people of all ages have difficulty sneaking away for more than five consecutive weekdays, these cruises are popular with everyone—young singles, professional couples, families at school break, retired folk. I have even encountered a few nuns on board having the time of their lives! It is a joy to see such a diversity of passengers on the one-week sailing taking advantage of seven days at sea. In just one week, passengers aboard the *Windward* or *Monarch of the Seas* from San Juan visit as many as six different secluded Caribbean islands for beach-side picnics and snorkeling.

Meanwhile, Regency Cruises offers a partial transit of the Panama Canal from Montego Bay, and you can study the flora and fauna in Mexico, the Galapagos and the Sea of Cortez, with Special Expeditions. Many cruise companies have port calls on private islands in the Bahamas and Caribbean (Princess Cruises **Princess Cays** and **Princess Bay**; Royal Caribbean Cruise Line's **Coco Cay**) that are featured in a one-week cruise (and many short sailings as well), an appealing feature for water sports enthusiasts.

In seven days, you can sail from New York to Bermuda and spend three full days in port, cruise either coast of Mexico and discover the beauty and history of the Northeast and Canada between New York and Montreal. One-week cruises between Vancouver and Whittier/Anchorage offer even more Alaskan glacial spectacles than the popular round trips from Vancouver, although most people extend the trip by taking inland tours. Seven days from Piraeus aboard Sun Line ships feature both Greek Islands and historical sites in Turkey, or in the same amount of time you can lazily float along a canal in Burgundy on the deck of a Premiere Selections hotel barge.

Before the value-conscious 90s, the world's most luxurious and expensive ships rarely offered short cruises, but the realities of tighter budgets affecting nearly everyone has resulted in companies like Seabourn Cruise Line offering an increasing number of one-week segments of longer voyages.

AUTHOR'S OBSERVATION

All cruise companies offer pre- and post-cruise hotel options. I can't urge you enough to invest in a pre-cruise package–air schedules are chaotic and you'll add at least a day's relaxation to the voyage when embarking after a good night's sleep and taking a leisurely ride to the ship. And, post-cruise hotel packages are an excellent way to avoid the mad rush for the airport with a thousand cruise passengers that afford time to explore the ship's home port, frequently overlooked with tight air schedules.

LONGER CRUISES

Longer cruises have mushroomed in popularity with more voyages than ever available in far-off places this year. But even closer to home, cruise companies are scheduling 10- and 11-day sailings stretching over two weekends that deliver a relaxing day or so more at sea and a greater number of ports.

Celebrity's *Meridian*, for example, departs from San Juan on a ten-day Friday-to-Monday itinerary (alternating with an 11-day schedule), with eight ports of call in the Southern Caribbean while Holland America's *Maasdam* voyages to the Eastern West Indies in the same duration of time. Many ships sail between Mexico and the Caribbean in 10 or 11 days for those seeking the thrill of a transit through the Panama Canal, including Princess Cruises' *Royal Princess* and Cunard's *Crown Dynasty.* American Canadian Caribbean Line takes nature lovers, scuba and snorkeling buffs to the Belizean coastline aboard the *Caribbean Prince* each winter on 12-day sailings, just the right amount of time to get an in-depth awareness of the barrier reef and its rich aquatic life. If your vacation time is limited to two weeks and an exotic destination beckons, 10-, 11- and 12-day itineraries make it feasible to fit a cruise in comfortably with air travel time. And, while it may not do justice to the locale, many more people are able to experience some of the world's most exceptional places within the confines of a two-week vacation. *Renaissance VIII* and Silverseas Cruises new *Silver Wind* both sail on 10-and 11-day itineraries between Kenya and The Seychelles. Crystal Cruises' *Crystal Harmony* and Royal Cruise Line's *Royal Odyssey* and *Golden Odyssey* ply the Mediterranean, Black Sea and Aegean on 12-day voyages from spring through fall. Seven Seas Cruise Line's *Song of Flower* explores exotic South Pacific Islands and Far East countries (including Vietnam) on 11- and 12-day voyages, and you can sail from Bombay to Israel on the *Seabourn Spirit* in just 12 days.

AUTHOR'S OBSERVATION

Those planning a two-week cruise can economize by combining two seven-day sailings on vessels that have one-week alternating itineraries and offer discounts of up to 50 percent for the second week.

Voyages of several weeks are still in vogue with those who seek a more in-depth look at exotic climes. In just 22 days, you can explore Vietnam, China and Russia's Far East aboard the *Ocean Pearl.*

VERY VERY LONG CRUISES

There are people who can and will spend 100 or more days on the same vessel as they circumnavigate the world, although one might think that they would have to be unglued from each other at disembarkation. A travel agent friend has a client who spends four months each year on one of the most deluxe vessels around. The commission on that booking alone will keep the agent in chocolates and nylons for a long time. Cunard's *Royal Viking Sun*, *Queen Elizabeth 2* and *Sagafjord* and Holland America's *Rotterdam* **circumnavigate the globe** this year and you can spend up to $150,000 on such a journey. Up to 80 percent of passengers select two- to three-week segments of the voyage, a perfect way to visit remote regions of the world other vessels don't visit, such as both coasts of Africa and the Indian Ocean. **South America** is very fashionable this year; one can circumnavigate the continent on the *Regent Sea* and *Britanis* in 71 to 80 days. The fancy new expedition ship *Hanseatic* kicks off the new year in Antarctica with a gala party. Those wishing to continue the adventure can stay aboard as she journeys to **South Africa**, up the east coast to **Mauritania** and the **Seychelles** and on to **Athens** (surely L.L. Bean is among the ship's boutiques), a very long time to be out of the office! This voyage will actually be offered in cruise segments, of course, but I hope one hearty soul is game for the whole experience.

SHIP'S SIZE AND PERSONALITY

Whether you choose a fun-and-sun cruise, an adventure or cultural cruise, or sailing for dramatic scenery, you should pay particular attention to the type of vessel that suits you best. If you're not fussy as long as the vessel sails to your destination, you have a choice of ships of varying size, shape, and nationality, but with so many in all areas of the globe today, you have the luxury of choice and should be picky. Remember, selecting a ship involves choosing not just a means of transportation, but a lifestyle and it will probably have more bearing on your overall enjoyment of the trip than the destination itself. If you wind up on a vessel that you feel is too formal and pretentious and you prefer laid-back and friendly, it can definitely detract from the enjoyment of the voyage. Conversely, a white-glove, reserved, aristocratic milieu may be more to your liking, and there are plenty of ships that pride themselves on a less formal experience.

AUTHOR'S OBSERVATION

The "personality" of ships and a general overview of passengers sailing on specific vessels is explored in "The Cruise Lines" and "Ships and their Ratings" sections–consult these chapters when you have specific vessels in mind.

One of the few generalities one can make today is that the smaller the ship, the more interaction there is between and among passengers and crew. For example, on a twelve-passenger luxury European hotel barge or a sailing ship where one may join the fun of hoisting sails, you may return home with new lifelong friends. While sailing aboard the 170-passenger *Star Clipper* this year, I found great camraderie among passengers from a variety of nations and ages that ranged from 30 to 75 by the second day. On a mega-liner, you may never converse with anyone except your sailing companion, unless you are naturally outgoing or join others in common interests such as bridge or sports. But if you opt for a mega-liner and still want to meet people, peruse the "Theme Cruise Calendar" and select a voyage where you know you'll meet people with a common bond.

AUTHOR'S OBSERVATION

On-board ambience (lively, subdued, high-brow, old, young, etc.) will be a key factor in your enjoyment of the cruise. Big ships have different personalities from the smaller ones.

In this age of mega-vessels, size has more bearing than ever on your cruise experience. While the *QE 2* and *Norway* are each in a class by themselves, one a floating city, the other a movable resort, some of the new ships being built today are programmed to carry around 2400 passengers. And, while there are more public rooms, the cabin sizes often get smaller and smaller: on RCCL's newest mega-ships, cabins average 130 square feet, although passengers don't take these vessels with the intention of spending much time there. On board, you won't feel crowded due to the enormous deck space and dozens of lounges and clubs, but disembarking in port (especially St. Thomas, where there are sometimes a half dozen vessels

arriving at once) can feel like Macy's the day after Thanksgiving. Many people love these behemoths. The smaller, ultra deluxe vessels (*Sea Goddess I* & *II*, *Seabourn Pride*, *Seabourn Spirit*, *Song of Flower*, and the new *Silver Cloud* and *Silver Wind*) are priced at the top per diem ($400-$750 per person, per day) and appeal to the 60+ well-heeled traveler who enjoys the ambience of a private yacht, with open-seating meals in elegant surroundings and the most exotic destinations.

They are subdued and refined, similar to a visit to the country club on a member's gala evening. The eight Renaissance ships, on the other hand, have the same amenities and size, but as destination-oriented vessels, carry passengers in a broader age range (30-80) at a lower per diem and there are no formal evenings. Swan Hellenic Cruises and *Ocean Pearl* offer in-depth educational and cultural experiences in the Mediterranean and Far East—in this instance, size and ship facilities are irrelevant to passengers eager to study what's ashore.

AUTHOR'S OBSERVATION

In general, passengers in the 25-40 age group tend to frequent the activity-oriented mega-liners and sailboats in the Caribbean, although a growing number of families are frequenting Alaska, Bermuda and New England/Canada cruises in summer. Passengers in the 55+ age group predominate on the more expensive ships, nearly all riverboats worldwide, as well as cruises in regions outside North America.

DIFFERENT AMBIENCE

Among larger upscale ships that boast more entertainment and facilities, both Crystal Cruises and Royal Cruise Line have very loyal followings, but a different ambience completely. Royal's passengers love the very outgoing and friendly Greek crews, the camaraderie that naturally develops between passengers over dinner at tables for eight. A voyage aboard the elegant *Crystal Harmony* is a more formal and reserved experience; a similiar milieu characterizes *Sagafjord*, *Vistafjord*, and *Royal Viking Sun*, but with a classical, white glove ambience. Paquet Cruise Line's *Mermoz* is French in flavor and the line's popular fine arts cruises draw a mixture of cultured, educated Americans and Europeans in the 60+ age group.

Holland America Line has one of the highest numbers of repeat passengers in the industry (my aunt sailed on the *Rotterdam* ten times), who love the classical, traditional ambience that harks back to the grand liners of the 30s and 40s. Generally in the 60+ age range, they come from a cross section of incomes and walks of life. Sun Line's long history in South America and the Mediterranean, the outgoing Greek crew and renowned lecturers attract educated, well-traveled passengers who like the warm, friendly ambience and educational enrichment. Regency Cruises' innovative Caribbean, New England/Canada and Mediterranean itineraries draw experienced cruisers in the 55+ age group who want a moderately priced traditional style of service. During the Mediterranean summer season, Costa Cruises passengers are 80 percent Europeans, but predominantly American (in the 35–60 age group) in the Caribbean.

A number of new ships launched in the past few years, including Celebrity Cruises' *Horizon*, *Meridian* and *Zenith* and Princess Cruises' *Regal Princess*, *Crown Princess*, *Star Princess* and *Royal Princess*, have raised the level of service, decor and cuisine frequently lacking in the Caribbean aboard mid-priced vessels. Their passengers are normally 45+, seeking a casually refined but unstuffy atmosphere, extensive fitness and spa facilities and an above-average dining service.

Norwegian Cruise Line and Royal Caribbean Cruise Line are moderately priced, attract a greater number of passengers in their 30s and 40s who are active, fun-loving sun-seekers, families with children, singles and young couples who seek plenty of lively entertainment and water sports at lower cost. Carnival Cruise Lines attracts many cruisers in their 20s and 30s (65 percent are first-timers), who keep the casino and disco hopping, a hard partying bunch who love on-board activities, such as pillow fights, beer drinking contests and hairy chest competitions, as well as more traditional fun.

A completely different experience is found aboard the ships of Clipper Cruise Line, Alaska Sightseeing/Cruise West, P&O Spice Island Cruises, Special Expeditions, American Canadian Caribbean Line and World Explorer Cruises. Appealing to naturalists and the ecology minded, these cruises fill a wonderful niche for those who want to explore the vanishing natural beauty of Alaska, Mexico, Canada, the Caribbean and South America in remote areas not frequented by other vessels.

You won't find a casino or disco aboard these ships (although very well-stocked libraries are the norm). As an executive of Alaska Sightseeing/Cruise West put it, "Our ice sculptures are outside." Swan Hellenic Cruises brings scholars on art and culture aboard European voyages for intellectual passengers who view travel as a rich learning experience.

SAILING SHIPS AND YACHTS

Cruising aboard a sailing ship is one of life's most glorious experiences for those who delight in watching the sails billow in the warm winds of the Caribbean, Mediterranean or Pacific and the relaxed lifestyle aboard. Crews are young and thrilled to be part of the romance of a large sailing ship that harks back to the time when clippers roamed the world. Windstar Cruises is at the upscale end of the sailing ships, with a small casino, cabins boasting color television and VCRs and affluent passengers in the 35+ age range. Those seeking another chic sailing adventure will love the sleekly modern 50-passenger *Le Ponant*, of Worldwide Travel & Cruise Associates, which sails from **Guadeloupe** in winter and **Nice** from May through October, and you can also sail aboard *Sea Cloud*, built by E.F. Hutton for his wife, Marjorie Merriweather Post. A delightful presence in Caribbean and Mediterranean waters are *Star Flyer* and *Star Clipper* cruising to pristine islands from **Barbados** and **St. Maarten** in the winter before the *Star Flyer* begins her summer season home porting in Cannes. The young at heart will love Zeus Cruises' small, lively sailboats in the Aegean, which chart a course for undiscovered Greek islands. *Club Med 1* and *2* carry the same lively atmosphere their land-based resorts do, including the GO's who ensure everyone is having fun while cruising in the **Caribbean** and **South Pacific**. Tall Ship Adventures' *Sir Francis Drake* is an authentic tall ship, built in 1917 as a working clipper, which has been lovingly restored and sails on 3-, 4- and 7-day cruises in the **British Virgin Islands**, a lovely historical adventure.

CARGO AND PASSENGER FERRY SHIPS

Europeans have always loved voyages aboard vessels that serve the dual purpose of transporting cars/cargo/mail while offering all the services and facilities of cruise ships, and a very casual, fun on-board ambience. On Bergen Line's Norwegian Coastal Voyages, for example, one can visit the charming villages of Norway's coastline and marvel at glaciers and fjords north of the Arctic Circle. A 23-day voyage between New Orleans and Buenos Aires can be found on Ivaran Line's *Americana*, carrying freight and very tony passenger accommodations. You'll visit fascinating ports along the way, with long stretches for reading and conversation.

EXPEDITION VESSELS

Plying the most exotic waters on earth, expedition vessels carry well-heeled, 60+ adventure-seeking passengers toting binoculars and a serious desire to gain a deeper appreciation of some of the world's least-explored peoples and regions. Abercrombie & Kent's *Explorer*, for example, cruises remote island groups of the Pacific, such as **Melanesia** and **Micronesia** before heading south to a season in **Antarctica**. On-board experts include geologists, marine biologists, ornithologists, geopolitical historians, glaciologists and veteran polar explorers who discuss topics such as global warming and the ozone hole. Special Expeditions' *Polaris* cruises the **Indian Ocean** and **west coast of Africa** in summer before journeying up the **Amazon** and **Orinoco** rivers in late fall while *Sea Bird* and *Sea Lion* chase whales in the **Sea of Cortez**. You can cruise both polar regions aboard Quark Expeditions' ice-breakers with passenger superstructure or a former Soviet research vessel converted for passenger use by Marine Expeditions.

RIVER CRUISES

"There is nothing in the world quite as much fun as messing around in boats."

Wind in the Willows

River cruises are expanding with every season along the rivers, lakes and canals of the world from the **Mekong** to the **Mississippi**, the **Nile** to the **Danube**, the **Orinoco** to the **St. Lawrence**. In 1995 you'll find two new companies—Victoria Cruises and Regal Cruises—with a total of nine European-style riverboats on China's Yangsee River. KD River Cruises of Europe represents elegant boats that ply the Rhine and has added cruises on the Danube and Elbe (the company's "Connisseur Collection" offers some of the finest dining and service found anywhere) as has Cunard EuroAmerica River Cruises.

EuroCruises has very innovative offerings, such as a one-week voyage along Portugal's Duro River and historic paddle-wheel steamers that meander Sweden's Gota Canal. Le Boat's self-drive houseboats through the scenic canals of France are a bargain and delightful escape for friends and families.

Abercrombie & Kent, French Cruise Line, Le Boat and Premiere Selections offer deluxe hotel barges, a lovely excursion with gourmet wine and food, bicycles, and pastoral scenes in France, Holland, England, Ireland, Germany, Austria, Hungary and Belgium from early spring through late fall. As you glide slowly past small towns and villages, your captain/host delivers wonderful meals and lessons in the food and wines of each region. Never mind such indulgent temptations, you can walk or bike off all the sumptuous courses while visiting local markets and historic sites and even guide your hotel barge through the many locks. The intimacy of the setting and the relaxing atmosphere foster great rapport among passengers. One entire group of Americans that sailed aboard a French Cruise Line barge (and never met before the voyage) is holding a reunion this year to relive the experience and renew strong friendships. The Mississippi has been a favored waterway for years (even a president vacationed there while in office) and both the *Delta Queen* and *Mississippi Queen* are a thrilling way to relive the lore of this great river. Less well known to cruise passengers are the historic Hudson, where so much of the Revolution was fought, and the beautiful Saguenay off the St. Lawrence, each summer cruised by the three vessels of American Canadian Caribbean Line. Out west, Alaska Sightseeing/Cruise West retraces the route of Lewis and Clark's exploration along the Columbia and Snake Rivers on a 1000-mile excursion from Portland to the Idaho border aboard the *Spirit of Glacier Bay* in the fall and spring. Clipper Cruise Line's *Nantucket Clipper* explores **Colonial America** and **Civil War battlefields**, cruising inland from Jacksonville, Florida to Washington, D.C.

THEME CRUISES

Special interest cruises enrich a vacation at sea for nearly everyone and there are very few hobbies and pastimes not available on one vessel or another. From scuba diving to basketball, symphony to square dancing, ecology to financial planning, murder mysteries to gardening, ancient civilizations and cuisine there are myriad opportunities to get together on a cruise with people from all walks of life who share your enthusiasm for a particular interest. Furthermore, special on-board performances, festivals and seminars are included in the price of a cruise, and you can frequently socialize with guest lecturers, artists, athletes, authors and other experts from the top echelon of their professions.

Theme cruises are subject to change, so be sure to confirm with the cruise company.

1995 THEME CRUISE CALENDAR

SHIP	CRUISE LINE	LOCATION	DATES
		ANTIQUES	
Actief	Abercrombie & Kent	Thames River, England	Apr. 23 & Oct. 22
		ART AND ARCHITECTURE	
Crown Odyssey	Royal Cruise Line	Mediterranean	Sept. 2, 26 & Oct. 8
Seabourn Spirit	Seabourn Cruise Line	"Architectural Digest Cruise" Cairs–Bali	Jan. 7
		ART HISTORY	
Crown Odyssey	Royal Cruise Line	Mediterranean	Apr. 23 & May 5
Star Odyssey	Royal Cruise Line	Mediterranean	May 20 & Oct. 23
		CURRENT EVENTS & POLITICS	
Crown Odyssey	Royal Cruise Line	Baltic	May 29, June 10, July 16, 28, Aug. 9 & 21
		Black Sea	Sept. 14 & Oct. 20
Royal Odyssey	Royal Cruise Line	Far East	Jan. 2, Mar. 15, 27, Apr. 5, 20, & 29
Seabourn Pride	Seabourn Cruise Line	"Art Buchwald on Current Events" Caribbean	Jan. 30
Star Odyssey	Royal Cruise Line	Black Sea Mediterranean Africa	June 1 Sept. 5 & 17 Nov. 4, 19 & Dec. 3
Seabourn Spirit	Seabourn Cruise Line	"Watergate & the World Today with G. Gordon Liddy" Baltic	Aug. 2
		CULINARY	
Royal Odyssey	Royal Cruise Line	New England/ Canada	Sept. 24, Oct. 18, 25 & Nov. 1
		Panama Canal	Nov. 10
Star Odyssey	Royal Cruise Line	Panama Canal	Jan. 25, Mar. 12, 20, & 30
		Mediterranean	Aug. 24
		FITNESS & HEALTH	
Crown Odyssey	Royal Cruise Line	Mexico	Jan. 4
Norway	Norwegian Cruise Line	Caribbean	Oct. 21
Royal Odyssey	Royal Cruise Line	Panama Canal	Dec. 3
		GARDENING	
Star Odyssey	Royal Cruise Line		July 19 & 31
		GOLF	
Club Med 1	Club Med Cruises	Caribbean	Jan. 1 & Mar. 25

SHIP	CRUISE LINE	LOCATION	DATES
Nantucket Clipper	Clipper Cruises	U.S. Intracoastal Waterway (Charleston to Jacksonville)	Nov. 12 & 26
		HISTORY	
Mississippi Queen	Delta Queen Steamboat Co.	Mississippi River Civil War	Aug. 16 & Sept. 28
		World War II	Aug. 2 & 9
		PERSONAL FINANCE	
QE2	Cunard Line	Transatlantic	July 10
		MURDER MYSTERY	
QE2	Cunard Line	Transatlantic	Apr. 28, May 3 & Sept. 28
		MUSIC & ENTERTAINMENT	
		Classical	
Crown Odyssey	Royal Cruise Line	Baltic	June 22 & July 4
Seabourn Spirit	Seabourn Cruise Line	Baltic Van Cliburn Piano Competition	July 5
Sagafjord	Cunard Line	New England/ Canada	Oct. 1
QE2	Cunard Line	Panama Canal	Jan. 6
Vistafjord	Cunard Line	Transcanal	Feb. 18
		Baltic	June 22
		Big Band	
Crown Odyssey	Royal Cruise Line	Panama Canal	Jan. 12, 30, Mar. 1, 14 & Dec. 6
		Hawaii	Feb. 13 & 19
		Transatlantic	Mar. 14
Mississippi Queen	Delta Queen Steamboat co.	Mississippi River	Jan. 23–Feb. 24, Aug. 2, 9, Sept. 2 & 9
Norway	Norwegian Cruise Line	Caribbean	Nov. 25
Royal Odyssey	Royal Cruise Line	Panama Canal	Sept. 10
		Comedy	
Norway	Norwegian Cruise Line	Caribbean	Juny 10
		Rock & Roll	
Cunard Countess	Cunard Line	Caribbean	Jan. 21 & Aug. 26
Norway	Norwegian Cruise Line	Caribbean	Sept. 9
		Country Western	
Cunard Countess	Cunard Line	Caribbean	Apr. 22, Oct. 22 & Nov. 26
Norway	Norwegian Cruise Line	Caribbean	Jan. 14 & Apr. 22

SHIP	CRUISE LINE	LOCATION	DATES
Royal Odyssey	**Royal Cruise Line**	**Alaska**	**Juny 28 & July 7**
		Jazz	
Cunard Countess	**Cunard Line**	**Caribbean**	**June 24**
Delta Queen	**Delta Queen Steamboat Co.**	**Dixie Land Fest Mississippi River**	**Feb. 6–Mar. 10**
Seabourn Pride	**Seabourn Cruise Line**	**"Classic Jazz Piano" Mediterranean**	**July 20**
Norway	**Norwegian Cruise Line**	**Caribbean**	**Oct,. 28**
Star Odyssey	**Royal Cruise Line**	**Panama Canal** **Caribbean**	**Feb. 4 & Mar. 1** **Feb. 15 & 22**
QE2	**Cunard Line**	**Transatlantic**	**Aug. 5**
		Opera	
Star Odyssey	**Royal Cruise Line**	**Mediterranean**	**Jul. 7**
Vistafjord	**Cunard Line**	**Black Sea**	**Sept. 11**
		Universal Studios	
Norway	**Norwegian Cruise Line**	**Caribbean**	**Aug. 5**
		Film	
Crown Odyssey	**Royal Cruise Line**	**"MGM Grand Film Festival"** **Mediterranean** **Canary Islands** **Transatlantic**	 **Mar. 23** **Mar. 30 & Apr. 11** **Nov. 15**
		Theater	
QE2	**Cunard Line**	**Transatlantic** **Mystery theater**	**May 2** **Setp. 28**
		NATURE & ENVIRONMENT	
Constitution & Independence	**American Hawaii Cruises**	**Hawaii whale watching**	**Feb. & Mar.**
Royal Odyssey	**Royal Cruise Line**	**Alaska**	**May 24, 31, June 7, 14, 28 & July 5**
Star Odyssey	**Royal Cruise Line**	**Amazon River**	**Jan. 3 & 14**
QE2	**Cunard Line**	**Transatlantic**	**Sept. 7**
		PHOTOGRAPHY	
Westerdam	**Holland America Line**	**Caribbean**	**Jan. 7, 14, 21, 28 & Feb. 4**
Rotterdam	**Holland America Line**	**Alaska**	**May 21, 28, June 4 & 11**
Royal Odyssey	**Royal Cruise Line**	**Alaska** **New England/ Canada**	**June 12, 19, 26, Aug. 5 & 17** **Oct. 4**

SHIP	CRUISE LINE	LOCATION	DATES
Noordam	**Holland America Line**	**Caribbean**	**Oct. 21, 28, Nov. 4, 11, 18, 25, Dec. 2, 9, & 15**
Star Odyssey	**Royal Cruise Line**	**Mediterranean**	**Apr. 19, May 1, June 13, Aug. 12 & Oct. 11**

PROFESSIONAL SPORTS

SHIP	CRUISE LINE	LOCATION	DATES
Norway	**Norwegian Cruise Line**	**Caribbean**	**Football Cruise: Feb. 18** **Tennis Cruise: Mar. 25 & Aug. 26** **Hockey Cruise: June 17** **Basketball Cruise: July 8** **Ski Cruise: Sept. 30** **Baseball Cruise: Nov. 11** **Motorsports Cruise: Dec. 2** **Volleyball Cruise: Dec. 9**
Dreamward	**Norwegian Cruise Line**	**Caribbean**	**Golf Cruise: Apr. 29 & Oct. 7**
Mississippi Queen	**Delta Queen Steamboat Co.**	**Mississippi River**	**Baseball: Jul. 8, 14 & Aug. 29**

SPECIAL EVENTS

Equinox

Equinox Sun Serpent at Maya ruins of Chichen Itza in Mexico, with *lecturers* on astronomy, Maya culture and archaeology

SHIP	CRUISE LINE	LOCATION	DATES
Stella Solaris	**Sun Line**		**Mar 12**

Great Steamboat Race

Delta Queen & Mississippi Queen compete with other paddle-wheel steamers in an annual race on Missippi River

SHIP	CRUISE LINE	LOCATION	DATES
Delta Queen *Mississippi Queen*	**Delta Queen Steamboat Co.**	**Mississippi River**	**June 24**

Kentecky Derby

SHIP	CRUISE LINE	LOCATION	DATES
Delta Queen *Mississippi Queen*	**Delta Queen Steamboat Co.**	**St. Louis**	**Apr. 28, May 2 & 7**

Valentine's Day

"Love Boat National Holiday"—Every February 14, some 4000 couples renew vows aboard all nine Princess Cruises' vessels, with ceremonies, special activities, games and contests.

WINE

SHIP	CRUISE LINE	LOCATION	DATES
Crown Odyssey	**Royal Cruise Line**	**Britain & France**	**May 17**
Royal Odyssey	**Royal Cruise Line**	**Australia/ New Zealand Panamal Canal**	**Jan. 14 & 29 Feb. 10 & 22 Nov. 21 & Dec. 11**
Star Odyssey	**Royal Cruise Line**	**Mediterranean**	**Sept. 29**

GUEST LECTURERS

From high-brow fine arts to kick-up-your heels fun, guest lecturers are popular today with many cruisers. And, while I usually like to leave my brain behind when cruising, so many fascinating authorities and experts sail on ships these days that one can return home with all kinds of inside tidbits to impress friends. One of my more memorable experiences was joining Isaac Asimov and a small group for cocktails aboard the *QE 2* after a lecture on the cosmos. (Thank goodness there were others at the table and I didn't have to try to carry the conversation alone.) Sun Line schedules scientists on its Amazon cruises and brings astronomers and anthropologists to its Mayan Equinox sailing. Passengers sailing betweeen the U.S. and Europe aboard the *QE 2* will find authors, celebrities, scientists, financial advisors, politicians and lecturers on everything under the sun. The *Crystal Harmony*'s Crystal Ball Enrichment Program features lecturers on all sailings who cover a wide gamut of topics, including investments, gems, stress and beauty and Swan Hellenic's Mediterranean voyages lure cerebral types from the halls of Oxford and Cambridge to discuss the antiquities of civilization. So many of the world's top chefs sail on ships these days that one wonders who's minding the kitchen back home—those sailing with Celebrity will find Michelle Roux, a three-star-rated Michelin chef, keeping tabs on operations during many voyages.

SPORTS AND FITNESS ABOARD

Norwegian Cruise Line lures many passengers who wouldn't sail otherwise with a roster of **professional sports stars** so one can lounge languidly on a deck chair while your spouse (who wouldn't dream of missing Monday Night Football) happily gets his or her sports fix at sea. Calling itself the Athlete's Fleet, NCL features a Sports Bar and Grill on the new *Dreamward* and *Windward* complete with banks of television broadcasting live ESPN, NFL and NBA broadcasts via satellite. In 1995, NCL SuperSport sailings feature stars from the NFL, NBA, hockey, golf, car racing, raquetball and tennis, volleyball, baseball and skiing seminars on several vessels. Those who love water sports will find that opportunities abound on dozens of vessels sailing to warm-water ports. Passengers on Royal Caribbean Cruise Line ships sailing to **Coco Cay**, an uninhabited island in the Bahamas, can snorkel or scuba to a replica of Blackbeard's pirate ship (which RCCL built and sank.) Princess Cruises' "New Waves" on *Crown Princess*, *Regal Princess*, *Star Princess* and *Sky Princess* Caribbean sailings features a **scuba certification** course and

snorkeling excursions. The barrier reef off Belize, where American Canadian Caribbean Line's *Caribbean Prince* winters offers divers some of the best facilities for **water sports**; Wind Star and Club Med vessels have a launching platform off the stern if you care to waterski from the ship's motorboats, and Star Clippers carry a full complement of equipment and instructors. Seabourn and Sea Goddess vessels and the *Queen Odyssey* have fold out marinas that lower to become sea-level, salt-water pools and transport sailboards, paddleboards, sailboats and powerboats for waterskiing.

Those intrigued by ancient civilizations can choose from dozens of vessels visiting Turkey, Israel, Tunisia and the Greek Islands; or sail the Nile on elegant river boats, such as those operated by Hilton, Sheraton, Abercrombie & Kent and Swan Hellenic. The secrets of the Western Hemisphere's most enigmatic culture, the **Maya**, are explored, as well, when the *Regent Spirit* calls in Honduras, Belize, Guatemala and Cozumel from January through April, with visits to the ancient pyramids of Tikal, Copan and Chichen Itza. The Stella Solaris has also scheduled a special Mayan Equinox cruise to view the extraordinary solar display at Chichen Itza during the March 21 vernal equinox.

The expedition ships of Abercrombie & Kent, Caledonia Travel and Special Expeditions journey to remote regions of the world for those interested in exotic cultures, eco-tourism, flora and fauna. World Explorer, Alaska Sightseeing, Spice Island Cruises and American Canadian Caribbean are perfect for nature-lovers who want more in-depth knowledge of the region, accompanied by scientists and culturalists who are experts in the regions visited.

SINGLES

Singles of all ages can have a wonderful time at sea on a wide variety of cruise vessels. Senior writer Mary B. McDowell has traveled alone on dozens of ships ranging from traditional cruise vessels to those carrying nature lovers and even a freighter leisurely winding down the coast of South America. She's of a certain age, always meets new friends, and I think her attitude contributes greatly to the fun of her seagoing adventures. She genuinely enjoys the company of people with a variety of interests from all walks of life and ages, can socialize easily and also relishes time alone. Mary's advice is to make friends at the beginning of the trip, before others form fixed cliques, and she reports the ship's social activities poolside, bridge, lectures, outdoor jacuzzi and cocktail lounges are the best venues for forming friendships. Also, book a table for eight at dinner. Mary re-

ports the very best place to meet passengers is in the jacuzzi (but skip those silly singles' mixers).

Young singles looking for action are almost certain to find it at sea on cruise vessels carrying a greater number of solo passengers in their age group.

Large-capacity passenger ships are best for the singles scene since these vessels carry more people in the 20-40 age group in smaller than usual spaces and offer a better opportunity for being thrown together in a storm. Try Carnival and Royal Caribbean Cruise Line's 2300-passenger vessels on seven-day cruises, among the others that sail from Miami. On ships with 1800+ passengers, there are constant social activities: deck games, parlor games, gambling, water sports, singles parties, fitness and aerobics facilities, not to mention discos that jump till dawn. Personally, I have found that water sports and other special interest activities naturally draw people of all ages into engaging conversation.

SINGLE TRAVEL ARRANGED

Singleworld, specializing in single travel for the 20-45 age group since 1957, has space allotments on a number of mid-priced vessels in the Caribbean and Europe and will arrange shared accommodations, if desired, to keep the cost down. Each Singleworld group has its own cruise director, dines collectively and has special on-board activities and shore excursions. Contact local agents regarding specific Singleworld cruises.

In general, the smaller and more informal the ship, the more people tend to converse and socialize with passengers other than their sailing companion, and people traveling solo in the 50+ age group will find a low-key conviviality conducive to meeting fellow passengers. The ships of Clipper Cruise Line, American Canadian Caribbean Cruises, Alaska Sightseeing/Cruise West and World Explorer Cruises transport those interested in nature and local culture where it's easy to join fellow enthusiasts in the enjoyment of the locale's special treasures. Ships from Windstar, Club Med and Star Clippers are sure bets for meeting people who love to sail from all corners of the world. Special interest programs, such as music and culinary festivals or sports activities, are also wonderful environments for meeting others who share a common bond.

Gentleman Hosts, dashing older men who are part of the cruise director's staff, are popular with single women in the 60+ age group who want a swing around the dance floor or a fourth for bridge. You'll find them aboard *QE 2*, *Sea Goddess I & II*, *Crystal Harmony*

and vessels of Regency Cruises, Royal Cruise Line and Seabourn Cruises.

When it comes to price, however, those traveling alone still get a raw deal from the cruise industry as a whole; the majority of ship lines add surcharges of 50-100 percent above double occupancy per person rates, and on some vessels, there are no single cabins available. Many lines will arrange a roommate share for singles, and the idea of occupying a small cabin with a stranger for a week or so may be acceptable to those who just left college dormitory life, but the concept is untenable to many vacationing solo.

Still, a few cruise companies do have better single rates. Cunard Line, for example, charges 15 percent above its per person, double occupancy rates on select *QE 2* cruises, and you may sail on some of the pricey boutique vessels at a lower single surcharge, including Seven Seas Cruise Line (25 percent), Seabourn Cruise Line (10-25 percent) and Orient Lines (10 percent).

Star Clippers has a guaranteed single occupancy fixed rate nearly equal to the per person, double occupancy standard cabin fare on a space available basis, a very good deal indeed.

AUTHOR'S OBSERVATION

Some of the better cruise-only travel agents may find you an unpublished bargain on a ship that isn't full during non-peak travel periods, so shop around. Ship lines prefer to sail with full cabins, even if it means being quietly flexible on their normal single rate policy.

LOVE AND ROMANCE ON THE HIGH SEAS

While I assumed lasting romance aboard ship happens about as often as it does over the vegetable bin at the local supermarket, I've been proven dead wrong. Moreover, while officers and crew seem to live by the Navy's credo—"It's any 'ole port in the storm"—more than a few serious romances have emerged at sea. For example, an executive of Royal Caribbean Cruise Line suggested his son join him on a cruise to discuss whether the son should break off his engagement to a woman he was ambivalent about marrying. Immediately upon sailing, dad (divorced at the time) suggested they scout out a nice mother and daughter duo during lifeboat drill. The son scored immediately with a dishy blonde and found the love of his life—they are still happily married six years later. In calling executives at cruise companies, there was a distinct "ho-hum" attitude—"oh, yea, my brother (father, cousin, secretary, boss) met his/her spouse on a cruise." Royal Cruise Line's Gentlemen Hosts are a big draw for the 60+ single female passengers; the company let it slip that a few have married their dance floor partners.

Nearly every cruise line has a vow renewal package (Royal Caribbean bakes 27,000 anniversary cakes a year aboard its nine vessels) and it's a cinch to get married aboard nearly any vessel.

TIPS ON FINDING ROMANCE AT SEA

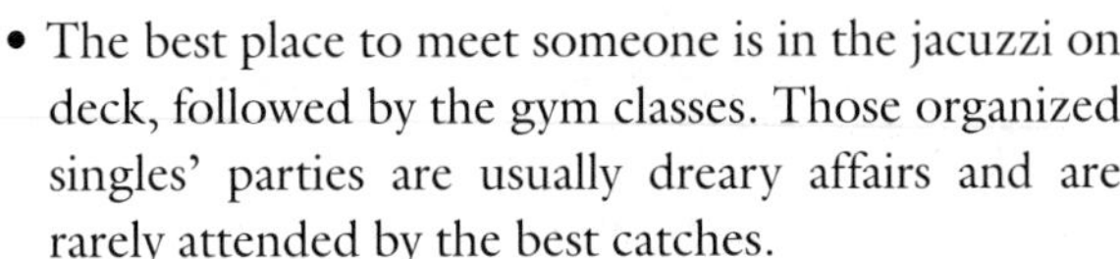

- The best place to meet someone is in the jacuzzi on deck, followed by the gym classes. Those organized singles' parties are usually dreary affairs and are rarely attended by the best catches.
- The most gorgeous single captains can be found aboard Royal Caribbean Cruise Line's *Nordic Empress* (Thomas Wildung, Scandinavian, early 40s), Seabourn's *Seabourn Spirit* (Erik Anderssen, early 50s, Norwegian) and Royal Cruise Line's *Royal Odyssey* (Emmanuel Psarrakis, late 40s, Greek).
- If sailing alone, book a dinner table for eight at second seating, and tell the maitre 'd you want to be seated with other singles.
- In general, when taking the smaller passenger ships and specialized cruises (nature, exotic culture, river, sail) the easier it is to meet people in a natural setting. The ship with the best pickins for men: Quark Expeditions' nuclear-powered icebreakers cruising both polar regions. Men on the prowl will find a wealth of single babes in the 20-40 age group aboard all Carnival ships and RCCL's *Monarch of the Seas*, *Majesty of the Seas* and *Nordic Empress.*
- Wealthy 55+ widows tend to frequent the Crystal Harmony and vessels of Seabourn, Royal Cruise Line and Holland America. Those whose tastes run to the 70+ age groups will find singles of both genders aboard any world cruise.
- Aways carry condoms, just in case. Some ships, such as Carnival, Royal Caribbean and Star Clipper sell them in their sundries shop, but you'll have to visit the infirmary (!!!) to obtain them aboard many vessels, especially those catering to passengers in

the 55+ age range. However, a butler aboard *Crystal Harmony* said he would "of course" deliver a condom to a stateroom at any time of the day or night (one assumes on a silver platter).

- Those seeking a romantic partner who shares a common bond (square dancing, cuisine, jazz, etc.) should check out the "Theme Cruise Calendar;" ask your travel agent to locate tour operators with blocks of cabins for special interest groups—whether you are gay, a retired teacher, or enthusiast of everything from square dancing to penguins, there is a company that has specialty cruises focusing on your interest, age group and lifestyle.

- Attractive single women under 40 will find Greek and Italian staff the most persistent and easy marks if your tastes run to men in uniform. A gay cruise passenger reports every ship holds excellent possibilities for romance.
- Never take a cruise specifically to find the great love of your life—you stand a better chance of it happening when you least expect it. While tales of dashing officers wedding passengers are legion, don't count on it. You stand a much better chance of simply being a replacement for a woman who tearfully waved goodbye as you boarded the ship.
- If it's a toss up between seeing a divorce lawyer or giving the marriage one more chance on a cruise, choose the former option. While ships are definitely romance enhancers for many, spending a week or so in close quarters with someone you can't stand is the pits.

FIELDING'S TOP TEN MOST ROMANTIC CRUISE EXPERIENCES

1. *Star Clipper/Star Flyer* (**Star Clippers**)

These new 180-passenger, 360-foot genuine clipper ships ply the most pristine waters of the Caribbean and Mediterranean. The ride is so calm there is nary a ripple in your champagne, and there is no better place for smooching than beneath the panoramic sky as the sails billow in a gentle breeze. Ages run from 30s to 70s with a range of nation-

alities. So romantic you may fall in love with yourself if nothing else turns up!

2. *Crystal Harmony* (**Crystal Cruises**)

   Modern elegance, outstanding cuisine, secluded private verandahs and more space per passenger than any ship afloat characterize this 960-passenger gem. Perfect for well-heeled burned-out 55+ couples seeking to rekindle a romance in subdued and refined surroundings.

3. **Seabourn Cruise Line**

   Love and money do go hand in hand aboard *Seabourn Pride* and *Seabourn Spirit.* There's plenty of beluga and champagne, dinner dancing and dishy officers, not to mention elegant new and old-monied passengers in tuxes and ball-gowns.

4. *Queen Elizabeth 2* (**Cunard Line**)
   Sail transatlantic between New York and Cherbourg/ Southampton with five glorious days at sea—the orchestra serenades, champagne flows and one can even wrap up in a comfy blanket while sipping bouillon on deck. Avoid the North Atlantic in early spring and late fall, however—seasickness is a definite turn-off.

5. **Windstar Cruises**

   Whether in the Caribbean, Mediterranean or sailing from Tahiti, Windstar's three motorized sail vessels are upscale and tres chic—romantic ports, pampering white-glove attendants and breakfast in bed is de rigeur.

6. **Premiere Selections/Abercrombie & Kent/ French Line/Le Boat**
   What could be cozier than a 10-passenger luxury hotel barge meandering the canals of Champagne or Burgundy. These companies represent the most elegant boats, boasting superb chefs, softly-lit cabins and stops at quaint villages and chateaux.

7. *Meridian/Horizon/Zenith* (**Celebrity Cruises**)
   These mid-priced, mid-sized ships are delightful for 45+ couples needing a break from the kids and everyday stress. Cuisine and service are tops, the decor soothing to the nerves and there are plenty of romantic lounges for cuddling.

8. **The "Love Boats" on Valentine's Day**
   Some 4000 couples renew vows on Princess Cruises' ships

every February 14. I'm told there was nary a dry eye aboard *Regal Princess* this year when Gavin MacLeod ("Captain Stubing") and a minister presided at a deckside ceremony.

9. *Song of Flower* (**Seven Seas Cruise Line**)
Carrying only 196 passengers, this gracious ship boasts subdued elegance, friendly, unpretentious staff and some of the world's best itineraries—the sunset in Borneo or Vietnam can be a real turn-on for many.

10. Crewed Yacht Charters
What could be more sublime than your own personal crewed yacht sailing warm-water ports from the Virgin Islands to the Mediterranean, South Pacific, Madagascar and every place in between. Check The Moorings and Sacks Yacht Charters for the best boats—frequently available for less than the cost of a traditional cruise.

"GET ME TO THE SHIP ON TIME"

Once you've landed that dashing officer, it's only normal to continue the theme by exchanging vows aboard ship. Today, weddings are very big business in the cruise industry and it's a rare cruise line that doesn't have a department to arrange every detail for you, from a wedding ceremony with all the trimmings (including minister) while the ship is in port, followed by a lavish reception (sometimes at sea when the entire guest list sails with the bride and groom). You just show up with the clothes and rings, the cruise company does the rest. Holland America's wedding department even pulled off a full wedding with some 80 guests aboard a ship docked in Los Angeles during the riots. Since a standard shore-side wedding can run from $10,000–$20,000 for the full dog and pony show, not to mention the wear and tear to the bride's parents, having your nuptials aboard ship can be a real bargain—most cruise lines charge a relatively moderate amount for the festivities.

While the majority of couples getting married on a cruise ship are first timers favoring the Miami cruise lines, we came up with a few chic alternatives for those trying matrimony on a second or third go-around in a small but ritzy milieu:

- The Biltmore Hotel in Coral Gables was built in the 1920s and boasts one of the most elegant courtyards in the U.S. After exchanging vows beneath towering stone arches, take a limo to Ft. Lauderdale and join the *Crystal Harmony* for an sybaritic 12-day transit of the Panama Canal.

- Book the owner's suite aboard the romantic *Star Clipper* or *Star Flyer*, elegant authentic clipper ships plying the Caribbean. While passengers are ashore, bring aboard a local minister and have nuptials on deck. (Be sure to invite the 70 staff and crew as witnesses—they'll be thrilled.)

- There's no city in the world more romantic than Venice and CIGA will take care of all the details of your wedding at the Gritti Palace, this city's most sublime hotel. The *Seabourn Pride* has six departures from Venice in 1995, enabling you to maintain the same ambience on a Mediterranean honeymoon cruise.
- Tie in a wedding at the Hotel Meurice in Paris with Cunard's package of a one-way *QE 2* crossing with air on the Concorde in the other direction.
- One can rent lavish private villas on Mustique—a simple ceremony at sunset on the beach followed by a crewed yacht charter is haute romance.

FINDING A TRAVEL AGENT YOU'LL LOVE

AUTHOR'S OBSERVATION

The single most important individual involved in the process of selecting a vacation at sea is a travel agent, and finding an experienced pro who specializes in cruises should be your top priority.

Travel agents book 95 percent of all cruises (in fact, some ship lines won't take direct reservations), have constant feedback about ships and companies from other clients and colleagues, and know what a good deal is and isn't.

Best of all, their services don't cost you a cent (the cruise line pays them a commission) and they are on *your* side as your representative in dealing with the company. Moreover, most people who return from a cruise enraptured with the experience will go again: you will become the loyal client of an agent who steers you right the first time.

The individual travel agent you select will not be the person who so expertly handles your corporate travel (although he or she may steer you towards an excellent cruise specialist). Look for a cruise agent as carefully as you would for a lawyer: a specialist in the affairs to be handled, with substantial experience and an unblemished reputation and who wins most cases.

Cruises have become so popular that a specialized breed of travel agency, the cruise-only agency, has been proliferating in recent years. As their name indicates, these retail outlets sell nothing but cruises and, as specialists, they obviously have to know their product well. However, the retail industry is still dominated by the traditional full-service agency, many of which have designated one or two persons on their staff to be cruise specialists, keeping abreast of all the pricing trends and industry changes and becoming thoroughly knowledgeable in the differences among the many ships available.

AUTHOR'S OBSERVATION

Buy a cruise only from a travel agent who specializes in them. Even if you think you know exactly what you want, the industry is so complicated today and so rapidly changing that it takes an expert who knows what is occurring inside—especially during the present climate of over-capacity and fierce discounting that may lead to more cruise line consolidation.

When selecting a travel agent, look at his or her industry affiliations. Cruise Lines International Association (CLIA), an organization of most cruise companies that sell in North America, has undertaken an extensive travel agency education program in recent years in an effort to keep the retail community as informed as possible about the products of its various member lines and the procedures of passenger handling and ticketing.

You can also find a cruise-only specialist through the National Association of Cruise Only Agencies (NACOA), a group of 1,000 agents nationwide who have continuous training seminars, require frequent ship inspections, have a higher level of industry experience and are also members of CLIA. To obtain a listing of member agencies in your region, send a self-addressed, stamped envelope to: NACOA, *113 W. Sunrise Highway, Suite R, Freeport, New York, 11520,* ☎ *516-378-8006.*

Dorothy Reminick, of Jean Rose Travel in Jupiter, Florida is my idea of another great agent: outspoken, opinionated and feisty, she will grill a client about interest and lifestyle, turn away business before steering someone to the wrong ship, fight like a tiger to get a better price and cabin upgrade, peruse details with the scrutiny of trial lawyer and shoot off a letter of complaint within an hour of hearing from a dissatisfied passenger. Carroll Paige of Carroll Paige Travel in Miami refused to book a major line because of complaints about dining room service (later resuming when hitches were resolved). For frantic clients whose nuptials in Jamaica were cancelled, she once arranged a wedding aboard a ship at the last moment complete with wedding cake from a local baker, and talked her *own* minister into sailing to conduct the service. (A footnote: the minister invited along a member of the congregation, they fell in love aboard ship and later eloped. Sometimes it *is* like "Love Boat" !) In short, a top cruise agent will go way beyond what is required and may get you much more than you pay for.

A personal recommendation is always excellent if the person directing you to an agent he or she adores has similar interests and lifestyle, and you know you'd be happy with the same seagoing experience. For example, the cruise your granddaughter was steered to and loved is probably not what you want.

While technically an agent can sell any vessel, they frequently specialize in certain types of cruises, such as mid-price or deluxe.

Aside from personal recommendations, how do you find a top-flight cruise specialist? Probably the worst way is just walking into any travel agency (like Russian roulette) and settling for whoever you find. Stick with the one who grills you about your personal preferences and lifestyles, openly admits vessels she personally knows or can obtain the real story from a colleague, gives you three or four cruise line brochures to peruse, advises you of all policies of the cruise company, handles documents expertly and advises you about tipping, weather, shore excursions and clothing.

Avoid an agent who tries to push one cruise line over another (it should be your choice, and this indicates the agent is only interested in getting the override, or extra commission paid by a cruise company), talk you into pre-paying shore excursions before departure or if the chemistry just isn't right. This is a service business and you should feel you are in reliable hands.

CHECK THESE ITEMS

You should scrutinize an agency with whom you are about do business and don't personally know:

- How long has the agency been in business (a minimum three years).
- How long has the agent been selling cruises (the longer the better).
- Ask for referrals from other clients.

- Inquire about membership in CLIA and NACOA.
- Check your local Better Business Bureau.

Cheryl Myerson of The Cruise Director in Arvada, Colorado advises steering clear of an agency that will not take your credit card when the cruise line will accept it as payment: this may indicate a cash-flow problem. She also reports that cruises have become the newest hook for scam operators to obtain your money: you receive a postcard stating you've won a prize, call the number listed and are asked for a credit card number. *BEWARE!*

Many cruise agencies do most of their business with four or five ship lines and get prefered rates for their volume of business, passing along the discount to you. They maintain long-standing relationships with the line's sales staff, which can facilitate the resolution of problems and may get you a cabin upgrade. While this is ideal if the ship you want is among those the agent sells, continue looking if the cruise counselor does not have an established rapport with your ship line of choice. On the other hand, the cruise line whose vessels you think you want may have problems (financial, service, sanitation) that the agent knows about.

If you are uncertain about which ship is best for you, discuss your lifestyle and interests with the cruise counselor.

AUTHOR'S OBSERVATION

When an agent recommends a specific vessel, inquire whether he or she is personally familiar with the ship and has booked other clients on it. If so, what was his or her experience? If an agent doesn't personally know the vessel you are interested in , he or she should contact a colleague who is familiar.

Other pertinent information to obtain includes:

- Size, type and age of vessel, passenger demographics (age range, income level).
- On-board atmosphere (lively, low-key).
- Itinerary (specific ports of call, including description and climate; visa and passport requirements).
- Square footage of cabins and location.
- On-board activities and entertainment; number of formal, semi-formal evenings.
- Rates & discounts (including advance booking).
- Specifics of air/sea program, including carrier.

- What's included in the fare?
- Method of payment (credit card or check), amount of deposit, final date of payment.
- Ship line policies on tipping, cancellation, on-board payment of expenses, dining room reservations.
- Special needs (dietary, handicapped, traveling with children, single, honeymoon).
- Transportation between the airport and pier.
- Cost and description of shore excursions, and advice on ports where they are necessary.

AUTHOR'S OBSERVATION

If you do know precisely what vessel you want, it's best to book with a travel agent who has an established professional relationship with the cruise line you choose. If you can't locate one, call the cruise company directly and ask for a local referral. However, don't let the reservation agent talk you into booking directly.

CRUISE INSURANCE

We've all experienced Murphy's Law, and while one hopes for only smooth sailing when taking a vacation at sea, purchasing travel insurance before departure can alleviate worries and help resolve problems, especially these days when so many of the best discounts are offered only in connection with a long-term advance booking and prepayment. While cruise lines offer trip cancellation insurance, NACOA's SafeSale Cruise Protection has additional coverage. For example, cruise company policies generally cover travel cancellation, interruptions or delays and lost baggage; NACOA's includes these features plus missed connections, emergency medical transportation and expenses, as well as accident coverage. SafeSale offers 24-hour hotline help.

A family of two or four are fully covered for $146 when taking a $3000 cruise; single rates for a $2000 voyage are $79. Contact NACOA (address above) or a local member-agent.

HOW MUCH DOES IT COST?

"The captain paid 8 drachmae, sailors and ship's carpenter 5, a skilled labourer paid the same as the captain, 8 ... common-law wives of army men were charged 20, and prostitutes no less than 108."

Passenger Rates From Egypt, A.D. 90
Travel In The Ancient World

Although it's generally true that the cost of the cruise is directly proportional to its length, there is nonetheless a huge variation in prices depending upon the type and quality of the vessel, the remoteness of its itinerary, the level of service on board, cabin size and location and a variety of other factors. To complicate matters further, it depends on when you buy your ticket and who you purchase it from. There is no regulation of rates in the cruise industry and you can easily find two travel agents on the same block quoting different prices for the same ship, date and cabin category!

At one time, a good way to evaluate the relative value of a cruise was to look at the per diem cost; however, don't be misled by the brochure price. Most cruise executives will readily admit that brochure prices have little relation to actual selling prices, except to serve as a standard from which discounts are calculated. For example, when checking per person, per diems for this book, one cruise executive asked if I wanted brochure rates or "reality" rates (in this company's case, the latter was $100 per person, per day lower.) However, specialty ships (many sailboats, expedition vessels, river boats) as well as those catering to special interest groups are usually sold at brochure price.

Over the past few years, cruise lines have come out with new pricing structures that offer a graduated scale of discounts that is steepest several months in advance of sailing and gradually increases to the brochure price by time of departure. You can save as much as 50 percent off brochure rates with these programs. They did this in an effort to re-educate the consumer away from the notion that a better fare will always open up at the last minute. In spite of this effort, however, some cruise lines continue to offer special fire sales as the sailing date approaches; especially popular are two-for-one rates.

AUTHOR'S OBSERVATION

If you do book under an advance purchase plan, be sure to ask your travel agent whether the line will protect you at the lowest available fare if it comes out with a last minute discount that undercuts the price you paid.

For example, some cruise companies state the advance rate is a protected lowest fare, but there may be loopholes: air fare may not be included or certain cabin categories excluded. Still, the advance purchase represents your best bet in saving up to 50 percent off the cruise fare without nail biting last-minute anxiety over space, price and vessel.

Last minute discounting continues, however, and in regions where there is an overcapacity of vessels (the Caribbean, Alaska, Mexico), fare wars start early each year. In 1994, the most expensive ships did the steepest discounting and these "fire sales" weren't in the newspaper—select travel agents got the deals by fax and passed savings along to their clients.

INSIDER'S TIPS ON BARGAIN HUNTING

- Check the yellow pages for travel agents, call those in the best areas and ask to be put on their mailing list—a great way to get inside deals that won't be advertised. If you are only inerested in a specific region, indicate this.
- Use some imagination. With a limited vacation budget you can a) travel aboard a not-so-hot ship you may not enjoy; b) find a great deal on a very good ship with some research; c) move to another type of water-bourne vessel (e.g., river boat, sailboat, expedition vessel); d) travel closer to home in a region that may warrant unexpected historic and natural surprises and e) shorten the duration of the cruise and combine it with a low-cost hotel stay.
- Always consult a cruise specialist, even if you see a newspaper ad discounting your favorite vessel—there are often loopholes in deals and you'll need a pro to explain the unvarnished deal.
- Air fare is often not included in last minute deals, and must be figured into the cost.
- If selecting a last-minute bargain, be prepared to compromise on cabin selection. The most desirable staterooms sell first, as do the lowest and highest categories.
- Fall and Spring positioning cruises (when a vessel moves from one cruising region to another) are frequently heavily discounted and you can sometimes

save 50% or more off vessels that would normally be out of your price range.

- Check local associations. AARP is very active in the cruise business and has wonderful group rates. Other organizations heavily involved in cruises include alumni associations, museums, zoos, horticultural and fine arts (opera,ballet, philharmonic) societies. You may have to pay a small membership fee, but the return can be substantial.

AUTHOR'S OBSERVATION

Travel agents with a large volume of cruise sales constantly receive word of rate cuts directly from the cruise line by fax; these unadvertised specials can be terrific deals! You may be able to sail aboard a vessel you never thought you could afford in an area of the world you never dreamed possible.

Don't jump at the chance to buy a last minute discount just because the price is cheap. Remember what we said before: selecting the right ship and going on an itinerary that satisfies your personal interest are more important than saving a few hundred dollars in terms of the satisfaction you'll derive from the cruise experience.

The most expensive ships did the steepest discounting in 1994 and if persistent, you may be able to procure a better rate or significant cabin upgrade from a cruise counselor who steers a lot of business their way. Contact the cruise companies directly and ask for an agent referral in your region if you know you'll love a vessel and discounts don't seem readily available.

A friend who is one of the best traveled and most savvy shoppers around decides precisely what she wants, visits three agents with her agenda and informs each she'll do business with the one who gives her the best price. She always finds a great deal on some very pricey ships!

AUTHOR'S OBSERVATION

The "hidden costs" of cruising are tips, shore excursions, port charges, on-board expenses (drinking, gambling, beauty parlor, massages and purchases). These are individually explored in the following chapters.

AIR-SEA PACKAGES

Air-sea packages are here to stay and are one of the reasons why the cruise industry is booming. One must remember, however, that unless the flight has been chartered by the ship line, air-sea passengers are at the mercy of the mess that airlines and airports have made over the past decade.

That means crowds, the possibility of delayed flights, lost luggage and the like. The only good news is that your cruise will wait if there are sufficient numbers of passengers delayed and the ship line will join the search for anything lost.

As the number of cruise passengers has grown, those traveling on air/sea packages sometimes find they are stuck with horrendous routing and connections even though the port of embarkation has plenty of non-stops from home. In this instance, cruise lines are at the mercy of the airlines, which determine your route.

TIPS ON HASSLE-FREE AIR TRAVEL

- Ask your travel agent to use the cruise line's "deviation desk," which will make special air arrangements for passengers who want to book specific schedules or airlines in advance—and who are willing to pay a surcharge beyond the normal air-sea price, if one applies, as well as a processing fee that usually runs about $25.
- Cruise executives point out that even though they generally get good deals from airlines for their air-sea programs, they don't always have the lowest air rates, especially when fare wars break out. So ask your agent to check out the option of booking a cruise-only fare and ticketing the air himself; he or she may be able to find a better deal than the cruise line is offering, such as Continental's "Peanut Fares". Continental also offers permanent savings of up to 75 percent off coach fares for U.S. and Caribbean travel to people aged 62 and over.
- You don't earn frequent flyer miles on an air/sea package, and it may be to your advantage to purchase a ticket separately, especially when cruising in far-flung destinations. For example, TWA, which has two daily non-stops between New York and Rome, awards 8,950 miles and frequent flyer mem-

bers can easily upgrade to business class. Don't forget you can always fly for free to your cruise if you have accumulated enough frequent flyer miles.

- Whichever option you choose, it always pays to select a pre-cruise hotel stay. You'll arrive the day before and board refreshed and relaxed.
- If purchasing air independently, check out additional costs such as taxis between the airport and pier (an air/sea package will include these transfers). It may be worthwhile purchasing cruise line transfers, especially in European ports like Rome, where the port is an hour's drive from the city.

When you sit down with your travel counselor to consider a cruise, measure carefully the advantages of all-inclusive air-sea packages. These feature cruise rate, reduced air fare, transfers from airport to ship, all at less than the cost of each component individually. This is certainly a worry-free way to travel, for you are met at the airport and transferred to the cruise vessel without even having to claim your own baggage. (It is transferred separately by the ship's personnel.) You don't have to live in a major metropolis to qualify. Every ship line today must offer convenient air-sea programs to enable anyone living anywhere to come aboard. It is one of the ironies of the travel industry that airlines once put transatlantic liners out of business yet today the two forces have joined to bring passengers to and from ports of embarkation. Air fare is often included in the passage, or a ship line will offer a low-cost add on. You do not have to accept either the included air fare or the add-on, as ship lines make every effort to be fair and offer rebates for those making their own air travel arrangements—persons who want to use frequent flyer award tickets, for instance.

FAMILY FUN AT SEA

During my teenage years, my parents thought it would be a marvelous idea for the whole family to vacation together in Yellowstone National Park. It is a bit of a drive from upstate New York to Wyoming, and furthermore, wouldn't it be fun to rent a trailer? Well, the experience didn't land me in interminable analysis, but the memory remains of the endless driving, battles with my brother (also a teenager), only to arrive and find there was nothing but *trees* and a few scrawny bears. *National Lampoon's Family Vacation* doesn't do it justice!

Some cruise lines take the torture out of family vacations by offering not only supervised activity programs for the kids but, in some cases, entirely separate facilities: clubs, discos, play rooms, computer rooms and so forth. The cheapest way to travel with your kids is to keep them in the same cabin you and your spouse occupy. However, squeezing five, four, or even three people into the same stateroom can make things a bit tight, even for the closest family. As an alternative, you might ask your travel agent to check for specials that feature discounts on the second room for children, frequently available during the summer months when cruise companies cater to families.

In order to get the best advice on traveling with children, I consulted two pros, friends Joan and Mark, who have been vacationing at sea since their kids were infants. (The oldest is now twelve.) Here are some hot tips from years of cruising with the children on a variety of vessels:

- Arrange for dining room seating on the first seating in advance of the cruise, so the kids can eat early and be able to watch the show after dinner. Kids like to participate.
- When you embark, book babysitters for a part of the day each day, so that adults can have some quiet time together.
- Bring plenty of diapers; cruise ships have limited supplies, and you don't want to spend a day in port searching for Pampers.
- Bring along enough games, books, toys for quiet in-cabin down time.
- Attend the kids orientation meeting on the first day, when children meet friends and counselors, to begin planning the week's activities.
- If traveling around an island on your own with children, it is helpful to head for a full-service hotel or resort with beach, rest rooms, and restaurants, so that back-up facilities are available.

AUTHOR'S OBSERVATION

If planning a shore excursion, choose a "child-friendly" tour (i.e., snorkeling, aquariums, submarines, glass bottom boat rides), rather than long bus rides.

They also report that although cruise lines that cater to families have children's menus, it's good to encourage the kids to experiment with cuisine they normally don't eat at home. Son Barry, for example, has always been adventuresome and seems to have developed a sophisticated palate. At age ten, he ordered escargots at dinner; when the waiter asked if this was his favorite food, Barry answered, "No, I prefer frog's legs!"

A cruise-only travel agent is always your best bet when planning a vacation at sea with children, especially in choosing accommodations in which you will all feel comfortable, air arrangements, dining reservations and special requirements. You should also inquire which shore excursions are best for the whole family, and get advice on attractions which are a must-see for kids during your itinerary.

AUTHOR'S OBSERVATION

Families with children from previous marriages must have a notarized letter from the absent parent giving permission for the child to travel–airlines and cruise ships can (and have) denied boarding without this!

BEFORE BOOKING

WHAT TO WEAR

With visions of seascapes and sunsets and dreamy days spent at the rail watching flying fish, not to mention dancing on the moonlit deck, you may wonder if you will need a new wardrobe for your cruise. Unless your closet has nothing but designer jeans, you can probably pack right now and not purchase one new item for shipboard life. Cruise clothes are simply resort clothes, and you'll need the same basic outfits that you wear at home when casual by day and off to cocktails and dinner in the evening. Some cruise vessels require more clothes than others, due to more activities on board and on shore and a greater number of port calls and climate changes. A more formal atmosphere prevails on Cunard's *Royal Viking Sun*, *Sagafjord*, and *Vistafjord* and Seabourn's vessels among others. On the other hand, life aboard the Swan Hellenic vessels and other specialty cruises like Special Expeditions and Star Clippers are very casual at night and hardly dictate black tie or elegant jewels.

For most cruises, you will want very casual and colorful wear during the day; no matter which vessel you choose, everyone wears the same "uniform"—shorts, tee or polo shirt and athletic shoes. One swimsuit and a coverup (for walking through the public rooms and having buffet luncheon on deck), along with a pair of rubber flip-flops are fine for a week's cruise. A pair of sneakers and espadrilles are perfect for walking on deck and sightseeing. (I never take expensive shoes for daytime wear because many of the interesting sites are dusty and the old winding streets in port can be dirty and slippery.) Short-shorts for everyone who looks good in them are perfect for lazy days at sea but are known to offend many inhabitants of host ports. In general, you should dress moderately on shore and save the strutting for the pleasure of your fellow passengers. In some ports, such as Rio, Naples and St. Peterburg, thievery is serious, and the cruise staff will advise you to leave all jewelry behind and dress as modestly as possible.

Many cruise ships request that male passengers wear a coat and tie in public rooms after 6 p.m., so if this is not your style you should find another cruise vessel. For women, the evening is time for high heels, silk blouses and romantic long skirts. Being on a cruise means getting dressed up almost every night on some ships. The first and last evenings spent on board are always casual—the first because you are probably tired from traveling, and the last because your suitcase is usually already packed and you dine in your onward-bound clothes. Generally, on a 7-day cruise, two nights will be formal, and on a 14-day sailing four nights will require party clothes. Most cruise brochures describe suggested attire.

AUTHOR'S OBSERVATION

Research the climate of the region you'll be visiting (most newspapers list temperature and rainfall in foreign cities). Despite the attire depicted in the brochures, in Alaska you'll undoubtedly find rain (Ketchikan is one of the wettest places in the world) and on a Baltic Sea cruise, you may never wear shorts once, even in August. In the Far East, be prepared for high humidity and bring light cotton, while the Greek Islands and Southern Mediterranean are usually blisteringly hot in August.

Just how formal you wish to be depends upon your taste, the ambience on board your vessel and the itinerary. Many cruise line spokespeople say that the night life in the Caribbean demands black tie or a dark suit at the Captain's parties. The reason: with many more days at sea in the Caribbean, passengers have plenty of time to primp; when islands are very close together, everyone is just too exhausted from visiting a port (and sometimes two) every day.

Your shipboard clothing should be fun to wear and should more or less take care of itself. Many vessels offer dry cleaning services, but most now also include self-service laundry facilities on board. (Salt air can cause many lovely fabrics to become limp and lifeless on board.) Silk or synthetic blouses are best, with a variety of pants and skirts to mix and match. You may want a simple but colorful gown for the captain's party and the traditional photo of your meeting with the master of the vessel. For a seven-day cruise, I take four outfits for the evening (which is far too many, but I like the feeling of choice).

AUTHOR'S OBSERVATION

I've noticed about half the men opt for a dark suit in lieu of a tuxedo on formal nights, even aboard the ritzier ships. While women still tend to get decked out, it's unnecessary to purchase a formal gown you'll only wear once. If you can't borrow something, dress up a long skirt with a dressy blouse and lots of glittery costume jewelry.

No matter in what sunny part of the world your ship is sailing, always pack enough sweaters and wraps for the air conditioning on board (it's freezing on most ships), the breezy evenings on deck and the early arrivals in port. You just never know and it's terrible to be clothed in nothing but filmy see-throughs. Along with an extra pullover, bring some inexpensive and lightweight rain gear such as a water-proof poncho or folding umbrella. Spring and fall are unpredictable the world over and my closet is full of umbrellas bought on vacations because I forgot to pack one. When you arrive in port, the purser will announce the weather forecast, as well as the present temperature. However, a comfortable-sounding temperature can be either warm or cool, depending upon wind and clouds and your tour bus may be air-conditioned, so always take an extra sweater.

AUTHOR'S OBSERVATION

If planning a winter cruise in the Caribbean, purchase bathing suits, cover-ups and sandles in summer. Away from warm climates they are impossible to find after September and you'll pay top dollar aboard ship and in port.

The best way to decide what to wear is to study the cruise news, the daily activity sheet slipped under your door during the night. It will suggest proper dress for shore excursions, as well as for the evening. If you're just beach-bound, you'll know what to wear; but you may need a windbreaker for an open boat ride across the bay.

SHIPBOARD FACILITIES

***Graceful sculpture adorns the pool aboard* Statendam.**

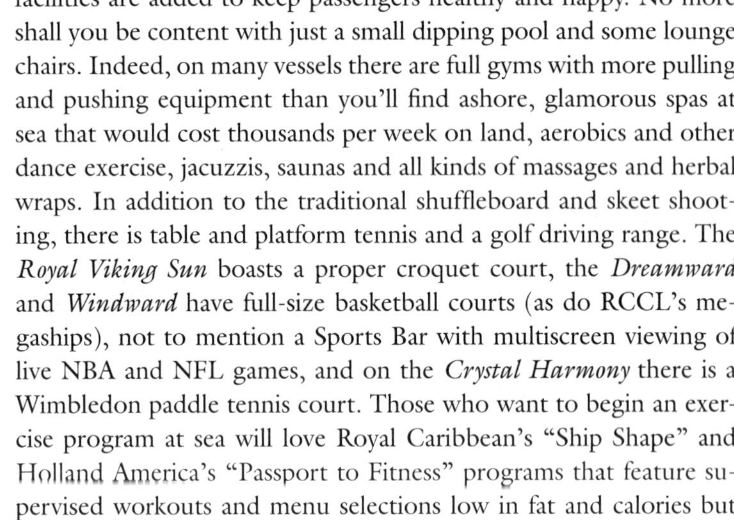

Cruise ships have truly become floating resorts, as more and more facilities are added to keep passengers healthy and happy. No more shall you be content with just a small dipping pool and some lounge chairs.  Indeed, on many vessels there are full gyms with more pulling and pushing equipment than you'll find ashore, glamorous spas at sea that would cost thousands per week on land, aerobics and other dance exercise, jacuzzis, saunas and all kinds of massages and herbal wraps. In addition to the traditional shuffleboard and skeet shooting, there is table and platform tennis and a golf driving range. The *Royal Viking Sun* boasts a proper croquet court, the *Dreamward* and *Windward* have full-size basketball courts (as do RCCL's megaships), not to mention a Sports Bar with multiscreen viewing of live NBA and NFL games,  and on the *Crystal Harmony* there is a Wimbledon paddle tennis court. Those who want to begin an exercise program at sea will love Royal Caribbean's "Ship Shape" and Holland America's "Passport to Fitness" programs that feature supervised workouts and menu selections low in fat and calories but rich in taste. On a recent cruise aboard Royal Cruise Line's *Crown Odyssey*, it seemed that everyone was engaged in some fitness program on deck during days at sea.

AUTHOR'S OBSERVATION

In general, the size of on-board health and fitness facilities and the variety of equipment tend to be directly proportional to the size of the ship. A serious fanatic considering a trip on an 800-passenger or smaller ship should inquire about what exactly is available in the so-called fitness center.

Joggers are found aboard nearly every ship these days and large vessels built in the past few years design running tracks just for passengers. One cannot run a marathon at sea, but several miles are possible. Most vessels make it easy for runners and post the number of laps around deck that make a mile. If you always run at 6:00 a.m., keep in mind that joggers are often requested to refrain from running until a reasonable hour, because there may be fellow passengers asleep underneath that thump, thump, thump. (Find a mega-ship with a separate running promenade if you can't bear to delay your jog a few hours.) If you prefer running in port, visit the local tourist office for a map and a good route. Running has become so popular all over the world, you will undoubtedly be in good company wherever the ship docks.

AUTHOR'S OBSERVATION

Joggers should inquire if the jogging track is all on one level and is relatively unimpeded by stairways, support pillars or other superstructure as may be the case on smaller ships.

Water and underwater activities are very popular on cruises in the Bahamas, Caribbean, Hawaii, South Pacific, Bermuda during the season and along both Mexican coastlines. Indeed, the beaches on some islands surpass any other attraction and passengers can delight in this fantastic underwater world along specified trails or on their own. Most ships can arrange this ashore, but first-timers are encouraged to attend classes in the ship's pool with a qualified instructor before they're allowed to take out the gear. The Caribbean is perfect for snorkeling, but if you're a real addict and want to dive in every port, be sure your cruise ship calls at St. Thomas, St. Croix, the Cayman Islands, Barbados, Belize, Cozumel, Nassau and Freeport, or even in Atlantic-bound Bermuda. You can also rent Sunfish in most of these (and other) ports, have a quick turn around the bay on water skis and do a little fishing.

The new and smaller vessels now carry their beaches and water sports with them. For example, Wind Star, Sea Goddess, and Seabourn vessels all boast aft platforms that descend into the sea so passengers can swim, waterski, windsurf, snorkel and the like from the safety of the ship. There is always someone on duty to watch over you and plenty of companions with whom to swim or snorkel. It's the closest thing to being a turtle, i.e., carrying your house and toys with you, that I have yet experienced!

Parasailing has become another addiction along beautiful beaches although it is not for everyone. On a recent Acapulco stop, however, the price was reasonable and well worth the experience! Alternatively, passengers who feel more comfortable in fresh-water pools may always head for a famous resort in port and have lunch and a dip. Cruise passengers have the best of both worlds!

AUTHOR'S OBSERVATION

Review ships recommended for water sports, golf and fitness in "The Best of 1995." These are selected not only by vessel, but also itinerary that offers the most opportunities for your passion.

Cruises are definitely a family affair today, so bring the young ones along. Many ship lines, such as the vessels of Carnival, Royal Caribbean, Norwegian Cruise Line, Celebrity and Premiere, have such extensive facilities for children of all ages that it is possible to park your offspring from after breakfast until dinnertime and everyone seems the happier for it! Youngsters have private club houses, coketail parties, separate menus and tours of the bridge while teens can dance in their own discos on some ships, play video games and take computer classes while you relax and enjoy your own colleagues. The *QE 2* hires proper nannies for the wee ones and offers cribs and playpens, and you'll frequently find ship's staff available to babysit on other vessels.

Take the plunge with Princess Cruises' onboard scuba diving program.

On the other hand, you'll want a ship with a sufficient number of quiet areas and lounges. The library is a good place to start, both for browsing through periodicals or for finding some light reading matter. If you wish to catch up on your correspondence, there is generally a good writing room (the Princess Grace room on the *Constitution* is perfectly lovely and a tasteful memorial). Bridge and backgammon aficionados will want to find the card room as quickly as possible and the social hostess will set up some good competition. Check out the public areas and cocktail lounges for nonsmoking areas, which are increasingly demanded by health-conscious passengers.

The list of activities on board can tire even the hardiest souls! Lectures abound all day long: financial advice, photography tips, graphoanalysis, fashion parades, wine tastings, cooking demonstrations, navigator talks and so it goes. Bingo, masquerade parties, handicraft clinics, feature films, horse racing, grandmothers teas (bring photos of the little ones), Rotary, AA and other organizations, as well as religious services are all featured on the daily programs.

However, if you intend to do nothing of the above but find a nice bar stool that is also fine. There are plenty of watering holes aboard a cruise ship and you will discover a favorite spot in no time. If you are a serious gambler, be sure your vessel has a full casino or you will be frustrated by a few slot machines tucked away in a dark corner. Some ship lines, like Carnival and Royal Caribbean, emphasize gambling although I noticed that even a tiny establishment, as on *Wind Song*, was good fun with good company.

SHIP SANITATION

Ship sanitation is sometimes a pain in the neck, but it is here to stay, and sometimes we're all better off for it. While one cruise ship suffered an outbreak of Legionnaires' Disease last year, it was not a result of sanitation and could have happened anywhere. Since July, 1975, after some serious intestinal outbreaks aboard cruise vessels, the Atlanta-based CDC instituted a federally funded program to ensure periodic inspections of all cruise ships calling in U.S. ports. A biweekly summary of these sanitation inspections is released and copies sent to anyone who wishes to read the results. Although ships are now graded (86 is passing) and many do not make the required amount, any score in the 80s or above should be considered adequate. There are some very low scores on the list, which I would tend to worry about. However, even the best ships get a below passing score from time to time and this may not reflect sanitary conditions at all. Sometimes CDC gives low marks because equipment or counter tops should be replaced and the following week the vessel receives a high score.

The inspection program has served a good purpose and you stand no more chance of getting an intestinal disorder than you do at any good hotel. An instance of illness aboard ship must be reported within 24 hours of arrival at U.S. ports. Everyone is aware of the necessity of sanitation these days and the kitchens of many vessels look like operating rooms. If you are interested in learning the score of a vessel you may sail aboard, contact: Chief, Vessel Sanitation Program, 1015 North America Way, Room 107, Miami, FL 33132.

BOOKING YOUR CABIN

"All the third-class passengers must gather up their luggage and go to the after part of the hurricane deck. All were busy collecting their luggage and preparing to go. Why do they want us to clear off this deck? We are getting on so well here. They want the space for two hundred bulls, to be taken aboard at Payta."

Bishop William Taylor, 1895.

Alas, the days are gone when you can study a deck plan and decide exactly which cabin you desire. Most ship lines today will only guarantee a cabin in the category you choose unless you insist upon the top suite and will settle for nothing less. The variations in your cruise fare will depend on the category of cabin you select, and since it can be complicated to decipher size, location and amenities, a travel agent who's a cruise specialist is invaluable.

Moreover, when weighing the pros and cons of one ship over another, the square footage of cabin size should be factored. It's no longer true that those who pay more will necessarily get a larger cabin. For example, Regency Cruises is frequented by budget-conscious travelers, but as the former grand transatlantic liners *Statendam* and *Gripsholm*, the *Regent Star* and *Regent Sea* have enormous staterooms by today's standards. Deluxe staterooms with verandas were added during a refurbishment of the *Norway* (the former *France*) but are smaller than the former first-class staterooms four price categories lower. While the ships of Carnival's fleet are in the budget end of the cruise industry, standard outside cabins on the newer vessels are 190 square feet, larger than is found on some vessels charging much higher rates.

AUTHOR'S OBSERVATION

Staterooms are measured in square feet, which is frequently not listed in the cruise brochure. And, keep in mind that the cabin size also includes beds, dressers, chairs, tables and nightstand.

The good news is: no matter what category your purse can handle, you and all other cruise passengers will enjoy the same facilities, food, activities, entertainment and get the same photo taken with the Captain. There may be some difference in cabin service but most cruise vessels have crew that serve all passengers equally and with the same happy face.

If you plan to use your cabin only to sleep and change your clothes, or share it with another single traveler, then by all means choose the lowest category and spend all your time out on the deck. However, if you and your spouse or companion plan to frequent the cabin or expect to entertain newfound friends, then spend a little more and book a larger, outside cabin that you will enjoy every minute. Request a cabin midships where the ride is certainly smoother if you're prone to motion sickness. It's also better to be midway between the upper and lower deck, especially on transatlantic crossings that may be stormy. Deluxe outside cabins on many new vessels today have outside balconies or floor-to-ceiling windows, while large picture windows are found in standard categories (the older ships still have port holes.) With the advent of air conditioning, inside cabins became comparable to those with a sea view (except for knowing what the weather is like).

But whatever your category, unless you have booked a lovely and very expensive suite, don't be shocked to find that your cabin is smaller than your kitchen (150 to 190 square feet is the norm in standard outside staterooms on mid-priced ships and some are smaller). Brochures are often misleading; the lovely cabins in their photographs are frequently in the more expensive categories and standard staterooms are made to appear more spacious with a wide-angle lens.

Lack of space in most cabins seems to have come full circle since the days of Charles Dickens. Dickens sailed to Boston in 1842 aboard the *Britannia* and was surprised to find his deluxe stateroom for three only a little larger than a closet. Dickens and his cabin mates agreed that their accommodation was indeed quite spacious, especially if they all turned around in unison!

AUTHOR'S OBSERVATION

You may pay a premium rate for an outside cabin only to find the view of a life boat or even worse, a stateroom located on a promenade deck, where joggers and late-night revelers can disturb sleep. A few deck plans indicate "obstructed view" (translate: a lifeboat is outside your window), but most forget to mention this feature in brochures. Your travel agent can tell by the deck plan layout.

You should be aware that some deluxe cabins on the *Sagafjord*, *Vistafjord* and *Norway*, for example have wonderful views of lifeboats; passengers in these cabins complain mightily, and some even try to transfer to lower deck.

When choosing a cabin, no matter what category, consider your habits. If you are in bed by 9 p.m., stay away from the disco (which doesn't begin popping until 10:30 every night). If walking is a problem, select a cabin near one of the elevators. Do you need a bathtub? Will a shower do just as well? Some showers are so small that if you drop the soap you've had it. Do you need extra space to work; does the cabin have a telephone; do you wish to have a great deal of privacy?

Of course, if you're purchasing a last-minute bargain there may be no choice, and it is usually unimportant on a three- or four-day escape, when a minimal amount of time is spent in a cabin. Personally, I would select a good-size inside stateroom at lower cost rather than an outside promenade-deck cabin with joggers or a parade of people from dawn until the wee hours of the morning disrupting my sleep and peace of mind.

Most newer vessels have sitting areas in all categories and beds that can be converted to queen size, but be sure to indicate your preference before departure. For example, I found suites on Royal Cruise

Line's *Crown Odyssey* that had single beds bolted to the floor; those set on a queen-size bed would have to change cabin category. Moreover, private verandas are found today on many new ships, but they come at a premium, so estimate how much time you'll actually use this lovely amenity. For example, on a one-week sailing, when five or six days are spent in port, you may have breakfast served on the balcony once or twice plus cocktails before dinner: a few hours use of this delightful feature may not warrant the extra cost. However, on longer voyages it is heavenly to recline on a chaise longue with a good book aboard your personal balcony overlooking the ocean, the sounds of the sea lulling your senses into sublime relaxation.

The enjoyment of your cruise experience does not necessarily depend upon the size of your cabin. I heard about a Norwegian family of four in a standard *Sovereign of the Seas* cabin (minuscule) and they were having a wonderful time! Even on *Sea Goddess I* and *II*, the cabin size does not match the per diem; Cunard does offer suites for those who wish to pay double for greater comfort.

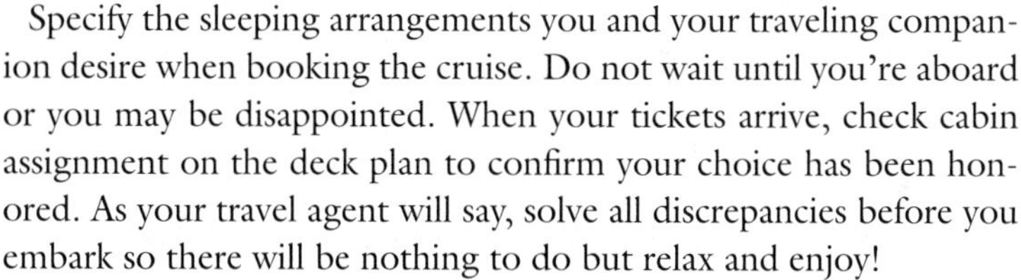

Specify the sleeping arrangements you and your traveling companion desire when booking the cruise. Do not wait until you're aboard or you may be disappointed. When your tickets arrive, check cabin assignment on the deck plan to confirm your choice has been honored. As your travel agent will say, solve all discrepancies before you embark so there will be nothing to do but relax and enjoy!

AUTHOR'S OBSERVATION

If you really can't stand your cabin (noisy neighbors, vibration from the engines on the lowest deck, joggers jarring you awake at 6 a.m.), contact the purser and asked to be moved.

Cruise staff usually try to accommodate a dissatisfied passenger with a reasonable complaint, and unless the ship is completely full, a request, if polite and valid, will most likely wind you up in better accommodations.

DINING ROOM RESERVATIONS

Dinner seating arrangements can be made by your travel agent when booking a ship with two dinner seatings; also specify your table preference (two, four or eight seats). The second seating tends to be most popular, except on vessels with a large number of families. While ship lines try to accommodate everyone, your reservation is rarely, if ever, guaranteed before embarkation. Ask your travel agent to send a request by fax to the cruise line with a copy for you. It carries more weight and at least you'll be assured your cruise counselor did his or her best.

AUTHOR'S OBSERVATION

One of my biggest gripes with most cruise lines is their refusal to confirm dining room reservations prior to departure even for those booking many months in advance. And unfortunately, lately it has become commonplace for experienced cruisers to tip the maitre'd or person confirming reservations at boarding to ensure they get the seating they prefer, even on the finest vessels a practice that is simply appalling. As one exasperated travel agent remarked, "We can put a man on the moon, but cruise lines can't seem to manage this one simple procedure!" Furthermore, many cruise ships (Princess Cruises' "Love Boats," for example) do not have tables for two; those who are set on this table configuration, especially honeymooners, may want to consider bypassing a vessel offering only tables for four or more. Remember, dining is a major event on board a ship and you should expect to be completely satisfied with the arrangements.

PRE-DEPARTURE RESERVATIONS

If you must have your hair fashioned before a formal evening, when shipboard beauticians are the busiest, ask your cruise counselor to book a salon appointment before departure. Massages are fashionable during days at sea and bookings fill quickly, so a pre-departure reservation will guarantee your preferred time of day. You can always cancel if you change your mind. But double check as soon as you board since pre-departure reservations don't always reach the ship.

PRE-PAYING SHORE EXCURSIONS

Keep in mind that shore excursions are a profit area for all cruise ships and you may feel pressured to purchase shore excursions during port briefings and through constant reminders in the daily program. Today, however, several lines are applying pressure to book before departure, a policy I dislike. The reasoning they use is that the best excursions book quickly, and it's easier to have it all arranged and paid for before departure. Last summer, friends sailing on a Baltic cruise received a high pressure sales pitch from the cruise line via direct mail extolling the need to pre-pay tours in every port. Fortunately, their travel agent knew they weren't necessary in three out of four ports of call (Copenhagen, Stockholm, and Helsinki were enjoyed on foot; St. Petersburg required a half-day tour). Moreover,

some cruise lines offer travel agents commissions on shore excursions they sell before departure—change agents if you feel pressured.

I deplore unsound pressure to purchase a shore excursion everywhere. In so many ports, the best sightseeing is frequently within walking distance of the ship. And, a cruise will be less than relaxing if you decide to spend hours each day on a bus puttering along bumpy roads! Granted, in many foreign countries (especially the Far East), tours add greatly to the enjoyment of the journey since the highlights are a distance from the ship. But getting away from the hordes on the buses, who are paying $30-100 per port to visit sites you may enjoy more on your own, can result in wonderful experience ashore.

AUTHOR'S OBSERVATION

You'll rarely need a shore excursion in the Caribbean and many European ports. Consult the tourist offices of the countries on your itinerary for lists of local sightseeing and city/port maps. Moreover, in most instances two couples can hire a taxi for the day with a negotiated flat rate and tour comfortably on their own for less than the price of an organized shore tour!

However, sometimes out-of-the-ordinary experiences are only available with a short excursion. Princess Cruises, for example, has land tours of the Caribbean led by local professional photographers for those who favor more than snapshots. Those aboard *Song of Flower* will find some very creative ventures ashore, such as visits to Bulgarian families and a private cooking class with the Hotel de Paris chef in Monte Carlo. If you have only a few hours in Rome, it's better to take a ship sightseeing excursion than try to get around on your own. And, some places are dangerous. For example, you are taking a real risk if you venture anywhere alone in Rio.

TIPPING

Tipping is like dust—it just never goes away. According to the hotel manager aboard *QE 2*, a *tip* derives from the habit of British businessmen paying a gratuity "To Insure Promptness" when giving letters to stagecoach drivers for delivery at the next stop. Today, it is also offered as a thank-you for services rendered. Some lines, like Holland America, have a "No Tipping Required" policy, but passengers do tip for the delightful service rendered.

On many of the new and higher-priced ships (Cunard's *Sea Goddess I* and *II*, Silver Sea Cruises, Seabourn Cruise Line and Seven Seas Cruise Line), a no-tipping permitted policy is in effect. However, on almost all cruise ships, tipping is expected, so add gratuities to your cruise budget well in advance. The good news is that many ship lines will accept credit cards (even personal checks) for tips. This is especially true on the Greek vessels, because it is mandatory to tip in bulk at the end of the cruise. The entire amount is then distributed to all members of the crew including those left behind the scenes.

Gratuities should be rendered to the cabin stewards or stewardesses, dining room stewards, wine steward, and bar. For wine and drinks, the usual 15 percent is acceptable. If you make arrangements to charge your wine and drinks, the ship line will often add the gratuity for you—a saving grace. For the cabin and dining room personnel, the cruise director will offer a suggested per passenger daily amount, which will average around $10 per person.

With a total of $7 to $9 per day, you are offering your cabin and dining room stewards about $3 each and the busboy between $1 and $1.50. Some ships suggest more, some less. It depends very much upon the ambience aboard and the nationality of the service crew. These amounts have not risen much in the past few years—more good news!

Although ship lines pay their service crew a pittance and expect the passengers to make up the rest, I consider tipping a very personal matter and wait until the final day to make any decision about amounts. It depends primarily on how efficient the service was, how genuine, and how much I prevailed on the crew for special favors (breakfast in bed, ice, more clean towels than usual, etc.). However, there are some ships where I know the service will be superb, and I am always prepared for tipping generously.

Consider gratuities to the crew as money well spent if you have enjoyed yourself and are disembarking with many happy memories. Above all, do not offer tips to officers or cruise directors. They have done their job only if your cruise was the best vacation ever. If you feel they have acted beyond the call of duty, commend them by letter to the ship line. Perhaps you will find your favorite first officer as a captain someday.

AUTHOR'S OBSERVATION

If traveling aboard a specialty ship in a foreign country, ask your travel agent to inquire with the cruise line about tipping. I've heard tales where staff on a European hotel barge suggested ten percent of the cruise fare at the end of the voyage (up to $300 per person!).

The Star Flyer *offers both Caribbean and Mediterranean itineraries.*

ANCHORS AWAY

"Of the gladdest moments in human lilfe, methinks, is the departure upon a distant journey to unknown lands. Shaking off with one mighty effort the fetters of habit, the leaden weight of routine, the cloak of many cares, and the slavery of home, many feel once more happy. The blood flows with the fast circulation of childhood ..."

Sir Richard Burton, 1856

When the cruise tickets arrive in the mail, you know you're on the way! It's a marvelous feeling just to grasp them and consider lazy days at sea, lunch on deck, adventuresome foods, personalized service, new ports and new friends. Not to disturb the reverie, but in order to increase the odds your cruise will be problem-free, several key items should be reviewed before departure.

CHECK ALL DOCUMENTS

An important part of your cruise counselor's job is to inspect all documents before delivering them to you, but you should double-check all details yourself. Since many ship lines do not assign cabins when you book but instead guarantee a certain category (and rate), check to see that the cabin number on your ticket coincides with the category you paid for (occasionally, it will even be a grade higher). Also, make sure the name of the ship is correct. Norwegian Cruise Line officials claim that many passengers who arrive for embarkation in Miami are not even aware what vessel they have booked, so don't laugh at this suggestion.

CRUISE CONTRACT

Read the passage contract carefully, for it details the ship owner's liability and cancellation charges. Ideally you have already asked about cancellation policies prior to making the deposit and bought travel insurance to protect against any last minute change of plans. The fine print in the brochure that you should always peruse closely before booking and in the passage contract specify that if you cannot use the ticket and do not give notice to the company within sixty days of departure, charges are levied (unless the space is immediately sold). If you decide not to sail less than five days before embarkation, the total fare may be forfeit unless the ship line is sympathetic to the calamitous happenings that prevent your traveling. In this instance, a top cruise counselor may be able to work miracles. However, once you embark and begin your cruise (and then get sick or whatever), there is no recompense. If the ship line must cancel, however, you will probably receive a full refund. This contract also states the cruise fare (with all inclusions), procedures describing how to settle your account for purchases on board, luggage restrictions, policy regarding cabin changes, instructions to safeguard valuables and a caution against carrying goods of a dangerous nature. These items are all detailed on, or along with, your ticket, in hope that no misunderstanding between passenger and ship operator will cause a future problem.

AUTHOR'S OBSERVATION

Never pack your tickets, passport, or any important items in your luggage-bags go astray; when traveling on an air/sea package they are delivered straight to your cabin from the airport. You will go through pre-embarkation on the pier and need your cruise ticket to board. (If you do pack them, things will be straightened out eventually, but with great delay.)

BAGGAGE TAGS

Baggage tags will accompany your tickets and you should transfer the information on your ticket to that required on the tags. Some lines have color-coded tags so porters will immediately recognize in which section of the ship your bags should be placed. If you're traveling on an air-sea program and are met at the airport for transfer to the vessel, you will probably be requested to tag your bags with the ship's labels before you check them at the airport. This enables the ship line personnel to claim your bags upon your flight's arrival and transport them to the ship. (Most companies send all baggage in bond straight to the ship, eliminating customs inspection.) If you neglect to follow these instructions, your cruise wardrobe may just sit in the baggage claim area until you begin to wonder why your cabin is so empty.

AUTHOR'S OBSERVATION

If you worry, as I do, about luggage not showing up on the ship after a connecting flight, go to the claim area and spot check your bags to make sure they didn't get lost in transit before being loaded on the bus.

Alternatively, if you fly into the city of embarkation on your own and did not follow thc instructions sent to you (and tagged your bags too soon), your cruise wardrobe will be sent straight to the ship while you run around the airport with visions of sailing away naked. Of course, bags do get authentically lost. If this happens to you, inform both the airline and the ship line at once, and don't leave the airport without filing a claim form and leaving your cruise itinerary (ports of call in order of appearance).

AUTHOR'S COMMENT

One big advantage of an air-sea program is that the cruise company has a contract with the airline, which must track your bags and deliver them to the next port. Furthermore, if bags are delayed, some cruise lines will give you an on-board credit for incidentals (Royal Caribbean Cruise Line's credit is $200).

PRE-DEPARTURE CHECK LIST

Here are items that you may want to double check:

- Cruise and Airline Tickets
- Credit Cards and Travelers Checks
- Driver's License and Photo I.D.
- Passport and/or Visas (if required)
- Information on Getting to Ship Terminal
- Address Book (for sending post cards)
- Business Cards (for meeting new friends)
- Camera and Extra Film (I take twice what I think I'll need)
- Travel Alarm Clock
- A Book (for the flight and reading on deck)

- Prescription Medication
- Aspirin, Alka-Seltzer and Suntan Lotion (to avoid high charges in ship's boutique.)
- Eyeglasses, Sunglasses
- Detailed Guide Book on the Region (Fielding's, of course)
- Toiletries
- Clothing (see "What to Wear")
- Shoes

LUGGAGE

Luggage can easily become a problem if you're not careful. Few of us can afford to rent the cabin next door just for our bags! One average-size suitcase and one carry-on bag should be sufficient for the normal seven-day cruise, especially if you plan to be casual by day. If your spouse or companion prefers a fold-over bag, all the better; you can sneak in a few garments. Ships were once famous for the huge amounts of baggage they could accommodate. No longer. Space is at a premium on most of today's cruise vessels. So just bring along what you can comfortably put in your cabin, either under the bed or in the wardrobe areas, because you don't want to fall over a suitcase every time you open the door. On ships offering longer cruises (more than a month or so), and most of the deluxe vessels, a proper baggage room for storage may exist. (Your cruise counselor can check this for you.)

AUTHOR'S OBSERVATION

Clothing will arrive wrinkle-free (I promise) if items are individually hung on hangers in dry cleaner's plastic bags and laid flat in the suitcase. I have rarely sailed on a ship that had enough hangers in the closets for a normal amount of clothing, so extras are a real plus.

IMMUNIZATION AND DOCUMENTS

If your cruise is confined to Caribbean, Mexico, Alaskan or European waters, you probably will not need any immunizations. But if you are sailing for the Far East, South America or Africa, be aware of requirements for smallpox, cholera, typhoid, tetanus, hepatitis and even yellow fever imposed by some of the countries your ship will visit. If you cruise within the Galapagos Islands and certain other parts of South America or along the African coastline, your doctor may advise that you take malaria-prevention medicine before and after your journey. Be sure your cruise counselor checks each country's requirement *before* you sail so that your own doctor can administer the immunization and your arms will return to normal before embarkation.

AUTHOR'S OBSERVATION

The Center for Disease Control has a new automated fax service that provides health warnings in foreign countries and immunization requirements. From a fax, call ☎ 404-332-4565, push 220022 for regional listings, or 000005 for the general directory.

You do not need a passport or visas for Caribbean, Alaska or Canadian cruises, but you must carry some proof of citizenship (voter's registration, birth certificate, or passport). Your cruise counselor should advise you of any visas necessary for the ports of call and will help you obtain them from the appropriate consulates.

AUTHOR'S OBSERVATION

When traveling to exotic locales always start the visa process as soon as you book—delays do occur, especially when dealing with consulates of some developing nations.

MONEY

All cruise lines today accept credit cards as well as cash/traveler's checks for final payment of on-board expenses. Cruises today are virtually cashless, and you will be asked to sign for everything, so you will be asked for a credit card imprint or cash deposit at the purser's office upon embarkation. Your on-board expenses include wine, drinks, masseuse, shore excursions and possibly boutique purchases. The purser's office often will convert your dollars into local currency at certain hours if the supply on board is adequate. But this is not a bank and the purser and his staff cannot reconvert your local currency into dollars. (So don't ask; they often get mad.) If the port officials are friendly and obliging, they will frequently allow a representative of a local bank to come aboard for several hours to handle passengers monetary transactions. This helpful courtesy saves much valuable time in port, so be properly grateful when it occurs.

AUTHOR'S OBSERVATION

In some foreign countries (such as Russia and Brazil), you can't convert local currency back into dollars, so always ask before you hand over dollars or travelers checks. Change a small amount and get more ashore at local banks or exchange bureaus if you need it. See "Shopping" regarding purchases in foreign countries.

ELECTRICAL APPLIANCES

Nearly all vessels built in the past few years have hair dryers in cabins, but if you are sailing on an older vessel, you may want to check if yours will work in the cabin. Most ship lines have the correct electrical fixture in the bathroom, but on some older vessels they may not function. If you travel with children, many vessels now have self-laundry/ironing rooms by popular demand. Although all ships offer laundry and pressing services, it is nice to know one can press out a crease quickly, if necessary. The newer vessels also offer dry cleaning services at reasonable cost.

EMBARKING

When it's embarkation time and you know that your cruise ship will be returning to the same terminal, be observant. The departure is usually a blur and the returning a hassle, but if you have memorized the terminal's layout and know where you parked your car or where the nearest taxi service is, your exit will be smooth.

For a 4:30 p.m. sailing, most ships begin embarkation around 1:30 p.m. If you embark on your own, do it early so you can relax and enjoy the getting underway. Lines of passengers waiting on the pier to get documents checked before boarding the ship seem unbearably long, especially in Miami, where a half-dozen ships depart at the same time. If you are arriving with luggage, local stevedores will carry your baggage onto the vessel and you will not see it again until it appears in the cabin. If you carry expensive camera equipment or a great deal of jewelry, stop by the customs office in port and declare your valuables prior to leaving the country. This saves considerable time and embarrassment upon return.

Once up the gangway, you will meet a steward who will show you the location of your cabin and introduce you to the cabin attendant. Since the Gulf War, ports still maintain airport-type security, and guests are not allowed to board, so large Bon Voyage parties are a thing of the past. But if you are sailing with friends and want a festive send-off with hors d'oeuvres or petits fours before departure, make arrangements in advance, since the crew is so busy at this time.

AUTHOR'S OBSERVATION

Upon boarding, dash to the dining room to confirm dining requests with the maitre'd and confirm your desired seating. Despite reserving this ashore, foul-ups do occur and one is most likely to get it corrected if done right away.

Plan to embark early enough to explore your new home, unpack at leisure, check out the pool area and deck chair situation, or even plot which side of the ship is better for a tan. And don't forget to locate your life jacket usually under the bed or on the top shelf of the wardrobe and study the deck plans on the back of your cabin door. Instructions for your lifeboat station and drill information also should be on the door. A drill will occur soon after sailing or early the next morning if the first day of your cruise is spent at sea. You will hear specific instructions on where to go prior to the alarm being sounded over the ship's public address system. Most ship lines take attendence, so don't fool around. The ship's photographer (whom you no doubt met upon embarkation) will record the event for posterity. You haven't been on a cruise until you have been immortalized in a life jacket!

PROTECTION FROM THE SUN

Medical authorities advise protecting yourself from the harmful rays of the sun, which can be quite a challenge on a cruise. Moreover, I recently heard a dermatologist claim that 70 percent of wrinkles are caused by the sun and all age spots—the worst damage happens within the first 20 minutes! Sunning oneself by the pool is almost as traditional as the midnight buffet, but I can't warn you enough not to overindulge. Many passengers forget that the tropical sun is more intense than that found in most parts of North America. Even with a strong sun block, visor and cover-up, I occasionally get burned, and once even had to consult the ship's doctor. Nowadays, upon boarding I'm frequently asked where I got my lovely tan in the dead of winter. Most of the time I respond truthfully—I put it on that morning before leaving for the airport (Estee Lauder, Body Shop, Lancome or whatever is at hand).

CAMERAS

Another danger may be to your camera; the sea spray can damage lenses, and sand is the end. The best advice is to visit your favorite camera shop with itinerary in hand and find out what lens, filters, film speed and type, and lens covers to use. Having the proper equipment is important if you're to enjoy taking your vacation photographs, especially at sea when so many elements are working together (and some against you) at the same time and you're moving besides!

AUTHOR'S OBSERVATION

Even if you are an avid photographer, the point-and-shoot models work best on a cruise and are great for snapshots of indoor and outdoor scenes.

Ashore, you may feel more secure in some countries if you aren't flashing around expensive photo gear, and best of all, if they fit in your pocket. Moreover, I always take twice the amount of film I think I'll use. Film is very expensive in ship's boutiques and in most ports.

SEASICKNESS

My own sufferings were short...but to be laughed at by crew, to hear a thousand prescriptions of salt pork and sea water.

Foreign Travel & Life At Sea, 1842

There is such a thing as *mal de mer*, simply, motion sickness that must be addressed immediately because the source is the ship's rock and roll. In the calm waters of the Caribbean or Alaska's Inside Passage, most people don't feel ill due to ship's stabilizers. But a bad storm on an Atlantic or Pacific crossing or even in the relatively calm waters of the Mediterranean or Baltic Sea can put everyone under the weather, even the crew.

There are many remedies available (pills, shots, patches, bracelets, etc.), but the best is the experience of being rewarded with one's sea legs. Most ship lines will dispense Dramamine (the old-fashioned remedy) along with aspirin and Alka-Seltzer from the on-board bars free of charge; however, they do charge for a better remedy (Bonine or Antivert), which does make you sleepy. If you do not wish to take pills, a friend recommends powdered ginger capsules, a natural remedy that works if you believe in it.

For serious cases, the shipboard doctor will administer a shot or suppository that sedates the nervous system and somehow makes one feel terrific again. The transderm patch, available through druggists, is popular but not terribly efficient as most victims do not follow the instructions properly. The patch must be applied behind the ear before you even step aboard, and it is effective for just 72 hours; then, it must be removed and a new one applied. Although you can eat or drink anything while wearing the patch, it is considered an appetite depressant and can cause both dryness of the mouth and blurred vision. With the shot, you should not drink coffee.

The natural, non-drug Sea Bands or acupressure bracelets that alleviate nausea within minutes have been tested by both the Royal British Navy and Australian Yacht Club. These are wrist bands into which a button is sewn; gentle pressure at a specific point on the wrist controls nausea. As no medication is involved, there are no side effects, so Sea Bands are safe for older passengers as well as pregnant women and do not have to be employed until nausea occurs. Your cruise counselor can help locate them.

Since I dislike anything stronger than a Vitamin C pill, my own cure for queasiness is a nice hot cup of consomme (usually available on deck at about 11 a.m.), some crackers (saltines are best) and deep breaths of sea air. One ship-line executive claims that the best antidote for *mal de mer* is preoccupation. Joining in the many on-board activities is the best way to forget about the roll of the ship. In fact, that queasy feeling will most likely disappear, forever!

Storms do occur, especially on the oceans of the world, and if it's bad enough you'll be asked to stay in the cabin for the duration. Some passengers ask crew for access to the lowest deck possible on the ship (below passenger accommodations) and sit mid-ships on the floor where there is the least amount of motion.

SAFETY AT SEA

A final warning on board ship is to treat the vessel with respect. Those railings are meant to keep you from falling overboard, but not if you are careless about safety. Children should not be allowed to play near the railings under any circumstances, and adults should not be foolish enough to sit on them. In one recent case, a passenger decided to sit on the railing after several drinks and fell overboard. He was lucky enough to be picked up immediately by a fishing trawler and was eventually returned to the vessel. But not for long; the captain threw him off the ship at the next port because his foolishness endangered the lives of all aboard.

SECURITY AT SEA

Security at sea is here to stay and all precautions undertaken are to passengers benefit. Many ship lines no longer allow visitors at Anchors Away and X-ray machines are a normal sight now on every pier. Both plain clothes and uniformed security are aboard many vessels whether you realize it or not. On many cruises, ID cards are issued to passengers for their own protection and must be shown to the gangway guard in ports of call. The best advice: Be aware of security yourself, and, if you become suspicious of a person or situation, report immediately to the purser's office. We live in a world in which our senses must be activated at all times.

AUTHOR'S OBSERVATION

When you disembark the ship in port, always take documents with you including passport, photo ID, and ship boarding card. It is always a good idea to have a copy or numbers of your ID on the ship in the event it is lost. Leave airline tickets in your cabin, as they can be difficult to have re-issued if misplaced.

TIPS ON VALIUM-FREE CRUISING

Yea, it's a great job, taking all those lovely ships for Fielding's *Cruises.* But professional travel writers probably make more dumb mistakes when traveling than novices. You get careless, or tired, and think, "boy, that can never happen to me." Add to that the stress of the small niggling things that plague us all when contending with weather, air travel and being stuck aboard a ship for a week or so that turns out to be less than the fantasy portrayed by the cruise company. But it's usually a pileup of the small stresses that make one the crankiest.

Here's a potpourri of assorted tricks garnered from countless screw-ups that save wear and tear on the heart valves and will make aspects of your cruise more enjoyable.

- When purchasing luggage, the most important criteria is wheels—trying to carry a heavy pullman plus carry-on and duty-free purchases through airports is torture. Since all bags look alike these days, wrapping a band of brightly colored tape around the suitcase handle helps identify it quickly on the carousel.

- Whenever possible, select a pre-cruise hotel stay in the city of embarkation. A good night's sleep after a tortuous flight and leisurely ride to the pier will add an extra day of relaxation to the voyage.
- If a major storm threatens your region and the cruise departs over a weekend, call your travel agent on Friday during business hours to get the cruise line's procedure on canceled or delayed flights for air/sea passengers; also obtain the cruise company's weekend hotline number.
- Depart for the airport an hour earlier than normal. Those check-in lines keep getting longer and slower and you'll stand the chance of getting a better seat assignment.
- If your heart is set on a double/queen bed, be sure to confirm this with your travel agent before departure. On some ships, even cabins in the highest categories have twin beds bolted to the floor that can't be reconfigured.
- Always carry documents in your handbag or suit jacket. One of us opted for a cute, small purse and put airline and cruise tickets in a small tote bag. Arrival at the hotel sans tote bag prompted a nail-biting dash back to Miami airport. A miracle did occur—someone found it lying on the floor next to the luggage carousel and turned it into lost and found. But this occurrence is rare.
- Never pack the following items in your luggage: jewelry, medication, reading glasses, money/traveler's checks, passport, air/sea documents or any item you won't mind losing forever in the event your luggage disappears.
- Photocopy your passport and stash the copy separately so you can reenter the U.S. easily if the document is lost. Also copy social security number,

driver's license and Medicaid/Insurance card and keep multiple copies in luggage.

- If you dislike your cabin (it's on promenade deck and revelers disturb your sleep or the family of six next door drives you crazy), ask to be moved. The same applies to assigned seating in the dining room— request a new table if you can't stand your waiter or fellow dinner companions.
- Never, never tolerate rude treatment aboard any seagoing vessel. You are paying for service and never allowed to forget that tipping is expected aboard most ships. If anyone treats you less than courteously, report them to the purser's office. Hotel managers, who oversee all service personnel, are generally a very conscientious bunch who want to know if there's a person on their staff with an attitude problem. However, even on the best ships people makes mistakes. If the error is rectified and staff is sincere in trying to make things right (which isn't always possible), there is probably no reason to raise a stink.
- Before sailing you've requested second seating in the dining room and end up in first, asked for a table for two and wind up at a table for eight (these arrangements are very rarely confirmed until you board). If necessary (and it usually is) have a $20 bill showing in your hand when you ask the maitre'd for a change. This usually works unless the ship is full.
- If food is not prepared to your liking, send it back and ask the kitchen to try again or select another dish. If you wind up on a ship and the food is generally lousy, select "spa" or "lean and light" menu options, which are frequently the best prepared.
- It's a rare ship that isn't over–air–conditioned at night (on one lovely ship in the Caribbean I slept in a sweatsuit when the outside temperature was 75 degrees). Bring a sweater or wrap for evening. And,

temperatures in Alaska, New England/Canada and the Baltic can be cold at any time, so always bring warmer daytime wear just in case.

- When planning a wintertime warm-water cruise, purchase incidentals like sandals, bathing suits and cover-ups in summer—these are impossible to find in the winter and you'll pay premium prices aboard ship and in port.
- During days at sea, stake your claim on the lounge chair of your choice by ll a.m. Ask if a live band will be performing nearby throughout the day, and scout out a quiet spot if seeking peace and quiet.
- When leaving port, don't stand forward and topside anywhere near the funnel—and ship's horn. If you survive the blast, you'll know your ticker is in excellent shape.
- You can make yourself very unpopular at the beginning of the cruise by pressing staff to board the ship before formal embarkation time. They may let you do it, but their time is so limited while turning the ship around in a few hours that you'll be branded a real pain in the butt.
- Ask specifics about shore excursions that sound enticing.

  For example, an attraction may involve a seven-hour bus ride over bumpy roads, with a hectic 30-minute stop at a less than inspiring site. You can nearly always travel more comfortably and cheaply by booking a local taxi with a few friends (confirm a flat hourly or half-day rate with the driver before you enter the vehicle and negotiate with several).
- On ships with VCR's in cabins, the best movies go first. Run for the video library the moment you board to procure your favorites and grab several.
- Do anything possible to avoid clearing U.S. Immigrations and Customs in Miami when you must also make a connecting flight.

The lines are impossibly long and slow, then you must dash to another ticket counter—which frequently seems about five miles away—to recheck your suitcases for the domestic flight. And, if you can't run fast enough, this airport is the pits when hanging out for the next available flight.

ON BOARD

A leisurely view of Mediterranean scenery from Swan Hellenic's **Orpheus**

Getting underway never fails to make my skin tingle, my eyes mist slightly and my knees feel a bit weak as I lift a glass of the bubbly in salute. Casting off and feeling the ship pull away from the pier is, indeed, one of the most exciting parts of being aboard. And the exhilaration exists whether you are sailing under the Golden Gate, past the Statue of Liberty, away from Dodge Island or into the bustling harbor of Piraeus. As familiar landmarks disappear and the sun dips into the horizon, you know that adventure lies ahead. To fully enjoy the sailing away, I always like to have unpacked and treated myself to a quick tour of the public areas, so I can be out on deck, glass in hand, to toast the leave-taking. Whatever the port of departure, it is always festive, with lots of streamers, music and waving to those on the pier below.

Some memorable leave-takings have been in the port of Piraeus at sunset, Nice at midday, Port Everglades in the early evening, New York past the famous Statue of Liberty, Honolulu at night and Miami in the afternoon. Indeed, the flotilla departing Miami is quite a sight; the decks are generally a sea of orange life vests as passengers prepare for their mandatory life boat drill! The modern cruise ship is a self-contained city. It has its own government and staff, communications, housing, recreation, food service, protection and fire department, water supply and garbage disposal. Coming aboard is like moving to a new town; you think you know how it will be, but the unexpected always happens! It takes some time to become accustomed to your new surroundings, which must be why some passengers request the same cabin and dining-room assignment year after year. (I have even heard of some loyal passengers who become upset over a new decor in their favorite stateroom.) And some sweet old things, who come aboard for world cruises or longer, are even allowed to bring their own bedspreads and other familiar accoutrements.

RESERVING A TABLE

If you have not already done so, be sure to take care of your table assignment and meal hour preference before you really settle in. At sailing time, the maitre'd (or someone on his staff) will be receiving passenger requests outside the dining room or in one of the public lounges, so seek him out speedily if you want a good choice of tables.

While most ship lines have two seatings for all meals, some are small enough to ensure that everyone can dine at leisure at open seating during all meals. *Song of Flower*, Royal Cruise Line's *Royal Odyssey, Star Odyssey* and *Queen Odyssey* and the vessels of Seabourn, Sea Goddess, Windstar, Star Clippers, Renaissance, Special Expeditions, American Canadian Caribbean Cruise Line, and Clipper (as well as other sailing ships, barges and river boats) provide a leisurely mode of dining. On the majority of vessels, your stomach is fed either earlier than it is accustomed to or later than satisfactory. Meal hours vary somewhat among the lines, but the first seating is around 7:30 a.m. (breakfast), noon (luncheon), and 6:30 p.m. (dinner). Second or late seating hours are generally around 8:45 a.m., 1:30 p.m. and 8:30 p.m. Since many people avoid these schedules by having breakfast in bed or out on deck in the morning, and partaking of the luncheon buffet that is usually served around the pool, dinner hour is the only real decision. If you have young children, you will be encouraged to consider the earlier time period. The later seating is more fashionable, of course, and more suitable to couples and swinging singles. Moreover, when dining later, there is more time to relax and freshen up after a long day in port before donning evening finery and having a few hours to lounge over a cocktail with new found friends.

AUTHOR'S OBSERVATION

On most ships you may request, and be very firm about, a table for two. If this is not possible, however, ask for a table for six or eight, because at a table for four you may get stuck with a completely incompatible couple.

Many ship lines claim that they are experts at putting people together in the dining room. I don't believe for one moment that any maitre'd or his staff can look at 700 different passengers in the space of an hour or two and match them perfectly. It's simply dumb luck, and if your luck doesn't hold and you find table companions not to be your type, then take your case back to the maitre'd . In most instances he will be obliging, but his hands may be tied if the ship is fully booked. If you are traveling alone or in a group of singles, you will want the largest table possible. Explain this in a gentle way to the maitre'd and he will do his best. After all, he wants everyone happy (and many a romance has begun at the table).

No matter how refined the vessel and creative the design, a dining room holding 700+ people is rarely intimate, and there are savvy cruisers who will only travel on smaller single-seating ships for this very reason. Several 1200-passenger cruise ships launched in the past few years have artfully solved this problem while maintaining two seatings. The *Dreamward* and *Windward*, for example, have four dining rooms (assignment by cabin location). Each is cozy, intimate, warm and reminds one of a fine shore-side restaurant. On the *Crystal Harmony* and the new *Crystal Symphony*, the main dining room serves superb international cuisine, and you can also feast on Italian specialities in Prego, or Japanese fare, such as tempura and sukiyaki, in Kyoto (or Chinese, when the Symphony is launched this May).

And, how does one get invited to dine at the Captain's table? That's simple, just be as rich as Croesus, or as famous as Madonna, on your 20th voyage aboard the vessel, the president of the cruise line (or about to buy it), a top-producing travel agent or the Captain's nationality!

EATING ABOARD

The staff of Celebrity Cruises rolls out the red carpet.

"Never eat more than you can lift."

Miss Piggy

More has been written about food on board cruise vessels than about itinerary, ambience, service, size of cabins or anything else. Because at least five meals are served daily, you can gorge yourself from early morning to late at night. For starters, you can rise early (good heavens!) and have coffee and assorted pastries on deck at 6:30 a.m. This may stimulate your appetite for the three choices of full breakfast available on most ships. You may return to your cabin for everything from the dainty Continental breakfast to kippers, assorted cheeses and hot chocolate. If you want the proper sit-down service that you paid for, head for the dining room where the waiter will keep hot java flowing and you may have everything on the menu. Or, you may have a pleasant buffet breakfast out on deck; although lighter than what is available in the dining room, this may include scrambled eggs, bacon and sausauge, English muffins, toast, fresh Danish pastries, juice, fruit and coffee/tea. There is usually a selection of healthy options as well, including yogurt and fat-free muffins. Hours for this repast will be posted in your daily program. For the real sleepyheads, coffee and Danish may be served in one of the lounges until 11 a.m. Deck service is now the norm on cruising vessels, and any repast in the open air is what cruises are all about, if you don't mind plastic service—it's a safety feature.

Not many ships continue the tradition of bouillon at 11 a.m., holdover from the grand old days of transatlantic travel. Bouillon, always good for warming the insides as you sat under a steamer rug on a deck chair in the misty air, was also an excellent antidote for queasy stomachs. In the Caribbean, you will probably not be served bouillon (instead you head for a cool, refreshing drink from the bar), but if you are cruising in the colder waters of Alaska, the Baltic, around the North Cape, or across the Atlantic, you can count on it (and it may be a lifesaver). Moreover, bouillion consumed before lunch will cut down on your appetite. American Hawaii Cruises features orange sherbert at 11 a.m. and it is very refreshing, indeed.

Before you have digested those waffles with whipped butter and rasher of bacon, lunch is being served. At sea (or in port) on pleasant days, a cold buffet is usually served near a swimming pool (and you may fill your plate while bikini-clad). Most ships also have hamburgers and hot dogs sizzling on a nearby grill. These ships often have full buffet restaurants next to the pool; some of the loveliest are aboard the *Statendam* and *Maasdam*, where food stations with separate courses are spread to avoid waiting in line. There is even an ice cream parlor and stations of lean and healthy fare for those who resist temptation. I always try to avoid the dining room at lunchtime in general, but one of my most memorable dining experiences at sea was lunch in *Song of Flower*'s restaurant, where we gorged on a buffet of king crab, prawns, shrimp and lobster, while everyone on deck had cold salads. Normally, however, even if the weather is on the cool side, it's refreshing to sit on deck and inhale the sea breezes. Aboard the *Stella Solaris* one spring, we sat on deck with some fruit and cheese from the cold buffet, shared a bottle of local wine with new-found friends and thought life was certainly splendid as the ship sailed away from Dikili and the ruins of Pergamum. Such a feeling would have been entirely lost in a packed dining room.

AUTHOR'S OBSERVATION

Dining under those colorful umbrellas at tables overlooking the sea is heavenly. Stake out a table just before the buffet opens or you may end up trying to juggle a plate of food and drink on your chaise longue.

Food takes top priority at sea for excellent reasons: it's included in the fare and you are obliged to do nothing but read the menu, order, and enjoy being served! If you wish to try a little bit of this and that, in addition to what you order no problem! Ship lines enjoy satisfied passengers, so if food is your yellow brick road to happiness, all the better.

Each Princess ship has its own pizzeria for tempting afternoon feasts.

Food is, however, a very personal taste, and what one passenger considers favorable, another will not. While the new megavessels never pretend to be gourmet experiences (there are just too many mouths to feed), some cruise lines have brought aboard star chefs to oversee their dining operations, and the results always show. Celebrity's *Horizon*, *Meridian* and *Zenith*, for example, have outstanding cuisine under the watchful eye of Michel Roux. The *Crystal Harmony's*, which boasts some of the best cuisine I've ever encountered on a ship, uses Michel Blanchet, formerly of L'Ermitage Restaurant of Los Angeles as a consultant. On Princess ships, fresh pasta is prepared to your liking at the table. Cunard's International Food Bazaar on selected nights in *QE 2's* transatlantic-class Mauretania Restaurant features four theme buffet tables, as well as four theme bars serving appropriate regional drinks. Dinner dancing on occasional evenings has also returned to sea, especially in the *QE 2's* Columbia and Mauretania restaurants, while *Statendam* and *Maasdam* passengers are serenaded by an orchestra as they dine. This is a splendid and festive touch, and hopefully, more ships will inaugurate these romantic traditions.

HEALTHY DINING AT SEA

The past few years have seen nearly every ship line introducing lean and light menu selections for those watching their fat and cholesterol intakes. In the past, the average passenger returned home a few pounds heavier, but the wonderful sauces and rich desserts were always worth it. No more! Royal Cruise Line's Dine To Your Heart's Content program has the blessing of the American Heart Association with dozens of healthy entrees, such as Melitzanes Papoutsakia (lean meat-stuffed eggplant) served on Greek Night. Holland America's Perfect Balance menu selections also meet AHA guidelines, so that your breakfast may include fare such as natural cereals and yogurt, muffins with oat bran and egg substitutes. On Crystal Cruises Perfect Harmony program, one can dine on basil pasta with prawns and scallops followed by an Alaskan cranberry tart. Healthy doesn't have to be boring! Ships that have extensive spas, such as the *Norway* and *QE 2*, feature spa cuisine at dinner so the tummy stays flat. Carnival Cruise Line boasts Nautical Spa Fare, healthy options in all courses for those restrained enough to maintain dietary regimens on a cruise.

The care and feeding of a shipload of passengers is no mean task, especially when two seatings are involved. The *QE 2* employs 239 waiters, 139 kitchen personnel, 50 beverage personnel, 14 bartenders, 16 bakers, and 18 wine stewards. The ice cream stocked for one transatlantic crossing would make 24,000 single-dip cones, and the caviar consumed (mainly from the Grills) is around 150 pounds. When the *Sovereign of the Seas* sails from Miami every week, 1500 bottles of champagne, 50 pounds of caviar, and 200 pounds of smoked salmon are stocked. Other impressive items on the grocery list are 2400 lobster tails, 2000 filet mignons, 1750 pounds of shrimp and 600 gallons of ice cream in 14 flavors.

Finally, you hightail it to the dining room as the first note of chimes is struck for your dinner seating. (Most cruise ships request that you enter the dining room not more than fifteen minutes after the meal has been announced when there are two seatings. This is a courtesy both to the kitchen and your table companions.) Most of these floating restaurants assume a new and enjoyable personality in the evening. The stewards are usually in a good mood because dinner is their favorite meal to serve, and their day is almost over. If the lights are low enough to hide your wrinkles still and you can find your plate, all the better!

FESTIVE GALA EVENINGS

Aside from the first and final evenings on board, which are casual and often awkward, your evenings in the dining room will be very special. You can expect a Captain's Welcome Dinner, as well as a Captain's Farewell Dinner plus any number of other galas. Often

featured are Spanish Night, Italian Night, French Night, Caribbean Night, Greek Night, American Night, Hawaiian Night, Norwegian Night and two or three galas depending upon the nationality of your crew and the length of your cruise. If you are aboard a Royal Cruise Line vessel, you will certainly enjoy the menu on Greek Night. For appetizers, the list reads: dolmadakia, taramosalata, tzatziki, amphissa olives, bourekakia, fried baby squashes and ouzo special. The soup specialty is Avgolemono, consisting of chicken broth, egg, and lemon all delicious! This is followed by: shrimps Microlimano style, baby lamb Roumeli style or veal liver, roast potatoes and buttered artichokes, Greek salad (cucumbers, tomatoes, feta cheese, onions, black olives, oil and vinegar), assorted Greek cheeses, and for dessert a choice of baklava, kataifi, galaktoboureko or kaimaki ice cream (or all four). And by the end of the meal, the sommelier has recommended a number of Greek wines.

And this is just one special evening! Royal Caribbean claims that you have a choice of some 1500 separate items on its weekly menus (but I suspect this includes all three meals). On some of the more elegant cruise vessels, you may order off the menu and have a steak every night if you wish. In Alaska, aboard *Song of Flower* we purchased salmon, caught a few hours before in port and the Austrian chef cooked it to our liking. Settle any special diet needs before you book your cruise, because some lines will not cater to individuals but do carry enough different types of foodstuffs so that you may work around the problem. Strictly speaking, I would say that the food on most cruise ships is good, and it's difficult not to overeat (especially when those luscious desserts come rolling in). Steaks, prime ribs, and fresh fish of all varieties are the best selections at sea. The presentation of salads and vegetables somehow misses at sea, except on the top-rated vessels. And don't expect mounds of caviar anymore because it is just too expensive for everyone's taste! Anyway, a little dab here and there is enough to make you feel like royalty especially if it does happen to be the best variety.

On the other hand, many fine and memorable dishes will keep you from becoming bored at sea. How about reindeer meat with juniper berries, real Russian borscht and piroshki, freshly grilled Alaskan salmon, grilled baby calves liver, duck a l'orange, and uncountable numbers of omelette surprises and special gateau! It's difficult not to indulge, so it's best to diet beforehand. Then, by the end of your cruise, you cannot complain that the sea air shrank your wardrobe.

In case you just can't make it to bed without another little snack, the midnight buffet begins about 11:30 p.m. and lasts until 1 a.m. or so. Here you will find deviled eggs, cold meats, cheeses, salads, lobster and shrimp, fresh fruit, and tempting little pastries. Some ships pay particular attention to this final meal of the day, especially in the Caribbean (Carnival Cruise Lines claims to have three different buffets on every vessel). If you happen to be sailing in Europe, you may not be honored with a buffet or you may find only a simple table of cheeses, bread and cold meats.

AUTHOR'S OBSERVATION

The sea air always stimulates my appetite; to keep calories in check, I eat salads ashore and skip the midnight buffet. Keeping fruit in the cabin also helps resist the temptation to order room service.

DRINKING ABOARD

"Three be the things I shall never obtain ...
envy, content and sufficient champagne."

Dorothy Parker

A captain of the *Dolphin*, a cozy vessel that cruises out of Miami twice weekly to the Bahamas, used to say the amount of alcohol consumed per day per passenger is directly related to the length of the cruise. He claimed that three- and four-day passengers drink more in each 24-hour period than do passengers on longer cruises. Well, for the getting underway, nothing beats those bubbles up your nose. It's traditional and popping that cork is good for the soul! Now, where to enjoy your champagne ... if you have a large cabin with terrace, you know where. Otherwise, out on deck to enhance every bittersweet moment of departure.

Most cruise vessels have several lounges with bars. Outstanding are the Royal Caribbean Cruise Line trademark Viking Crown Lounge, ten stories up and cantilevered from the smokestack, and the *Norway*'s Club International, one of the most elegant lounges afloat and a lovely hangover from French Line days. Once the vessel is underway and you have time to explore, you'll be surprised how many little nooks are tucked around where you can have a preprandial cocktail, waker-upper or putter-to-sleeper. With the exception of the Club International (which concentrates solely upon itself), I always venture toward the best view and find my spot for the duration of the cruise (a true creature of habit). Most vessels have some type of glass-enclosed lounge located on a high deck, so that you can be on top of (yet a part of) the sea below. On the *Stella Solaris*, the glassed-in Piano Bar has a panoramic view and the *Mississippi*

Queen's two-story, glass-enclosed Paddlewheel Lounge is among the most dramatic. On the Princess vessels, the view is best from the Starlight lounges. Every vessel has at least one spectacular public area, a quiet bar, and plenty of spots where the action congregates.

AUTHOR'S OBSERVATION

When transiting the Panama Canal, the lounges on the highest deck make the most comfortable spots for viewing (unless you want to stand ten deep on deck in the hot sun and humidity of the Canal Zone).

Drinks on board ship, no longer as inexpensive as they were, are are often comparable to what is found on dry land (with all this rampant discounting the cruise companies have to make it up somewhere). There are plenty of juices, sodas, and designer waters in the $1 plus range, as well as beer in the can, bottle or on tap for $1.50 or so. It has become very popular now to obtain a variety of wines by the glass at the bar and mixed drinks range from $3.50 and upwards. Daily specials, Bloody Marys, Cuba Libres, screwdrivers, etc., are posted around the pool. There are also special concoctions in glasses you take with you for $6 and up (if you can decipher what you are drinking). The types of drinks served depend upon the cruise ship and where you are sailing; few passengers begin the day with a rum punch aboard *Vistafjord's* North Cape cruise!

If you enjoy wine with your dinner, you'll love being at sea. The wine list is usually interesting, especially if you're aboard a Greek- or Italian-flag vessel and wish to try the many local brands at reasonable prices. Greek white wines might be retsina, Robola, Santa Elena, Hymettos, Santa Laura, Demestica; red wines of the same type are Chevalier de Rhodes, Naoussa, Monte Nero, Santa Laura, Demestica and Lava. On Italian vessels, Soave Bolla seems to be the popular brand, along with Verdicchio, Frascati and the straw-covered Chiantis. The more expensive French white and red burgundies, Beaujolais, California names and even Blue Nun are on most wine lists, plus champagnes from sparkling German wines to vintage French. The *QE2* boasts a cellar of some 20,000 bottles ranging from prize-winning vintages to vin ordinaire. And if you prefer domestic American wines, many brands from California and Washington have found their way on cruise-ship lists. Wine prices have escalated greatly in the past few years aboard cruise ships. No longer is that fun bottle of Greek or Italian nectar to be enjoyed for just a few dollars!

Expect prices just barely below a good restaurant. Ship lines are using liquor and wine sales as serious sources of on-board revenue these days as an antidote to the drastic discounting occurring in the marketplace. If you wish to order wine, advise your dining room steward as soon as you are seated, for the sommelier can become very busy as the evening progresses and may not have time to chill or uncork the bottle properly. He knows the cellar and can offer worthy suggestions if you catch him before he is beckoned away and you have to wait forever for your choice. Most cruise vessels post the menus in advance and allow you to order your dinner wine early for more efficiency—a fine idea.

AUTHOR'S OBSERVATION

If you are a teetotaler, take heart: there are plenty of festive concoctions on bar menus sans alcohol so you can join in the merriment and not have to struggle with a hangover the next morning. Those in twelve-step programs will find daily AA meetings aboard nearly every cruise ship above a 400-passenger capacity, but confirm this with the cruise line before departure.

SHIP'S PERSONNEL AND SERVICES

Officers of Crystal Symphony *look forward to taking the helm of the new ship.*

The most important people in your personal shipboard life are your cabin attendants and the dining room staff assigned to your section. The names of your cabin attendants should be posted and visible as you enter your cabin for the first time, and in fact, he/she, or they should be waiting to greet you and offer any assistance. These stewards or stewardesses are your link with the rest of the cruise vessel, for they know what time meals are and what to do about laundry, pressing, ice or extra glasses for cocktail parties. They will clean your cabin when you depart in the morning and should have a sixth sense about what you might want upon your return from a long day in port or up at the pool. If you enjoy breakfast in bed, your cabin steward or stewardess will collect your order in the late evening and bring the tray at the appointed time the following morning. If there is a small service you wish to have performed each day (like tea at 4:00 or the ice bucket filled at 5:00), inform him or her as you get settled (and a small tip then may help). Your cabin attendants are chosen for their cheerful attitude and willingness to serve. If you find them to the contrary and it threatens to ruin your cruise, discuss the situation with the chief purser. If there is space elsewhere on the ship, the chief purser may move you to another cabin. If there is not, you may have to settle for his reprimanding the proper person. I have had excellent cabin attendants and a rare few less excellent. If you have strong feelings about your cabin service either way, reflect it in your tips (good service should be rewarded well).

The same goes for the dining room personnel. If the maitre'd has placed you at a table of stimulating people, the sommelier has suggested the most perfect wines each evening, and the stewards have been attentive and gracious at every meal, they should all be tipped appropriately. And don't forget how many times you have requested additional favors, like an extra dessert, a birthday cake for your husband or farewell champagne for the table. You will have found your own favorite barman who, within a few hours of sailing, remembers your favorite brand and how much ice to add. If he also remembers your names, you belong to an exclusive club, indeed. And don't be surprised if your favorite steward or stewardess serves at other functions, like the luncheon buffet around the pool, afternoon tea in the lounge, or a private cocktail party. A good waiter is in demand throughout the vessel.

Other service personnel you may wish to know are the deck steward, the pool attendants (indoors or out), the gymnasium attendant, and any children's counselors. On deck, you may need assistance with setting up the chaises, getting proper towels for swimming, and the accoutrements of deck games, such as shuffleboard or table tennis. If you use the indoor pool, another set of attendants will service that area as well.

KEEPING IN SHAPE

This year, you will find gyms and spas beyond anything imaginable a while back. You'll find 12,000 squre feet of fitness/spa facilities on Carnival's newest ships; *Majesty of the Seas* and *Monarch of the Seas* boast some of the largest fitness facilities afloat and Royal Caribbean's Ship Shape regimen runs the gamut from basketball to gut-buster exercises to aquadynamics. In fact, nearly every vessel above 1000-capacity built in the past five years has an excellent fitness facility, the best equipment and a full-time trainer.

AUTHOR'S OBSERVATION

If you are not in shape, be cautious about starting a strenuous exercise regime aboard ship.

ENTERTAINING THE KIDS

If you are sailing with the children, you will be delighted to know that they are entertained in their own part of the ship and you may not see them from breakfast to dinnertime (after that, it's your responsibility). Many ships have separate children's playrooms and also add a set of young counselors to their service personnel during school vacation periods and the summer months.

Young passengers have their own games, are tended while swimming, get their favorite junk food for lunch (hamburgers, hot dogs, french fries and sodas), watch movies geared to their age and even have their own tea parties. Children love shipboard life and they are a pleasure to watch at play. On many ships, the young people have their own video arcade (the grown-ups video is now known as a Computer Center and available widely at sea). Both Royal Caribbean and Cunard's *QE 2* have teen discos. A Christmas/New Year's sailing up the Amazon aboard the *Stella Solaris* had a substantial children's complement and it contributed greatly to the festive atmosphere. Because children are so well cared for during the day, families will enjoy the evening meal with them and it is suggested that they dine at the early sitting. Afterward, if parents wish to enjoy the late hours, arrangements with the purser and cabin stewards to baby-sit are always acceptable (for the usual sitting fee, of course).

SPAS AND SALONS

If you wish to use the beauty/barber shop and spa facilities found on most cruise ships, make your appointments well in advance and make several of them to be sure (you can always cancel later). Beauticians and barbers on board have excellent reputations and will give you a new hairstyle for less than it costs at home (haircuts are especially reasonable for men). Most of these shops also offer pedicure/manicure treatments on availability. Make appointments especially early for evenings that feature a gala, because space in these shops is limited. The same goes for sauna or massage appointments. The price of such pampering is not included in the cruise fare, so you may wish to consider whether you really need a massage. Since the answer is usually yes, book early for a mid- or late-cruise treatment. Directly after a strenuous port tour is the best time and it will make you feel like a new person.

GLAMOROUS EVENINGS

After you have learned the ropes of wining, dining, exercising and pampering yourself with a manicure and massage, you may either collapse in a deck chair for the rest of the voyage or attend marathon activities. Foremost in your schedule should be the Captain's Welcome Aboard Cocktail and Dinner Gala on the evening of your first full day at sea. This is the most formal event of the cruise, and just how dressy you should be will depend upon your particular ship line. If you enjoy dressing for dinner, you will love these special gala evenings. On a seven-day cruise, there will be just one, since the farewell dinner is a little less formal. If you are on longer sailings, there will be many more formal evenings that dictate black-tie and long gowns. It all depends upon your own comfort and the type of ship you have chosen. Your travel agent should be able to advise the type of evening clothes suitable. If you enjoy wearing black tie and long gowns, bring them along; if you prefer dark suits and short dresses be as comfortable as you wish. This is your vacation.

MEETING THE CAPTAIN

At the Captain's Welcome Aboard evening, the cruise director (or directrice) will ask your name and then introduce you to the chief purser and the captain. It's easy to tell which one is the *captain*, or master of the vessel, because he wears the most gold on either shoulder (usually four wide bars). The *chief purser*, who deals with the day-to-day running of the cruise and is general information officer, wears three gold (sometimes silver) bars on either shoulder and an insignia that looks like a clover. After you have been introduced to these two men and photographed by the ship's professional shutterbug (the photos will be on display and sale later), you are offered a drink (martini, Manhattan, juice, champagne) and an hors d'oeuvre or two.

When all the passengers have been received, the captain introduces the rest of his staff. This will consist of the *chief engineer* (four stripes and a propeller) who makes everything work properly, the *chief radio operator* (three stripes and a radio signal), the *chief electrician* (three stripes and some electrical current) and the *doctor* (three stripes with red or three stripes and a caduceus). And then the *cruise director* will introduce his or her staff, and you are invited to the dining room for a splendid seven-course meal. On a few ships, champagne and caviar are still part of the traditional welcome dinner.

The cruise director is a very special being and the range in personalities and talent is quite incredible. Some of the more impressive beings we have encountered lately have been Fernando de Oliveira of Royal Cruise Line and John Butts of Cunard all professionals and among the hardest working individuals at sea. The cruise staff is generally dressed alike, so it is impossible to miss them around the ship. They handle all the activities on board and must always be upbeat when dealing with any problems, complaints, etc. Frankly, the staff assigned to the young people have the best jobs. It's like being the pied piper because so many small devotees follow them around all day long!

The person responsible for the entire hotel function of your cruise vessel is the hotel manager. He also wears four gold bars. The *hotel manager* is a fairly new position aboard ship (it is thought that Holland America started it about 20 years ago), but his responsibility is enormous. On his shoulders are all the cabins, all the stewards, all the food and drink and even the entertainment. Some are the most popular of all the shipboard personnel because they manage to keep everyone happy at the same time. It takes a special personality to be a good hotel manager, as well as a strong dose of humor and patience.

The chief purser and the cruise director report directly to the hotel manager and are your most evident contact with what is happening behind the scenes. The chief purser and his staff handle all money transactions, stamps, and stationery; clear you through customs at ports of call; and provide general information. Whatever you need to know about the vessel and any scheduling you will find at the purser's office, which is open daily from about 9:00 a.m. and is usually situated in the middle of the main public deck. Should you need the doctor, you will find his hours posted as well, and you will be advised what numbers to call in case of emergency. If you need to send a message or make a ship-to-shore phone call, the radio room is open to passengers at certain hours (but always closed by law in port). Communication with office or home is very expensive, so be prepared to pay plenty for the privilege. Most communication is excellent and swift, so there is nothing to fear about being way out at sea, and most cruise ships now advertise their use of satellites for telephone calls, placed in the privacy of your cabin. (It's called Progress when you can't even get away from it all on a cruise!)

AUTHOR'S OBSERVATION

Talk is not cheap when calling from a ship–the cost of a phone call is around $15 per minute, and it's always better to use pay phones on shore, which are are nearly always found on piers.

If you plan to cruise aboard *Sovereign of the Seas*, you can do most of the above with your fingertips, via an interactive state-of-the-art television system called Cruise Control. This video-viewing system enables you to preview on-board activities, review bar tabs, order room service and even wine with dinner from the privacy of your cabin. It sounds truly modern, but what happened to the interaction with other persons, which is what a cruise is all about?

ACTIVITIES

"Two things change the monotony of an ocean trip: Sometimes, alas! you ship a sea, And sometimes see a ship."

Foreign Travel and Life At Sea, 1842

Your cruise director, responsible for the daily passenger activity list, will invite everyone to the main lounge on the morning of the first full day at sea to explain the myriad happenings that is called a cruise. He will run down the basics like the library, cardroom, and writing room (for books, bridge, and backgammon) and offer the outdoor crowd such sports as shuffleboard, golf driving range, table or deck tennis, badminton and volleyball (although not every ship offers every sport). He will also explain rules around the pool areas: what to do about towels, how to get and keep a deck chair, how to get beverage service. Then he will probably begin to check off special activities, like skeet shooting, wine tasting parties, lectures, ice carving lessons, art auctions, dance lessons, trapshooting and concerts. And we must not forget bingo, which is still everyone's favorite pastime and the stakes can become very high! Just remember that bingo like slot machines and the casino would not be offered if the ship line did not make a bundle from the operations.

Keeping fit aboard the Norway *in a spirited basketball game*

EVENING ENTERTAINMENT

Entertainment at sea these days is quite overwhelming and, like the food, almost too much to digest in a short time. Many ship lines, such as Royal Caribbean, advertise Big-Name Talent, which is marvelous for those that remember them when they *were* big. I often think good heavens, is he or she still around? Frankly, the Big Names are sometimes a bust whether they have written books or made millions in show business. I prefer the average-size (even the small) names; they try harder and are much more personable around the ship. Nonetheless, there is some sort of evening entertainment for everyone, and if you find the spectacle in one lounge too noisy, there is always an alternative. Highbrow, lowbrow, middlebrow entertainment is very personal. according to taste and mood, but cruise ships offer good variety and many different venues. Those who want the best evening floor shows will find the most lavish entertainment aboard Royal Caribbean and Crystal Cruises.

DAYTIME ENRICHMENT

Cunard started it all with the "Festival of Life" series over a decade ago and today the cruise cup runneth over with daytime offerings. Ship lines are always busy creating other wonderful reasons for you to enjoy a cruise and an event, such as an eclipse. So, in between worldwide celebrations of centennials and natural phenomena, ship lines are inviting you aboard to participate in more enrichment topics than one dreamed possible. Intrigue is *in*. So is chili, photography, music, square dancing, cooking demonstrations, ecology, art auctions, wine, eclipse of the sun, graphology, amusing psychiatrists and behind-the-scenes lectures on just about anything. Forget financial experts (if they really knew what they pretend to know, they would own their own yachts by now), fashion coordinators, hypnotists and the like. Languages are sometimes offered and great fun to learn. Music is always soothing from jazz to classical and passengers are always welcome at informal rehearsals.

GAMBLING ON THE HIGH SEAS

Tempting Lady Luck in Royal Caribbean's lively Casino Royal

Unless you are aboard one of the very serious and intellectually stimulating cruises, your shipboard life will also feature elaborate evening entertainment and gambling. The latter ranges from a few slot machines to a full casino, complete with bunny club type croupiers. Here you can play roulette and blackjack to your heart's content and some of these casinos are open from twelve to fourteen hours per day. (Just keep in mind that the house usually wins more than you do.) Slot machines are the more casual form of tempting Lady Luck and some vessels also go in for horse racing (using films in one of the lounges and accepting big bets on who will win). The jackpot does overflow from time to time, so if you're in the mood for a little gambling, you will not be disappointed. Carnival and Norwegian Cruise Line pride themselves on the biggest and splashiest casinos afloat. Most companies franchise their casinos and take a pre-determined piece of the action. But if gambling is your main passion in life, go with Carnival. (I'm told there are even high rollers betting thousands aboard this company's fleet.)

MOVIES AND PERFORMANCES

Aside from the races and travel shorts, you can also find full-length feature films that are first-rate. Times and titles are posted in the bulletin daily; if you have a cabin with TV you can watch the film in privacy while relaxing or dressing for dinner. Many ship lines also offer news broadcasts via satellite and Crystal has an arrangement with Cable News Network. Cabin VCRs are also popular in the top-rated cabins on many vessels, as well as on the newer ships and video lending is available in the library or purser's office. (On the Windstar fleet, the cassette is charged to your account until returned; on the *Song of Flower* and Sea Goddess ships, the honor system prevails.) Cruise ships have excellent theaters although some of them are way, way down below and religious services are held here as well. The *Rotterdam* theater is known for weddings from time to time! *Norway's* Saga Theatre is famous for its Broadway productions, live concerts with stars and a Las Vegas-style revue spectacular that even the most jaded enjoy.

LATE NIGHT FUN

Royal Odyssey ***passengers are welcomed by Greek dancers in Crete.***

A little less spectacular, but equally enthusiastic, entertainment is offered in the largest lounge after the evening meal. This is one of the day's big events and a wonderful way to wind down. The shows are always energetic and some are topnotch (so enjoyable that you would even pay to see them). Some of the best evening entertainment can be usually found aboard the ships cruising in the Caribbean. And you are soon aware if a ship line pays particular attention to its entertainment. For example, Royal Caribbean boasts that you never see the same act twice, as it shuttles groups between ports and its vast fleet. But however good a professional group can be, I always prefer the traditional cruise staff talent show to anything (probably because the faces are familiar).

This is where the Norwegians, Greeks, Italians and other nationalities distinguish themselves in native dances, colorful costumes, a little clowning and some singing. If you enjoy dressing up and being someone else for a few hours, bring along a splendid costume and be the show stopper if your ship has a masquerade party. (I think you also win a bottle of something that goes by the name of champagne.)

Late in the evening, the main lounge continues to keep some passengers contented with soft music and dancing, while others scatter around the ship. This is the time I choose a quiet moonlit nightcap and my cabin. Elsewhere the action continues in a discotheque and doesn't even break while the midnight buffet is served. After all, the hours fly by, and A Club Called Dazzles aboard the *Norway* actually advertises a closing at 3 a.m. Oh well, that leaves just enough time for a short rest before early bird coffee at 6, and then the fun begins all over again!

GLOSSARY OF NAUTICAL TERMS

No one wants to sound like an Old Salt, as they say, but learning some of the language of the sea will make you feel like an experienced sailor—especially if this is your first cruise. Study a few of the nautical terms listed below and you'll be surprised at how quickly you will begin to say port and starboard without giving it another thought. Port, of course, is the left side of your ship (both words have four letters so that's easy to remember) and starboard is the right side.

ABEAM—means perpendicular to the point halfway between bow and stern; forward of the beam; aft of beam.

ACCOMMODATION LADDER—a lightweight ladder made of wooden slats or aluminum, that is slung from the ship to a dock or small boat. Pilots and other officials use this ladder to come aboard while at sea. Passengers use this ladder at some ports as well, when the vessel is anchored out and tenders are the only available transportation between ship and shore.

AFT—toward the rear of the vessel, or to the stern.

ALLEYWAY—any passageway or narrow corridor of a ship. Sailors also use this term ashore to describe the narrow street behind port.

AMIDSHIPS—in the middle of the vessel; halfway between port and starboard.

AWNING—the same term as on land. Any canvas covering strung over an open deck area for protection from sun and rain.

ASTERN—behind the rear or stern of the ship; often refers to something in the wake.

ATHWART—across the width of the ship.

BALLAST—weight placed in the ship to keep her on an even keel when empty. Calle Cristo, Old San Juan's most famous street, is paved with adoquines—bluish-tint bricks formerly used for ballast in Spanish ships.

BAR—sandbar, caused by current or tide near the shore.

BEAM—width of ship at her widest point.

BEARING—compass direction, expressed in degrees.

BELOW—under the deck or on a subsequent deck farther down in the ship. Can also mean "at rest" or "off duty" for crew member.

BELLS—sounding of the ship's time, at half-hour intervals, from one to eight, beginning at 4:30, 8:30, and 12:30 anew.

BERTH—nautical term for bed, means where vessel docks in port as well as the beds in your cabin.

BON VOYAGE—French expression for Happy Voyage or Journey. When you tell your friends you are taking a cruise, they will say Bon Voyage!

BOW—the forward, or foremost, part of the ship.

BRIDGE—ship's command center, where all navigation and navigational decisions are made. It is located above and forward of the passenger areas, much like the cockpit of a 747 aircraft. This is the domain of the captain and his officers; passengers are admitted only by special invitation.

BULKHEAD—wall-like construction inside a vessel for subdividing space or strengthening the structure; partition wall.

BUNKERS—a large bin or receptacle for storing fuel. Also refers to the fuel itself.

CABIN—your bedroom or sleeping accommodation aboard ship. Also called a stateroom, depending upon size and situation.

CABLE—the heavy iron chain used for the ship's anchor.

CLASS—first, cabin, and tourist were the three classes passengers booked across the Atlantic for years. Under my definition, Cunard Line has the three-class system on the *Queen Elizabeth 2* transatlantic run (although they only admit to having two classes).

COLORS—refers to the national flag or emblem flown by the ship.

COMPANIONWAY—interior stairway leading from deck to deck.

COURSE—ship's heading—laid down by pencil. Even though computers do most of the work now, the navigator is responsible for whether the ship is on course.

CROW'S NEST—the lookout cage high up on the foremast.

DAVIT—the apparatus that secures the lifeboats at sea and from which they are launched. (Pronounced day-vit.)

DECK—each floor of a ship.

DISEMBARK—to go out from a ship. Opposite of embark.

DOCK—where the ship ties up. Also called pier, wharf, quay.

DRAFT OR DRAUGHT—the amount of water a ship draws or needs to keep out of trouble. The draft is calculated from the lowest point of the ship to the waterline.

DRILL—any exercise ordered by the master of the ship, like the lifeboat drill the first day out.

EMBARK—to board a ship. Opposite of disembark.

FATHOM—a measure of six feet; used in determining the depth of water by soundings. This term is familiar to many Americans, because Mark Twain, the pen name of Samuel Clemens (who spent his youth as a pilot on the Mississippi River), means "two fathoms sounded."

FIX—to obtain a geographical position by any method (sextant, radar, satellite navigator).

FLAGS—ships talk to each other with flags in an international code of signals that all nations understand. While the flag hoisted on a private yacht might say "Come over for a drink," the signals on a large ship leaving port will show if a pilot is aboard, whether a medical doctor is in attendance and what type of cargo is carried. Signal flags are never flown at sea, except when a vessel is in distress. The ship's country of registry is flown from the stern in port; on the gaff from the mast at sea. The company flag is on the foremast. A courtesy ensign is flown on the starboard side of available halyards when ship is approaching a port. This ensign can be at a height equal to (but no higher than) the ship's national flag.

FREEBOARD—the outer part of a ship's hull between the waterline and main deck.

FREE PORT—a port not included in customs territory, or free from import taxes. For example, St. Thomas in the U.S. Virgin Islands is a free port and a favorite stop for Caribbean cruise shoppers.

FUNNEL—the smokestack, or chimney, of the ship.

GALLEY—the kitchen.

GANGWAY—a portable accommodation for entry/exit from the ship. Used to be known as a gangplank.

GMT—standard of time as designated at the Observatory in Greenwich, England. Used in England and as a basis of calculation elsewhere.

GROSS REGISTER TON—a measure of the size of a ship. One hundred cubic feet equals one gross register ton.

HATCHWAY—wide openings on deck allowing access to a holds or lower deck.

HAWSER—a rope of sufficient size and strength to tow or secure a ship.

HEAD—toilet.

HELM—the entire steering apparatus of the ship. The expression "at helm" means whoever has charge of the ship's course at that time.

HOLD—the area below deck where cargo is stored.

HOUSE FLAG—the company flag or symbol flown from the mast, or a design on the funnel that designates who owns the ship.

HULL—also called hulk, the body of the ship.

ISTHMUS—a narrow strip of land bordered on both sides by water.

JACOB'S LADDER—a rope ladder usually with wooden rungs.

JONES ACT—the Jones Act of 1886, designed to protect American shipping interests, forbids foreign-registered ships from carrying passengers between U.S. ports. It is often strictly enforced by the U.S. Bureau of Customs. Puerto Rico and the U.S. Virgin Islands and some others are exempted.

KEEL—the backbone of the vessel. To be "on even keel" means to be in balance, or steady.

KEELHAULED—seamen's expression for giving someone a good "telling off." Originates from the days of wooden ships and iron men (instead of the opposite nowadays) where miscreants were punished by literally having ropes tied to hands and feet and being hauled under the keel of the ship. Never mind the drowning, barnacles, wood splinters and all would do the job.

KNOT—a unit of speed for a ship. One knot is equal to one nautical mile (6080.2 feet), or approximately 1.15 statute (land) miles per hour. The speed of a ship is measured in knots.

LATITUDE—angular distance measured in degrees north and south of the equator. One degree equals about 60 nautical miles.

LEAGUE—a unit of distance. In English-speaking countries, a league is approximately 3.45 nautical miles.

LEEWARD—the direction toward which the wind blows.

LETTING THE CAT OUT OF THE BAG—has nothing to do with secrets or gossip. Meant impending punishment, as seamen were whipped with something called "a cat-o'-nine-tails."

LIFEBOAT—a small launch designed to carry passengers in an emergency. Lifeboat stations are noted in every cabin. Lifeboat drills, mandatory on all vessels, require passengers and crew to don their life vests and proceed to their boat stations (listed on back of cabin door).

LOG—the daily record in which details of navigation, weather, engine performance and other aspects of ship's progress are kept. The log is also a device for measuring speed.

LONGITUDE—angular distance measured east and west of Greenwich, England. One degree varies according to the earth's curvature. all degrees of longitude are widest at the equator and merge at the true poles.

MANIFEST—list of ship's passengers, crew, and cargo.

MASTER—the captain of the ship.

NAUTICAL MILE—6080.2 feet (land mile is 5280 feet).

NOON—when sun reaches its highest point.

PITCH—the rise and fall of the ship in rough seas, as opposed to the "roll" or rocking motion from side to side. Pitch is also the angle of the propeller blade.

PORT—the left side of the ship looking forward, also indicated by red navigational light; harbor.

PORTHOLE—the round window in your cabin. Deluxe cabins have large, rectangular windows, which are not portholes.

PROW—another word for bow or front of the ship.

QUAY—dock, berth, pier. (Pronounced "key.")

RAILING—something to keep you from falling off the ship; good to lean on in the moonlight or while watching flying fish.

REGISTRY—certificate of ownership. The country of registry is denoted by the national flag flown at the stern of the vessel. The port of registry is written on the stern of the ship.

ROLL—the sideways motion of the ship, as opposed to the "pitch" or up and down motion.

RUNNING LIGHTS—the colored lights required on all vessels at night to indicate their direction or course.

SAFETY AT SEA LAWS—according to the International Convention for the Safety of Life at Sea of 1960, all ships embarking passengers in U.S. ports must comply with the strict standards set forth at this convention.

SHE—yes, ships are always considered members of the female gender. It's an old tradition that even feminists have to accept. Longtime men at sea have their own reasons . . . but here are two. "It's not the initial expense that breaks you, it's the upkeep." "Because she shows her topsides, hides her bottom, and when coming into port, heads straight for the buoys."

SHIP TO SHORE—communications with land by radio telephone. Some ships now use a telephone link by satellite, which is faster.

SHIP'S TOTE—want to spend a dollar? Guess how many nautical miles the ship has steamed in a given time. The cruise staff announces the daily tote.

SKIPPER—slang for captain. This term is not used on cruise ships, as the more formal "master" is generally employed.

SPLICING THE MAIN BRACE—any sailor who ran up to splice or repair the main brace in the heat of battle received an extra tot of rum!

STABILIZER—a retractable fin extending into the water on either side of the vessel to ensure smooth sailing in rough seas. Most vessels are now equipped with stabilizers of the Denny Brown type from England.

STACK—funnel or chimney of the vessel.

STAGE—a walkway protruding from the front of a "steamboat," that can be raised while cruising or lowered to embark passengers and/or supplies.

SOUNDING—see fathom.

STARBOARD—the right side of the ship looking forward, also indicated by a green navigational light.

STATEROOM—a sleeping accommodation aboard ship.

STERN—the aft, or extreme rear section of the ship.

SUPERSTRUCTURE—the structural part of the ship above the main deck.

TENDER—a smaller vessel, sometimes a lifeboat, used to carry passengers from ship to shore and vice versa.

TIME AT SEA—nautical time is like Navy time, based on the 24-hour clock. Hence, 8 a.m. is 0800 and 8 p.m. is 2000 hours.

UNCHARTED—anything (rock, reef, canyon) that does not appear on a chart of the area.

UNDER WAY—indicates the ship is set to sail, the anchor has been brought up, and the lines let go.

WAKE—the trail a ship leaves behind in the water, the foam churned up by the propellers.

WATERLINE—the painted line dividing the ship between the portion that should remain above water and the section that is below.

WEIGH ANCHOR—to raise the anchor and prepare to get under way, a command given from the bridge.

WINCH—power-operated machine used to work the ship's cranes and/or davit.

WINDWARD—the direction from which the wind is blowing.

WINDLASS—a device for raising the anchor.

YARDARM—either outer arm of the yard (beam) of a square sail. The expression "when the sun is over the yardarm" now means that cocktail time is approaching. However, the sun is over the yardarm in the morning.

YAW—to deviate from the ship's course, usually caused by high seas.

ABBREVIATIONS

MS—Motor Ship

MTS—Motor Turbine Ship

MV—Motor Vessel

TSS—Turbine Steamship

SS—Steamship

USS—United States Ship

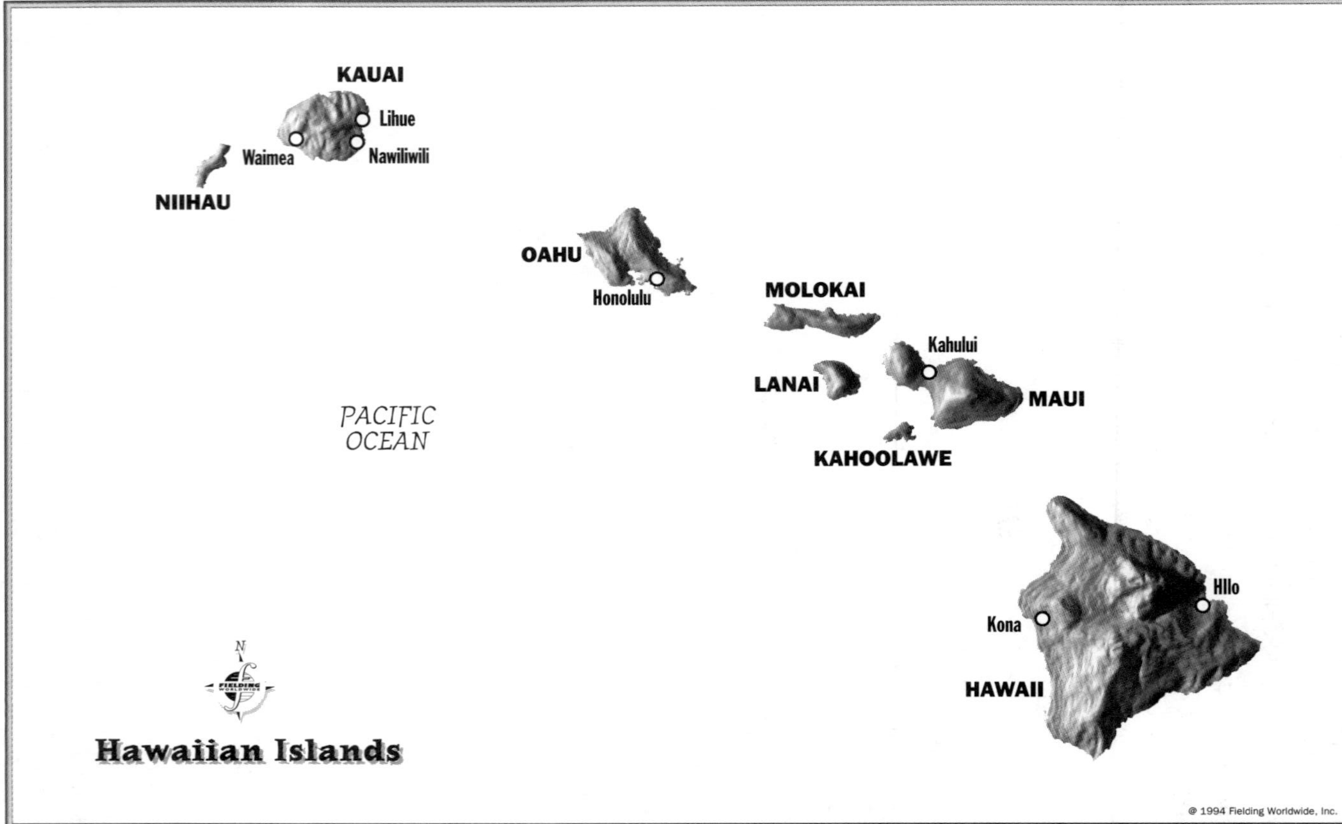

KAUAI
Lihue
Waimea
Nawiliwili
NIIHAU
OAHU
Honolulu
MOLOKAI
Kahului
LANAI
MAUI
PACIFIC OCEAN
KAHOOLAWE
Hilo
Kona
HAWAII
N
FIELDING WORLDWIDE
Hawaiian Islands
© 1994 Fielding Worldwide, Inc.

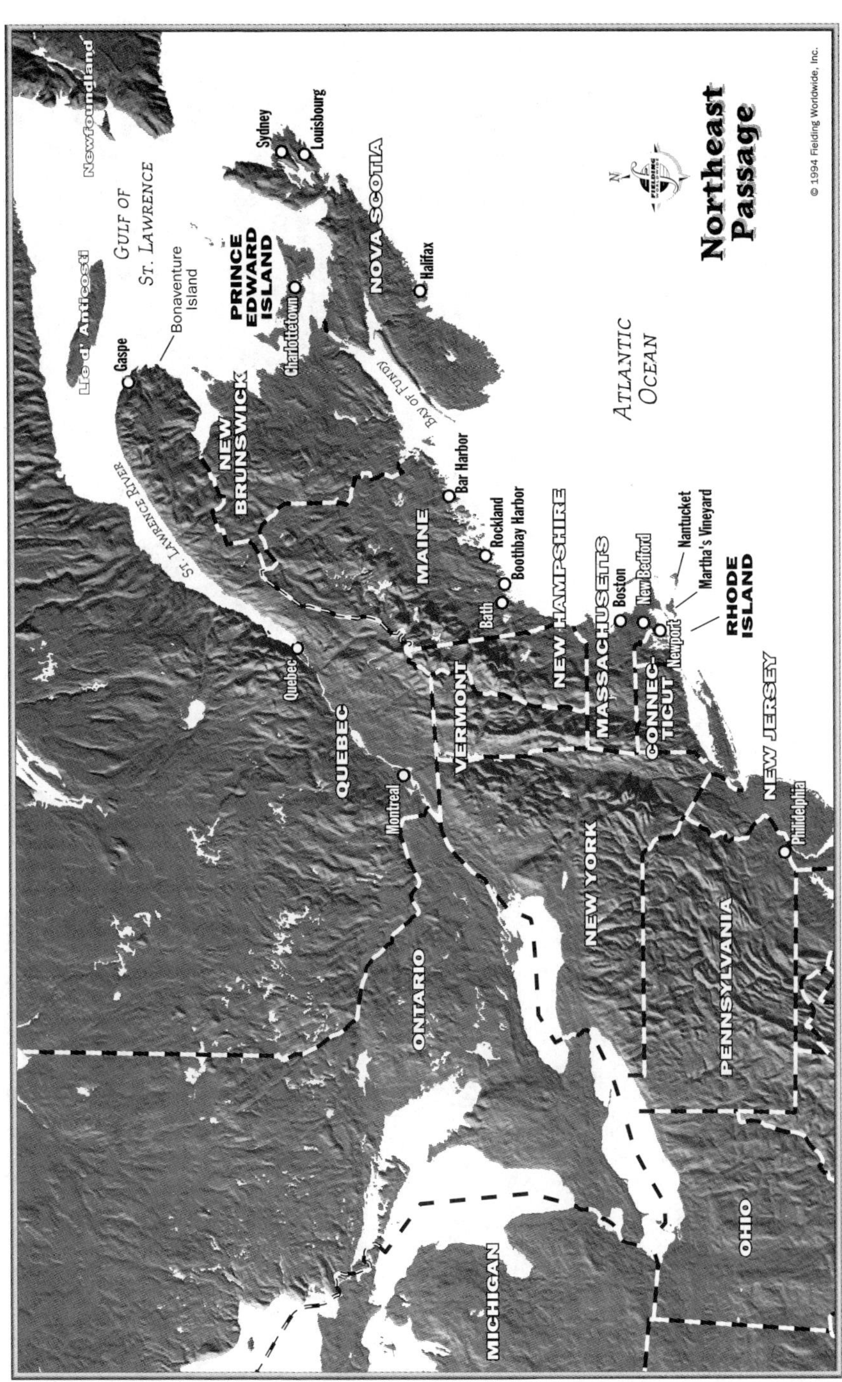
Northeast Passage
Newfoundland
Lle d' Anticosti
Gulf of St. Lawrence
Bonaventure Island
Gaspe
Sydney
Louisbourg
Prince Edward Island
Charlottetown
Nova Scotia
Halifax
Bay of Fundy
New Brunswick
St. Lawrence River
Quebec
Quebec
Montreal
Atlantic Ocean
Bar Harbor
Rockland
Boothbay Harbor
Bath
Maine
New Hampshire
Vermont
Massachusetts
Boston
New Bedford
Nantucket
Martha's Vineyard
Rhode Island
Newport
Connec-ticut
New Jersey
Philidelphia
New York
Pennsylvania
Ontario
Ohio
Michigan
© 1994 Fielding Worldwide, Inc.

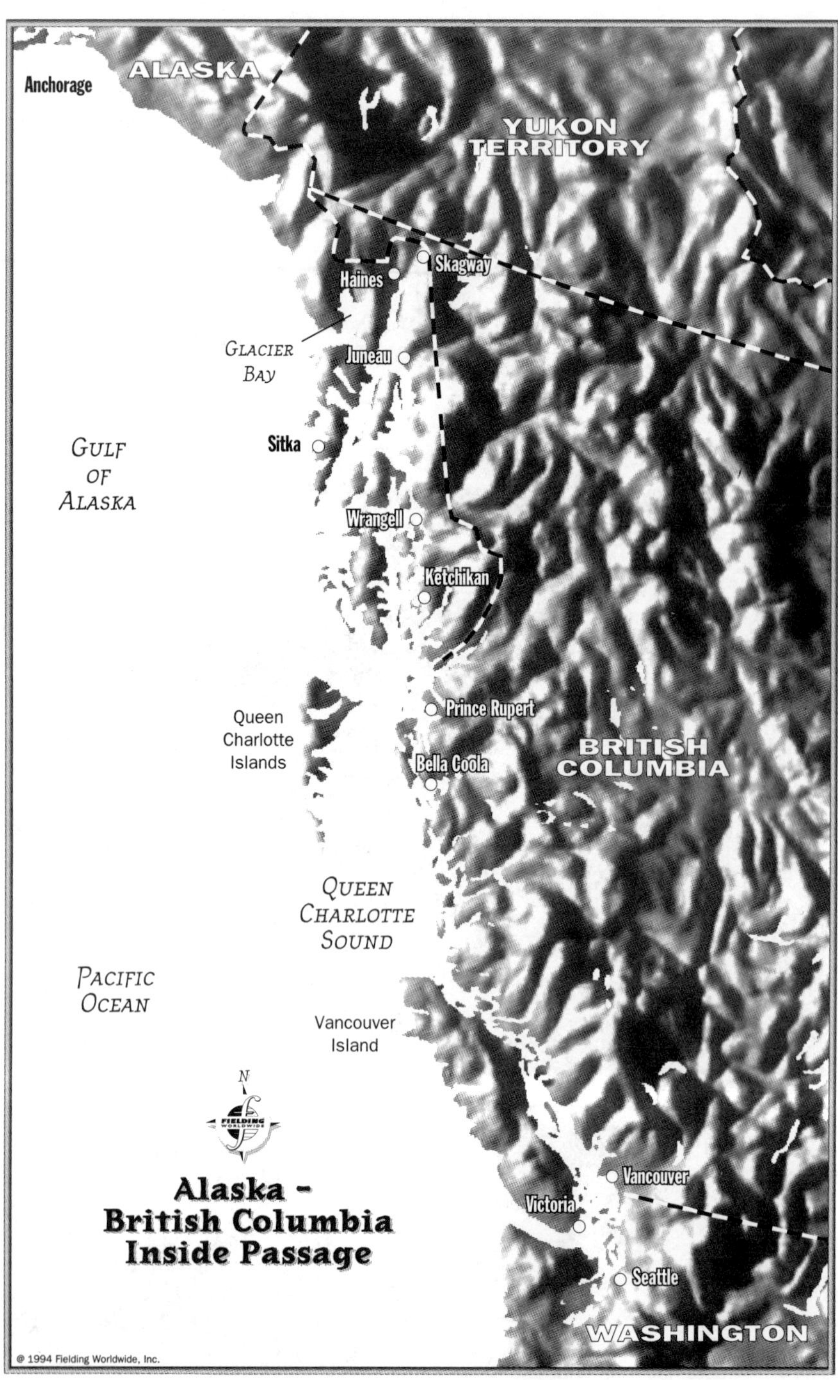
ALASKA
Anchorage
YUKON TERRITORY
Skagway
Haines
Glacier Bay
Juneau
Sitka
Gulf of Alaska
Wrangell
Ketchikan
Prince Rupert
Queen Charlotte Islands
Bella Coola
British Columbia
Queen Charlotte Sound
Pacific Ocean
Vancouver Island
N
FIELDING WORLDWIDE
Alaska - British Columbia Inside Passage
Vancouver
Victoria
Seattle
WASHINGTON
© 1994 Fielding Worldwide, Inc.

UNITED STATES OF AMERICA
Los Angeles
San Diego
Ensenada
ATLANTIC OCEAN
BAHAMA ISLANDS
Miami
Galveston
New Orleans
GULF OF MEXICO
Baja Peninsula
Cabo San Lucas
Mazatlan
MEXICO
Puerto Vallarta
PACIFIC OCEAN
Manzanillo
Ixtapa
Zihuatanejo
Acapulco
Playa del Carmen
Cancun
Cozumel
CUBA
CAYMAN ISLANDS
JAMAICA
BELIZE
GUATEMALA
HONDURAS
CARIBBEAN SEA
NICARAGUA
EL SALVADOR
COSTA RICA
PANAMA
Mexico
© 1994 Fielding Worldwide, Inc.

MINNESOTA
MICHIGAN
WISCONSIN
St. Paul
Wabasha
La Crosse
Prairie du Chien
Dubuque
NEW YORK
PENNSYLVANIA
Pittsburgh
IOWA
OHIO
INDIANA
Nauvoo
ILLINOIS
Gallipolis
Cincinnati
Madison
Hannibal
Ripley
WEST VIRGINIA
St. Louis
Evansville
Louisville
VIRGINIA
KANSAS
Cairo
KENTUCKY
MISSOURI
NORTH CAROLINA
TENNESSEE
OKLAHOMA
Memphis
SOUTH CAROLINA
ARKANSAS
MISSISSIPPI
GEORGIA
ALABAMA
Vicksburg
LOUISIANA
Natchez
TEXAS
St. Francisville
Baton Rouge
Houmas House
Oak Alley
New Orleans
GULF OF MEXICO
FLORIDA
N
FIELDING WORLDWIDE
Mississippi River
© 1994 Fielding Worldwide, Inc.

Far East
FIELDING WORLDWIDE
N
RUSSIA
MONGOLIA
CHINA
JAPAN
NORTH KOREA
SOUTH KOREA
Pacific Ocean
Tokyo
Yokohama
Kyoto
Kobe
Pusan
Beijing
Tianjin
Soochow
Shanghai
East China Sea
Taipei
TAIWAN
Guangzhou
Hong Kong
Macao
South China Sea
BURMA
LAOS
THAILAND
VIETNAM
Bangkok
CAMBODIA
Ho Chi Minh City
Manila
PHILIPPINES
BRUNEI
Penang
Kuala Lumpur
MALAYSIA
SINGAPORE
INDONESIA
PAPUA NEW GUINEA
Komodo
Surabaya
Bali
Jakarta
Yogyakarta
AUSTRALIA
© 1994 Fielding Worldwide, Inc.

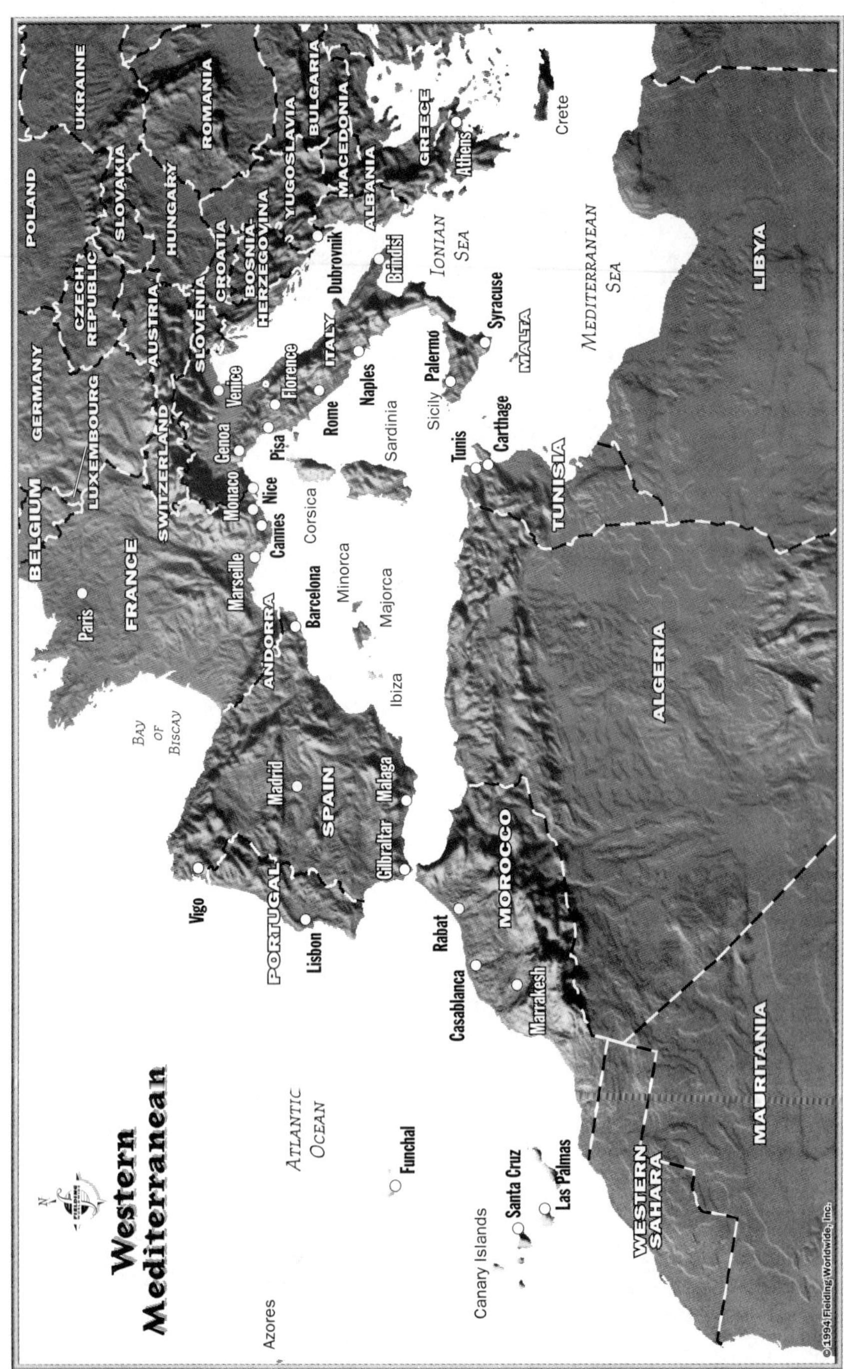
Western Mediterranean
Azores
Atlantic Ocean
Funchal
Canary Islands
Santa Cruz
Las Palmas
Western Sahara
Mauritania
Morocco
Casablanca
Rabat
Marrakesh
Algeria
Tunisia
Tunis
Carthage
Libya
Portugal
Lisbon
Vigo
Spain
Madrid
Gibraltar
Malaga
Bay of Biscay
Andorra
Barcelona
Ibiza
Majorca
Minorca
France
Paris
Marseille
Cannes
Nice
Monaco
Corsica
Sardinia
Belgium
Luxembourg
Switzerland
Germany
Genoa
Pisa
Venice
Florence
Rome
Naples
Italy
Sicily
Palermo
Syracuse
Malta
Mediterranean Sea
Ionian Sea
Brindisi
Dubrovnik
Austria
Slovenia
Croatia
Bosnia-Herzegovina
Czech Republic
Poland
Slovakia
Hungary
Yugoslavia
Albania
Macedonia
Greece
Athens
Crete
Romania
Bulgaria
Ukraine
©1994 Fielding Worldwide, Inc.

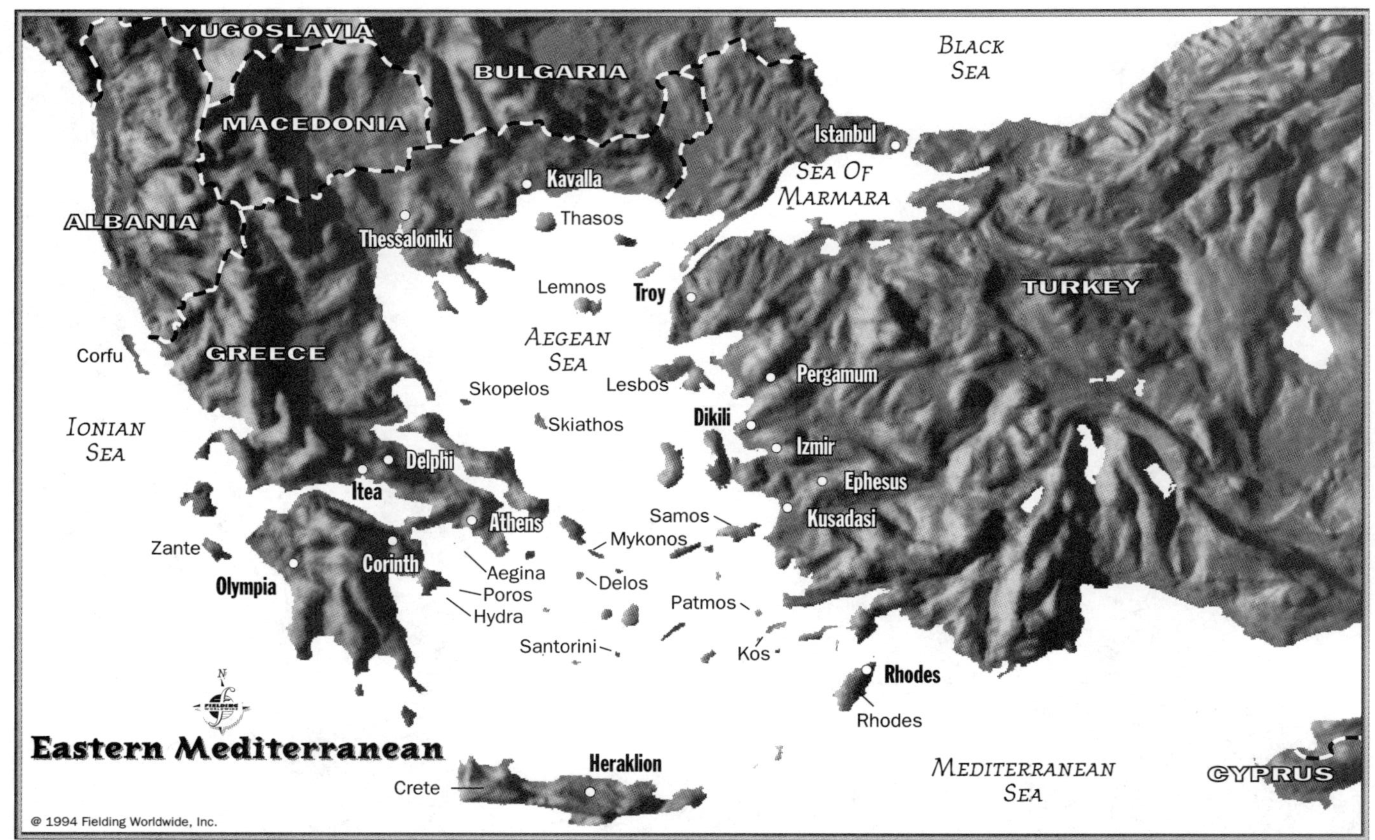

Eastern Mediterranean
© 1994 Fielding Worldwide, Inc.
YUGOSLAVIA
BULGARIA
MACEDONIA
ALBANIA
GREECE
TURKEY
CYPRUS
BLACK SEA
SEA OF MARMARA
AEGEAN SEA
IONIAN SEA
MEDITERRANEAN SEA
Istanbul
Kavalla
Thasos
Thessaloniki
Lemnos
Troy
Corfu
Skopelos
Lesbos
Pergamum
Skiathos
Dikili
Izmir
Delphi
Ephesus
Itea
Athens
Samos
Kusadasi
Mykonos
Zante
Corinth
Olympia
Aegina
Poros
Hydra
Delos
Patmos
Santorini
Kos
Rhodes
Rhodes
Heraklion
Crete

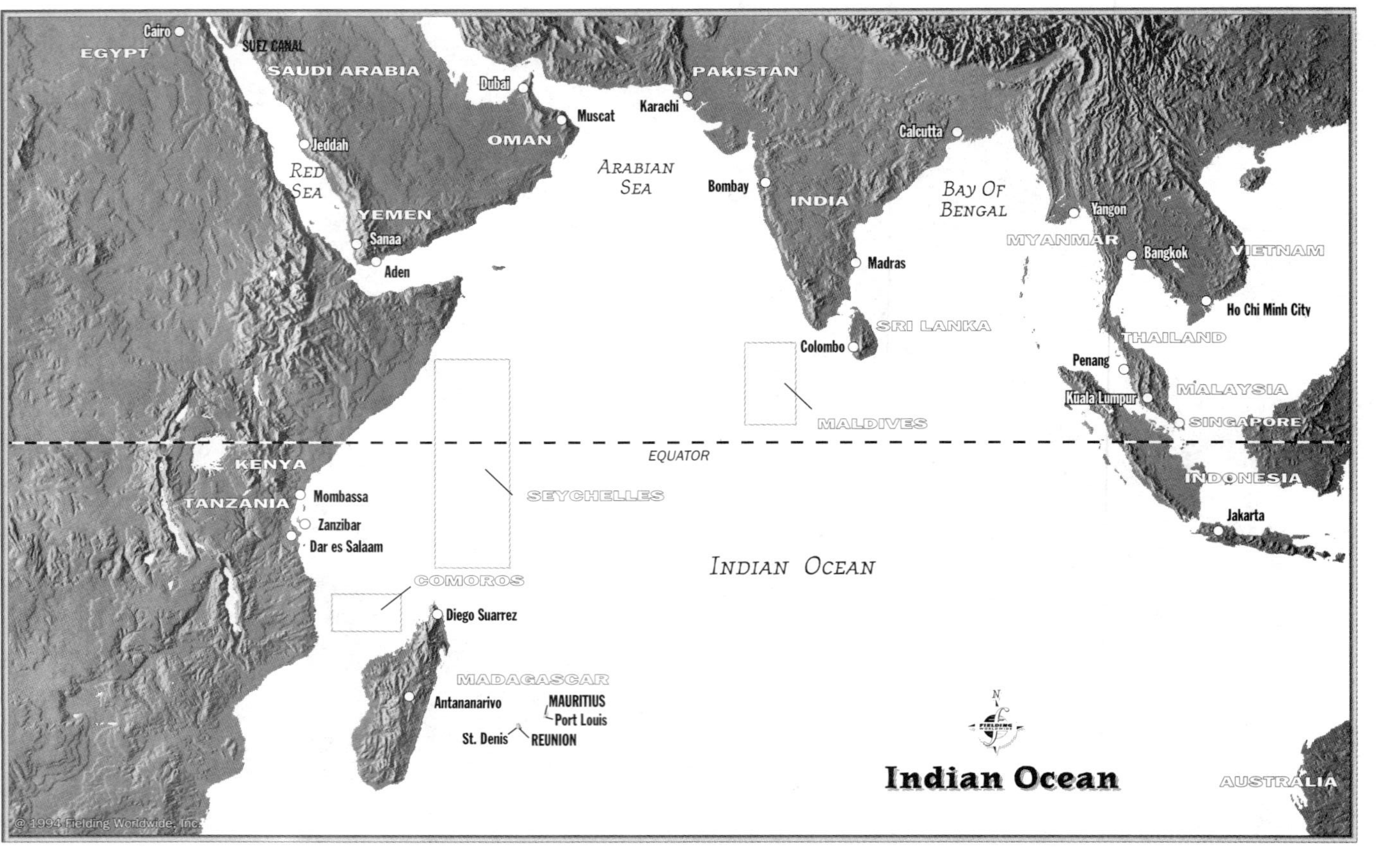
Indian Ocean
EGYPT
Cairo
SUEZ CANAL
SAUDI ARABIA
Jeddah
RED SEA
YEMEN
Sanaa
Aden
OMAN
Dubai
Muscat
ARABIAN SEA
Karachi
PAKISTAN
Bombay
INDIA
Madras
Calcutta
BAY OF BENGAL
SRI LANKA
Colombo
MALDIVES
MYANMAR
Yangon
Bangkok
THAILAND
VIETNAM
Ho Chi Minh City
MALAYSIA
Penang
Kuala Lumpur
SINGAPORE
INDONESIA
Jakarta
AUSTRALIA
EQUATOR
INDIAN OCEAN
SEYCHELLES
COMOROS
Diego Suarrez
MADAGASCAR
Antananarivo
St. Denis
REUNION
MAURITIUS
Port Louis
KENYA
TANZANIA
Mombassa
Zanzibar
Dar es Salaam
N
© 1994 Fielding Worldwide, Inc.

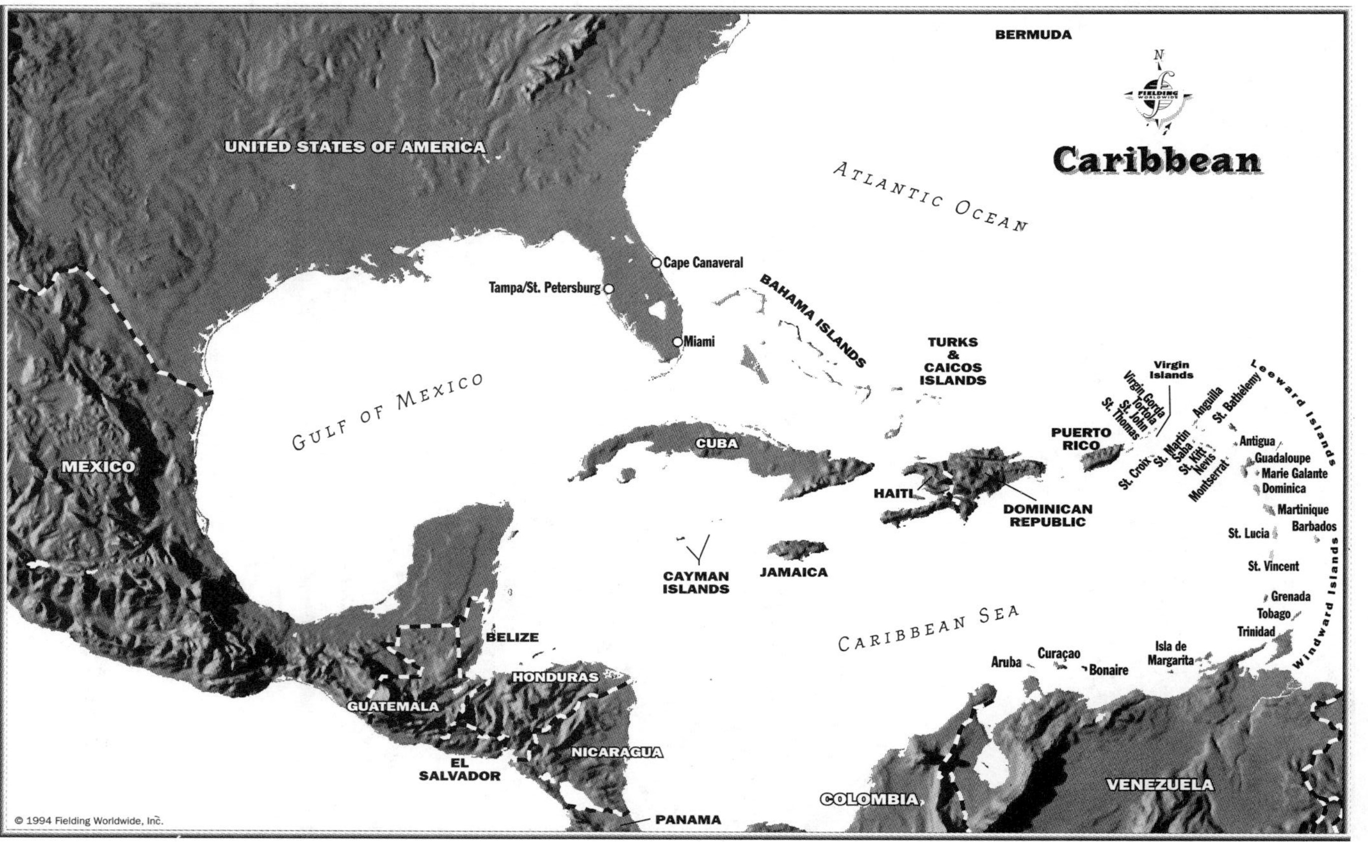
BERMUDA
Caribbean
Atlantic Ocean
UNITED STATES OF AMERICA
Cape Canaveral
Tampa/St. Petersburg
Miami
BAHAMA ISLANDS
TURKS & CAICOS ISLANDS
Gulf of Mexico
MEXICO
CUBA
HAITI
DOMINICAN REPUBLIC
PUERTO RICO
Virgin Islands
Virgin Gorda
Tortola
St. John
St. Thomas
St. Croix
St. Martin
Saba
St. Kitt
Nevis
Montserrat
Anguilla
St. Bathelemy
Leeward Islands
Antigua
Guadaloupe
Marie Galante
Dominica
Martinique
Barbados
St. Lucia
St. Vincent
Grenada
Tobago
Trinidad
Windward Islands
CAYMAN ISLANDS
JAMAICA
Caribbean Sea
Aruba
Curaçao
Bonaire
Isla de Margarita
BELIZE
HONDURAS
GUATEMALA
NICARAGUA
EL SALVADOR
PANAMA
COLOMBIA
VENEZUELA
© 1994 Fielding Worldwide, Inc.

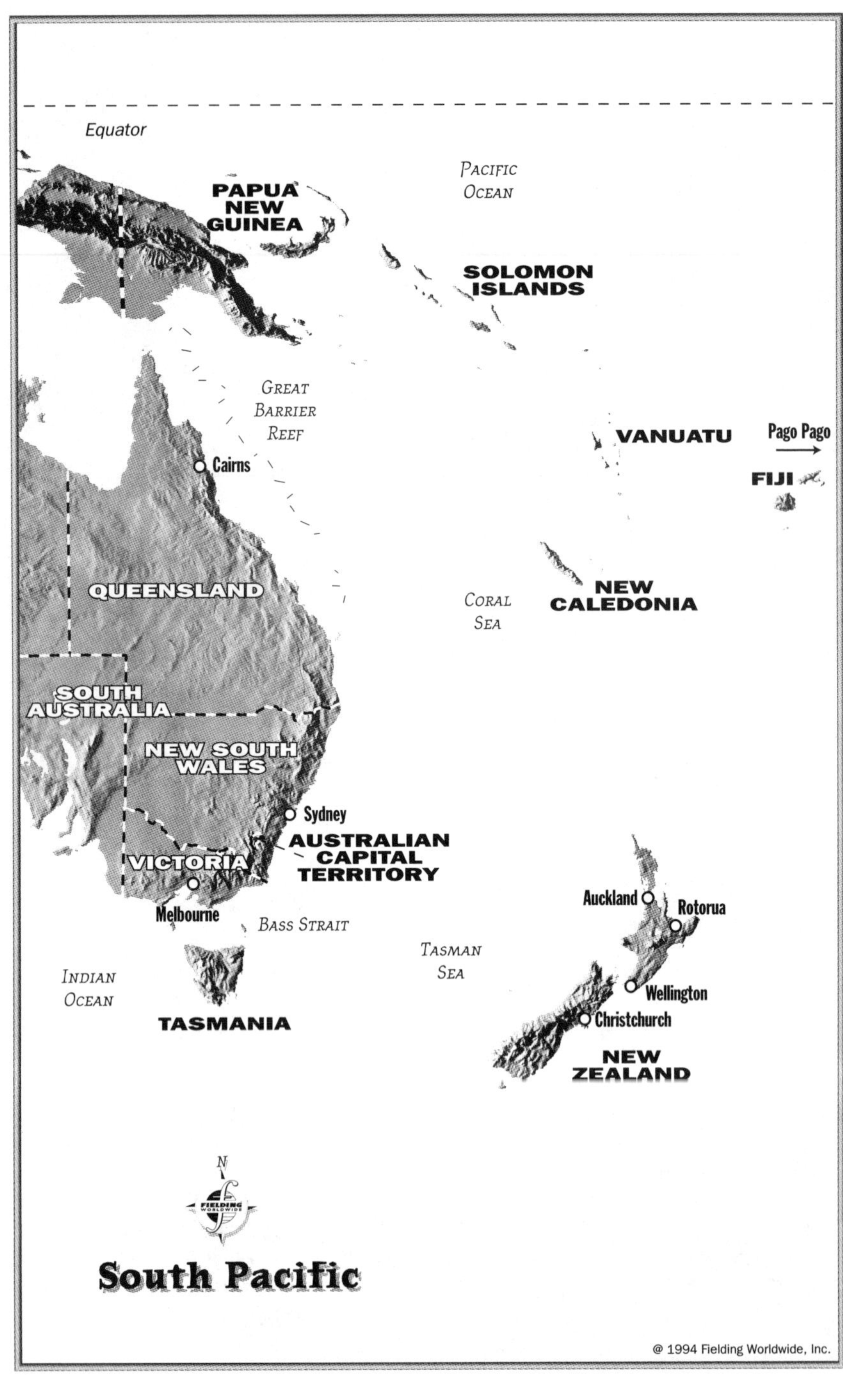

Equator
PACIFIC OCEAN
PAPUA NEW GUINEA
SOLOMON ISLANDS
GREAT BARRIER REEF
Cairns
VANUATU
Pago Pago
FIJI
QUEENSLAND
CORAL SEA
NEW CALEDONIA
SOUTH AUSTRALIA
NEW SOUTH WALES
Sydney
AUSTRALIAN CAPITAL TERRITORY
VICTORIA
Melbourne
BASS STRAIT
Auckland
Rotorua
TASMAN SEA
INDIAN OCEAN
Wellington
Christchurch
TASMANIA
NEW ZEALAND
N
FIELDING WORLDWIDE
South Pacific
@ 1994 Fielding Worldwide, Inc.

Caribbean Sea
Panama Canal
Cartagena
Caracas
TRINIDAD & TOBAGO
PANAMA
VENEZUELA
GUYANA
SURINAME
FRENCH GUIANA
Bogota
COLOMBIA
Quito
Equator
ECUADOR
Manaus
Guayaquil
Amazon
Recife
PERU
BRAZIL
Lima
Salvador
BOLIVIA
Pacific Ocean
CHILE
PARAGUAY
Santos
Rio de Janeiro
Porto Alegre
Atlantic Ocean
Valparaiso
Santiago
ARGENTINA
URUGUAY
Buenos Aires
Montevideo
Puerto Montt
FALKLAND ISLANDS
Strait of Magellan
SOUTH GEORGIA (FALKLAND)
N
South America
© 1994 Fielding Worldwide, Inc.

N
FIELDING WORLDWIDE
British Isles
Shetland Islands
Orkney Islands
Lewis
Harris
Hebrides Islands
NORTH SEA
SCOTLAND
ATLANTIC OCEAN
Edinburgh
NORTHERN IRELAND
Belfast
York
Hull
Dublin
Holyhead
Liverpool
Conway
GALWAY BAY
ENGLAND
IRELAND
Waterford
Stratford-upon-Avon
WALES
Oxford
London
Windsor
BANTRY BAY
ST. GEORGE'S CHANNEL
Dover
Calais
Southampton
Plymouth
ENGLISH CHANNEL
Le Havre
Channel Islands

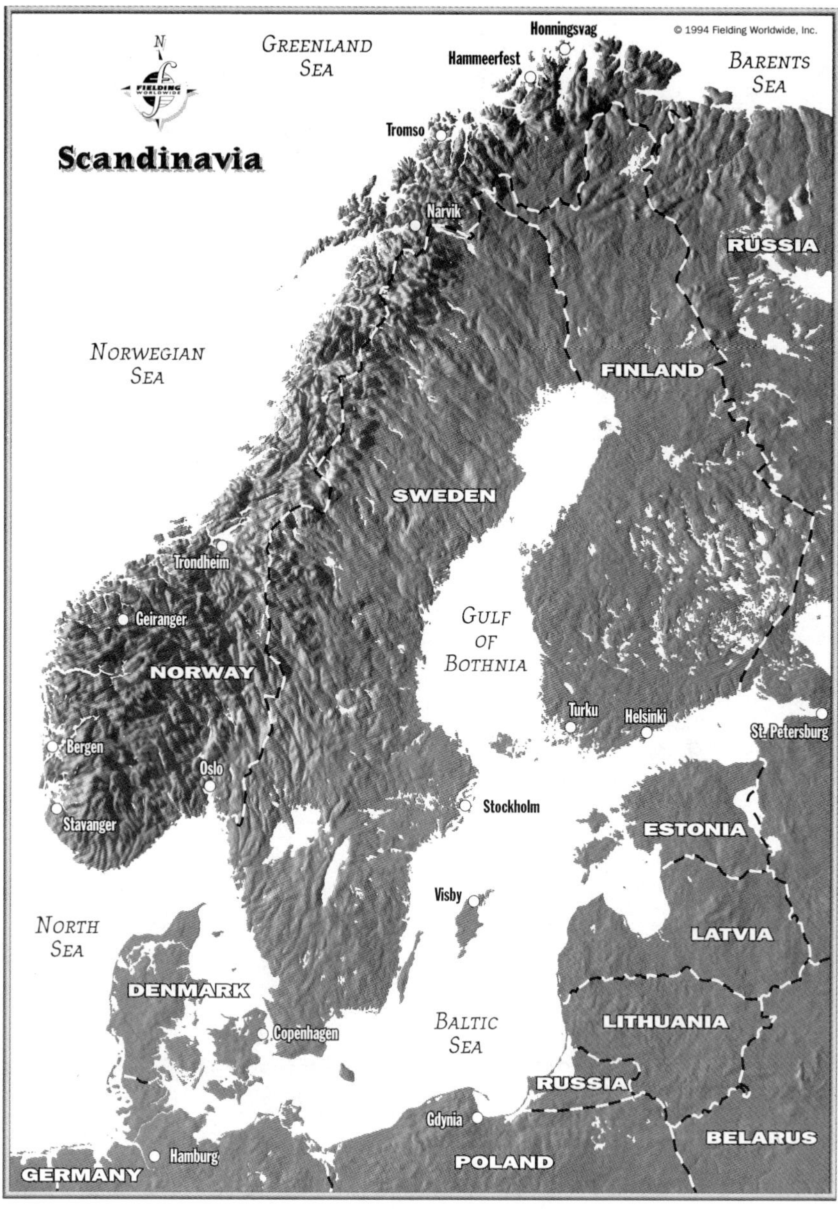

Scandinavia
© 1994 Fielding Worldwide, Inc.
Greenland Sea
Barents Sea
Norwegian Sea
North Sea
Gulf of Bothnia
Baltic Sea
Honningsvag
Hammeerfest
Tromso
Narvik
Trondheim
Geiranger
Bergen
Oslo
Stavanger
Stockholm
Turku
Helsinki
St. Petersburg
Visby
Copenhagen
Gdynia
Hamburg
RUSSIA
FINLAND
SWEDEN
NORWAY
ESTONIA
LATVIA
DENMARK
LITHUANIA
RUSSIA
BELARUS
POLAND
GERMANY

SHOPPING

Shopping for duty-free bargains aboard the Westward

Browsing through the local markets and shops is definitely an important pastime on travels. Just consider how the art of shopping introduces us to the local people, products and specialties of the land. I never fail to come away with something unusual and enjoyable by spending a little time looking at what is available both aboard ship and in ports of call. In addition to the usual souvenirs or remembrances of where I was through T-shirts, hats and accessories, perfumes and other paraphernalia, there are fragrant spices for a song, as well as flavorful liqueurs in interesting bottles and charming works of art that make memories linger long after the cruise is over.

SHIPBOARD SHOPPING

AUTHOR'S OBSERVATION

Cruise ship stores are in direct competition with merchants ashore, and very often you'll find the best deals on perfumes, china and crystal at sea. And, some will match any price you find in port–a good deal in the Caribbean, where there really aren't all that many bargains now.

A great deal has changed in the past few years in shipboard shops, so I never fail to check them out in my annual inspection tours. Although many are run by outside franchises and have a certain amount of junk merchandise that shouldn't be allowed valuable space, most of the shops these days have excellent buys in jewelry, handbags, scarves, perfumes and cruisewear. Shipboard shopping has become a multi-billion dollar business and warehouses in south Florida are brimming with goods from all over the world to be loaded onto cruise ships sailing the Caribbean. According to shop managers, Gucci handbags are the number-one seller afloat followed by perfumes and fancy watches. But don't be surprised to see fox and mink joining the ranks of Hummel and Majorcan pearls!

When the newly-refurbished *Queen Elizabeth 2* returned to service in May 1987, she boasted a $7 million shopping arcade filled with Gucci, Dior, Louis Feraud, Aquascutum, Pringle, etc., and with prices to match. The Garrard jewelry shop featured a $250,000 graduated diamond necklace in case one of you wins big at the tables. In the Dunhill shop, men's blazers are a mere $500-plus (compared to $750 on land). One shop rents and tailors tuxedos for men, while another sells such English delicacies as smoked salmon and Stilton cheese, as well as jams and a variety of tea. It is a lovely arcade and a wonderful place to browse especially on a transatlantic voyage when the foghorns can be heard in the distance. The shopping arcade aboard the Crystal Harmony is especially chic. Crystal will match any prices found ashore and merchandise can be returned if there is a problem later.

The *Norway* has a two-level emporium, Le Drugstore, on one deck (sundries, paperbacks, cigarettes and liquor) with Upstairs at the Downstairs above, where unusual gift items, china, crystal and porcelain, as well as a selection of fine watches are displayed. The Golden Touch has fine jewelry; Dimensions has chic cruisewear for women, and the Islander caters to the male ego. Faces and Fragrances sells cosmetics and perfumes, and Norway Nights is a new boutique featuring evening wear and furs for both sexes. At the end of the promenade is a conveniently located ice cream parlor (adjacent to the children's computer room), where you can satisfy your soul with one of Sven's favorite flavors.

Onboard the 74,000-ton *Sovereign of the Sea*, a total of eight different boutiques line the shopping area known as Shops of Centrum. The arcade's designer calls it London's Bond Street/Miami's Bal Harbour/Los Angeles Rodeo Drive collectively. Among the fancy storefronts are Gucci, of course, a fabulous perfumerie, a Scandinavian shop featuring Orrefors crystal, local crafts and Blue Fox fur jackets. A jewelry shop, a boutique full of elegant evening clothes, and an all-purpose sundry/reading material/liquor/cigarette, etc., complete the Centrum Mall.

The sailing region of ships is a clue to what the shops may feature. For example, Royal Cruise Line, which travels around the Greek Islands from spring through fall, stocks lovely Greek gold in its shops including pieces from the famed jeweler, LaLaounis. I saw a lovely necklace for about $7500! On board *Wind-Song* in French Polynesia, one shop featured the distinctive black pearls of the South Seas—beautiful but costly! Nonetheless, we all had a good look and a drool.

Holland America's vessels have terrific shopping areas, with cases full of Waterford, Royal Worcester and Royal Copenhagen, as well as the usual handbags and scarves, watches and jewelry. The *Nieuw Amsterdam's* shopping arcade is named Perel Straet after the Dutch Colony's center of import-export activity, so plan to buy your Dutch chocolates here. This same area is known as Canael Street on the *Noordam*, and the shops reflect the ship's east/west theme of exploration and discovery.

Muumuus and aloha shirts are the most popular items in the *Independence* and *Constitution* shops, and they disappear rapidly from the racks when Hawaiian night occurs on each ship! Even though each line attempts to "theme" its shops with items relating to itinerary and clientele, the world is small and products will pop up from just about anywhere! As on land, consider the price carefully and if you still love it buy it as a wonderful memento of your cruise.

SHOPPING AT PORTS OF CALL

AUTHOR'S OBSERVATION

In the old days, cruise directors made a bundle by getting kickbacks from shops they recommended in shore excursion lectures. Many cruise lines decided to get in on the act and now get "tips" as a matter of course from local merchants. How can you tell? When the port lecture includes recommendations for purchasing in specific stores, there's a deal already set. I take aside ship's staff and ask them where they shop, and if there's anything worth checking out in port (in the Caribbean, they usually direct me to a local crafts shop or advise me to stick to tee shirts).

Enticements lie around the corner of every street and lane in your current port of call! Tax-free temptations may seem too hard to resist, but bring the price of your favorite perfume, china and crystal—you may find a bargain, but prices are frequently better in the ship's shops (or at home!) these days. On several visits to **Bermuda** I have managed to collect an entire set of Herend hand painted china from Hungary at 40 percent below New York prices. Other good and frequent purchases from Trimingham's and Smith's and Cooper's include Shetland pullovers in beautiful colors, Liberty of London prints, and Bermuda bags with cedar handles. After I check Blucks once again to convince myself a new piece of Herend has not snuck into the shop, I never fail to feed another addiction. I pay a call on the island's artist laureate, Alfred Birdsey, to add a few more watercolors to my collection. No one has brought the spirit of Bermuda to paper so well as Birdsey. (I have called him an eccentric elsewhere and I shall continue to do so, because he loves it!) If your cruise vessel is **Bahamas**-bound or if you just pop over for the weekend out of Miami, you will want to save a few pennies to spend at the Straw Market in Rawson Square for bags and hats and such. This is about the only fun shopping left in the Bahamian capital, as Bay Street is no longer very interesting (unless you have a hankering for American fastfood-chain chicken or hamburger).

In the Caribbean most cruise vessels aim their bows straight for **St. Thomas**, USVI, and do not even bother to pass go. But the chaotic town of Charlotte Amalie (where there may very easily be 10,000 cruise passengers in port the same day) is no longer the bargain center. Professional photographers report they find the best prices on cameras in the world in some specialty stores, so bring along a discount catalogue (47th Street Photo in New York, is tops) and compare prices.

Throughout the Caribbean you can buy some lovely handcrafts. Puerto Rico has Santos (small religious wooden figures that are handcarved and very traditional), a Bacardi Rum factory, and a Hathaway shirt outlet in the center of the shopping district. In fact, San Juan has excellent outlet stores, including a Bass Shoe shop and a two-story Ralph Lauren boutique where bargains abound for both sexes. I don't recommend Barrachina, which has promised free piña coladas (a thimbleful) and two-dollar rides to the airport. When I went, the place was dirty and overpriced (and extremely rude when I refused to buy). You can find delft jugs and orange liqueur in Curacao, lovely filigree jewelry and Dunhill pipes in Trinidad, perfumes and French crystal in Martinique, and straw items wherever your cruise calls. Silver jewelry in **Mexico** is not the bargain it once was but prices are better than they have been for a few years. Take lots of cash if you plan some purchases—discounts abound with greenbacks. Mexico is also the home of Aca Joe for casual wear, and there are some good Polo outlet shops with pullovers, slacks, etc., for quite a savings. **Alaska** has fur boots, ivory curios, gold nuggets, totem-pole souvenirs and packaged fish products. It also boasts some fine local artists, so check out the galleries wherever you go. A recent call in **Costa Rica** brought a gold mine in coffee at $1 a pound! as well as hand-carved salad bowls, trays and some lovely handcrafts at the museum in San Jose. If I had a place to park one of the colorful hand-painted ox carts, that too would have been a memorable purchase.

South America Shopping

AUTHOR'S OBSERVATION

When traveling aboard ships bound for Brazilian ports, expect to find gem merchants as fellow passengers. These fellows can't pitch you aboard ship, but will schmooze and entertain "pigeons," offering a free car with driver for local sightseeing in Brazilian cities. A slight hitch, however, you must stop by our lovely showroom for a short look-see. If you bite, these merchants will nail you in the shop, and few escape without spending a bundle.

If your cruise includes ports in South America, you will have even more fun shopping. Hans Stern, who lives in **Rio de Janeiro**, is a jeweler known throughout the world for his good and sometimes gaudy designs featuring gold and Brazilian semiprecious stones. His stores will literally follow you around South America, and he has also opened in the U.S., Paris, Lisbon, Madeira, Frankfurt, Tel Aviv and

Jerusalem. The stores are reputable, as far as I can gather and the tag prices prevail (no bargaining). In Buenos Aires you will find some of the best shopping on the continent, especially when the dollar is in your favor. I once bought an extra suit case to lug home ten cashmere sweaters, six pairs of shoes, custom fitted buttery leather in every piece of clothing imaginable and a dyed nutria jacket—all bought for a steal. Be sure to check the shops along Rua Sui Pacha for great prices and styles. In **Caracas** you can buy jewelry made from cacique coins, the familiar Hand of Fatima, *chinchorros* (hammocks), handbags, and sandals.

If your vessel calls at **Montevideo**, you may want to pick up a few amethysts (they are considered the best in the world here), a suede or antelope jacket and nutria or seal coats. Or perhaps a nice gaucho hat with boots to match. **Chilean** specialties include colorful, handwoven ponchos, vicuña rugs, and artisan copper work. Chilean contemporary art is extremely interesting, and the rock shops feature locally mined lapis lazuli, jade, amethyst, agate and onyx. Although Lima overflows with silver and gold, you should also look for the many Indian items available, such as baskets, gourds, textiles, and rugs of alpaca and llama fur. When you get to **Ecuador**, you have landed where the very finest Panama hats are made. Ecuador has some lovely early Indian artifacts and some fine contemporary painters gain their inspiration from the pottery. The country has presented an artistic medal of honor to Olga Fisch, who turns out oneof-a-kind carpets and wall-hangings with early Indian motifs. They are worth every penny.

Sailing slowly along the **Amazon** will do wonders for your cruise diary and photo album, but don't expect to complete your Christmas list with all the exotica for sale. Other than some attractive round baskets (that fall apart on the way home) and some bowls made from gourds, there is not much available in the native inventory. **Manaus**, the former boom town 1000 miles up the Amazon, is a so-called free port but the shops are full of electronic goods and little kids sell fake perfumes on every street corner. There is one local handcraft shop, House of the Hummingbird, where everyone stops and rainmakers (a grass tube filled with sand) can be brought for about a dollar.

If your ship sails to the heart of the **Pacific Islands**, pick up some macadamia nuts in Honolulu, some sarongs in Tahiti, finely woven placemats in Samoa and a few baskets in Suva. Although koala bears are not for sale in Sydney, Maori carvings are the thing to buy in **New Zealand** (along with anything wooly, of course).

Hong Kong

If you're bound for the Far East, head straight for Hong Kong; it has everything anyone has ever wanted, and for the best price! While not the idyllic shoppers paradise it once was, Hong Kong is still the number one shopper's call on world cruises. Singapore tries to match Hong Kong as a free port but has never succeeded (there is less choice in products and the prices are slightly higher, probably because the shelves are cleaner). It's simple to spend money in Hong Kong as it's rather difficult to find anything else to do. Your ship docks right at Ocean Terminal, itself a huge shopping complex and only a short walk from the Nathan Road area where buying and selling is practically a religion. Here you can still have a silk dress made in forty-eight hours (but don't expect it to fit like standard-size clothes), find a setting for your new stones, buy photographic and stereo equipment and even pick up a Camcord at prices lower than many places outside New York (if you pay cash).

AUTHOR'S OBSERVATION

If you insist upon using a credit card, the shop may charge you an additional percentage to cover the carrying charges.

However, it is pretty hard to beat Hong Kong's prices if you shop carefully and follow the advice of the free *Stop and Shop Bargain Guide* (issued by the Hong Kong Tourist Association), which outlines licensed dealers for every type of equipment and product sold and gives suggested retail prices (which I have always found to be quite accurate). It is especially important to follow this guide for photographic equipment purchases. I am still staggered that my husband recently got more trade-in allowance for a lens than I originally paid in Hong Kong eight years ago. Such is Hong Kong.

AUTHOR'S OBSERVATION

A word to the world traveler. Avoid the fancy European designer shops–they are rather expensive and often more than what you would pay at home (especially when local merchants have good sales). Stick to what Hong Kong is famous for -Chinese-made goods and wearing apparel.

The tourist association has a good list of factory outlets (with maps and taxi instructions) that are great! Here you can buy lovely silk pants suits, shirts, lounging outfits and plenty of designer dresses. The labels are often missing but who cares?

If you plan to skip the **People's Republic of China**, you can make do with one of the many terrific Chinese department stores, completely owned and operated by the PRC and often offering better prices than in Guangzhou (Canton) or Beijing (Peking). These department stores market lovely silks and embroideries, carpets, jade, Ming dynasty-style vases and gold (the gold is only 9-karat, I believe). The best department store, China Arts and Crafts, has a Kowloon branch catty-corner to the Star Ferry Building (the one with the clocks), on the left-hand side as you walk from Ocean Terminal to Nathan Road. Hong Kong has also become quite a diamond center, but check first with the Hong Kong Tourist Association for their list of reputable dealers. And never pay attention to people on the street who offer you gold watches and such. They think they can always spot a victim, so prove them wrong!

If your Far East cruise does include China, spend some time shopping in this fascinating country. The Chinese now accept traveler's checks as well as some credit cards in the government-run Friendship Stores. You may browse in other stores, of course, such as the famous Number One Department Store in Shanghai, which has a money exchange on the top floor and is quite accustomed to foreign guests. If you enter the smaller shops, be certain to have plenty of *Renminbi* with you. The most popular items are Mao jackets and hats that now come in extra large sizes to fit the Western figure. Silk pajamas and lounge suits abound but often the prices are better in Hong Kong, where there is more competition. If you get into a government-controlled antique shop, you will be staggered by the prices; take care in what you buy. Nothing really old is allowed out of China these days, so you may be the owner of an authentic reproduction (despite the dynasty chart the sweet little girl explains to you in great detail). Good buys in China are jade (if you have lots of money with you), embroidered silks and linens, souvenirs like sandalwood fans or hand-painted silk fans and handkerchiefs. The silk fans are my favorite item, however, for they make wonderful spur-of-the-moment gifts and only cost about the equivalent of thirty cents. If you're lucky enough to visit a silk fan factory, buy them there and save a penny.

Japan Shopping

Shopping in **Japan**, a subtle and sensitive art form, includes the play of nimble fingers over an abacus to finish every deal. Although prices remain out of sight, the Japanese make some of the most beautiful things in the world. This is the land of pearls, woodblock prints, happy coats and kimonos, exquisite lacquerware, and imaginative folk crafts. Mingei (folk art), found primarily in paper, wood, and pottery, make the local shops seem like art galleries, they are so bursting with charming designs. The tape recorders and computer products are better bought in Hong Kong, where fierce competition keeps the prices low. For the real experience of shopping Japanese-style, stick to the arts and crafts of Japan.

Elsewhere on your Far East cruise, you will find brilliant silks in **Thailand**, as well as shops full of rings set with semiprecious stones. **Singapore** is a clean version of Hong Kong, and **Penang** has little but Malaysian batiks. Indonesia offers beautiful, rich brown and blue batiks (and the antique irons used to make them are wonderful bookends). Buy dolls of old coins in **Sumatra**, *wayang* puppets in Bandung (wonderful souvenirs) and art (paintings, carvings, sculpture) in Bali. In the Philippines you will find the wonderful pina fiber (made from pineapples) that the barong tagalog shirt and ladies pantsuits and dresses use (but no matter how interesting they look, beware; they can be very hot!). **Taiwan** is a shopper's paradise for brass, baskets, and tailoring at low prices. Semiprecious stones sparkle in **Sri Lanka**, which has sapphires, chameleonlike alexandrites, cat's eyes, rubies and aquamarines. And if your vessel calls at **Bombay**, seek out some lovely saris and exquisite Moghul miniatures (that are mostly fakes, but never mind if you don't pay too much).

Shopping In Europe

European and Mediterranean waters bring you into contact with many familiar items, but before long you realize that many of your favorite things are actually cheaper at home. The U.S. dollar is not strong enough these days that you can count on great buys.

AUTHOR'S OBSERVATION

Most European countries have Value Added Tax (VAT), which raises the price of luxury items by as much as 33.33%. Unfortunately, this tax is unavoidable if you buy less than $100 at a time and carry the item back on board. The Scandinavian countries have among the highest goods taxes in Europe (Iceland 23.5%, Sweden 22.3%, Denmark 22%, Norway 20%) but have instituted a cash return of the tax paid before you sail away (be sure to check with the local customs at the pier).

AUTHOR'S OBSERVATION

Watch out in St. Petersburg. Those lovely enamel boxes are often fakes. You can tell by taking the lens of a camera and looking closely at the design. If you see dot matrix, it's not the real thing.

It is almost impossible to get the VAT returned from shops in **France** and **England** without some reminder, especially if a considerable amount is involved. **Spain** and **Portugal** are still wonderful countries in which to shop and Lisbon is a popular shopping port call. But if you have the luck of stopping by **Madeira**, you are very fortunate. Here amid a floating garden, are wonderful wicker products, exquisite hand-fingered embroideries and plenty of the local wine.

Specialties along the shores of the **Mediterranean** include whatever you can find in the famous souks of Morocco, wonderful white filigree birdcages from Tunisia, scarabs from Egypt, as well as busts of Nefertiti and jellabas and caftans. Actually, the most popular Egyptian souvenir is the cartouche, an insignia bearing a pharaoh's name in hieroglyphics; you can buy it as a necklace, in gold or silver. If you would rather have a Muslim charm, the Hand of Fatima is here, too.

On a **Greek island** and **Turkey** cruise, you will be tempted by rugs, rugs and more rugs. All are fascinating and if you buy one, carry it home. The covered bazaar in Istanbul is a wonderful place to get lost and you will be approached time and time again by people pushing rugs. (I even had an offer of a flying carpet.) Turkey also has wonderful brass and copper items, spices, leather coats and jackets and meerschaum pipes. But I've been warned by cruise staff that one should never purchase a carpet in Istanbul that can't be carried home—those who request shipping frequently never see it. And, Tangier can be a shopper's nightmare. A colleague mildly admired an "antique" rug initially offered at $3000. The merchant chased her down the street with rug in tow, trying to get $200 for the carpet. Everything in Greece is a temptation, and I have a very hard time resisting, especially among the various island ports. Crete offers impressive red rugs (they're best as wall hangings), and Mykonos displays the most splendid-looking handmade sweaters in the world, and Rhodes (glorious Rhodes) has just about everything. I buy all my gold jewelry in Rhodes, among the shops just off the Palace of the Knights, and I always dream about the pieces left behind!

Souvenir items in Greece include fine reproductions of pottery found in the ancient tombs hand-painted and very reasonably priced. Black Sea ports are back in favor, but there is very little to buy yet in these ports.

U.S. CUSTOMS

Sailing Through Customs is a Norwegian Cruise Lines catchphrase for declaring all your new purchases. According to the U.S. Customs laws, each returning resident may bring back up to $400 worth of acquired merchandise (including gifts), duty free, every thirty days. The only exception is from the U.S. Virgin Islands, American Samoa, or Guam, where the allowance is $800 (if you return directly and at least half of your bundle was purchased there).

Original works of art and antiques (at least 100 years old) are exempt from duty, as are any items made on these U.S. territories (perfume, clothing, jewelry, and handbags). If you travel as a family, the duty-free allowance lets you pool your purchases, which means that a family of four has a combined allowance of $1600. If your acquisitions exceed this (and the customs officials are very lenient), a flat rate of 10% is assessed on the first $1000 over the limit. After that the rate of duty reverts to the old laws and varies widely. If all your purchases were made in U.S. territories, the flat rate is only 5% for the first $1000 worth of goods over the allowance.

AUTHOR'S OBSERVATION

If you plan to return with tobacco and liquor, first check your state laws, for federal and state regulations differ widely.

DUTY FREE LIMITS

California residents should be aware that importing more than one bottle of wine is illegal. Basically, your duty-free limit is two cartons (400) of cigarettes per person. Each U.S. resident (age twenty-one and over) is also allowed two quarts of liquor duty free. Cruise passengers returning from the U.S. Virgin Islands may import one gallon (five fifths), provided at least four fifths were bought in St. Thomas. It is also forbidden to bring any live plant, piece of fruit or vegetable, plant cutting or seeds, or unprocessed plant product into this country. Other items banned include ivory items, alligator products and any articles made from the skins of endangered species. Trademarked products may be imported now for personal use only; the limit is one item.

If you plan to send gifts from abroad, restrict yourself to one per address and no more than $25 worth, duty free ($40 if sent from St. Thomas) to stay within the limit. When you send presents through the mail, be careful which countries you choose; know the regulations and be certain to insure the packages properly. Write in large letters on the outside of the wrapping, Gift enclosed, value under $25 ($40 if from St. Thomas).

The Generalized System of Preferences, instituted in 1976 to help developing countries improve their financial or economic condition through export trade, provides for duty-free importation of certain products from certain nations. Many of these are tourist items. The list, which is renewed each year, includes 107 nations, 32 dependent territories and approximately 2700 items—Turkish rugs, loose semi-precious stones, rattan (other than furniture), shell products (except from the Philippines), toys (except from Hong Kong and Taiwan), wigs (except from South Korea) and local handicrafts from many countries to name a few. If your cruise encompasses a great many calls in developing nations and territories, you may wish to check which potential purchases might be duty free. Under the Trade Act, however, certain items like most footwear, textiles, watches, some electronic products and some glass and steel products are specifically excluded from any GSP benefits. The U.S. actually prohibits importation of many articles, such as many types of ivory, skins from endangered species, plants and animals, and foodstuffs that could carry contamination. If you feel a buying spree approaching, contact your nearest U.S. Customs office for updated information. Or write to: Department of the Treasury, U.S. Customs Service, Washington, DC 20229 for *GSP & the Traveler* and *Customs Hints—Know Before You Go*. If you contemplate purchases of ivory, skins, fur, etc., contact the U.S. Fish and Wildlife Service, Department of the Interior.

AUTHOR'S OBSERVATION

Because cruise traffic has grown so rapidly in recent years, returning to U.S. ports is no longer the simple procedure it once was. Chances are your luggage will be placed on the pier according to the first letter of your surname.

Alas, confusion is rampant as you collect all your baggage and lug it over to the nearest Customs official for clearance. I have great respect for Customs officials and make a point of making their day as pleasant as possible. With the very generous duty-free allowances that we Americans receive, there is no reason not to make the clearance process hassle-free.

The only time Customs officials will spend more than the time to say "Welcome home" is when you traveled in hot drug- and diamond-smuggling spots. Since most cruise vessels don't frequent such areas, there is little to worry about. I have been scrutinized beyond the call of duty twice—once returning from Amsterdam and the other from Ecuador but both arrivals were at JFK Airport in New York City.

If you are on an overseas air-sea program, you will return to the U.S. through a major gateway like New York City. The rule worldwide is the first point of earth you touch in any country is where you must clear both Customs and Immigration. Personally, I would do nearly anything to avoid Miami airport when a connecting flight is involved. The lines at customs and immigration are horrendous and one must dash for what seems miles to reach the connecting airline check-in.

GOING ASHORE

Shopping is a main ingredient of many shore excursions.

A friendly male voice left a message on my telephone answering machine the other day, requesting that I consider giving stars to shore excursions. It's a wonderful idea and I do appreciate his concern for making this book better; however, it is quite impossible. We all understand that there are good shore excursions and there are the antithesis dreadful! What's more, there are good and dreadful ones on the same route in the same week. And, unless a cruise vessel staff member is on each bus of each tour, there is no immediate control concerning guide courtesy, value information, relation of shopping stops versus seeing the sites, etc.

In my opinion, most shore excursions begin too early. After all, we are supposed to be on vacation! However, moving large shiploads of people is a tedious task and time in port is restricted. To visit the ancient city of Pergamum during a Greek Island cruise several years ago, we embarked the tenders around 7 a.m., but still savor memories of every moment we spent ashore in Dikili, Turkey.

Thank goodness the Greek Islands/Turkey are back in favor because the shore excursions in this area of the cruise world are some of the best, even if you abhor ancient ruins. There is plenty to do on every island, from shopping for local handicrafts to just sitting in the sunshine (with a glass of ouzo at your elbow) watching the scenery go by. The Greek Islands are a favorite with Scandinavians seeking the sun after their long winter, and the sight of those lithe, tanned Vikings (of both sexes) is something to behold!

Some people never go ashore. They just love ships, sailing, and the whole concept of a cruise; they feel no need ever to set foot in port. However, most of us eagerly await each port of call and, in fact, we often choose our cruise holidays as much by the itinerary offered as by the passenger vessel. Ship lines are cognizant of passenger preferences and pay particular attention to what ports receive the highest praise and offer the most rewarding cruise call experience. Ship lines also consider integration of on-board and onshore activities, convenience and comfort for passengers, availability of sightseeing attractions and shopping opportunities, and rigid navigation safety standards. It is safe to assume that what happens ashore affects your entire cruise experience. The physical facilities for every potential port of call must meet stringent standards and offer adequate vessel accommodations. Most ship lines prefer ports with dockside berthing, since it is more convenient for passengers to walk ashore. Most lines also seek ports that have sufficient emergency facilities (doctors, dentists, hospitals, ambulances), just in case.

I pay particular attention to destination, hours spent in each port, arrival time and day of the week (are the shops open, is it a holiday, is there a strike of some sort?). These questions are very important, because I try to plan as much exploration time as possible, while also calculating how much time to allow for shopping and indulging in local specialties. Thus, it can be most disappointing if the program changes without your knowledge. Often the changes are to passengers benefit; however, your travel agent should be advised of any last-minute alterations to the schedule and she or he should inform you. Ship lines are responsible and can always verify their notification of travel agents, so check carefully into such matters before any complaints are registered.

AUTHOR'S OBSERVATION

Modern technology has indeed made the world a smaller place. You can obtain cash with your bank card on most Caribbsean islands as well as many corners of the globe. In Europe, machines use a four-digit code, and your local bank can give you a new number before departure if necessary.

PORTS OF CALL

Long before each port of call looms over the horizon, a member of the cruise staff will give an on-board briefing detailing the latest information on arrival and departure times (they tend to vary according to sailing conditions and any unforeseen circumstances), the vessel's mooring plans, dress suggestions considering local custom and weather, currency rates, shore excursions (if you have not already bought the full package) and free time. If you plan to do any exploring alone or in a private group, you will also wish to know taxi and other transportation rates, where to eat and shop and how long it takes to get from place to place. The briefings may even include a short film or slide show to acquaint you with the location of famous sights. However, most of these port talks provide only adequate information and you may want to supplement them. A map is always helpful, whether you join the organized tour or not. Most ships sell maps in the purser's office (but the supply is limited, so get there early). The best maps have famous sites sketched on them, so that even if the taxi driver cannot read English, he can at least recognize the monument (this was a godsend in China). The best advice is to obtain one from tourist offices before departure. Your travel agent can give the number of their U.S. office.

Historical novels are a good source for atmosphere, and since port cities were often the first settled or colonized, plenty has been written about most of them. Friends and colleagues may offer tips, and perhaps your travel agency has its own cache of materials. If you are booked on a serious cruise (Swan Hellenic or Special Expeditions) you may receive a reading list to prepare yourself for the sights and sounds ahead. And if you're really lucky, you may discover some picture books and such in the ship's library. Advance preparation, your local library, museum publications and videos from a favorite shop are the best ways to enjoy your cruise. In addition, I try to have some local currency ready so I can purchase a book or two in port. Although many are not bound very well and tend to fall apart with use, the local books, usually written by native scholars, are a good primary source.

SHORE EXCURSIONS

If you have booked a cruise operated by some of the specialty companies or on many of the lovely barges in Europe, the shore tours are all-inclusive (and how excellent they are).

The average shore excursion, developed between the ship line and a local tour operator in each port of call, is generally well organized and well managed. You don't have to worry about safety or buses running out of fuel, because the ship line plans carefully. What the company cannot control is the turnover in tour guides, some of whom are in it only for the money.

AUTHOR'S OBSERVATION

Beware of guides who put green dots on your collar or flowers in your buttonhole for identification. Guides may use these symbols to tip off shops that you are a wealthy tourist. (It's an old trick and still used worldwide.)

If you feel your guide has not fulfilled her/his duties gracefully or has attempted to obtain extra charges from the bus group, complain at once to the purser's office. You deserve a hassle-free experience in return for the price paid.

Shore excursions are expensive for many reasons. Today, they are a major profit center for cruise companies to make up for the rampant discounting. Moreover, the ship line must deal with countries where the cost of fuel and vehicles is almost prohibitive. Add this to the greed that tourism breeds and you have inflated prices. I understand that tour guides in the Caracas area want $500 a day, which explains why a short morning tour of Caracas from La Guaira costs far more than it is worth. Then, remember that you buy the tour from the ship line, which buys from the tour organizer, which buys from someone else. Each party marks the price up. Actually, ship lines claim that they only add a little to the price to cover the expenses (and commission to the travel agent). However, ship lines would not have tour-desk personnel if they did not make their salaries.

AUTHOR'S OBSERVATION

You rarely need a shore excursion in the Caribbean, and even when traveling distances, it's usually more economical and comfortable to hire a taxi for a flat rate. Many cities in Europe are best explored by foot and street maps can be obtained from tourist offices in the U.S., or the local tourist office, which frequently is located near the pier.

Despite the cost, the morning spent at Ephesus will remain one of the great travel memories in my husband's and my album. There are many others: a late evening gondola ride through the back canals of Venice; the magnificent mosaics in Ravenna best viewed with a proper guide and torch; a barbecue at the Tropicale Hotel in Santarem under the stars; a tour of the great houses in Newport, Rhode Island; wine tasting in the chateaus of Bordeaux.

Some areas in the cruise world demand price be damned shore excursions. These include China (where it's obligatory for the most part), North Africa, the Red Sea (especially to Petra), some South American, Far East and Alaska calls. For example, one of the most popular but very expensive excursions on Alaskan cruises is a seaplane tour which, if it includes lunch at the charming Taku Lodge, could be well over $100 per person. A forty-five-minute helicopter tour of Sitka Sound, St. Lazari Island National Bird Reserve, Mt. Edgecumbe and a quick landing nearby to see goats, seals, whales, and bears costs almost as much. But, all who take this short ride say it is the highlight of the entire Inside Passage sailing. Unfortunately, there are places plagued by crime and you won't want to travel without a group (Kingston, Jamaica, and Rio, to name a few).

ON-YOUR-OWN SHORE EXCURSIONS

AUTHOR'S OBSERVATION

You can save by touring many ports on your own, especially if they have few tourist sites and are more renowned for their beauty and fine beaches than their costlier attractions.

Try the Mexican Riviera or many of the Caribbean Islands (especially Puerto Rico and St. Thomas) for this. Toss aside frantic sightseeing tours of these ports and indulge in a leisurely catamaran cruise in the harbor or a stroll through the narrow back streets to reward yourself. Tours around the Hawaiian islands are excellent as there is much beauty and drama to see here. However, if you are as allergic to buses as I am, you may prefer to rent a car or hire a taxi and swim off less-congested beaches. American Hawaii Cruises packs tasty picnic lunches.

AUTHOR'S OBSERVATION

In the 50 states, Bermuda, Bahamas and Caribbean islands, the rental car agencies (Budget, Avis, Hertz, etc.) all have good road maps. Any driver's license of the fifty states is valid, of course. Know what is available before you go; some of these agencies will offer a bargain weekly rate and have a car waiting at each port call in the islands.

In so many port cities, tourist information, a good map and a friend to help share taxi expenses make for a thrifty and enjoyable exploration, especially in the the Caribbean and Europe. Some voyages sailing the Orinoco River or transiting the Panama Canal, for example are exciting enough in themselves, and you never need to go ashore. However, I would not miss the temple tour in Bangkok, the Japanese garden tour in Kyoto or any tour of that Morning of the World island, Bali. And, if you spend the time and energy to sail up or down the Nile, you must take every tour of the temples and monuments no matter what the temperature or the hour!

Many of the local cruise and beach tours around the Caribbean sound splendid and some ship lines even arrange their own. Norwegian Cruises has offered a very successful beach party in the Caymans. Its other vessels have dropped anchor off one of the uninhabited Berry Islands and the *Norway* uses Little San Salvador to treat its passengers to sun, sail, waterski, and snorkel between rounds of beer and soda, hamburger and hotdogs. Snorkeling is a popular pastime at many calls in the Caribbean and should be included in your shore excursion budget, for it's pretty hard to beat the beauty and excitement of this underwater world. Activities like these also present a wonderful way to meet other people on the ship with shared interests. You may even make lasting friendships. Often, passengers will become friendly during an organized tour in one port and decide to share expenses and explore together during the next call.

On the new, smaller vessels such as the *Sea Goddesses* and *Windstar* fleet), you don't need to bother with local beaches because unique stern platforms allow watersport amenities then and there. The platforms are lowered when the ship is at anchor, for swimming, water skiing, jetskiing, windsurfing, sunfish sailing, snorkeling, or just hitching a Zodiac ride. These platforms are a wonderful invention and a great way to spend a few hours especially if the majority of passengers have disappeared on a shore excursion!

AUTHOR'S OBSERVATION

If you do decide to explore alone, pay particular attention to checking off and on the ship and allowing plenty of time for coming back aboard. (Many cruise staff personnel insist they will not wait for returning passengers.)

If the port is small and lacks the proper facilities, your vessel may have to anchor out. This means tendering in, which cuts your time in port considerably; remember it is your responsibility to know the times of the last tender. Frequently, the boats leave the ship every fifteen minutes or so for the first hour and then make returns every hour on the half hour. Ship lines often leave a crew member on the pier to check your boarding tag numbers, especially if you opt for the last launch back, to prevent anyone's being left behind. But you never know. The port calls and shore periods have been carefully planned by the ship line for passengers fullest enjoyment. But don't miss the boat—you'll have to catch up with the ship at the next port on your own!

CHANGES IN ITINERARY

If weather or some other unforeseen circumstance prevents your cruise ship from completing the full itinerary in the time allotted, you can do nothing but accept the situation gracefully. A monsoon in the South China Sea is an act of God, so we can't hold the ship line responsible. If this happens to you, be grateful for the competency of the captain and thank him when it's all over. On the other hand, if the boilers break down and the entire cruise is ruined, you will probably receive some recompense that may be a considerable refund, a discount on a future cruise, or both. Since happy passengers take future cruises and even tell their friends, no ship line will let you down the gangway discontented!

THE CRUISE LINES

ALASKA SIGHTSEEING/CRUISE WEST

4th and Battery Building, Suite 700, Seattle, Washington 98121
☎ (206) 441-8687, (800) 426-7702

If one name is synonymous with the development of tourism in Alaska it is Chuck West, who began a small tour operation to the territory in 1946. When Westours was sold to Holland America Line for the development of its extensive shore excursion program, West decided to start his own cruise operation offering an experience that separated his company from the giants. Looking around for a home port, West selected Seattle for it's good air connections, and launched Alaska Sightseeing/Cruise West in 1973 with the 143-foot *Spirit of Alaska* (the former *Pacific Northwest Explorer*).

His spunky little vessel proved so popular, its cruises a one-of-a-kind experience, that the family-run business has mushroomed into four ships that are nearly sold out at the season.

Alaska Sightseeing, now headed by son Dick West, is proud of the fact that all ships are American-made and fly the U.S. flag. In addition to the 82-passenger *Spirit of Alaska*, the fleet of excursion-type vessels now includes the 58-passenger *Spirit of Glacier Bay* and the 82-passenger *Spirit of Discovery*. In 1993, the company launched its largest ship, the 101-passenger *Spirit of '98*. Designed in the style of a historic coastal steamer, it boasts turn-of-the-century Victorian decor. A new vessel, the 72-passenger *Spirit of Columbia*, joins the fleet in 1995.

Alaska Sightseeing vessels visit wilderness areas and inland waterways that are inaccessible to large ships in **Alaska**, **British Columbia** and on the **Columbia River**, including Vancouver Island, the San Juan Islands and Puget Sound. Their brochures claim no port is too small, no lock too narrow and nature lovers normally see bears, moose, caribou, seals and whales, not to mention a close-up view of glaciers, on a typical cruise.

Passengers, generally in their 60s, find life aboard is delightfully unpretentious, four star cooking served in open seating, very casual attire the norm, a movie night when popcorn is served, and young, knowledgeable naturalists who enthusiastically discuss the rich flora and fauna found in the region. The modest cabins have lower beds, small bathrooms with showers and sufficient closet space for the casual clothing worn on ships.

After a few hours spent ashore, passengers may be welcomed aboard by crew distributing warm chocolate chip cookies. As Dick West says, "Our ice sculptures are outside."

In 1995, May through September itineraries include eight-day round-trip cruises from Seattle to **British Columbia** and the **San Juan Islands**, visiting Desolation Sound, Campbell River, Princess Inlet, Frasier River, with stops in **Victoria**, **Vancouver**, **La Conner** and **Port Townsend**. Cruise-only rates begin around $1295 per person, double occupancy, depending upon cabin and departure dates.

Ten-day Alaska sailings aboard the *Spirit of '98* between Seattle and Juneau feature port calls in **Sitka**, **Petersburg**, **Ketchikan** and **Misty Fjords** with cruising on the **Inside Passage**. Extensive land tours from Anchorage are also available. The company launches new itineraries this year, including full-season weekly cruises, 1000-miles roundtrip on the Columbia and Snake rivers aboard the new *Spirit of Columbia* (rates start at $1395). New seven-night cruises from **Sausalito** to **Napa**, **Sacramento** and **San Francisco** will be available September through November aboard the *Spirit of Alaska*, priced from $1395 including shore excursions.

AUTHOR'S AWARD

If you are content to forego the standard cruise experience, view wildlife and regions rarely visited by tourists, Alaska Sightseeing/Cruise West offers an intimate experience of our 50th state and British Columbia at moderate cost.

AMERICAN CANADIAN CARIBBEAN LINE, INC.

461 Water Street, P.O. Box 368, Warren, RI 02885
☎ (401) 247-0955, (800) 556-7450

American Canadian Caribbean Line (ACCL) has been operating cruises along the New England coastline and the inland waterways of Canada, as well as throughout the Caribbean, for just more than a quarter century, and its small vessels have sailed many more than a million miles.

It all began when Luther Blount (now in his 70s), inveterate mariner, explorer, ship designer and builder, and native Yankee, took groups of friends on informal mini-cruises along the historic Erie Canal. These social expeditions became a business, aboard small ships designed and built at Blount Marine located on the Warren River in Rhode Island. ACCL's three cruise ships depart from the Blount dock on their summer itineraries, along with a popular dinner boat, *Vista Jubilee*, which cruises Narragansett Bay to fashionable **Newport**, **Rhode Island**, and returns.

The three ACCL ships in operation attract middle-aged folk who have experienced the dress-up, larger vessels and are seeking a more informal and intimate atmosphere. Repeat business is more than 70 percent and ACCL adds new itineraries each winter season so repeaters need not repeat a cruise! At a time when other small ship companies have gone out of business, ACCL enjoys great success due to its special itineraries and the TLC with which passengers are treated. The entire ambience is of a family, as this is a family-run business.

All ACCL vessels ply the **Erie Canal/Saguenay River** on 12-day schedules throughout the summer and the ever-popular 15-day intracoastal routes from **Warren**, **Rhode Island** to **West Palm Beach** in November; the reverse schedules operate in April and early May.

ACCL now has three vessels, the *Caribbean Prince*, with a capacity of 84, the *Mayan Prince* (launched in 1992) holding 92 and their newest, the *Niagara Prince*, introduced in 1994. The latest addition is an 82-passenger riverboat with wraparound windows on the second deck, affording maximum visibility as she cruises the inland waterways; in the fall of 1995, cruising regions include **Central America**, **Venezuela** and **Chile**.

In December 1983, Luther Blount inaugurated the 80-passenger *Caribbean Prince*. The 160-foot vessel has a spacious, ultramodern interior with a yacht-like ambience. Air-conditioned cabins have large picture windows, private facilities, teakwood trim, and a choice of sleeping arrangements (twin or double). For the economy-minded, there are six cabins without portholes below. The *Caribbean Prince* also boasts the Blount specialty, a ramp that goes down from the bow and allows passengers to walk right off the ship onto the beach. Blount calls it his Bow Ramp design, a feature that enables the vessel to stop at off-beat places that other ships may not be able to reach.

During the winter season, the *Caribbean Prince* offers a unique 12-day itinerary to the large barrier reef off Belize where the snorkeling is supposed to be superb. Passengers fly to and from Belize to pick up the boat. Swimming, snorkeling, bonefishing, sailing (the ship carries small boats), and collecting shells are the order of the day, but tours to the local ancient sites are also available. Life is very casual onboard. The cabins are rather small, so luggage should be kept to a minimum. Days are spent playing in the water or walking on the beach, and in the evening you are left to your own entertainment devices. The dining room seats all passengers at one time, and meal service is family style, with menus geared to American taste buds (and now very much on the light side if you so desire). There is no need to dress up; a nice sports shirt for men and a long cotton skirt for women are appropriate. The brochure advises to BYOB (bring your own bottle), although sodas are supplied. No money on board is necessary other than any gratuities you wish to present at the end of your wonderful cruise.

The *Mayan Prince* will winter in the Caribbean for several cruises to remote areas of **Aruba**, **Bonaire** and **Curacao**, very popular with water sports enthusiasts due to the vessel's bow ramp, shallow draft and Luther's glass-bottom boat invention. Travelers can visit inaccessible areas and take advantage of fantastic snorkeling in hidden coves. She then proceeds to cruises in the Virgin Islands followed by an itinerary combining Trinidad with Venezuala's Orinoco River. Summer is spent sailing between Rochester and Georgian Bay. The new *Niagara Prince* cruises on 12-day **Panama/San Blas Islands/Pearl Islands** and **Darien Jungle** tour before a summer season cruising between **New Orleans** and **Chicago**.

American Canadian Caribbean Line is a family-run company; Luther Blount's daughter, Nancy Palumbo, is Director of Operations. The ship line's philosophy is *cruising areas that are uncommon, unhurried and unspoiled.* While the ships are small and cabin space cramped, passengers find a big welcome and most friendly atmosphere onboard. Rates are also among the lowest in the cruise industry, an incentive for repeaters.

The venerable Luther Blount has also designed and built in his shipyard the restaurant day-cruisers *Spirit of New York*, *Boston* and *Chicago*, as well as the *Spirit of Norfolk*. The boats are very comfortable and are a wonderful way to spend a few hours seeing a skyline by water. His latest invention, we are told, is a head (toilet) that flushes silently on one pint of water! Per person per diem rates begin around $100, a *very* good deal.

AMERICAN HAWAII CRUISES

550 Kearny Street, San Francisco, CA 94108

☎ (415) 392-9400, (800) 765-7000

American Hawaii Cruises has just celebrated 14 years of sailing among the God-given islands of our 50th state. The ship line experienced some rough weather in its start-up days, and barely escaped bankrupcy in 1993. Rescued by Delta Queen Steamboat Company, a healthy and prosperous company, American Hawaii now has the capital necessary to upgrade the fleet.

The *Independence* underwent a $28 million refurbishment in the fall of 1994 and the *Constitution* will get a similar face lift in 1995. There is new life and vitality today as the company continually adds new features like theme cruises and intriuging shore excursions. American Hawaii offers a consistent itinerary and a most beautiful one so that passengers know what to expect and where they are going.

It all began with the famous *Independence*, a 30,000-ton vessel built at the Bethelehem Quincy shipyard in Massachusetts as a former member of American Export Lines fleet. An American group of investors formed American Global Line and Congress approved her return to U. S. registry. It was a wonderful idea and, although the Tung Group is no longer involved and Chinese/American businessman Peter Huang is, the idea has proven successful.

The 30,000-ton *Constitution*, a true sister ship of the *Independence* and also built at Bethlehem Quincy Shipyards in Massachusetts in 1951 for American Export Line, was also returned to U.S.-flag status by executive order in the early months of 1982. At inauguration, the late Princess Grace of Monaco smashed a bottle of champagne against the ship's bow in Kaohsiung, Taiwan, where the vessel was being refurbished for inter-Hawaiian-island cruises. The *Constitution* was always a favorite of the Princess. As Academy-award-winning movie star Grace Kelly, she sailed aboard the *Constitution* to her fairy-tale wedding and principality on the Cote d'Azur. She later boarded the vessel with her Monarch-of-Monaco husband, Prince Rainier, and then took an additional voyage alone.

Deluxe staterooms, public rooms and cabins are designed by a Honolulu firm, and cabins feature prints by Hawaiian artist Pegge Hopper. In addition to routine maintenance while in dry dock, the vessels receive bridge and lifeboat equipment, as well as a careful U. S. Coast Guard inspection.

The *Constitution* and *Independence* sail in tandem every Saturday at 9 p.m. from the Aloha Tower near **Honolulu's** famed Waikiki Beach and it is a glorious sight to see. Both vessels spend the first day at sea, cruising slowly among the beautiful islands. Both visit the same islands and ports, but in reverse order, and both spend a night on **Maui**. Other port calls are **Hilo** and **Kona** on the big island of Hawaii and **Nawiliwili** on Kauai. The vessels then meet outside Honolulu harbor to return together to the Aloha Tower.

New a few years ago and very popular are the 3- and 4-day cruises aboard the *Constitution*, which may be taken with or without resort stays on one of the islands for golf, tennis or just beach time. There are several different itineraries available in this Cruise and Resort program, including honeymoon and anniversary packages, with air supplements from North America. All-inclusive prices are very reasonable (especially from the west coast), and popular with the younger/more active set who wish to try their sea legs before committing to a full week's sailing. Once on board, this group finds plenty of activities in the fitness center/health spa and super-healthy menus just like home!

During the summer months, both the *Constitution* and *Independence* are terrific for families and there are plenty of counselors and activities on-board for all age groups. To encourage families traveling together, American Hawaii offers the free kids program for up to two children (16 and under) sharing a cabin with two full-fare adults year-round, except July through August 14, when children sail for $129. The ship line's youth directors guide special programs for the young passengers such as pool activities, treasure hunts and video games during summer holidays. American Hawaii Cruises is committed to supporting the humpback whales that migrate from Alaska each winter to breed in the warm Hawaiian waters. Ship line chairman Peter Huang has made a personal commitment to the preservation of the humpbacks through benefits and donations. He also added a Whale Gallery to each vessel, featuring color photographs of the mammals, as well as migratory details and current research data. Other photos of humpbacks hang throughout the corridors of the ships.

One-week cruises in February and March are designed to generate humpback whale awareness through lectures, slide presentations and shore excursions on **Maui** with experts. Researchers, photographers and marine biologists are on-board. One-week cruises begin at $995 per person, double occupancy!

BERGEN LINE

505 Fifth Avenue, New York, NY 10017
☎ (212) 986-2711, (800) 323-7436

The original Bergen Line steamship/mail cargo system dated from 1851 in Bergen, Norway, and provided reliable and regular service between key Norwegian coastal cities and major ports. In 1985, Bergen Line became a subsidiary of Kosmos Group, a Norwegian travel and transportation conglomerate and today markets several European steamship companies and other travel-related firms with sailings through Northern Europe, Scandinavia and the Baltic. It represents 28 vessels including those of Norwegian Coastal Voyages, with crossings between Sweden and Finland, Baltic cruises to Russia, and overnight services between Germany and Norway.

The company's most popular product, Norwegian Coastal Voyages, begins in **Bergen**. The Voyages cover 1250 miles of Norway's spectacular western coastline via a fleet of 11 mail cargo vessels calling in dozens of villages and towns enroute to **Kirkenes**, which is well above the Arctic Circle. The working steamers sail year-round and offer unpretentious but comfortable accommodations plus three hearty meals a day. Passengers may sign up for organized shore excursions or disembark on their own. In the **Arctic Circle**, the experience of viewing Midnight Sun in summer and the Northern Lights in winter is unforgettable.

Bergen Line also represents Silja Line, Baltic Express Line, Color Line, Gota Canal and Scandinavia Seaways. Silja Line has a very comfortable overnight car/ferry service linking **Finland**, **Sweden** and the **Baltic States**, with overnight connections serving **Helsinki**, **Stockholm**, **Turku**, and **Marienhamn**, as well as Travemunde (Germany). Short cruises across the Baltic to St. Petersburg, Tallinn (Estonia), or to the medieval city of Visby on the Swedish island of Gotland are also available. Additional 4- and 6 day cruises from Helsinki and Stockholm to St. Petersburg are offered through Baltic Express Line. Reservations can also be made on Color Line's six car/passenger vessels, which sail year-round connecting Norway with the Continent and England on four routes: Oslo or Kristiansand, **Norway**, to Hirtshals at the tip of Jutland in **Denmark**.

Through Bergen Line you can book Scandinavian Seaways seven car ferry/ passenger ships with year-round North Sea crossings and daily connections between **Oslo** and **Copenhagen**. Gota Canal's scenic inland 4- and 6-day cruises sail across Sweden between **Stockholm** and **Gothenberg** aboard three vessels from May through September.

Life aboard these ships is laid-back and fun. Although this is a relatively new concept for Americans, Europeans have flocked to these delightful cruise experiences for decades, and it's a marvelous and inexpensive way to visit small towns in some of Europe's most scenic and unspoiled regions. Best of all, you may take that new Mercedes you just purchased along for the ride!

CALEDONIA TRAVEL

P.O. Box 1421 Stamford, CT 06904-1421
☎ (203) 866-2220

Caledonia Travel, formed in 1982 and operating for a time with the defunct Salen Lindblad Cruising, is the U.S. representative of the expedition ship *Caledonian Star*, a hearty vessel that visits some of the most exotic places on earth. Those seeking an in-depth experience of Borneo, New Guinea and Aqaba, for example, should look no farther. Originally operated by Salen Lindblad Cruises as the *North Star*, this 110-passenger ship was constructed in 1966 and last rebuilt in 1987, when civilized amenities such as TV/VCR's were added.

In January 1995, *Caledonian Star* spends a full month exploring the Spice Islands, New Guinea and Borneo before moving to the Indian Ocean for two-week cruises to the Seychelles, Madagascar, Comores and Frigate Isles.

Spring through Fall is spent in the Mediterranean, Western Europe and Great Britain followed by a Kuwait to Bombay positioning voyage and a Christmas cruise to ports in India.

CARNIVAL CRUISE LINES

3655 N.W. 87th Ave., Miami, FL 33178-2428
☎ (305) 599-2600, (800) 327-9501

Carnival Cruise Lines has grown in the past two decades from a mom and pop organization with two vintage vessels to a giant in the industry—*the giant*. Carnival carries more than 25 percent of all cruise passengers recorded, with occupancy levels exceeding 100 percent (based on two to a cabin) and impressive revenue levels. Passenger levels for 1994 are expected to reach the one million mark, and I'm sure the company won't stop there. The ship Line went public in 1987, offering some $400 million in shares, and is considered a multi-billion-dollar company involved in cruises, gambling casinos, related resort properties and an airline. The ship line currently operates a series of 3-, 4-, and 7-day cruises aboard ten large vessels, with three more expected over the next four years, to the **Bahamas** and **Caribbean** from south and central Florida; to the **southern Caribbean** from San Juan and to **Mexico** from the West Coast.

Carnival launched the first of its soon-to-be super fleet with the flagship *Mardi Gras* in 1973. This 27,250-ton vessel carrying an easy 906 passengers, was the former *Empress of Canada*. A year later Carnival developed the Fun Ship theme, which soon became associated with sparkling white exteriors and a red, white, and blue smokestack that is recognized in every Caribbean port. In 1976, the ship line launched the *Carnival*, the former *Empress of Britain*, sister ship of the *Mardi Gras*. Both vessels were converted from North Atlantic sailings to full-time Caribbean cruising, and through continual refurbishment, the old-world ambience and dark woods have been replaced to reflect Caribbean lifestyle and colors. These ships do well, catering to the night-owl set, who love to eat, drink and be merry on into the wee hours. The *Carnival* set occupancy records since her launching, carrying well above the 950-passenger complement forecast.

Then, the 38,175-ton *Festival* joined the fleet in 1978. The former SA *Vaal* and *Trans-Vaal Castle* carries just more than 1400 passengers and has done very well since her relaunching as a Caribbean cruise ship.

Carnival introduced in 1982 its much-touted ship of the 80s to cruise clientele in the Caribbean. Called the *Tropicale*, the $100 million, Danish-built vessel has a capacity for 1200-plus passengers and quickly became the top fun ship of the then four-vessel fleet. The vessel was well-designed, with plenty of deck space for the swinging crowd, an enormous casino, and just enough spit-and-polish to be vaguely impressive. Cabins are comfortable and, with the exception of twelve veranda-suites on Veranda Deck, all are the same size with large windows, closed-circuit color television, and twin beds that can be joined for a king-size treat. Emphasis is on having a good time and dropping lots of money in the casino or at any of the several bars.

The 46,000-ton *Holiday* entered Caribbean service mid-July 1985, carrying 1452 passengers and a normal crew size of 660. The vessel, constructed in Denmark, with public areas and cabins under the design supervision of Joe Farkis, represents a definite departure for Carnival in on-board ambience. While the cabins are standardized and easily convertible from L-shaped twin configuration to together-beds, there are some interesting public areas. The two dining rooms offer a much more gracious meal experience than ever before found on a Carnival ship, and such spaces as the Carnegie Library and Rick's Cafe American (piano bar) are pleasantly relaxing, indeed.

A year later, the 1500-passenger *Jubilee* entered service in the Caribbean and was followed in March 1987 by sister ship *Celebration*. Both vessels boast 48,000 tons and created a new concept in cruising for Carnival, which touted itself as the mega-vessel company. So, Carnival ordered three more to be even bigger and more glitzy and astounded the industry with their names...*Fantasy, Ecstasy, Sensation*! Alas, the shipyard in which this superliner trio was to be constructed, underbid the contract and fell into grave financial difficulties that Carnival was forced to help rectify. The first of this new generation of cruise ships at 70,000 tons, *Fantasy* was a bit delayed but arrived in Miami in February 1990 complete with 12 miles of neon tubing installed in its walls and ceilings (that change color, of course, throughout the day) and a 20-foot-tall kinetic sculpture among other accoutrements.

Sister ship *Ecstasy* arrived in June, 1991, followed by 2600-passenger mega liners *Sensation* (November, 1993), *Fascination* (1994) and *Imagination* (1995). And, just when we thought ships couldn't possibly get any bigger, Carnival announced construction had begun on the largest ever built, a 100,000-ton behemoth (unnamed) that will hold around 3000 passengers, set for delivery in 1996.

Meanwhile, Carnival Cruise Lines has not been resting upon the laurels of its success and its cash-rich basis. Anxious to be respectable in this crazy industry, Carnival purchased the travel and tourism activities of Holland America Line and all its subsidiaries Westours, Westmark Hotels and Windstar Cruises for approximately $625 million in January 1989. This marked the company's move to the upscale end of the market; in 1991 Carnival purchased 25 percent of Seabourn Cruise Line and it's latest investment was acquiring 43 percent stake in Epirotiki in 1994.

Carnival carries the lion's share of first-time cruisers (around 70 percent) and I m sure Kathy Lee Gifford's glittery presence on Carnival's constant TV ads is a big factor in attracting a large number of vacationers under the age of 35 to these vessels. The slot machines are functional at 8:00 a.m., and everyone stays in a party mood throughout the day: the energy and the noise level are high, with cocktails flowing and the on-board activities at times a bit high-spirited. During the inaugural of the *Sensation* this year I sailed with Joe Farkis, the brainchild designer responsible for Carnival's distinctive ships. He called the ships' startling interiors "entertainment architecture," designed to energize passengers and encourage participation in the "Fun Ship" experience. But glitzy and bargain prices don't necessarily mean cutting corners. Those who are paying Carnival's modest prices will find surprises: at around 190 square feet, cabins aboard the new ships are large by industry standards and fitness/spa facilities aboard the *Sensation*, *Ecstasy* and *Fantasy* are some 12,000 square feet of every treatment and facility one could dream of. The company does beautifully with children (and carries some 86,000 annually) with separate facilities for all age groups in the summer and holiday season. If you like Las Vegas, enjoy frenetic energy and all that neon doesn't make your hair stand on end, Carnival may be your cup of tea.

Carnival will move the *Holiday* to Los Angeles in June, 1995, where it will operate year-round 3- and 4-day cruises to **Catalina Island** and **Ensenada**.

Year-round itineraries of Carnival's fleet: the *Festivale* sails on seven-day cruises from San Juan to **St. Thomas**, **St. Maarten**, **Dominica**, **Barbados** and **Martinique**; the *Ecstasy* and *Fantasy* on 3- and 4-day **Bahama** cruises from Port Canaveral and Miami; the *Sensation* on 7-day sailings from Miami to **Nassau**, **San Juan** and **St. Thomas**, alternating with **Playa del Carmel**, **Cozumel**, **Grand Cayman** and **Ocho Rios**; the *Tropicale* on weekly cruises from Tampa and New Orleans on Western Caribbean itineraries; the *Jubilee* on 7-day cruises from Los Angeles to **Cabo San Lucas**, **Mazatlan** and **Puerto Vallarta**. The *Celebration* sails from Miami on 7-day cruises to San Juan, St.

Thomas and St. Maarten. Average cruise-only per person, per diem ranges from $120 to $145 before "Super Saver" discounts.

CELEBRITY CRUISES

5200 Blue Lagoon Drive, Miami, Florida 33126
☎ (305) 262-8322, (800) 437-3111

Like many other ship lines, Chandris Inc. has not stood still in the past few years, but few have transformed its fleet and image to the degree this company has. This family-owned company has indeed been busy. It concluded that, in addition to the Chandris Fantasy Cruise fleet in the Caribbean and Mediterranean, it needs a more upscale product to offer loyal passengers. Hence, Celebrity Cruises was announced mid-1989 by John Chandris. Today the popular Celebrity fleet consists of three vessels—the 30,000-ton *Meridian* (ex-*Galileo*) and the new 45,000-ton sister ships *Horizon* and *Zenith*. Celebrity Cruises is quite a departure for the Chandris Group, which was founded in 1915 with cargo business, but known the last 15 years or so for its Fantasy Cruise value sailings. In 1993, the two cruise lines under the Celebrity banner became part of a joint venture between Maritime Overseas Corporation and the Chandris Group. The *Britanis* and *Amerikanis* are still in the Fantasy Cruise division, popular with the budget-conscious traveler.

The 1160-passenger *Meridian*, with an international crew of 480, was completely reconstructed in Germany from the former *Galileo*. The $70-million rebuilding created structural changes in the public areas, as well as some cabins, with floor-to-ceiling windows and suites with skylights. The 1354-passenger *Horizon* and *Zenith*, built at a combined cost of $400 million, were launched in 1990 and 1991 respectively. Both were designed by a consortium of well-known ship architects, including the famed husband-and-wife Katzourakis team, whose fine work appears on so many other vessels.

In 1993, John Chandris announced a major fleet expansion, the addition of three new 70,000-ton, 1740 passenger vessels designated for the line's new Century series. The *Century* is scheduled for delivery in 1995, the second and third to follow at one-year intervals. The new ships, will boast an active sports area of 62,000-square feet, as well as 120,000 square feet of interior entertainment facilities. Following the *Century's* christening on December 20, 1995, she will sail from Ft. Lauderdale on seven-day cruises.

From Miami, the *Britanis* sails year round on two- and five-night itineraries (a weekend party cruise and Mexico/Key West port calls) and each year makes a circumnavigation of **South America**. The *Amerikanis* winters in the Caribbean on one-week cruises from San Juan to the eastern **Caribbean**; from April through fall, she moves to Europe for a season of **North Cape**, **Baltic**, **Mediterranean** and **Canary Island** sailings.

Celebrity sails from New York to **Bermuda** with the *Horizon* calling at Hamilton and St. George and the *Meridian* at the West End on a weekly basis from May through October. During the winter, both vessels cruise from San Juan. The *Horizon* offers a deep Carribean itinerary of seven nights to **Martinique**, **Barbados**, **St. Lucia**, **Antigua** and **St. Thomas**. The *Meridian's* 10- and 11-night Ultimate Caribbean itineraries include port calls at **La Guaira**, **Grenada**, **Barbados**, **St. Lucia**, **Martinique**, **St. Maarten** and **St.Thomas** on the 10-night cruise; the 11-night cruise features a partial transit of the **Panama Canal**, the **San Blas islands**, **Curacao**, **Martinique**, **St. John** and **St. Thomas**. The *Zenith* cruises year-round from Ft. Lauderdale on alternating one-week itineraries: the **eastern Caribbean** cruise includes visits to San Juan, St. Thomas, St. Maarten and Nassau; the **western Caribbean** cruises visit Montego Bay, Grand Cayman, Cozumel and Key West.

What sets Celebrity apart from other cruise companies is wonderful attention to detail, especially in the all-important areas of food and service. These ships are stunning, but it's rare to find cuisine of these standards and such attentive on-board service in a moderately-priced line. Celebrity's culinary consultant, Michele Roux, has brought a superb level of dining to the three vessels by overseeing recipes and service and providing menus; he makes surprise visits to the vessels every six weeks to ensure quality and consistency of dining remains high. This three star Michelin chef takes his job very seriously—not only creating new recipes, but ensuring it is prepared and served to his liking. His favorite dish follows:

Back of Salmon on Crisp Slices of Fennel (serves 4)

For the salmon:
1-1/2 lbs salmon fillet, skinned and boned
1 large bulb of fennel, leaves still attached
1/2 cucumber
1 tblsp olive oil
For the sauce:
1 tblsp. olive oil
1-1/2 oz. shallots or onions sliced
Fennel Trimmings, roughly chopped
1 sprig Thyme
4 pieces of leaves of basil
8 oz. fish stock
1 tblsp Pernod or Ricard
7 oz. heavy cream
2 oz. butter
Salt & freshly ground pepper

Preparing Salmon: Cut the salmon into 4 pieces across the filet and then cut each piece into 3 lengthwise, making 12 portions of equal length. Store in refrigerator. Wash the fennel and cut off top leaves, leaving the most attractive leaves to use as a garnish. Remove the outer layers of the fennel, and keep the trimmings for the sauce. Thinly slice the fennel lengthwise and fry for 30 seconds in very hot oil so the fennel remains crisp. Season with salt and pepper and keep in a warm place. Peel the cucumber and cut in half lengthwise. Use a teaspoon to remove the seeds from the center, then cut the two halves into very thin stripes. Refrigerate.

Cooking the sauce: Heat the olive oil in a saucepan, add the shallots or onions, fennel trimmings, thyme and basil and cook until the vegetables turn a light, golden brown color. Add the fish stock and Pernod (or Ricard) and reduce to a syrupy consistency. Then add the heavy cream, bring to a boil, and reduce again to a sauce consistency. Pass through a fine sieve into a clean saucepan. Whisk the butter into the sauce and season with salt and freshly ground black pepper to taste. Keep Hot.

The salmon—Season the stripes of salmon and briefly fry in a little olive oil around 45 seconds on each side. The salmon strips should still be pink in the middle.

Serving: Sprinkle an equal quantity of crisp, sliced fennel on four warmed plates.

Place 3 pieces of salmon on each plate and pour the sauce around them.

Scatter the thin strips of cucumber on tip and garnish with the reserved green fennel leaves. Serve immediately.

During winter cruises, Celebrity's passengers are in the 45+ age range; during summer months, *Meridian*'s Bermuda cruises are popular with families due to the ship's extensive roster of special activities for children. The onboard atmosphere of all three vessels is low-key, casual and refined, the high number of repeat passengers (around 50 percent) delighted to be aboard such lovely, well-run ships.

AUTHOR'S AWARD

The Horizon, Meridian *and* Zenith *stand out from the pack in decor, service and cuisine, an outstanding value in the mid-price range of Caribbean/Bermuda cruise ships.*

CLASSICAL CRUISES

132 East 70th Street, New York, N.Y. 10021
☎ (212) 794-3200, (800) 252-7745

Classical Cruises' marriage of a high-brow cultural and learning experience with exotic ports has proved so popular that this company's expansion has been rapid. George and Vasos Papagapitos, who founded Classical's parent company, Travel Dynamics in 1969. Devoted to providing educational experiences abroad, Classical Cruises was launched in 1990 with specialized itineraries on the *Illiria*, followed three years later by the elegant *Aurora I & II*, built specifically for the company's exotic itineraries and superb on-board lecturers. In 1994, however, Classical dropped its long term charter of all three vessels (*Aurora I* & *II* are now floating casinos in Malaysia!).

In 1995, the company has part- or full-charter arrangements for individual cruises on a variety of ships ranging from budget to deluxe throughout the world.

Those who seek a learning experience at sea will find the itineraries and guest lecturers unbeatable (joining the ranks of scholars will be Bill Moyers and Roger Mudd). In September 1995 & 1996, for example, Classical explores the Marquesas, Tuamotus, Pitcarin and Easter Island aboard the

World Discoverer. You can explore pre-historic caves of Dorgogne and the vineyards of Burgundy and Provence aboard the river boat *Arlene*; the ancient cultures of Indonesia, Borneo, Vietnam and Cambodia during a cruise of the *Bali Sea Dancer* and the flora and fauna of the Aleutians, Priboilots and Russian Far East on the expedition vessel *World Discoverer*. Classical's customized programs at sea are pricey, but this company does an unbeatable job of enriching the regions visited.

CLIPPER CRUISE LINE

7711 Bonhomme Avenue, St. Louis, MO 63105
☎ (314) 727-2929, (800) 325-0010

It might occur to you that St. Louis is a rather funny home base for a cruise line whose fleet is intended to sail both coasts of North America and the Intracoastal Waterway, and then spend the winter season among the lesser-visited Virgin, Leeward, Windward and Grenadine Islands. The reason: Clipper Cruise Line is owned and operated by St. Louis-native Barney Ebsworth, who also owns and operates the much-respected and highly successful tour company known as INTRAV, also based in his hometown. The two function as wholly separate sister companies that benefit from a single headquarters for all of their operations, hotel, sales and marketing departments. The St. Louis locale also provides fertile territory for Clipper's recruitment of its well-scrubbed, young American shipboard staff who offer the kind of personable service that's hard to find elsewhere.

Clipper operates highly maneuverable, shallow-draft, yacht-like vessels, on which 100-138 passengers can explore places of natural beauty and historic interest that, for the most part, are inaccessible to conventional cruise ships.

The line attracts sophisticated passengers who have done it all elsewhere but come aboard for a different view of America the Beautiful. These vessels are not for people who need a casino, disco, midnight buffet or nightclub shows.

One is encouraged to enjoy the best of American cuisine, walking tours with naturalists or historians when the ships are in port, and quiet evenings with a recap of the day's activities or local entertainment. During the day there are excellent lectures relevant to the destinations, and ever-changing scenery, since the ships are never far from shore.

In the past few years, Clipper has greatly expanded its cruise destinations to provide loyal passengers with ever more adventure. Since 1992, the company has chartered the legendary, 138-passenger expedition ship *World Discoverer* to explore **Antarctica** and **South America's West Coast**. The company has dropped the charter agreement, and after April, 1995, will no longer market the ship in the United States.

Closer to home, Clipper takes full advantage of the small size and shallow draft of its two wholly-owned ships to go into such places as **Alaska's Inside Passage**, the Northwest **Columbia River** and even California's **Sacramento River**. Other destinations include the **St. Lawrence**, the **Orinoco**

River and lovely **Costa Rica**. Wherever they sail, the Clipper fleet does it with style, and passengers love the experience and time on-board.

The *Nantucket Clipper*, built in 1984 in Jeffersonville, Indiana carries a total of 102 passengers each in 51 small but comfortable cabins, while the newer and sleeker *Yorktown Clipper* accommodates 138 passengers and was constructed at Clipper's own First Coast Shipbuilding Company near Jacksonville, Florida. It began cruising the scenic waterways of the Eastern Seaboard in April, 1988.

The *Nantucket Clipper* carries on the East Coast tradition from spring through fall, cruising the coastline on historically-focused cruises from Florida to **Montreal**. It then repositions to the **Virgin Islands** for the winter season, sailing weekly from St. Thomas. The *Yorktown Clipper* sails among the **Windward**, **Leeward** and **Grenadine Islands** and ventures as far south as Venezuela's **Orinoco River** in the winter, combining natural with cultural history. From early spring through fall, the *Yorktown* hugs the West Coast on in-depth, nature-oriented voyages to **Costa Rica** and the **Darien Jungle**, Mexico's **Sea of Cortez**, the **Sacramento** and **Columbia Rivers**, the **San Juan** and **Gulf Islands** of the Pacific Northwest and Alaska's **Inside Passage**.

Wherever they cruise, these two vessels offer the unusual in secluded coves, coming so close to shore that passengers can just reach out and touch something. Passengers are usually 60+ and fascinated by local culture, flora and fauna. Clipper's on-board lecturers are top-notch.

COMMODORE CRUISE LINE

800 Douglas Road, Suite 700, Coral Gables, Florida 33134

☎ (305) 529-3000

Commodore Cruise Line is owned by EffJohn International, a shipping group combination of the Johnson Line of Sweden and Effoa of Finland, which are two of the largest ferry operators in the Baltic. This company has undergone so many changes, just in 1993 alone, that it's a challenge to keep abreast of developments.

In May the 17,000-ton *Caribe* was chartered by a group of investors and now sails as the *Regal Empress*. According to *Tour and Travel News*, in April 1993, while the vessel was still sailing with Commodore as the *Caribe*, an outbreak of illness sickened some 200 passengers and crew, which the Centers for Disease Control blamed on severe sanitation problems on the ship, including warm refrigerators and unsanitary food handling.

In April, Commodore's *Enchanted Isle* was moved to Russia, where it was to become a floating hotel in St. Petersburg. At present the company operates the *Enchanted Seas* on year-round 7-day cruises from **New Orleans** to **Montego Bay**, **Grand Cayman** and **Playa del Carmen**; alternating weekly sailings include visits to **Key West**, **Playa del Carmen** and **Cozumel**.

COSTA CRUISE LINES

World Trade Center, 80 S.W. 8th Street, Miami, FL 33130-3097
☎ (305) 358-7325, (800) 462-6782

Costa used to boast that it was the largest cruise line in the world, and it was, without doubt, during the early years of the North American cruise industry. Costa is also one of the oldest privately owned maritime firms in Italy, established in 1924 with the purchase of the freighter *Ravenna*, although the Genoa-based family has been in the olive oil business since 1860. More than a century ago, Giacomo Costa and his brother began importing the oil from Sardinia, refining it,and exporting it throughout Europe. To do so, they needed vessels, and a soon-booming cargo business led to passengers and cruises. By 1935, seven more freighters joined the Costa fleet. Following World War II, Costa was left with just the tiny ship *Lagano*, but bounded back quickly with some 12 vessels flying the house flag from 1946 to 1948. Passenger service between Genoa and South America began in early 1948, with the 850-passenger *Anna* (air-conditioned, too, so they claim!).

Three more passenger vessels were added to the fleet—the *Andrea C.*, *Giovanna C.*, and *Franca C.* The 1200-passenger *Frederico C.* (now *Star/Ship Royale*) was constructed in the late 1950s, and the new flagship *Eugenio C.* began service between Italy and South America in 1966. The *Enrico C.* (formerly the *Province*) was also placed on this run.

In the late 1960s, Costa acquired the *Carla C.* (former *Flandre*), the *Fulvia* (former *Oslofjord*), and the *Flavia.* During the 1970s, Costa operated eight of its own vessels and chartered six others, with a fleet deployed in the Mediterranean, Caribbean and along the eastern coastline of South America. The company claims it pioneered Caribbean cruises from San Juan in 1968.

Costa undertook a massive fleet expansion in the 1990s, launching four new ships: the 772-passenger *Costa Marina* in 1990; the 800-passenger *Costa Allegra* and 1300-passenger *Costa Classica* in 1992, followed by sister ship *Costa Romantica*, in 1993. With the debut of *Costa Classica* in 1992, the company inaugurated an upscale "EuroLuxe Cruises" promotional campaign that touted the new vessels as offering the greatest elements of European style and service. But in response to very vocal negative feedback from passengers and travel agents who sailed aboard the new vessels, the EuroLuxe theme was dropped in 1993 and Costa returned briefly to more modest claims in its brochure.

Costa apparently does not want its ships reviewed by *Fielding's Cruises.* Company executives could not have been more accessible when mere information was requested for this guide in 1994; when it came time to sail aboard these ships for the purpose of a review, numerous phone calls were never returned, written queries never answered. I have only to assume there's a good reason. The company's 1994 brochures once again carry the luxury theme and claim Costa is "the most elegant fleet in the Caribbean. It's the honest truth."

In 1993, a joint venture called American Family Cruises was formed between Costa Crociere of Genoa and Costa Cruises' former president president, Bruce Nierenberg. Two vessels *American Pioneer* (ex-*Costa Riviera*) and *American Adventurer* (ex-*Eugenio Costa*) were planned to offer the very first vacation exclusively dedicated to families. The *American Adventurer* was launched in late 1993 and the company floundered eight months later.

CRYSTAL CRUISES

2121 Avenue of the Stars, Los Angeles, CA 90067
☎ (310) 785-9300, (800) 446-6645

Crystal Cruises launched the 960-passenger *Crystal Harmony* into the sea of luxury vessels in 1990 and never looked back. Filling a niche for well-heeled travelers who can afford the tiny yacht-like boutique vessels but prefer more activities and facilities, this 49,400-ton vessel charts a global course and is very successful indeed. Crystal Cruises is a subsidiary of NYK (Nippon Yusen Kaisha) Line, headquartered in Tokyo, which announced a $1 billion total investment in the passenger ship industry. The *Crystal Harmony* is so successful that a sister ship, the *Crystal Symphony*, enters the world of luxury cruising in May, 1995 (and one hears murmurs of a third being built down the road).

The Crystal Harmony *makes a grand entrance in Venice.*

Unlike other ships in Fielding's five star plus category, the *Crystal Harmony* schedules more days at sea due to passengers desire for a more leisurely voyage and enough time to be pampered aboard. With the highest space ratio of any ship afloat, the 960-passenger vessel gives the impression of owning one's own luxury liner. *Crystal Harmony* is also Fielding's first ship awarded the highest rating with two-seating dining. Two separate open seating restaurants provide delightful choices during a cruise. From breakfast served on one's private veranda to snuggling under a down comforter with a video at night, there is a full roster of activities and guest lecturers; but the tranquil ambience captures even the most hyper passenger, and sitting on a padded chaise lounge by the pool is the most one can usually manage. Indeed, few companies match Crystal Cruises with the attention to detail affecting all areas of operations that make one almost wish the ship would never dock. And, while there are many beautiful ships from which to choose and itineraries around the globe that make the mouth water, it is always service that sets cruise ship apart.

Crystal's executives frequently begin a sentance "Our guests want ..." They have listened to the point where sister ship *Crystal Symphony* was widened two feet to give extra closet and bathroom space in the lowest-category staterooms. Crystal has also increased deck space and the number of private verandas to 57 percent, added to the capacity of the two alternative dining rooms and enlarged some popular public rooms.

In 1995, *Crystal Harmony* cruises to South America followed by a series of 10- and 11-day transcanal sailings; from May through October the ship cruises in the **Baltic** and **Mediterranean** before returning to the Panama Canal. Following the May 9, 1995, christening of *Crystal Symphony* in New York, the new ship proceeds to a summer season of 11- and 12-day Alaska cruises round-trip from San Francisco followed in September with a series of **Far East**, **Australia** and **New Zealand** itineraries.

CUNARD LINE

555 Fifth Avenue, New York, NY 10017
☎ (800) 221-4770

Cunard Line, which started life as the British and North American Royal Mail Steam-Packet Company more than 150 years ago, was the first to offer regular transatlantic passenger service and has remained the last. The visionary behind such an undertaking was a merchant from Halifax, Nova Scotia, named Samuel Cunard, who took an idea to London in 1839: scheduled mail service on the North Atlantic was possible. A few passengers could come along too, he added. Cunard cajoled a mail contract out of the British Admiralty, and a year later he launched the *Britannia*, which left Liverpool on July 4, 1840. The voyage to Boston took fourteen days and eight hours, and the *Britannia* received a tumultuous welcome. The Boston citizenry were so proud of this new service that they presented Cunard with an enormous sterling silver loving cup as a memento. Miraculously, the cup has survived 150 years of stormy seas and wars, and is on view just as you enter the Columbia Dining Room of the *QE2*.

The *Britannia* was a wooden paddle steamer of 1150 tons with a 207-foot hull. She carried noteworthy passengers including novelist Charles Dickens, who sailed to Boston in 1842 and was shocked to discover his stateroom was nothing more than a closet, even though he had booked deluxe accommodations. He called it utterly impractical, thoroughly hopeless, and a profoundly preposterous box. However, he and his two roommates finally agreed that the cabin could be quite spacious, especially if they all turned around in unison!

In 1847, Cunard added the port of New York to the transatlantic itinerary, and the Admiralty agreed to increase his mail subsidy. By the end of the decade, the fleet had doubled and the North Atlantic was becoming crowded, Cunard cried. After all, this not-too-minor body of water was already known as Cunard's Pond. But in 1856, he launched the biggest ship ever, the *Persia*, twice the length of the *Britannia*, with paddles that were no less than forty feet in diameter, a capacity for three times more passengers than before, and a record speed of fourteen knots. Although Cunard Line never formally recognized the famous Blue Riband, the award to the fastest ship on the Atlantic service presented from the 1880s to the end of the 1960s, the launching of the *Persia* began a racetrack atmosphere.

Hence, the history of passenger service on the North Atlantic closely parallels the development of Cunard Line (its denouement in the early 1970s and its renaissance in the 1980s). At the end of the 19th century, Cunard was building ships in pairs, following specifications laid down by Lloyds and decorating them in the manner of the day—Victorian with velvet drapes, stained-glass cupolas and the wooden paneling. The 20th century brought the turbine engine and such sister ships as the *Carmania* and *Caronia*, *Mauretania* and *Lusitania*.

THE FAMOUS QUEENS

But the most famous of all Cunard's vessels are, undoubtedly, the *Queen Mary* and *Queen Elizabeth*. These two ships were planned with dollar signs in the eyes of company officials, so that every week of the year (with the exception of brief overhaul periods) one *Queen* would depart Southampton, the other New York, at a speed of about 28-1/2 knots. The *Queen Mary* was launched in 1937 and, by the next year, was the fastest ship in Atlantic service. The *Queen Elizabeth* did not fare so auspiciously at first, but began life stealing across the North Atlantic under the cover of wartime gray. The vessel did not carry any paying passengers until after the war. During the war the two *Queens* had together transported more than a million troops back and forth across the seas. Of this service Winston Churchill commented, "The world owes them a debt that it will not be able to measure."

In the postwar years when Europe was again reachable, life was heady for Cunard Line. The two *Queens* were the most prestigious ships on the transatlantic run, not for their cuisine especially but for their traditional British style service of afternoon tea and violins among the palms and for all the elegant people (not to mention the misplaced royalty) who sailed aboard them! But within two decades, the dream faded. In September 1967, the *Queen Mary* tooted to her younger sister, the *Queen Elizabeth*, for the last time as they passed midway across the Atlantic. Less than one year later, the *Elizabeth* was retired and on her way to an ignominious end to be ravaged by fire in Hong Kong harbor.

Cunard was not without a Queen for long. In the spring of 1969, Queen Elizabeth II used the same pair of gold scissors to cut the launching cord of the *QE2* that her mother and grandmother had used while christening the two ships named after them. It was a lovely beginning for the splendid new 67,107-ton vessel filled with the latest in transport technology. Her 1700 passengers have thirteen decks and fourteen public rooms through which to roam, as well as four swimming pools, two gymnasia, several saunas and a complete hospital. One can get lost but not bored on the *QE2*. And the grand dame hangs in there, offering the only regular passenger service from New York to Southampton between April and December, interspersed with more lucrative short cruises. From January to April she circumnavigates the world sometimes in as little as eighty days, just because she's the only ship that can do so.

As one of the most publicized vessel afloat, the *Queen* does splendidly in the 1990's. Her two dozen or so transatlantic crossings each year have a healthy passenger complement and why not? With such enticements as riding the Concorde for a song, putting up at the Ritz in London, as well as discounts on Cunard's new European riverboat cruises, it's absolute madness to stay at home. The Queen is among the most sophisticated ships at sea, and it is amazing how quickly the days pass between Southampton and New York harbor.

MAJOR REFURBISHMENTS AND CORPORATE RESTRUCTURING

To ensure the *QE2* a place in history well into the 1990s, she undergoes a $45 million refurbishment in the fall of 1994 that will improve flow of public areas, refurbish all cabins plus add art and nautical memorabilia from the era of Cunard's renowned transatlantic liners. Additions will include a traditional English pub seating 100, a new shopping plaza and lido for casual lunch and dinner buffet, an observation lounge and enlarged Grand Lounge, among other modifications.

Cunard Line continues to diversify and enlarge its fleet. With the demise of Royal Viking Line in 1994, Cunard purchased the 758-passenger *Royal Viking Sun* and established the upscale Cunard Royal Viking division; the company's other high-end vessels—*Sagafjord*, *Vistafjord*, *Sea Goddess I* & *II*—comprise this new brand name, while *QE2* remains in a class by herself.

Royal Viking Sun will retain the same staff and crew while continuing the 1995 schedule established by Royal Viking Line; she joins *QE 2* as one of the few ships making world cruises in early 1995; sails the Baltic, Western Europe and Mediterranean from June through October and makes a full 53-day circumnavigation of South America beginning Oct. 28. Cunard Line acquired the top-rated *Sagafjord* and *Vistafjord* in late 1983 and both ships continue to have a fiercely loyal following. The 696-passenger *Vistafjord* undergoes a $15 million refurbishment in late 1994 before cruising the Panama Canal, the west coast of South America, Caribbean and European waters. The *Sagafjord*, scheduled for complete refurbishment in 1996, continues with her annual world cruise each year, and summers in Alaska on 10- and 11-day voyages. Following trans-Canal and New England/Canada itineraries *Sagafjord* makes a 34-day soujourn to Europe, sailing round-trip from Ft. Lauderdale Oct. 22-Nov. 25. *Sea Goddess I and II*, Cunard's small yacht-like vessels, originally constructed by the now-bankrupt Wartsila Shipyard in Finland for Sea Goddess Cruises, were designed for just 116 discerning passengers who didn't mind paying a premium for good service, excellent food, complimentary champagne (plus all drinks) and caviar, and cabins that are a bit of a squeeze (including a tiny bathroom). Both vessels spend the season in the Mediterranean, for which they are ideally suited. During the winter months, *Sea Goddess I* plies the Caribbean's most pristine islands, voyages up the Amazon and joins her sister ship in the Mediterranean. *Sea Goddess II* winters in Asia with positioning voyages through the Indian Ocean before a return to European waters.

Cunard has kept up the standard of Sea Goddess Cruises original intent, without the fancy clientele. Leave grandmother's jewels at home, believe me, no one else on board has any! Life on *Sea Goddess I and II* still offer the ultimate cruise experience.

MID-PRICED CRUISES

In 1993 Cunard expanded its fleet to create the Cunard Crown group of mid-priced ships. Under a joint agreement between Trafalgar House and EffJohn Group, Cunard markets the 800-passenger sister ships *Crown Jewel* and *Crown Dynasty*, launched in 1992 and 1993. *Crown Jewel* cruises year-round from Port Everglades on alternating weekly itineraries to San Juan, Puerto Plata, St. Thomas, St. John and Nassau, alternating with Ocho Rios, Cozumel, Grand Cayman and Cancun. *Crown Dynasty* sails on 10- and 11-day Panama Canal voyages between Port Everglades and Acapulco through April, then moves to Alaska for weekly cruises between Vancouver and Seward.

Completing the Cunard Crown group are two warm-weather, short-cruising vessels, the *Cunard Countess* and the *Cunard Princess*, carrying 800 passengers. *Cunard Countess* cruises year-round from San Juan on alternating itineraries: the "Caribbean Capitals" calls in **Tortola**, **Antigua**, **Martinique**, **Barbados** and **St. Thomas** while the "7-Plus" sailing visits **St. Maarten**, **Guadeloupe**, **Grenada**, **St. Lucia**, **St. Kitts** and **St. Thomas**. The two can be combined for La Grande Caribbean, a 2-week cruise featuring 12 different ports. Prices are reasonable and cruises can be booked as a Sail and Stay program for an extra week at either Wyndham Morgan Bay on St. Lucia or Heywoods on Barbados. A familiar presence in the Canary Islands, *Cunard Princess* caters primarily to a European crowd, sailing from Malaga to **Tangier**, **Lanzarote**, **Las Palmas**, **Santa Cruz de Tenerife**, **La Palma**, **Funchal** and **Gibraltar** from March through November; the remainder of the year *Cunard Princess* cruises in the Eastern and Western Mediterranean and Black Sea.

CUNARD EUROPAMERICA CRUISES

In 1993, Cunard expanded its European cruise operation through an agreement with EuropAmerica Cruises to represent three river cruise vessels and added two additional vessels in 1994. The *Mozart* and *Danube Princess* cruise the Danube; the *Prussian Princess* sails the Rhine; the *Princese de Provence* journeys through the French wine country while the *Dresden* cruises the Elbe. Cunard EuropAmerica River Cruises are offered at savings of 50 percent when combined with a *QE 2* transatlantic crossing.

DIAMOND CRUISES

600 Corporate Drive, Suite 410, Ft. Lauderdale, FL 33344
☎ (305) 776-6123, (800) 833-3333

Diamond Cruise Ltd. was announced to the American public in May 1990 but was actually formed in Helsinki, Finland, in November 1986 by Captain Offe Nyblin and his partner, Christian Aspegren. The two Finnish entrepreneurs seemed to know their minds and engaged the respected Rauma Yards in Rauma, Finland, to construct a $125-million vessel with a revolutionary design technology called SSC (Semi-Submersible Craft). At first glance, the vessel looks like a catamaran because it is lifted above the water on two large struts that are attached to two submerged hulls that provide buoyancy.

The 18,400-ton *Radisson Diamond*, launched in 1992, carries a passenger complement of 354 and a crew of 170, with average cruise-only prices per person, per diem in the $500-$600 range (including tips and house wine with dinner). Managed and marketed by Radisson Hotels International, the vessel was originally intended to attract the meetings and incentive market, as well as well-heeled individual travelers, hence the large areas designed for board meetings and a conference center. The focal point is a five-story atrium with glass elevators, as well as a grand staircase. The all-suite accommodations feature terraces, as well as state-of-the-art amenities and communications technology for the executive class, to which the Radisson Hotels caters. The dining room is open-seating and the eight-deck lounge has panoramic sea views. Recreational features include an outdoor swimming pool and Jacuzzi, pool, health and fitness center, jogging track and floating marina at the stern of the vessel.

During 1995, *Radisson Diamond* cruises the Panama Canal before commencing 3-, 4- and 7-night Caribbean cruises; the vessel summers in the Mediterranean on one-week sailings between Istanbul and Athens.

DOLPHIN CRUISE LINE

901 South America Way, Miami, FL 33132
☎ (305) 358-5122, (800) 222-1003

Dolphin Cruise Line has come a long way since it was formed in 1984 to take over the marketing of 3- and 4-day cruises aboard the *Dolphin IV*, a 590-passenger vessel relinquished by Paquet Cruises. In 1989, Dolphin expanded into the one-week cruise market with acquisition of the *SeaBreeze* (former Starship *Royale* of Premier Cruise Line), on which it spent $5.5 million in refurbishment, and entered the *OceanBreeze* into service as well. The company painted all three ships white with a blue-on-blue stripe and put an adorable dolphin logo on the smokestacks. In 1992, the company made a big splash in the industry by forming an upscale sister company, Majesty Cruise Line, and built the $220 million elegant *Royal Majesty*, currently on 3- and 4-day sailings from **Miami**. Meanwhile, Dolphin does quite nicely with bargain-hunters on its modest vessels. I understand that at least two weddings a week are held aboard the *SeaBreeze* from **Miami**. The *Dolphin* caters to families: Fred Flintstone and Yogi Bear frequently sail to entertain the kids.

The *OceanBreeze* cruises year-round from **Aruba** on alternating one-week Southern Caribbean and Panama Canal itineraries. *SeaBreeze*, based in **Miami**, offers alternating weekly cruises to the Eastern and Western Caribbean and the *Dolphin* continues its 3- and 4-night sailings from **Miami**.

EPIROTIKI LINES, INC.

551 Fifth Avenue, New York, N.Y. 10176
☎ (212) 599-1750, (800) 221-2470

The name *Epirotiki* is synonymous with Greek island cruising. The line has been a presence in the Mediterranean since 1946, but in 1991 suffered a major blow with the sinking of the 7554-ton *Oceanos* in the Indian Ocean near South Africa during a severe storm. The foundering of a vessel at sea today is among the rarest of events due to the high safety standards of maritime shipping, One cannot find a more secure travel experience than a cruise.

According to news media, Epirotiki's officers and crew fled the vessel on lifeboats as soon as problems arose. The vessel's Captain jumped aboard the first helicopter, abandoning *Oceanos's* 361 passengers. The ship's British entertainers assumed control of the rescue operation, assisting in the airlift of passengers into helicopters and there were no casualties. In 1994, Epirotiki suffered its fourth mishap, when the *Pallas Athena* caught fire in Piraeus, Greece, harbor; no one was injured, but the ship burned for six days and there has been no word on whether the vessel will resume service.

In 1994, Carnival Cruise Lines acquired a 43 percent share of Epirotiki and installed a new president, who has stated the company's major concern is safety. Moreover, we have rated Epirotiki's ships one star until there is enough evidence the company's vessels are brought up to U.S. safety standards.

Epirotiki's fleet consists of the 706-passenger *Triton*; the 536-passenger *World Renaissance*; the 452-passenger *Odysseus*; the 184-passenger *Neptune*; the 272-passenger *Jason* and the 850-passenger *Olympic* (ex-*Mardi Gras*).

GALAPAGOS CRUISES

c/o Adventure Associates, 13150 Coit Road, Suite 110, Dallas, Texas 75240
☎ (214) 907-0414, (800) 527-2500

Galapagos Cruises, a division of Metropolitan Touring of Quito, Ecuador, was the pioneer in offering pleasure cruises to the **Galapagos Islands**. Ecuadorean Eduardo Proano, president of Metropolitan Touring, is deeply concerned with both promoting and preserving these enchanted islands.

He brings in most (if not all) of the allotted twelve thousand tourists annually. Proano opened the area to tourism in 1968.

Flagship of Galapagos Cruises is the 1500-ton *Santa Cruz*, a 90-passenger, all first-class vessel built in Spain in 1979 especially for these cruises. The *Santa Cruz* offers a 3-, 4-, or 7-day program among the islands, but the best is a 7-day itinerary (a combination of the 3- and 4-day), with flights to and from the ship. In addition, the company operates the new *Isabella II*, a 40-passenger yacht (which Galapagos National Park regulations restricts to a capacity of just 34) on 7-night itineraries from Baltra to Plaza, Hood, Floreana, Barrington, Santa Cruz, Tower, Isabela, Fernandina, James and Bartolome islands. The 166-foot yacht has 20 outside twin cabins, each with two lower berths and private facilities, as well as a salon/bar, spacious dining room and separate reading and games rooms. It carries a crew of 17, including two multilingual naturalist guides.

Metropolitan Touring also operates a series of smaller yachts accommodating from 6 to 14 passengers each—the *Merak, Encantada, Mistral, Nortada, Amigo I*, and *Beagle III*—and develops itineraries to suit your needs. Introduced in 1989 were inexpensive hotel and day cruise packages utilizing the 36-passenger motor yacht *Delphin II* and the Hotel Delfin, built around a tidal lagoon in Academy Bay on **Santa Cruz Island**. Travelers can choose as many days as they like of the package, but the itineraries are designed with guaranteed air space from **Guayaquil** on the 3-, 4-, or 7-night cruises. During the various Galapagos programs that highlight the most popular islands, guides trained by the Darwin Research Station come aboard each vessel. Metropolitan offers more than 60 different tours within mainland **Ecuador**, ranging from city sightseeing and visits to Indian markets to countrywide itineraries, mountain climbing, trekking, birdwatching, a look at the equator marker, etc.

Galapagos Cruises also operates the three-deck, 56-passenger flotel *Orellana* on Ecuador's **Napo River** for 2- to 4-night jungle cruises. The 2- to 4-berth cabins all have private facilities, and the flotel has a large sun deck, salon and dining room. Shore excursions into the rain forests in motorized dugout canoes travel to such places as the **Jivino River**, **Monkey Island**, **Primavera**, **Limoncocha** and **Lake Taracoa** are not for the timid, but worth it for the colorful scenery and thousand new sounds.

GALAPAGOS, INC.

7800 Red Road, Suite 112, South Miami, FL 33143
☎ (305) 665-0841, (800) 327-9854

This Florida-based company represents the *Galapagos Explorer*, a vessel carrying 100 passengers in air-conditioned comfort around the **Galapagos Islands**. Like the *Buccanero* before, the operators say this is the largest cruise ship operating in the islands. The ship boasts such amenities as a swimming pool, solarium, spacious dining room, two bar areas, and music for dancing. Five naturalist guides, who studied at the Charles Darwin Research Station, are also aboard, and the 3- and 4-night cruises can be combined to a full week. Flights from **Guayaquil** carry passengers to **San**

Cristobal to catch up with the Explorer. The Wednesday to Saturday or Saturday to Wednesday departures are year-round. Galapagos Inc. also offers yacht cruises of the islands aboard the first-class *Dorado,* tourist-class *Yolita* and *San Pedro,* economy-class *Darwin, Albatros, Poderoso, San Antonio,* and *Aida Maria,* as well as some charter boats upon request.

HOLLAND AMERICA LINE

300 Elliott Avenue West, Seattle, WA 98119
☎ (206) 281-3535, (800) 426-0327

The beginning of Holland America Line fits into modern history. The future of Rotterdam as a port looked rather bleak in the early 1870s because ship owners seemed to prefer rival Amsterdam. Therefore, to try to develop some necessary trade between Holland and America, two young Dutchmen commissioned the SS *Rotterdam,* an iron vessel of 1700 tons that could carry eight passengers in first-class accommodations and 380 in steerage, as well as 1500 tons of cargo. Her maiden voyage took place in October 1872, and her subsequent voyages were so successful that the two young partners joined with a third to form the Netherlands-America Steam Navigation Company in April 1873. It became known simply as Holland America Line in 1896.

From the very beginning, Holland America's flagship has been named the *Rotterdam,* one in a fleet that features such names as *Nieuw Amsterdam, Westerdam, Ryndam, Noordam, Maasdam,* and *Statendam.* In addition to weekly service between Rotterdam and New York, the company began cruises to Copenhagen as early as June 1895 aboard the *Rotterdam* (the second). Another cruise offered during the first decade of the 20th century, aboard the *Statendam,* included a visit to the Holy Land. A few years later the company ordered a new 32,000-ton *Statendam,* which was destined to become a giant among passenger vessels, but alas, never carried a paying passenger. The ship, launched just as World War I broke out, was fitted to transport troops, only to be sunk at sea, a U-boat victim.

Another new *Statendam,* ordered in the mid-1920s, sailed on her maiden voyage in April 1929, arriving in New York on the 300th anniversary of the landing of the Dutch ships that carried the founders of the settlement once known as New Amsterdam. The decade of the 1930s was a slump time for shipping, due to the world economic situation. By May 1940, Germany had invaded Holland and Dutch shipping ground to a standstill. At this time, however, Holland America transferred its headquarters to Curacao in the Dutch West Indies, where it remains.

AFTER THE WAR

In the postwar period, Holland America launched the 15,000-ton *Ryndam* and the *Maasdam.* The former *Statendam* (fourth of her name), launched in 1957, now sails as *Regent Star.* In 1958, Queen Juliana launched the fifth Rotterdam; her maiden voyage took place a year later. Both vessels easily converted to one-class cruising ships to accommodate the demand of the past few decades.

The 1075-passenger *Rotterdam* is the grande dame of the Holland America Line fleet. Worldly and gracious, the *Rotterdam* has a loyal following and has circumnavigated the globe some 25 times, the last one in 1993 when HAL management decided the long cruise market was passing away. But times change quickly and the *Rotterdam* voyages around the globe in January, 1995 followed by 16-day fall and spring Hawaiian Island cruises and a 34-day journey to the South Pacific in the fall.

Two 32,000-ton sister ships, the 1214-passenger *Nieuw Amsterdam* (1983) and *Noordam* (1984) have proved successful for Holland America, as they are well suited to short **Caribbean** cruises during the winter months, as well as the **Alaska** season in summer. Both vessels are beautifully designed and decorated. The *Nieuw Amsterdam* has the ambience of a 17th-century sailing ship and over $1 million in nautical artifacts, while the *Noordam* received an 18th-century interior and also $1 million in lovely antiques.

Fourth and largest of the fleet is the 52,000-ton *Westerdam* (former *Homeric*), which received a $65-million expansion and redesign in the Papenburg, West German, shipyard where she was originally constructed (1986). The insertion of a 130-foot section increased the ship's passenger complement to 1476 and her length to 798 feet. Another million dollars in 17th- and 18th-century art and antiques to reflect Dutch exploration were also added.

Holland America, whose motto is "Tradition of Excellence," is known for its Dutch officers and Indonesian crew trained at a special school in Jakarta (Filipinos have since been added). The line is also known for its No Tipping Required policy, the spirit of which seems to work well as the crew all appear to have happy faces. However, exceptional service is not expected to go unrewarded, so tipping aboard HAL ships is not a bad word; it's just not a continual word!

Holland America, through its Westours subsidiary, has been a major force in Alaska and the Yukon territory for four decades. It also operates Gray Line of Alaska, Westmark Hotels and Inns, several large excursion boats and the McKinley Explorer glass-domed railway cars. Holland America places four vessels in Alaska for the summer season and offers more than 70 Inside Passage cruises, with cruise/tours being a top seller for those who wish to extend their visit with enticing land programs. In 1987 and 1988, Holland America acquired half and then full interest in Windstar Cruises, and its small vessels *Wind Star*, *Wind Song* and *Wind Spirit*. In January 1989, Carnival Cruise Line completed acquisition of Holland America Line, which is treated as a wholly owned subsidiary. Before the end of that same year, the two companies announced an order for four new Holland America vessels to be constructed at Italy's Fincantieri shipyard. In 1993, Holland America added two vessels to the fleet—the 1266-passenger sister ships *Statendam* and *Maasdam*; the third sister ship, *Ryndam*, launched Oct., 1994, is sure to be among the most popular ships cruising Alaska. The fourth identical vessel, *Veendam*, will commence service in 1996. *Statendam*, *Maasdam* and *Ryndam* continue the company's tradition of designing vessels that are reminiscent of the grand old liners of yesterday: wonderful art collections, larger cabins and use of marble, polished wood and fine fabrics throughout. In 1995, Holland America vessels offering multiple trans-canal sailings include *Maasdam* and *Nieuw Amsterdam*; one-week Caribbean itineraries are available on *Westerdam*, *Maasdam*, *Noordam* and *Nieuw Amsterdam*, while 10-day Caribbean voyages are scheduled for *Statendam* and *Ryndam*. *Rotterdam* begins the new year on an 85-day world cruise, followed by two 16/19-day Hawaii sailings. Following an Alaska season, a 34-day "Grand South Pacific Voyage" takes this vessel to some lovely exotic isles. The company remains a major presence in Alaska with marvelous cruise tours offering extended land excursions in the 50th state and British Columbia. Vessels deployed to Alaska in 1995 include *Nieuw Amsterdam*, *Noordam*, *Statendam*, *Ryndam* and *Rotterdam*. Equally popular are Holland America's spring through fall cruises in the Baltic, Western Europe and the Mediterranean, this year scheduled aboard the *Maasdam*

IVARAN LINES, INC.

Ivaran Agencies, Newport Financial Center
111 Pavonia Avenue, Jersey City, NJ 07310-1755
☎ (201) 798-5656, (800) 451-1639

The Oslo-based Ivaran Lines is no stranger to the East Coast of the United States nor South American ports. For nearly 70 years, Ivaran has been sending its cargo vessels and a few passengers on these routes. But in 1988, the company launched the *Americana*, a beautiful 19,500-ton passenger/container vessel, constructed in Korea, for 46-day sailings from New Orleans to **South America**. The concept is a reincarnation of the famous Grace Line cargo liners that departed the West Coast and made two-month voyages around South America.

Ivaran Lines offers excellent service aboard the 88-passenger *Americana* and a new passenger vessel is rumored in the works. Passenger facilities found on the *Americana* are well designed and beautifully maintained, matching those found on any traditional cruise vessel; Norwegian officers and crew, and the young, enthusiastic South American staff nicely complement cruise passengers who are in the 60+ age group and are experienced travelers.

The southbound 46-day itinerary between **New Orleans** and **Buenos Aires** includes port calls in Baltimore, Norfolk, Savannah, Jacksonville, Miami, San Juan, the Brazilian ports Fortaleza, Salvador, Ilheus, Rio de Janeiro, Santos, Paranagua, Itajai, Rio Grande de Sul and Montevideo, **Uruguay**. Full-voyage air/sea rates range from $4230 to $6100 per person, double occupancy, with discounts available on certain sailings.

MAJESTY CRUISE LINE

901 South America Way, Miami, Florida 33132-2073
☎ (305) 358-5122, (800) 532-7788

Built at a cost of $220 million, *Royal Majesty* was launched by sister company Dolphin Cruises as an upscale ship in 1992 and has proved popular with both first-time passengers, who traditionally sail on shorter voyages, and experienced cruisers who seek a brief respite at sea. The decor is tastefully colorful, with a proliferation of brass, polished wood, marble and quality fabrics, as well as nautical prints.

During evening hours, the Observatory Bar's pianist serenades those having a quiet cocktail and a sports bar with 24 TVs, brings live college and pro games. *Royal Majesty* offer a first non-smoking dining room and 25 percent of cabins are designated for non-smokers.

While the ship initially received rave reviews, we experienced a slacking off in service and cuisine on a recent cruise. Sailing from Miami, *Royal Majesty* visits **Nassau** and **Royal Isle**, a private island in the Bahamas on 3-night cruises; the 4-night itinerary includes port calls in **Cozumel** and **Key West**.

MARINE EXPEDITIONS

13 Hazelton Avenue Toronto, Ontario, Canada M5R 2E1

☎ (416) 964-2569, (800) 263-9147

Those seeking a true learning experience of some of the world's most remote regions aboard a hard-working former research vessel may be intriuged by Marine Expeditions' *Akademik Ioffe*. This 79-passenger ship offers a rare and authentic field study of both polar regions and the Great Lakes.

The *Akademik Ioffe* was commissioned by the Academy of Sciences of Moscow and constructed in Finland's Holming Shipyard in 1989 as an ice-rated oceanographic research vessel. The crew is Russain, assisted by a cruise staff of North Americans and Europeans. All cabins are outside, with writing desk, couch and mini-bar and most have en-suite bathrooms. Meals are prepared by European chefs and are waiter served. Open access to the command bridge, with its highly sophisticated communication, navigation and monitoring equipment, is a highlight while cruising. Other facilities include a small pool, sauna, library, a mud room, chart room, meterological lab and a bird identification lab. In remote regions, transportation ashore is by Zodiacs.

This ship carries scientists and naturalists as lecturers. Prices are among the most reasonable for expedition cruising to polar regions: a 14-day Antarctica cruise is available from $2995 per person, double occupancy including round-trip airfare and all shore excursions.

During 1995, the *Akademik Ioffe* winters in Antartica, visiting the Falklands, Tierra del Fuego and the Magellan Straights. Exploration of the Arctic region departs from London and visits Spitsbergen, the Lofoten Islands and Tromso.

During summer, two 8- and 10-day cruises through the Great Lakes (the first since the mid-1970's) cruise to secluded areas of Lake Superior, Lake Huron, Lake Erie and Lake Ontario for a study of flora and fauna and Indian settlements, with plenty of time for fishing and swimming.

NORWEGIAN CRUISE LINE

5 Merrick Way, Coral Gables, Florida 33134
☎ (305) 445-0866, (800) 327-7030

It seems a long way from hauling coal around Scandinavia at the turn of the century to buying one of the most famous ships afloat and converting her into a fun-filled resort called the *Norway*, but that is just the history of the family Kloster. The *Norway* was a coup for the grandson of the original Kloster ship owner, Knut Utstein Kloster, who bought his first steamer of 830 tons in 1906. Today, the company cruises in the Caribbean, Alaska, the west coast and Mexico.

While parent company Kloster Cruise Limited has been plagued by servere financial problems over the past few years, its debt reaching a reported $1 billion, a recent restructuring has eased the pressure substantially.

In order to raise capital for the purchase of vessels, Kloster Cruise planned a $100 million stock offering in late 1987 that was postponed due to stormy weather on Wall Street since the October market crash. In 1993, the company issued $300 million in bonds to restructure its long-term debt; according to *Tour and Travel News*, the delivery of the *Windward*, already enroute to the U.S. for its maiden voyage, was contingent upon consummation of that bond offering. Kloster assured a very nervous industry that NCL is financially solvent. In 1994, Kloster dissolved NCL's sister upscale cruise company Royal Viking Line, selling the *Royal Viking Sun* to Cunard Line for $170 million and transferring the *Royal Viking Queen* to Royal Cruise Line, where it will sail as the *Queen Odyssey*. In streamling NCL's older vessels, Kloster sold the *Southward* to a British firm and transferred the *Westward* to Royal Cruise Line, where the ship underwent a major refurbishment and now sails as the *Star Odyssey*.

Its first venture into the cruise business occurred in 1966 with the introduction of the *Sunward* on 3- and 4-day cruises to the **Bahamas** from Miami. The original *Sunward* (now retired) was soon followed by the 16,000-ton *Starward*, and in subsequent years, the *Skyward*, *Southward* and *Sunward II*. NCL's own Out Island in the Bahamas was called Great Stirrup Cay; it is now known as Pleasure Island.

During these years, Kloster bought real estate in Jamaica so passengers aboard the *Starward* could enjoy a cruise-and-stay holiday at Jamaica Hill near Port Antonio. Unfortunately, the 44-villa resort on an old estate with acres of lawn, tennis courts and a swimming pool has not been a success and is no longer a part of the NCL package. Kloster's boldest move was the purchase of the SS *France*. Despite some severe problems, the company transformed her into the *Norway*, a very popular ship with those who want the activities found aboard a mega-ship and the chance to recapture the experience of a grand old liner; she underwent a $23 million facelift in 1993.

Kloster made steps towards upgrading NCL's elderly fleet with the construction of the 1246-passenger *Dreamward* in 1992, followed a year later by her sistership, the *Windward*.

In 1995, the 1504-passenger *Seaward* sails year round from Miami on 3-day cruises to the **Bahamas** and 4-day cruises to **Key West**, **Cancun** and **Cozumel**; from October through April, the *Windward* cruises on weekly alternating itineraries: **Barbados**, **Martinique**, **St. Maarten**, **Antigua** and **St. Thomas** alternating with **Aruba**, **Curacao**, **Tortola**, **St. John** and **St. Thomas** before beginning cruises in **Alaska**, May through September; from fall through spring, the *Dreamward* sails from Ft. Lauderdale on 7-day voyages to **Grand Cayman**, **Playa del Carmen**, **Cozumel**, **Cancun** and **Pleasure Island** and will offer 1-week Bermuda voyages from New York May through October. The *Starward* cruises year round on weekly voyages from San Juan to **St. Kitts**, **Grenada**, **Tobago**, **St. Lucia**, **St. Barts**, **St. John** and **St. Thomas**. The *Norway* sails year-round from Miami to **St. Maarten**, **St. John**, **St. Thomas** and **Pleasure Island**.

While Kloster's aim is to transform NCL into an upscale cruise line, the company has a way to go, despite sexy TV commercials depicting glamour that is far from reality. However, the *Dreamward*, *Windward* and *Norway* are excellent choices for those seeking comfortable, well-kept ships at moderate price. NCL stands out in theme cruises (sports and jazz) and services and facilities for children.

OCEANIC CRUISES

5757 West Century Blvd., Los Angeles, CA 90045

☎ (310) 215-0190, (800) 545-5778

Cruise Japanese Style aboard the *Oceanic Grace*, says the attractive brochure. Oceanic Cruises is another of the booming Japanese companies to enter the industry with a luxury vessel. The company is owned by Showa Line, one of the six largest steamship companies in Japan involved with commercial shipping worldwide. According to Showa's corporate profile, the company operates containers, liners, tankers and transport and bulk carrier services, involving 113 different owned or chartered vessels. To enter the cruise/leisure industry seems a logical extension of such success.

The 120-passenger *Oceanic Grace* was built in Japan and began service in April 1989. It was designed by the Studio Yacht group of Holland and closely resembles the *Sea Goddess I* and *II*, except the chairs are shorter, the beds are harder and the bathtubs are only four feet long! While the vessel caters primarily (80 to 90 percent at this writing) to the Japanese market, we understand that Americans and Europeans are very welcome and the Japanese passengers on-board are such that they are eager to interface with westerners.

For the 1995 season, *Oceanic Grace* offers 2- to 9-night cruises from **Nagasaki**, **Yokohama**, **Tokyo**, **Kobe**, **Hakodate** and **Niigata**. She is the only vessel sailing exclusively around the Japanese archipelago so extensively, and her 5000-ton size allows visits to both large and small ports. Sounds wonderful, and we wish her well!

ODESSA AMERICA CRUISE COMPANY

170 Old Country Road, Suite 608, Mineola, New York 11501
☎ (516) 747-8880, (800) 221-3254

Odessa America Cruise Company (OdessAmerica) was formed in 1991 as a Ukrainian-American joint venture between Black Sea Shipping Company of Ukraine and International Cruise Center of New York. Established in 1833, Black Sea Shipping Company is the largest cruise company in the former Soviet Union and owns 15 passenger ships and river boats ranging from 100 to 650 passengers.

Black Sea launched Russian style cruising to North Americans in the 1970s and 1980s when ex-Soviet vessels *Maxim Gorky*, *Kazakhstan* and *Odessa* sailed regularly from New York, Los Angeles, New Orleans, Baltimore, Vancouver and Montreal. OdessAmerica launched the 450-passenger *Gruziya* (which means Georgia) in 1991. Owned by Black Sea Shipping Company and registered in Odessa, Ukraine, the *Gruziya* underwent a $20 million refurbishment in Bremerhaven, Germany, in 1992 and began weekly cruises along the **St. Lawrence** and **Saguenay**, where she cruises today from June through October, visiting Montreal, ports of St. Pierre et Miquelon, the Gaspe peninsula, Prince Edward Island and Quebec City; from October through April, the *Gruziya* charts a route to the ancient Maya, with port calls in **Honduras**, **Belize** and **Cancun**. Passengers will find this ship a unique experience, with activities including Russian language lessons, ancient Tea Ceremonies, Ukraine and Russian entertainment and a ship boutique with handicrafts from the home land.

Even more exotic are river cruises aboard OdessAmerica's 288-passenger *Andropov*, on a 14-day itinerary through lakes, canals and rivers which connect **Moscow** and **St. Petersburg** from May through September. The 300-passenger *Glushkov*, with all outside cabins, has weekly cruises between **Kiev** and **Odessa** on the Dnieper River; the vessel also sails on the Danube from Passau, Germany, visiting **Vienna**, **Budapest**, **Bratislava**, **Nikopol**, **Bucharest**, **Izmail** and into the Black Sea ports of **Yalta** and **Istanbul**.

OdessaAmerica also represents the London-based CTC Lines *Kareliya*, cruising the Baltic to Iceland and the Norwegian coast line to the North Cape, and the *Azerbaydzhan*, sister ship of the *Gruziya*, which cruises to **Lisbon**, **Nice**, **Casablanca**, **Dublin**, **Tangier**, **Malaga** and **Palma** from spring through fall.

Don't look for luxury or refined service aboard these vessels, but a unique cultural experience. As they say in the Ukraine, Laskavo Prosymo !

ORIENT LINES

1510 S.E. 17th Street, Fort Lauderdale, Florida 33316
☎ (305) 527-6660, (800) 333-7300

Orient Lines was founded in 1992 by British entrepreneur Gerry Herrod, former head of Pearl Cruises and Ocean Cruise Line, to offer cruises to exotic destinations at affordable prices. In November, 1993, the company launched the 800-passenger *Marco Polo* with a very ambitious itinerary: a

24-day **Argentina** to **New Zealand** voyage that included a partial circumnavigation of Antarctica.

The 20,500-ton vessel is the former *Alexandr Pushkin*, built in 1965 as a cruise ship with troop transport capabilities, and rebuilt at a cost of $75 million. Of the total 425 cabins, 286 are outside; the ship's facilities include two restaurants, four lounges, a casino, swimming pool, health club and beauty center, as well as three Jacuzzis and a helipad on the top deck.

Priced are around $245 per person, per day, *Marco Polo* cruises in the **Far East**, **South Pacific**, **Africa** and the **Indian Ocean**; from January through April, 1995, a series of **Australia** and **New Zealand** cruises are scheduled.

P & O CRUISES

c/o Princess Cruises, 10110 Santa Monica Blvd., Los Angeles, CA 90067
☎ (310) 553-1770, (800) 568-3262
or
97 New Oxford Street, London WC1A 1PP
☎ (01) 831-1234

The Peninsular and Oriental Steam Navigation Company, England's largest and most prestigious passenger and cargo line, began in the early 1800s and grew steadily in the 19th and 20th centuries through a series of astute acquisitions (and some romantic seafaring history). The company flag, a combination of the blue and white national colors of Portugal quartered with the red and yellow colors of Spain, symbolizes the highest of honors that both countries bestowed upon the ship line in the 1830s, commemorating valuable services rendered to Queen Maria of Portugal and Queen Isabella of Spain. Another interesting episode in the annals of P & O history dates to the opening of service between Egypt and India, which added a new word to the English language: Posh appeared stamped on certain steamship tickets to indicate that the passenger had bought the best (and coolest) cabin which happened to be Port Out (to India), Starboard Home. Since this cabin was in the most expensive category, the new word began to connote wealth and elitism.

According to company correspondence, P & O Line had such a fine reputation in the Victorian 19th century that even its shipwrecks were considered the best of any passenger fleet! In a letter dated 1863, from a Mrs. Dulcimer to her friend, Laura, the writer advises, "If you are ever shipwrecked, do contrive to get the catastrophe conducted by the Peninsular and Oriental Company. I believe other companies drown you sometimes, and drowning is a very prosaic arrangement fit only for seafaring people and second-class passengers. I have just been shipwrecked under the auspices of P & O, and I assure you that it is the pleasantest thing imaginable. It has its little hardships to be sure, but so has a picnic, and the wreck was one of the most agreeable picnics you can imagine." What a recommendation!

P & O Cruises, which celebrated its 150th anniversary as a passenger ship company in 1987, is part of a huge conglomerate of companies in

Britain involved in cargo/container shipping, as well as construction and real estate.

In passenger services, P & O owns and operates Princess cruises of Los Angeles (*Royal Princess, Island Princess, Pacific Princess, Fair Princess, Sky Princess, Crown Princess, Golden Princess, Star Princess, Regal Princess*), as well as the Swan Group (Swan Hellenic Cruises aboard the *Orpheus*, Nile cruises aboard *Nile Star*) and P & O Spice Island Cruises (expedition ships in the Indonesian archipelago) and markets the last of the great ocean liners, *Canberra*.

The 44,807-ton *Canberra* was built in Northern Ireland in 1961, but has been refurbished twice in the past decade to bring her up to 1980s standards. She carries 1400 passengers (double occupancy), as well as a crew of 805 that represents the far reaches of the former British Empire—British officers with Indian (Goanese), Pakistani, and Chinese deck and engine crew. Many cabins still do not boast complete private facilities (WC and showers are down the hall a bit), but the Great White Whale, as she is so affectionately termed by her loyal passengers, is certainly the last of a breed. She is very popular with a wide range of English-speaking nationalities, and makes a world cruise every winter, as well as round-trip sailings from Southampton to ports throughout the Mediterranean, Black and Baltic seas, never repeating an itinerary if she can avoid doing so!

P & O SPICE ISLAND CRUISES

c/o Esplanade Tours, 581 Boylston Street, Boston, MA 02116
☎ (617) 266-7465, (800) 426-5492

P & O Spice Island Cruises can be a heavenly experience for the intrepid adventurer seeking exotic cultures, rare wildlife and volcanoes rarely visited by Westerners. The company's three ships sail the Indonesian archipelago, calling on villagers who see very few outsiders, and ports inaccessible to all but the tiniest vessels. Represented in the United States by Esplanade Tours, which also markets the high brow Swan Hellenic Cruises, this cruise line's two custom-built catamaran ships with a shallow draft give passengers access to the intriguing South Pacific cultures little touched by the outside world.

The *Spice Islander* and *Island Explorer* carry between 35 and 40 passengers. Life on-board these vessels is casual; their passengers are the adventuresome sort who love exploring jungle rivers by Zodiacs, snorkelling and diving to coral reefs, and delight in participating in island ceremonies and celebrations. In the fall of 1994, the company adds a third ship, the 150-passenger *Sea Bali Dancer*, the former *Illyria*, for 3- and 4-day sailings from Bali.

The 120-foot *Spice Islander* and 130-foot *Island Explorer* cruise Indonesia year-round on three itineraries. The eight-day Volcanoes and Rain Forests excursion sails round-trip from Jakarta with port calls in **Krakatau**, with an early morning climb to the smoking crater of *Anak Krakatu* volcano, which last erupted in 1883 and was the largest explosion in recorded history. Additional port calls include the 200,000-acre Ujung Kulon Game Reserve and rain forest on Java and an elephant training center on Sumatra.

The alternating eight-day Sandalwood and Dragons Expeditions cruise between Bali and the island of Timor, with visits to Komodo, home of the 10-foot prehistoric Komodo lizard; to Kilo, where pony carts transport passengers to villages and markets; and to Sumbawa's buffalo race and the Solor Islands, where locals meet the vessels with welcoming gifts of palm leaf cigars and tuak toddy.

PAQUET FRENCH CRUISES

6301 N.W. 5th Way, Suite 4000, Fort Lauderdale, Florida 33309
☎ (305) 772-8600, (800) 556-8850

Paquet French Cruises returned to the North American scene in 1990 after an absence of several years. The French-based company, known as Compagnie Francaise de Crossieres in Paris, is owned by two large conglomerates—Chargeurs S.A. and Accor (owners of both Novotel and Sofitel hotels). Paquet was originally founded by Nicolas Paquet in 1860 as a merchant shipping operation between Marseilles and Morocco and has survived several diverse lives since then.

Today, the company owns the 530-passenger *Mermoz*, which flies the Bahamian flag but features French officers (and a large 50+ percent European clientele). Her annual Music Festival At Sea, held each August or September in the Mediterranean, attracts world-renowned classical performers, dancers and lecturers and on positioning cruises, one can take a **French language course**.

In 1995, the *Mermoz* cruises around the globe sailing the **Mediterranean** and **Baltic** from May through October.

PEARL CRUISES

6301 N.W. 5th Way, Suite 4000, Fort Lauderdale, Florida 33309
☎ (800) 556-8850

Pearl Cruises, a division of Costa Crocieres S.p.A. following an alliance formed between Costa and Paquet in May 1993, was formerly owned by Paquet French Cruises. The 480-passenger *Pearl* was constructed in 1967 as the *Finlandia* and sailed as a car/passenger ferry vessel in the Baltic. She underwent a multi-million dollar renovation in 1984 to convert her to a cruise ship, and another in 1988 when she made her debut as the *Ocean Pearl.* Today she is the most familiar vessel in the Far East, her lengthy itineraries popular with those who seek an in-depth experience in the region.

Pearl Cruises combines itineraries with in-depth pre- and post-cruise land tours, and the *Pearl's* most popular programs are frequently three weeks in duration, although several 14-day cruises are planned this year. Based year-round in the Far East, her cruises provide more time in port, and some of the most enticing itineraries in the region. In 1995, for example, three 17-day cruises/tours are devoted entirely to Vietnam and *Pearl* is the only vessel focusing exclusively on this country. Other popular programs include "Burma & Siam," "Great Cities of Asia," "Spirits of New Guinea," "China Dynasty" and "Classical Japan." Pearl Cruises' cruise tours combine pre- and/or post-cruise land stays with cruise; itineraries vary from 14 to 23 days at rates starting at $2295. per person, double occupancy. Low-cost air add-ons are offered from the U.S. and advance purchase savings of up to $1200 are availble for those booking 90 days in advance.

PREMIER CRUISE LINES

400 Challenger Road, Cape Canaveral, FL 32920

☎ (407) 783-5061, (800) 327-7113 (outside Florida)

While Premier Cruise Lines is no longer the official cruise Line of Walt Disney World, the company is still popular with families seeking a lively short vacation at affordable price. The Dial Corporation-backed ship line is managed by two co-executives whose ambition to offer 3- and 4-day cruises to the Bahamas from Port Canaveral that would appeal not only to families but to anyone young at heart is sound and very successful. Today, Bugs Bunny, Daffy Duck, Sylvester and Speedy (Looney Tunes pals) greet families aboard these ships. Today, family travel is one of the most competitive areas of the cruise industry (with the American Family Cruises surviving only eight months), but Premier's new arrangement with Warner Brothers Worldwide Consumer Products ensures the kids will be properly entertained by costumed cartoon characters while parents have sophisticated fun. This is truly the best way for all generations to enjoy the same holiday, and family-size cabins accommodate as many as five people (providing that three are small ones).

Premier Cruise Lines made its debut in March 1984 with the 21,000-ton *Royale*, the former *Frederico C.*, which was sold to Dolphin Cruise Line and became the *SeaBreeze*. The company brought the well-known 40,000-ton *Oceanic* into service in late April 1986, followed by the former *Atlantic* and the former *Sun Princess*. These are now known as *Star-Ship Oceanic*, *Star-Ship Atlantic* and *Star-Ship Majestic*. Premiere has cancelled a long-term charter agreement and the *Majestic* departs in February, 1995; the company claims it is seeking a larger vessel. Premier's vessels are painted with Premier Cruise red on the hull, and the *Oceanic* has been nicely refurbished by the husband and wife team, Agni and Michael Katzourakis, who brightened interiors and added a number of kiddie and adult play areas casino, teen center, video game room, fitness center, etc. Cabins were not paid much attention, although Premier did add some double beds for the younger crowd. Also for the grown-up contingent is name entertainment, decent food, some excellent bars and good company among the passengers. After all, other people who bring their children along on vacations have to be okay! Premier inaugurated "edutainment" for children aboard its vessels that are hand-on programs focusing on the ocean; for example children and their parents learn about things like angelfish and the jet stream.

Premier offers the ease of a 3- or 4-day cruise to the **Bahamas** from Port Canaveral aboard the *Oceanic* and *Atlantic*, including the line's exclusive facilities in the **Port Lucaya** section of Freeport.

PRINCESS CRUISES

10100 Santa Monica Boulevard, Los Angeles, CA 90067
☎ (310) 553-1770, (800) 568-3262

The **Star Princess** *in Bermuda*

Princess Cruises was founded by Seattle industrialist and entrepreneur Stanley B. McDonald in 1965, when he pioneered cruising to Mexico's west coast aboard the 6000-ton ferry vessel named *Princess Patricia.* Two years later he brought the *Princess Carla* into year-round service that combined the Mexico cruises during the winter with Alaska sailings all summer. McDonald sold his company to Boise Cascade in 1968 but bought it back again (for a song) in 1970. Four years later McDonald sold the company once and for all to P & O, who promised to retain the Princess name.

At the time (and to this day), the prestigious Peninsular and Oriental Steam Navigation Company (P & O) prided itself on having invented leisure cruises when William Makepeace Thackeray took a series of P & O vessels around the Mediterranean in 1844 and wrote *From Cornhill to Grand Cairo* which enticed other writers (Kipling, Forster, Trollope) to follow in his wake. With the union of Princess Cruises and P & O in 1974, the popular *Island Princess* was purchased outright and so was sister ship *Pacific Princess.* P & O's new *Spirit of London* became *Sun Princess* so that by the end of 1975 Princess Cruises boasted a three-vessel fleet. In November 1984, Her Royal Highness the Princess of Wales christened the company's trendsetter in superships, the 45,000-ton *Royal Princess*, which carried her complement of 1200 passengers in all outside cabins, many with terraces. The Princess Cruises family expanded to five members in December 1986 with the addition of *Sea Princess* (former *Kungsholm*), formerly operated by P & O in Australia/Europe trade.

Not to rest on well-known laurels, Princess Cruises/P & O bought out the competition Sitmar Cruises in July 1988 and acquired three vessels in operation (*Fairwind, Fairsea, Fairsky*), as well as three under construction. The 925-passenger *Fairwind* was renamed the *Fair Princess.* The 1200-passenger *Fairsky* is now *Sky Princess.* The 1470-passenger *Star Princess* was christened by the lovely Audrey Hepburn in Port Everglades in March 1989, and the 1590-passenger *Crown Princess* received her blessing from actress Sophia Loren in New York harbor in September 1990. Her sister ship, *Regal Princess,* was inaugurated 1991 and christened by the former British Prime Minister, Margaret Thatcher.

Princess Cruises is one of the industry's most agressive and prosperous cruise lines and can boast a fleet of nine vessels carrying more than 430,000 passengers worldwide each year. During the summer season, Princess Cruises is quite a presence in Alaska, with some 102 departures on six different ships from May to September. The 7- and 10-day itineraries feature the Inside Passage and Gulf of Alaska from San Francisco, Vancouver and Seward.

Princess vessels can also be found in Europe, the South Pacific and Orient, through the Panama Canal, to the Mexican Riviera, the Caribbean, South America, Canada/New England, India, Africa, Hawaii, the South Pacific and Holy Land. Since launching its newest jewels, *Star Princess* (1989), *Crown Princess* (1990), and *Regal Princess* (1991), the company has become a major presence in the premium cruise market. They are among the most stunning vessels afloat, with a wide appeal for nearly everyone who appreciates quality at a great price, approximately $225 per person, per day with airfare. Princess will expand its capacity by some 70 percent over the next four years with the launching of the 1950-passenger *Sun Princess* in 1996, followed by a sister ship in 1997 and whopping 100,000-ton, 2500-passenger ship in 1997.

Princess is the cruise line that said yes to "Love Boat," the long-running television program that brought the idea of taking a cruise to millions. *Pacific Princess* is the original Love Boat, but the series sailed and filmed aboard *Royal, Island, Pacific, Sky* and *Sea Princess.* In syndication, the series has been translated into 29 different languages and viewed by millions in some 93 countries. Now that "Love Boat" is no longer in production, Princess has contracted the familiar face of Gavin MacLeod as its spokesperson just in case you miss the show.

Today, Princess Cruises attracts a growing number of passengers on Caribbean sailings in their 35+ age range due to special sports and recreational activities. The New Waves Scuba and Snorkeling Program, offered on *Regal Princess, Crown Princess* and *Star Princess* Caribbean sailings, features full scuba certification, with classes and lectures on ship and in port. In Focus features shore tours led by accomplished local photographers with specialized itineraries for serious photo-buffs.

Cruisercise is a personalized workout program with daily walk-a-mile and aerobics, stretch and tone plus aquacise classes.

While Princess is best known for its Alaska and Caribbean presence, several ships journey in far-flung locales. In 1995 Island Princess visits the South Pacific, Asia, the east coast of Africa and Indian Ocean while *Pacific Princess* voyages to South America and the South Pacific. *Golden Princess* visits Australia, New Zealand and Asia before commencing 10 Hawaii/Tahiti itineraries in Spring, 1995. *Crown Princess, Star Princess,* and *Regal Princess* sail on one-week Caribbean cruises through April while *Royal Princess* cruises between San Juan and Acapulco on 10- and 11-day trans-canal crossings. *Fair Princess* continues its weekly Mexico itinerary.

During the spring through fall, Princess continues its strong presence in Alaska, deploying *Regal, Crown, Star, Golden, Sky* and *Fair* to the region while the Baltic and Mediterranean are cruised by *Pacific Princess, Island Princess* and *Royal Princess.*

QUARK EXPEDITIONS

980 Post Road Darien, CT 06820
☎ (203) 656-0499 (800) 356-5600

Macho boys and girls take note: here's the opportunity to venture forth where no other cruise passengers have ever traveled. Launched in 1990, Quark Expeditions offers hearty cruises of the Arctic, Antarctic and Down Under aboard a fleet of reconstructed former Soviet icebreakers and scientific research vessels. Quark Expeditions' six ships have been converted for passenger use with the construction of a Finnish-built superstructure. The icebreakers are *Kapitan Dranitsyn, Kapitan Khlebnikov* and *Yamal*; Quark's ice-strengthened research vessels include *Alla Tarasova, Professor Khromov* and *Akademik Shokalski.* All but the latter two vessels cruise the Arctic in Summer and the Antarctic in Winter.

The icebreakers can plow through 16 feet of ice. For example, you can summer at latitude 90 degrees aboard the 100-passenger *Yamal*, breaking out a bottle of bubbly when you officially reach the North Pole (see if your friends can top that!). The *Yamal* was the second vessel ever to sail across the Arctic Ocean via the North Pole. You can cruise the Northeast Passage from Finland to Alaska with landings on glaciers via helicopter on the icebreaker 106-passenger *Kapitan Khlebnikov.* Why not winter at the South Pole while navigating the Ross Ice Shelf, a floating barrier of ice the size of France? Or, go for broke and circumnavigate this contintinent on a voyage from Hobart, New Zealand to Ushuaia, Chile, stopping in Dumont, the South Magnetic Pole.

Quark's South Pacific cruises aboard oceanographic research vessels *Akademik Skokalski* and *Professor Khromov* are equally exotic. From March through April, 1995, seven voyages will include port calls in Micronesia, Polynesia, Melanesia and Easter Island. In April, you can swim among the whale sharks with Ron and Valerie Taylor on dives off the coast of Western Australia.

Quark doesn't claim these vessels rival the creature-comforts found aboard a conventional cruise ship, but the ships have been converted to incorporate the basic necessities. For example, the *Kapitan Dranitsyn*, has 53 cabins (all with private facilities), lounges, an indoor heated swimming pool, gym with sauna, library, hospital and dining room. The ships are staffed by Russian officers and crew, European chefs and cabin attendants. Lecturers from the scientific community accompany all voyages and landings are made by Zodiacs and helicopters.

All this high adventure comes at a price: a 25-day Antartica expedition ranges from $10,000 to $15,200 per person, double occupancy, including all shore excursions.

REGENCY CRUISES

260 Madison Avenue, New York, NY 10016
☎ (212) 972-4774, (800) 388-5500

Regency Cruises was founded in November 1984 and completed its initial stock offering in June 1985 becoming the first cruise Line to go public without having a ship in operation. The new cruise company began service in November, 1985 with the 722-passenger *Regent Sea* (former *Gripsholm, Navarino*), sailing from from Montego Bay every Sunday.

Founded by the late, respected industry veteran William Schanz, one of the founders and former president of Paquet French Cruises, Regency has carved its niche as a great buy for bargain hunters seeking European on-board ambience, above average cuisine and out-of-the-ordinary itineraries. While its ships are far from elegant, many experienced cruisers flock to Regency's fleet of former transatlantic liners, which boast exceptionally spacious cabins.

With the acquisition of a third vessel in December 1988, the former *Royal Odyssey/Doric*, renamed *Regent Sun*, Regency began to diversify its Caribbean itineraries for its loyal passengers. Montego Bay is still home port for the *Regent Star* for the winter season, offering Regency's signature cruises of a partial transit of the **Panama Canal** on weekly sailings. In 1993, the company tripled its fleet, adding the *Regent Rainbow* on 3- and 4-day cruises from Tampa, the *Regent Spirit* and the *Regent Jewel* (re-named the *Regent Calypso* and scheduled for Far East cruises).

From January through Spring, 1995, the *Regent Spirit* offers one-week Land of the Maya cruises from Cozumel to **Belize**, **Guatemala**, **Honduras** and **Roatan Island** while the *Regent Sun* winters in San Juan offering one-week cruises to **St. Croix**, **St. Kitts**, **St. Lucia**, **Barbados** and **St. Maarten**, alternating with weekly voyages to **St. Barts**, **Antigua**, **Martinique**, **Grenada** and **St. Thomas**. The *Regent Star* sails from Montego Bay to Costa Rica, Cartagena and Aruba with a partial transit of the Panama Canal on weekly cruises. Regency adds full trans-canal crossings with 9- and 14-day cruises of the *Regent Sea* between Montego Bay and a choice of San Diego and Los Angeles. During the summer months, Regency sends three of its vessels to Alaska—*Regent Sea*, *Regent Rainbow* and *Regent Star*—on one-week sailings between Whittier (Anchorage) and Vancouver; the *Regent Sun* begins its fourth season of popular summer New England/Canada cruises between New York and Montreal

RENAISSANCE CRUISES

1800 Eller Drive, Suite 300, P. O. Box 350307, Fort Lauderdale, FL 33335-0307

☎ (305) 463-0982, (800) 525-5350

Renaissance Cruises' eight small, intimate ships are focused on delivering unique, destination-oriented itineraries. Launched in 1989, two years later the company was sold to a partnership established between the Cameli Group in Genoa, Italy and Luxury Liners, Ltd., controlled by Edward Rudner.

Renaissance Cruises features destination-oriented vacations to unspoiled, exotic locations often inaccessible to other vessels. Modular itineraries allow guests a choice of 7-, 14-, or 21-day vacations without revisiting ports or repeating so much as a single dinner menu.

These yacht-like ships sail to six areas of the globe: The **Mediterranean**; **Scandinavia**, **Western Europe** and **Russia**; **Asia** and **India**; the **Caribbean**; the **Seychelles Islands** and **East Africa**.

Renaissance I-VIII carry from 100-114 passengers, and feature a casually elegant, relaxed atmosphere onboard. Renaissance prides itself on personal service with a well-trained, attentive European crew and a high staff-to-guest ratio. All staterooms are outside suites ranging from 210 to 287 square feet, delightfully appointed with refined Italian craftsmanship. Many cabins have verandas and all come with separate seating area, TV/VCR, stereo and refrigerator bar. The bathrooms are unusually spacious, with marble vanities and teak floors; beds can be made into either queen or twin configuration and there is ample closet and storage space.

The small size of the vessels and the focus on Renaissance's unique destinations tends to foster a great sense of camaraderie among passengers, who tend to be in a wide spread of ages. The atmosphere is casual and the entertainment tends to revolve around social interaction of passengers. While most men wear jacket and tie to dinner, it isn't required, although women tend to get dressed in the evening. Cuisine has an international flavor and caters to Americans preferences for lighter, healthier preparation. Breakfast and lunch buffets are served on deck and in the open seating dining room in the evening. Facilities include an intimate piano bar, lounge with music for dancing, library with books and videos, a water-sports platform and equipment, small saltwater pool and freshwater Jacuzzi and full promenade deck for strolling. The Captain welcomes passengers aboard the bridge for a chat throughout the day and night.

While Renaissance Cruises is best-known for its wonderful itineraries, especially the **Seychelles/Africa** cruises, rates are very attractive for a small, all-suite vessel.

While nearly identical in size and offering lovely itineraries wherever they roam, there are inconsistencies from one ship to another. While Renaissance cruises in the Caribbean and Mediterranean are overall of high quality, we experienced hitches in the Seychelles this year, including the risky practice of off-loading 65 years-old-plus passengers into zodiacs to go ashore in heavy surf (Renaissance's Miami office had no idea this was being done). Moreover, the company has an outrageous tipping policy that one only discovers in printed matter distributed aboard ship (it's not mentioned in the brochure): recommended gratuities for waiters are $12-$15 per person per day, stewards $5-$8 per day. Renaissance also advises: "You may wish to show your appreciation to individual staff members (such as Galley Staff in the case of passengers who have availed themselves of our flexibility in food preparation, or Guest Services)" This is way beyond industry norms, and I hope no passenger believes he or she has to comply.

ROYAL CARIBBEAN CRUISE LINE

1050 Caribbean Way, Miami, FL 33132
☎ (305) 539-6000

In the highly competitive world of cruise companies based in Miami for sailings for the Caribbean, Royal Caribbean Cruise Line consistently earns top honors in quality of its ships, itineraries and on-board amenities. The ship line was founded in 1969 as a partnership of three respected Norwegian companies, long experienced in offering solid products worldwide and is now owned by Anders Wilhemson A/S of Oslo, Norway, the Pritzker family of Chicago and is a publicly traded company on the New York Stock Exchange. While Royal Caribbean's headquarters and fleet is registered in Norway its North American headquarters is Miami.

RCCL has not been idle in the 1980s and 1990s. In January, 1988, the French-built *Sovereign of the Seas*, largest cruise ship afloat at that time, made her cruise debut from Miami to great acclaim. The vessel proved so popular with loyal RCCL passengers that two larger mega-liners, the 2354-passenger sister ships *Monarch of the Seas* and *Majesty of the Seas*, entered service in 1991 and 1992 respectively. The ships boast some of the largest casinos at sea, name entertainers on each voyage and enough fitness and spa facilities to keep the whole NFL busy. And, it all works beautifully: passengers have no difficulty locating facilities and cabins, the design ensures there is never a crowded feeling and staff manages to keep the active 30s and 40s passengers quite happy. The Viking Crown Lounges, which completely encircle the vessels smoke stacks, are the highest ship lounges in the world.

In 1990, Royal Caribbean entered the 3- and 4-night cruise market from Miami to the Bahamas when the 1600-passenger *Nordic Empress*, the first vessel designed and built specifically for shorter cruise vacations, was launched. The design of the ship was the result of research ensuring that the layout of the vessel's public rooms and activity areas would accommodate the unique requirements of short voyages. Also in 1990, sister company Admiral Cruises' *Stardancer* was transferred to the RCCL fleet, upgraded and renamed *Viking Serenade* and the following year underwent a total reconstruction, which increased its passenger capacity to 1512 and added a new dining room, indoor-outdoor cafe and Viking Crown Lounge.

But Royal Caribbean was doing much more than building new ships and adding new itineraries; it was actually creating new destinations. The line built a private destination called **Labadee** on the secluded north coast of **Haiti** for the exclusive use of passengers; the facility is currently not in use due to political conditions. Royal Caribbean's very popular private island in the **Bahamas**, **CocoCay**, is used by the cruise line's passengers.

In 1993, further expansion continued when Royal Caribbean became a public company and began trading on the New York Stock Exchange, only the second major cruise line to go public. Apparently nine vessels aren't enough for this prosperous company. RCCL announced that three new vessels are under construction at Chantiers de l'Atlantique in St. Nazaire, France. Two 70,000-ton sisterships will carry 1800 passengers: *Legend of the Seas* enters service in April, 1995 and *Splendor of the Seas* in March, 1996. In addition, a 1950-passenger ship has been ordered for delivery in November 1996 with an option for a second 1950-passenger ship in late 1996.

The public rooms on all Royal Caribbean vessels are "themed" after hit Broadway musicals. The *Song of Norway* features The King and I, My Fair Lady and South Pacific lounges; the *Nordic Prince* boasts Camelot, Carousel and Showboat; HMS Pinafore, The Merry Widow,and Annie Get Your Gun can be found on the *Sun Viking*; and the three mega-ships inaugurate Can Can, Oklahoma and Guys and Dolls. Deck space is superb on all RCCL vessels and outdoor pools are among the best afloat. Dining room service is excellent and, once again, each night of the week is "themed" with different table settings and menus. Waiters seem to be hired as much for their ability to take orders as for their ability in singing and entertaining guests.

Royal Caribbean's attention to quality is evident in its highly rated food and service, entertainment that rotates weekly among the fleet, and cabin cleanliness. Passengers report that breakfast arrives promptly every morning when requested, ice and fruit are replenished daily, covers are turned down with soft lights turned on, and a chocolate is on every pillow before bedtime. And, in order to appeal to the lowered average age of clientele on all RCCL vessels, shipshape programs and family cruising are part of the experience.

Cabin size is my major gripe with RCCL, and how they expect two, let alone four, passengers to enjoy those boxes is beyond me. These are the ships on which I always say travel with someone friendly because you will lock knees when you sit down in the cabin! However, passengers don't seem to mind because RCCL keeps everyone too busy to think about the small space provided for their private lives. In addition, the ship line takes such good care of passengers and their travel agents from start to finish that only praises come forth.

Those who are avid fitness buffs will find more programs and equipment on *Nordic Empress, Sovereign of the Seas, Majesty of the Seas* and *Monarch of the Seas* than nearly any other vessel. RCCL's ShipShape program offers aquadynamics, basketball free-throws, aerobics, Gut-Buster exercises, morning walk-a-thons, advanced challenge workouts and triathalon. Seniors Sit to be Fit exercises are done while seated and Vitality Unlimited is for mature travelers and those out of shape. Cuisine low in fat, cholesterol and calories is available in all courses. Royal Caribbean's Kids, Tweens, Teens programs provide supervised activities in age groups, special children's menus and private discos for teenagers on some vessels. Golfers will find great packages and lovely itineraries for their game on *Monarch of the Seas* cruises and *Song of America* sailings between New York and Bermuda in the summer.

In 1995, RCCL adds 10-, 11- and 12-night cruises, moves larger ships on extended length voyages, adds a second ship in Europe and begins Hawaii and Far East cruises. During the summer season, the 1012-passenger *Nordic Prince* will replace the *Sun Viking* on 10- and 11-night Alaska cruises sailing round-trip from Vancouver. In the fall, the new Legend of the Seas replaces the *Song of Norway* on 10- and 11-night Panama Canal sailings between Acapulco and San Juan; *Sun Viking* will join *Song of Norway* for 12-night Europe cruises and *Legend of the Seas* sails in Alaska during summer followed by two 10-night cruises to the Hawaiian Islands in the fall, RCCL's first itineraries in the 50th state. From Miami, the *Nordic Empress* sails year-round on 3- and 4-day Bahamas cruises; *Sovereign of the Seas* offers weekly cruises to San Juan, St. Thomas and CocoCay and *Majesty of the Seas* cruises to Playa Del Carmen, Cozumel, Grand Cayman, Ocho Rios and CocoCay on 7-day voyages. From San Juan, *Monarch of the Seas* charts a weekly eastern Caribbean course to Martinique, Barbados, Antigua, St. Maarten and St. Thomas while *Song of America* sails on alternating 10- and 11-day cruises from San Juan to St. Thomas, St. Maarten, Martinique, Trinidad, Dominica, St. Kitts, St. Croix, CocoCay and Miami; the following week she departs from Miami and sails to CocoCay, St. Kitts, Dominica, Trinidad, Martinique, St. Martin, St. Thomas and San Juan. *Song of Norway* sails on 10- and 11-day trans-canal cruises between Acapulco and San Juan. Sun Viking, also on weekly cruises from San Juan, visits St. Croix, St. Barts Guadeloupe, St. Maarten, St. John and St. Thomas. From Los Angeles, *Viking Serenade* offers 3- and 4-night Mexican/Baja cruises and the *Nordic Prince* on 1-week Mexican Riviera cruises from Los Angeles. From spring through fall, *Song of America* offers weekly cruises from New York to Bermuda.

The company's biggest news in 1994 was the deployment of the *Sun Viking* to the Far East, where she will be based year-round. Commencing November, 1995, *Sun Viking* will operate five 13- and 14-day itineraries with port calls in China, Malaysia, Thailand, Vietnam, Hong Kong, Japan, Korea and Indonesia. Per person, double occupancy rates for a two-week cruise will begin at $3000 before discounts; low-cost air add-ons are $99 from the Pacific states, $199 from the central U.S. and $299 from the East Coast.

ROYAL CRUISE LINE

One Maritime Plaza, San Francisco, CA 94111
☎ (415) 956-7200, (800) 227-5628

Royal Cruise Line, founded in Greece by chairman Pericles S. Panagopoulos in 1971, was acquired in 1989 by Kloster Cruises Ltd. a company that owns Norwegian Cruise Line, and until the company was dissolved in August, 1994, the prestigious Royal Viking Line. Royal Cruise Line is the up-market division of Kloster as its vessels, itineraries and personnel are good quality and operate in the Mediterranean, Scandinavia, South America and Caribbean with great success.

For the first decade of its existence, Royal operated a single vessel—the 10,500-ton, 450-passenger *Golden Odyssey.* The vessel was built in Elsinore, Denmark, in 1974 under the direction of Tage Wandborg, one of the world's leading naval architects. After a lengthy search for more tonnage, Royal purchased the former *Doric* (Home Lines) in late 1981 and spent some $20 million transforming her into the *Royal Odyssey.* The vessel was very popular with Royal's loyal clientele, but the ship line sold her to Regency Cruises, where she has been sailing as the *Regent Sun* since December 1988. The sale was to pave the way for the $178-million *Crown Odyssey,* a 34,250-ton vessel accommodating 1000 passengers, which was built in Papenburg, Germany, and delivered to Royal Cruise Line in June 1988.

In December, 1991, the 750-passenger *Royal Odyssey* (formerly the *Royal Viking Sea*), joined the Royal Cruise Line fleet. Named after the ship RCL operated from 1982 through 1988, the *Royal Odyssey* debuted in Singapore and her current itineraries include the Mediterranean, Australia and New Zealand and the Orient. Royal Cruise Line retired the grand *Golden Odyssey* in May, 1994, and launched the 750-passenger *Star Odyssey* (former *Royal Viking Star,* which sailed as Norwegian Cruise Line's *Westward* for two years) following a $30 million refurbishment that reduced the passenger capacity by 75 and restores the single-seating dining configuration.

Royal Cruise Line begins 1995 with yet another new vessel—the all-suite 212-passenger *Queen Odyssey,* defunct Royal Viking Line's revered *Royal Viking Queen.* Royal's newest addition will sail with Royal Viking's superb staff and new itineraries in the Caribbean during the winter; she cruises the Mediterranean on 12- and 14-day itineraries. Rates remain in the $750+ per person, per diem range, but Royal offers discounts on 1995 cruises: those booking by March 31 may bring the second person free.

Royal is also continuing its successful host program of inviting distinguished gentlemen aboard cruises to act as unofficial hosts, serving as dinner, dancing and card partners. They also escort groups of single ladies ashore, to cocktail receptions and other shipboard activities. They are onboard strictly to mingle and not favor any one lady. Meanwhile, the ladies love the program! Royals' vessels have all-Greek crews and a solid reputation for helpful and attentive service. Royal Cruise Line is proud of its Dine To Your Heart's Content program, featuring meals prepared in accordance with the guidelines of the American Heart Association. A special on-board booklet describes everything you have ever wanted to know about keeping a healthy heart, along with a number of luncheon and dinner dishes recommended for their sensible nutrient content. Also popular onboard is the invigorating New Beginnings lecture series, regarding health of the body, mind and spirit.

In 1995, Royal Cruise Line's successful theme cruises continue, with big band and jazz cruises a big favorite. Shore excursion provide another example of Royal Cruise Line's attention to detail. These are under the very expert and personable care of John Tirrell, who travels the world to ensure that Royal Cruise Line passengers receive memorable times ashore in every port.

Royal enters the mid-1990s with three ships featuring single-seating dining (*Royal Odyssey*, *Star Odyssey* and *Queen Odyssey*), and itineraries that stand out from the pack. But the "soul" of Royal Cruise Line will always be its outgoing, charming Greek crew; they may lack the polish of the Northern European staff found aboard luxury vessels, but give Royal's cruises a "family" feeling.

SEABOURN CRUISE LINE

55 Francisco Street, San Francisco, CA 94133
☎ (415) 391-7444, (800) 929-959

Seabourn Cruise Line was founded in 1986 by Norwegian investors interested in the super luxury resort/cruise business. They brought the highly respected veteran of the top-quality cruise business, Warren Titus, out of retirement from Royal Viking Line to CEO the new company. Titus did an excellent job in launching *Seabourn Pride* (December 1988) and *Seabourn Spirit* (November 1989) and has now moved up to chairman of the company. The twin vessels, with all-suite accommodations and spacious public areas, have created a special place in the cruise industry and appeal to a discriminating clientele.

In 1992, Seabourn became another feather in Carnival Cruise Lines' hat when Carnival acquired 25 percent of the company, with an option to increase this to 50 percent.

The $50-million (each), 10,000-ton *Pride* and *Spirit* carry a maximum of 212 passengers in beautfully appointed staterooms/suites that feature five-foot seaview picture windows with automated shades (if you can find the button!) Deck space is crowded during days at sea but a generous Spa/Fitness Center overlooks the sea. So does the beauty salon. Walk-in closets with a private safe and a marble bathroom with tub and two sinks are also well-considered amenities for such an exclusive vessel. Seabourn's

vessels carry guest lecturers; when anchored, the ship's fold-out marina platform becomes a protected salt-water pool and passengers may go water skiing from the ship's motorboats. Air/sea per person, per diem is in the $1000 range; there is a no tipping permitted policy but drinks and shore excursions are not included in the rate.

Watersports "Seabourn" style—waterskiing from the fold-out marina

In 1995, *Seabourn Pride* winters in the Caribbean/Panama Canal then sails on 14- and 16-day itineraries between Ft. Lauderdale and the Amazon while *Seabourn Spirit* cruises in the Far East and South Pacific. From April through September, both ships proceed to Europe, for a series of 7- and 14-day Mediterranean, Black Sea and Baltic Sea/North Cape cruises.

SEVEN SEAS CRUISE LINE

333 Market Street, Suite 2600, San Francisco, CA 94105-2102
☎ (415) 905-6000, (800) 285-1835

While it may seem difficult to separate one exclusive yacht-like vessel from another, Seven Seas Cruise Line has done just that with well-heeled travelers who want the best of everything and a bargain to boot. Since starting operations in 1990 with the launching of the 172-passenger *Song of Flower*, the company has carved a niche for itself by creating distinctive itineraries in the **Far East** and **Mediterranean**, maintaining the highest levels of service and offering more of everything at a better price. But what sets this ship apart from other chic "boutique" vessels is the warm, unpretentious staff and crew, who immediately make everyone feel like family.

Song of Flower, formerly owned by the Scandinavian firm of Fenly and Eager and leased to the (now defunct) Exploration Cruise Lines of Seattle, Washington, was top of the line for the small ship company. Sold in 1989 to Tomoko Uenaka of Japan (whose fortune comes from the lucrative wedding industry), the vessel now sails for Seven Seas Cruise Line, a joint venture of Japan's K Line and the Meiyo Corporation of Japan. The marriage of Ms. Uenaka's own personal good taste with experienced cruise professionals who manage the operating company has made this vessel very popular indeed.

Moreover, Seven Seas is offering its faithful passengers a new experience in 1995 with the launching of the 170-passenger *Hanseatic*, a 9000-ton luxury vessel that cruises Antarctica. If you've always dreamed of celebrating New Year's Eve among the bergs in elegant style, this is your chance. Built in 1993 in Rauma Ship Yard in Finland, the 188-passenger (crew of 125) ship has an A1 ice rating (just below an ice breaker) and all the refined accoutrements of her sister ship—a no tipping policy, complimentary airfare, liquor and many shore excursions with a per person, per diem in the $450 range. In March, the *Hanseatic* proceeds to the east coast of Africa, calling in South Africa, Mauritius, Reunion and the Seychelles, followed by a voyage through the Indian Ocean and the Suez Canal to Athens.

In the meantime, *Song of Flower* winters in the **Far East**, visiting Vietnam, China, Borneo, Malaysia and a host of little-known ports, before heading east to **India** and a **Suez Canal** transit, then to **Europe**, where she cruises the **Mediterranean**, **Black Sea**, **Baltic** and **Scandinavia** from April through August. Per person, per diem rates begin around $450 (depending on departure date and cabin) including round trip airfare, tips, wine and spirits and shore excursions on Far East itineraries, an unbeatable price if this sort of cruise experience suits your fancy. In the Mediterranean, the cruise-only per person, per diem without shore excursions begins around $400.

AUTHOR'S AWARD

Those seeking a lovely cruise experience with a refined, unpretentious ambience will adore Song of Flower. *The best value in the Far East, South Pacific and Australia.*

SILVERSEA CRUISES

110 East Broward Boulevard, Ft. Lauderdale, FL 33301
☎ (305) 468-4770, (800) 722-6655

In 1994, Silversea Cruises launched two new 15,000-ton vessels to the crowded club of all-suite, yacht-like vessels. Silversea Cruises owners, the Lefebvre family of Rome and the Vlasov Group of Monaco, were part owners of Sitmar Cruises before its merger with Princess Cruises in 1988. *Silver Cloud* began service in May, 1994 and was followed by sister ship *Silver Wind* this December. They are designs of Petter Yran and Bjorn Storbraaten of Oslo, whose credits include the vessels of *Sea Goddess, Seabourn, Renaissance* and *Royal Viking Queen.* The 296-passenger vessels have 148 suites ranging from 240 to 1085 square feet, 75 percent of which have verandas; cabin features include walk-in closet, marble bath, TV/VCR and bars. Dining is single-seating and the ships are giving the small, luxurious yacht-like vessels a literal run for the money; included in the starting per person, per diem of around $480 are nearly everything: airfare, tips, insurance, liquor consumed on-board and select shore excursions. Add to that some of the dreamiest itineraries around, and the verandas lacking on the "boutique" ships costing twice the price and I predict these ships will make a big splash.

In 1995, *Silver Cloud* cruises to South America, including an **Amazon** and **Orinoco River** voyage, and the Caribbean. *Silver Wind* sails on 7- and 14-day voyages between **Mombasa**, **Kenya** and **Mahe**, **Seychelles**, with an Abercrombie & Kent African safari extension.

SPECIAL EXPEDITIONS

720 Fifth Avenue, New York, NY 10019
☎ (212) 765-7740, (800) 762-0003

Special Expeditions was founded in 1979 by Sven-Olaf Lindblad (son of Lars-Eric Lindblad) and has been dedicated to the spirit of discovery ever since. The company caters to small groups (10-100 passengers) of intellectually-curious individuals who share an interest in ornithology, marine biology, geology, culture and history. Special Expeditions operates the 80-passenger *Polaris* (formerly known as the *Lindblad Polaris*), a most comfortable vessel equipped with a fleet of Zodiacs, as well as a specially designed glass bottom boat outfitted for both day and night viewing, enabling passengers to explore the rich and colorful world under water. *Polaris* has both Swedish and American command and boasts a pleasant ambience, with lounge/bar, quiet library, good deck space, sea view restaurant, sauna and cabins in a variety of configurations. Lindblad refers to his company as one of the pioneers in the expedition cruising field; his passengers are well-heeled 60+ folks with a craving for travel experiences that enrich and stimulate the mind.

These voyages accounted for around 90 percent of Special Expeditions business until the late 1980s, when the company acquired two smaller vessels that were constructed near Seattle, in 1981. Formerly part of Exploration Cruise Line's fleet, the 70-passenger *Sea Bird* and *Sea Lion* were completely refurbished. These small ships can navigate small rivers, such as the **Columbia** and **Snake** rivers, closely explore **Alaska's Coastal Wilderness** and offer an exploration of the flora and fauna of and the **Sea of Cortez**. Operating the *Sea Bird* and *Sea Lion* allows Special Expeditions to position the *Explorer* in **Europe** during the summer and **Central** and **South America** in the winter.

In 1995, Special Expeditions offers a slew of exotic itineraries, including **Exploring Coastal Iberia**, **France** and **Britain**; the **Islands of Indonesia**; **Impressions of an Arctic Summer**; the **Amazon** and **Orinoco** rivers; the **North Cape** and the 9- and 12-day voyages that explore the eastern coast of **Central America** from the Panama Canal to Belize. During Baja and the Sea of Cortez sailings, passengers will discover up to 122 varieties of birds; fish (108), plants (68) and 14 varieties of marine mammals (including six species of whales). These are very special expeditions indeed, for those who enjoy the company of naturalists, historians, artists, photographers and writers, all of whom accompany voyages.

SUN LINE CRUISES

One Rockefeller Plaza, New York, NY 10020
☎ (212) 397-6400, (800) 872-6400

Sun Line Cruises is owned by Keusseoglou family interests. The company was founded in 1958 by the late Ch. A. Keusseoglou, who remained chief executive until his passing in May 1984. A former executive with Home Lines, Keusseoglou launched the *Stella Maris I* as Sun Line's first vessel for Aegean cruises from the port of Piraeus. In 1963 the *Stella Maris II* replaced her namesake, and the *Stella Oceanis* became a Sun Line ship in 1967. Flagship and pride of the fleet, the *Stella Solaris*, made her maiden voyage in 1973. Isabella Keusseoglou supervised the interior design of all three Sun Line vessels and still takes an active part in the day-to-day housekeeping from the family home in Monaco and a New York City pied a terre. President of the company is M. P. Pilli Keusseoglou, who lives in Athens; vice-president is younger brother, Alex Aleco, who manages the marketing aspect from New York City. Mrs. K. is rightfully proud of her two sons.

Sun Line has always been considered one of the premier cruise lines in the Mediterranean/Aegean. From spring through fall, Sun Line offers 3-, 4-, 7-, 14-, and 21-day sailings from **Piraeus**, **Venice** and **Nice** aboard *Stella Maris, Stella Oceanis* and *Stella Solaris.* From May to October, the *Stella Oceanis* sails from Piraeus on 3- and 4-day **Greek Island/Turkey** cruises. The baby *Stella Maris* makes one-week Greek Island/Turkey cruises in April-May and September-October from Piraeus, then transfers to **Nice/Venice** for weekly departures in June, July and August of her Around Italy program. The *Stella Solaris* sails every Monday, alternating between **Greek Islands/Turkey** and **Greek Islands/Egypt/Israel/Turkey**. The two cruises can be combined for a lovely 14-day experience that encompasses the best of this region.

The 18,000-ton *Stella Solaris* was built in 1973 and carries just 620 passengers, an intimate vessel by current standards. She has none of the razzmatazz of modern cruise ships, but her 330 Greek crew members epitomize warm and personal service. Many of them have been with the company for years and love to see returning passengers. The same is true of the smaller vessels, the 5500 ton *Stella Oceanis*, which carries only 300 passengers and the yachtlike *Stella Maris* with her 175 passenger complement. Indeed, it is quite usual and very flattering for staff members on any of these vessels to make an effort to remember not only your face but your name as many as five years hence! But, that is the Sun Line trademark and it is very special.

The 4000-ton *Stella Maris II* is the baby of the fleet and everyone's favorite. Carrying not more than 180 passengers and a crew of 100, the vessel sails from Piraeus on 3- and 4-day **Greek Island/Turkey** cruises beside the *Oceanis* during the spring and fall months. During the summer, she offers one of the best itineraries in the Mediterranean on weekly sailings between **Nice** and **Venice**. This popular cruise is sold out early, so hurry! While this ship needs an overhaul, service is superb and there is a wonderful feeling of "getting to know you" among the passengers and crew.

During the winter season, only the *Stella Solaris* repositions to the Western Hemisphere to offer its popular **South American** cruises between Ft. Lauderdale and Manaus, Brazil, with on-board authorities on the flora and fauna of the Amazon. From March through April, she cruises in the **Caribbean** on a partial transit of the Panama Canal and Mayan Adventure sailings from Galveston to **Grand Cayman** and **Cozumel** before returning to Europe for the Mediterranean season.

SWAN HELLENIC CRUISES

c/o Esplanade Tours, 581 Boylston Street, Boston, MA 02116
☎ (617) 266-7465, (800) 426-5492

The prestigious London Travel firm of W.F. and R.K. Swan has been operating Mediterranean cruises since 1954 on a regular schedule and Nile cruises since 1960, in addition to the quality tours arranged to more than forty different countries since the 1930s. In 1980, R.K. Swan inaugurated **Around Britain** cruises. For the first time in 25 years, he repeated an itinerary. This was an earth-shattering event, for Swan prided himself on never duplicating cruise itineraries. Although Swan sold the company to P&O in 1983, he still remains an active consultant and nothing has changed with the company or its program. Expect the same high quality as ever.

Swan Hellenic Cruises is more than just cruises. The ship is transportation coupled with mini-courses in the archaeology, history and culture of the area visited; the cruises attract travelers who wish to learn as much as possible from their experiences. Lecturers on board each cruise, drawn from the corridors of Cambridge, Oxford and other notable universities (even from Princeton and Yale) entertain and enlighten passengers on what they are about to see and do. Although this may sound a little too cerebral, it's really not, because R.K. Swan has remembered that his clients are on holiday, after all. You can just as well sit in a deck chair with a beer, or you can listen to the lectures in the privacy of your cabin. But the high-caliber lectures are well worth the effort to attend.

R.K., as he is known to his colleagues, believes in delivering as much value for the money as possible to his passengers. Included in the cruise fare are all port taxes, shore excursions, site fees, gratuities and literature. And the literature is superb! Each cruise has its own special handbooks with maps, a quick reference of selected dates and historical events, a short description of each place visited, and a glossary of technical terms. All cruises are aboard Epirotiki's 240-passenger *Orpheus* because she does so well with passengers. The ship is comfortable and simple, but during eight months of the year, is full of spirit and intellectual pursuits as she cruises around the Hellenistic World of the **Aegean**, **Mediterranean**, **Black**, **Red** and **Adriatic** seas. The all-Greek crew is carefully picked because there is a no-tipping policy aboard. All gratuities are included in the reasonable cruise fare. In fact, just about everything is included in the cruise rate except personal bar and laundry expenses. Life on-board is relaxed and friendly and passengers need not worry about a thing except having a wonderful experience, making many new friends and learning a great deal about the ancient and modern world.

Jacky Keith is U.S. general sales representative for Swan Hellenic Cruises, and she is extremely knowledgeable about the programs and can arrange tender, loving care for all passengers traveling to London from North America to embark the *Orpheus.* The brochure is enticing and a list of guest lecturers is announced for every sailing. The map of the Mediterranean ports of call is mind boggling. Many of the Hellenic cruises have a special interest such as botany, ornithology or marine biology with experts in those particular fields traveling with passengers. To attract younger passengers, the company offers 50 percent discounts on certain sailings when they travel with an older relative or friend paying full fare. This is a wonderful marketing ploy and should result in many future Swan Hellenic fans. In 1995, Swan Hellenic schedules a port calls in Beirut and Libya but Americans still aren't allowed to disembark in these countries.

Swan Hellenic also has **Nile** and **Rhine** river cruises, as well as **Natural History** and **Art Treasures** tours of the world. These are programs for the young in mind at any age!

WORLD EXPLORER CRUISES

555 Montgomery Street, Suite 1400, San Francisco, CA 94111
☎ (415) 393-1565, (800) 854-3835

World Explorer Cruises is a name now synonymous with **Alaska** as its one and only vessel, the *Universe*, has been offering in-depth sailings along the coastline of our 49th state for considerably more than a decade. Alaska has been called one of the top destinations of the 1990s, and this is an Alaskan cruise for passengers who value their money and their time. More is explored and accomplished on these two-week voyages than aboard any of the more luxurious, glitzy vessels. The ship line offers a total of nine ports of call on every cruise, as well as excellent lecturers and guides, 44 different optional shore excursions (the expensive flight-seeing tours seem to be the most popular), and vacation extensions in **Vancouver** or **Seattle** either before or after your cruise.

World Explorer Cruises operates the 550 passenger *Universe*, a modest vessel with Chinese officers and crew but American cruise staff and lecturers. Twice a year, in September and January, the *Universe* does perform as a seawise university on **around-the-world** voyages. These sailings can accommodate 500 students, who receive credit for the semester at sea, and return home very enthusiastic for the world they have experienced! World Explorer Cruises also offers extension credits to Alaska passengers in conjunction with California's Chapman College. Courses are taught on-board, and there is no pre-registration requirement. There is, in addition, a 12,000-volume library on-board for browsing or writing a serious paper!

From May through August, the *Universe* can be found in Alaskan waters, departing from Vancouver every two weeks. The vessel is quite unique in the world of cruising, and rave reviews occur after every sailing from a wide range of passengers. So, leave your fancy clothes behind and discover Alaska!

RIVERBOATS AND HOTEL BARGES

Residents of Antarctica greet the arrival of the Explorer.

"Russia is celebrated for its internal navigation. Canals and rivers enable St. Petersburg to receive produce from China...it requires three years to accomplish it."

Universal Traveler, 1848

AUTHOR'S OBSERVATION

Companies that specialize in excursions by riverboats and hotel barges are described below. Cruise companies also offering journeys on the inland waterways of the United States and South America include Alaska Sightseeing/Cruise West; American Canadian Caribbean Line, Special Expeditions and Clipper Cruise Line, profiled in The Cruise Lines.

ABERCROMBIE & KENT INTERNATIONAL, INC.

1520 Kensington Road, Suite 212, Oak Brook, IL 60521
☎ (708) 954-2944 or (800) 323-50521

Abercrombie & Kent has been a premiere tour operator for three decades. First love and area of expertise is the Africa of safaris, but A & K has extended its tours to feature such inland waterways as the Nile River, barge trips in France, England, and Holland/Belgium, and China's Yangtze River. Other cruises offered are along the Turkish coastline, and in the Galapagos Islands. Additional cruises aboard the *Explorer* are offered in Antarctica, the South Pacific and Easter Island; A&K also offers cruises on a variety of vessels along the Turkish coast, the Galapagos and China's Yangtze River. The company is owned by Geoffrey and Jorie Butler Kent, two intrepid travelers whose picture cannot be missed in every brochure. Geoffrey confesses that he added the Abercrombie only to ensure an early listing (the As) in any travel agent compendium!

A & K offers extensive barge cruises on the delightful rivers and canals of **France**, **England**, and **Holland/ Belgium**. It is simply the best way to travel, according to Gerard Morgan-Grenville, author of several books on the subject and owner of two very special charter barges, *Virginia Anne* and *Fleur de Lys*, both marketed by A & K.

The 7-passenger *Fleur de Lys*, considered the flagship of the A & K fleet, is the most elegant and spacious vessel on any inland waterway. Her accommodations boast a suite with king-size bed and bathroom with full tub and twin sinks. There is a baby grand piano in the antique-filled main salon and a heated swimming pool on the aft deck. (As yet, no other charter barge features such impressive amenities although *The Princess*, industrialist Ludwig's 10-passenger charter vessel, is not far behind.) Three-, 6, or 9-day charters are available throughout the season in Alsace, between **Nancy** and **Strasbourg** in northeastern France. Prices are stiff but include gourmet meals, wines and bar drinks, all excursions and the loving care of the crew. Passengers are transported to and from *Fleur de Lys* from train, plane or hotel in the area. I sampled the Fleur de Lys, an experience extraordinaire.

The six-passenger *Virginia Anne* is a charter barge with a different character, a period vessel originally built of iron in 1911. One of the pioneers of this popular way to travel, she is the subject of *Barging into France* by her owner/author Gerard Morgan-Grenville. *Virginia Anne* spends the season

(April through October) in the Nivernais region of Burgundy on 3-, 6-, and nine-night cruises between **Auxerre** and **Dirol**.

Also well known as a charter vessel is the 48-passenger *Mark Twain*, which cruises on three routes in Bordeaux and Midi. The *Mark Twain* has four twin cabins, plus a spacious wood-paneled salon and sundeck with traditional ambience from a Dutch 19th-century origin. The Bordeaux cruises are between **Moissac** and **Castets**. In the Midi, *Mark Twain* covers the area between **Toulouse** and **Carcassonne** or **Carcassonne** to **Agde**. The fourth charter barge in the A & K fleet is *Alouette*, converted in 1986 to a canal boat for 6 passengers. *Alouette* offers cruises from April to November throughout **Burgundy** and the **Loire valley**.

Hotel barges generally carry more passengers (in smaller cabins) and are individually booked. They include the 22-passenger *L'Abercrombie* on three-to nine-night cruises in **lower Burgundy**, the 20-passenger *Litote* (Understatement) on six-night cruises in **central Burgundy**, and the 22-passenger *Lafayette* in **Sancerre** and the **Upper Loire Valley** for three or six nights. Hotel barges are less pricey and great fun. Antoinette DeLand took *Litote* about ten years ago and had very fond memories. Travelers are met in Paris, usually at the Hotel Lutetia-Concorde on the Left Bank, for transportation to the barge. During the cruise, ballooning may be available for an extra charge of about $200 per person. Drifting slowly over the vineyards of France is a sensation worth the money!

The 12-passenger *Actief* is A & K's offering on English waterways. Converted from a Dutch clipper in 1977, the *Actief* cruises the River Thames between **Windsor** and **Shillingford Bridge** (a few miles from Oxford). The three- or six- night cruises along the so-called Queen's Waterway feature the playing fields of Eton, the spires of Oxford University and some charming little villages. The *Actief* is a comfortable vessel with a total English atmosphere. In the low countries, the 17-passenger *Rembrandt* offers a choice of cruises round-trip from **Amsterdam** or **Amsterdam/Bruges**. The Dutch owned-and-managed *Rembrandt* has six twin staterooms, the Van Gogh and Rembrandt suites and one single cabin. The Holland cruises visit **Kaag**, **The Hague**, the famous cheese town of **Alkmaar** and **Marken**. (When we were aboard a few years ago, a rijstaeffel farewell dinner was a nice complement to the hearty Dutch food served daily!) The Amsterdam to Bruges itinerary features **Haarlem**, **Delft**, the other famous cheese town of **Gouda**, **Hansweert**, **Ghent** and **Bruges**.

In addition to **Galapagos Island** cruises aboard the 34-passenger *Isabella II* (which other tour operators also utilize), A & K offers travelers 4- or 7-day sailings along the **Turkish coastline** in the Gulf of Fethiye aboard the 30-passenger M.Y. *Halas*. A former Bosphorus Sea ferry recently converted to a private yacht, *Halas* boasts three French double, eight standard twin, two large twin and two sumptuous suites (Lycian and Bridal), as well as a crew of 26 to cater Turkish/Continental cuisine, local wines, two well-stocked bars and all water sports equipment. The *Halas* also boasts such modern amenities as cellular telephones and fax machines!

In 1995, Abercrombie & Kent expands its vistas in **China** with the new Regal China Cruises's European-style riverboats. Regal's three 289-passenger sister ships, the *Princess Sheena*, *Princess Jeannie* and *Princess Elaine*, were built in Germany in 1992 and have modern facilities such as an exercise room, sauna, restaurants, lounges, dry cleaning and beauty salon. They are offered as four-day cruises with A&K's 18-day China tours.

The 96-passenger *Explorer*, Abercrombie & Kent's excursion vessel, was conceived and built by Lars-Eric Lindblad in 1969 and was part of the Society Expeditions fleet. Following a complete refurbishment in 1992, she now journeys to some of the most remote regions of the globe. In 1995, her itineraries include **Melanesia**, **Polynesia** and the Wake of the Bounty voyage from **Tahiti** to **Easter Island**, with stops in the Austral, Marotiri and Gambler islands plus Pitcairn, Henderson and Ducie islands and a season in **Antarctica**.

CRUISE COMPANY OF GREENWICH

31 Brookside Drive, Greenwich, CT 06830

☎ (203) 622-0203, (800) 825-0826

Cruise Company of Greenwich has been offering hotel barging holidays since 1976 through veteran John Liley, whose book *France-The Quiet Way* is definitive on the subject. The 14-passenger, 6-crew *Luciole* was completed under Liley's direction and cruises the waterways of western Burgundy the canals de Bourgogne and Nivernais between **Dijon**, **Auxerre** and **Nevers**. Passengers visit the famous vineyards and historic sites of the region on daily excursions. Included in the price of the trip is the personally escorted service between Paris and Montbard via high speed TGV train.

Cruise Company also represents Shannon Barge Line's *Bona Spes* with cruising, golfing and fishing holidays on the **River Shannon**, the longest inland waterway in the British Isles. The cozy 10-passenger barge meanders through a 160-mile region steeped in history with dozens of castles, monasteries and monuments on shore. For fishermen, the river, lakes and tributaries offer a huge variety of pike and coarse fish habitats. For golfers, Bona Spes is a floating hotel that cruises from golf course to golf course and there are seven golf clubs, such as Hodsons Bay Harbour, less than 15 minutes from the river.

In England, the twin barges *Barkis* and *Peggotty* cruise through **Cambridgeshire** countryside on weekly excursions from April to October. On the upper reaches of the **River Great Ouse**, passengers may explore country gardens, village greens, quaint inns and churches dating back a millenia. Excursions on *Barkis* and *Peggotty* may also be combined with walking tours of stately homes and gardens. *Le Sans Egal* cruises six nights on the Thames between **Windsor** and **Oxford** via Cookham, Henley on Thames, Sonning, Goring, Streatley and Shillingford. Day trips are delightful pub lunches, visits to **Blenheim Palace**, an art gallery and historic mill.

CUNARD EUROPAMERICA RIVER CRUISES

555 Fifth Avenue, New York, New York 10017-2453
☎ (212) 880-7500, (800) 221-4770

In 1993, Cunard Line extended its fleet by adding three of Europe's best known riverboats, *Danube Princess, Prussian Princess* and the *Princesse de Provence*, which meander the **Danube**, **Elbe** and **Rhone** rivers on seven- and 11-day cruises from March through November.

Owned and operated by Peter Deilmann-Reederei, they boast the services and amenities of a seagoing vessel and are one of the most delightful ways to view scenery, castles, vineyards and small villages while relaxing on deck or a comfy chair in the main lounge. Passengers sailing trans-Atlantic aboard *QE 2* receive 45 percent discounts off river boat rates.

The *Danube Princess* cruises nearly 2000 miles through eight countries from the black forest to the Black Sea along the Danube River. Seven-day sailings round-trip from Passau, **Germany** include visits to Vienna, Durnstein, Melk and Grein, **Austria**; Bratislava, **Slovakia**; Budapest and Esztergom, **Hungary**. An 11-day Black Sea itinerary sails between Passau and Constanta, **Romania** cruising through the Iron Gates Passage, a gorge cradled among four countries, Romania and Russe, Bulgaria; Belgrade and Bezdan, Yugoslavia; Budapest, Hungary; Vienna, Melk and Grein, Austria.

Since the reunification of East and West Germany, cruises along the Elbe River are once again popular. The *Prussian Princess* makes 7-day cruises between Hamburg and Dresden, with stops in Meissen, Wittenberg and Worlitz.

The *Princesse de Provence* sails round-trip from **Lyon** up the **Saone River** and then down the **Rhone River**, past the vineyards of Burgundy and stopping in Tournus, Chalon Sur Saone, Avignon, Arles, Trevoux, Tournon, Vienne and Macon.

DELTA QUEEN STEAMBOAT COMPANY

30 Robin Street Wharf, New Orleans, LA 70130
☎ (800) 543-1949

The Delta Queen steamboats are as much fun to think and write about as they are to sail upon. As two of the only paddle wheel overnight boats left in America, they are charged with the glorious mission of keeping alive a more than 150-year tradition as they cruise more than 35,000 miles each along the Mississippi, Arkansas and Ohio rivers, at the speed of some eight miles per hour. These two paddle wheelers visit a dozen states each year, as well as hundreds of large and small river towns.

The company celebrated its centennial year in 1990 to much fanfare, as it is the oldest surviving cruise line in America and has operated some 29 steamboats on the Mississippi River and its tributaries. The company began in 1890 when a young river pilot, Gordon C. Greene, bought his first steamboat and ran it with his wife, who also had her master's license. Their son, Tom (born aboard an ice-bound steamboat), would later bring the *Delta Queen* to the Mississippi River from California.

The *Delta Queen*, last of the old-time steamboats, was constructed in 1926 with no expense spared in the teakwood handrails, stained glass windows set with copper instead of lead, brass fittings and posts, and paneling of either oak or mahogany. These irreplaceable features cost $850,000 at the time. During World War II the U.S. Navy commissioned the *Delta Queen* to ferry wounded and healthy troops across San Francisco Bay. In 1946, she was sold to the president of Greene Line Steamers (the former name of the Delta Queen Steamboat Company) who had the paddle wheeler towed home to New Orleans. (It was a long journey down the Pacific Coast, through the Panama Canal and across the Gulf of Mexico, even if in a crate!) From there, the *Delta Queen* traveled to Pittsburgh for a thorough remodeling and refitting. She began her new life on the Mississippi River in June 1948.

For the next two decades this steamboat cruised slowly up and down the main arteries of the Midwest, offering her passengers the treat of experiencing American river life. Then the controversy began. A new Safety at Sea law required all vessels carrying more than 50 passengers overnight to be constructed entirely of steel. Facing threats that the venerable old lady might be forced to retire, her loyal subjects rallied and not only obtained six subsequent exemptions from the law, but also enjoined the Department of the Interior to list the *Delta Queen* in the National Register of Historic Places. The current exemption was extended by President Reagan in August 1986. And watch for much fanfare in 1995 when a third paddle wheel steamer is launched! The brand new *American Queen*, Delta Queen's 30th riverboat, is meld of modern technology and victoriana. While the boat's plans call for a swimming pool, elevators and many other "newfangled" amenities, a steam engine will propel the *American Queen's* 60-ton paddlewheel; since steam technology has long been obsolete, the company searched for and found an antique steam engine that originally drove a steam dredge. At 420 feet long, six decks high and accommodating 420 overnight passengers, she is the largest overnight passenger vessel built in a U.S. shipyard since the S.S. *United States* in 1953.

The *Delta Queen* follows an itinerary of 3- to 12-night cruises that stop along the Mississippi and Ohio rivers from February through December. The final sailings of the season are round-trip from **New Orleans** with an old-fashioned holiday atmosphere. A popular annual summer event for the sister Queens is the Great Steamboat Race during the 11-night Mississippi Explorer itinerary from New Orleans to St. Louis (in June). Steamboat racing was a colorful pastime on American rivers during the last century, and the Delta Queen Steamboat Company was able to revive the tradition a few years ago. The two Queens vie for the coveted Golden Antlers Award, which passes between them quite fairly from year to year. The annual Races are a colorful occasion, as both boats perform 11-day cruises from New Orleans to St. Louis via **Natchez**, **Vicksburg**, **Memphis** and **Cairo**. It's wonderful fun with races between the steamboats and contests between the complement of passengers. Streamers, shouting, clapping, New Orleans jazz and nonstop libations add to the excitement.

While some aficionados prefer spring and others wouldn't miss the fall foliage, any time of the year on the river is special, for life is relaxing and the livin' is easy aboard these boats. I suggest comfortable sportswear for both men and women, and good walking shoes are helpful for visiting plantations, small towns and such along the way. Jackets and ties, although not required for dinner, are in good taste for the formal evenings on board. There are two seatings for each meal, and shore tours are arranged at most stops. The cruise director will advise you of all activities in the daily *Steamboat Times*, so nothing will pass you by. Service on board both Queens is special. The average age of the crew is about thirty years old and all are totally dedicated to their work on the river. During the summer you may find occasional students who have joined the staff hoping to get a flavor of life on the Mississippi, but all are perfectly professional and should be treated with the same courtesies (that means tips) as the crew aboard a large cruise ship.

The enthusiastic entertainment on board both steamboats is strictly river-oriented (that's what you came for), sweeping you up with singalongs, Dixieland jazz bands, barbershop quartets, and concerts of river songs. How long has it been since you've heard "Bill Bailey," "My Old Kentucky Home," "Camptown Races," and everyone's favorite tune "Ole Man River?" As the entertainment fires up spontaneously at times, you may find yourself the recipient of a tableside serenade at dinner, which by the way, is strictly American fare. Expect the menu to offer such items as southern fried catfish from Arkansas (an old Mark Twain favorite, they say), creole dishes, peanut butter soup and cornbread in all disguises. And whether you ve ordered them or not, you ll probably find grits with your scrambled eggs at breakfast. Wines tend to be domestic and the Bloody Marys are famous for being hot and spicy.

Life on board the *Mississippi Queen* is slightly more formal because of her size, her greater luxury and her well air-conditioned public rooms (which means more dressing up). Personally, I prefer the *Mississippi Queen*, because she has a small whirlpool and exercise gym, as well as 14 spacious veranda suites up on Promenade Deck. The newest stern-wheeler, launched in 1976 (at a final cost of $27 million) and old world in concept is a thoroughly splendid and modern machine. In appearance, the two boats are similar, although the *Mississippi Queen* is much larger by approximately 100 feet and almost 3000 tons. But both have the same layer-cake look and both seem to cruise along the rivers leading with their tongue, or stage that sticks straight ahead. The *Mississippi Queen*, however, has benefited from the most advanced technology, for her huge 35-by-25-foot paddle wheel is turned by a four- cylinder horizontal tandem compound condensing steam engine. Her automatic boilers (which use oil like everything else) and her steam turbine generators can provide enough electricity to power a small city. Inside, her moldings, mirrors, polished steel, brass and chandeliers all evoke the past in 19th- century detail, but nothing is made of wood. Even her calliope, considered to be the world's largest and lustiest, is computerized so that both professionals and passengers can play onto a digital tape, push a button, and hear it all come back. And if you happen to be sitting on the top deck near the whirlpool, you really hear it!

Both cruises offer **Bodacious Steamboatin'** with ongoing programs Music of the Rivers, River Heritage, and Crafts, Food and Folklore. Theme vacations are also an annual event—The Great Steamboat Race, Big Bands, Mardi Gras, Mark Twain Celebrations, Fall Foliage Vacations, Cajun Christmas/Shopping Spree, Taste of the Mississippi and American Anthology Vacations. There are also annual Feature Cruises—Memorial Day/Civil War, Antiques, Mystery Cruises, Victorian Lifestyle, even Women in Politics.

Chattanooga, Tennessee was added as a new port city a few years ago and and in 1994, the company began service on the Arkansas River. *Delta Queen* offers a series of port city packages for passengers before or after the cruise. The 2- or 3-night packages are available in New Orleans, Memphis, St. Louis and Minneapolis/St. Paul on the Mississippi River sailings; Cincinnati and Pittsburgh on the Ohio River; and Nashville on the Cumberland River. What a wonderful way to see the heartland of America!

EUROCRUISES

303 West 13th Street New York, N.Y. 10014
☎ (212) 691-2099, (800) 688-EURO

EuroCruises is a cruise tour operator specializing in **Scandinavia**, **Russia** and the **Baltic Sea**, representing more than 70 ships, most indigenous to Europe and little known here, including Kristina Cruises, Viking Line, Baltic Express Line, Estline, Polferries and the Northwest River Shipping Company. Capitalizing on the new interest in the former Soviet Union and the opening of the Baltic States to American tourists, the company has created some of the most provocative itineraries in this regions.

EuroCruises' most popular offerings are 4-, 5- and 7-day "visa-free" cruises betweeen Stockholm or Kiel, Germany and St. Petersburg aboard the modern riverboats *Konstantin Simonov*, *Anna Karenina* and *Ilich*. Available from February through early December, they are priced from under $75 per person, per day, including all meals, plus entertainment and a English-speaking staff, one of Europe's best bargains.

EuroCruises Baltic States itineraries feature ten Baltic ports. The 220-passenger Finnish owned and operated *Kristina Regina* makes a 12-day cruise from Copenhagen to Helinski, stopping at Lubeck and Rostock in **Germany**; Gdansk in **Poland**; Kaliningrad and St. Petersburg in **Russia**; Klaipeda in **Lithuania**; Riga in Latvia and Tallinn in Estonia. Cruises depart in June and August, with rates beginning around $2750.

Arctic exploration on the 8-day Realm of the Polar Bears cruise to Norway's northernmost archipelago, **Spitsbergen**, aboard the 25-passenger *Polarstar* will guarantee you round-the-clock sunshine, glaciers, polar bears, Arctic foxes, seals and birds. Special departures are designated for English-speaking passengers, although staff and guides are English-speaking on all voyages. For a shorter peek, a three- and four-day Spitsbergen Cruise is enough time to voyage along the coastline of The Seven Icebergs to the launch point for Arctic expeditions and visit a Russian mining town aboard the 36-passenger *Rembrandt Van Rijn*.

EuroCruises also offers excursions on the Sweden's Gota Canal aboard three vintage steamers, the *Diana*, *Wilhelm Tham* and *Juno*. These historic steamers are a novel and affordable way to visit fortress ruins, medieval cloisters, royal palaces, picturesque hamlets and lush Swedish forests while tasting local delicacies like fresh salmon, sherried herring, caviar-stuffed eggs and reindeer meat! Accommodations are quite modest aboard these historic vessels, but the four- to six-day cruises are hidden treasures for those seeking a taste of Sweden few Americans ever discover on their own.

From St. Petersburg to Siberia, the waterways of Russia are plied by EuroCruises' modern riverboats. The 280-passenger *Sergei Kirov* sails between St. Petersburg and Moscow and one can cruise the Yenisey River from Dudinka (240 miles north of the Arctic Circle) to Krasnoyarsk in the South through Siberia aboard the *Anton Tchekhov*. River cruises between Kiev and Odessa are offered aboard the *Taras Shevchenko* and *General Lavrinenkov*. The 160-passenger *Delta Star* cruises the Danube round-trip from Vienna to ports in Hungary, Slovakia, Austria and Germany on 8-day itineraries.

The company recently launched river cruises on Portugal's River Douro with seven-night cruises of the *Lady Ivy May*, a lovely way to visit the port wine region and the Spanish Sierras.

AUTHOR'S AWARD

EuroCruises' itineraries are among the most creative in Europe—from Scandinavia to the Arctic Circle, St. Petersburg to Siberia, the Baltic to the Black Sea, these affordable cruises comfortably transport you to regions few ever discover.

FRENCH COUNTRY WATERWAYS, LTD.

P.O. Box 2195, Duxbury, MA 02331
☎ (617) 934-2454, (800) 222-1236

French Country Waterways, Ltd. has blossomed through the marketing and management of the *Nenuphar*, *Horizon II*, and *Liberté* (former Horizon Cruises vessels), as well as the *Esprit*, which is owned and operated by FCW owners Jim and Pat Tyng. The lovely *Esprit* was completed in 1986 under the supervision of Charlie Pope, a veteran hotel barge captain formerly with Horizon and Continental Waterways, who commands the 18-passenger vessel. *Esprit* cruises from April to October between **Nancy/Strasbourg**, **Strasbourg/Montreux-Chateau**, **Montreaux-Chateau/Dole** and **Vandenesse/Auxonne**. Under such fine tutelage, passengers aboard *Esprit* can enjoy a very special experience and plenty of information on the cruising areas.

Horizon II is the flagship of Horizon Cruises, a company owned by Chicago attorney Rex Carr. The three-barge fleet is now in the good hands of the Tyngs who will market and manage the vessels with loving care. *Horizon II* accommodates a dozen passengers and a crew of six on Canal de Bourgogne cruises through the popular Cote d'Or (golden coast) Burgundy wine region between **Pouilly-en-Auxois** and **Dijon**. *Horizon II* is decorated with oriental carpets and antiques and features one suite, one double, and four twin cabins, all air conditioned.

The *Nenuphar* (water lily) also accommodates 12 guests and a crew of six in air-conditioned comfort with all luxurious suites furnished in French antiques. *Nenuphar* cruises the northern section of Canal de Bourgogne between **Montbard** and **Tonnerre**, with escorted visits to the 18th-century Forges de Buffon, the 12th-century Abbaye de Fontenay, and the 16th-century d' Ancy- le-Franc, as well as the vineyards of Chablis.

The 10-passenger *Liberté* explores the romantic Canal du Nivernais between *Auxerre* and *Villiers*. This area produces France's famous chablis wines and ballooning over the vineyards is an option (approximately $225 per person) on *Liberté* and other French Country Waterways cruises. The three Horizon Cruises vessels all depart on Sundays (the *Esprit* on Saturdays) from April through October. Passengers are escorted to and from Paris to their luxury hotel barge.

K.D. RIVER CRUISES OF EUROPE

Rhine Cruise Agency, 170 Hamilton Avenue, White Plains, NY 10601
☎ (914) 948-3600, (800) 346-6525
or
323 Geary Street (West of Mississippi), San Francisco, CA 94102
☎ (415) 392-8817, (800) 858-8587

KD German Rhine Line is well on to its 167th anniversary in operating high quality passenger services on the river that flows through the very heart of Europe. The Rhine has often determined the course of European history. It flows from the romantic Alps of Switzerland and France to the rugged North Sea, 820 miles of important trade routes, historic towns and cities, and cultural monuments that give a fine taste of the civilizations that developed here for several centuries. The river touches upon the banks of four European countries, **Switzerland**, **France**, **Germany** and **Holland**, and the variety of scenery you pass through and impressions you receive will seem endless. It's exhilarating to cruise along this stalwart waterway trying to absorb almost 2000 years of art and history.

This is the rich and romantic Rhine, where the famed Lorelei reclined some 433 feet above, combing her locks and singing a siren song that lured fishermen to the rocky shores. Here Caesar's legions bridged the floodwaters and General Eisenhower battled the army of Hitler. Industrial areas spew saffron smoke into the air, a stark contrast to the castles dating from the 12th century when you could almost see the dragons who inhabited the cliffs. Wooded hills, vineyards and the spire of a distant church all tease the senses.

Arriving in Cologne aboard a KD River Cruise boat

KD River Cruises of Europe operates some 24 different passenger vessels, including 12 comfortable river boats: the *Deutschland*, *Britannia*, *France*, *Austria*, *Italia*, *Helvetia*, *Europa* on the **Rhine**, **Moselle** and **Main**; the *Clara Schumann* and *Theodore Fontane* on the **Elbe**; French Cruise Lines' *Normandie* on the **Seine** and *Arlene* on the **Rhone** and **Saone**. The ships average about 330 feet long and 40 feet wide, and sail about 10 miles per hour upstream, 16 miles per hour downstream. Vessels carry 100 to 200 passengers in clean and simple all-outside cabins, which have a sofa-bed and folding bed, a large window and private facilities. The public areas feature a spacious observation lounge with double-length windows for uninterrupted views of the river and a cozy bar, reading room, dining room and shopping arcade.

All the ships have large sun decks and five have a heated outdoor swimming pool. The cuisine on board favors Continental specialties, with plentiful wines at moderate price; on some vesssels, simple dining offers buffet breakfasts and 3-course luncheons and dinners. This, instead of served breakfasts and 5-course meals the rest of the day, results in lower prices (by about 30 percent) as compared to ships with more elegant service.

RHINE-MAIN-DANUBE CANAL

KD River Cruises of Europe also offers weekly cruises on the **Danube** and new **Rhine-Main-Danube Canal**, which was completed in 1992 and now connects Europe's river systems from the North Sea to the Black Sea. Cruises are aboard the 110-passenger *Ursula III* (which KD will rename) on a 106-mile journey from Bamberg on the Main to Kelheim on the Danube, rising and falling 800 feet through 16 locks that lift it over the Franconian Alps. Launched in 1991, KD's Elbe voyages between eastern **Germany** and **Czechoslovakia** are four to eight days in duration and cover the most popular portions of the river: Hamburg to Dresden, Dresden to Wittenberg (Martin Luther's city), Wittenberg to Prague and Prague to

Hamburg. All Elbe cruises call at **Wittenberg, Dresden, Meissen** and **Torgau** and are aboard two new 124-passenger vessels, *Clara Schumann* and *Theodor Fontana*, built specially for Elbe cruises.

Along its traditional route on the Rhine from **Switzerland** through **France** and **Germany** to **Holland** and return, KD offers deluxe and moderately-priced programs. The high-end voyages include a 5-day cruises from Basel to Amsterdam; Amsterdam to Strasbourg; Cologne to Basel and three-day Strasbourg to Cologne excursion. Three- and four-day **Magic Triangle Cruises** combine the Rhine with the Main, Frankfurt's river, or the Main and the Moselle, the winding tributary of the Rhine. The line also operates a variety of cruises with a geography theme or season as a special focus: a seven-day Five Country Cruise, an eight-day Floating Wine Seminar and seven-day **Christmas and New Year's cruise**. Thirteen cruises scheduled from early July through mid-September will feature The Rhine in Flames celebration, which illuminates the river and surroundings with fireworks.

KD River Cruises of Europe also represents the two boats of French Cruise Lines: the *Normandie*, on seven-night River Seine cruises between **Paris** and **Honfleur**, and the *Arlene*'s one-week voyages on the Saone and the Rhone in **Burgundy** and **Provence**, between Avignon and St.-Jean-de-Losne, near Dijon. The ships, built in 1986 (*Arlene*) and 1989 (*Normandie*), each accommodate 100 passengers in twin-bedded, outside cabins with color TV, hair dryer and tiled bathroom with shower.

The *Normandie* docks right at the Eiffel Tower, and during an overnight at the beginning or end of the trip, a gala dinner party is staged aboard as the ship cruises amid Paris' spectacular illuminations. Ports of call between Paris and Honfleur, gateway to the D-Day beaches of Normandy, include **Vernon**, opposite Giverny, **Monet's house** and gardens; **Rouen**, where Joan of Arc was burned at the stake; and **Les Andelys**, set beneath Chateau Gaillard, the most famous castle on the Seine. Among the stops on *Arlene*'s cruises on the Saone and the Rhone between St.-Jean-de-Losne and the palaces of Avignon are **Arles**, with its Roman ruins; **Lyon**, home of French gastronomy and the medieval town of **Vivieres**.

I cruised aboard the *Deutschland*, a luxurious 184-passenger riverboat, from Basel to Amsterdam this summer. Sitting deckside on a comfy lounge chair or floating in the pool, medieval castles and vineyards floated serenely by along the banks of the Rhine. Stops along the way include Cologne, Strasbourg, Heidelberg and Koningswinter, where KD transports you by motorcoach to the best sightseeing areas. The *Deutschland* and sistership *Brittania* are part of KD's Connisseur Collection of cruises. Both boats have small but comfortable twin-bedded cabins with television, private bath and shower, outstanding cuisine served in open seating restaurants, a bar, observation lounge with sofas and comfortable chairs, reading room, boutique and heated outdoor pools.

AUTHOR'S AWARD

KD River Cruises of Europe's Connoisseur Collection offers five star plus service and cuisine along the most scenic regions of the Rhine and Danube.

HILTON INTERNATIONAL

P.O. Box 257, Cairo, Egypt
☎ (800) 445-8667

The Nile Hilton in Cairo operates two of the most popular boats that cruise the Nile River—the 270-foot, 90-passenger twin vessels, the *Isis* and *Osiris*, and the new 100-passenger *Nephtis*, which sail between **Luxor** and **Aswan** on four-night/five-day excursions year-round. These vessels are alike, simple but very comfortable, and are considered as floating hotels of Hilton International standards. A number of top-quality tour operators who specialize in Egypt use the twins. The vessels were overhauled recently and are very popular for short Nile cruises.

The *Isis* and *Osiris* have four passenger decks and are fully air conditioned. The cabins, small and simple, can sleep from one to three persons in all outside accommodations with private facilities. On the top, or Bridge Deck, are a good swimming pool, open sitting area with awning, and enclosed lounge. The first deck has a pleasant dining room with bar, a lounge and a small boutique. The front office and beauty salon are located on the main deck, along with passenger cabins, and the lower deck is all accommodations. Although Egypt bills itself as a year-round destination, the best time for cruising along the Nile falls between September and the end of May, when the days are sunny and warm and the nights cool. From December through February the weather is also pleasant, although the evenings can be chilly. June through August should be avoided if you cannot take heat and bone-dry air (the vessels are well air conditioned, but the monuments are not). At all times of the year, though, the sightseeing excursions occur only during early morning and late afternoon hours, because the Egyptians fully agree that only mad dogs and Englishmen are crazy enough to sit in the midday sun.

The ships alternate sailing every five days from **Luxor** to **Aswan** and vice versa. The Luxor/Aswan itinerary includes the great temples of Luxor, Karnak and Abydos. You will visit the Temple of Hatour, Thebes Necropolis, Valley of the Kings and Tomb of Tutankhamen. The Temple of Queen Hatshepsut at Deir al Bahri, the romantic Valley of the Nobles, the Valley of the Queens, the Temple of Medinet Habu and the famed Colossi of Memnon will awe you. Then, an early morning departure for Esna takes you to the Temple of Esna and on to the Temple of Horus (237 B.C.), the most complete example of the remaining Egyptian temples. During your last day you will see the Ptolemic Temple of Kom Ombo, with its beautiful murals, fascinating reliefs and fine view of the river. A morning sailing to

Aswan includes a visit to the Botanical Island and Mausoleum of Agha Khan by feluccas (small native sailing craft).

LE BOAT, INC.

215 Union Street Hackensack, NJ 07601

☎ (800) 992-0291 or (201) 342-1838

Le Boat represents several fine European hotel barge companies but its main focus since 1979 is chartering boats of all sizes for private use. Among Le Boat's most unique offerings are small family-size river boats and barges that ply the canals of England and France, presenting an inexpensive way for everyone to join in the fun of navigating, tying up, pushing off or just keeping everything shipshape while cruising at a leisurely four miles per hour along scenic countryside. Some 30 percent of those chartering the boats have never been near one before, and full instructions are given prior to departure.

In England, Black Prince Holidays's narrow boats (similar to barges), range from 38 to 70 feet, with a passenger capacity from two to eight. All have cabins with bed linens, communal bathrooms with shower, kitchen with utensils and a dining/lounge area. They cruise narrow canals throughout England, through easily-navigable locks and it's one of the loveliest ways to visit small towns, as well as the more popular sightseeing areas, such as **Stratford-upon-Avon** and **Cambridge**.

In France, Crown Blue Line's fleet of 400 self-drive house boats accommodate two to ten cruisers in double and twin cabins. All have full bathrooms complete with showers and hair dryers and modern galleys equipped with refrigerators, gas stoves and cooking utensils—everything but food and wine, which is purchased in local markets enroute. Departing from a choice of 16 bases, passengers will cover some 90 miles in a week of leisurely cruising along the most scenic canals of **Champagne, Alsace Lorraine**, **Loire Valley, La Touraine**, **Burgundy** and **Bourgogne**. Before departure you are given a full course in operating the boats and navigating canals, plus details on sightseeing, restaurants and local markets. A nominal fee is charged for bikes; one-week boat charter rates range from $970 to $3575, depending on the size and cruising period, with diesel fuel approximately $200 extra. The popular 8-passenger Classique category, for example, is priced at $2850 per week in May, June and September.

Le Boat caters to those who wish to charter a sleek yacht or sailboat for a cruise in the Mediterranean or to feel at home among the vessels moored in Monte Carlo. I'll take the10-passenger, 192-foot sailboat *The Other Woman*, with a grand piano in the main lounge, outdoor pool, original works of art by Picasso, Matisse and Chagall, master bedroom with his-and-her marble baths and crew of 11. Of course most vessels are quite a bit more modest, and Le Boat has bareboat charter vessels in the Caribbean, New England, South Pacific, Kenya and South East Asia as well.

AUTHOR'S AWARD

Le Boat represents one of Europe's best kept secrets: Crown Blue Line's self drive houseboats, the most scenic way to see the real France at bargain prices. A great find for families and groups of friends.

PREMIERE SELECTIONS

Tourpak International Inc., A Kemwel Company
106 Calvert Street, Harrison, N.Y. 10528
☎ (800) 234-4000

Premiere Selections, a fairly new addition to the Tourpak/Kemwel travel conglomerate, is headed by Jennifer Ogilvy, one of the most knowledgeable people around about deluxe hotel barges. During her years with the now-defunct Floating Through Europe, I learned to love this gloriously serene cruise experience.

Premiere selections caters to those who know better and like it. Not everyone is suited to the spirit and intimacy of barge travel but those who are certainly enjoy cheerful cabins (albeit tiny) and memorable meals. They are also pleased with the well-planned excursions in the barge's own mini-bus, which miraculously appears at every mooring. Premiere's barge fleet is all individually owned and operated, frequently by the captain and his family, and there is no stinting on cuisine, comfortable accommodations, good private facilities and charming public areas. Most barges are 100-128 feet long and carry six to 12 passengers, have English-speaking crew, sundecks with tables and chairs, and cabins with full-size or larger bed and private facilities. Chefs are professionally trained, many at La Varenne or Cordon Blue; fresh produce is purchased almost daily from local markets, and you can count on plenty of interesting cheeses, patés, breads and salads, not to mention the local bottled grape that is carefully chosen to complement the menus.

Cruising from mid-March to mid-November on six-night schedules, Premiere's barges ply the charming rivers and canals of **Burgundy**, **Alsace Lorraine**, **Bordeaux** and **Canal du Midi**, Languedoc in France; the **East Anglia** and **Thames** in England and regions of **Holland**.

In the Champagne region of France, on the lovely *Meanderer* which cruises the River Marne, enjoy tasting in the famous houses **Moet et Chandon**, **Laurent Perrier** and **Ruinart**, and visit the Abbey of Hautvillers where **Dom Perignon** discovered the secret of the Bubbly, the tranquil American Cemetery, a grand chateau and the great Gothic cathedral. In Burgundy, the new 8-passenger *Who Knows*, once a movie star's Parisian home, cruises in the **Cote d'Or** from Pont d' Ouche to Chagny, stopping at stately chateaus, **Dijon**, a 12th-century Benedictine abbey and lovely vineyards, where one can go hot-air ballooning; other barges cruising this beautiful region include *Lady A*, *La Reine Pedauque* and *Niagara*.

In the south of France, the 12-passenger *Athos* cruises between **Carcassonne** and **Port Beziers**. Passengers are met in Montpelier and escorted to their hotel barges moored on the Canal du Midi just above Carcassonne. Historic and beautiful places en route are **Minerve**, **Narbonne** and **Adge**. In Bordeaux, the Valley of the Garonne is explored on the six-passenger Berendina cruising from **Agen**, famous for its paintings by **Goya** and the impressionists to **Nerac**, **Meilhan** and **Chateau de Roquetaillade**.

In Alsace Lorraine, the 8-passenger *Stella* cruises between **Strasbourg** and **Nancy** along the Canal de la Marne au Rhin. Stops along the way include Waltenheim, Saverne, Lutzelbourg, Niderville and Einville. There are lovely drives through this beautiful scenery, as well as wine tastings of the refreshing white of the Alsace region. There are plenty of tow paths for walking, cycling or jogging, and there is plenty to see, satisfying everyone's taste.

The *Stella* also cruises through **Holland** and **Belgium** in tulip time and guests may view the exquisite blossoms of Keukenhof Gardens, as well as the glorious canvases of **Van Gogh**, **Rembrandt** and **Rubens** in the magnificent museums en route.

For those who wish to extend their stay in the lap of luxury, Premiere Selections will arrange custom-designed chateaux and inn stays and chauffeur- driven or self-drive car tours to complement the cruises.

REGAL CRUISES OF CHINA

(See Abercrombie & Kent)

SHERATON NILE CRUISES

Sheraton Hotels P.O. Box 125, Orman, Giza
Egypt, or any Sheraton reservations center

Sheraton Hotels in Egypt operates four identical hotel barges year-round on the Nile River between Luxor and Aswan. These 89-cabin vessels built in Scandinavia, named the *Tut*, *Aton*, *Anni*, and *Htop*, have a total of about 25 sailings each month of either four or seven nights. The 235-foot barges carry 178 passengers in two-berth cabins (some have an additional berth for a third person). All accommodations have private facilities, air conditioning and lots of wardrobe space. In addition, each barge has a large restaurant and lounge/bar that converts to a disco in the evening. Live entertainment, a swimming pool and a sun deck that is popular at cocktail time provide pleasant distractions. Two meal seatings offer lunch at noon or 1:15 p.m. and dinner at 7 p.m. or 8:15 p.m. All meals, plus afternoon tea, shore excursions, and entertainment are included in the cruise fare.

The four-night cruises visit the temples at **Luxor** and **Karnak**, the Valley of the Kings, Esna, Edfu, Kom Ombo and **Aswan**. The seven-night itinerary features **Luxor** and **Karnak**, Thebes, Nag Hammadi, Abydos, Dendera, Esna, Edfu, Kom Ombo and Aswan/Elephantine/Kitchener/**Aga Khan Mausoleum**, as well as the High Dam/Old Dam, granite quarries and Philae Temple. The order of sites reverses when the barges sail from **Aswan** to **Luxor**. These are spacious vessels perfect for travelers who enjoy having a little leg room.

VICTORIA CRUISES

57-08 39th Avenue Woodside, New York 11377
☎ (800) 348-8084 or (212) 818-1680

Victoria Cruises was launched in 1994 to operate and manage six new European-style boats on China's Yangtze River. A joint venture between a large Chinese transportation company and an American firm, the river boats were built exclusively for cruising the world's third largest river by Chongqing Changjiang Shipping Company. Sister ships *Victoria I, II, III* and *IV* entered service in 1994 to be followed by *Victoria V* and *VI* in 1994.

The 154-passenger *Victoria* boats have shallow drafts (8.5 feet) and double-bottom hull constructions. All 77 outside cabins and suites have two lower berths, close-circuit television and private bath. Western-style amenities on four decks include single-seating dining room, three bars, library, panoramic observation deck, several cafes, a nightclub, outdoor jacuzzi, beauty salon, fitness center and business center. Shipboard programs range from feature films shown in cabins and lectures on local history and culture to taiji classes, painting and calligraphy, live entertainment and local performances of traditional Chinese arts. Cuisine ranges from Chinese to Western and fresh-baked French bread and croissants. The ships carry a crew of 112, including English- and Chinese-speaking cruise directors and tour guides.

Cruises along the Yangtze River (meandering almost 3500 miles from the Tibetan highlands to Shanghai) include the five-day voyage between Chongqing and Wuhan and the ten-day itinerary between Chongquing and Shanghai. Both cruise the famous Three Gorges and allow passengers to experience local life along the river, including visits to farms, markets, fisheries and villages.

SAILING SHIPS AND YACHTS

Cruising the Caribbean aboard Le Ponant

CLUB MED CRUISES

40 West 57th Street, New York, N.Y., 10019
☎ (212) 977-2100, (800) CLUB-MED

Club Mediterranée, the famous French resort company, joined forces with three French banks to construct two 386-passenger, $100 million sail cruisers with five masts and 2990 yards of sail. The vessels, which entered service in 1990 and 1992, are sister ships ordered from Societe Nouvelle des Ateliers et Chantiers du Havre, the same shipyard that was responsible for three 150-passenger Windstar cruisers.

Club Med 1 and *2* have been designed with eight decks, are 617 feet long, 66 feet at beam, and have a draft of 16 feet. The 193 cabins are outside and 188 square feet, with television, radio, minibar, telephone and private bath. Passengers are 65% European (including 35% French) and 35% American, with English-speaking crew.

Club Med 1 and *2* have two restaurants one buffet style, and complimentary wine is served with lunch and open-seated dinner (dress is recommended as semi-formal in the evening). There are five bars, two swimming pools and a sports platform on the stern. Officers and crew are French and 63 Club Med GOs (gentle organizers) are aboard to ensure everyone has fun. A spa program on Club Med 1 includes sybaritic seaweed baths, massages of all kinds and jet showers.

In 1995, *Club Med 1* winters in Martinique on 7-day varying itineraries to the French West Indies, British and U.S. Virgin Islands and Grenadines, before a May-October series of 3-, 4- and 7-day Mediterranean cruises. From January through March, 1995, *Club Med 2* cruises the South Pacific to islands in New Caledonia with port calls in Vanuatu; the remainder of the year, 3-, 4- and 7-night itineraries from Tahiti to Bora Bora, Huahine and Moorea are planned. Cruise-only rates are around $1925 for one-week Caribbean sailings (with air/sea packages available), depending on departure date; there is no tipping.

THE MOORINGS

19345 U.S. Hwy 19 North, 4th Floor
Clearwater, FL 34624
☎ (813) 535-1446, (800) 535-7289

With a fleet of nearly 700 bareboat (sail them yourself) and crewed (captain & chef) yachts in the Caribbean, Mediterranean and South Pacific, The Moorings is recognized as the largest yacht chartering and management company in the world. Bareboats are offered in 30 locations worldwide; crewed yachts are available in the British Virgin Islands, St. Martin, Guadeloupe, Martinique, St. Lucia, Grenada and Tahiti. The Moorings also owns three small Caribbean hotels marketed as Club Mariner water sports resorts, at which one can combine a hotel stay with a yachting holiday.

The combination hotel/yacht package, for example, includes four nights hotel stay with breakfast, dinner and complimentary water sports and three nights on a shared 50-foot yacht; aboard the yacht, accommodations are in a double cabin with private lavatory, and all meals, bar beverages and watersports are included. During low season (March–December), the per person, double occupancy seven-night package price begins at $825; peak season (December–April) rates begin at $1149.

But chartering one's own private crewed yacht is obviously chic. A cruise from Tahiti aboard a 50-foot yacht sleeping six is priced from $8330 for the week, including captain, chef, most meals, bar beverages and snorkel gear. In the Greek Isles, full-week charter aboard a 50-foot yacht with crew can be found for $4690, while the Caribbean has a range of prices. Sailors with deep pockets can pick up a lovely 82-foot sloop in Martinique that sleeps six plus crew for $17,815. Those who want to do their own thing and are experienced can select a bareboat charter of a 35-foot sloop sleeping four priced from $1792 per week (includes linens, fuel, snorkel gear, motor dinghy and airport transfers).

NAUTICAL RESOURCES, INC.

666 Fifth Avenue, New York, N.Y. 10103
☎ (800) 398-6244

Nautical Resources, a corporate and private yacht charter firm, now offers cruises for individual passengers on three of its most elegant sailing ships, the *Colombaio Star*, *Colombaio Sun* and *Colombaio Sky*. These identical 38-meter sailboats have six double staterooms and 12 passengers are pampered by a crew of seven including chef and two stewardesses. Cabins are identical and have twin/double bed configuration, telephone, stereo, marble bathrooms with shower. *Colombaio Star* operates on a fixed itinerary during the winter in Baja, California and two of the three ships will summer along the Italian Riveria and Eastern Mediterranean.

A three-week cruise sailing round-trip from Acapulco transits the Panama Canal, visiting secluded ports such as Tobago Cays, Los Roques, Colon and Balboa. The per person, per diem rate is $357. In the Mediterranean, per person, per diem prices will be $550.

SACKS YACHT CHARTERS

1600 Southeast 17th Street, Suite 418
Ft. Lauderdale, FL 33316
☎ (305) 764-7742

Sacks Yacht Charters is a Fort Lauderdale-based charter firm that has been arranging yacht charter vacations for some ten years. One look at this company's brochure—resplendent with elegant, formally attired couples in the most opulent surroundings—and you know this is the high end of charters. Some 60 fully-crewed sail and motor boats, ranging from 53- to 166-feet in length, are available in all corners of the globe, although most are based in the Caribbean and Mediterranean. But they'll also set you up nicely in the Marquesas, the Cook Islands and Thailand, among other distant locales. Wedding charters are popular in Florida, and Sacks has an in-house events coordinator who will arrange every detail—you just show up with dress and bride/groom. A four- to six-hour event charter is priced from $1500 to $5000 plus food, beverages, service and all the extras.

STAR CLIPPERS

4101 Salzedo Avenue, Coral Gables, Florida 33146
☎ (800) 442-0551

Star Clipper's owner and president, Mikael Krafft, was raised next door to a ship yard on the Stockholm archipelago and his childhood romance with tales of the early clipper ships led to the creation of two unique sailing vessels. Trained in maritime law, he founded White Star Group of Belgium, parent company of Star Clippers, and commissioned the design and construction of his two bona fide sister-ship clippers, *Star Flyer* and *Star Clipper*, launched in 1991 and 1992 respectively. The tallest (226 feet to the tip of each mainmast) and swiftest clipper ships ever built, the Star Clippers ships are among a handful of authentic clippers constructed since the 19th century, and carry 180 passengers on one of the loveliest seagoing vacations around. The four masts, with 36,000 square feet of sails, carry the ships through Caribbean and Mediterranean waters, although motors are available for nagivating in port. Life aboard these vessels is relaxed and informal, with one-seating dinner in the mahogany and teak Clipper Dining Room, cocktails on deck or the Piano Bar. Caribbean itineraries are ideal for water sports (there is no charge for snorkeling or "banana boat" rides; scuba dives and lessons are reasonably priced) and both ships carry instructors. During voyages, passengers board Zodiacs to view the ships under full sail.

Star Flyer cruises from St. Maarten to Anguilla, St. Thomas/St. Croix, Tortola, Norman Island, Virgin Gorda and St. Barts; alternating with cruises to Saba, St. Kitts, Antigua, Iles Des Saintes, Nevis and St. Barts. *Star Clipper* cruises from Barbados to Saba, St. Kitts, Antigua, Iles Des Saintes, Nevis and St. Barts, alternating with sailings to Iles Des Saintes, Martinique, St. Vincent, St. Lucia and Dominica.

Star Flyer summers in the Mediterranean and home ports in Cannes on alternating one week itineraries cruising to Corsica, where three stops are made at Star Clipper Island (near Sardinia), Elba and St. Tropez; the alternating voyages from Cannes include Corsica, Sardinia, Giglio, Portovenore and Monaco. One-week rates begin around $1296 in the Caribbean and $1345 in the Mediterranean. Singles get an excellent break. Star Clippers has a guaranteed single occupancy rate of beginning at $1605 in a cabin to be assigned upon arrival.

TALL SHIP ADVENTURES

1010 South Jolliet Street, Suite 200, Aurora, Colorado 80012
☎ (303) 341-0335, (800) 662-0090

While today's sailing vessels are reminiscent of the great era of tall ships, the *Sir Francis Drake* is the real thing. Built in 1917, this three-masted schooner is among the less than 100 remaining tall ships (those built originally to transport under sail only) remaining in the world. Originally the S.V. *Landkirchen*, she transported copper around Cape Horn and later plied the Baltic as a trading ship. In 1988, she found her way into the loving hands of entrepreneur Eckart Straub and his partner, Captain Bryan Petley, a New Zealander who has been sailing since the age of 13. They lovingly restored her, and renamed the ship *Sir Francis Drake* after the famous admiral. The 165-foot, 28-passenger ship has 14 cabins, all with private toilet and shower; a library and salon, where meals are served. While not as refined as the Star Clippers and Windstar fleet, passengers sailing aboard the *Sir Francis Drake* are in for a real historical maritime experience.

The *Sir Francis Drake* sails year-round to the British Virgin Islands from her home port of St. Thomas on 3 , 4 and 7-day cruises. Per person, double occupancy rates begin at $995 for a one-week cruise; $450 for 3-day or $585 for 4-day sailing.

WINDSTAR CRUISES

300 Elliott Avenue West, Seattle, Washington 98119
☎ (206) 281-3535, (800) 258-SAIL

It seems like yesterday, but it was December, 1984, when an invited group of friends and press gathered at the New York Yacht Club to hear plans of this new and unusual company to operate a series of 150-passenger sail-cruise vessels, originally designed by Kai Levander of Finland's famed Wartsila Shipyard near Helsinki. The four-masted, computerized sailing vessels would be constructed in France at the Societe Nouvelle Des Ateliers et Chantier du Havre for 1-week sailings in the Caribbean, Mediterranean and French Polynesia.

Cruising the South Pacific at full sail aboard the **Wind Spirit**

The principal figure and chairman of this young cruise line is a creative and dynamic 42-year-old Finn named Karl Andren, descendant of a proud Aland Islands seafaring family, who arrived in America as a young boy and was soon smitten with the hurly-burly vibrance of New York harbor. It did not take Karl long to combine an MBA with his love of the sea. He bought Circle Line and developed the sail-cruise concept. Along the way, he acquired a notable partner, Norwegian ship owner and fellow entrepreneur Jacob Stolt-Nielsen, and well-known cruise industry figure Jean Claude Potier as company president. Potier has been associated with French Line, Sun Line and Paquet French Cruises.

Other Scandinavian shipping friends joined the group to offer advice and help develop the concept. Parisian designer Marc Held worked with Louise Andren on the interiors; Tom Heinan is credited with designing the spectacular clover-shaped bathroom, and his wife assisted in selecting the contents of each library. The result of everyone's endeavors, Windstar Cruises ships are objects of breathtaking beauty inside and out, complete with state-of-the-art technology and creature comforts to complement the unstructured ambience of sailing. To sit on deck watching the white sheets unfurl and feeling the vessel respond to wind conditions is akin to understanding the drama and sense of adventure that compelled such writers as Herman Melville and Joseph Conrad to share their seagoing experiences.

The first vessel, *Wind Star*, was christened by Louise Andren in the fall of 1985 at the French shipyard and made her sailing debut in the Caribbean, December 1986. The second vessel, *Wind Song*, arrived in New York harbor in the spring of 1987 and was christened by Nadia Stolt-Nielsen, wife of the vice chairman. *Wind Song* made her debut in French Polynesia that summer, on a year-round program every week from Papeete, Tahiti. The third vessel, *Wind Spirit*, was christened in Monaco's tiny harbor by Clara van der Vorm, wife of the then chairman of Holland America Line, in April 1988, and sailed the following day on her inaugural cruise of the French and Italian rivieras. Since all these festivities occurred, Holland America Line went from half-interest owner in Windstar Cruises to full ownership, and then Carnival Cruise Line acquired Holland America Line and Windstar in the bundle!

All three vessels are alike in design, concept and spaciousness although the main lounges of each have been gradually improved (one learns by experience). The cabins are cozy, cheerful and roomy enough for two (honest), without losing the effect of being aboard a sailing vessel. The bathrooms, however, receive more comment and praise than any other area on board! Cabin and bathroom amenities include: TV/VCR; refrigerator with minibar; state-of-the-art telephones; twin/queen beds; wall safe; gray terrycloth robes with matching towels; a shower designed for two friendly people; hair dryer; Roger Gallet soaps and shampoo, as well as a small atomizer of Evian water (for the skin, not the stomach).

The atmosphere on board Windstar Cruises is deliberately unstructured and aimed at sports-minded young or young at heart. These vessels are suited to newlyweds as well as those celebrating their silver anniversary; they are not suited to the single passsenger who cannot make his or her own entertainment. There are few activities of a group nature, and meals are casually elegant; you dine when you wish (within certain hours) and sit where you please. There are no assigned tables and nighttime entertainment is minimal—a small band in the lounge for after-dinner dancing, a library, a casino, and lots of video tapes available at the purser's office.

The vessels anchor out of port as much as possible, so that passengers can enjoy the wonderful sports platform aft, which sits atop the sea for swimming, water skiing, wind surfing, etc. The platform is also convenient for embarking boats for water tours, as the one offered up-river in Raiatea. Another friendly design features a navigation platform aft for passengers, as well as the open wheelhouse forward. Indeed, passengers are encouraged to absorb the entire sailing experience, and I know one energetic passenger named Bob Gates who doesn t feel the vessel should leave harbor unless he is within the vicinity of the wheelhouse!

These vessels are absolutely for people who enjoy a casual, elegant environment, a young and energetic crew, good food and drink, lovely vistas and the feeling of *sailing* for it is the sailing experience that makes Windstar different from any other cruise line.

Wind Star winters in the Caribbean and summers in the Mediterranean. What could be more glamorous? She sails on one-week cruises from Barbados from October to April then moves to 7 and 14-day voyages between Athens and Istanbul. *Wind Song* continues her successful year-round departures from Papeete, Tahiti, through the Society Islands (Huahine, Raiatea, Bora Bora, Moorea). *Wind Spirit* cruises on a year-round Far East itinerary, sailing between Singapore and Bangkok, with visits to islands in Malaysia and Thailand.

WORLDWIDE TRAVEL AND CRUISE ASSOCIATES

400 S.E. 12th Street, Ft. Lauderdale, FL 33316
☎ (305) 463-1922, (800) 881-8484

Worldwide Travel and Cruises represents some very tony sailing ships. President James Castle, a former ship captain, oversees the diverse operation of chic ships that cruise the Mediterranean, Caribbean and Great Barrier Reef of Australia.

The 64-passenger *Le Ponant*, a 300-foot motorized sailing ship launched in 1992, is French in flavor and spirit, her interiors modern and elegant and cabins equipped with minibars, bathrobes and beach towels, fresh flowers and beds that convert to doubles. Fresh food is brought aboard each day and those dining al fresco may find rack of lamb at lunch or a roast suckling pig at dinner. Dining is open-seating, and everyone sits at the captain's table once during a voyage. She winters in the Caribbean, cruising from Guadeloupe to Saintes, Dominica, St. Martin, Anguilla, St. Barts and Antigua (rates begin around $1210 sans air); in summer, she sails from Nice to coves around Corsica at rates from around $2160.

Those bound for Down Under have a choice of sailing vessels and catamarans for cruises on Australia's Great Barrier Reef. The *Atlantic Clipper*, built in 1987, is an unpretentious 34-passenger sailing ship; *Royleen Endeavor I* and *II* and *Double Force* are catamarans with small, modest cabins and plenty of water sports gear for viewing the world's most famous underwater panorama.

ZEUS CRUISES

566 Seventh Avenue, New York, New York 10018
☎ (212) 221-0006, (800) 447-5667

While most Americans believe they are limited to conventional cruise ships for visiting the Greek Islands and Turkey, Zeus Cruises offers small motorized sailing vessels that call at some of the most charming, little-known ports in the Aegean. Under the aegis of Zeus Tours, a travel company established in 1948 specializing in tours in the Mediterranean, Zeus Cruises matches yacht capacity to group size, switching from one to another of seven vessels when bookings demand it.

Six vessels (*Zeus I, III* and *V, Nicholas A, Argonaut* and *Viking Star*) are motor-sailers with passenger capacities ranging from 26 to 49; *Zeus II* is a motoryacht carrying 40. Cabins are small, with twin beds (most with private facilities), and the on-board ambience is young and lively with passengers dining on home-cooked traditional Greek cuisine at one seating or reveling ashore when the vessels are in port many evenings. These vessels are modest, but everyone has a wonderful time partying with Greek officers and exploring quaint villages undiscovered by the hoards of tourists found on the better-known isles.

From May through September, one-week sailings depart from Rhodes, Corfu and Piraeus on itineraries such as "Greco-Turkish Mystique," with port calls in Simi, Kos, Lipsi, Samos, Kusadasi, Patmos, Kalymnos and Chalki. Per person, double occupancy cruise-only rates range from $925 to $1150.

THE SHIPS AND THEIR RATINGS

In the 1995 edition of Fielding's cruises we begin a new system of rating vessels against each other. Conventional cruise ships continue to be awarded stars, while "specialty ships" receive anchors. Fielding's is the only cruise guide book which reviews all vessels intended for leisure travel—cruise ships as well as sailboats, riverboats, freighters, paddlewheel steamers, excursion and expedition ships. The criteria that lends to the enjoyment of a cruise ship vacation varies from those of a specialty vessel. In the first instance, the focus of the vessel is the destination itself; with specialty ships, however, the enjoyment is found outside the vessel (e.g., nature, a more port intensive experience) or the experience of the ship or boat (such as sailboats). And, as we continue to add exciting and unusual discoveries each year, the need to make this distinction between one type of vessel and another is increasingly important.

The factors comprised in the rating of a cruise ship include the flow (or layout) of public rooms and their decor; cabin size, amenities and general decor; standards of cuisine and service and the overall passenger satisfaction level. When rating specialty ships, these same factors are taken into account; but equally important, how well does the vessel and its staff deliver the promised experience? In both cases, while feedback from passengers and travel agents have been considered, the final decision in all cases is that of the author. It is important, however, not to let the stars and anchors be the sole determinant when choosing one vessel over another. It is important always to remember that these are objective ratings that stack up vessels against each other.

Even my own personal favorite (don't ask!) does not have a five star/anchor plus rating. Pay very close attention to onboard facilities, services, the age and lifestyle of passengers, atmosphere and "theme cruise" programs that reflect your lifestyle and special interests. These should also be factored into the decision as well as itineraries and price.

CRUISE SHIP STARS

A refined and elegant cruise experience with the finest service, food and amenities; extraordinary attention to detail and ships perfectly maintained. Rates start around $400 to $1000 per person, per day.

A luxurious cruise experience; ships have two seatings in dining room (except on very small vessels), but don't expect kilos of Beluga caviar upon request; facilities and service excellent, cabins well appointed and very comfortable (but not necessarily large). Rates vary by vessel.

A ship outstanding in decor, flow of public rooms, a high level of personalized service and above average cuisine with nice presentation, although often provided by a catering service. The vessels are frequently larger, with more facilities and services. Cabins but comfortable and well appointed. Varying rates.

A very good cruise experience; cabins may be quite small on the newer vessels and showing their age on the older ships; cuisine and presentation, while not gourmet, is enjoyable, and service is cordial and friendly although may not be overly efficient. Varying rates.

Don't expect luxury and refined service. The older ships may need some sprucing up, but overall are comfortable, clean and efficiently run. Cuisine is plentiful and ranges from mediocre to very good. Cabins may be larger on older ships and often very small on newer ships, lacking many amenities. Can be a real find if itinerary is outstanding and price is a bargain.

A very modest vessel. Cuisine is mediocre and service may not be up to standard. Cabins are bare bones and lacking amenities. Rates are budget.

Bypass this ship for a better vessel in its price range.

N/R

Not reviewed by the author.

SPECIALTY SHIP ANCHORS

⚓⚓⚓⚓⚓+

This vessel meets the highest standards of comfort, service and cuisine while delivering the ultimate experience of its kind. If there are lecturers, they are the best in their field; staff and crew are hand selected to enhance the enjoyment of the journey.

⚓⚓⚓⚓⚓

An outstanding seagoing experience, enhanced by above average accommodations, cuisine and service. This vessel is often tops in its destination or type.

⚓⚓⚓⚓+

A good, all-round vessel with none of the frills, more than adequate accommodations, cuisine and service. Delivers a wonderful experience of the region.

⚓⚓⚓⚓

While this vessel may need some sprucing up in public areas, and cuisine is not outstanding, a very satisfactory seagoing holiday, especially in remote regions where it presents a one-of-a-kind vacation.

⚓⚓⚓+

Clean, efficient and adequate food and service, although accommodations and public areas may be cramped. Generally an older vessel that could use a refurbishment.

⚓⚓⚓

Don't expect refinement in public areas or accommodations. Staff is adequate, there may be insufficient material necessary to the enjoyment of the experience outside.

⚓⚓⚓⚓⚓

AMERICANA

Ivaran Lines; Norwegian registry and crew; built in Korea in 1988; 19,500 tons; 578 feet long; 85 feet at beam; 88 passengers; crew of 52; cruising speed of 20 knots; 5 decks.

This lovely vessel combines carrying cargo with luxury space for passengers on the leisurely 29-day New Orleans to Buenos Aires run or a longer 44-day voyage; Ivaran also offers cruise segments. The concept is certainly reminiscent of the once familiar Grace Line vessels that departed from the West Coast every two weeks on their South American journeys. The *Americana* departs from New Orleans to South American ports with as many as 88 passengers on board to ensure priority berthing and an ability to keep on schedule. Built at South Korea's Hyundai yard, the ship has space for over 1100 containers of 20 feet each, and the passenger space is prefabricated components from Scandinavia and Japan, as well as other countries. The result is impressive, modern and bright, and passengers will not be disappointed with their environment.

Public rooms include a lounge/bar, swimming pool with lido area, one-seating dining room with large picture windows and adjustable tables, library, a few slot machines, health club and hairdresser. The spacious cabins feature telephones, closed circuit VCRs, safe and minibar. Some of the bathrooms boast bidets (as though anyone ever uses them). There are 22 double cabins, eight deluxe (four with private balconies), two suites, eight single outside and 12 single inside (convertible to double) accommodations. Entertainment is the do-it-yourself variety, and shore excursions along the east coast and South American ports will focus on the cultural with a minimum of 12 hours spent at each call (but you'll have two full days to explore lovely Salvador).

Passengers are primarily of the retired and well traveled sort who seem to know more about the South American ports than others on board and are happy to share their knowledge.

Sailing southbound from New Orleans, ports of call include Houston; Puerto Cabello and La Guaira, Venezuela; Rio de Janeiro and Santos (Sao Paulo), Brazil. Those sailing northbound from Buenos Aires visit Montevideo, Uruguay; Rio Grande, Itakai, Paranagua, Santos, Salvador and Fortaleza, Brazil; Bridgetown, Barbados; San Juan; and Veracruz and Tampico, Mexico. Rates are not cheap—Ivaran has 22- to 29-day air/sea programs from New Orleans to Buenos Aires or vice versa priced from $4400 to $9860; a full 49-day round-trip voyage ranges from $10,140 to $15,390. It really depends upon whether you want a slow boat to South America or a faster one!

★★

AMERIKANIS

Celebrity/Fantasy Cruises; Panamanian registry; Greek officers and international crew; built in 1952 as *Kenya Castle*; rebuilt in 1968 by Chandris and renamed *Amerikanis*; last refurbished 1987; 20,000 tons; 576 feet long; 74 feet at beam; 606 passengers; crew of 400; cruising speed of 16 knots; 8 passenger decks.

If anyone mentions a Chandris (now Celebrity Cruises) vessel, the *Amerikanis* will receive affectionate responses and for good reason. Built as a one-class vessel for the round-Africa service, she was acquired by Chandris in 1968 and rebuilt as a cruise vessel sailing for Chandris and then on charter to Costa Line for many years. Since the return of the *Amerikanis* to Celebrity Fantasy Cruises, the vessel was spruced up and was most recently refurbished in June 1987 (including complete interior carpeting). Cabins aboard the *Amerikanis* are spacious and old-world with fine wooden details and plenty of closets. Bathrooms are very old-fashioned, a pleasure to turn around in! (No problems with dropping the soap here.) Of the total 306 cabins, 212 are outside and 67 boast double beds. The 54 mini-suites are approximately 250 square feet and even the lowest priced cabin is not smaller than 165 square feet. This ship represents the good old days, folks, although closed circuit TV has been added to all cabins.

The large Galaxy Disco is located up on Sun Deck and, before hopping begins, is a splendid gathering place for private parties. Below on Athens Deck are the large Neptune Casino, shops and small rooms, the Mayfair Ballroom (main lounge) and Rendezvous Bar. The 360-degree Rendezvous Bar commanding this spacious room is very popular and a good place to become acquainted with fellow passengers at cocktail time or after dinner and before things begin to awaken in the disco.

The Silver Carte and Silver Leaf restaurants are located below on Rome Deck and offer a nice, cozy feeling. There are two seatings for all meals; if traveling with friends, be sure to book the same dining room at the same time.

Food and service have been improved by the new, tough management that puts up with no nonsense. (Any complaint from passengers is immediately rectified.) A gym/sauna is located on Lisbon deck, the cinema on Ottawa deck.

The Amerikanis *sails year-round from San Juan, departing for the lower Caribbean every Monday. The one-week cruises call at St. Thomas, Guadeloupe, Barbados, St. Lucia, Antigua, and St. Maarten during the winter/spring season, and St. Thomas, Martinique, Grenada, La Guaira, and Curacao during the summer/fall months. Special 6- and 8-day cruises are also available during the holiday season. Per person, per diem is in the $100-$260 range.*

AUTHOR'S NOTE

Necessary Expenditures

Port Charges—Notice in the small type in your brochure that this may add up to $100 to the cost of a cruise.

Tipping—Between cabin steward and waiter, the industry standard is about $9 per passenger per day.

Shore Excursions—These are not mandatory, but are frequently purchased. Costs can run from $30 to $150 extra per port. Ask your travel agent to advise you on ports where these excursions are really unnecessary

Travel Insurance—This is a worthwhile investment that covers medical, lost luggage and trip cancellation. Most people don't bother but *should.*

Visa—Check if it is necessary for your destination.

★★★+
STAR/SHIP ATLANTIC

Premier Cruise Lines; Liberian registry and Greek officers; international crew; originally built in 1982 for Home Lines; acquired by Premier and refurbished 1988; 36,500 tons; 671 feet long; 90 feet at beam; 1068 passengers; crew of 550; cruising speed of 24 knots; 7 passenger decks.

The *Atlantic* is a very sturdy ship, as she was built for Home Lines, and has a high degree of spaciousness; Premier has not tampered with the passenger configuration. While not so elegant in design as the *Oceanic* especially the exterior the vessel is a very pleasant one and suited to all ages. A jogging track has been installed on Sun Deck, around the Magradome (sliding roof) of the Riviera pool and terrace on Pool Deck below. This deck also boasts the Satellite Cafe for buffet breakfasts and lunches, as well as the Seasport Fitness and Health Center, two bars, an ice cream parlor, and the Calypso Pool aft.

Lounge Deck, below, features superior cabins with queen-sized beds, as well as Club Universe (for evening shows), Lucky Star Casino, shops and photo gallery, Space Station teen center and the Junkanoo Club/Bar. Forward on the deck below is Pluto's Playhouse children's recreation center and pool. The Galaxy dining room is a few decks down next to the infirmary.

Star/Ship Atlantic *sails from Port Canaveral every Friday and Monday for Nassau and a private beach on Bahamian Out Island. Per person, double occupancy rates are in the $148-$308 range.*

AUTHOR'S NOTE

Optional Expenditures

Items listed below are common extras you may want to factor in your vacation budget:

- **Gambling/Bingo**
- **On-board beverages**
- **Hairdressing**
- **Boutique items**
- **Laundry/dry cleaning**
- **Postage, postcards**
- **Car rental**
- **Medication**
- **Toiletry items**
- **Taxi to pier**
- **Telephone calls, faxes**
- **Souvenirs**
- **Excess baggage**
- **New luggage**
- **Cruise clothing**
- **Travel guides**
- **Books to read**
- **On-shore shopping purchases**

★★+

BRITANIS

Celebrity/Fantasy Cruises; Panamanian registry; Greek officers and international crew; 26,000 tons; originally built in 1932 in Quincy, MA, and formerly named *Monterey, Matsonia* and *Lurline*; refitted in 1971 and renamed *Britanis*; last refurbished in 1987; 26,000 tons; 638 feet long; 82 feet at beam; 926 passengers; crew of 530; cruising speed of 20 knots; 8 passenger decks.

The *Britanis* has a great history in American passenger service. She was built by Bethlehem Steel Company in 1932 for the Matson Navigation Company and sailed that romantic route between San Francisco and Honolulu as the *Lurline* before the war, the *Matsonia* following. But life was never the same, and the ship became the *Monterey*; however, the U.S. government decided (wisely) to no longer subsidize the salaries of U.S. crew aboard leisure passenger vessels, so the ship and company went out of service.

The vessel was purchased by Chandris Inc. (today Celebrity Cruises) in 1971 and converted from a transpacific liner to one-class Caribbean cruising. She is no glamour puss but a traditional vessel with old-world ambience, and is among the most worthy ships afloat. When it was suggested to young John Chandris that he replace the *Britanis* with another known vessel, he replied astutely, "Why should I buy that ship whose boilers are always blowing up? The *Britanis* has six sound boilers and never a problem!" Well said.

The 926-passenger *Britanis* has a total of 463 cabins (of which 87 are rock bottom value because they share facilities). Double cabins top at 225 square feet and large suites are about 405 square feet. Public rooms are located on Promenade Deck, with a large casino, several bars, the ballroom and shopping arcade. The outdoor swimming pool with bar area (becomes late night disco) is located on Upper Deck; a gym and library/card room are forward on Main Deck. The Waikiki (they never changed the name, it seems) and Coral dining rooms are on Barbados Deck (with sauna way, way forward) and the theater is on Dorado Deck. Although modest and far from luxurious, the vessel is well maintained and is in fine form for such a grande dame. The food on board is good quality, especially for the price, and there are two excellent musical groups for dancing and serenading.

This vessel offers good value for your dollar and an interesting itinerary, with an interesting passenger mix of Americans, Canadians and Europeans.

In September 1995, the Britanis *makes her eighth annual circumnavigation of South America, and there is no reason to stop now! Passengers love the long, leisurely cruise aboard such a great lady. For the rest of the year, Britanis sails from Miami on 5-night cruises to Key West, Playa del Carmen, and Cozumel every Sunday, and 2-night Fantasy Champagne Weekend cruises every Friday to Nassau. Per person, double occupancy rates are in the $100-$260 range.*

AUTHOR TIP

Are you in the market for new luggage that is durable, affordable and easy to use? Luggage companies have some very user-friendly selections available today. Your best bet in a large-size suitcase has wheels and is made of heavy-duty vinyl or rip-stop nylon. Detachable pulling straps can be easily lost, so make sure the strap is attached and can be snapped in place when you check in at the airport. And, while airlines all require a baggage tag, it is always a good idea to tape your name, address and phone number on the inside of the suitcase in the event the outside tag comes off.

You may want to explore the new carry-on models equipped with wheels and fold-down handles that can be rolled easily down the concourse. But be sure to ask if the model meets the airline's size specifications for carry-on luggage. Many airlines today are installing sizer boxes at the departure gates. If your carry-on suitcase doesn't fit into the sizer box, airline personnel will require you to check the bag.

⚓⚓⚓⚓+

CALEDONIAN STAR

Caledonia Travel & Special Expeditions; Bahamian registry; Scandinavian officers and international crew; formerly known as *North Star*; built in 1966 and refitted and refurbished 1987; 3095 tons; 295 feet long; 46 feet at beam; 110 passengers; crew of 70; cruising speed of 13.5 knots; 5 passenger decks.

The *Caledonian Star* (former *North Star*) is a hearty expedition vessel, marketed in the U.S. by Caledonia Travel and Special Expeditions. The ship is frequently chartered by organizations, but both companies offer specific itineraries to individuals. Seeking an in-depth experience in Borneo or New Guinea? You'll probably want to hop aboard the *Caledonian Star* for a lengthy voyage back in time to a '90's version of a Margaret Mead adventure. On board everything is casual but comfortable, with small but all outside, adequate cabins (refurbished to feature TV/VCR and refrigerator), a main lounge/bar/lido bar and small swimming pool with plenty of deck space, a small library, theater and enlarged dining room that now seats all passengers. There is also a small boutique (where I bought a beautiful watch a few years ago), as well as the famous Baby Star tender and a fleet of Zodiac landing craft.

Caledonian Star is a sturdy ship (she was originally built in Bremerhaven in 1966 and employed as a German fish factory vessel) and well suited for expedition cruises. I had a wonderful week aboard (as *North Star*) from Gothenburg, Sweden, into the spectacular Norwegian fjord country, and felt very happy in my cabin on Upper Deck with its single bed and convertible sofa. The two windows were perfect for viewing the passing scenery over early morning coffee and yogurt, nicely delivered by the young Scandinavian stewardess.

In 1995, Caledonian Star *sails in the Far East before a series of voyages along the east coast of Africa and the Seychelles. From fall through spring you'll find her in the Mediterranean, Baltic and British Isles. This ship is perfect for the hearty traveler interested in nature, local culture and an in-depth experience of ports from onboard experts. Exotica is not cheap—per person, per diem rates are in the $250-$500 range.*

⚓⚓⚓⚓

CARIBBEAN PRINCE/MAYAN PRINCE/NIAGARA PRINCE

American Canadian Caribbean Line; American registry and crew; designed by Luther Blount and built in Warren, Rhode Island, in 1983, 1994; 100 tons; 160 feet long; 35 feet at beam; 72-92 passengers; crew of 15; cruising speed of 12 knots; 3 passenger decks.

The *Caribbean Prince*, *Mayan Prince* and new *Niagara Prince* are the distinctive creative designs of shipbuilder Luther Blount, who superbly describes his company: "we first seek out unusual places and then build the ships to take us there." Blount specializes in small vessels with shallow drafts and a bow that folds down right onto the beach! Hence, the cruise line's philosophy and itineraries are rather like those of a private yacht. The ships have three passenger decks, with 32 spacious picture window cabins and six economy cabins without portholes. All have private facilities, and the Sun/Main deck cabins have a choice of sleeping arrangements (double or twin configuration). The dining room and main lounge are located on Main Deck, and both spaces seat all passengers. Setups and hors d 'oeuvres are served in the lounge at cocktail time, when passengers bring their own bottles. The meals are prepared by world-class chefs but served family-style around round tables seating six guests each.

The Caribbean Prince *cruises in the Caribbean from mid-November to mid-April on a series of 12-day itineraries featuring Guatemala and the Belizean coastline where the famous barrier reef is well known with those who snorkel or scuba. It's a fascinating area that includes plenty of unusual flora and fauna, time for beaching and snorkeling, as well as visiting two famous Mayan ruins Altun Ha and Quiriqua plus a side trip to Tikal before or after the cruise.*

In early May, the *Caribbean Prince* sails up the eastern seaboard on a 15-day cruise to Warren, Rhode Island, for the summer season. The popular 12-day, one-way Saguenay River cruises are scheduled all summer, followed by two 12-day Fall Foliage sailings between Rhode Island and Montreal. These summer cruises offer a wonderful itinerary through Narragansett Bay and Long Island Sound to South Street Seaport in New York City, up the Hudson River to the Erie Canal, along the St. Lawrence Seaway through the Thousand Islands and into the Saguenay as far as Cape

Trinity and the Bay of Eternity (for a Bow Landing!). The cruise ends in Montreal, from whence passengers return to Rhode Island by bus (or vice versa). More fall foliage can be enjoyed on the 15-day repositioning cruise from Rhode Island down to West Palm Beach in November. This winter the *Mayan Prince* cruises to little-known areas of Aruba, Bonaire and Curacao on 12-day cruises followed by a captivating 12-day voyage between Trinidad and Tobago and Venezuela's Orinoco River, with naturalists aboard to point out flora and fauna. During the summer, this ship sails round-trip from Warren on 6-day "New England Islands" voyages visiting Cuttyhunk, Nantucket, Martha's Vineyard, Block Island and Newport and then proceeds to a Rochester/Georgian Bay schedule. In 1995, ACCL launches the new *Niagara Prince*, boasting wraparound windows, so Luther can offer a wonderful 12-day Panama Canal itinerary. Sailing between Panama City and Balboa, the itinerary features the San Blas Islands, Pearl Islands, Darien Jungle and a visit to the Choco Indians. A 12-day "Mundo Maya" cruise to Guatemala and Belize precedes cruises between New Orleans and Chicago. If this laid-back, low-key mode of cruising appeals, you'll be delighted at ACCL's per person, per diem which is in the $100 to $173 range.

AUTHOR TIP

Planning a 10-day plus cruise in a foreign cruising region can present real packing challenges. Of course, men have it easiest, since dress attire for evening can be mixed and matched easily. Women have a tougher task in planning sufficient dressy clothes for evening while not overpacking. The solution? Dressy separates work best and give the most versatility. One or two fancy evening jackets may be worn with long or short skirts and dressy pants in a variety of ensembles. Accessories change everything—a chiffon scarf draped around the neck, glittery costume jewelry and several dressy blouses can stretch the furthest in having a versatile evening wardrobe.

★★★

CARNIVALE

Carnival Cruise Lines; Bahamian registry; Italian officers and international crew; originally built in 1956 and entered service as the *Empress of Britain*; also cruised as *Queen Anna Maria*; last refurbished in 1989; 27,250 tons; 640 feet long; 87 feet at beam; 950 passengers; crew of 550; cruising speed of 21 knots; 9 passenger decks.

The *Carnivale* entered service as a Caribbean cruise ship in 1976, and was the first vessel on which interior designer Joe Farkis of Miami worked. In fact, this began Farkis's longstanding association with Carnival Cruise Lines. Cabins aboard the *Carnivale* are similar to the *Mardi Gras*, her sister ship. They are larger than the Caribbean style of other 7-day vessels, and all now have 110 AC current to coincide with what passengers find on land.

There is a large complement of inside cabins, approximately 265 to 217 outside cabins. Many have double and king-size beds, and there is a large percentage of 4-person cabins for singles and couples with children. But passengers are not expected to spend much time in their cabins anyway! The Riverboat Club Casino and Lounge is placed prominently in the center of Promenade Deck. In fact, no one is supposed to miss it!

Forward of the casino are the Mardi Gras Night Club and the Fly Aweigh Discotheque, with a library in between. Aft is the cinema and Showplace Lounge, as well as children's playroom and shops. There are three separate outdoor pools plus a children's wading pool on Sun Deck and an indoor pool/gymnasium down on Riviera Deck. The International dining room is located down on Main Deck. Three full meals, two evening buffets and several daytime snacks are the quantity if not the quality of food served aboard.

A much-needed $10-million refurbishment improved the cabin areas and hallways, the Showplace Lounge, Promenade, Mardi Gras Lounge, International dining room, Lido Bar, Sun Deck (which received a 16-person-capacity whirlpool) and Children's Playroom. The general ambience of the vessel received a more Caribbean look, and the old-world decor was replaced from necessity in most areas.

The refurbishment took place just prior to Carnivale's *reposition to Port Canaveral for Thursday and Sunday sailings to the Bahamas that can be combined with central Florida attractions and complete air-sea programs. Average per person per diem rates range from $120 to $145 (after Super Saver discount).*

AUTHOR TIP

If planning a cruise on an expedition vessel, here are some incidentals you won't want to leave behind—binoculars, insect repellant (in tropical regions), plenty of sun block, a sturdy canvas hat and very comfortable, rubber-sole walking shoes, plenty of warm, comfortable daytime wear such as sweat pants, a hooded, waterproof parka and a notebook. On the other hand, it usually is unnecessary to lug along specialty books, as most expedition vessels have very well-stocked libraries covering history and flora and fauna of the region.

★★★

CELEBRATION

Carnival Cruise Lines; Liberian registry; Italian officers and international crew; built in Malmo, Sweden, and entered service March 1987; 48,000 tons; 733 feet long; 92 feet at beam; 1486 passengers; crew of 670; cruising speed of 21 knots; 9 passenger decks.

The *Celebration* is one of three superliners built especially for Carnival Cruise Lines in Malmo, Sweden. She is sister ship to the *Holiday* and *Jubilee*. While the *Holiday* has a fantasy theme and the *Jubilee* a nostalgia theme, the *Celebration* has a futuristic theme.

Cabin configuration and suites are identical to the other two vessels as are all public areas. Only the names have changed. The main showplace is the Astoria Lounge. The dining rooms are named Vista and Horizon. The piano bar is the Red Hot and across the way is Admiralty Library. Instead of a Bus Stop or Gazebo, there is now a Trolley. The casino is known as the Rainbow Club; the disco is Galax Z; and the Lido deck restaurant is Wheelhouse Bar & Grill. People places are Holiday Square, Mardi Gras Square and Bourbon Street. The coffee area is the Bistro and the aft showroom for late night cabaret is Islands in the Sun.

The public areas are Joe Farkis (the architect/designer who does all Carnival products) glitzy, but that is what Carnival is all about and it works for them. Very well. Effort has been made, however, to present a dining room that is restful and pleasant. The food gets mixed reviews, however, more so than on any other ship line.

There are two outdoor adult swimming pools and one wading pool, and plenty of deck area for bikini watching or other sporting events. The vessel boasts a health spa with whirlpool, as well as plenty of shops and people watching along the promenade area Bourbon Street, Holiday Square, Mardi Gras Square. Cabin size is good (for the price) and all twin beds are convertible to queen-size. Bathrooms are modular-standard and on the small side-strictly one person at a time, and it helps if you are a midget.

The Celebration *sails every Saturday from Miami at 4 p.m. and spends Sunday and most of Monday at sea. The vessel arrives in San Juan at 6 p.m. on Monday for just the evening; she arrives in St. Thomas at 8 a.m. on Tuesday, spends Wednesday in St. Maarten, and the next two days at sea. This is definitely a cruise for people who like to sun on deck, gamble and drink things that come in different colored liquids on a tray. Average per person per diem rates range from $120-$145 after Super Saver discounts.*

N/R
CONSTITUTION

American Hawaii Cruises; American registry (returned) and mostly Hawaiian crew; originally built in the U.S. in 1951 and named the *Constitution*; previously owned by the C. Y. Tung conglomerate but placed under American custody for cruising in Hawaiian waters; now owned and operated by Peter Huang, Chinese-American businessman; 30,090 tons; 682 feet long; 89 feet at beam; 800 passengers; crew of 320; cruising speed of 20 knots; 9 passenger decks.

A true sister ship to the *Independence*, an identical twin as it were, the *Constitution* was built at Bethlehem Steel Corp.'s Ford River Shipyard in Quincy, Massachusetts. The vessel made a 23-port gala 60-day maiden voyage to the Mediterranean in April 1951. The ship was built for express liner three-class service between New York and Italy, with calls at Gibraltar and Cannes. Quickly popular with the celebrity set, the American Export Line vessel was among the fastest and safest U.S. flags afloat. First-class passengers included politicians, diplomats, and film personalities, which explains why Grace Kelly chose to sail aboard the *Constitution* with her wedding party in 1956 to become a princess in Monaco.

When American Export Isbrandtsen Lines ended transatlantic service in 1967, the *Constitution* was laid up at Jacksonville, Florida until purchased (jointly with the *Independence*) by the C.Y. Tung Group of Hong Kong in 1974. She joined the Hawaiian Islands itinerary in June 1982, following a complete refit and refurbishment in Taiwan where she was also rechristened by *Princess Grace of Monaco*. The *Constitution* is the only American-flag vessel to receive royal (even minor as it is) sponsorship. As a remembrance of the late princess, a beautiful writing room on board has been dedicated to her memory.

The *Constitution* is a comfortable vessel—one that offers passengers a feeling of safety. Although constructed in 1950-51, she is extremely modern in design and decor and one of the first to boast air conditioning throughout! A recent multimillion dollar refurbishment scheme has added a tone and color scheme more suitable to cruising in the Hawaiian Islands. Among the vessel's refurbishments is the addition of a 2-room Owner's Suite with deluxe amenities and adjoining 2-berth inside cabin for children/nanny, etc. A full-size gymnasium has been installed in the former Starlight Lounge on Sports Deck, there is a new phone system on board, and the public restrooms have been redecorated. The cabins are spacious and well planned for the early 50s, but only the few suites aboard have full bathrooms with tubs. Even in the deluxe cabins, which have plenty of closet and moving about space, it is just possible to turn around in the bathroom. And if you drop that sliver of soap in the shower, forget it!

Public rooms aboard the *Constitution* are attractive and spacious, especially the Constitution Lounge with the smaller Princess Grace memorial room aft portside and the Friendship Lounge on the starboard side. Captain Harry T. Y. Wu, the master of the vessel, welcomes passengers in the Tropicana Showplace where the nightly shows are also performed. Behind the nightclub is a pleasant bar with good sea views, called Tradewinds Terrace. Below, on Upper Deck, are the shopping and photo arcades, as well as some electronic games set up. There is a spacious Lahaina Landing lounge with plenty of outdoor tables and lounges around the swimming pool. This is where most of the daytime action occurs, from a sumptuous buffet breakfast (7–9 a.m.) to refreshing scoops of sherbet served at 11 a.m, and a deck buffet luncheon (11:45 a.m.–1 p.m.).

If you prefer a quieter area, ascend two flights to Sun Deck and the Beachcomber Bar. This is the former first-class swimming pool and outdoor bar, and it seems to catch the best rays of sun. There is a large Conference Center aft on Main Deck, very suitable for the many seminars aboard, and two dining rooms on Aloha Deck. The captain, hotel manager and chief engineer dine in the Hibiscus, while other officers have tables in the Bird of Paradise room. The food is excellent, especially if you like plenty of fresh fruits, seafood and steak, and homemade ice creams. Service has come full circle since the cruise was inaugurated and is quite suitable to the type of clientele the vessel attracts. As one passenger said, "Food and service aboard the *Constitution* are equal to the best of ships sailing from Miami." And if you are interested in ship history, contact Greg Abbott, the chief purser.

Captain Wu is a charming fellow who definitely enjoys his work. He is more visible than many other captains and holds a series of small champagne parties for selected passengers throughout the cruise. He also invites a different group to his dinner table each night. Despite the social schedule, Captain Wu is known for running a very tight ship, indeed. His safety standards are very high, evident from the detail of the lifeboat drill.

The all-American crew is hired in Honolulu; hence they are mainly islanders. They are a young and energetic group who seem eager to please.

However, under Peter Huang's management style, both vessels have been upgraded and a great deal of money has been spent on them. Menus are better, the dining room is more attractive and the service crew has new uniforms. This refurbishment program does not detract from the American/casual atmosphere on board; rather, it is enhanced. (It also helps when competition is arriving in the form of another ship.) More attention has also been focused on local Hawaiian talent in decor and entertainment.

The 1-week, 4-island itinerary of the Constitution *departs Aloha Tower at 9 p.m. on Saturday, cruises all day Sunday, calls at Maui on Monday, Hilo and Kona on Hawaii (Tuesday and Wednesday), Nawiliwili (Kauai) on Thursday and Friday, and returns to Honolulu Saturday at 7:15 a.m. Per person, per diem is in the $100-556 range.*

N/R

COSTA ALLEGRA/COSTA CLASSICA/COSTA ROMANTICA/COSTA MARINA

(See Costa Cruises in "The Cruise Lines")

AUTHOR TIP

Be aware that you pay for a certain category of cabin, but in some instances have no control over which one you actually end up in within that category. See the purser or hotel manager, who will probably make an effort to move you (explain your reasons nicely and never demand—they aren't required to do anything).

AUTHOR TIP

Read the fine print in the brochure—nobody does. A cruise company can do pretty much as they please, including bypassing a port because of weather, politics or whatever. Again, contact your travel agent upon return and lodge a complaint—you may get recompense (but don't count on it).

★★★★

CROWN DYNASTY/CROWN JEWEL

Cunard Line; Panamanian Registry; European officers and international crew; Built in Union Naval de Levante, Valencia, Spain; Launched 1993 (*Dynasty*) and 1992 (*Jewel*); 19, 500 tons; 537 feet long; 74 feet at beam; 800 passengers; crew of 320; 8 passenger decks.

From the moment one steps aboard the *Crown Dynasty* and *Crown Jewel* there is a sense of being in a lovely Mediterranean villa, and that one must get the name of the interior designer. The 800-passenger sister ships arrived in 1992 and 1993 with beautiful art and attention to detail that sets them apart in decor from other vessels cruising the Caribbean.

Crown Dynasty and *Crown Jewel* joined the Cunard fleet under a long-term marketing agreement with Crown Cruise Line in early 1993. Constructed in Union Naval de Levante Shipyard, Valencia, Spain, and designed by Petter Yran of Oslo, they boast lovely art (such as *Crown Jewel's* murals of South American locales and French Impressionist-style Parisian street scenes) adorning walls in public areas. The four-story atrium with floor-to-ceiling glass and the frequent use of skylights contribute to the warm atmosphere.

The ship's piéce de résistance are the circular 413-seat dining rooms, decorated in peach wallpaper with burgundy borders. The three-tiered design, Doric columns and panoramic ocean views lend an exceptionally spacious, genteel ambience, where one likes to linger as long as possible after a leisurely dinner. In my opinion, they are among the most relaxing, beautiful dining rooms found aboard any vessel in the mid-price range.

The Marco Polo Cafe, a buffet restaurant for casual breakfast and lunch, is a tropical-Moorish design, with teak floor, dark green rattan furniture and a champagne bar. However, it is located two decks below the pool, and a bit inconvenient for those who like a light lunch with only a cover-up after a dip in the pool.

Those who work out will find only a dozen or so pieces of equipment in the fitness center and it may be a bit crowded, but the facility boasts a lovely Jacuzzi beneath a skylight, floor-to-ceiling windows and padded aerobics/ stretching floor. The large outdoor pool area has three Jacuzzis and a wading pool, with glass panels to reduce wind.

Public entertainment areas include the Rhapsody Lounge for evening shows, which is multi-tiered for excellent viewing throughout; Alexander's Lounge is lovely, with a green and aqua marble bar, but located next to the casino which is not enclosed. What seems like an ocean of slot machines adjacent to the boutiques in the public area is incongruous with the tasteful decor of the ship. Quiet conversation is next to impossible and quiet lounges could not be found which I find unappealing. Late night disco is found in the Kit Kat Club, with banks of televisions projecting videos. Both ships have tiny libraries, card rooms and toddlers play areas, but no separate facilities for children above the age of five.

Cabins aboard *Crown Dynasty* and *Crown Jewel* average 124 square feet and although a few staterooms in the higher categories have balconies, all bathrooms have tiny showers and no bathtubs. The decor of the pastel colored staterooms is cheerful and the accommodations are comfortable for a 7- day cruise. Midships outside cabins on Deck 6 and 7 have views of lifeboats.

I was introduced to *Crown Jewel* at her christening in New York in July, 1993 and haven't had a chance to sail on her; a number of travel agents report their clients enjoy the *Crown Dynasty* and one can assume her sister ship will be just as popular. The 800-passenger size is right for those who dislike the megavessels and want a more intimate, although lively, atmosphere; the cuisine and service have both received mixed reviews from colleagues.

In 1995, Crown Dynasty *cruises 10- and 11-day Panama Canal voyages between Port Everglades and Acapulco. She summers in Alaska on 7-day cruises between Vancouver and Seward and returns to the Panama Canal itinerary in late September.* Crown Jewel *sails year-round from Port Everglades on alternating 7-day itineraries, visiting San Juan, Puerto Plata, St.Thomas, St. John and Nassau, alternating with Ocho Rios, Cozumel, Grand Cayman and Cancun. Per person, per diem begins around $156.*

★★★★+

CROWN ODYSSEY

Royal Cruise Line; Bahamian registry and Greek crew; built in Papenburg, Germany, and began service in June 1988; 40,000 tons; 614 feet long; 92 feet at beam; 990/1052 passengers; crew of 470; cruising speed of 22 knots; 10 passenger decks.

Royal Cruise Line's *Crown Odyssey* resembles a spacious contemporary hotel with gleaming surfaces and abstract sculptures transporting active 60+ passengers who seem constantly busy cramming in every activity in they can manage. While there are ample lounges for quiet pre-dinner cocktails and conversation, those who seek a full roster of fitness activities and nightlife may find this fits the bill.

Carrying a comfortable capacity of 1000, *Crown Odyssey* was launched in 1988 and is the only modern vessel in Royal's fleet. While not in the deluxe end of cruising, there is no sign of five years' of wear and tear, the result of constant upkeep of public areas and staterooms. My favorite design aspect of this ship is the lavish deck space that spreads over many levels and allows one the choice of joining other passengers poolside during days at sea or securing complete solitude. It also lends perfectly to Royal's popular fitness programs—early mornings are bustling with dozens of hearty souls jogging along Promenade deck or trying an aquacize class, some confessing this is their first fitness effort ever.

The heart and soul of any Royal Cruise Line ship is the Greek crew. They lack the polish and fine points of service found aboard many vessels in this price range, but those who want outgoing, friendly and charming personnel who genuinely seem to enjoy passengers will discover an added joy in cruising with Royal. They smile, flirt openly with women of all ages and love to engage in conversation. Many of Royal's repeaters claimed they cruise because of "Yannis," "Nico," "Fernadez;" Greek Night, when waiters don native attire and the crew entertains in the Odyssey Show Lounge is wildly popular with passengers and staff alike. Royal's captain and senior officers, who dance with passengers, attend evening shows and social events, seem to enjoy themselves immensely.

My favorite public room is the Top of the Crown boasting lovely seating areas (one section is rattan, the rest decorated in navy and deep rose) and 360 degrees of floor to ceiling windows—wonderful for escaping the direct sun during a Panama Canal crossing, a pre-dinner cocktail or evening swing around the dance floor.

Cruising the Greek Islands aboard "Crown Odyssey"

The Monte Carlo Court on Lido Deck reflects salmon and burnt orange from mirrored surfaces, a harpist serenading in one corner as those on the other side of the bar sip cocktails and watch fellow passengers win and lose in the casino. A wide circular staircase with enormous stained glass ceiling panel leads down to Marina Deck. Here one find's the Purser's Office and a large lobby with golden pine walls, rust-colored carpet and a modern revolving statue of a globe (I think!). A long, narrow hallway with lighted shelves holding reproductions of ancient Greek art leads to the two-seating dining room. Decorated in Wedgewood blue and dusty rose, with stained glass and large picture windows, it is comfortable and roomy (table configurations are 6, 8 and 10) at dinner. Additional public rooms include the Yacht Club, popular for afternoon tea and evening dancing, the Odyssey Show Lounge for evening cabaret, a large cinema, full gym/salon and library.

Among the design statements aboard Crown Odyssey are bay windows (with computerized shades) complementing all Superior Deluxe cabins on Riviera Deck. One deck above, the Penthouse Apartments boast large terraces, separate sitting rooms and whirlpool tubs. These accommodations are very spacious, and each one features a different decorative theme from tartan to contemporary to oriental (I presume that passengers can specify the desired decor if booked well in advance). In all, there are 18 categories of accommodations, most with large windows, large bathroom vanities and more than ample closet/drawer space. Cabins lack several amenities standard aboard modern ships in this price range, including television (a corporate decision intended to encourage passengers to seek their enjoyment from the ship) and hair dryers, which can be obtained from room stewards. In some cabin categories twin beds are bolted to the floor and those who want a queen-size bed must change the grade of stateroom (confirm your preference before departure).

A congenial Host Program, providing appropriate aged gentlemen for dancing, dining and bridge/backgammon, as well as "New Beginnings" seminars featuring motivational guest lecturers are a major draw with the 60+ passengers. During my cruise, cuisine was one important area that needed work—while Greek specialties and pasta were always good, entrees of beef, lamb and chicken were frequently over- or undercooked, vegetables were often mushy and desserts usually tasteless.

In 1995, Crown Odyssey *cruises the Panama Canal from January through March; 12-day Baltic, Western Europe, Mediterranean and Black Sea sailings are slated from March through October. As is the case of all Royal ships,* Crown Odyssey *has a marvelous lineup of theme cruises scheduled throughout the year. (Consult Fielding's Theme Cruise Calendar in the chapter devoted to "Choosing Your Cruise.") Per person per diem rates range from $150 to $725.*

AUTHOR'S NOTE

Especially when booking small ships (under 300 passengers), a large group (Society of French Horn Players, Cleveland Rotary or whatever) can be disruptive. Ditto a celebrity—despite what you think, Madonna and her entourage or Gerald Ford and a large contingent of Secret Service can disrupt the ambience enormously. Ask your travel agent to get the inside scoop on any booked groups before you pay your deposit. (Keep in mind, the cruise line has the right not to divulge this information to an agent—it's strictly a courtesy.)

★★★★+

CROWN PRINCESS/REGAL PRINCESS

Princess Cruises; Italian registry; Italian officers and European crew; constructed in Monfalcone, Italy, for July 1990 and Summer 1991 delivery; 70,000 tons; 804 feet long; 115 feet at beam; 1590 passengers; crew of 630; cruising speed of 19.5 knots; 12 decks.

On a bright day in August, 1991, Margaret Thatcher, the former Prime Minister of England, exploded a bottle of champagne over the bow of the *Regal Princess.* Earlier that same summer, Sophia Loren arrived via horse and carriage to christen sister ship *Crown Princess.* These two additions to the Love Boat chain are aimed at the top end of cruise passengers, and Princess pitches hard to keep that image. For the most part, they succeed.

Rich with a collection of art that would please the post picky of patrons, this contemporary collection represents, among others, Robert Motherwell, David Hockney and Helen Frankenthaler, gathered at a cost of more than $l million.

Designed in the studios of Renzo Piano, Italy's very "in" architect, the Dolphin-like look of the ships is no accident. Sleek and curving, they ply through the waters like lovely and graceful creatures of the sea. Built in Monfalcone, Italy, a crew of 696 provides comfort and TLC for 1590 passengers in the Caribbean, Alaska and on trans-canal crossings.

The interiors are beautiful as well as functional. The tiered reception/lobby area is my candidate for one of the most dramatic and beautiful afloat. Soaring the height of three decks, it has wraparound balconies and a walkway around several duty free shops. This is the ships' "Main Street," the Town Square where all the action is. A center staircase fills one end of the vast room, great for making a dramatic entrance in dressy attire. It is a Greco/Roman agora concept, done in light, bright colors and plenty of chrome.

Comfortable low chairs and tables group together for easy conversation and people watching. Passengers really use this grand and inviting space; there is always something going on in the area, from the constant activity of the reception and tour desks to La Patisserie, serving coffee, wine, pastries and hors d'oeuvres. A magnificent carpet ties the whole space together and carries in its pattern all the predominant colors of the room: hues of green, corals and gold. A young woman in flowing chiffon plays the harp each day at tea time. On one of the upper levels is tiny Bacchus Bar, serving wine, champagne and six different kinds of caviar. The Dome, topside and forward, soars 19 feet high and is surrounded with curved glass windows. This cantilevered space gives one a real sense of being on the "high seas."

The International Show Lounge rises three full tiers. Acoustically outstanding, its pink and sand wallpaper and cool green fabrics make a soothing background for the two glittering floor shows held each evening. The ship's casino is one of the most appealing afloat, with cozy seating and low lighting, it lacks the normal glare of most gaming rooms. Lounges and watering holes are scattered throughout these ships, including the 240-seat Stage Door, popular for its cabaret and disco; the art-deco Adagio lounge and Bengal Bar, reminiscent of the Raj in India with its large wicker chairs and ceiling fans. I came away with the feeling of "music, music everywhere" on the *Regal Princess*: singers, dancers and pianists perform throughout the day, a great steel band keeps the tempo lively around the pool and violinists serenade during dinner on some evenings.

Those who like to keep fit will find extensive facilities including a jogging deck, Princess' "Cruisercise" program of walk-a-mile, high and low impact aerobics, and enough stretching and pulling equipment that the gym is not overly crowded. However, the massage room is low in the ship, and I felt that I didn't get much benefit from what was to be a relaxing experience because of all the banging and thumping right under the table. Overall, the ship was noisy with the sound of joggers and engine noise.

Crown Princess

Crown Princess and *Regal Princess* each have 795 spacious cabins, a substantial number with private veranda. The 430 standard outside cabins without balconies are 190 square feet while 134 outside cabins with verandas are 210 square feet. All cabins have a twin/queen bed configuration and TV, safes, refrigerators and comfy terrycloth bathrobes. My cabin had a veranda that was nearly unusable due to the thick indoor-outdoor carpeting which remained sopping wet. Insulation between cabins is minimal and mercifully my neighbors were quiet.

ing which remained sopping wet. Insulation between cabins is minimal and mercifully my neighbors were quiet.

Aboard the *Regal Princess* there were food problems, with inconsistencies in both processing and presentation. Too much food was crammed onto plates and it looked as if dumped there. One night, roast lamb was so heavily seasoned that it could have been anything. And, I found the dining room itself less than inspiring, impersonal, noisy and crowded. This ship's two seatings presented problems for those who had requested late seating and boarded to discover they were dining early. Everyone who was unhappy about their seating assignment was summoned to a meeting (about 70 showed up) and some were literally offering money to buy places at the late seating. It was a touchy, competitive scene and not a nice way to begin a cruise.

I discovered that Princess really excels in the handling of its shore tours. They are well led and managed, above average in quality and reasonably priced. Princess Cays in the Bahamas is the company's private island, and we spent a lovely day on a pristine beach with all the watersports one could imagine a few feet away.

In 1995, Crown Princess *and* Regal Princess *cruise from Ft. Lauderdale on identical alternating 1-week itineraries. The Eastern Caribbean sailings include port calls in San Juan, St. Maarten, St. Thomas and Princess Cays (the company's private island); Western Caribbean ports include Princess Cays, Montego Bay, Grand Cayman and Cozumel. From May through September, both vessels cruise on 7-day Alaska itineraries between Vancouver and Seward. The average per person, per diem is $225, including airfare.*

AUTHOR'S NOTE

You've requested second seating and wind up in first, asked for a table for two and land at a table for eight. Unfortunately, when booking a ship with two seatings, you can only request a time and table configuration and won't know until you board the ship what the outcome is. If necessary (and it usually is), have a $20 bill showing in your hand when asking for a change—this usually effects a satisfactory outcome unless the ship is full.

★★★★★+

CRYSTAL HARMONY

Crystal Cruises; Bahamian registry; European officers and hotel staff; built in Nagasaki, Japan, launched in 1990; 49,400 tons; 791 feet long; 97 feet at beam; 960 passengers; crew of 505; cruising speed of 23 knots; 8 passenger decks.

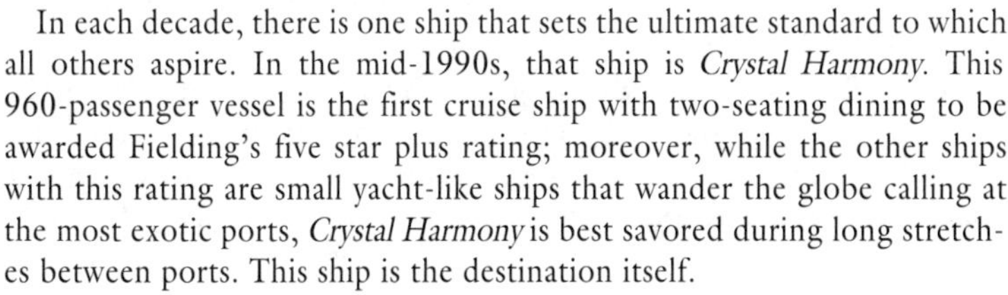

In each decade, there is one ship that sets the ultimate standard to which all others aspire. In the mid-1990s, that ship is *Crystal Harmony*. This 960-passenger vessel is the first cruise ship with two-seating dining to be awarded Fielding's five star plus rating; moreover, while the other ships with this rating are small yacht-like ships that wander the globe calling at the most exotic ports, *Crystal Harmony* is best savored during long stretches between ports. This ship is the destination itself.

If the 200-passenger ships of *Seabourn* and *Sea Goddess* evoke the experience of being aboard a personal yacht, cruising aboard *Crystal Harmony* is closer to an ocean liner—if the *QE 2* should ever retire, this ship would be the perfect replacement on transatlantic service. It seems nearly impossible that so much space can exist on a seagoing vessel, and even when sailing full, passengers often wonder where all their fellow sailing companions are hiding. In fact, this is not an illusion—other ships in the 50,000-ton range very comfortably carry 300 additional passengers. Not only are cabins wonderfully spacious (some 54 percent with private balconies), but enormous public rooms seem to stretch on forever, each with a contemporary and warm decor.

Elegant touches are evident throughout: oriental carpets in elevators and poolside bathrooms, down-filled comforters and butlers in tails serving caviar, to name just a few. And, while there are constant activities available and enough recreational and entertainment facilities to suit the needs of the most active passenger, *Crystal Harmony* has an aura that nearly forces one to wind down, relax and do as little as possible (I noticed a few passengers who were busily working poolside with laptop computers the first day soon abandoned all cares of work, content to just gaze at the ocean).

Crystal knows that first impressions set the tone. One is greeted curbside by white-glove staff sporting braided greeting uniforms. The entry aboard ship is dramatic as one steps immediately into the light-filled two-story Crystal Plaza atrium lobby stretching the width of the ship. The focal point is a cut-glass statue of graceful dancers next to a waterfall; a wide brass and plexiglass circular staircase leads up to a shopping arcade of four boutiques and enclosed casino, and down to the mahogany purser's desk and plant-filled lobby with overstuffed leather chairs that features the soft tinkling of a pianist in the background.

As opposed to one frantic and crowded seating for everyone, Crystal offers two elegant and unhurried seatings (6:30 and 8:30 p.m.) in the Crystal Dining Room. However, (and this is a big however), the alternatives to dinner in the main salon are so attractive, and so well done that they may very well set a new trend for shipboard dining. Tucked away on the starboard side are the elegant open-seating Prego and Kyoto restaurants, dining requiring reservations; open each evening they are available at no additional charge. As the names indicate, one restaurant is Italian and one Japanese, and each is an extension of the tasteful decor that is a hallmark of the entire ship. Those dining in Prego will find soft, blond woods and warm crimson and ivory fabrics; in Kyoto, pools of light reflect the black lacquer tables, creamy beige and grayish walls, all softened by eye-cathching oriental flower arrangements.

The food in each restaurant is superb, on par with Executive Chef Hubert's superbly high standards in the main salon, and service in each is impeccable. The Crystal Dining Room's configuration includes plenty of space and a large selection of tables for two bathed in the glow of cut crystal and brass lamps. The restaurant's decor is soft and romantic, with pale mauve and peach curtains draping large picture windows.

Crystal Harmony's cuisine is superb, a gourmet dining experience at sea. One of my favorite dishes was Brie and Crab soup, so rich one could skip all other courses. Chef Hubert shares his recipe:

BRIE AND CRAB SOUP
2 Onions (peeled and chopped)
2 oz. Butter
2 oz. Flour
4 cups Heavy Cream
8 oz. Brie Cheese
16 oz. Crab, Lobster, or Fish Stock
5 oz. Crab Meat
Chopped Chives
Salt
Pepper
Garlic To Taste

Cook onions, butter and flour for a few minutes, add Crab/fish stock. Cook for 20 minutes over low heat. Add cream, garlic, salt and pepper to taste. Mix in Brie cheese with mixer until the soup has a nice texture. Put the chopped crab meat in a bowl and top with the soup, sprinkle with chopped chives. Serves ten people.

Luncheon buffet is served at the Lido Cafe, adjacent to the pool. You can carry out your tray to the aft deck to watch the wake of the ship while sipping morning coffee (just like in the magazine ads!); poolside there are plenty of tables with umbrellas for alfresco dining. Those seeking an evening's respite from dressing up can order a pizza and popcorn and watch a video in the cabin (watch out—creme brulee is on the room service menu!)

When reviewing dozens of vessels in the course of a year, public rooms frequently become a blur; several aboard *Crystal Harmony* are unforgettable. The Palm Court is one of the most beautiful lounges afloat, an airy, plant-filled tropical oasis stretching the width of the ship. Boasting floor to ceiling windows, soft grey carpet and polished pine dance floor, sumptuous green and coral fabrics adorning rattan furniture, it is tranquil for afternoon tea and romantic for after-dinner dancing. The adjacent three-tiered Vista Lounge is futuristic (Captain Picard would feel right at home if this room were beamed aboard the Enterprise!) with white reclining leather chairs, a ceiling of twinkling "stars" and 270 degrees of floor to ceiling windows: delightful for watching entry into port or a quiet nightcap. A small wine bar, with crystal stemware and lovely vintages, separates the two areas. While watering holes abound, the Avenue Saloon is a favorite of many passengers. It resembles an elegant private club with its soft green leather banquettes, oriental carpets, overstuffed armchairs, sofas and tables for two which overlook the sea. An oval bar is central in the room and guests are serenaded by a pianist who favors tunes from the 40s and 50s. For the late night crowd, a choice of Stars Disco or Club 21 are open until the last passenger shouts "uncle" and heads for bed. Caesar's Palace At Sea (operated by Caesar's Palace of Las Vegas) is the ship's elegant casino, with more than enough gaming tables and slots for the ships' passengers. Crystal stages lavish Broadway-calibre entertainment each evening in the 270-seat Hollywood Theatre. Additional facilities include a well-stocked library with plenty of reference and travel books, plus popular fiction and nonfiction. The complimentary video lending library has plentiful new and old favorites. There is even a small children's playroom, used primarily during holiday season. The ship's "Avenue of the Stars" has elegant stores stocked with distinctive merchandise. Crystal is one of the few companies that does not use a concession but selects its own stock.

Drop dead gorgeous is the 948-square feet Crystal Penthouse, the ship's largest, with living room, dining room, huge jacuzzi tub next to a floor-to-ceiling window, extra wide veranda and the only bathroom I've seen with an ocean view window (talk about water, water everywhere!). In case you think the accommodations are all down hill from here, they're really not. Penthouse Deck has 26 Penthouse Suites (492 square feet) and 32 Penthouses (360 square feet), all with large private verandas, white-glove butler service, walk-in closets and heavenly marble baths; tubs have whirlpools, there are two sinks and a separate shower. In addition Crystal Harmony has 198 outside deluxe staterooms with verandas (271 square feet), 201 outside deluxe staterooms (198 square feet) and 19 inside cabins (183 square feet); in these lower categories, I found drawer space inadequate for lengthy cruises, even in Category C. All cabins have VCR/TV with CNN

& ESPN, mini-refrigerators, safes, bathrobes, hair dryers and direct dial telephone. However, bathrooms in some of the smaller cabins on decks 5, 6, 7, and 8 are disappointing, considering the superb planning of the rest of the ship. The doors open inward and, when open, it is virtually impossible to turn around. Two people could not share the bathroom together at the same time unless they bathed together, and that's not likely given the average age.

Crystal Harmony has superb fitness facilities—the 3000 sq. ft. Crystal Spa, complete with personal fitness trainers, overlooking the sea; there is a full array of steps, weights, pulleys and oars. Join the Jazz exercise or aerobics class, then head for the sauna or steam room, followed by a choice of massages. Deck space is bountiful, with two large pools and jacuzzis, and there is never a feeling of being crowded; there are many secluded areas for those who wish to be alone. Ambitious fitness buffs will find a full jogging promenade, a Wimbledon paddle tennis court, golf driving range. I also loved the Bistro Cafe, reminiscent of a European sidewalk cafe, where cappucino and croissants are great companions for perusing daily papers and magazines.

The young European hotel staff is exceptional. Rarely have I met a staff so appreciative of the ship they're working aboard; they are obviously well treated by Crystal Cruises and extend this to their "guests," as passengers are always called. There is an unpretentious, friendly eagerness to ensure each passenger is well taken care of, and I never once felt I was a "pigeon" for a good tip.

Sister-ship *Crystal Symphony* will be launched in May, 1995, and retains the same "look" and atmosphere of *Crystal Harmony.* Crystal Cruises avidly seeks the feedback of its guests and has modified this new vessel to expand popular areas. Built in Kvaerner Masa-Yard in Turku, Finland, *Symphony* will be two feet wider just to allow more bathroom and closet space in the lower grade cabins. All staterooms will have 15 drawers and nine feet of hanging space, double sinks and telephones in bathrooms; the company is doubling the size of the Crystal Plaza by 50 percent. The two small existing business centers will be combined with the library; Caesar's Palace at Sea Casino will be increased to 4400 square feet and feature five blackjack tables, one roulette table, one craps and one baccarat table plus 125 slot machines. The two alternative restaurants will be enlarged, the Jade restaurant with Chinese cuisine replacing Kyoto, and popular Prego continuing to offer wonderful Italian fare. Open deck space will be expanded and will feature two pools, one with a magradome. *Crystal Symphony's* captain is Helge Brudvik, one of the most charming and personable masters at sea.

No ship in the world is perfect for everyone and those who eschew a classy, elegant milieu and relaxing days at sea should look elsewhere. Moreover, there are those who frequent the under 300-passenger ships with single, open seating who will never settle for two-seating dining. There is always a tradeoff, and all that spaciousness found on a large ship sometimes necessitates tendering into port while bypassing some very chic places that are inaccessible to a large vessel. *Crystal Harmony* is the destination itself, necessitates tendering into port while bypassing some very chic places that are inaccessible to a large vessel. *Crystal Harmony* is the destination itself, not a chic means of transportation from one exotic port to another. The ship's average per person, per diem is $434.

In 1995, Crystal Harmony *cruises down the east coast of South America to Buenos Aires before a March through May season of Panama Canal sailings. She summers in the Baltic, Europe and Mediterranean before returning to the Canal in October. Following her May 10, 1995 christening in New York,* Crystal Symphony *cruises to San Francisco for a season of 12-day Alaska voyages followed by Far East, Australia and New Zealand sailings from September through December.*

AUTHOR'S NOTE

In the end, the ship you choose is up to you. If you wind up on a vessel that doesn't meet your specific life-style and interests or is less than the brochure promised, it means you didn't do enough research on the particular ship. However, if you have valid, specific gripes, you'll find many cruise companies offer some type of recompense such as credit toward a future sailing.

★★★

CUNARD COUNTESS

Cunard Line; Bahamian registry and British officers, international crew; built in Denmark and outfitted; christened in 1976; 17,600 tons; 537 feet long; 75 feet at beam; 796 passengers; crew of 350; cruising speed of 18.5 knots; 8 passenger decks.

One of two sister ships especially designed for short, warm-weather cruises and high passenger capacity, the *Countess* was christened in San Juan in August 1976 by Janet Armstrong, wife of former U.S. astronaut Neil Armstrong, who was the first man to walk upon the moon. Although all Cunard vessels have been christened by prominent women, most of the ships extended the honor to British subjects and members of the royal family. The decision to invite Mrs. Armstrong was prompted by America's 1976 bicentennial celebration and was in keeping with the contemporary concept of the vessel and the astro-theme interior. Not to mention the fact that Cunard predicted (accurately) that the majority of *Countess* passengers would be Americans. Huge photos taken from space decorate the Splashdown Bar on Sun Deck (adjacent to the swimming pool), as well as other sections. (At least two of these photos were taken by Neil Armstrong.) The ship also has the Gemini Dining Room; Nova Suite, a theater/conference center; Galaxy Lounge and Club Aquarius; and Starlight Lounge, which is adjacent to the casino.

Like the *Princess*, the *Countess* has 259 outside and 121 inside cabins, all with private facilities and all very small. The beds fold over to make sofas by day, but this doesn't help the lack of space very much. I found the cabins very plastic and prefab, so be rather careful about slamming dresser drawers and such, or you may jolt your next door neighbor right out of bed (this happened to me)! However, the deluxe cabins have now been fitted with twin beds that make up into a huge king-size version wonderful! But there is plenty of public space, both in the lounges and on deck. In addition to using the swimming pool/Splashdown Bar area on Sun Deck, you can shape up at the putting green/driving range and on the paddle tennis court.

The calls for the two seatings in the dining room are harbingers of food that could be improved. Expect to have one Medieval night. The English breakfasts include kippered herrings, Nova Scotia salmon, steamed finnan haddie, and even French onion soup—a quick antidote for the morning after. Or you can breakfast alfresco at the charming cafe on Five Deck, which also serves hamburgers at lunchtime. The food is generally below par, no matter how often passengers complain about it.

The indoor/outdoor theater-in-the-round-plus-disco is located in the nightclub area. This is also where the captain holds his Welcome Aboard party and the setting is very impressive. The pool area features a Jacuzzi whirlpool and there is a gymnasium aboard. The Milky Way video arcade is for the youth (but expect to find parents there, too). The Meridian restaurant is lovely in subtle beige and complementary colors. The ship also offers a Vitality Shipshape health and fitness program. I also like the Cinema/meeting room, which can be expanded to include the Potpourri Room for larger conventions/seminars.

In 1995, Cunard Countess *cruises year-round on seven-day alternating weekly Caribbean voyages from her home port of San Juan. The 7-Plus schedule includes port calls in St. Maarten, Guadeloupe, Grenada, St. Lucia, St. Kitts, St. Thomas. The Caribbean Capitals schedule features visits to Tortola, Antigua, Martinique, Barbados and St. Thomas. Cunard Countess' per person, per diem begins around $170.*

AUTHOR TIP

Photocopy your *passport* and stash the copy separately so you can re-enter the U.S. easily if the document is lost. Also copy social security number, driver's licence and Medicaid/Insurance card and keep multiple copies in your luggage.

★★★

CUNARD PRINCESS

Cunard Line; Bahamian registry, British officers and international crew; built in Denmark and outfitted in Italy; christened in March 1977; 17,600 tons; 537 feet long; 75 feet at beam; 802 passengers; crew of 370; cruising speed of 18.5 knots; 8 passenger decks.

The *Cunard Princess* had the distinction of being the first passenger vessel ever christened in New York harbor. The late Princess Grace of Monaco did the honors in 1977, and a lovely portrait of the former actress hangs in the main stairwell of the vessel. The *Princess* is identical to the *Countess*, with private facilities in all 259 outside and 121 inside cabins. Be careful about engaging in loud conversations or slamming drawers in your cabin, as everything can be heard next door (see *Cunard Countess*)! Your sleeping quarters become sitting rooms by day, with beds that make up into sofas, but as on the *Countess* you won't want to spend much time here since the spaces are rather small. There are some nice outside deluxe cabins, with bathtubs, color TVs that receive films, and side-by-side twin beds that can with a little imagination be considered king-size! They are excellent value and definitely for those passengers who enjoy being alone!

Passengers aboard the *Princess* are now well acquainted with an extensive refit that included a new indoor/outdoor center, refurbished cabins, Jacuzzis up by the pool, redecorated Meridien restaurant, Outrigger cafe (for buffet breakfasts and lunches) and Topsail lounge. The casino was enlarged behind the Indoor/Outdoor cafe, and the shopping arcade was improved although the goods in the shops were not. (Can you believe I couldn't find anything to buy!) The theater was refurbished and is located just behind the Outrigger and between the card rooms. There are two seatings in the attractive restaurant, and the food is the same as aboard Countess, below par.

The atmosphere on board *Cunard Princess* seems to be far friendlier than her sister ship, primarily because her Bahamian flag has allowed management to staff the vessel as it feels best. There are several Costa Ricans among the crew, who are like Filipinos and Indonesians in their helpful and caring attitude. Unfortunately, many of the staff who ran the vessel so well are no longer on board, having been promoted to loftier positions.

Having sailed all over the map looking for cruise passengers, Cunard Princess *is now stationed in Europe, where we hope she will find a deserved happy home. From mid-November to mid-March, she sails along the Canary Islands on ten-day cruises round trip from Malaga to Tangier, Lanzarote, Las Palmas, Santa Cruz de Tenerife, La Palma, Funchal and Gibraltar. From May through October, Cunard Princess cruises on alternating 10- and 11-day itineraries. The Egypt/Israel schedule between Venice and Athens includes visits to Katakolon, Alexandria, Ashdod, Limassol, Rhodes, Bodrum and Kos; the alternating program between Athens and Venice includes port calls in Mitilini, Istanbul, Kusadasi, Patmos, Rhodes, Mykonos, Katakolon and Corfu. Per person, per diem begins around $170.*

AUTHOR TIP

When planning a *winter-time warm-water cruise,* purchase incidentals like sandals, bathing suits and cover-ups in summer—these are impossible to find in the winter and you'll pay premium prices aboard ship and in port.

AUTHOR TIP

If you're a fitness fanatic who hates to miss a good workout on your cruise vacation, ask your travel agent to find out: (1) Whether the ship has a jogging track all on a single deck, unimpeded by any stairs, handrails, etc., and whether the cruise line limits runners to specific hours (as some do, to prevent the thump-thump-thump of runners from waking those under the deck who prefer to sleep in; (2) Exactly what kind of equipment is available in the ship's health club; they range from quite lavish facilities with everything that's in your home gym to meager little rooms with a stationary bicycle or two.

★★★★

DREAMWARD/WINDWARD

Norwegian Cruise Line; Bahamas registry and international crew;sister ships built in Chantiers del Atlantique, St. Nazaire, France and launched 1992 (Dreamward) and 1993 (Windward); 41,000 tons; 624 feet long; 94 feet at beam; 1,246 passengers; crew of 482; 10 decks.

Norwegian Cruise Line's new identical sister ships, the *Dreamward* and *Windward*, are wonderful entries into the mid-priced range of vessels plying the Caribbean, Alaska and Bermuda. Unique public room and deck design, quality fabrics and materials (such as fine wood and marble), and abundant facilities for sports and fitness buffs ensure these vessels will be very, very popular with passengers seeking quality ships at moderate cost. The atmosphere on board is lively and fun, but you won't find slot machines in public areas and the hard-partying crowd that frequents many Caribbean vessels. And, while there are plenty of facilities for sports and entertainment of all kinds, there are relaxing lounges for quiet conversation.

There is a light, spacious ambience in public rooms created by floor to ceiling windows, pale aqua, blue and peach decor, mirrors and high ceilings. Designed by Bjorn Storbatten, who also planned Seabourn's vessels and the *Royal Viking Queen*, the two ships boast a distinctive terraced design that provides a sense of roominess in public areas and deck space. The upper decks cascade down (both forward and aft) offering unobstructed views from dining rooms, lounges and the midships pool area. The use of pale colors, mirrors and an impressive collection of modern art speak of tasteful interior design.

The *Dreamward* and *Windward* have several unique features. There are four dining rooms (assignments based on cabin location) ranging in capacity from 76 to 282 passengers, which lends an uncrowded atmosphere to each. My favorites are the Terraces Dining Room, located on International Deck, and Sun Terraces Dining Rooms on Sun Deck. Both are tiered, extend the width of the vessel with floor to ceiling windows overlooking the sea and offer above average space between tables. The Four Seasons Dining Room is decorated in soft peach and blue, with pink marble and brass finishing. The Cafe, the only restaurant not open for dinner, has a clubby ambience, and is also used for wine tastings and afternoon tea.

Public rooms have a marvelous flow, and there are ample lounges with different ambience to please everyone's taste. The 635-seat Stardust Lounge, in a lavender and coral color scheme, is the setting of the musical "George M!" and Sea Legs Circus at Sea on the *Windward.* The Observatory Lounge on Sports Deck is circular and offers panoramic views by day and serves as a disco at night. The most distinctive lounge is the Sports Bar and Grill, decorated with sports memorabilia, where passengers watch live ESPN, NBA and NFL games from a bank of televisions. While not a sports fan, even I found it fun and lively.

Both vessels cater to families with children during the summer and facilities include separate clubs, one for teenagers and another for youngsters, both supervised with ship's staff.

The *Dreamward* and *Windward* have two outdoor pools: one is midships with terraced teak levels of chaise lounge seatings where a lively atmosphere prevails during the day and calypso bands entertain. A more tranquil setting is found at the smaller pool aft on International Deck. In keeping with Norwegian Cruise Line's Athlete's Fleet theme, there is a full basketball court (also used for volleyball games), golf driving range and large gym, complete with free and standing weights, separate mirrored aerobics room and massage facilities.

Cabins are lovely; all have separate seating areas, twin or queen beds, wood dressers and counters, color television for closed circuit movie viewing. The majority are 160 square feet, some with floor to ceiling windows, others with large picture windows or portholes. Pale fabrics and the separate sitting area give a sense of roominess. Bathrooms have hair dryers, all but the top category are shower only, but there is virtually no vanity space for storing toiletries. Bathrooms and closets are very tiny, and two people may find storing clothing for a week quite a creative endeavor.

Passengers selecting a cabin on Promenade Deck should be aware that the ship's full length jogging track is located here, which may disturb sleep in the morning; Category 4 staterooms located midships on Norway deck have obstructed views of lifeboats.

During the winter, the Windward *sails from San Juan on seven-day alternating weekly itineraries: Barbados, Martinique, St. Maarten, Antigua, St. Thomas. The second week she sails to Aruba, Curacao, Tortola/Virgin Gorda, St. John and St. Thomas. From May through September, a one-week Alaska itinerary is planned. The* Dreamward *cruises in the Caribbean in 1995 from Ft. Lauderdale, on a one-week schedule that includes Grand Cayman, Playa del Carmen, Cozumel, Cancun and NCL's private Bahamas Island. From May through October, a series of one-week Bermuda sailings from New York are scheduled. Per person, per diam rates range from $185 to $485. These are very good ships in the mid-price range, especially with NCL's discounts*

⚓⚓⚓⚓⚓+

DELTA QUEEN

Delta Queen Steamboat Company; American crew and registry; built in 1926; most recently refurbished 1986; 1650 tons; 285 feet long; 58 feet at beam; 176 passengers; crew of 74; 12 miles per hour maximum speed; 4 passenger decks; listed in the National Register of Historic Places.

Prior to becoming one of two official steamboats of the Louisiana World Exposition a few years ago, the *Delta Queen* had an interior facelift that made 14 new deluxe staterooms and two superior staterooms on Cabin Deck. The spacious new accommodations are all outside, with large picture windows, and furnished with Governor Winthrop desks, Chippendale armchairs and Goddard chests. Cotton-sateen drapes blend with the emerald green or spiced rose Saxony carpeting. The windows have stained glass inserts and the mirrors are of beveled glass. There are Stobard prints of great steamboats of the past on the walls, and brass headboards with porcelain spinnings.

The Orleans Room, the dining and entertainment area aboard the old *Queen*, has also been refurbished. Old New Orleans brass finials support silkscreened linen draperies, and the dining chairs are upholstered in a margaux-colored velvet. The Siamese bark floor, known as ironwood for its strength and durability, has been polished and returned to its natural color.

The Forward Cabin and Texas lounges were refurbished a few years ago, and the air conditioning throughout was upgraded to compensate for those lazy, hazy summer days along the river.

With so much history and with a cozy passenger capacity, the *Delta Queen* is an intimate paddle wheeler. Not many minutes will pass by after you board before old friends are reacquainted and new ones made.

Since the *Delta Queen* began steamboating life on the rivers of America in 1927, this carefully preserved and beloved antique entered into the National Register of Historic Places in 1970, has cruised more than 30,000 miles annually, and has visited more than 14 states from her home port in New Orleans. While watching the banks drift by is still the favored pastime, passengers can also enjoy spontaneous sing-alongs, kite flying over the paddlewheel, calliope playing contests, locking through on the Upper Mississippi and Ohio rivers, first run films in the lounge, lectures by staff members and visiting guests on river history and commerce, and boat tours.

The Delta Queen *sails from New Orleans, Cincinnati, St. Louis, Pittsburgh, Memphis and St. Paul on 3- to 12-night cruises along the Mississippi and Ohio rivers. The cruises emphasize a Heart of Dixie, Show Me Showboatin', Kentucky Derby, Ohio Valley, Steamboatin Sampler, White Lightning, Yankee Steamer, Frontier Adventure, Mississippi Explorer, Great Steamboat Race, New Orleans Express and Heart of America. Per person, per diam rates range from $250–$590, but discounts are available.*

ECSTASY

(See Fantasy)

AUTHOR TIP

Do anything possible to avoid clearing *U.S. Immigrations and Customs in Miami* when you must also make a connecting flight. The lines are impossibly long and slow, you must dash to another ticket counter—which frequently seems about five miles away—to re-check your suitcases for the domestic flight. And, if you can't run fast enough, this airport is the pits when hanging out for the next available flight.

AUTHOR TIP

Ever wonder about the quantities of food and materials necessary for supplying cruise vessels? Here are a few figures from Royal Caribbean Cruise Line, which operates a fleet of nine ships: the company purchases over 1 million rolls of toilet paper, enough to encircle the globe; in one year the company serves 224,000 gallons of ice cream, 40,000 gallons of syrup, 16 million eggs, 800 tons of beef steak, sells 800,000 T-shirts and bakes 27,000 anniversary cakes.

⚓⚓⚓⚓⚓

EXPLORER

Abercrombie & Kent; Liberian registry; European officers and international crew; built in Finland in 1969 as *Lindblad Explorer*, refitted in 1985 as *Society Explorer* and refurbished in 1992; 2398 tons; 238 feet long; 45 feet at beam; cruising speed of 13 knots; 96 passengers; crew of 60; 6 passenger decks; 8000 mile cruising range.

The *Explorer* has long been famous as an expedition vessel, transporting passengers to the world's most remote regions first as the *Lindblad Explorer* and later, the *Society Explorer*, of the now-defunct Society Expeditions Cruises. Abercrombie & Kent invested $1 million in refurbishment, redecoration and repair on all areas of the vessel, from the superstructure to passenger cabins and crew areas and relaunched her in 1992.

The ship has 50 outside cabins with two lower beds and private facilities. Staterooms are small but adequate and nicely redecorated by Abercrombie & Kent. In addition to the single-seating dining room, the ship has a gymnasium and ample lounge areas. Don't pack an extensive wardrobe as space is limited and life on board quite casual and family-like. Expect to have your smallest wish delivered. Fellow passengers are flexible and eager to gain in-depth knowledge of the most exotic and far flung places on earth, and a genuine camaraderie develops on these exciting excursions. The ship's small size permits staff to be flexible enough to concoct a hot-chocolate-and-whipped-cream (and rum, if desired) drink and serve it out on deck so passengers need not sacrifice the scenery to have a drink.

Explorer *cruises in Antarctica from November through March on voyages ranging from 15 to 23 days in duration. Lecturers include scientists involved in research projects, including geologists, marine biologists, ornithologists, geopolitical historians, glaciologists and veteran polar explorers. The vessel's laboratory is always the busiest place aboard! In 1995, South Pacific cruises are planned during August and September visiting ports in Melanesia and Polynesia, as well as a voyage from Tahiti to Easter Island, with port calls in the Austral and Marotiri Islands and Pitcairn .*

★★★

FAIR PRINCESS

Princess Cruises; Liberian registry; Italian officers and European crew; originally built as *Fairsea* in 1971; renamed by Princess Cruises in 1988 and refurbished in 1989; 25,000 tons; 608 feet long; 80 feet at beam; 890 passengers; crew of 430 cruising speed of 19 knots; 11 passenger decks.

Fair Princess, formerly operated by Sitmar Cruises in North American waters, was acquired by Princess Cruises in 1988 when Princess Cruises bought Sitmar. It has a homey and friendly reputation and a loyal following. Princess spent considerable millions redecorating the ship, using the same design firm that was responsible for the ship line's new *Star Princess.*

The public areas received special attention, including the nightclubs and the South Pacific and Caribbean lounges, where new sound and lighting systems were added. New furniture and drapes are featured in the dining rooms, Grosvenor/Lancaster, and the shopping areas were remodeled to reflect the architectural and design features. Cabins also received attention and were rewired with 110 volt current to allow for the use of passengers hair dryers and other small appliances (formerly, one was obliged to visit the hair dryer room on each deck). Computer and satellite systems were also added on board to offer passengers more options on the televisions in the four suites and 26 mini-suites.

Of the total 503 cabins, there are 238 outside and 235, inside a high ratio of inside cabins which reflects the age of these vessels (originally built in 1956 by the famous John Brown shipyard on the River Clyde in Scotland). In addition to a library, casino, lounges and three outdoor swimming pools, each vessel boasts a youth center and the popular pizzeria, where authentic Italian chefs tempt passengers of all ages. These have become family-oriented vessels and children have a wonderful time.

During the summer season, Fair Princess *can be found in Alaskan waters offering one-week cruises between Vancouver and Whittier (for Anchorage); the ship spends the winter on the Mexican Riviera, sailing round trip from Los Angeles on 7- and 10-day cruises to Cabo San Lucas, Mazatlan, and Puerto Vallarta, with Zihuatanejo/Ixtapa and Acapulco added on the longer voyages. The average per person, per diem is $200 including airfare.*

★★★★

FANTASY/FASCINATION/ECSTASY/SENSATION

Carnival Cruise Lines; Bahamian registry and international crew; designed and built in Kvaerner-Masa Shipyard, Helsinki, Finland and launched 1990s (*Fantasy*), 1991 (*Ecstasy*), 1993 (*Sensation*) and 1994 (*Fascination*); 70,367 tons; 855 feet long; 104 feet at beam; 2040-2600 passengers; crew of 920; cruising speed of 21 knots; 9 passenger decks.

When Carnival Cruise Lines launched *Fantasy* in the 1990s, the first in a series of 70,367-ton ships, the formula proved so successful that these behemoths roll out of Finland's Kvaerner-Masa Shipyard on an average of one per year (*Imagination* and a sixth unnamed ship will arrive in 1995 and 1996 respectively). Except for individual "theme" decor, all are identical, and have proved so successful in making Carnival the largest (and most profitable) cruise line in the world—in 1994, the company reached the one million passenger mark, roughly one-fifth of all cruise passengers in the world.

Fantasy, *Fascination Sensation* and *Ecstasy* have been designed by Carnival's own Joe Farkis, and the interiors are in themselves fantastic, ecstatic and sensational! I had the good fortune to sail with Joe aboard the new *Fascination* this year and he termed the outrageous decor of these ships "entertainment architecture." In fact, sailing aboard this new megaliner was like having one big fraternity party, dining at Planet Hollywood, strolling the Galleria Shopping Mall and staying in a glitzy Atlantic City casino hotel all rolled into one. Expect nonstop action, late night antics, colorful boozy concoctions with umbrellas that could knock out an elephant, miles of blinking lights, hot colors and more facilities than are found in many medium-size cities and you have the "Fun Ship" experience. There really is something for everyone (except those who seek a tranquil milieu), and I found eighty-something folks cavorting with their grandchildren, singles on the prowl and married folks of all ages.

Some 30 percent of Carnival's passengers are under age 35, many first timers lured by perky Kathy Lee's constant presence on television. Carnival's per person, per diem averages $120–$145 (factoring in Super Saver advance purchase discounts), a bargain so many middle-Americans can't resist.

Not only are these 2040-passenger ships enormous to see, but everything inside is larger than life. A six-deck-high atrium is central to each ship and there are theme bars spread throughout. Hollywood is the theme of the new Sensation, with bars appropriately named Bogey's Cafe, Puttin' On The Ritz, Beverly Hills, Coconut Grove and Passage To India (on Fantasy, they're called Cats nightclub, Cleopatra's Bar, etc.). You'll find the largest casino and spa/fitness centers on the high seas—12,000 square foot Nautica Spas have no less than six treadmills, a separate jogging track, huge aerobics studio and every sort of massage therapy known to mankind.

Two dining rooms hold around 650 passengers each in two seatings and boast dramatic entrances and sea views. Cuisine was very mediocre on my cruise, so I stuck to the spa menus for food that never disappointed. In keeping with the needs of today's younger passengers, menus have been devised that promise more health-conscious meals and circular salad bars. Cabins aboard these ships are far more spacious than on other mass market vessels (averaging 190 square feet), and suites boast plenty of space plus whirlpools. Cabins have TVs, as well as wall safes (so sensible, because the boxes in the purser's office are a great walking distance!).

Carnival carries around 86,000 children each year, and there are few vessels better equipped to handle kids of all ages. "Camp Carnival" employs 46 permanent child counselors fleet-wide who arrange morning to night activities in four age categories: toddlers (2-4); Juniors (5-8); Intermediate (9-13) and teens (14-17). Facilities include playrooms, video arcades, children's wading pools, 15-foot high, 114-foot long water slides and teen clubs.

No matter which vessel you choose, be prepared for non-stop shipboard activities designed for nearly everyone. For the fitness oriented, there are classes for all age groups in aerobics and calisthenics plus group walking. You'll find a pillow fighting contest, a sex, love & romance trivia quiz, a grandma's and grandpa's party and the more traditional pasttimes of bingo, trapshooting, limbo contests and afternoon tea. On these ships, the slot machines are operative from 8:00 a.m. to "whenever" while the library is open from 2:00 to 3:00 p.m.

We've included a recipe for a Carnival cocktail for those who want to get in the mood before departure:

"Especiales Fiesta Marina"
Ingredients:
l oz. Vodka
l l/2 oz. white 80 proof rum
1/4 oz. Apricot Brandy
1/4 oz. Amaretto
6 oz. Fruit Punch

Fill hurricane (or very large) glass with ice, blend all ingredients together in a mixing cup, pour over ice. Little papumbrella is optional.

The Fantasy *is popular with 3- and 4-day Bahamas market from Port Canaveral;* Ecstasy *sails from Miami on three-day Bahamas and four-day Key West/Cozumel sailing;* Sensation *sails seven-day alternating Eastern and Western Caribbean cruises from Miami and* Fascination *is based in San Juan on seven-day Southern Caribbean itineraries. Average per person per diem rates range from $120 to $145 with Super Saver discounts.*

AUTHOR TIP

Here are a few home remedies for those who suffer from *mal de mer.* First, realize that it is often psychological, especially with first-time cruisers. An executive of Holland America said he's seen people getting sick waiting in line on the pier before they even embark! An ex-Navy officer now with Fielding advises sitting on the top deck and staring at the horizon if you feel ill. He also recommends fresh air, munching on soda crackers and sipping a little water; avoid alcohol and greasy food. Fresh air can make all the difference. And, common sense prevails—the oceans of the world are where you are most likely to experience some discomfort. The Baltic and North Sea can also be rough (many of the passenger/ferry vessels sailing along the coast of Norway have velcro under plates in the dining room; chairs are chained to tables!). You are least likely to experience any motion in the Caribbean aboard 400-passenger or above capacity.

FASCINATION

(See Fantasy)

AUTHOR TIP

When *purchasing luggage*, the most important criteria is wheels—trying to carry a heavy pullman plus carry-on and duty-free purchases through airports is torture. And, since all bags look alike these days, wrapping a band of brightly-colored tape around the suitcase handle helps identify it quickly on the carousel.

AUTHOR TIP

When *leaving port*, don't stand forward and topside anywhere near the funnel—and ship's horn. If you survive the blast, you know your ticker is in excellent shape.

★★★

FESTIVALE

Carnival Cruise Line; Bahamian registry, Italian officers, and international crew; originally built in 1961 and formerly named the S.A. *Vaal*; refurbished in 1978 and launched as the *Festivale*; 38,175 tons; 760 feet long; 90 feet at beam; 1146 passengers; crew of 612; cruising speed of 22 knots; 9 passenger decks.

When Carnival Cruise Lines bought the S.A. Vaal, which had transported passengers between Southampton and South Africa, she became the third and largest of the fleet. The 38,000-ton vessel was transformed into a Caribbean cruiser through a $30 million refit in a Japanese shipyard under the direction of architect Joe Farkis. The vessel entered Caribbean service in 1978 and, at the time, was both the largest and fastest vessel sailing weekly from Miami.

No doubt due to the lucrative South Africa trade, the *Festivale* boasts a top deck of some splendid old-world cabins with full bathrooms, sitting areas and some 10 with verandas. The remaining 272 outside and 309 inside cabins are located on Empress, Upper, Main and Riviera decks and are more spacious than average on the Caribbean run but less than elegant.

The *Festivale* has two outdoor pools for adults and a wading pool for children. She also has a children's playroom, health/massage center, Fanta-Z discotheque, Le Cabaret nightclub, Carnivale lounge and bar, Tradewinds Club, Copacabana Lounge and, of course, the Glasslight Club Casino and Saloon located smack center on Promenade Deck. Don't miss it, folks this is Carnival's profit center! The unwindowed Continental restaurant is located down on Main Deck and seats 700 people in each of two meal services.

The Festivale *sails from San Juan to St. Thomas, St. Maarten, Barbados, Dominica and Martinique and the first Carnival vessel to offer passengers four port calls. Full sea days are Wednesday and Saturday. Cruise rates include free round-trip air fare from more than 95 continental U.S. cities to San Juan. Pre- and post-cruise packages are available at the El San Juan Hotel (boasting one of the largest casinos in the Caribbean) or the Clarion Hotel & Casino. Average per person, per diem rates range from $120 to $145 with Super Saver discounts.*

N/R
GOLDEN PRINCESS

Princess Cruises; Bahamian registry; European officers and international crew; built at Wartsila Shipyard, Helsinki, Finland, in 1973 as *Royal Viking Sky*, stretched with a 93-foot midsection from 1981-83, refurbished 1991, 1993; 28,000 tons; 674 feet; 83 at beam; 830 passengers; crew of 410; cruising speed of 21 knots; 8 passenger decks.

In June, 1993, Princess Cruises added the *Golden Princess* to its fleet to replace the retiring *Dawn Princess.* She is on long-term charter from Birka Lines, where she sailed as the *Birka Queen* in Europe; originally built by Royal Viking Line in 1973, she had an illustrious life as the *Royal Viking Sky*, one of the more elegant vessels of her day. I have not sailed aboard the ship since she entered service with Princess Cruises, but assume she retains many of the aristocratic appointments and charm of her glorious past.

Public rooms on *Golden Princess* include the Observatory Lounge on Sun Deck, where early risers get the best view of arrival in port; Venus Lounge, where nightly cabaret and dancing is featured; the 600-passenger Stardust Lounge, the main showroom for nightclub acts; a late night disco and large casino. Seven Seas Dining Room, with large picture windows, has two-seating dining and casual breakfast and lunch can be found at the outdoor Pool and Deck buffet.

The 830-passenger ship's fitness facilities include a full-size basketball court, paddle tennis court, golf driving range and fitness center with Lifecycles, rowers, steps and free weights. Children will find a video arcade and Kids' Korner playroom.

By today's standards, the *Golden Princess* staterooms are large: 289 outside cabins are 168 square feet, and deluxe cabins are 240 square feet. Most have bathtubs, all have spacious closets and color television.

In 1995, Golden Princess *will sail on seven-day Mexico cruises from Los Angeles, with port calls in Puerto Vallarta, Zihuatanejo/ Ixtapa; Acapulco; Mazatlan and Cabo San Lucas. She will summer in Alaska on 7-day cruises sailing round-trip from Vancouver. The average per person, per diem is $200 including airfare.*

★★★

HOLIDAY

Carnival Cruise Lines; Bahamian registry; Italian officers and international crew; built in Aalborg, Denmark, for Carnival and entered Caribbean service July 13, 1985; 46,052 tons; 728 feet long; 92 feet at beam; 1452 passengers; crew of 660; cruising speed of 21 knots; 9 passenger decks.

The *Holiday* was the first of three superliners constructed for Carnival Cruise Lines in Scandinavia. When all three (*Holiday*, *Jubilee*, *Celebration*) were in place at the end of 1987, Carnival became the largest of the worldwide cruise lines (at least for a while) and boasted over a half million annual passengers. The *Holiday* is a definite departure in design attitude and onboard atmosphere for Carnival, and the vessel presents a new image for the rest of the Carnival fleet.

Cabins are more or less the same, however, with more spaciousness than usual in the standard categories and all L-shaped twin configuration convertible to togetherness sleeping arrangements. There are 10 veranda suites that feature bathtub Jacuzzis; 431 outside twins and 252 inside twins. There are six outside and 27 inside upper/lower berth cabins.

One startling design departure for Carnival on the *Holiday* is formal meal service, featuring two separate windowed (at last!) restaurants, the Seven Seas and the Four Winds. Both are located on America Deck but reachable by separate stairwells. Both are very attractive, with tables for eight, six, four and (a very few) two dressed in pink. Chairs in the Four Winds are upholstered in a copper-colored, basket weave velvet pattern, those in the Seven Seas are in burgundy velvet. The decor certainly enhances the setting, but meal presentation needs a lot of work. The Seven Seas restaurant is also the site of the gala Midnight Buffet.

My favorite room on board the *Holiday* is the Carnegie Library, which has been endowed with a classical decor and really does have some books. Large glass doors can enclose the space during the day for quietude or private parties; in the evening, music from Rick's American Cafe across the corridor turns the library into a pleasant cocktail lounge, the only intimate space aboard. Rick's is a 90-seat piano bar (passengers are encouraged to pretend they are in Casablanca) connected to the casino by a spiral red staircase. Of course.

The Gaming Club casino seats 250 and is supposed to be the largest afloat (at this time). There are 21 blackjack and two roulette tables, three for craps, and a wheel of fortune. Add to this more than 100 electronic slot machines. Starboard of the casino is the Bus Stop cafe, through which the 1:30 a.m. mini-buffet is served. It is a renovated 1930s vintage bus, with a bar/cafe adjacent to satisfy the late night crowd.

Forward of Bus Stop is Times Square, a full-width-of-the-ship area featuring sculptured figures in stainless steel and acrylic to represent performing artists. Times Square flows into the top section of the enormous Americana Lounge, which spans two decks and accommodates more than 900 passengers. With a stars-and-stripes motif, this lounge is the site of full theatrical and cabaret presentations.

Broadway is another enclosed promenade space with a simulated brick sidewalk that takes passengers into the Bus Stop area. Broadway also has Cappucino's, where special coffees and sweets can be bought. Behind the coffee house on port side is the Tahiti lounge, decorated in Polynesian style. The 78 hand-carved mahogany totems that line the walls were, however, carved by a Bahamian named Henry Fernander. The room also serves as a small meeting area, and is equipped with a movie screen concealed in the ceiling.

Reflections Disco functions as a meeting room by day and a swinging disco place at night. The aft Blue Lagoon lounge is the second showroom aboard the *Holiday* and features a midnight special every evening, as well as cocktails and dancing before and after dinner. The decor of the room suggests an undersea grotto and is obviously an acquired taste. Directly above Promenade Deck is the Wharf bar and grill, which serves buffet breakfast and lunch. It happens to be the mechanical room of the vessel, but ducts and such are concealed behind a tugboat called Sweetness and the usual paraphernalia one expects on a wharf.

Forward of the two restaurants, Carnegie Library and Rick's Cafe on America Deck, is Union Square another enclosed promenade with seats of rattan on the port side, easy chairs on the starboard. The Galleria shops adjacent offer gifts and sundry items, a boutique and duty-free liquor store. Artworks throughout the vessel are indicative of the media in which Americans are working. A six-foot fountain created by San Francisco artist Helen Webber, with 400 sculptured tiles and a sea fantasy theme, is located in the Purser's Lobby so passengers pass by at least twice per cruise.

The *Holiday* also has a children's playroom, a game room, a large health club with whirlpool, massage and gym on Veranda Deck and two adult swimming pools. On a hot day at sea, these pools are hardly adequate for the full passenger complement. It was people to people the last time I looked out at the very crowded pool aft on Lido Deck!

The Holiday *sails every Saturday at 4 p.m. from Miami for Sunday at sea, Monday at Cozumel/Playa del Carmen, Tuesday at sea, Wednesday at Grand Cayman, Thursday at Ocho Rios, Friday at sea, and return to Miami at 8 a.m. on Saturday. The itinerary may be reversed on certain sailings. Average per person, per diem rates range from $120–$145 with Super Saver discounts.*

★★★★★

HORIZON

Celebrity Cruises; Liberian registry; Greek officers; international crew; built in Papenburg, Germany, for delivery in May 1990s; 46,811 tons; 682 feet long; 95 feet at beam; 1354 passengers; crew of 642; cruising speed of 21.5 knots; 9 passenger decks.

The *Horizon* is a wonderful surprise, and Chandris was justly proud of its first new vessel in the Celebrity Cruises line! She is a beauty with her futuristic exterior and space-age smokestack emblazoned with the new Chandris logo, an X riding the waves. Indeed, the white and blue-hulled vessel has an outward character quite apart from the boxlike designs that seem to appear with such regularity these days. The *Horizon* is sleek and understated, a refreshing delight.

The interior of the vessel is also understated and in excellent taste. Four international design firms shared the responsibility for the interiors, including the famed husband-and-wife Katzourakis team of Greece, who must have conceived the Horizon Lobby (entry hall), as it reminds me of the Agora, the marketplace of Athens in classical times. The pastel colors were a bit of a shock at first sight, but one becomes quite enamored with this busy area, and the doric-style columns above add a certain stability and peace.

While the ship is fairly large and will most likely always be filled to capacity, there is plenty of space for everyone. Fantasy and Galaxy decks provide the public areas, although the America's Cup Club with panoramic views on Marina Deck seems to be the most popular preprandial meeting place. Fantasy Deck features the Zodiac Club/Gemini Disco aft, with the Casino Royal/Plaza Bar and Mall shops (where merchandise could be more worthy of the prices) midships, and the second tier of the Palladium Show Lounge forward. Along the Panorama Gallery on Fantasy Deck are display cases featuring reproductions of ancient Cycladian artifacts, no doubt, a Chandris family personal touch. Other artwork on the *Horizon* is contemporary, and complements very well the decor throughout the ship.

Galaxy Deck boasts the large Palladium show lounge forward, a cozy Rendezvous Lounge/piano bar midships (with a library and card room portside), and the Starlight restaurant where the menus are under the direction of noted French chef Michel Roux (who has earned a few Michelin stars from two restaurants in the London area). Food and service in the dining room are certainly well above cruise fare, and passengers do not seem to be streamlined through the two seatings. The menu and wine list offer plenty of variety, and compliments were heard all around.

The breakfast and luncheon buffets in the Coral Seas Cafe are also well presented (I was impressed that real china was utilized), and there were many fine comments about the plentiful supply of coffee and tea throughout the afternoon. In between meals, there are two lovely pools and plenty of lounge chairs on Marina Deck, as well as a whirlpool, jogging track, Fantasia (teen room), Olympic Health Club and small Mast bar up on Sun Deck. Children have their own playroom down on Florida Deck next to the Steiner beauty salon (where complimentary facials were offered on Friday). And if there is an organized tour of the Bridge, take it, it's quite unique, as the Captain likes to boast, with its fantastic four-color radar equipment and enclosed wings!

Cabins aboard *Horizon* are spacious and feature radio and TV (with feature films). There are 2 Presidential suites and 18 Horizon suites, 40 double-bed cabins, and 469 twins (all outside); inside cabins number 32 double-bed and 112 twins. There are also two cabins set aside for wheelchair passengers. The pastel colors in all accommodations are pleasant and restful. Cabin service is excellent, with European stewardesses in the higher categories. Fresh linens, ice and water need never be requested. Room service is also impressive and very swift.

During the summer season Horizon *is one of just four cruise ships allowed regular calls in Bermuda. From April through October, she sails every Saturday from New York to Hamilton. From November to April, Horizon is based in San Juan for one-week cruises every Saturday to Martinique, Barbados, Mayreau, Antigua and St. Thomas. Average per person, per diem rates are $275.*

N/R
INDEPENDENCE

American Hawaii Cruises; American registry and crew; originally built in the U.S. in 1951 and named the *Independence*; extensively refurbished in 1989; 30,090 tons; 682 feet long; 89 feet at beam; 800+ passengers; crew of 320; cruising speed of 20 knots; 9 passenger decks.

Former flagship of American Export Lines, the *Independence* was a three class vessel carrying some 1000 passengers across the Atlantic and on long cruises throughout the world. She was retired in 1967 when travel by ship became outmoded, and was laid up near Baltimore, Maryland. The vessel was purchased by Atlantic Far East Lines, a subsidiary of the C. Y. Tung group of Hong Kong in 1974 and placed into service as the *Oceanic Independence*. Five years later, the vessel was transferred to American Global Lines (another subsidiary of the C. Y. Tung group) and once again flew the U.S. flag by act of Congress. She began operating weekly cruises from Honolulu around the Hawaiian Islands on June 21, 1980. In the fall of 1994, American Hawaii's new parent company, Delta Queen Steamboat Company, will give this grand liner the facelift she deserves with a $28 million overall.

Many public areas, including the Independence Lounge, will be "opened up" to give passengers a better view of the sea and islands, creating an indoor-outdoor "Lanai" environment. The Sports Deck Solarium, which is currently the Fitness Center, will be converted into passenger suites.

Additional staterooms will be added on Boat Deck and Main Deck. All cabins will be redecorated with a Hawaiian motif. On Upper Deck, the buffet will be expanded, creating indoor-outdoor cooking and eating areas on the ship's fantail.

American Hawaii has recently added Kumus (Hawaiian teachers) to educate passengers about the culture and history of Hawaii. A "Kumu's Study," with historic artifacts, will be added off the central lounge.

The Honolulu-based Bishop Museum will create hands-on displays to be added in the lounge area. Large three-dimensional exhibits will allow passenger to learn about Hawaii through ancient games and arts and crafts displays. The centerpiece will be a three-dimensional map of the Hawaiian Islands chain—from sea floor to the top of the highest volcanic peak with moveable ship pieces.

The *Independence* has 20 suites (including a two-bedroom owner's suite), 27 deluxe cabins, 107 outside cabins with two lower beds, 8 outside with double beds, and 6 outside with upper/lower berths. There are 141 inside cabins with 2 lower beds, 17 inside with double beds, 60 inside doubles with upper/lower berths, and 11 inside singles with lower berths. All cabins have private facilities and are definitely larger than average for cruise space. Onboard facilities include two outdoor swimming pools, the Barefoot Bar overlooking the Sun Deck pool, and Latitude 20° with a glass wall over the Upper Deck pool. The Palms dining room, down on Aloha Deck, does not have sea views but is divided into smoking and non-smoking sections. What was once another dining room on Main Deck is now a conference center, booked in advance on many cruises for groups who wish to combine business with pleasure. Midships on Promenade Deck is the Independence Lounge, while the huge Pacific Showplace (for evening entertainment) and the Commodore's Terrace are aft. The Hunt breakfast is served on deck, and morning sherbet and afternoon tea are available in the Parisian-style Sidewalk Cafe on Upper Deck, which also houses shops and the children's playroom. A cinema is down on Coral Deck.

There is a popular Youth Recreation Center, with jukebox, dance floor and soda fountain aboard the vessel and there are excellent local shows of traditional Hawaiian music and song.

During the summer season, when a more youthful set of passengers is aboard, underwater sports are popular, and there are excellent scuba and snorkeling tours planned. All this, plus tax deductible seminars at sea make these cruises something to consider. The itinerary is so marvelous and the atmosphere so infectious that just about everyone ends up buying an Aloha shirt or a Muumuu, the native dress. American Hawaii has also added whale watching theme cruises during February and March and numerous music cruises. A new singles program is an added bonus—inside deluxe staterooms are offered for single occupancy for a $100 supplement.

The Independence *sails every Saturday at 9 p.m. from Aloha Tower in Honolulu, along with the* Constitution. *Sundays are spent at sea, cruising among the islands. On Monday at sunrise, the* Independence *arrives at Nawiliwili, Kauai; Tuesday is spent at Kona and Wednesday at Hilo, both on the big island of Hawaii; Thursday morning to Friday evening is at Kahului, Maui (everyone's favorite), and on Saturday morning the* Independence *sails in tandem with the* Constitution *back to Aloha Tower in Honolulu. Kids free (in same cabin with two full-fare adults) during the summer vacation months are standard American Hawaii Cruises offerings. Per person, per diem rates range from $145–$556.*

⚓⚓⚓⚓

ISLAND EXPLORER/SPICE ISLANDER

P & O Spice Island Cruises; Indonesian flag and crew; built in 1985; 859 tons; 130 and 120 feet long; 42 feet at beam; 35 and 40 passengers; crew of 25; cruising speed of 16 knots; 3 passenger decks.

P&O Spice Island Cruises is a meld of intriguing factors—former dive boats converted to comfortable passenger ships, the interest in eco-tourism that today sends people thousands of miles in search of meaningful natural adventures, a dash of entrepreneurial spirit and good government contacts.

The company's two 35-passenger expedition ships, *Spice Islander* and *Island Explorer*, both constructed in 1985, explore some of the most remote and intriguing islands of the more than 13,000 that comprise the Indonesian archipelago. They are the only vessels visiting islands still unspoiled by tourism and modern development. The result is a highly educational and rewarding glimpse of the exotic. In 1995, P&O Spice Island Cruises adds a third vessel, the 150-passenger *Sea Bali Dancer* (the former *Illyria*), offering three- and four-day cruises from Bali for those with time for only a glimpse of the exotic.

The ships sail on 7- and 14-day alternating itineraries to some 15 islands that are home to hundreds of different ethnic groups. Passengers discover colorful dances, ceremonies, religious events and animist ceremonies, the dragons of Komodo (large foul breathed monitor lizards that can reach 12 feet), snorkel in pristine coral reefs and climb extinct volcanoes. These are places impossible to explore on one's own, and few Westerners even know of this region, which boasts the last preserve of the Javan rhino, the Way Kambas elephant preserve and some of the best diving in the world.

You may be a bit disheartened when first viewing *Spice Islander* or *Island Explorer.* Tucked between rusting Chinese freighters in Jakarta's or Bali's harbor, the first impression is of a barge. While P&O's brochures call these "cruise ships," it is something of a misnomer. They are tough expedition vessels and resemble a cross between a car ferry and excursion boat.

Some 120 feet in length, these ships are small and squat. With a cruising capacity of only nine knots, there is a sideways rocking motion rather than the typical rolling most cruise passengers encounter. Be forewarned: you will feel plenty of motion when hitting swells or large waves; during my cruise aboard the *Island Explorer* we encountered a cyclone and were flipped from beds like a pancake. We traveled in December, however, not the best time for savoring this part of the world. From a weather standpoint, the best cruising time is April through June, September and October (I cruised during monsoon season!).

But once aboard, I discovered the compact ship worked beautifully for exploring these remote regions. The main lounge area is akin to your favorite uncle's living room. Large, lived-in, so, couches and chairs are amply scattered around. There is a feeling of clutter, with everything from spears to bongos tucked into every nook and cranny. The ship's library has a mixture of pulp paperbacks and scientific and cultural books on Indonesian arts, crafts, wildlife and culture.

The dining room, where all dine buffet style in a single seating, is comfortable with floor to ceiling windows, enhanced with carved motifs. Topside, the small sun deck, with comfortable folding deck chairs, affords great views of sunsets and the large aft deck is used for barbecues and diving platforms. While not haute cuisine, the quality of food was consistently good, with plenty of fresh fruit, hearty breakfasts and well- planned dinners. The last night, all stops are pulled when the Dutch/Indonesian ristaffel is prepared in a grand smorgasbord banquet.

On *Island Explorer* there are 18 cabins, including six suites. Standard cabins are utilitarian and sparsely furnished, a bit cramped for anyone over 5'll', but beds were quite comfortable. Showers are a daily reminder that one is not aboard a cruise ship—the trick of using one's hip to push the shower water tap is quickly passed on by crew and other passengers. In standard cabins, one of the two beds is a foldout couch and those who seek the comfort of a queen-size bed should book a suite.

The great enjoyment of the voyage was the camaraderie and shared experiences that are fostered aboard a small ship with high adventure each day. After a short hesitation, I learned to love the close atmosphere and after the first hour got to know my fellow passengers—we were instant friends. Fellow passengers were seekers of the exotic who included Americans, Australians, German, British and Dutch. Ages ranged from late twenties to seventies plus several young children. All were here for the experience, were educated and well traveled. There were no complaints about weather, food or even the horrendous seas we encountered.

The 32 Indonesian crew outnumbered passengers on my cruise and their enthusiasm and personal interest in the happiness of those sailing was evident throughout. Every request was executed with gusto; the crew speaks fluent English and learns your first name and favorite drink quickly. The crew is superlative in their genuine desire to make each cruise the best. Shore excursions were handled expertly, and special requests (such as diving from a specific reef) were easily arranged.

The real focus of a Spice Island cruise is the remarkable potpourri of exotic islands, each sporting unique flora and fauna and experiences that are as diverse as one will find anywhere on the globe.

But if I were to issue a warning, it would be to anticipate the onshore experience as both enlightening and at times disturbing. In Sumatra, we were invited into a home in the midst of preparation of a wedding, the proud parents carefully showing us gifts, the rooms lavishly decorated for the wedding night. A Chinese man read our fortunes in an ancient temple and we laughed and cheered as we raced each other while being transported by three-wheeled tri-shaws called beceks. We spent a day climbing Krakotoa, an extinct volcano, in the company of an eminent Indonesian volcanologist and botanist. But there was also the other side of Indonesia, which includes poverty and filth. The elephant preserve at Way Kambas may disturb some—it is a training center (really a reform school) for wayward elephants and treatment at times appeared brutal; don't expect a tranquil nature preserve. Bird sanctuaries are also smelly swamps.

This is a voyage for those who want to experience it all directly. The itineraries can be spur of the moment—bad weather, upcoming marriages, local festivals and an unscheduled eruption of a volcano can result in a change of course.

Spice Island Cruises offers a choice of itineraries: 7-day "Dance of Welcome" cruise from Kupang, with a new stop at Rote, a traditional center of palm culture; the 8-day "Sandalwood and Dragons" cruise from Lompok after a short flight from Bali and the 14-day "Ring of Fire" cruise sailing round-trip from Bali. In 1995, per person, double occupancy rates for a standard cabin with transfers begin at $2,400 for an 8-day cruise and $4,250 for a 14-day voyage. Pre- and post-cruise hotel nights are available at very reasonable cost.

Spice Island Cruises' exotic excursions are certainly not for everyone, especially those who seek the creature comforts of a modern cruise ship and limited exposure to exotic cultures. These tiny expedition vessels are modest but comfortable, and well suited for the exotic itineraries. The crew was outstanding, and the shared camaraderie of kindred explorers made the journey unforgettable.

★★★★

ISLAND PRINCESS/PACIFIC PRINCESS

Princess Cruises; British registry and crew (with Italian dining room personnel); sister ships built in West Germany and launched in 1970 (*Pacific Princess*) and 1972 (*Island Princess*); 20,000 tons; 553 feet long; 82 feet at beam; 610 passengers; crew of 350; cruising speed of 19 knots; 7 passenger decks.

The *Island* and *Pacific Princess* rank high in the most attractive cruise ship category; with the distinctive Princess Cruises logo atop their smokestacks, both are among the luxurious vessels in the P & O family. Although identical in design and ambience, they differ somewhat in decor. However, once you find your way around one of these *Princesses*, you'll feel right at home aboard the twin. You'll also be very pleased with your choice of vessels!

Although Princess has expanded its fleet in recent years with such glamorous attractions as *Royal Princess*, *Star Princess* and *Crown Princess* (not to forget *Regal Princess*, in the shipyard), many loyal passengers still prefer what they now consider the babies of the family; they love the intimacy of the smaller vessels and the fact that meeting and making new friends is so much easier here than on the 1200 to 1500-passenger newer ships. Both *Island Princess* and *Pacific Princess* are justly famous as they were featured in the Love Boat series, which is still enjoyed by millions of viewers worldwide (in syndication).

With a total of 13 different public rooms you feel the spaciousness aboard these vessels from the gracious Purser's Lobby, with its dramatic staircase and galley to the romantic Starlight Lounge in the forward section of Sun Deck. This lovely hideaway has wraparound windows that allow wonderful views of the sea and sky. On Riviera Deck the Carib/Pacific lounge, bar and club; the Princess Theater; and the Carousel lounge and bar offer a variety of entertainment. And if you're a night owl, the Skal Bar turns into a disco at midnight. For games and more serious pursuits, you can seek out the Bridge and International lounges or the library/writing room one deck below. Both vessels have the Coral Dining Room (located on Coral Deck) with two sittings for luncheon and dinner, and two swimming pools. The Crystal Pool on Sun Deck is the most glamorous, with its Sun Dome for inclement weather (of course, it is rarely needed).

Pacific Princess

Accommodations aboard both these *Princess* vessels are splendid. The deluxe suites are spacious and delightful. The sitting areas are perfect for private gatherings, and you can find large beds in cabins 346, 348, 349 and 350. The deluxe outside twin cabins are as large as minisuites, and the standard twin gains space by day with one bed that folds into the wall while the other becomes a sofa. The crew aboard both vessels is friendly, attractive and helpful; and the British officers are stunning in their short white uniforms and knee socks! In the dining room, the Italian chef and stewards dish up a cuisine that has both a fine reputation and sex appeal. Needless to say, the food is another outstanding feature on these two vessels, so plan to enjoy yourself and forget about calories.

Both ships offer Princess Cruises most exotic itineraries in 1995. From January through March, Pacific Princess *cruises the South Pacific and Far East; she then sails from Bangkok to Athens before commencing 12-day Mediterranean/Black Sea cruises from May through October.* Island Princess *visits the South Pacific, Australia and New Zealand from January and February, followed by Amazon cruises and a Buenos Aires to Barcelona voyage. From May through October, the ship cruises the Mediterranean with visits to North African ports. The average per person, per diem of both ships is $275 including airfare.*

★

JASON

Epirotiki Lines; Greek crew and registry; built in Italy in 1965; refurbished and launched as *Jason* in April 1968; 5250 tons; 346 feet long, 61 feet at beam; 268 passengers; crew of 112; cruising speed of 15 knots; 6 passenger decks.

The *Jason* has 134 cabins situated among four decks, and all but 30 have outside views. All have private facilities with stall showers. The only full baths found on the ship are in suites A1 through A6 on Apollo deck. The cabins, small but very pleasant, have fold-over sofa arrangements for day.

Large murals reminiscent of the island of Thira and curtain designs that feature shields of ancient Greek heroes make the rooms even more pleasant.

Up on Jupiter Deck an unusual fountain supplies fresh seawater to the Argo Pool, while the mosaic tabletops in the adjoining Argonaut Bar reflect the designs of ancient warrior shields. Below, in the Orpheus Nightclub (a disco after 10 p.m.), a life size bronze and copper figure of Orpheus plays his lyre. On Dionysos Deck (also called Main Deck), the Jason Bar stands out with its tapestry of Jason yoking the wild bulls in the sacred field of Ares, and the corridor to the Golden Fleece Lounge boasts a monumental brass sculpture, Sunburst, which is said to be the largest bronze work cast in Greece since the classical age.

The Jason *cruises from Piraeus. The vessel's most recent itinerary featured ports in Turkey, Egypt, and Israel, as well as the Greek Islands of Rhodes and Patmos. The ship can also be found on charter in the Caribbean during the winter season.*

AUTHOR TIP

If a major storm threatens your region and the cruise departs over a weekend, call your travel agent on Friday during business hours to get the cruise line's procedure on *cancelled or delayed flights* for air/sea passengers; also obtain the cruise company's weekend hotline number.

★★★

JUBILEE

Carnival Cruise Lines; Liberian registry; Italian officers and international crew; built in Malmo, Sweden, and entered service in July 1986; 48,000 tons; 733 feet long; 92 feet at beam; 1486 passengers; crew of 670; cruising speed of 21 knots; 9 passenger decks.

The *Jubilee* called at New York en route to homeport of Miami and made a terrific impression on all who stopped by to visit. For starters, the *Jubilee* completely dwarfed two other ships in port—the *Nordic Prince* and *Stella Solaris*—as the second of three superliners to join the Carnival fleet within an 18-month period. With the arrival of the *Celebration* in March 1987, all three superliner sister ships were in place for Carnival, and the ship line prepared its new generations of superliners *Fantasy* (which arrived in Miami in February 1990), *Ecstasy* (1991), and *Sensation* (late, 1993). Life keeps sailing ahead at this company!

The *Jubilee* is identical to the *Holiday* but rather more subdued and sophisticated in its interior. While the *Holiday* design jumps out and is "themed" to suggest throngs of people—Union Square, Broadway, Bus Stop, Times Square—and the *Jubilee* does have Trafalgar Square, Park Lane and Tivoli Square, the art work is not so three-dimensional and always getting in one's way. Colors are also better in most of the public areas.

Cabins are standardized and spacious for new construction in the 7-day market. Large picture windows dominate in the outside accommodations, and the L-shaped bed configuration can be changed in all cabins to simulate the king-size variety. Bathrooms are still small, but subdued tilework has been added, to give a more homey feeling. Ten suites on Veranda Deck have terraces and are attractively decorated with TV/bar console, walk-in closets with small safe, and bathtubs.

A small gymnasium/fitness center is also on Veranda Deck and overlooks a Lido Deck pool so watch out, girls! There are two pools on Lido Deck, with the air-conditioned Funnel Bar and Grill between. This is a most attractive room for buffet breakfasts, lunch and afternoon snacks, with tables for six on which there are posters of old liners and now extinct steamship companies. Funnels line the bulkheads and the whole area looks as though it works well.

The Burgundy and Bordeaux dining rooms on Atlantic Deck are joined by a common galley and replicas of the Holiday restaurants. Both are very attractive, with pink tablecloths, a raised center, some booths, and both round and rectangular tables. Carnival does not promise gourmet food, but is making an attempt to make dining more memorable. The dining room staff wears white gloves on special occasions, which is supposed to make it taste better!

Adjacent to the Burgundy dining room is Churchill's Library and the Speakeasy Lounge the most incongruous combination one can imagine, but it works in the evening because cocktail service is available in the library, away from the piano bar. Neither room is quite so attractive as respective counterparts on the *Holiday*. Forward is Trafalgar Square, the shopping area, children's video game room and the lower level of the large Atlantic Lounge.

Promenade Deck is total public space, with a children's pool aft (the children's playroom is one deck below). There are: Terraces in the Grove Lounge, with a dance floor that can become a raised stage; the Oz discotheque; Smuggler's Lounge, decorated with sidings from an old barn in Sweden; the Espresso's Cafe, where exotic coffee drinks can be purchased; the vast Sporting Club Casino; the Gazebo with bar; Tivoli Square and the upper section of the Atlantis Lounge.

The *Jubilee* was constructed of some 23 different prefabricated sections and boasts a massive red, white and blue winged stack. Interior architect Joe Farkis tried to create an overall feeling of nostalgia, and created many, many spaces in which 1500 to 1900 passengers can play. As one visitor said, "Carnival is not so much in the cruise business as in the vertical integration business." Whatever that means.

Jubilee *departs the west coast every Sunday afternoon for Puerto Vallarta, Mazatlan and Cabo San Lucas. Average per person, per diem rates range from $120 to $145 with Super Saver discounts.*

⚓⚓⚓⚓⚓

LE PONANT

Worldwide Travel & Cruise Associates; Matu registry; built in France, 1990; French officers and crew; 850 tons; 300 feet long; 39 feet at beam; 67 passengers; 30 crew; cruising speed 14 knots; 3 passenger decks.

I don't know a mizzen mast from a telephone pole, but I do recognize a gorgeous sailing vessel when I see one, and the three masted *Le Ponant* is sensational, and very French. Let's hit the language bit head on, for everyone asks about it up front. If you are a bit anxious, and wondering how, or even if you will communicate with your fellow French speaking passengers and staff read on. On my cruise, only eight out of 67 passengers were Americans. But not to worry unduly, for by the second day out there was a pretty good rapport. A language barrier is there, it does exist, and it must be addressed for any ship with a strong national and/or ethnic identification. Those who don't want to commingle simply don't, and that's OK. On *Le Ponant*, one cannot expect to plunk down next to an interesting looking person and carry on a sustained conversation—it just doesn't happen unless you're fluent in French. But those who stayed to themselves, and to their own language exclusively, missed out on a great multi-language experience. We eight Americans smiled a lot, and said "d'accord," from time to time, and disembarked having made some new friends. But it depends entirely on your attitude and flexibility. All announcements on the ship are made in both French and English, and every evening we were given an English briefing of the next day's activities by our young and energetic Social Director.

Zut alors! (the French say that a lot), imagine sailing on a cobalt Caribbean during breakfast, mooring near a tiny, quiet island for a morning swim and perhaps a walk on the beach, then back to the ship for lunch. When the wind snaps at these delicate sails, your eyes go up, and up to the top of the tallest mast, and it's rather like looking up into the vault of a towering cathedral. Built just outside of Paris in 1991, this 290-foot long beauty has a unique itinerary that appeals to travelers who have seen something of the Caribbean and are ready to explore more deeply, see different islands and new ports.

Some cabins are amazingly spacious for such a small ship. My stateroom, A-8, was a generous 160 square feet, with lots of shelf space and drawers. Check carefully before booking on Antigua deck since many cabins (at 140 square feet), are small and cramped. They have port holes overlooking the Promenade Deck, and the only access to the room is via a heavy outside sea door. All rooms have mini-bars, safes and twin beds that can be converted to queen. Hair dryers and hand-held showers should be standard on a ship of this calibre, and they weren't; bath towels could also be thicker. Moreover, cabin sanitation could be better—some litter on the cabin floor was there on embarkation, and still there at the end of the trip. And, there is no room service, not even a cup of coffee, before 8:00 a.m.

A small nook tucked behind the reception area houses a few bookshelves and a large TV set. There is another TV in the main lounge, a multipurpose room that is oddly and uncomfortably designed and doesn't lend itself to small groups for conversation. Decorated in pale blue and chrome, it is a series of four squares built into settees in the four corners of the room. A dance floor was never used on our trip, but people did use the aft deck for dancing on "Caribbean Night." A sports platform got a lot of use, for swimmers too lazy to board the tender for the beach. The supervision of watersports on Le Ponant is excellent, with knowledgeable and patient instructors. While the ship has a good supply of beach gear, snorkeling equipment needs to be replaced.

Cuisine is very good and very French. On this ship you gormandize, and holding back means one misses a lot of the total experience of the voyage. Al fresco lunches served on the deck were spectacular. Half the deck is protected from the wind and the sun. We always choose to sit outside, at tables set for six and eight. Chairs with bright aqua canvas backs, pink tablecloths, bottles of chilled rose wine and baskets of crusty, fresh-baked bread made the whole scene look a cover from *Gourmet* Magazine. Lunch was always a grand affair—one day it was a whole roasted baby lamb, on another, slices of tender beef from whole tenderloins or broiled salmon. When creme brulee is an everyday staple, it can spell deep trouble. And that's only lunch! Dinner is a sit-down affair in the dining salon, a room disappointingly dark and lifeless, badly lighted with a harsh glare that bounces from wood paneled walls. Louvered windows make the room feel "caged in," and chairs with chrome frames, again, harshly reflect light.

The brochure presents this ship as having just about the most elegant service afloat. But keep in mind one is aboard a sailboat, not a luxurious cruise ship—staff does not patrol the deck to see if you would like a towel or drink. Service staff is energetic and enthusiastic, are willing to do anything you request, but there is a lack of polish and finesse. Casualness goes with the territory, but it's worth your life to get a drink from the tiny lounge bar before lunch or dinner to avoid a long line. And, several people complained about having to stand in line for both breakfast and lunch. We stopped at Sandy Island, a tiny uninhabited dot near Cariacou, in the Grenadines. Our day and picnic lunch there should have been perfection, but weren't. The langouste was overcooked and tough, and another cruise ship off-loaded its passengers for the day, making this lovely scene overcrowded (surely our schedule and theirs was made in advance).

Le Ponant has a lot of motion, and while true sailors revel in the pitch and roll of the sea, some less hearty souls were uncomfortable. One windy day we were having lunch on deck and suddenly glasses, wine bottles and bread were flying around while napkins blew off into the sky. And, it was a strange feeling to be talking to someone across a table and suddenly see him slide across the deck in his chair mid-sentence (particularly when this fellow weighed around 250!). But those who adore sail don't mind this experience a bit.

Le Ponant *winters in the Caribbean, sailing from Guadeloupe on weekly alternating itineraries: the Northern route includes visits to St. Barts, the British Virgin Islands, Anguilla, St. Kitts and Nevis and the Southern cruise calls in Les Saintes, St. Lucia, Bequie, Mayero, Tobago, Cariacou and Martinique. Positioned in the Mediterranean during summer, the ship sails from Nice to tiny villages of Corsica, Sardinia and Elba. One-week Caribbean rates are around $2600 per person, double occupancy while Mediterranean cruises are in the $2200 range.*

AUTHOR TIP

Always carry *documents* in your handbag or suit jacket. One of us opted for a cute, small purse and put airline and cruise tickets in a small tote bag. Arrival at the hotel sans tote bag prompted a nail-biting dash back to Miami airport. A miracle did occur—someone found it lying on the floor next to the luggage carousel and turned it into lost and found. But this occurrence is rare.

AUTHOR TIP

If you can book early, the advance purchase deals are the best security in garnering a decent cabin and good price. But whether you are pursuing one of these programs, a published rate or an exclusive deal from your travel agent, always tally up the *real* cost. For example, does the reduced cruise fare include free airfare or a low-cost add-on? If the airfare isn't included your final vacation tab may be significantly higher. Also check if you are assured of a cabin that is adequate (not located next to the boilers, with a view facing lifeboats or on a heavily-trafficked promenade deck).

MAASDAM

(see Statendam)

AUTHOR TIP

Never pack the following items in your luggage: jewelry, medication, reading glasses, money/travelers checks, passport, air/sea documents or any item you won't mind losing forever in the event your luggage disappears.

AUTHOR TIP

Scrutinize both air and sea tickets the moment you receive them so your travel agent has enough time to make corrections. Carry all documents, including passport and valuables, on your person (one can easily forget a tote bag). Never, never pack documents in your suitcase!

★★★★

MAJESTY OF THE SEAS/MONARCH OF THE SEAS

Royal Caribbean Cruise Line; Bahamian registry; Norwegian officers and Norwegian/international crew: built at Chantiere de l'Atlantique, St. Nazaire, France; launched 1991 (*Monarch*) and 1992 (*Majesty*); 73,941 tons; 880 feet; 106 at beam; 2354 passengers; crew of 822; cruising speed 22 knots; 14 passenger decks.

When passengers surveyed indicated they wanted more activities and choices aboard ships, Royal Caribbean Cruise Line certainly listened. These identical sister megaships, built at a cost of $300 million each, have more activities and places to do them in than most small cities and it all works very nicely.

One assumes that Lauren Bacall and Queen Sonja of Norway had very large bottles of bubbly when they christened, respectively, *Monarch of the Seas* in 1991 and *Majesty of the Seas* the following year. Holding more passengers than any cruise ships in the world, these behemoths make most other vessels in port look minuscule by comparison. Boasting some of the largest casinos afloat and the most extensive fitness facilities and outstanding entertainment, there is a greater selection of everything than is imaginable.

The most impressive aspect of *Monarch* and *Majesty* is how passenger friendly these vessels are in terms of finding one's way around. Entering the second level of The Centrum, a five-story atrium, reminds one of a well-designed modern hotel, its large sweeping, brass trimmed staircases leading to shops and lounges on ascending decks. Two glass enclosed elevators shuttle passengers amid a backdrop of fountains, foliage and art. Public rooms are light, airy and tastefully decorated, with pale colors and floor to ceiling windows beautifully embellishing the modern decor.

Fitness buffs will have a hard time finding greater facilities on any ship. Bridge Deck's enormous workout rooms include state-of-the-art equipment, weight rooms, a large aerobics center and seven massage cubicles. RCCL's Ship Shape program features activities ranging from aquadynamics to basketball free throws, sunrise stretch class, Gut-Buster exercises, dance classes and walk-a-thons. Mature passengers enjoy Vitality Unlimited, a class specially designed for senior citizens.

Monarch and *Majesty* have some of the largest deck space found at sea, with two pools, many whirlpools and bars. The adjacent Windjammer Cafe is popular for casual breakfast and luncheon buffets. RCCL's Kids/Tweens/Teens Programs offer activities for the 5 to 17 age group, attracting many families in the summer and holiday season. Supervised activities for youngsters include masquerade parades, talent shows and their own dinner menus. Teenagers have their own disco, and festivities such as the Dating Game, Sea Cruise Investigations, pizza parties, movies and videos.

Other facilities include a lovely 2000-volume library, 225-seat cinema and an exceptional shopping arcade with a dozen or so boutiques.

Las Vegas-style revues feature headline entertainers, such as, Jerry Lewis, Connie Stevens, Lou Rawls, Diahann Carroll, Vic Damone and Jerry Van Dyke. They perform on every sailing in the two-deck, terraced, 1050-seat A Chorus Line Lounge of Life on *Majesty* and Sound of Music Lounge on *Monarch*. Both vessels have seagoing video walls with 50 television monitors on moveable banks that complement live performances. The tastefully decorated 350-person nightclub is lively until the wee hours of the morning, as are the smaller lounges located throughout the ships, including the Touch of Class bar, designed in art nouveau style, where couples congregate for a glass of champagne or wine. RCCL's signature Viking Crown Lounge is 150 feet above the water and encircles the smokestack, the most popular place for watching arrival in port and after dinner nightcaps. Casino Royal, the largest casino afloat, completes the nighttime entertainment.

Monarch of the Seas

RCCL never brags that its cuisine is gourmet, but it's plentiful and well-prepared all-American fare, and menu selections of courses low in fat and cholesterol are available. Two dining rooms, holding between 663 and 700 people each in two seatings, are located on Main and A deck.

Both ships have 1177 cabins (732 outside; 445 inside) that average around 130 square feet small, but passengers on these vessels are aboard for the nonstop fun found on decks above. All have telephone, color television, three-channel radio and twins that can be converted to doubles.

Those seeking a classical cruise experience with intimate service and a subdued environment would probably not enjoy these vessels. But if your interests are Las Vegas-style entertainment, gambling, extensive fitness facilities, water sports, great children's activities and a very lively ambience at a very good price, these behemoths may be just right.

Monarch of the Seas *sails year-round from her home port of San Juan to Martinique, Barbados, Antigua, St. Maarten and St. Thomas.* Majesty of the Seas *cruises from Miami on a Western Caribbean itinerary, with port calls in Playa Del Carmen and Cozumel in Mexico; Grand Cayman, Jamaica and RCCL's private island, CocoCay, in the Bahamas. If you are a water sports enthusiast,* Majesty's *port calls will give you some the best scuba and snorkeling regions in the Caribbean.*

AUTHOR TIP

During days at sea, *stake your claim on the lounge chair* of your choice by 11:00 a.m. Ask if a live band will be performing nearby during the day and scout out a quiet spot if seeking peace and quiet. Book your salon appointment the moment you board the ship if planning to get gussied up for formal night (you can always cancel).

AUTHOR TIP

Discussion on ports of call and whether or not you need shore excursions is the norm with a good agent. Some cruise lines offer agents commissions on shore excursions purchased before departure, so be wary if you feel pressured—they can always be selected aboard ship.

N/R

MARCO POLO

Orient Lines; Bahamian Registry; European officers and Filipino crew; Built 1965 in Wismar, Germany, rebuilt 1992; launched October, 1993; 20,502 tons; 578 feet long; 77 feet at beam; 850 passengers; crew of 350; cruising speed of 19 knots; 12 passenger decks.

Designed for lengthy voyages and some of the most exotic itineraries available, including a circumnavigation of Antarctica, the 850-passenger *Marco Polo* has unique structural features, such as an ice-strengthened hull and helicopter landing pad. Rebuilt under the supervision of naval architect Knud Hansen with interior design by the well-known A & M Katzourakis team, the vessel's $60 million refurbishment has extended to cabins and public areas.

Public rooms include the Palm Court, Ambassador Lounge, Polo Lounge and Charleston Club. The balconied Seven Seas Restaurant boasts a Tiffany-style ceiling, etched glass panels and art deco sconces; passengers may also dine in Raffles, featuring Oriental specialties. Additional facilities include a health club, saltwater pool and three Jacuzzis, library, casino, boutique and movie theater where lectures are also held.

The 426 cabins (131 inside; 289 outside) have mirrored dressing table and television. Higher categories have large picture windows and tubs, others, a shower and porthole.

In 1995, Marco Polo's *itineraries include the Far East, including Vietnam and China, the South Pacific, Australia and New Zealand. We haven't cruised aboard* Marco Polo *and are unable to report on facilities, food and service but several travelers have passed along favorable comments about* Marco Polo. *Per person, double occupancy rates begin at $245.*

★★★★★

MERIDIAN

Celebrity Cruises; Bahamian registry; Greek officers and international crew; originally built in 1963 in Trieste and known as *Galileo Galilei* of Lloyd Triestino Line; sailed as *Galileo* for Chandris Fantasy Cruises; completely refitted in 1989 and relaunched as *Meridian* for Celebrity Cruises in April 1990; 30,440 tons; 700 feet long; 94 feet at beam; 1106 passengers; crew of 500; cruising speed of 24.5 knots; 8 passenger decks.

Chandris spent $55 million on the former *Galileo* to bring the vessel into the Celebrity Cruises fleet and the results are wonderful. Without disturbing the traditional lines of the exterior, the modernization has given new life to a ship so familiar in ports around the world. The new blue-and-white hull is topped with the now trademark Celebrity Cruises smokestack on which the X of Chandris is riding the waves.

The *Meridian* has a passenger complement of 1106 in 553 cabins, of which 258 are on the inside. Of the 295 outside cabins, there are eight large suites on Captain's Deck (just aft of the Bridge) that feature picture windows as well as skylights! There are 47 deluxe cabins with separate seating areas on Atlantic Deck, and the outside cabins on Horizon Deck boast sea views from floor to ceiling windows. Two cabins have been adapted for wheelchair passengers. All accommodations have radios and telephones but no TV, refrigerator or mini-safe, even in the suites.

Among the structural changes on the *Meridian* are an entirely new sun deck area with three whirlpools, plenty of lounge seating and a bar. Below on Lido Deck is a new swimming pool, as well as the Marina Cafe, serving buffet breakfast and lunch plus tasty barbecues. At night, the interior of the cafe becomes the Marina Disco fantasyland through the use of hundreds of twinkling lights and appropriate music. The main public rooms are located on Horizon Deck: the Zodiac Club, intimate Interlude Bar, Monte Carlo Casino, Rendezvous Lounge with piano bar and Celebrity Showroom. Along the sides are shops and card room, as well as the refurbished Palm Court and Promenade reminiscent of the good old transatlantic days.

The Four Seasons restaurant on Bermuda Deck (with exposed Wine Cellar) is under consultancy of Michel Roux, a renowned French chef who has earned several Michelin stars for restaurants in the London area. Roux's role is to create some special recipes, design menus, and train restaurant staff. The result is some of the finest cuisine afloat, and service that makes the *Meridian* a standout from other cruise ships sailing the Caribbean. A two-level cinema and a small chapel, both retained from the original vessel, complete the public spaces.

From June through September, the *Meridian* sails on one-week cruises from New York to King's Wharf, Bermuda, with a season-long program for families. Children and young adults will find a special daily program of activities to choose from, all supervised by Celebrity's staff. Youngsters can paint and draw, learn special songs and dances and participate in scavenger hunts, among other activities. The Young Mariners program introduces children to operations of the vessel, including a lesson from the Captain on navigation. For sporting kids, there's Celebrity Junior Olympics, with volleyball, water basketball, putting, ping pong, shuffleboard and kit flying.

From November through March, the Meridian *cruises on 10- and 11-day alternating Caribbean voyages from San Juan. The 10-day cruises include port calls in Aruba, La Guaira (port of Caracas), Grenada, Barbados, St. Lucia, Martinique, St. Maarten and St. Thomas; the alternating 11-day sailing visits La Guaira, Panama Canal, San Blas Islands, Cartagena, Martinique, St. John, St. Thomas. She is a very popular presence on the New York-Bermuda circuit from spring through fall. Average per person, per diem rates are $265.*

AUTHOR'S OBSERVATION

The Meridian's 10- and 11-day Caribbean cruises are an excellent value, offered at the same price as Celebrity's seven-day itineraries.

★★★+
MERMOZ

Paquet French Cruises; Bahamian flag; French officers and international crew; originally built in 1956 as *Jean Mermoz*; relaunched in 1970 as *Mermoz*; last refurbished 1984; 13,800 tons; 491 feet long; 61 feet at beam; 530 passengers; crew of 320; cruising speed of 16 knots; 5 passenger decks.

The *Mermoz* is a compact vessel on which cuisine, under the direction of head chef Jean Abauzit, is very important; the French definitely have a flair for such things. For such a small vessel, the *Mermoz* boasts an assemblage of 52 chefs, cooks, pastry chefs and bakers, not to mention all those who do the washing up! There is one sitting for all meals (dinner begins at 8 p.m.) either in the Restaurant Massilia (cabin category 7 to 15) on Delos Deck or the Renaissance Grill (cabin category 1 to 6) overlooking the Roman Bath pool. There is also a self-service buffet in the Lido Ancerville, adjacent to the sun deck pool.

Other amenities include four bars, the Gibraltar Cinema (showing both French and English films) on Gibraltar Deck, Galapagos Club/Disco on Galapagos Deck, the Grand Salon Mermoz, a small casino, complete health club with hydrotherapy/sauna/massage, and a small but classy boutique. There are 15 different cabin categories, including 17 cabins available for single passengers only.

The Mermoz *sails the world around South America, Easter Island, Galapagos/Panama/Florida, Florida/Antilles, the Caribbean, transatlantic from Guadeloupe to Rouen, France (during the 15-day crossing, Berlitz will immerse you in the French language for a few hundred dollars extra); the Baltic, Fjords of Norway and Spitsbergen, Iberian Shores (from Le Havre to Toulon), Music Festival at Sea (Toulon/Toulon) now entering its 35th and 36th years, Mediterranean Shores, Greece/Cappadocia, en route to Yemen (Heraklion, Crete to Djibouti), India/Ceylon (Djibouti to Port Victoria, Seychelles), and Seychelles to South Islands (Mauritius). All this and a plethora of shore excursions and cruise land-extensions!.*

⚓⚓⚓⚓⚓+

MISSISSIPPI QUEEN

Delta Queen Steamboat Company; American crew and registry; built by Jeffboat in Jeffersonville, Indiana; launched July 1976; refurbished in 1984 and 1989; 4500 tons; 382 feet long; 68 feet at beam; 398 passengers; crew of 150; 8 miles per hour maximum speed; 7 passenger decks.

When the *Mississippi Queen* was commissioned on July 25, 1976, in Cincinnati, Ohio, it was the culmination of a ten-year project that cost $27 million and involved the craftsmen of both England and America. This *Queen* was the largest and most spectacular riverboat ever built, and special arrangements were made for her to be constructed in Jeffersonville, Indiana, where nearly 5000 steamboats had been born during the 19th century.

The *MQ* is more than 100 feet longer, ten feet wider at beam, and almost 3000 tons larger than her venerable sister, the *Delta Queen.* She also carries twice the passenger and crew capacity. Her exterior was devised by James Gardner of London, who also participated in the design of Cunard Line's flagship, the *Queen Elizabeth 2.* The exterior was somewhat altered during the 1989 refurbishment program. Fluted twin smoke stacks appeared, along with filigree and wrought iron trim around open decks and the pilot house. At the stern of the vessel, the great paddle wheel was painted a brilliant red, and the two-story glass windows behind it outlined in stark white. The interior of the vessel has been conceived very carefully to offer every nuance of the ambience of 19th-century river life, without breaking the Safety at Sea Law that states all materials must be as nonflammable as possible. Although none of the fine old polished woods of the *DQ* are possible here, the moldings, mirrors, highly polished steel and brass everywhere, and the plush carpeting throughout the public areas certainly recall the opulence of the great steamboat era.

The *MQ* has 145 outside cabins, of which 94 have private verandas just like the good old days. The cabins are well-designed, some with pullman-type berths, and 79 are on the inside. All cabins-staterooms now have names and have been redecorated, including the 14 deluxe suites with large picture windows and private verandas added to Promenade Deck. All are extremely spacious, with king-size beds, full baths and sitting areas, and the forward two suites have the same wonderful view as the captain's! Nothing was spared in decorating these accommodations, from silk draperies and custom sculpted carpets to hand crewel bedspreads, black iron and brass beds, ebony-colored dressers, Stobart prints of old steamboats on the walls, and other brass-and-glass furnishings.

Public areas of the *MQ* have also been refurbished, and the prominent colors are ruby, lapis, emerald and gold tones. The Grand Saloon has lapis upholstery on the banquettes; the Library has deep emerald and lighted bookcases of glass-and-brass; the Center Bar has lapis and almond hues in upholstery; the Gift Shop has emerald walls and carpeting and brass-and-glass cases; the dining room has new carpeting and window shades in all the colors. Even the two Paddlewheel Lounges, upper and lower, have lapis, emerald and ruby accents now.

At the other end of the Observation Deck is the Dining Saloon, with windows so large the river is always at your elbow. There are two sittings for all meals, the only awkward aspect of the entire program. The Dining Saloon opens onto the Upper Paddlewheel Lounge, overlooking a double-tiered space sheathed in glass just forward of that ever-churning red paddlewheel. The lounge is where the day's fun usually begins and ends: Dixieland, barbershop quartet and jazz are all live continually as the libations flow on. You will always meet new friends in this lounge and find old ones!

Promenade Deck aft is the location of the famous Calliope (claimed to be the largest in the world) and the Calliope Bar. Passengers try their talent on the steam pianna throughout the cruise, and it's even computerized so sour notes can be heard again. Midships on Promenade Deck is a small Jacuzzi pool, open year-round and heated to suit the temperatures of the day, as well as a small gym, massage areas and sauna. A library is the most recent addition to Observation Deck, and history lovers will enjoy the many books covering steamboating and the Old South. The library provides quiet and relaxation; next to it on the port side is an expanded Steamboatique, with more than 400 selections of gifts and souvenirs from porcelain dolls to riverboat gambler sets. The main body of the Paddlewheel Lounge is located aft on Texas Deck. The Purser's Office, Forward Lounge and embarkation/disembarkation areas are forward on Cabin Deck and boast new carpeting, softer lighting and new valances on the floor-to-ceiling windows. The theater and beauty shop have gone, but two elevators still remain and have been rebuilt with Victorian mahogany walls and brass handrails.

The *MQ* has a loyal following and attracts a more active and energetic crowd than those devoted to her elder sister. The captain and his fine American crew are young and enthusiastic and make the voyages very special for all on board as the paddlewheeler transverses the heart of America. Life aboard ship revolves a great deal around the Paddlewheel Lounge, and there is plenty of local entertainment in the Grand Saloon or up in the Calliope Bar. Kite flying, exercise sessions, riverboat bingo, calliope contests, lectures, shore gazing, pilot house turns, locking through the Upper Mississippi and eating well are all part of onboard life.

The Mississippi Queen *sails from New Orleans, Memphis, St. Louis, Chattanooga, and St. Paul on a series of cruises from 3 to 11 nights. Highlight of the summer schedule is the annual Great Steamboat Race from New Orleans to St. Louis. The* Mississippi Queen *has been a part of the river for a full decade now, offering such enticing-sounding steamboat adventures as Mississippi Explorer, Heart of Dixie, The Tom Sawyer, Yankee Steamer, Frontier Adventure, Southern Comfort and Mississippi River. Throughout the year there are also special theme vacations on board Big Band Cruises, Southern Celebration, Civil War, Mark Twain Celebrations, Fall Foliage, Dixiefest, and Old Fashioned Holidays. Pre- and post-cruise tours in Cajun Country are also available. Per person, per diem rates range from $250–$580 before advance purchase discounts.*

AUTHOR TIP

Ask specifics about *shore excursions* that sound enticing. For example, an attraction may also involve a seven-hour bus ride over bumpy roads, with a hectic 30-minute stop at the site. Most places you can travel cheaper and more comfortably by hiring a taxi with a few friends. However, always establish the price before leaving the pier.

⚓⚓⚓⚓⚓+

NANTUCKET CLIPPER/YORKTOWN CLIPPER

Clipper Cruise Line; American registry and crew; ships built in Jeffersonville, Indiana; launched December 1984, June 1988; 100 tons each; 207 feet long; 37 feet at beam; 100 (*Nantucket Clipper*) and 138 (*Yorktown Clipper*); crew of 28; cruising speed of 10 statute miles per hour; 4 passenger decks.

It always amuses me that Clipper Cruise Line, the very name of which evokes images of the open sea and tall masted ships, is based in St. Louis, Missouri. Cruising on one of these two lovely ships (they both, incidentally, run under power, with nary a sail in sight!), is not unlike being invited on to a friend's beautifully cared for private yacht. Only you pay for it! These ships are not cheap, but for this traveler, it is value received, all the way.

Nantucket Clipper and *Yorktown Clipper* are informal ships, with many, many repeaters, people who really do consider these their own yachts, passengers who have sailed on any or all of them so many times that they know the crew, down to the last cook and busboy and who come back to their own particular cabin much like homing pigeons. People meet and intermingle from the first happy hour in the lounge. The Dining Room has single, open seating for all meals, which helps in the mix and match process and encourages passengers to change around as they like, breakfast, lunch and dinner.

These vessels are not for people who need a casino, disco, midnight buffet or nightclub shows. They attract sophisticated passengers who have done it all elsewhere but come aboard for a different view of America the Beautiful. They explore the historic towns that have grown up along America's waterways, and during the day there are excellent port lectures. The scenery is ever-changing since the ships are never far away.

The common rooms on both ships can be easily described as warm, cozy, inviting and very hard to leave at the end of the voyage. A small bar is tucked into a corner of the only Lounge/sitting room and it serves as the local pub, card room, game and reading space. Brightly patterned chintzes in warm and inviting colors cover comfortable chairs and sofas; different size tables are at hand for cards, drinks, snacks or writing post cards. The whole room is wrapped with large windows. There is a lovely feeling of welcome and homeyness, reinforced by a wonderfully energetic staff and crew. This cheerful and hard working group is really amazing—they all wear so many hats and seem to have double and triple duties and responsibilities, carried out with good will and a lot of banter back and forth. They all seem able to organize tours, mix drinks, swim, snorkel, man the Zodiacs, wait on tables and tidy up the cabins, all done with interchangeable ease.

Cabins on *Nantucket Clipper* and *Yorktown Clipper* are all outside twins, small, but perfectly adequate since there is no need to pack formal, or even semiformal clothes. A couple of skirts and dressy tops and a nice pantsuit or two for the ladies and the ubiquitous navy blue blazer for men is the norm. Staterooms have large picture windows, plenty of closet space and are decorated with pleasant light woods. But I have one big complaint—there are no passenger operated laundry facilities aboard, which can mean having to go ashore to wash clothing on a trip of more than a week and possibly missing something wonderful.

I found food on these ships superior. The chefs are trained at the Culinary Institute of America and the cuisine is American at its very best. This is no caviar on command regime, but lots of fresh fish and vegetables and salads, simply and carefully prepared and served. A very special treat: Clipper Chocolate Chippers, served warm from the oven every afternoon at tea time.

Again, just like going to visit Grandma: the chef shared the following recipe with us. Be forewarned, they are the most addictive cookies I have ever eaten:.

CLIPPER CHOCOLATE CHIPPERS
(Preheat oven to 325 degrees)
3/4 cup packed light brown sugar
3/4 cup granulated sugar
1cup butter, softened
1 Tsp. baking soda
1 Tbsp. Frangelico
1Tbsp. Tia Maria
1/2 Tsp. salt
1Tbsp. vanilla
2 eggs
2 1/2 cups all purpose flour
4 cups milk chocolate chips
1cup walnut halves (optional)
1/2 cup pecan halves (optional)
1/2 cup macadamia nuts (optional

Cream butter, sugar, vanilla, Tia Maria and Frangelico until light and fluffy. Add eggs; beat well. Combine flour, baking soda and salt; gradually beat into creamed mixture. Stir in chocolate chips and nuts. Mix well. Place in storage container and refrigerate overnight. Drop by teaspoonful onto ungreased cookie sheet. Bake at 325 degrees for approximately 10–13 minutes or until golden brown. Cool slightly and serve immediately. Makes 3-4 dozen.

The itineraries of *Nantucket Clipper* and *Yorktown Clipper* enable passengers to have many special experiences. One of my fondest was a cruise through the British Virgin Islands, when we went ashore to have a picnic lunch on a tiny uninhabited island. Mid afternoon, while some of us were shelling, a small well-weathered sailboat anchored only a few feet from our beach and the five who came ashore were a mother and father and three children who were on the last leg of a round the world trip. They had been gone for more than a year and were headed back home to Boston. They seemed as anxious to share tales of their adventures as they were to share our food and drink and what tales they had to tell! These are the kinds of chance encounters that just don't happen when traveling on large ships where the schedule must be made up months in advance and pretty much adhered to.

In 1995, Nantucket Clipper *carries on the East Coast tradition from spring through fall, cruising the coastline on historically-focused cruises from Florida to Montreal. It then repositions to the Virgin Islands for the winter season, sailing weekly from St. Thomas. The* Yorktown Clipper *sails among the Windward, Leeward and Grenadine islands and ventures to Venezuela's Orinoco in the winter. From early spring through fall, the* Yorktown Clipper *hugs the West Coast on nature-oriented voyages to costa Rica and the Darien Jungle, Mexico's Sea of Cortez, the Sacramento and Columbia rivers, the San Juan and Gulf islands of the Pacific Northwest and Alaska's Inside Passage. Per person, per diem rates begin at $350.*

Yorktown Clipper

★

NEPTUNE

Epirotiki Lines; Greek crew and registry; built in 1955 in Denmark; refurbished and relaunched as *Neptune* in April 1972; 4000 tons; 300 feet long; 45 feet at beam; 190 passengers; crew of 97; cruising speed of 14 knots; 6 passenger decks.

The *Neptune* is the smallest of the Epirotiki fleet. The vessel has only 96 cabins (of which 24 are inside), all with private facilities and a fold-over sofa arrangement for daytime use. You will find full baths in only three Special Staterooms (HS, HS1, HS2) located on Hera Deck, just inside the observation area. The cabin decor features murals depicting the underwater Palace of Poseidon (Neptune), with curtains on which happy waves seem to play in blues and greens or gold and brown tones. As on all Epirotiki vessels, interior designer Maurice Bailey and artists Arminio Lozzo and Russel Holmes have integrated the mythological tales of the ship's namesake throughout.

The vessel has *Poseidon* painted in Greek on the stern, but *Neptune* in Roman characters on the bow (for the American passengers, no doubt). However one calls this fellow, he was Lord of the Sea; and this ship's tapestries, mosaics, brass sculptures and other artworks indicate this. The Lounge of the Tritons, the main public area, has three large tapestries of Neptune with his trident. Next door in the Poseidon Bar, a large, swirled mosaic made me think of the "Poseidon Adventure" (which I doubt was the intention). In the passageways, handmade brass lamps represent the house of Poseidon, and more tapestries hang in the Dining Room of the Sirens, a cheerful restaurant in purples and pinks that seats the full complement of passengers. The large viewing windows also add to the pleasant effect.

Another nice spot is up on Hera Deck in the solarium, located between the swimming pool and the Mermaid Bar. Here you can catch a bit of the sun, enjoy the excitement of the sea, and appreciate the highlight of this floating art gallery—the magnificent mosaic by the swimming pool. And while you're up here, try a Neptune Wave, the ship's specialty that consists of one ounce tequila, two ounces fresh orange juice, and one-quarter ounce Grenadine.

The Neptune *is often positioned on the 3- and 4-day Greek Islands itinerary, departing Piraeus every Friday for Mykonos, Rhodes, Kusadasi (for Ephesus) and Patmos. Every Monday the vessel sails for all of the above plus Santorini and Heraklion (Crete).*

★★★★★

NIEUW AMSTERDAM/NOORDAM

Holland America Line; Netherlands Antilles registry; Dutch officers and Indonesian-Filipino crew; both built at St. Nazaire in France; *Nieuw Amsterdam* commissioned July 1983, *Noordam* April 1984; 33,900 tons; 704 feet; 90 feet at beam; 1212 passengers; crew of 542; cruising speed of 22 knots; 11 passenger decks.

These two $150/$160 million vessels designed and built by Holland America Line were planned to return passengers to the old ocean liner philosophy of the good old days. Both public rooms and staterooms have old world touches that are obvious even to the neophyte. A great deal of thought and good taste was applied, and money was spent on good materials and craftsmanship. Polished rosewood, teak and other high-quality woods are used on the interior and decks and beveled corners are impressive even to the experienced eye. There is a comforting lack of chrome, plastic, vinyl and bright colors.

Public areas are expansive without being overwhelming, and staterooms are far more spacious than one would anticipate on a cruise ship built in the 80s. Every cabin has touches of grained-wood paneling and dressers. Even the mirrors are trimmed in wood. There is plenty of counter and storage space and every cabin boasts a color TV. The modular bathrooms seem to be the only bow to the modern age; they are smallish but cheerful and well lit, and the deluxe cabins have good-size bathtubs.

Each vessel has 194 spacious inside cabins; the *Nieuw Amsterdam* has 411 outside staterooms and suites, the *Noordam* two more with 413. The most luxurious accommodations are 20 suites in a special area on Navigation and Boat decks, with large picture windows and king-size beds. (As on many ships, watch out for accommodations on these decks because of partially obstructed views due to the lifeboats.) Nonetheless, for those who prefer the ultimate in privacy, it is rather difficult to find these cabins. But these are two vessels where even the inside twin cabins are pleasant, according to a travel agent friend who found himself in one. And, as a result of restoration during a recent drydocking, both vessels now boast four staterooms with bathrooms accessible by wheelchair. These are Category C #100, 101, 102, 103 on Boat Deck of both vessels.

The *Nieuw Amsterdam* and *Noordam* are indeed sister ships, with identical exteriors and layout. But the interior of each has been planned with a difference. The *Nieuw Amsterdam* is "themed" to reflect the Dutch influence in the New World. It has the Manhattan dining room (two seatings), Stuyvesant Lounge and Minnewit Terrace, Hudson and Explorers lounges, Peartree Club and Partridge Bar, The Big Apple disco, The Wampun casino and Perel Straet shopping area. There is a fine collection of antiques and paintings aboard that recall the 17th and 18th centuries, when Holland was so prominent in the New World. According to HAL, a leading Dutch historian, an antique dealer spent two years seeking the appropriate items throughout Europe and the United States and most of the purchases are of museum quality. Certainly, the artworks are an integral part of the overall ambience of the vessel.

The theme of the *Noordam* is also the 17th and 18th centuries, but expanded to reflect the influence of the Dutch East India Company throughout the world. Established in Amsterdam in 1603, the company was one of the premier traders in both the East and West. Hence, the Noordam has the Amsterdam dining room, Admiral's Lounge, Tasman Terrace, Piet Heyn (well-known admiral), Explorers Lounge, Horn Pipe Club, Shanty Bar, Big Dipper, De Halve Maen (name of the ship Henry Hudson sailed up the Hudson River in 1609) and Canael Straet shopping area.

Both vessels have the Crow's Nest late night lookout on Sun Deck, a fabulous Ocean Spa, supervised by the Sheraton Bonaventure Resort & Spa of Fort Lauderdale, for exercise and sports, two outdoor swimming pools, as well as a heated whirlpool, a card room and a library, and the Lido Restaurant, where buffet breakfasts and lunch are served. There are a myriad of activities and entertainment available day and night, beauty/barber shop, attractive boutiques and round-the-clock food. Communications with the outside world are excellent, plus daily news/stock quotations via UPI. All the 80s and 90s vessels are claiming the latest in navigation facilities, and the *Nieuw Amsterdam/Noordam* system is known as INMARSAT, established by the International Maritime Satellite Organization.

Officers are Dutch; the service crew is Indonesian-Filipino and some of the friendliest and most helpful afloat. While there are occasional language problems, their eagerness to please is quite overwhelming and no one disembarks a Holland America vessel without the memory of a warm and caring atmosphere. The No Tipping Necessary policy works, and although passengers do wish to offer gratuities, none of the cruise staff suggests a daily amount. As a result, there is a friendly hole in one's pocket at the end of the cruise and everyone is happy!

Food service aboard both vessels is excellent and there are plenty of places to consume calories! The self-service Lido restaurant offers buffet breakfast and lunch, as well as 24-hour coffee and its own ice cream section. Hamburgers and hot dogs are prepared on deck at noon for the fast-food crowd. Dinner is in the two-seating dining rooms is gracious, and the tables are placed so there is considerable privacy and quietude among passengers. The company instigated a lighter menu recently and it works well.

Just in case anyone thinks he is going to lose weight, special desserts can be prepared at table at least once during the cruise.

During the summer season, *Nieuw Amsterdam* and *Noordam* join the rest of the fleet (*Rotterdam* and *Westerdam*) in Alaskan waters for a series of sailings from Vancouver through the Inside Passage. Ports of call are Ketchikan, Juneau, Glacier Bay and Sitka, as well as cruising in Glacier Bay during the one-week round-trip sailings. The cruises are available in conjunction with Westours motorcoach land arrangements of Alaska's interior and stays at Westmark Hotels throughout the state. Both Westours and Westmark are subsidiaries of Holland America Line, a formidable presence in our 49th state.

Panama Canal transits are another important feature of both these vessels, especially at spring and fall repositioning cruises both excellent times to be cruising between the west coast and south Florida. During the winter months *Nieuw Amsterdam* and *Noordam* are in the Caribbean on warm weather programs.

The Nieuw Amsterdam *sails from Tampa on weekly cruises to the western Caribbean, calling at Key West, Playa del Carmen, Ocho Rios, and Grand Cayman. The* Noordam *sails from Fort Lauderdale (Port Everglades) on 7-day itineraries to eastern and western Caribbean islands. The average per person per diem of the* Nieuw Amsterdam *in the Caribbean is $303; in Alaska the rate is $370. In the Caribbean, the* Noordam's *per person, per diem is $309 and in Alaska, $360.*

★★★★+

NORDIC EMPRESS

Royal Caribbean Cruise Line; Liberian registry; Norwegian officers and international crew; constructed at Chantiers de l'Atlantique shipyard, St. Nazaire, France, for June 1990 delivery; 45,000 tons; 673 feet long; 100 feet at beam; 1610 passengers; crew of 640; cruising speed of 19.5 knots; 12 passenger decks.

Those who think they must sacrifice quality when selecting a cruise under a week's duration will find *Nordic Empress* a delightful surprise. Designed and built specifically for the three- and four-day cruise market, this ship has a formula that works very well. Launched in 1990, *Nordic Empress* offers top quality weekend or midweek escapes for couples, singles and families. First-time cruisers who want to test the waters of a seagoing holiday will find excellent value for the money.

From the moment embarkation begins, everything seems to take place effortlessly, no simple task when loading 1600 passengers. Boarding directly into the ship's Centrum, an atrium soaring the height of nearly nine decks, the white marble floors and sparkling polished brass railings convey the spacious and light-filled effect characteristic of this ship. Huge palms surrounding a white baby grand piano give a garden effect that is a wonderful first impression. While there are plenty of low-key nooks and crannies when one wants a quiet drink, three major public rooms covering no less than two levels give a wonderful feeling of openness.

The Carmen Dining Room has an upper and main level connected by brass staircases that lead to a podium of white marble and a white baby grand piano surrounded by palm trees. At the stern, two decks of picture windows give wonderful views of the sea and add to the airy atmosphere. For all its spaciousness, the dining room was noisy and a bit too busy at times as passengers and staff moved about. The Strike Up the Band Lounge is a very pink affair and very Las Vegas. Shows with feathered costumes, lavish audiovisual effects and Broadway-style musical reviews were always packed.

The Viking Crown Lounge is a two-level club, which at midnight turns into a disco, located aft of the smoke stack. While the effect is "21st century," it isn't gaudy and is one of the best late night clubs at sea or on land for those who like to party hard.

The Carousel Pub is a quiet getaway, decorated in soft greens and blues. Boasting a circular bar and brightly painted carousel horses, it was popular for pre-dinner cocktails. My favorite bar is the High Society Lounge decorated in modern deco, its statues reminiscent of Erte; the wood paneling with deep pastel fabrics presents a tranquil oasis from the hectic pace found elsewhere. If you love Las Vegas, *Nordic Empress'* casino will make you feel right at home, and here the action never lets up. It is the cruise industry's first two-deck, three-level gaming facility, located near the ship's shopping arcade.

The center of activity throughout the day is found on Pool Deck. Two large pools and three jacuzzis, graced with sail-like canvas canopies provide a welcome relief from the sun. Forward of the pool is the Windjammer Lido Cafe where breakfast and lunch buffets are served for those who wish to dine casually, and with three separate food stations, there was virtually no time spent in line. Late afternoon tea is served here as well, and along with delectable tea sandwiches, salads and ice cream sundaes, fresh omelets made to order were whipped up by staff, an impressive option for a late afternoon snack.

Those who want to maintain—or begin—a fitness regimen will find RCCL's "ShipShape" program an added bonus. Facilities include a spacious fitness center with the full range of modern exercise equipment, sauna and massage.

This ship has wonderful facilities for the large number of families who sail year-round. The 495-square foot Kids' Konnection playroom is designed in the theme of a space station for children age 5 to 12. There are huge enclosed tubes of brushed aluminum that are lighted and carpeted inside, and mirrors reflecting a moonscape mural and dance floor shaped like the ringed planet Saturn. Teenagers have their own dating game, and the ship boasts children's menus for several age groups.

The quality and presentation of food was a wonderful surprise. It is not gourmet, but the equivalent of fine hotel food. While there are no surprises, just basic fare, the quality remained consistent wherever one dined. Staff, who must feed 800 people at one sitting, were well-trained and friendly.

Royal Caribbean is known for its minuscule cabins, and those aboard *Nordic Empress* are no exception. They are approximately 130 square feet, tiny by industry standards, but on a short cruise when one spends so little time in a cabin, it is not a handicap. Decorated in soft pink and blue pastels, it was comfortable, and a large picture window gave a greater sense of openness.

Standard amenities include TV, 3-channel radio and twin beds that convert to double. Of the 800 cabins, a large number (329) are inside, which must be very claustrophobic.

Most passengers found the cruise highlight was a day spent at Royal Caribbean's private island, Coco Cay, located between Freeport and Nassau in the Bahamas' Berry Island chain. With some 140 acres of pristine beaches and coconut palm groves, there was plenty of space for those who sought a nap in a swinging hammock. Water sports of all types were very popular with most passengers, and we had a memorable barbecue set up at two different locations to avoid lines.

Nordic Empress *sails from Miami every Monday and Friday year-round. Three-night cruises call at Nassau and CocoCay, are priced from $579 per person, double occupancy; four-night cruises add a stop in Freeport, and begin at $719. Advance purchase discounts lower the price, making this a very good deal indeed!*

AUTHOR TIP

On ships with *VCRs* in cabins, the best movies (and X-rated films, when available) go first. Run for the video library the moment you board to procure your favorites...and grab several.

★★★+

NORDIC PRINCE

Royal Caribbean Cruise Line; Norwegian registry and officers, international crew; built in Wartsila shipyard in Helsinki and originally launched in 1971; refitted and lengthened in 1980; 23,000 tons; 635 feet long; 80 feet at beam; 1012 passengers; crew of 400; cruising speed of 16 knots; 8 passenger decks.

Second of the famed RCCL fleet to be stretched, the *Nordic Prince* gained 85 feet and 4500 tons, allowing space for 310 more passengers and 80 additional crew. As a result of this process, the ship now has 339 outside and 180 inside cabins, all with private facilities. The size of the cabins has not changed, there are just many more of them. However, the dimensions of the public areas are much larger, especially the Camelot dining room, the Showboat Lounge (and theater), and the Carousel Lounge. In addition, the Midsummer's Night Lounge on Promenade Deck and the pool area with a new pool cafe for luncheon buffets have both increased considerably in size. Food and service aboard the *Nordic Prince* is on par with the other RCCL vessels, and the entertainment is exactly the same. Royal Caribbean uses the same nightclub attractions on all its ships and flies them from port to port, so you see each act only once. In short, this vessel is another fine RCCL product. The only differences are the names of the public areas and the ports of call, which are generally in Caribbean and southeastern coastal waters.

During the summer season the Nordic Prince *cruises on 7-day Alaska itineraries. When* Nordic Prince *returns to Mexico, the vessel is on a series of 7-day Mexican Riviera cruises. Per person, double occupancy rates begin at $1199 for one-week Mexico cruises and $999 for weekly Alaska sailings.*

★★★★
NORWAY

Norwegian Cruise Lines; Bahamian registry and Norwegian officers, international crew; originally built in France in 1962 and launched as the flagship of French Line; relaunched in 1980 as the Norway; $40-million refurbishment in 1990; 75,000 tons; 1035 feet long; 110 feet at beam; 2044 passengers; crew of 900; cruising capacity of 18 knots; 9 passenger decks.

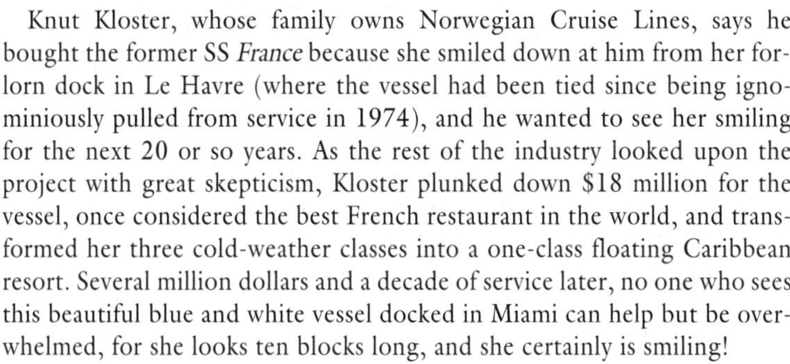

Knut Kloster, whose family owns Norwegian Cruise Lines, says he bought the former SS *France* because she smiled down at him from her forlorn dock in Le Havre (where the vessel had been tied since being ignominiously pulled from service in 1974), and he wanted to see her smiling for the next 20 or so years. As the rest of the industry looked upon the project with great skepticism, Kloster plunked down $18 million for the vessel, once considered the best French restaurant in the world, and transformed her three cold-weather classes into a one-class floating Caribbean resort. Several million dollars and a decade of service later, no one who sees this beautiful blue and white vessel docked in Miami can help but be overwhelmed, for she looks ten blocks long, and she certainly is smiling!

Danish naval architect Tage Wandborg, who has more than 30 modern cruise ships and more than 100 conversions to his credit, supervised the reincarnation and left behind his distinctive and stylish trademark. For the decoration of the public areas, Kloster hired the late interior designer Angelo Donghia of New York, who had some famous clients and was a familiar figure in the new hotel and nightclub circuit. Since the initial refurbishment, the *Norway* has undergone several extensive renovations, including a $23 million overhaul in 1993.

The *Norway* is virtually a destination itself and offers myriad activities and facilities during three heavenly days at sea on a one-week cruise. This ship attracts passengers in a wide range of ages and interests, and NCL is adding more service enhancements in an effort to attract a more upscale clientele.

However, unlike the current NCL ad campaign that suggests chic and sophisticated travelers, the majority on my sailing were not like those depicted on TV. To a degree many of NCL's improvements went unnoticed by this crowd, comprised of first time cruisers, families with children and many hard partying revelers. For example, there were a lot more participants at poolside Olympics and Calypso Night than attended the daily art auction or the elegant high tea offered by white-gloved waiters.

Since she was built as a two-class transatlantic liner more than 30 years ago, the ship structurally does not lend itself to a smooth passenger flow. There are long lines for most buffets and the more popular activities, such as NCL's new "Chocoholic Buffet."

What the *Norway* lacks in efficiency she makes up for in ambience. This ship is loaded with character, extraordinary art deco touches, some of the largest cabins around and deck space that seems endless. And, this ship offers some of the best and most varied entertainment of any cruise ship, including a Broadway show with a cast that did justice to the New York production of "Will Rogers Follies."

The *Norway's* immense size—1035 feet long—is overwhelming to some when first boarding, but distinctive color schemes that change amidships help one get a sense of forward and aft fairly soon. The original First Class Promenade on International Deck serve as the center of the *Norway's* major public rooms and most activities. The promenade has been transformed into a tree-lined boulevard that circles the International Deck with marquees, cafes, shops, entertainment, lounges, a purser's office and an ice cream parlor. The starboard side is named Champs Elysee and the port side is Fifth Avenue.

Much of the *Norway's* "soul" remains the Club International, part of the France's original first class public areas. If you enjoy violin music, afternoon tea and ballroom dancing, then this is your spot (although only a handful of passengers actually showed up for these glamorous events). Club International is refurbished in gold and pale green with the original deco look intact. A huge statue of Neptune adorns the white columned room and a mirrored bar adds to the flavor of a grand hotel.

The more informal and intimate piano lounge is the Windjammer Bar, its deep green and warm wood paneling evoking a nautical theme. Checkers is a large club featuring cabaret, contemporary dance music from the 50s and 60s and serves as the setting for NCL's Sport Celebrity Programs and daily art auction. Decorated in a checkerboard motif, it attracts a crowd in their 30s and 40s looking to dance, flirt and have fun without having to resort to a disco environment. I adore the Ibsen Library which is practically a museum itself, its decor unchanged since the ship's first launching.

The Windward Dining Room has the traditional grand staircase that spans the breadth of the ship. Above the dining area is a huge dome that gives the effect of being outdoors under a starlit night sky. Spectacular, original art work adorn the dining room walls, including murals in gold and bronze and mirrored walls with etched glass designs. Originally designated as the tourist class dining room, the Leeward section has been upgraded to understated elegance. The two-tiered burgundy and off-white room has a spiral chrome staircase leading from the upper balcony and a metallic sculptured chandelier.

Dining room service, while not polished, was warm and generally efficient. Staffed exclusively by European waiters, cuisine has been upgraded recently by NCL, with quality and presentation quite good. Recent additions include a Viking theme meal with Norwegian delicacies and a toast of Aquavit. Room service menus have been completely revamped, offering a greater selection and the elimination of that pesky $2.00 surcharge. I had a goose pate appetizer that was magical and miniature raspberry and blueberry tarts during high tea that were inspired.

When selecting a cabin, it is important to note that the best are not the most expensive. A refurbishment added modern cabins with verandas in the highest-priced category. Vacuum flush toilets and a corporate look characterize the 124 staterooms now located on the new top decks. Be advised, however, that the veranda partitions are not true partitions and the balconies lack privacy. My outside stateroom (Nl62) was originally a first class stateroom on the France with many of the original art deco touches, including a vanity with three-sided movable mirrors that was right out of a Fred and Ginger movie. Best of all, it had several traditional portholes and a full tub. You'll need an excellent travel agent to land the perfect cabin with this fairly complicated deck plan, but I recommend midships on Viking Deck.

However, stay clear of those located beneath Checkers as the evening cabaret and morning joggers can disturb sleep. Cabins on Fjord Deck are some of the nicest and offer good value, but many have obstructed views due to life boats.

A terrific addition is the Roman Spa, a 6000 square foot facility with the best in beauty and health programs, including herbal treatment, hydrotherapy baths and a cardiovascular exercise area. The health club has floor-to-ceiling windows, state of the art equipment, a 360 degree jogging track, a 12-person Jacuzzi and plenty of classes for the energetic. NCL's Sports Afloat program is one of the best fitness regimen's at sea, with classes ranging from beginners to advanced levels.

Kids have a wonderful time on the *Norway*, with plenty of space in which to play. They have their own *Cruise News* daily, their own activities area (Trolland), that wonderful ice cream parlor, and even special shore excursions. When the vessel calls at NCL's Pleasure Island, treasure hunts and relay races are arranged and, of course, there are nonstop hamburgers at lunchtime! Grownups go for these as well, I noticed.

The Norway *sails every Saturday from Miami with three days at sea, and calls at St. Maarten, St. John/St. Thomas and Great Stirrup Cay, NCL's private island, where the ship line delivers a cookout, limbo contest, Calypso band and treasure hunts. Passengers may take advantage of the fine Dive-In program here, which includes snorkeling equipment and instruction on the ship and a special underwater trail off the island.*

★★★+

STAR/SHIP OCEANIC

Premier Cruise Lines; Panamanian registry; Greek officers; international crew; built in Trieste in 1965; refurbished 1986 and rechristened by Minnie Mouse; 40,000 tons; 671 feet long; 96 feet at beam; 1180 passengers; crew of 550; cruising speed of 26 knots; 8 passenger decks.

Premier bought the *Oceanic* from Home Lines for $20 million in the fall of 1985 and spent another $10 million in refurbishing the public areas. The result, under the direction of Agni and Michael Katzourakis, is very impressive. This renowned husband-and-wife team from Athens did not tamper with the existing design of the vessel, which has worn well over two decades as both classic and modern, but concentrated on brighter colors and an effective use of mirrors to lighten the interior. More than 30,000 square yards of carpet were woven in England, especially for the vessel's eight passenger decks. Furnishings and what new beds were brought in (there are now 167 double beds) are from Finland, the chairs are Italian, and the new deck teak is from Nigeria. The refurbishing was completed in this country.

The Katzourakis team did not tamper with the sculptures in the stairwells, which are essential to feeling at home in the *Oceanic*. They did change the entire atmosphere of the glass-domed pool area, however, with the use of striped yellow awnings, white furniture, yellow lamps a la Bourbon Street and plenty of foliage. All other areas—the Satellite cafe, Galaxy disco, Starlight Cabaret, Tropicana Club, Mars Bar, Lucky Star Casino, Heroes & Legends Pub (resembling a British pub and the only dark area on the ship) and Seven Continents restaurant—are attractive and cheerful.

The Broadway Showman has very uncomfortable seating arrangements, but Premier promises all kinds of scintillating entertainment here. It's a splendid idea, especially after the children are fast asleep and dreaming of Mickey, Minnie, Goofy and lots of ice cream cones!

Children's facilities on board are excellent. This is truly a ship for the whole family. There is a spacious Teen Activity Center and a large Children's Recreation Center with arts and crafts room, splash pool and outdoor supervised activities for ages 2 through 12. Adult playrooms include the Seasport Fitness Center, complete with gym and eight-lap jogging track, and Lucky Star Casino, conveniently adjacent to a beautiful shopping arcade.

The hull is now Premier red and (bravo) the great lady is back in service and looking better than ever! As Minnie Mouse said at the rechristening, "We wish her well and all those who sail with her!"

The Oceanic *departs Port Canaveral every Monday and Friday for Nassau and Salt Cay, an Out Island. Hurry!.*

★★★★+

OCEANIC GRACE

Oceanic Cruises; Japanese flag and crew; constructed in Japan and launched in April 1989; 5050 tons; 336 feet long; 50s feet at beam; 118 passengers; crew of 70; cruising speed of 19.6 knots; 5 passenger decks.

Designed in Holland and constructed in Japan, *Oceanic Grace* is the oriental version of Sea Goddess Cruises. The 59 all-suite vessel features accommodations that are approximately 185 square feet with twin or queen-size beds and large windows. All cabins are located midships and are nicely decorated. For western tastes, the beds are rather hard and the bathtubs are somewhat on the short side, but these are minor complaints (take showers). There is one wheelchair-access stateroom. Other amenities include phone, radio/TV/VCR, refrigerator and minibar, personal safe, toiletries and hair dryer. Athletic and health features on board are a jogging track, gym, saunas, freshwater pool and Jacuzzi, as well as water sports equipment in the marina, or water-level platform for skiing, snorkeling, parasailing, windsurfing and scuba diving offered on a complimentary basis. The company hopes to have real diver enthusiasts on board and will furnish as many as six trained and certified instructors/buddies.

Food on board *Oceanic Grace* is considered some of the best afloat as the chefs were trained at the famed Palace Hotel in Tokyo, and Japanese-style dishes are designed from the freshest ingredients possible and presented to the diner as works of art. Breakfast and lunch are served buffet style in the Day Lounge or by the swimming pool and feature both western and oriental items. Dinner is served from 7 to 10 p.m. in the Main Restaurant, where seating is not assigned. Many shore excursions suggest local restaurants where passengers can enjoy specialties of the region for a price (!). Wine and drinks are expensive on board (and ashore), but beer is complimentary during the day and sake is reasonable by the bottle.

In addition to the Day Lounge on pool deck, there is the Main Lounge one deck below, which is very attractively decorated and utilized for musical entertainment. As on Sea Goddess and Seabourn Cruises, there is no formal entertainment on *Oceanic Grace*, as passengers are expected to relax and entertain themselves. The ship attracts sophisticated and educated Japanese executive couples who speak English and enjoy meeting and conversing with westerners. In fact, Oceanic Cruises would like to have about 30 percent Americans/westerners on every cruise to offer a good mix.

The cruises (some of which can be embarked for only three or four days) sail from Yokohama, Nagasaki, Tokyo, Kobe, Hakodate, and Guam. The Guam/Marshall Islands/Micronesia itinerary is new in 1994 and features calls at Palau, Rota, Saipan, Truk Lagoon, Ulithi, Woleai and Yap. A 1-week cruise for an American couple, including air fare, is approximately $10,000, but the good news is there is no tipping on board Oceanic Grace, *and even the photographs are free!*

★

ODYSSEUS

Epirotiki Lines; Greek registry and crew; formerly known as *Aquamarine*; acquired by Epirotiki in early 1988 and extensively refurbished; 12,000 tons; 483 feet long; 61 feet at beam; 452 passengers; crew of 190; cruising speed of 18.5 knots; 7 passenger decks.

When last seen this vessel was languishing in Hong Kong harbor, while Greek banking interests searched for a new owner. As the *Aquamarine*, this vessel was operated by a member of the Kavounides family (the now defunct K-Lines) on China cruises between Hong Kong and Kobe in 1978/79. It was a great idea, but badly operated, and the program went bankrupt.

Epirotiki acquired and renamed this vessel *Odysseus* in early 1988 and hired Italian/American designer Armenio Lozzi for the interior decor. Deck names are now standard with all Epirotiki ships—Apollo, Jupiter, Dionysus, Poseidon, Hera, Venus and Chronos while public rooms are named after the adventures in the *Odyssey*. Sirens, Circe, Naussica, Aeolian Winds, Penelope, Lotus-eaters and Ithaca will all be found on board. The public areas include a grand salon, a second lounge/bar, a writing room, reading veranda, disco, boutique, casino, dining room and taverna, as well as swimming pool and Lido area. A gym/sauna and movie projection area have also been added.

Cabins are large on this vessel, approximately 90 percent have an outside configuration, and almost all have a separate seating area. All cabins feature private facilities (albeit very old-fashioned ones), plus plenty of wardrobe and drawer space. There are some pleasant cabins aft on the top deck, as I recall.

★★★★
ORPHEUS

Swan Hellenic Cruises; Greek flag and crew; originally built in 1952 as the *Munster*; rebuilt in Greece in 1969 and renamed the *Orpheus*; refurbished in 1983; 5000 tons; 353 feet long; 51 feet at beam; 300 passengers; crew of 139; cruising speed of 15 knots; 6 passenger decks.

The *Orpheus* is a comfortable Greek vessel that has learned to speak English, according to the Swan Hellenic company that has chartered the ship from Epirotiki for several seasons. Swan carries fewer than the 300 passenger complement in a less-than-ritzy but very sociable atmosphere. There are no fixed seating arrangements in the cozy Dionysus restaurant, and there is light evening music in the Lounge of the Muses. Other public areas include the Apollo Lounge and the Jason Taverna, where buffet lunches are served at sea. There is a small shop aboard, a British registered doctor, a hairdresser and laundry. There is also a superb reference library because these cruises are for those who enjoy intellectual stimulation.

Swan Hellenic's passengers adore the *Orpheus* as she glides from one European port to another. Cultural and historical enrichment programs are perfectly suited aboard a vessel with such an old-world atmosphere; the company's roster of high-brow but unstuffy lecturers adds a deep understanding of the countries visited that is rarely found aboard a standard cruise. Many of the Hellenic cruises have a special interest, such as botany, ornithology or marine biology, with experts in those particular fields traveling with you. Swan Hellenic also has Nile and Rhine river cruises, as well as Natural History and Art Treasures tours for the young in mind at any age!

PACIFIC PRINCESS

(see Island Princess)

AUTHOR TIP

A good agent will cover all the basics necessary for your on-board happiness: preferences for first or second seating and preferences for twin versus double/queen bed. The pro will avoid booking you on a promenade deck or in an outside cabin with a lifeboat for a view. Expect to discuss the pros and cons of purchasing an air/sea package versus making separate air arrangements.

⚓⚓⚓⚓+

PEARL

Pearl Cruises; Bahamian registry; Scandinavian and American officers; European hotel management; Filipino crew; originally built in 1967 in Finland and named *Finnstar*; rebuilt in 1982 and rechristened the *Pearl of Scandinavia*; extensively refurbished in 1988 and rechristened *Ocean Pearl*; 12,400 tons; 514 feet long; 66 feet at beam; 500 passengers; crew of 225; cruising speed of 20 knots; 9 passenger decks.

While the *Pearl* is a traditional cruise ship, we have listed the vessel in the "specialty ship" category due to the intensive focus on the history and culture of ports. A cruise aboard the *Pearl* is geared toward those who want in-depth exposure to the Far East and is above all a rich educational experience. There are standard cruise ship amenities, but the real focus is the countries visited.

The former *Pearl of Scandinavia* was acquired by Ocean Cruise Lines in the spring of 1987 and, following a multimillion dollar refit, was rechristened *Ocean Pearl* (in 1994, she was renamed the *Pearl*). Her passenger complement is 500, in 11 different cabin categories. Public rooms are decorated in oriental motifs, two new bars have been added, as well as a fitness center and 24 more cabins (two inside cabins included). Several public rooms have been renamed: the Orchid Room restaurant (now overlooking the bow area and sea); Raffles Cafe and Discotheque (including outdoor buffet and barbecue); and the aft decks have been reteaked. A popular Piano Bar is in the former restaurant space, and the main Marco Polo Lounge and Explorers Bar are much improved and very impressive. There is also a Skylight Lounge and Card Room located on Sky Deck (just aft of the bridge), which has a quiet atmosphere, sea views and Singapore-style rattan decor that offers the nuance of colonial times.

The ship is bright and clean, with service both helpful and friendly. The Filipino stewards get high marks, and everyone adores the darling bar hostesses. This is one vessel where the lounge stewards do not ignore passengers thirsts! Port material and briefings are very important on this type of cruise, and passengers are pleased by the comprehensive material that awaits them in the cabin. Cruise staff on board is especially helpful in answering questions and well experienced in the whys and ways of the Far

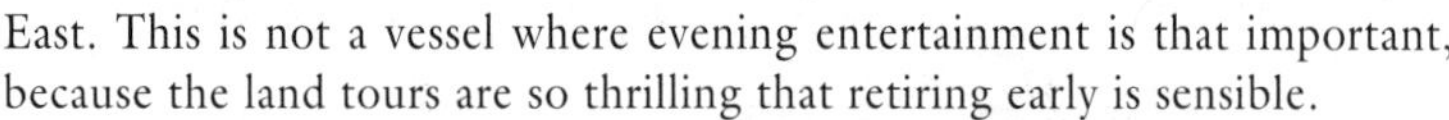

East. This is not a vessel where evening entertainment is that important, because the land tours are so thrilling that retiring early is sensible.

Pearl *sails year-round in the Far East on 12-23 day cruises with port calls in China, Vietnam, Hong Kong, Russia, Bangkok, Japan, Korea and Indonesia. If you have a hankering to visit Vietnam before McDonalds and Hilton arrive, Pearl offers a 17-day all-Vietnam voyage that delivers the most in-depth program available. The company offers cruise tours, which include pre-cruise hotel stays with sightseeing in the port of embarkation. Rates are very reasonable for this area of the world: for example, a 23-day "Great Cities of Asia" cruise/tour is priced from $3550, including a three-day pre-or post-cruise hotel stay in Hong Kong and a five-day pre- or post-cruise stay in Singapore and Bangkok. Advance purchase discounts offer savings of up to $1200 and round-trip air add-ons are available from $595, depending on date and departure city.*

AUTHOR'S AWARD

The Pearl *offers superb Asian itineraries at moderate cost in the Far East for those seeking an in-depth experience of history and local culture.*

⚓⚓⚓⚓+

POLARIS

Special Expeditions; Bahamian registry and Scandinavian officers; international crew; built in Denmark in 1960 as overnight ferry; rebuilt 1982 as *Lindblad Polaris*; became simply *Polaris* in 1988; 2214 tons; 238 feet long; 43 feet at beam; 80 passengers; crew of 40; cruising speed of 16 knots; 4 passenger decks.

Packing for a voyage on the 2214-ton Polaris is a breeze! A medium size suitcase filled with slacks, shorts, sweaters and sweats, all suited to layering, is all one needs for an extraordinary journey to some of the most intriguing parts of the globe. Add walking shoes, binoculars and a camera and you're ready to jump into a waiting Zodiac.

Built originally as a ferry boat, the expedition vessel *Polaris* today carries some 80 passengers and a crew of 51. There is no pool, no elevator, and the steps connecting the inside passenger levels are steep. One goes aboard this ship to learn and explore, and every day there are lectures on wild life, history, flora and fauna, photography and even, I'm told, wine tasting and local cooking. While there are group tours of villages, cathedrals, castles and museums, one is encouraged to go off on one's own and explore. Passengers are mostly older, retired and well-traveled. The staff is mostly young, well-educated, enthusiastic and passionately committed to the environment.

Public rooms reflect the laid-back, homey and scholarly feeling of the ship. A small library is inviting and cozy, with deep, well-used comfortable chairs and couches. Tucked into one corner of the room is a small, well-stocked snack bar where you help yourself to coffee, tea, cookies and fresh fruit. The Lounge is a large, rectangular room with window walls port and starboard, and a bar nestled in one corner. Banquettes along the walls are deep and comfortable and small swivel chairs pulled up to tables encourage cozy conversation, reading or viewing. A very able pianist plays his heart out with pre-dinner renditions and everyone gathers here for pre- and post-dinner cocktails. There is also a very well-equipped shop should you forget a heavy jacket or sweater, your bird book or binoculars—they seem to have thought of everything for your exploring comfort and enjoyment. The ship's "art" is magnificent photography of birds, polar bears and whales taken by staff and former passengers. They share a wall with posters dispensing practical advice such as the procedure when you find yourself nose to nose with a huge Polar bear, and the art of boarding Zodiacs.

The dining room has peach table linens, fresh flowers, attractive china and flatware, and the single, open seating encourages people to mingle. Wide windows on three sides provide a wonderful panoramic view while dining. The food is very good, simple, tasty and fresh. Breakfast and lunch are large buffets and dinner is served by a very efficient crew. There is no room service unless one is ill.

Cabins on the *Polaris* come in a variety of shapes and sizes, the largest at 258 square feet. Most are a standard 124 square feet, with large windows, twin beds, a desk/dressing area and two small, but adequate, closets (you don't need much clothing on these trips). Bathrooms are equipped with Evac toilets, a basin and shower. The operative word is casual. One is told when boarding the ship that Polaris is a "keyless" vessel, and I never once felt uncomfortable leaving my cabin unlocked. Cabins #103 and #104 deep in the ship are roomy and probably the most stable.

Deck space is limited since the Zodiacs take up a lot of room and used for observing what's ashore or dolphin/whale spotting. The Captain maintains an open bridge policy and seems to enjoy visits from interested passengers.

Land tours from the *Polaris* are first class, and not limited exclusively to nature and the environment. In Spain, on our visit to Santiago de Compostela, we visited the rococo Cathedral and wound up in the courtyard of a historic vaulted hall. We joined together for a marvelous sit-down luncheon of steak, salad, green vegetables and thick Spanish bread, all washed down with a good local wine that flowed profusely.

This ship does indeed deliver what is promised—you do hop into Zodiacs, visit remote spots, have in-depth land tours and find topflight lecturers.

There were inevitable hitches, but even at the hefty per person, per diem of around $450, it's worth every cent.

Sailing areas for the Polaris *are Central America (especially Costa Rica), the Panama Canal, Coastal Iberia and France, the British Isles, the North Cape and the Arctic, Canada's Maritime Provinces and the Bay of Fundy, Atlantic Seaboard, A Thousand Miles up the Amazon, the Orinoco River and lower Caribbean islands and from the Caribbean to the Pacific Ocean.*

★★★★★

QUEEN ELIZABETH 2

Cunard Line; British registry and crew; built on the River Clyde and launched in 1967; christened by Her Majesty the Queen; maiden voyage in 1969; last major refit 1987; 67,139 tons; 963 feet long; 105 feet at beam; 1864 passengers; crew of 1025; cruising speed of 32.5 knots; 13 passenger decks.

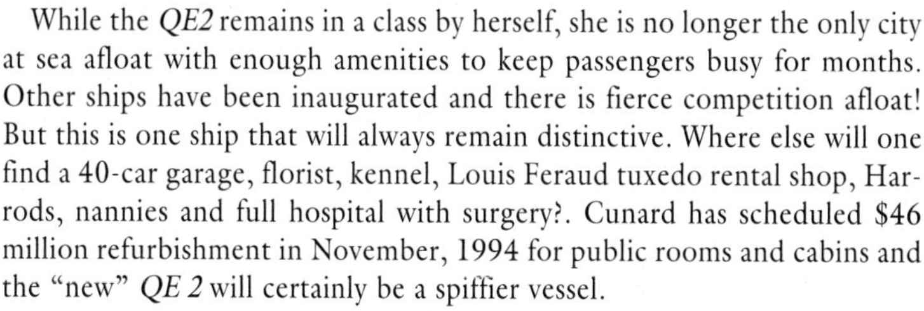

While the *QE2* remains in a class by herself, she is no longer the only city at sea afloat with enough amenities to keep passengers busy for months. Other ships have been inaugurated and there is fierce competition afloat! But this is one ship that will always remain distinctive. Where else will one find a 40-car garage, florist, kennel, Louis Feraud tuxedo rental shop, Harrods, nannies and full hospital with surgery?. Cunard has scheduled $46 million refurbishment in November, 1994 for public rooms and cabins and the "new" *QE 2* will certainly be a spiffier vessel.

Passenger flow will be greatly improved (it takes a full five days to find one's way around), public decks renamed and throughout the ship will be memorabilia from the era of the great liners.

Sports Deck will be renamed Sun Deck, its bar enlarged, and new freshwater showers added for use by sunbathers. First class passengers will find their own facilities on Boat Deck, with the addition of four new ultra-deluxe cabins; the card room will be enlarged; a new "Observation Lounge" with sweeping views of the ocean added; the Queens' Grill will be refurbished and enlarged and a new business center will offer faxes, computers and business publications. On Upper Deck, where most public rooms are located, the Columbia Restaurant will be relocated and renamed the Caronia Restaurant.

Cunard will also add the "Golden Lion," an authentic British pub with dart board and draft beer and game room while expanding the casino and Yacht Club bar, and relocating the Shopping Promenade.

On Quarter Deck, the Midships Bar will be refurbished and "themed" as a Chart Room Bar utilizing charts and nautical instruments while both Princess Grills will be refurbished. The Mauretania Restaurant will be relocated from Upper Deck while the Queen's Room will be revamped and will become a ballroom entertainment area. A new teen club will feature pinball and video games plus disco area with large TV.

Some 20 cabins will be designated as handicapped staterooms and all staterooms aboard ship will be refurbished, including new bathrooms, carpets, upholstery and curtains.

The *QE 2* was the first ship to launch an extravagant shopping arcade and its stores will remain elite—Harrods, H. Stern and Tiffany, to name-drop a few.

The Grande Theater will boast tiered seating and a state-of-the-art entertainment center. It is a large room, but it has none of the cold glitz associated with other spacious showrooms afloat. As an added bonus, those upstairs buying Gucci and Pucci or renting a black tie for certain transatlantic nights, can watch the shows or other activities. Behind the Grande Theater is the bright and airy Yacht Club, which overlooks paddle tennis/volleyball court by day and is properly romantic at night with a Lucite-covered baby grand piano/and bar. Adult, teenage, and children's games rooms are near the Yacht Club, so the various generations can keep track of each other.

The theater remains among the best afloat, with comfortable seating, a balcony section and a convenient location (how many times have you scratched a good program because the theater was several decks down?).

Intellectual pursuits on board include an extensive series of lectures generally, something for everyone classical and popular concerts, the *QE2* Network, or view from the bridge on television in every cabin (VCRs in first-class and above accommodations), a mini-version of the *International Herald Tribune* delivered beneath your door, and telephones that wake you up (when they work) and will get you anywhere on earth or above.

ELEGANT RESTAURANTS

The *QE2* boasts the famous Spa at Sea which includes a whirlpool bath and thalassotherapy pool with high-powered jets for relaxation, an inhalation room with moist, negatively ionized seawater or herbal mist, French hydrotherapy bath treatment and massages of every kind. A popular jogging track can be found on Boat Deck; there is weight training equipment and four Jacuzzis, as well as saunas and trained masseuses. Most everything is complimentary, except the massage and hair and beauty treatments.

Accommodations on board the *QE2* range from Super Class suites to inside cabins with upper and lower berths, and your dining experience depends upon the category you choose. The 8000 category suites are lovely in good weather, but all that glass looking out on a nasty, gray sea can be gloomy. On transatlantic crossings, the B category accommodations offer the traditional seagoing ambience and retain their coziness even when the North Atlantic acts up. However, passengers who choose the lower categories have just as much fun as everyone else provided they do not expect to be pampered. For the ship is a floating city and there are so many daily activities available, there is little time to dream up a list of complaints (although a certain percentage manage to do so on every sailing).

Several years ago Cunard created the ultimate travel experience by offering SS-ST superliner/supersonic between the U.S. and London, as well as other major world ports. The result is that Cunard has become one of the largest charterers of British Airways Concorde service and offers the sea/air packages at hefty but decent rates. And it's a great way to go! During the scheduled transatlantic crossings between April and December, Cunard offers a series of escorted European tours, as well as discounts at Trafalgar House properties.

Cunard's new European riverboats are also discounted, and you can cruise on nearly every major river of the continent. From January through April, QE 2 *circumnavigates the globe on a 100-day world cruise to six continents; in addition to regularly scheduled transatlantic service between New York and Southampton, scheduled throughout the remainder of 1995, occasional cruises are offered in the Mediterranean, Baltic, New England and Bermuda. Wonderful special interest programs are scheduled on nearly all transatlantic crossings. Cunard has dozens of discount options. Brochure per person, per diem rates range from $270–$950.*

AUTHOR TIP

When buying a cruise package to Europe, don't be misled by the number of days advertised. Some companies promote "eight-day" vacations that involve only six nights abroad, for example. How can this be? They count the day you leave the U.S. as the first day; most eastbound flights to Europe operate overnight, so your second day (i.e., day of arrival) is really your first night in Europe. They also count the day of your return flight as the eighth day. Add it up and you have eight days of travel but only six nights on the ship.

★★★★★+

QUEEN ODYSSEY

Royal Cruise Line; Bahamian registry and Greek crew; 10,000 tons; built by Schichau Seebeckwerft Shipyard, Bremerhaven, Germany; commissioned February, 1992 as *Royal Viking Queen*, entered Royal Cruise Line's fleet in August, 1994; 212 passengers; 140 crew; 62 feet at beam; cruising speed 19 knots; 6 passenger decks.

With the demise of Royal Viking Line, parent company Kloster Cruises moved the tony *Royal Viking Queen* to Royal Cruise Line's fleet where she will sail as the *Queen Odyssey* in January, 1995. This 212-passenger ship was one of the most recent entries into the elite world of yacht-like vessels combining understated elegance with exotic itineraries most commonly associated with expedition vessels. Palm Beach society turned out en masse to help christen the $86 million vessel in 1992, and she has sailed to some of the world's most remote and glamorous locales ever since. As *Queen Odyssey* will keep her superb RVL staff and crew, with Royal adding its best Greek captain and senior officers; RVL's no-tipping policy has been eliminated.

The all-suite accommodations, the smallest measuring 277 square feet, all boast five-foot-wide windows, large marble bathrooms, walk-in closets with ample storage for several weeks of clothing, TV/VCR, refrigerators, bars with the guest's personal favorites (stocked at time of sailing), plush furniture, a coffee table that converts to a dining table (for those who wish to dine in their cabins) and twin beds that convert to queen-size. Six suites have balconies: two have been designated as Owner's Suites; four have been renamed the St. Paul de Vence Suite, the Mykonos Suite, the Venezia Suite and the Seville Suite.

The focal point of the ship is a three-foot glass and mirrored globe located at the base of a circular stairwell that connects all six decks. A skylight atop the ship projects natural light down the stairwell creating the illusion of the world's surface in the area below.

The *Queen Odyssey* has the ambience of a very exclusive private yacht, with public rooms exquisitely furnished in luxurious fabrics and materials. For example, the pale aqua observation lounge, is wonderful for watching arrival in port, and the Portofino Bar is a relaxing place to meet friends for an after-dinner cognac, as is the large lounge. Other public areas include a well-stocked library, boutique and casino. A Board Room holds computers and international calling telephones.

The Queen's Restaurant, with open seating, is among the most elegant dining rooms afloat. Calories can be burned off in the spacious health and fitness center with aerobics room, weights, Lifecycles, sauna and massage. Additional facilities include a sun deck with swimming pool, jogging track and two whirlpools. After a dip, casual lunch is served in the lido cafe. Like Sea Goddess and Seabourn vessels, the Queen Odyssey has a floating marina which, when the ship is at anchor, permits passengers to swim in a specially constructed marine pool, boat or water ski right from the ship's stern.

Royal's itineraries in 1995 include 7-day Caribbean itineraries which can be combined for 14- and 21-day cruises with no duplication of ports. From spring through fall, Queen Odyssey *cruises the Mediterranean on 12- and 14-day itineraries, which may be taken in shorter segments. Royal will introduce "Odyssey Discovery Day" at surprise locations selected for their beauty, privacy and range of attractions. On these special days the ship will be anchored, its self-contained marina deployed, and guests invited to snorkel, explore the local and in some cases, go fishing!.* Queen Odyssey's *rates are still among the highest in the industry (starting around $750 per person, per day, depending on cruising region) but Royal makes it easier to sample the good life by offering a special pricing structure. Those booking by March 31, 1995 at brochure rate can bring a second person free of charge.*

★★★★+

RADISSON DIAMOND

Diamond Cruises; built in Finnyards OY in Rauma, Finland; launched in 1992; International staff and crew; 20,000 tons; 410 feet long; 105 feet at beam; 354 passengers; 192 crew; cruising speed 12.5 knots.

Originally intended as an upscale meeting and incentive vessel, *Radisson Diamond* seems to be trying to shed that image and join the ranks of the topflight deluxe cruise ship. Revolutionary is the term most often used to describe this double-hulled, 354-passenger ship. She is the first and only ship of Diamond Cruise Line, part of Radisson Hotels International.

From certain angles, the ship looks like a prehistoric behemoth, measuring 410 feet in length and 105 feet in width (the *QE 2* is only two feet wider).

The company claims this is "the most stable cruise ship afloat," but there seems to be some controversy to this claim. I sailed with Thoumas Routa, in charge of concept and product development for Diamond Cruises. He explained the structure's merits: because the working machinery of the ship is built deep into the pontoons (in other words, way below the water line), there is less noise and vibration—and this is true. On a conventional ship, the whole hull of the ship comes into contact with the water. On *Radisson Diamond*, however, because of the enormous space between the hulls, only a small part of the ships' surface comes into contact with the rise and fall of the swells.

If that explanation helps Thoumas and a handful of other passenger to combat motion sickness, so be it. But it didn't help me, and it didn't help a lot of other passengers while on board. On a recent Caribbean voyage we had some fairly rough seas. Most of us felt a lot of motion, at least as much as on other medium-size or larger ships. In my experience, it seems that in mildly rough seas she has about the same pitch and roll as other ships.

Since a prime reason for going on a cruise is to look at the ocean, I found this ship's interior a hinderance. There is a "closed in" feeling, and it begins when you enter a low-ceiling reception area with dark woods, dark floral carpeting and subdued lighting. A lovely brass and glass stairway curves upward around the elevators which, unfortunately, are designed with the cables and wires and works exposed on all floors. If this is part of the design, it doesn't work (the elevators look as though under repair). I have a problem with the 230-seat entertainment lounge, called Windows. On three levels, including a small balcony, the room is decorated in blue-grey leather with a lot of chrome and glass. Advertised as offering "breathtaking views of the ocean," the view is there, but only if you are standing up, or kneeling on one of the banquettes.

The *Radisson Diamond* is full of stunning art. A frieze depicting sea scenes made of ceramic tiles encircles the Grand Dining Room. This room is one of the most spectacular dining rooms afloat. During the day, sun streams through the floor to ceiling windows while the aqua, coral and green decor brings this room alive. Support columns designed to look like palm trees break up the space in this huge room, and give it an intimacy that belies its size. Comfortable chairs are upholstered and barrel-backed, and there is plenty of space between tables. While you may request a specific table from the maitre'd, there is open seating at tables for two, four, six and eight.

Complimentary red and white wines are served with dinner each night (choices lean toward Merlots, Zinfandels, Carbernets and Chardonnays, with premium wines available at a surcharge). All of the above, plus a crackerjack dining room staff, makes dining on the ship a very pleasant experience. The Grill, adjacent to the decks and near the outdoor swimming pool, is an alternative to dinner in the Dining Room. Italian to the core, it is festive with red checkered table cloths and an open kitchen so you can watch all of the culinary action.Every day at the lunch buffet a special, such as sushi or pasta, is offered. The appeal of a colorful salad bar was somewhat diminished by bottles of Kraft salad dressing on the table (nothing against Kraft, but a nicely mixed dressing would be better). There is no midnight buffet, but room service is available 24 hours a day.

The art deco Club Lounge is eye-catching white, mauve and purples, with subtle light gleaming from wood-paneled walls. The room seats 60 in a subdued and elegant setting, and is furnished with some of the most uncomfortable furniture I've ever wrestled with. A piano bar is tucked into one corner and there is a small dance floor. The Constellation Center, a 150- seat conference center has state-of-the-art audiovisual facilities; but for a ship that advertises itself as "corporate conference and incentive group" oriented, it was a bit of a shock to find only one computer, which was constantly in use on days that it functioned. Chips Casino is located amidship, a small, low-key operation. The fitness center has 12 machines, classes and sauna/massage. There was an odd potpourri of lectures on my voyage, including "International Narcotics, Challenge of the '90s," "The War in Afghanistan, the Soviet Union Defeated" and "Today's Art World."

The 177 staterooms are really more like suites. Private balconies are available in 123 cabins and the rest have floor-to-ceiling windows. Each is a generous 243 square feet of space, decorated in soft rose and blue; light woods and lots of mirrors reflect the light. All are well furnished with a complimentary bar, refrigerator, 13" TV/VCR, safe, terrycloth robes and seating area with two chairs, a sofa and small table. Bathrooms are spacious and well designed, although tubs are smaller than one might like.

I found carelessness on deck, some of it a bit frightening. Hoses and ropes were left unattended on decks where passengers could easily (and did), trip over them. Some of the deck crew seemed to have little concern for safety of the passengers. One afternoon, while walking across the aft deck, a crew hand, without a glance in either direction, slid a chair across the deck.

It missed hitting a passenger only because she jumped out of the way. While passengers gasped, seconds later he tossed a second chair. While the cost of docking a ship is exorbitant, I was surprised that a vessel in this price range always tendered passengers ashore. In St. Thomas, we did dock in Crown Bay, a taxi ride to town, instead of Charlotte Amalie, where all the action is and the offloading port of nearly every cruise ship. "Heavy scheduling" ... "peak season," etc., just doesn't cut it.

In 1995, Radisson Diamond *winters in the Caribbean on 3-, 4-, 5-, 6- and 7-night itineraries. Sailing from San Juan, the shorter cruises primarily visit St. Thomas and St. Maarten, while 7-day itineraries are a bit more imaginative. This ship cruises in the Mediterranean between Athens and Istanbul from May through October. Per person, per diem rates begin at around $450, including tips, en-suite alcohol and wine with meals.*

Radisson Diamond

REGAL PRINCESS

(See Crown Princess)

AUTHOR TIP

Most ships sailing on Caribbean itineraries stop in St. Thomas, dispensing 1.2 million cash-laden passengers each year who eagerly flock to duty free shops in Charlotte Amalie. But this self-proclaimed "American Paradise" could become a potentially hellish experience due to an increase in **crime against tourists**. The U.S. Navy cancelled all port calls to the island following a series of attacks on sailors in public. Many port lectures aboard ships now urge passengers to avoid going solo and to select a shore excursion, even for shopping. It's not necessary to bypass this port, but passengers may want to opt for a day in nearby St. John, a tranquil nature preserve a short ferry ride away, or head for Marigot Beach, one of the best in the Caribbean.

N/R
REGENT RAINBOW

Regency Cruises; Panamanian registry; European and international officers and crew; rebuilt in 1992 and relaunched in January, 1993; 25,000 tons; 599 feet long; 84 feet at beam; 960 passengers;crew of 420; cruising speed of 19 knots.

The *Regent Rainbow* joined Regency Cruises fleet in 1993, and was the company's entry into the two- and five-day market. The 960-passenger vessel is the only ship offering short cruises from Tampa, with children's activities during holidays and summer months, for those combining a brief vacation at sea with Florida's west coast sightseeing attractions.

Public rooms are decorated in soft pastel colors, including the Starlight Lounge on Bridge Deck, where late night dancing is popular; the Regency Showroom, which boasts evening cabaret and Las Vegas-type revues; Monte Carlo Court, Casino Royale and a number of lounges. The two-seating Chanterelle Dining Room has an orchestra balcony and casual breakfast and lunch are served in Le Bistro, adjacent to the pool. Children's facilities include a Junior Cruisers Clubhouse with supervised activities for kids of all ages.

There are 484 staterooms, all with color television, radio and hair dryers in bathrooms, many with tubs. Superior and deluxe outside staterooms have private sitting areas, and a choice of twin or double beds.

I haven't cruised on the Regent Rainbow, *but she has received overall high marks from travel agents. Regency's cuisine and service are well above average, and the onboard ambience is more subdued than is found on the typical short-cruise vessel. Sailing from Tampa, where one avoids the crowds who flock from Miami, is a plus with those who also like exploring local attractions, such as Busch Gardens. Through April 28, 1995,* Regent Rainbow *offers 4-day cruises to Playa del Carmen and Cozumel; the alternating 5-day itinerary calls in Playa del Carmen/Cancun, Cozumel and Key West. In May, the Regent Rainbow inaugurates a season of weekly spring through fall Alaska cruises. Per person, per diem begins around $105 before "SmartFare" discounts.*

★★★

REGENT SEA

Regency Cruises; Bahamian registry; Greek officers and European crew; originally built in 1957 and sailed as *Gripsholm* for Swedish America Line; refurbished in 1975 and renamed *Navarino* for Mediterranean cruises; refurbished in 1985 and renamed *Regent Sea*; 22,000 tons; 631 feet long; 83 feet at beam; 722 passengers; crew of 365; cruising speed of 18.5 knots; 8 passenger decks.

Since the former *Navarino/Gripsholm* rebirth as *Regent Sea*, all reports have been excellent for onboard services and food and itineraries. As a vessel, she is one of the most comfortable afloat, with old-world spaciousness in accommodations and public areas and a feeling of stability. Karageorgis (a wealthy Greek shipper and the former owner) transformed the ship into a cruise-style vessel, added a theater and some suites. (I understand from a former *Gripsholm* purser that his ex-cabin is now a top-grade accommodation which says something about the treatment of officers on Swedish America Line!)

The ship was designed with all outside cabins, so the 23 inside-variety are courtesy of Karageorgis. The rest of the accommodations are so spacious that passengers are immediately impressed by the fact that they do not run into each other or themselves in the bathroom. Many have double beds, multiple closets and most boast a bathtub, as well as shower. Single travelers are matched with a colleague (of the same sex) and even upgraded if necessary.

Public areas on board *Regent Sea* are attractive, and all paths lead midships on Veranda Deck to the Regency Lounge. Forward of the main lounge is a shopping arcade, card room, Casino Royale, the lime green/white rattan Riviera Veranda, romantic Rendezvous Lounge with live mood music, popular computer room, and Ruby Lounge (where video cassettes can be seen). Aft of the main lounge is the library and Lido Cafe/Veranda/Disco where food, music and dance action takes place from buffet breakfasts until sandwiches and pizza in the wee hours of the next day. A lovely swimming pool is aft on Veranda Deck; a fitness center with whirlpool area is located down on Dorado Deck.

The Caravelle dining room (one for smoking, one for non) on Allegro Deck is a place of great enjoyment for *Regent Sea* passengers, not only for its pleasing decor, but for the pleasing menus provided by topnotch caterers. Here, as elsewhere on the vessel, the European-style service is apparent and enjoyed by the "well-cruised" clientele. For it is the experienced set that Regency appeals to, at prices that everyone can afford but hardly believe! A very comfortable theater is located forward of the dining room.

The Regent Sea *spends the summer in Alaska and winters in the Caribbean, cruising every Saturday from Montego Bay on Land of the Maya voyages to Belize, Honduras, Guatemala and Cozumel, with wonderful shore excursions to Tikal, Copan and other Maya antiquities. In my opinion, the most impressive archaeological ruins in this hemisphere.*

During the summer, Regent Sea *can be found in Alaska sailing every Sunday from either Vancouver or Whittier (Anchorage) for College Fjord/Columbia Glacier, Sitka, Lynn Canal, Skagway, Juneau, Ketchikan and all-day cruising of the Inside Passage. Each fall the* Regent Sea *makes a full circumnavigation of South America.*

AUTHOR TIP

Some of **the best deals are never advertised** but available through travel agencies that are part of a nationwide franchise. They commonly book large blocks of cabins on specific sailings and offer their clients savings of up to 50% off brochure rates. Check your local newspaper and yellow pages for local travel agencies, call and ask to be added to their cruise mailing list. Specify if you have a specific interest, such as children's programs or preferred geographic regions. You may wind up sailing aboard a ship you couldn't afford otherwise.

★★★
REGENT STAR

Regency Cruises; Bahamian registry and European crew; built in Holland in 1957 and sailed as *Statendam* until 1982; refurbished and renamed *Rhapsody* by Paquet; 24,500 tons; 642 feet long; 79 feet at beam; 950 passengers; crew of 450; cruising speed of 19 knots; 9 passenger decks.

With the rebirth of the *Statendam* as *Regent Star*, the vessel gained some new diesel engines and improved maneuverability via a bow thruster. The *Star* is another classic vessel, with plenty of space for passengers. Regency did not change much of the decor when it assumed operation during the summer of 1987, as Paquet had already spent money on that. The vessel has 487 spacious accommodations, of which 187 are inside.

The main public rooms are located on Promenade Deck, with its Regency Lounge, Lido cafe and bar that opens onto the outdoor swimming pool area, the Starlight Lounge/disco, Casino Royale, library and card room. The Cordon Bleu dining room is located on Bolero Deck, a theater on Concerto Deck, and indoor pool/fitness center on Domino Deck. Rather far down, but that is the way these vessels were built in the good old days.

The *Regent Star* is a handsome and comfortable vessel that offers good value, without being as elegant as others in the Regency fleet.

During the winter months she is based in Montego Bay for Sunday departures on the original Regency schedule. The 1-week cruises feature Costa Rica, Aruba and Cartagena, Colombia and a partial transit of the Panama Canal through Gatun Lock to Gatun Lake. From late May to September, the Regent Star *sails Whittier and Anchorage on 7-day Alaska cruises.*

★★★+

REGENT SUN

Regency Cruises; Bahamian registry and European officers and crew; originally built in 1964; and former names were *Hanseatic, Shalom,* and most recently *Doric* and *Royal Odyssey*; last refurbished in 1982; 25,500 tons; 627 feet long; 81 feet at beam; 836 passengers; crew of 410; cruising speed of 19 knots; 9 passenger decks.

The 836-passenger *Regent Sun* enjoyed a very happy life as the *Doric* for Home Lines. When she was sold to Royal Cruise Line in 1982 and became *Royal Odyssey*, the vessel underwent an extensive refit under the loving care of interior designers A. and M. Katzourakis, who created colorful schemes throughout. In fact, practically nothing was left of the former *Doric*. A great deal of money was spent and the result is quite impressive. Regency Cruises acquired a ready to sail vessel and has made her its flagship.

The multi-tiered Regency Lounge, where theatrical entertainment occurs in the evening, has an Italian parquet dance floor designed by David Legno, as well as a reportedly spectacular lighting system. Both indoor and outdoor pools have been refurbished and tiled with French Briare ceramics. The Cordon Rouge Dining Room has been opened up, with windows to the sea, and Greek-designed tapestries and mirrored abstracts grace landings and corridors. Regency does exceptionally well in areas of food and service, outshining some ships which are twice the cost. Staterooms are unusually spacious in nearly all categories, accented with silkscreen panels, and a contemporary decor.

The *Regent Sun* boasts a total of 422 cabins: 22 superior deluxe suites, 33 junior suites, 290 outside cabins and 75 inside cabins. Bathrooms have been modernized and many have tubs as well as showers. All cabins have individual air conditioning, American electrical outlets, twin beds, full vanities with long mirror, music and telephone for 24-hour room service. In addition to the five lounges, the vessel is equipped with cardroom, casino, library, theater, gymnasium, sauna and hairdresser. She is well organized and spacious enough for the full complement of passengers.

During the summer season Regent Sun *cruises between New York and Montreal on very popular 7-day New England/Canada voyages a wonderful route for history buffs and families. From October through April, the vessel is based in San Juan for 7-day Gems of the Caribbean cruises.*

★★★★+

RENAISSANCE I-VIII

Renaissance Cruises; Italian registry; Italian officers and European crew; all eight ships built in La Spezia, Italy, 1989-91; 4500 tons; 290/297 feet long; 50 feet at beam; 100/114 passengers; crew of 67/72; cruising speed of 15 knots; 6 passenger decks.

These six vessels are identical except for a few modifications as noted above. Some of the Renaissance ships will carry another 14 passengers, five more crew members, and be some seven feet longer—hardly noticeable even among the experts! The vessels feature all-outside suites ranging in size from 220 to 290 square feet, with queen- or twin-size beds (convertible), color TV/VCR (remote controlled if you can figure it out), bar/refrigerator, which has been stocked to your preference, security lock-drawer, etc. The decor is refined with good use of dark wood panels and mirrors that offer a yacht-like ambience. The sitting area furniture is covered in suede. The teak floor bathrooms have stall showers with a seat, marble vanity, plush towels, terrycloth robes—built-in hair dryer and designer toiletries. Starboard cabins are for nonsmokers; portside for those still with the habit. Suite stewardesses are Scandinavian.

Onboard amenities include the Lounge Club with piano bar and small casino, library, boutique, outdoor pool and spa with Jacuzzi, sauna and beauty salon, and a sports platform with Zodiacs, sunfish and snorkeling equipment. Life on board Renaissance is low-key, with planned activities other than enrichment lectures a rarity. Dress is comfortable elegance and passengers are sophisticated travelers who know what to expect. The restaurant offers tables for two to eight and guests are free to dine as they wish, from 7:30 to 10 p.m. Breakfast and lunch are informal and served buffet style al fresco, with hot items cooked to order. Continental breakfast and an international menu are available in the suites.

Destinations are the primary focus of these small vessels, with an emphasis on itineraries that other ship lines are just now "discovering." For example, cruises through 1995 are planned in the Far East, Mediterranean, Scandinavia, Black Sea, East Africa (Mahe, Seychelles to Mombasa, Kenya) and Caribbean.

Renaissance ships, while identical in size, amenities and wonderful destinations, are very difficult summarize as a fleet in terms of staff and quality. Standards vary significantly from one cruising region to another, and each vessel seems to operate by its own rules. The Caribbean and Europe offer consistently high standards. But this winter when I cruised in the Seychelles with Renaissance there were several surprises. A week-old tray of moldy food was under my bed. The ship unloaded its 70+ passenger on Zodiacs into heavy surf, a very unnerving adventure for these unsuspecting passengers. Renaissance Cruises office had no idea disembarkation was being handled this way in the Seychelles, and said it would put a warning in its next brochure. And, as has been stated in the company's profile, we find Renaissance Cruises' exorbitant tipping policy (which is not outlined in the brochure) to be completely unreasonable. Per person per diem ranges from $185 to $785.

AUTHOR TIP

Most experienced cruisers know that taking the **inaugural sailing** of a new ship will include some glitches. Multiply these problems by a hundred if you choose the inaugural of a ship that has just left the yard after a total refurbishment, especially when the vessel has changed cruise lines. FCI recently experienced such a voyage: passengers encountered problems such as plumbing leaks, lack of water and a stabilizer malfunction that resulted in a sudden 35 degree roll (there were no injuries, but plenty of breakage). Your travel agent should warn you against inaugural sailings, but always ask. And, it's generally wise to avoid the first sailing after a ship has left its annual dry dock since construction is frequently unfinished.

★★★★★

ROTTERDAM

Holland America Line; Netherlands Antilles registry, Dutch officers and Indonesian crew; originally built in the Netherlands in 1959 and christened by former *Queen Juliana*; last refurbished 1989; 38,000 tons; 748 feet long; 94 feet at beam; 1070 passengers; crew of 603; cruising speed of 21 knots; 10 passenger decks.

They don't build ships like the *Rotterdam* anymore. Her sleek black and white hull exudes confidence and comfort and a seaworthiness that is hard to find these days. She has an old-world charm that grew on me, even though I thought she got left behind in the beauty and glamour department. However, this vessel has some very fine features and a very loyal following. Among the ship's finest assets are her interior woods, many of which are rare today, the artistry of which has been lost forever. This and the spaciousness throughout offer a certain grace that can never be repeated on most of the newer vessels.

The *Rotterdam* has some wonderful public areas, and you can get rather lost going from forward to aft. You enter the vessel via Main Deck, near the front office and beauty parlor. Two flights up is Promenade Deck, which extends from the vast swimming pool area to the 450-seat theater in the forward section. In between are the pleasant Lido Terrace, a large Lido Restaurant for breakfast and buffet luncheons, a card/game room, the Lynbaan shopping center, the Ocean Bar and the Queen's Lounge with a bust of Juliana surveying all those who enter. One deck up are two nightclubs, the Ambassador Room and the Ritz Carlton, the latter of which has an elegant winding staircase up to a terrace and open deck area. But one cannot bypass the smoking room, the Tropic Bar, more shops and a pleasant theater balcony that seats 160 passengers. The dining rooms down on B Deck are called Odyssey and La Fontaine. In the tradition of vessels designed for the transatlantic run, these dining rooms do not have a sea view, but they are very well planned and comfortable. The vessel also has indoor swimming pool/sauna/massage areas, casino and self-service laundry with ironing facilities.

During her most recent refurbishment, a $15-million renovation completed in 1989 in Portland, Oregon, back-of-the-house equipment, as well as passenger amenities received attention. The public rooms, especially the Sky Room, Ritz Carlton Lounge, Ambassador Lounge, Queen's Lounge, Library, and both Ocean and Tropic bars were freshened. The Lido area (restaurant and deck) received a facelift and Upper Promenade Deck was extended. All staterooms boast new decor, as well as some bathrooms. Even the Casino was on the list with an additional 31 slot machines and two blackjack tables!

The *Rotterdam* has 304 outside cabins and 246 inside, all with private facilities. While not glamorous by my standards, the accommodations are sturdy, functional, and spacious, nothing tacky or prefab about them. The crew is eager to please, friendly, and forever smiling, offering gracious service. Holland America runs its own training school in Djakarta for crew aboard three of its vessels, and does a fine job. There is a No Tipping Required policy on board, which does not mean that some gratuities aren't rendered but the crew does not go around with palms extended, a refreshing change from most cruise ships.

Many of her loyal followers will be delighted to learn Rotterdam *once again voyages to distant lands. She begins 1995 with an 85-day world cruise between Los Angeles and New York; following a popular Alaska season, she makes a 34-day South Pacific voyage sailing round trip from Los Angeles. The* Rotterdam's *average per person, per diem ranges from $295 to $308, depending on cruising region.*

★★★+

ROYAL MAJESTY

Majesty Cruise Line; Panamanian registry; Greek officers and international crew; built in 1992 in Finland; 32,400 tons; 568 feet; 91 feet at beam; 1056 passengers; crew of 500; cruising speed 21 knots.

Royal Majesty was launched by Dolphin Cruises as a luxury ship in the 3- and 4-day cruise market, a vessel for those seeking a brief escape at sea on a vessel with refined decor, casual yet sophisticated atmosphere, and lovely cuisine. For a while she delivered, and was a refreshing alternative in this region.

Royal Majesty's decor is a tasteful nautical theme throughout the public rooms, with quality materials, such as brass, marble, elegant fabrics, floor-to-ceiling windows, as well as a good flow of public rooms. *Royal Majesty's* lounges are relaxing and plentiful. The Royal Observatory Panorama Bar, with intimate group seating, is lovely for watching sunsets and departure from port; other favorites are the Polo Club, where those having an after-dinner aperitif are serenaded by a pianist, and the wood-paneled Rendezvous Lounge, with marble bar and plush, comfortable chairs. The Palace Theatre, which features evening entertainment, has terraced seating; Frame 52, the late night disco, has wraparound windows and special lighting. *Royal Majesty* has the first nonsmoking dining room, so the palate is never affected by the odor of nicotine.

Fitness facilities are found in Bodywaves Spa, ample for the 1000-passenger capacity. There is sufficient deck space for sunning adjacent to the outdoor pool and two whirlpools; the secluded, quiet Crown Deck has a sunning area for those who prefer more privacy. Cabins are small, as the ship was designed specifically for 3- and 4-day cruises (outside standard staterooms measure 125 square feet), but very well appointed with soft decor, terrycloth robes, color television and hair dryers in bathrooms. Some 25 percent have been designated for nonsmokers.

I sailed with friends aboard Royal Majesty last Christmas and there were a number of areas which disappointed. Cuisine ranged from mediocre to fair and service was a problem throughout. While others had no complaints about their waiter, ours was incompetent and hostile. In general, there seemed to be disorder throughout the ship. A sleepless, harried cruise director tried to do everything from making announcements from the bridge to leading kids around in Christmas carols—and let it slip that she was the fourth in her position in a few months. One of our group asked a crew member to unlock the library 15 minutes after the designated opening time; reeking of liquor, he told her to turn the light on herself when she said she couldn't reach it. Since then, I've heard mixed reviews. It's my guess Dolphin decided to cut costs in the two most critical areas—food and service.

In 1995, Royal Majesty *cruises year-round from Miami on a 3-day itinerary to Nassau and Royal Isle, a private island where water sports are plen-*

tiful; 4-day cruises visit Playa del Carmen, Cozumel and Key West. Per person per diem rates range from $100 to $195.

AUTHOR TIP

Never, ever, ever take a new camera that you haven't used before. If it's complicated, it probably won't work properly or even at all. You'll not only get frustrated, but you also won't get any pictures. The new computerized automatic everything jobs can be delicate—not on the outside, but in the inner workings—and frequently dislike the typical cold and dampness of Alaska.

AUTHOR TIP

Photography buffs who want to get shots of beach scenes and water that are a notch above the rest should be advised to take along a polarizing filter for their 35mm SLR cameras; used properly, it will eliminate the glare or reflected sunlight off the surface of the water, bringing out the many hues of blue in the tropical water. Favorite film: Kodachrome 64—slow enough for rich colors in the sunlight, but fast enough to be useful on cloudy days as well.

★★★★+

ROYAL ODYSSEY

Royal Cruise Line; Bahamian registry; Greek officers and crew; originally built in 1983 as *Royal Viking Sea*; relaunched in 1991 as *Royal Odyssey*; 28,000 tons; 676 feet; 83 feet at beam; 750 passengers; crew of 410; cruising speed 21 knots; 9 passenger decks.

Royal Cruise Line has taken a venerable lady of the waves, the *Royal Viking Sea*, and imprinted its own distinctive signature on this popular ship. A renovation transformed her into a very 90s vessel with lovely public rooms and cabins, but the real spirit of the ship is RCL's warmhearted Greek ambience and crew that are beloved by the company's loyal following.

Maintaining the single-seating dining experience uncommon today in vessels above 300 passengers, the *Royal Odyssey* embodies a classic cruise style with the elegant lines and spacious layout of the former Royal Viking Line ship. The design team of A & M Katzourakis created a warm Mediterranean ambience with elegant fabrics, art and lovely public rooms that are gracious and intimate.

Stateroom fabrics are a blend of chintz and chenille in stylized floral prints and softly shaded graphic patterns. Among the 399 staterooms, 357 are outside, many with large picture windows, bathtubs and showers; the ship boasts 49 single-occupancy cabins, an unusually high number today. All cabins include television, telephones, three-channel radios, security lock-drawers; many have refrigerators and wall-mounted hair dryers. Nine superior deluxe apartments have art from ports of call the line visits. Outside cabins range from 160 to 240 square feet; deluxe apartments are 440 and 550 square feet.

The Penthouse Deck's public areas are devoted to casual gatherings and informal dining: aft are whirlpools, an informal bar and grill, and deck space for informal lunches and open-air dancing at night. On Deck Nine, the Penthouse Lounge, with soft biscuit wall coverings, striped curtains and brightly upholstered chairs, has a glass partitioned bar and lounge area with dance floor for lectures, bridge games and evening cocktail parties and dancing. The Panorama Lounge and Bar is popular for casual luncheon buffet and afternoon tea.

The *Royal Odyssey's* fitness center, located on Riviera Deck, has a gym with full time fitness director and supervised workouts.

A paracourse, paddle tennis court and golf driving range complete the facilities on Horizon Deck. A large pool on Odyssey deck is wind-sheltered and adjacent to Yianni's Hearth, where fresh-baked cinnamon buns are a morning tradition.

On Promenade Deck, the Ports of Call Lounge and Disco, used for tea and buffets during the day, becomes a popular disco bar at night; portside is the ship's casino. Also located on Promenade Deck are the purser's office, library, writing room and game room, as well as a cardroom equipped with felt-topped tables.

The Royal Restaurant on Odyssey Deck has wonderful touches, such as Aubusson tapestry-like carpeting and well-spaced tables fitted in damask linens. The adjacent Odyssey Lounge, where *Royal Odyssey's* evening entertainment is held, has upholstered sofas and chairs. Named for the familiar flying horse of Greek mythology, the Pegasus Bar is a gathering place for cocktails before and after the show.

The ship is indeed lovely, but Royal Cruise Line's large number of repeat passengers return again and again for the classical cruise experience and the renowned warmth and friendliness of the Greek officers and crew. At dinner, tables for eight are very popular with the outgoing 50s+ crowd who enjoy the camaraderie aboard the vessel. RCL's gentlemen hosts, who serve as dance partners, are among the ship's most popular features for women traveling alone.

Royal Cruise Line's Dine To Your Heart's Content menu is also a big hit with health-conscious passengers who want to keep calories, fat, cholesterol and salt in check. On Greek Night, for example, one can safely indulge in fare, such as Melitzanes Papoutsakia, lean meat-stuffed eggplant and rice-stuffed tomatoes. On a Mediterranean cruise last summer, however, cuisine in general was not up to the standards it should be in a vessel of this caliber. Per person, double occupancy rates range from $150 to $620.

In 1995, the Royal Odyssey *voyages to Australia, New Zealand and the Far East stopping in Vietnam, China and Japan. From May through August, 7-day Alaska cruises are scheduled, followed by New England/Canada sailings and late fall Panama Canal crossings. Royal has a marvelous lineup of theme cruises scheduled for this ship (consult Fielding's Theme Cruise Calendar in "Choosing Your Cruise").*

★★★★+

ROYAL PRINCESS

Princess Cruises; British registry and officers; European/British crew; completed in November 1984 in Wartsila Shipyard, Helsinki; christened in Southampton by HRH the *Princess of Wales*; 45,000 tons; 757 feet long; 106 feet at beam; 1200 passengers; crew of approximately 500; cruising speed of 20 knots; 9 passenger decks.

The *Royal Princess*, a decade old and still going strong, is very royal indeed and a real beauty. Designed and constructed at the famous Wartsila shipyard in Helsinki, the $150 million vessel has all outside cabins and a passenger complement of 1200. The ship's two-story atrium resembles a hotel, but the rest of the ship is extremely open and airy.

All 600 cabins have nice picture windows, wonderful light for reading, twin beds that convert to doubles, queens or kings, spacious bathrooms with both tub and shower (but no hair dryers, which should be a standard amenity aboard a ship of this caliber), individual climate control, refrigerators and color TV. Fire resistant woods have been used in the cabinets and closet areas. Suites, deluxe cabins and some standard cabins have private terraces.

A cruise aboard the *Royal Princess* is a real experience. The ship is large and boasts a variety of places to play and plenty of quiet lounges. The Lido pool area with its Jacuzzis is a pleasant spot in which to sun and read. There is another outdoor pool above. The ship has a total of 10 decks, four swimming pools, a Promenade Deck for joggers, and a full health spa with massage and sauna, just for starters. The Horizon lounge on Sun Deck is perfect for sunsets and early evening, but gets very busy as the night moves along.

Because the cabins are on the upper decks, one goes down to public areas and one is always aware of being at sea due to floor through ceiling windows, a delight at tea time.. The Crown Casino, Riviera Club, Terrace Room, Princess Court, library, theater, bridge room and International Lounge are all located on Riviera Deck. Below on Plaza Deck are the Continental dining room, Purser's Lobby and beauty salon. The dramatic Princess Court, a two-story space winding down by spiral staircase to the Plaza entrance hall, is the focal point of the vessel. The artwork is impressive, as it is on all Princess vessels. The largest and most dramatic piece is "Spendthrift" by British artist David Norris. With a height of more than 11 feet, it features three groups of gray-green bronze seagulls in flight and is located in the Plaza, the heart of the ship. There are enamel and ceramic murals, as well as a tapestry wall hanging in the public rooms. Staterooms have seven original lithographs, commissioned for *Royal Princess* from artists Paul Hogarth, Chris Corr, Alistair Crawford and Paul Benjamin.

Breakfast on your own terrace is a must; buffet luncheons are popular on Lido Deck, with the usual hamburgers, salads, fruit and pastries; dinner is a formal affair in the two-seating Continental dining room. The Italian chefs and stewards enjoy making special pastas, as well as flaming desserts for passengers, and are well rewarded for their services. Overall, I found the cuisine excellent, although at times uneven; dining staff was cheerful, helpful and responsive. There is 24-hour cabin service, and with your own small refrigerator in which to keep snacks, no one is likely to ever experience hunger pangs aboard!

Officers and hotel crew are British and very charming. I was impressed that the staff captain stopped by to explain lifeboat procedures personally (as we had embarked after the cruise had begun). This ship is wonderful, but could use a facelift—new carpets and fabrics would bring sparkle to this lovely ship. Shore excursions were extremely well organized but for my taste, too much time was spent on a bus. I was surprised that Princess charged for shuttle service between the pier and town. During my Baltic cruise, passengers were generally 55+ and most experienced travelers.

In response to consumer demand, the Royal Princess *is spending her summers in Europe, with 13-day sailings in the Baltic Sea—ah, romance! The* Royal *cruises the Panama Canal from fall through spring on 10- and 11-day sailings between San Juan and Acapulco, and Canada/New England during fall foliage season. The average per person, per diem is $275 including airfare.*

★★★★★+

ROYAL VIKING SUN

Cunard Line; Bahamian registry and European crew; 38,000 tons; built by Wartsila Marine Industries in Finland for service entry December 1988; 740 passengers; crew of 460; 673 feet long; 95 feet at beam; cruising speed of 21 knots; 8 passenger decks.

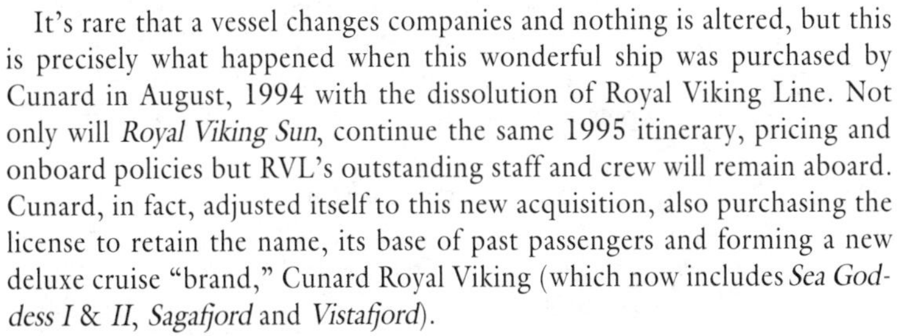

It's rare that a vessel changes companies and nothing is altered, but this is precisely what happened when this wonderful ship was purchased by Cunard in August, 1994 with the dissolution of Royal Viking Line. Not only will *Royal Viking Sun*, continue the same 1995 itinerary, pricing and onboard policies but RVL's outstanding staff and crew will remain aboard. Cunard, in fact, adjusted itself to this new acquisition, also purchasing the license to retain the name, its base of past passengers and forming a new deluxe cruise "brand," Cunard Royal Viking (which now includes *Sea Goddess I* & *II*, *Sagafjord* and *Vistafjord*).

The *Royal Viking Sun*, a $125-million vessel, boasts more space per passenger than almost any cruise vessel ever built except *Crystal Harmony*. The 370 staterooms all have walk-in closets and average about 200 square feet, with 96 percent outside and 39 percent of these with private verandas. In addition, accommodations offer TV/videos, convertible beds, and refrigerator/bars. There are 18 penthouse suites named for explorers (Cook, Amundsen, Columbus, Nansen, Tasman, Eriksson, Drake and Magellan, for instance) and an ultra-luxurious Owner's Suite on Sky Deck, all with convertible king-size beds, private verandas and Jacuzzi baths, as well as exclusive butler service. Also on Sky Deck is the Stella Polaris Room, an observation lounge forward.

Another set of penthouse suites is located on Bridge Deck (Vasco da Gama, Bougainville, Palmer, Heyerdahl, Cartier, Cabot, Bering, Amerigo Vespucci, Vancouver and Balboa). The Garden Lounge and Garden Cafe (informal dining during the day) are located on Bridge Deck, as is the Royal Grill a la carte restaurant seating 60 persons (with advance reservations) and offering both continental and nouvelle cuisine in an intimate ambience. The supper club-like setting features live music, and the menu will be prepared by the world's best visiting chefs on a rotating basis. Paul

Bocuse, who has become a mini-corporation, is the consulting chef for Royal Grill and has planned its menus.

Other public area amenities are the Oak Room, wood-paneled lounge with fireplace (reminiscent of the former Smoking Room men-only lounges on such glamorous vessels as the *Normandie*), two swimming pools (one with a swim-up bar), Royal Viking Spa with sea views, located near the lap pool, Norway Lounge with state-of-the-art sound/light equipment, multipurpose Starlight theater with flexible seating, cardroom, Compass Rose Wine Bar and piano lounge, the Casino and Midnight Sun Lounge (the ship's nightclub). Most of the public rooms are on Norway Deck, including the Dickens Library and Royal Arcade shopping area.

The open-seating Royal Viking dining room is surrounded by large picture windows and divided into three sections to maximize the sea views. Alternate dining is available in the Garden Cafe and Royal Grill. There are eight passenger decks in all, with deluxe cabins on Discovery Deck and other accommodations on Scandinavia, Atlantic and Pacific decks.

Other interesting features of the vessel include rubber-mounted engines, automatic window washing equipment, excellent soundproofing in all cabins, an open Promenade Deck, custom-designed tenders and a croquet court! This is definitely a first for cruise ships and although a scaled-down version of a professional croquet court (not the backyard variety), it has proved to be very popular. Already, there have been several croquet cruises of note.

Royal Viking Sun *starts her year in grand style—a 108-day world cruise between Ft. Lauderdale and San Francisco visiting 19 countries. Her May through October season in the Mediterranean, Black Sea and Baltic includes 2-week sailings that may be taken in 7-day segments, convenient for those who lack the time or funds for a full itinerary. In late 1995, a circumnavigation of South America is planned. Per person, per diem begins around $400.*

★★★★+
SAGAFJORD

Cunard Line; Bahamian registry; Scandinavian officers and European crew; launched in 1965; refitted in 1979 and 1984; 25,147 tons; 620 feet long; 82 feet at beam; 589 passengers; crew of 352; cruising speed of 20 knots; 7 passenger decks.

The *Sagafjord* became a quarter of a century old in 1990 and, unfortunately shows it—Cunard has a major refurbishment planned 1996. Passengers paying her still hefty per person, per diem, will find the wear and tear on this great classic disheartening. However, her age alone enhances, rather than detracts from, the quality of cruise life one finds aboard, and there are still loyal passengers who couldn't imagine skipping an annual voyage aboard *Sagafjord*, despite the need for a major overhaul. The vessel was built for Norwegian America Line at a time when sailings were still great happenings with lots of flowers, champagne and steamer trunks. Hence, cabins are large (no locked knees when you sit down on these beds) and there is plenty of closet space. There are also a record 54 singles for those traveling alone. Pampering begins at once, with such cabin amenities as terrycloth robes and fragrant soaps. Men get a *Sagafjord* cap, while ladies receive a tote bag that is light and very useful both on board and ashore. From time to time, other remembrances appear in your cabin. It's all part of the process of being pampered.

The *Sagafjord* has always been one of my favorite ships afloat. The ship's two-tiered nightclub, double-height windows in the dining room and two dozen suites were added a dozen years ago and have become part of the furniture.

While other vessels now boast state-of-the-art this and that, even five-story glass elevators, the *Sagafjord* remains a true seagoing vessel with traditional values. She truly is a home away from home for many loyal passengers, with a warm and caring ambience fostered by a staff that seems to have been there forever. The *Vistafjord* may be a touch prettier, and you may find more caviar on the Sea Goddess ships, but the cruise experience aboard *Sagafjord* heralds back to the era of the grand liners. The average age on board is retired, those who seek this kind of old-world attentiveness to detail and pampering.

Although the ship's registry is now in the Bahamas, officers remain Scandinavian and the crew is Northern European (with some charming western Canadians added to the cabin stewardess roster). By day, life aboard the *Sagafjord* is not casual chic, it's just plain casual and do as you please. But every evening is an event from (black tie) formal to dress-up for an elegant restaurant. On a cruise last year, the quality of food had declined with the rest of the ship, and I hope Cunard restores this to the memorable experience it once was.

However, what can compete in one's memory with the sight of those handsome officers in dress uniforms walking down the double staircase into the dining room? Only the parade of 50 stewards on the same staircase with platters of flaming Norwegian Surprise! Per person per diem rates range from $250 to $500.

AUTHOR TIP

If you are traveling on an air/sea package, the airline is responsible for finding your luggage and delivering it to the next port. But if you arranged your own air it's your problem—always have a well-fixed baggage tag plus ID taped to the inside of your luggage. Keep track of claim tickets and give the airline a detailed itinerary.

⚓⚓⚓

SANTA CRUZ

Galapagos Cruises of Quito, Ecuador; Ecuadorean crew and registry; designed and built in Spain exclusively for Galapagos cruises; launched December 1979; 1500 tons; 230 feet long; 90s passengers; crew of 35; cruising speed of 15 knots; 4 passenger decks; American Bureau of Shipping highest international safety classification.

The *Santa Cruz*, accommodating 90 passengers in 45 cabins, is among the best of the vessels cruising the Galapagos Islands. All twin and triple cabins are outside, and five single, inside cabins are on Main and Upper deck. All cabins have private facilities and are well designed with comfortable beds and a feeling of spaciousness. The vessel has a large sun deck, a pleasant one-seating dining room and an attractive lounge area with bar. The bar hours are flexible to passengers wishes, and bartender Pepe makes terrific Pisco Sours, the local cocktail. Mixed drinks are rather expensive since most supplies are imported by air, and wine can run to $20 per bottle. Beer and cigarettes cost about $2 each. The food on board is good, but not gourmet to my taste.

Breakfasts are wonderful (omelets, pancakes, fruit and fresh juices), but my coffee was powdered Nescafé. The dinners of fresh fish and fresh lobster tails are superb.

Life on board the *Santa Cruz* is decidedly casual, as each passenger is restricted to 20 pounds of luggage. Men are required to wear nothing more formal than a short sleeve pullover, while woman may want a more dressy outfit for the evening. After all, the charming Carlos, captain of the *Santa Cruz*, may invite you to dine at his table! Per person, per diem ranges from $180 to $260.

⚓⚓⚓⚓⚓

SEA BIRD/SEA LION

Special Expeditions; American registry and crew; built near Seattle, Washington, in 1982; formerly known as *Majestic Explorer* and *Great Rivers Explorer*, respectively; refurbished and renamed in 1990; 100 tons; 152 feet long; 31 feet at beam; 70 passengers; crew of 25; cruising speed of 12 knots; 4 passenger decks.

These two vessels are well suited to Special Expeditions cruises and one (or both) have been chartered by Sven Olaf Lindblad previously for his programs. They are now on long-term charter to his company and have been nicely refurbished to carry just 70 passengers in all-outside cabins with lower beds, private facilities and individual climate controls. Most accommodations also feature a large picture window.

The vessels have a shallow draft of eight feet and bow thrusters that provide maximum maneuverability into small coves and access to unreachable waterways. A fleet of rubber landing craft are also on board. These are expedition vessels and life on board reflects this. There is a bar/lounge, dining room and sun deck.

The vessels can be found on the Columbia and Snake rivers (in the wake of Lewis and Clark), exploring Alaska's coastal wilderness and voyaging to the Sea of Cortez around Baja, California, to observe migrations of whales and other animals. In summer, they venture to Europe and the Arctic for polar bear spotting. All expeditions are led by naturalists. Per person, per diem ranges from $250 to $500.

N/R

SEA CLOUD

Special Expeditions; Malta registry; built in 1931 in Germany, last refurbishment 1993; German officers and crew; 2517 tons; 360 feet long; 50 feet at beam; 67 passengers; crew of 50; cruising speed 12 knots; 3 passenger decks.

Those who want to know what it feels like to be really rich can discover the experience aboard *Sea Cloud*, an engagement present from E.F. Hutton to his bride, Marjorie Merriweather Post. Built in the Germania shipyard in Kiel, Germany in 1931, Ms. Post's yacht is the largest and most opulent sailboat ever built, cruising the world with royalty, heads of state and the cream of society as Post's personal guests. Upon separating from Hutton, Post married the Ambassador to the Soviet Union, who turned *Sea Cloud* into a floating ambassadorial palace in Leningrad's harbor. At the start of World War II, the vessel was patriotically leased to the U.S. Navy for one dollar, and served as a weather observation ship in the North Atlantic.

Sea Cloud's first and second owner's staterooms still have many of the original furnishings, including Louis-Philippe chairs and Ms. Post's antique white French bed with gold leafing; bathrooms and fireplaces in these cabins are Carrera marble. While other cabins are less grand, all have private facilities and twin bed configurations although I've heard some are the size of a broom closet (be sure to check square feet when booking). The ship's restaurant is in the former wood-paneled salon, where dinner is open-seating and always an event.

A number of companies sell this yacht, which is frequently on charter.

From November through April, Sea Cloud *offers 7-day cruises from Antigua to secluded coves in the Caribbean's less populated islands; she summers in the Mediterranean, cruising from Piraeus and Kusadasi to Greek Islands and ports along the Turkish coastline.*

★★★★★+

SEA GODDESS I AND II

Cunard/Sea Goddess; Norwegian registry; Norwegian officers; European/American crew; custom built in Wartsila Shipyard, Helsinki; inaugurated April 1984 and May 1985, respectively; 4250 tons; 344 feet long; 48 feet at beam; 118 passengers; crew of 89; cruising speed of 17.5 knots; 5 passenger decks.

Sea Goddess I and *II* were christened by Princess Caroline of Monaco. The 118-passenger vessels do, indeed, have the ambience of a private club. The all-suite accommodations are 205 square feet (including full bathroom) and decorated in top quality pastel fabrics. Many have convertible twin/double beds. The wall units of white oak contain a superlative stereo/video system, as well as a well-stocked complimentary bar (replenished daily). Frankly, the cabins are quite small (the ship was designed by a fellow who only knew yachts) and miniscule bathrooms. Since the only complaints about the vessel deal with the size of accommodations, Cunard has opened up several cabins into connecting suites and the result is spectacular.

However, cabin amenities are lovely fresh flowers and fruit, ice and your choice of drinks in the refrigerator, and a programmable wall safe–hurray! (I presume that anyone gauche enough to demand caviar daily would receive it.) Bathroom amenities include lovely terrycloth robes, fragrant soaps, shampoo/conditioner, and both pre- and post-tanning lotions. Closet space is quite adequate (except the hangers are too big) and there are plenty of full-length mirrors. The ship line also offers playing cards and a few books to peruse in the cabin.

Public areas on these charming vessels include a large sport deck, off which an aft platform into the water is used for water skiing, wind surfing, snorkeling, etc. There is also a health center, attractive outdoor pool with hot tub, tropical greenhouse, and outdoor cafe for al fresco buffet breakfasts and lunches. A spacious library/card room is for passengers who prefer some quiet time. The library has a good assortment of books, as well as a few hundred video tapes for viewing in the privacy of your cabin (sorry, I did not notice any X-rated).

Throughout both *Sea Goddess I* and *II* are beautiful floral bouquets and elegant touches in brass and wood. The dining salon on 2 Deck has the atmosphere of a fine restaurant, with flowers and crystal and leather-bound menus. Passengers are encouraged to dine as they like between 8 and 10 p.m. and order their fancy, with complimentary Russian caviar and complimentary wines especially selected for that particular menu. Tables are not assigned, so couples may mix and match, or ask to sit by themselves. Soft piano music is played throughout the meal. Dinner means coat or jacket every evening, with black tie suggested at Welcome and Farewell parties.

Breakfast and lunch on deck are very, very lovely on board *Sea Goddess* because they are personal and no one has to stand in line with a tray and plastic fixtures. The blue-rimmed Villeroy & Bosch china is a splendid way to enjoy one's repast in the fresh air. Breakfast and lunch are also served in the restaurant for those who require formal service. The food on board is excellent (but not outrageously delicious) and there is definitely an overabundance of caviar available. I believe that Dirk Pons, chief steward on *Sea Goddess II*, said that passengers consumed several kilos of Beluga caviar each week. Dirk's attention to detail on board is quite overwhelming; my impression is that he delivers to passengers more than many can appreciate. These are very special ships and people should go on with a group of very dear friends.

Evening entertainment features a casino, as well as dancing in the Main Salon. More intimate is the Piano Bar or Club Salon. Passengers enjoy such thoughtful details as subdued lighting in all public areas after dark. But the most relaxing aspect of *Sea Goddess I* and *II* is the lack of planned activities. Passengers do not feel obliged to be somewhere at a certain time which often makes a cruise more tiring than staying at home! I enjoyed a fine Scottish singer on our *Sea Goddess II* cruise and he entertained just enough to be delightful but never was he overpowering in such a small space.

Both Sea Goddess vessels spend the posh summer season in the Mediterranean, where they definitely belong, because the kitchen can stock good stores and the ability of being yacht-like in ports of call enhances the on board ambience. The sports platform is a fabulous feature in the beautiful waters of the Mediterranean Sea and Greek islands. (Those who do not do well on small vessels should avoid transatlantic crossings, however.) During the winter months Sea Goddess I *cruises the Amazon and Caribbean between St. Thomas and Barbados, calling at such places as Palm Island, Mustique, Antigua, Virgin Gorda, St. Barts and St. John in one week. Longer holiday sailings are available.*

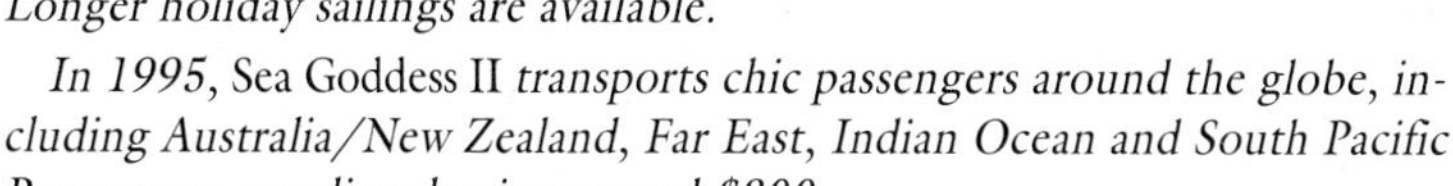

In 1995, Sea Goddess II *transports chic passengers around the globe, including Australia/New Zealand, Far East, Indian Ocean and South Pacific Per person, per diem begins around $800.*

★★★★★+
SEABOURN PRIDE/SEABOURN SPIRIT

Seabourn Cruise Line; Norwegian registry and officers; European hotel staff; built in Bremerhaven for December 1988 and 1989 service, respectively; 10,000 tons; 439 feet at beam; 202 passengers; crew of 140; cruising speed of 18 knots; 6 passenger decks.

The $50 million (each) *Seabourn Pride* and *Seabourn Spirit*, identical sister ships, are at the very top end of exclusive yacht-like cruise vessels catering to those seeking the ultimate in pampering, cuisine, service and a dramatic entry into the world's most glamorous ports. These sleek, modern 202- passenger ships are right at home in Monte Carlo and Corfu parked next to the private yachts of the rich and famous.

Now in their fifth and sixth years of service, *Pride* and *Spirit* are contemporary inside and out. A brass and plexiglass circular staircase flooded with natural light connects all passenger decks. Fabrics and furnishings are sumptuous, but colors are a bit too cool—white, pale blue and beige—for my personal taste. While one may assume a smaller ship necessarily means limited space, public rooms are plentiful and exceedingly spacious. My favorite, the large, circular observation lounge, has floor to ceiling windows, an electronic map with the ships' course and soft blue leather sofas and comfy chairs. It is wonderful for early coffee and fresh croissants, afternoon tea and watching entry into port. Seabourn stages excellent evening cabaret with a few, very accomplished entertainers in the show lounge while late night cocktails and dancing to a small combo was found in the soft beige Club, adjacent to a small casino. Additional entertainment and recreational facilities include a spa/fitness center with supervised aerobics and sufficient machinery for pulling and stretching, a beauty salon, well-stocked library with complimentary videos and small boutique with standard shipboard merchandise. On deck there is a saltwater pool and three jacuzzis.

Sun bathing during days at sea was crowded, with chaise lounges crammed too close to each other on the small open deck space. If you're lucky, a Seabourn cruise may include the use of the ships' foldout marina and the thrill of watersports from the bow of the ship. High speed boats and zodiacs pull waterskiers, inflated inner tubes and "banana boats." Seabourn adds to the experience with a band and buffet on starched white linens.

Cabins aboard *Seabourn Spirit* and *Seabourn Pride* are all-suite and predominately the Category A configuration, measuring 277 square feet. Decorated in soft beige, they boast a five-foot wide picture window, TV/VCR, mini-bar stocked with complimentary liquor, sofa and chairs, writing desk (with personalized stationary), twin or queen-size beds and large mirrors.

There are walk-in closets with safes but drawer space is inadequate for even a one-week cruise. The marble bathrooms have two sinks, hair dryer, designer toiletries, terrycloth robes and all but four handicapped cabins have tubs. Private verandas are one sybaritic delight absent from all but four larger staterooms (three with obstructed views). Stewardesses are superb in keeping the cabins always tidy and well-stocked with fresh flowers.

On my cruise, passengers included new and old-monied 60s+ experienced travelers from the U.S., Europe and South America; a Middle East sheik plus the 50 or so passengers sailing with a pharmaceutical sales incentive group in their 30s and 40s, many first-time cruisers. All mixed very well together due to the easy camaraderie fostered by staff and the informality found aboard a small vessel. Since Seabourn appears to be moving into the incentive market (disembarking from the cruise before mine were a 50-person or so contingent of car dealers), you may want your agent to inquire about groups on your cruise if you want only the real monied sort as sailing companions.

Seabourn distinguishes itself with some of the most outstanding food and service available on the high seas today. The young European staff all seemed to know my name and drink preference from day one, to anticipate all my needs before I was aware of them myself. There is a natural enthusiasm and desire to excel (this is a "no tipping permitted" ship, which eliminates the factor of good service for extra money). It is always the fine points that are most memorable. For example, during dinner the first night, I mentioned to my waiter that I like creme brulee; during the remainder of the voyage it was always among my dessert options. Passengers routinely receive invitations to dine at officers' tables, a wonderful way to become personally acquainted with fellow passengers and staff in a leisurely fashion. During my Rome to Venice cruise aboard *Seabourn Spirit*, Captain Erik Anderssen, surely one of the most outgoing and gracious masters at sea, charmed and flattered passengers and was always present at social affairs.

Open seating dining in The Restaurant was the highlight of each day, with food cooked to perfection. While one can order dishes not listed on the menu, it would be difficult to pass by entrees such as roast tenderloin of milkfed veal with wild sundried tomato sauce; breast of guinea fowl with grapes, or seared sesame crusted tuna steak with wasabi sauce, a chilled pineapple and yogurt soup or raspberry souffle. Fresh produce is loaded in each port, where the young executive chef visits vegetable and fish markets for the evening meal. During formal evenings, when everyone tends to dine at one time, service can be slow and the quality slipped slightly. Those who care to dine in suites may order from the menu and are served by course.

The Veranda Cafe, with alfresco breakfast and lunch overlooking the sea, had a marvelous buffet with pasta and other hot dishes prepared to order. And if one should ever tire, beluga caviar may be ordered in cabins for breakfast, lunch or dinner and any time in between. Seabourn shared one of its recipes for those who want to sample culinary delight before departure:

STUFFED POTATOES WITH CAVIAR BEURRE BLANC SAUCE
For the Potatoes:
4 large potatoes
1fine chopped tomato
1 fine chopped shallot
1????? fine chopped mushrooms
1 Egg Yolk
1 teaspoon chopped chives
Light salt and pepper

Beurre Blanc Sauce
1/4 cup dry white wine
2 tbsp white wine vinegar
3 fine chopped shallots
1cup cold butter, cut in small chunks
Salt & pepper
1tbsp Beluga caviar

Boil potatoes with skin until they are soft. Cut off top quarter, scoop the inside out and chop it fine. Saute shallots and mushrooms and add together with tomatoes, chives and egg yolk. Refill the potato with the stuffing, wrap in foil and bake in the oven for about 15 minutes.

For the Beurre Blanc Sauce, bring wine, vinegar and shallots to boil and reduce until l-l/2 tablespoon is left. Reduce the heat and whisk in the butter until it melts and becomes creamy. Add the caviar and pour over the potatoes. Be cautious with salt.

All this luxury comes at a price, naturally: a per person, per diem air/sea rates start at $1000. Seabourn Pride *and* Seabourn Spirit *sail nearly everywhere on the globe one could wish to visit. Both vessels summer in the Mediterranean, Baltic and Western Europe. In 1995,* Seabourn Spirit *cruises in the Far East, including China and Vietnam, Australia and Indonesia while* Seabourn Pride *visits the Caribbean, Panama Canal and Amazon River. These ships, which rarely ever repeat an itinerary, are available in seven-day segments, making it easy to add together several weeks of exotic ports.*

There are always trade-offs when taking a very small ship. While there is ample space in public rooms for 200 passengers so one doesn't feel crowded, there is very little to do when not in port. For example, if one eschews sunning on the overcrowed deck during a day at sea, there are no other options available except watching a video in the cabin, reading or bridge. The absence of private balconies in cabins of this price range is a flaw. In my opinion, when one is paying a thousand dollars per day, top flight port lecturers who are experts on the history and culture of regions visited should be standard on every cruise. And, while mini-bars are stocked with the passenger's preferred spirits at the beginning of the voyage, it is simply cheap not to offer at least a good-quality complimentary wine with dinner; all wine and spirits consumed on-board should be included in the fare of the priciest cruise ship in the industry.

It's difficult to leave after only one week, and I envied those passengers who, once aboard, decided to stick around for a while longer. Per person, per diem on an air/sea package begins around $1000.

AUTHOR TIP

If you miss the ship's departure and are traveling on an air/sea package, the airline will rearrange flights to join the ship. However, if you are traveling "cruise only" and have arranged your own air you are responsible for additional costs and flight changes. However, if while in port you don't return to the ship in time or miss the last tender, it's always your nickel to catch up at the next port. Don't be late!

★★

SEABREEZE

Dolphin Cruise Line; Bahamian registry; Greek officers and international crew; originally built in 1958 as *Federico C.* for Costa Line; refitted and rechristened in 1983 as *Starship Royale* for Premier Cruise Line; refurbished in 1988 and renamed *SeaBreeze*; 21,000 tons; 606 feet long; 74 feet at beam; 840 passengers; crew of 350; cruising speed of 22 knots; 8 passenger decks.

You wouldn't recognize this vessel from her sailing days as *Starship Royale* for Premier Cruise Line. Replacing the startling red hull is a temperate white with attractive blue stripes, a charming *SeaBreeze* painted in script on the prow, and a playful Dolphin on the smokestack. In 1988 $5.5 million was spent by Dolphin Cruise Line to refurbish the ship, much of it in the cabin areas, where radios and telephones were installed; some lower deck cabins were gutted and rebuilt.

The names of the decks have been changed and reflect everyone's favorite operas (or characters in them) Aida, La Boheme, Carmen, Daphne, Electra, Fidelio, La Gioconda, Isolde and Juliet (note that the names of the decks correspond to their letters). Public rooms have received the low-key treatment, with blue Dolphin logo carpeting. Facilities on board include the Four Seasons Observatory, Water Music Whirlpool and Prelude Bar, Royal Fireworks Lounge (which should temper the works because it is surrounded by deluxe cabins), surprise Casino, Carmen Lounge and Pastorale Cafe (buffet breakfast and lunch served here), La Mer pool, Slim Gym Center, Serenade Bar and the Bacchanalia Restaurant. There is also a small children's corner/recreational area, Intermezzo Theater and Agitato Disco. Food and service are on a par with a 3-star vessel.

The SeaBreeze sails every Sunday from Miami at 4 p.m. to Grand Cayman (Tuesday), Montego Bay (Wednesday), and Playa del Carmen/Cozumel (Friday). The Sunday departures are convenient to honeymooners, as well as young families. The ship is popular with both groups, especially during the summer months. Per person per diem begins around $200.

★★★+

SEAWARD

Norwegian Cruise Line; Bahamian registry, Norwegian officers, and international crew; built in Finland for service June 1988; 42,000 tons; 700 feet long; 96 feet at beam; 1534 passengers; crew of 624; cruising speed of 21.5 knots; 10 passenger decks.

The $120-million *Seaward* was christened in New York harbor by Greta Waitz, famed marathon runner and Olympic champion, in a ceremony that raised money for the U.S. Olympic Team. Mrs. Waitz is a Norwegian citizen but seems to spend some time in North America, mainly winning the woman's division of marathons in New York City.

Seaward has 767 cabins, of which 67 percent are in the outside configuration. According to the published rate list, there are 13 different cabin categories ranging from deluxe suites on Norway Deck to standard inside with upper and lower berths on Atlantic/Biscayne decks. At this writing, rates range from just under $300 a day per person down to just over $200 a day per person.

Facilities on board include diversified dining in two dining rooms—Seven Seas and Four Seasons—with strolling musicians, plus a 92-seat Palm Tree Restaurant that offers a more intimate atmosphere, an à la carte menu, white-glove service, sea views and a $35+ charge. The Palm Tree is by reservation only. Less formal meals can be enjoyed in the Big Apple Cafe and East/Wet Side Patios, which serve from breakfast to midnight buffets. There is also an ice cream parlor on board called Lickety Splits.

International Deck is the main public area, with its Cabaret Lounge, Stardust Lounge, Everything Under the Sun shopping arcade, Oscar's Piano Bar, Monte Carlo Casino, photo shop and cardroom. Boomer's Nightclub is located on Norway Deck. Pool Deck features the Indoor/Outdoor cafe, bar and ice cream parlor. Sun Deck boasts the Palm Tree restaurant, as well as Gatsby's wine bar, an observatory lounge, fitness center and Coconut Willy's forward outdoor bar. The ship features Broadway-type entertainment and the well-known NCL Dive-In Program, with double-deck, catamaran-style tenders (embarked from #1 Deck) carrying passengers to shore when docking facilities are not available.

The Seaward *sails year-round from Miami on 3-day cruises to the Bahamas and 4-day cruises to Key West, Cancun and Cozumel. Rates range from $559 to $1527 for 3-day sailings and $689 to $1649 for 4-day itineraries.*

AUTHOR TIP

Give serious thought to purchasing cruise protection insurance. No one can predict a health situation or job loss that may result in the need to cancel a trip. Furthermore, you have no recourse if weather conditions should cause your flight to be canceled.

SENSATION

(See Fantasy)

AUTHOR TIP

While some cruise companies have wonderful activities and facilities for kids, on some ships you'll find nothing. Look carefully at the brochure—if everyone has grey hair and no children are depicted, bypass that ship. The best course is to have your agent suggest only vessels that are child-friendly.

N/R
SILVER CLOUD

Silversea Cruises; Italian registry; European officers and crew; built in 1994 at Marrotti Yard, Genoa; 16,500 tons; 514 feet long; 70 feet at beam; 296 passengers; 185 crew; cruising speed 20.5 knots; 6 passenger decks.

The new 300-passenger *Silver Cloud*, launched by Silversea Cruises this May (to be followed by the identical *Silver Wind* in January, 1995) enters the fray of elegant, yacht-like ships at the very top end of the industry.

Competing head-to-head with Seabourn and Sea Goddess in the $800+ per person, per diem range, Silversea Cruises offers these ships serious competition. Silversea targets the affluent cruiser who is price conscious and also seeking the penultimate in luxurious amenities and service plus enticing itineraries.

With a starting per person, per diem of $480, Silverseas claims to be the only "all inclusive" line in the business; this is nearly true. They day you make your final payment, a travel insurance plan goes into effect. The list of included features is impressive: round-trip airfare, tips, spirits consumed onboard and pre- and post-cruise hotel stay. Selected shore excursions are also included, but these are offered only once per cruise.

The 300-passenger *Silver Cloud* has all the intimacy and comfort of her 200-passenger tony cousins and a lion's share of the amenities and services of the larger (more than 1000-passenger) vessels. In my opinion, her size is just about perfect for those who feel that a smaller ship can become too "cliquish" and exclusive, and that bigger ships are too impersonal. Moreover, a wonderful feature is the availability of private verandas in 75 percent of staterooms, a sybaritic delight absent from all but a very few cabins aboard the 200-passenger ships. There is a lot of ship here: wide hallways that open into spacious sitting areas and seemingly acres of uncrowded deck space.

The Dining Room, with single, open seating, has a small dance floor and dinner dancing is encouraged. Slate blue and peach fabrics and carpets, large windows and etched glass doors contribute to the beautifully relaxed ambience. Comfortable, curved back chairs and lots of space between tables, subtle lighting, fresh flowers, snowy linen, heavy Christofle flatware and Limoges china are part of the elegance of this room. Table configurations are primarily four or six, although tables for two can be negotiated as can larger settings for up to ten, upon request.

The bright, plant-filled Terrace Cafe is a nice alternative to the formal Dining Room. Open for buffet breakfast, lunch and the occasional "theme dinners," the room is lush with greenery, brass and dark wood. The Bar (that's its name), off the Casino and Entertainment Lounge, boasts glowing mosaics lining the walls of the room with art "themed" from the sea. Central to the room is the long bar flanked by seating areas with low tables and chairs near windows for gorgeous views of the sea. A jazz combo plays at night, making it a natural gathering place for late night get-togethers. The Panorama Lounge overlooking an aft deck has soft blue, coral and beige tones in striped draperies, printed fabrics and leather chair covers. It is a light and airy gathering place for afternoon tea and cocktails.

The Venetian Lounge, the ship's main entertainment area, with bright, classy and colorful decor in tangerine and teal with trompe l'oeil panels is a splendid place for evening entertainment and port lectures. The small casino, with two black jack tables, one roulette table and 19 slot machines has green plants and a bright chandelier to add glitter. The Library has excellent reference books, a wide selection of current hardback books, an extensive VCR lending library and computer for passenger use. *Silver Cloud's* Spa is upbeat, with a vivid blue carpet, lively music and an energetic young trainer/instructor who leads group aerobics and exercise classes. Equipment consists of a Nordic track, four Lifecycles, one Liferower and three Life Stride treadmills.

Cabins are all-suite, most with verandas. The smallest are Vista suites, at 240 square feet, and Veranda Suites are sightly larger, at 295 square feet. All cabins offer twin beds that may be converted to queen size, a sitting area with comfortable chairs and a table that expands for in-suite dining; TV/VCR; telephone, mini-bar and refrigerator, wall safe, walk-in closet and dressing table. Lighting is good, and lots of mirrors add to a feeling of space and airiness. Room service is available 24-hours per day and bathrooms, some of the roomiest afloat have peach marble walls. Amenities include terrycloth robes, hair dryers and plenty of designer toiletries. Other cabin categories include the 528 sq. ft. Silver Suite, the Owner's Suite, at 887 sq. feet and the two-bedroom Grand Suite with 1085 sq. feet.

I sailed this June only a month after this's ships' christening and found cuisine consistently very good. You may start your day with a breakfast menu as long as your arm, followed by a hearty lunch in the dining room or Terrace Cafe (where the chef prepares pasta and other fresh dishes to order).

Dinner is always lavish, with a choice of three appetizers, a pasta dish, three soups, two salads and a choice of four entrees. A separate dessert menu plus sweet tray and wine flowing courtesy of the line, ensure dinner is always a highlight.

Following her inaugural Mediterranean season, *Silver Cloud* heads for west for New England/Canada cruises, voyages to South America and the

Caribbean. A return to the Mediterranean and Baltic is scheduled for the summer of 1995. In 1995, identical sister ship *Silver Wind* will cruise between Mombasa, Kenya and Mahe, Seychelles next January, followed by Mediterranean and Baltic Cruises and New England/Canada fall sailings.

When I sailed on *Silver Cloud* she was a brand new ship and Silversea is a new line. To give this ship a specific rating at this particular time in her young life would be unfair. Within this ship are the makings of a top of the line vessel. There is much potential here, but a lot of tightening needs to be done. Company officials seemed willing to listen, appeared to be sensitive to passenger complaints and suggestions. My "nitpick" list includes the following: smoking and nonsmoking areas on the ship should be more carefully monitored, particularly in the Dining Room; at mealtimes, service was very slow between courses, the food whisked away before one was finished.

The crew was mostly smiling and friendly, sometimes less so; all of the decks and public rooms should be checked more often to remove used glasses, ashtrays. There was also a throb, a lurch, to this otherwise extremely stable ship. There is not enough acoustical insulation between cabins. TV sets in some cabins are poorly positioned, not conducive to viewing from bed. And, hand-held showers should be standard equipment in all bathrooms.

Silverseas has a wonderfully attractive ship, fabulous itineraries, very appealing prices and those heavenly verandas. It is so close to being superb and the company knows how to fix it—and a starting per person, per diem of around $480 makes this a very good deal indeed!

N/R

SIR FRANCIS DRAKE

Tall Ship Adventures; Panamanian registry; International officers and crew; built in 1917 on the river Weser, Germany and refurbished in 1988; 450 tons; 165 feet long; 23 feet at beam; 34 passengers; crew of 14.

Those enthralled by the romantic era when clipper ships roamed the globe carrying passengers and cargo across the seven seas will find Tall Ship Adventures' *Sir Francis Drake* a genuine historical experience. The 450-ton ship is among the less than one hundred remaining tall ships (those built originally to transport under sail only) in the world. Constructed on the river Wesel in Germany in 1917, this three-masted schooner (first named the S.V. *Landkirchen*) originally transported copper around Cape Horn between the western coast of Chile and Europe. After about a decade, a motor was added and the ship spent the next 40 years in the Baltic and North Seas as a trading ship. In 1979, she was renamed S.V. *Godewind* (Divine Wind) and cruised the Caribbean, catering to Europeans who relished her seagoing heritage.

In 1988, she found her way into the loving hands of her new owners, Eckart Straub, an international entrepreneur, and his partner, Captain Bryan Petley, a New Zealander who has been sailing since age 13. They refurbished the ship and renamed her *Sir Francis Drake*, after the famous admiral, buccaneer and circumnavigator of the globe.

The 165-foot tall ship carries 34 passengers to secluded Caribbean ports on 3- , 4- and 7-day cruises in a very casual, relaxed ambience. The mahogany panel lounge with bar, stereo, video, television and library serves as the social center of the ship, although passengers are frequently topside, lending assistance in hoisting the sails or relaxing with a rum punch.

All staterooms have air conditioning and private bathrooms, and configurations include upper/lower bunks, twin beds and double bed with upper twin and one suite. Meals are taken in the lounge or on deck and passengers join in the fun of beach picnics or barbecues under the stars. Watersports equipment, including Sunfish, sailboats, windsurfing and snorkeling gear, is free of charge. Unlike some other wood sailing ships in the Caribbean, the Sir Francis Drake is U.S. Coast Guard certified.

In 1995, Sir Francis Drake *departs from St. Thomas on 7-day cruises calling in St. John-Cruz Bay, Caneel Bay, Francis or Trunk Bay, St. James Island, Tortola, Jost Van Dyke, Sandy Cay, Norman or Peter Island; 4-day itineraries include visits to Tortola, Jost Van Dyke, Sandy Cay and Norman or Peter Island and 3-day cruises feature port calls in Caneel Bay, Trunk or Francis Bay and St. James Island.*

I have yet to sail aboard the Sir Francis Drake. I wouldn't expect luxurious accommodations and refined service but rather a fun, very casual ambience, plenty of secluded coves for scuba and the thrill of sailing aboard a grand old lady who has already earned her keep!

AUTHOR TIP

Don't think you can escape the harmful rays of the sun just by getting dressed. According to *Traveling Healthy*, a white cotton T-shirt is about SPF 7 when dry and SPF 5 when wet. Stretching fabric also lessens protection—a polo shirt stretched across the shoulders has only an SPF of 9 when dry. Opaque, dark and tightly weaved fabrics are best for sun protection (denim has an SPF of 1000).

★★★★

SKY PRINCESS

Princess Cruises; Liberian registry; Italian officers and European crew; built in France in 1984 as *Fairsky* for Sitmar Cruises; renamed in 1988 by Princess Cruises and refurbished in 1989; 46,000 tons; 789 feet long; 98 feet at beam; 1200 passengers; crew of 535; cruising speed of 19 knots; 11 passenger decks.

The newer of the three vessels in the Sitmar fleet, which Princess Cruises acquired in 1988, the now-named *Sky Princess* began her life in Alaska in May 1984 to great success despite what we all considered her overwhelming size (how times change)! *Sky Princess* is now considered mid-size and a very attractive vessel.

More than a million dollars was spent on the Showroom aboard *Sky Princess*, which included a new stage, intimate bar area adjacent with full view of the entertainment, multi-tiered seating and new furnishings. The Starlight Disco, Veranda Lounge and Promenade Lounge also received attention, and small personal safes were installed in all cabins. *Sky Princess* has some splendid facilities, including a large library, cardrooms, greatly expanded casino, Rainbow Bar and the glass-encased Horizon Lounge forward on Riviera Deck. Aft on Riviera Deck is the Starlight Disco, reachable only from the aft stairway on Promenade Deck.

Although the public areas on Promenade Deck flow well, attempting to reach your dining room—Regency or Savoy on Aloha Deck—is a major problem the first few days on board. This vessel is a challenge to even the best of scouts! There are also two swimming pools, a spacious spa with whirlpool and gymnasium on Sun Deck, and a large area for children and teens aft on Aloha Deck. The ever-popular Pizzeria is conveniently located amidships on Promenade Deck. There is also a proper two-tiered theater for movies and meetings.

The 606 cabins aboard *Sky Princess* are spacious, with 388 outside (including 10 veranda suites and 28 mini-suites). All cabins boast color TV, plenty of storage space and showers that one can turn around in! However, as on other former Sitmar vessels, there is a high percentage of inside cabins.

In 1995, the Sky Princess *sails on trans-canal cruises. During the summer season* Sky Princess *returns to Alaska on 7-day cruises between Seward/Anchorage and Vancouver, where Princess Cruises is another major presence! Average per person, per diem rates are $225, including airfare.*

AUTHOR TIP

Those planning a honeymoon cruise or who simply prefer to dine in romantic seclusion should look closely at the dining room configuration of prospective ships. On some ships—Princess Cruises' "Love Boats," for example—you'll find no tables for two and the experience may be decidedly unromantic if you're stuck with six or eight uncongenial souls.

★★★+

SONG OF AMERICA

Royal Caribbean Cruise Line; Norwegian registry and international crew; built in Wartsila Yard in Helsinki and launched in 1982; 37,500 tons; 705 feet long; 93 feet at beam; 1390 passengers; crew of 500; cruising speed of 16 knots; 12 passenger decks.

With the inaugural service of the *Song of America* on December 5, 1982, and the christening by opera star Beverly Sills (also known as Bubbles), Royal Caribbean Cruise Line became a 4-fleet company, but not for long. The ship has a total of 707 cabins plus 21 deluxe staterooms and one super suite, all with Scandinavian decor and complementary Caribbean colors. The walls are off-white and natural tones. All cabins have 100-volt current for American-made hair dryers, curlers and electric shavers, in addition to modular bathrooms with showers.

The *Song of America* boasts the well-recognized RCCL trademark, the cantilevered Viking Crown Lounge. However, this one encircles the funnel stack some 12 decks above sea level and offers a complete 360-degree panorama. On a clear day, you can see some 20 miles (so they say). The lounge also holds about 140 passengers comfortably, almost three times more than those above the rest of the fleet, and an elevator whisks you into the center with nary a hair out of place! This is a popular spot when the *Song of America* sails away from port as the panoramic views from the Viking Crown Lounge at any hour looking back to land are both spectacular and romantic! The vessel also has a proper theater for first-run films on Cabaret Deck.

Other public areas include the CanCan and Oklahoma lounges on Cabaret Deck, and the main dining room on Main Deck. This large facility is divided into the Madame Butterfly restaurant, the Ambassador Room and the Oriental Terrace, all of which will change settings and specialties at each dinner service. In addition to the Welcome Aboard dinner, there is French Night, Italian Night, a Spanish dinner and a Caribbean dinner. The Captain's Gala Dinner on Friday is followed by America the Beautiful night, and don't forget the impressive looking Midnight Buffet! The late night spot can be found in the Guys and Dolls Lounge on Promenade Deck. Sun-seekers will love the two huge pools, with bar and outdoor Veranda Cafe on Sun Deck, and fitness buffs should not miss the gymnasium and saunas on Bridge Deck. The Mast Bar and Sun Walk are located up on Compass Deck.

The Song of America *sails on 10- and 11-day cruises from San Juan to St. Thomas, St. Martin, Martinique, Trinidad, Dominica, St. Kitts, St. Croix and Coco Cay to Miami. The alternate schedule is from Miami to Coco Cay, St. Kitts, Trinidad, Dominica, Martinique, St. Martin, St. Thomas and San Juan, and is popular on Bermuda cruises from New York during the summer.*

AUTHOR TIP

Your interest and life-style are the most important criteria for narrowing the field to one or two vessels—ships are vastly different in terms of the amenities and services they offer as well as itineraries and the age and socioeconomic profile of passengers. Take a very close look at your own personal preferences and compare them to the vessel you are considering.

★★★★★+

SONG OF FLOWER

Seven Seas Cruise Line; Norwegian registry; Norwegian and Japanese officers; European crew; and Japanese built in West Germany in 1986 and refurbished in 1989; 8282 tons; 409 feet long; 52 feet at beam; 172 passengers; crew of 144; cruising speed of 17 knots; 8 decks.

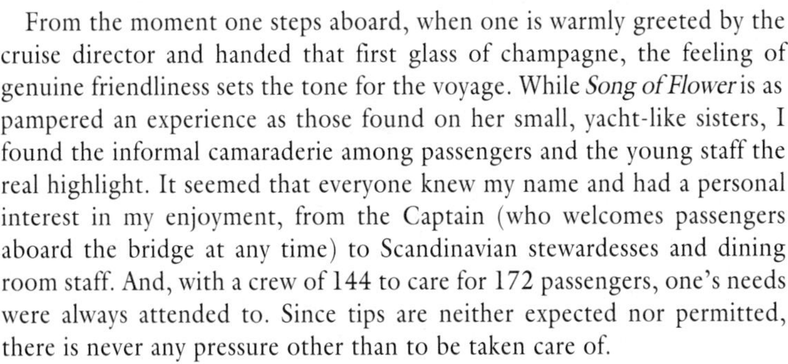

From the moment one steps aboard, when one is warmly greeted by the cruise director and handed that first glass of champagne, the feeling of genuine friendliness sets the tone for the voyage. While *Song of Flower* is as pampered an experience as those found on her small, yacht-like sisters, I found the informal camaraderie among passengers and the young staff the real highlight. It seemed that everyone knew my name and had a personal interest in my enjoyment, from the Captain (who welcomes passengers aboard the bridge at any time) to Scandinavian stewardesses and dining room staff. And, with a crew of 144 to care for 172 passengers, one's needs were always attended to. Since tips are neither expected nor permitted, there is never any pressure other than to be taken care of.

Song of Flower is a very lovely vessel. Ms. Tomoko Uenaka, who purchased the ship, personally supervised the refurbishment; decor was redone by the same company that made Sea Goddess and Seabourn cruise ships so glamorous. It is unpretentious, but tastefully refined throughout with pastel fabrics, beige marble and polished wood. *Song of Flower* features all-outside staterooms with TV/VCR, well-stocked complimentary mini-bars and refrigerators, deluxe bathrooms with hair dryers and designer toiletries. All cabins have comfy terrycloth bathrobes, slippers and sun visors; fresh orchids adorn the vanity and one's favorite spirits are replenished daily (drinks and wine are included in the fare). There are several categories of staterooms (standard are 200 square feet), all with large sea view windows and ample closet space; deluxe staterooms have private verandas.

Public rooms include the Observation Lounge, with its cozy leather furniture and floor-to-ceiling windows—my favorite place to chat with friends and read—the nightclub with cabaret which, on my cruise, featured a superb Filipino singer. The Galaxy dining room has open seating at unassigned tables, the atmosphere relaxed and elegant, conducive to lingering long after dessert. I thought the cuisine was wonderful; one of my most

memorable meals aboard any vessel was a luncheon buffet of the freshest King Crab, prawns, lobster and mussels (I consumed an embarrassing amount). Several times in port I purchased fish caught a few hours before, and the Austrian chef prepared it to my liking.

Other amenities are a library with 1000 art, history and popular books, as well as a selection of 300 complimentary videos, small casino, large sun deck with swimming pool and Jacuzzi, a tiny fitness facility and sauna, massage and rental facility for designer evening wear. In the Royal Flower Boutique, Hermes scarves were 40 percent below U.S. prices as were perfumes and cosmetics. On my voyage, entertainment was excellent for a small vessel wine tasting, a fashion show, a lecture by famous ship historian Bill Miller and a very knowledgeable discussion of ports culture and history by a local expert; at night we enjoyed a good cabaret and singer. The most fun was found at a costume party (wigs and clothes provided), where everyone let down his and her hair and donned outrageous attire.

A water sports platform is used when the ship is at anchor, and a 120-passenger *Tiny Flower* excursion vessel takes passengers into tiny coves and inlets.

Seven Seas Cruise Line's itineraries are among the most enticing in the Far East, where Song of Flower *cruises from November through March; the Mediterranean/Black Sea and Baltic from spring through fall. Shore excursions are especially creative. In Europe, for example, one can visit families and private homes in Bulgaria, have a private culinary demonstration with the chef of the Hotel de Paris in Monte Carlo and visit a working farm and winery on the Channel Islands. Shore excursions are included in the cruise price on Far East sailings. The per person, per diem (beginning around $450) makes this ship a real bargain for those choosing a cruise experience on a ship with the ambience of a private yacht.*

AUTHOR'S AWARD

Song of Flower *is the top bargain among five plus star vessels, especially in the Far East, where the cruise fare includes airfare, drinks, tips and all shore excursions beginning at $450 per person, per diem.*

★★★★

SONG OF NORWAY

Royal Caribbean Cruise Line; Norwegian registry and officers, international crew; built in Wartsila shipyard, Helsinki, and originally launched in 1970s; refitted and lengthened by 85 feet in 1978; 23,005 tons; 635 feet long; 80 feet at beam; 1040 passengers; crew of 400; cruising speed of 16 knots; 7 passenger decks.

The *Song of Norway* was the firstborn of the RCCL fleet and she remains one of the most popular. Following eight years of success, the vessel was returned to Wartsila shipyard in Helsinki for a stretching, which added 85 feet to her midsection and increased her passenger complement by 30 percent. Public rooms were also increased in size, and the vessel has one of the most beautiful sun-and-pool areas afloat.

Like all RCCL vessels, the *Song's* public rooms have been named after hit Broadway musicals. There is the King and I dining room, the My Fair Lady forward lounge, the South Pacific aft lounge. The famous cantilevered Viking Crown Lounge on the funnel stack still accommodates only 67 passengers comfortably, and the panorama is impressive. The Lounge of the Midnight Sun nightclub was enlarged and has simultaneous slide shows happening on several wall areas, so it's best to stay sober and enjoy! Entertainment quality is very high, as on all RCCL ships, and passengers never see the same nighttime attraction twice. The dining service is "themed" each night, with costumes for the waiters and different table settings, as well as menu offerings.

The *Song of Norway* has a total of 535 cabins, most of them rather small but compact. Third and fourth persons in them make it very cozy, indeed. The stretching of the vessel, however, allowed for several new outside deluxe and larger cabins (13 even have bathtubs). Onboard amenities are excellent, and the ship has a reputation for being beautifully managed and maintained. There is plenty to occupy the days at sea and plenty of space in which to be active.

The Song of Norway *cruises on 10-day and 11-day trans-canal sailings between San Juan and Acapulco. She then voyages to Europe for a summer season of 12-day Baltic Sea and Mediterranean cruises.*

★★★★

SOVEREIGN OF THE SEAS

Royal Caribbean Cruise Line; Liberian registry; Norwegian officers and international crew; built at Chantiers de L'Atlantique, St. Nazaire; maiden voyage January 1988; 74,000 tons; 880 feet long; 106 at beam; 2282 passengers; crew of 750; cruising speed of 16 knots; 14 passenger decks.

The world's largest cruise vessel of its time arrived in Miami on schedule for viewing by a cast of thousands and christening by former First Lady Rosalynn Carter. It seems that the Carters have enjoyed one or two RCCL cruises since their abdication, and the ship line thought it would be a nice gesture to invite Rosalynn as godmother. In return, RCCL made a $25,000 donation to the Carter Library in Atlanta and invited over a dozen family members, as well as the Secret Service to the festivities held dockside and then afloat for a week.

It is quite awesome to sail aboard this $185-million-dollar vessel one of the largest designed, built, and afloat! *Sovereign of the Seas* is a big ship; there is no doubt about it, and it represents a departure from what has become the traditional cruise vessel. Upon entry, the familiar purser's square has become an overwhelming Centrum with multilevel sweeping staircases and glass elevators that go up and down five stories. "Is this a cruise ship or have we turned the wrong corner into a Hyatt Regency Hotel?" is the primary reaction of most passengers. Located in the Centrum is the purser's office, as well as shore excursion office and entrance to the Kismet dining room. The duplicate Gigi Dining Room is located one level below on Main Deck where serenaders perform during the cocktail hour. One deck below Main, if you can find them, are Cinema I and II (they were offering some tempting feature films when I was on board, but it seemed like too much of a struggle to make the show). It seems outdated to place theaters on the lowest deck possible especially when ship lines are expecting to entice meetings and conventions on board.

The design of the vessel features most cabins forward and public rooms aft. Of the 1141 cabins, 722 are outside configuration and a staggering 419 are inside. There are 124 three-berth and 88 four-berth cabins. All are standard RCCL small, with the exception of those located on Bridge Deck, which are considered deluxe staterooms and suites. Aft on Bridge Deck, by the way, is a large and impressive health center with gymnasium and sauna and Jacuzzi. It should become one of the most popular places on board.

Public areas are enormous, and passengers do feel at times that they are not afloat but in New York City's convention center. The Folies, Finian's Rainbow and Music Man lounges are huge; so is the Casino Royale and Anything Goes Discotheque. However, there are a few little hideaways for people who prefer more intimate settings. The Champagne Bar is an oasis in the midst of activity, nestled between the handsome library and card-room/conference center. The Champagne Bar was not offering the bubbly when I was aboard, but on display was a sovereign of Taittinger champagne the largest bottle ever made and offered by the wine firm for the christening of the *Sovereign.* Also offering some quietude is the 360-degree Viking Crown Lounge, which features nice ship and sea views from high above. But why doesn't it turn? The lounge overlooks the swimming pool area, which will certainly resemble a so-called meat market when the sun is shining high. The pool area flows into the Windjammer Cafe forward, where breakfast and lunch buffets are served; aft of the pool area is a kids/teen/ video games hideout.

There is plenty to see and do on board *Sovereign of the Seas* from sunrise stretch classes at 7 a.m. down through dance music in the Music Man Lounge until 1:30 a.m. Evening entertainment in the many lounges is quality stuff, if you like theatrical glitz. You can also walk the four miles of corridors, ride the 18 elevators on board or play every one of the 170 slot machines. The vessel is as high as the Statue of Liberty (171 feet) and its four giant engines are floated on rubber mountings to ensure smoother sailing. Captain Stangeland calls the vessel surprisingly easy to handle and a dream come true.

Sovereign of the Seas *sails every Saturday from Miami to Coco Cay, San Juan and St. Thomas. Up front discounts are offered on certain sailings; all rates include airfare. Despite all the comments about this behemoth of a vessel,* Sovereign of the Seas *has proved to be so successful that RCCL ordered two more!* Sovereign II *began San Juan sailings in late 1991 and* Sovereign III *arrived in 1992.*

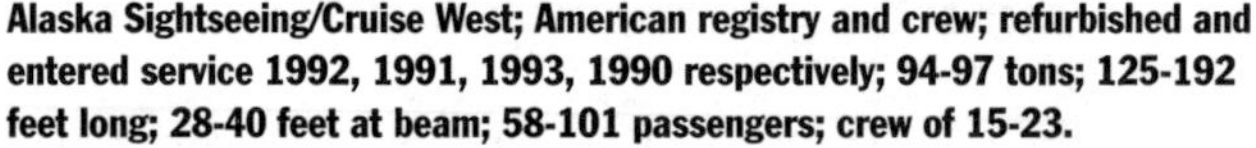

SPIRIT OF '98/SPIRIT OF ALASKA/SPIRIT OF DISCOVERY/SPIRIT OF GLACIER BAY

Alaska Sightseeing/Cruise West; American registry and crew; refurbished and entered service 1992, 1991, 1993, 1990 respectively; 94-97 tons; 125-192 feet long; 28-40 feet at beam; 58-101 passengers; crew of 15-23.

Alaska Sightseeing/Cruise West's small, shallow draft ships carry between 58 and 100 passengers with an all-American crew of about of around 20. They are excursion/expedition ships that have a loyal following for those who seek the real flora and fauna of Alaska, British Columbia, the Pacific Northwest and leisurely voyages along the Columbia River in a very casual, family-style environment. The focus and enjoyment is outside these ships; you won't find a show lounge, bingo or any other standard shipboard activities. Alaska Sightseeing/Cruise West's loyal passengers (these ships sell out early, with nary a discount) love the informality and camaraderie between fellow passengers and the young energetic crew, and the chance to experience natural wonders virtually impossible to find by any other means.

The Pacific Northwest is one of my favorite places and has the most beautiful coastal scenery imaginable outside of Alaska—much of it accessible only by small boat. Since, like most people, I don't have a boat of my own, I did the next best thing—I sailed to the San Juan Islands on Alaska Sightseeing/Cruise West's *Spirit of Discovery*, a vessel that can go practically anywhere. I found it the perfect way to appreciate the wonders of Mother Nature and to get up close and personal with waterfalls and wildlife.

Almost immediately, the infectious exuberance of the young crew members filtered down to the most staid among us. Being aboard *Spirit of Discovery* is like being part of a large extended family that includes the annoying cousin, assorted brothers, sisters, parents, maiden aunts and grandparents. The crew were the adoring grandchildren and everyone was quickly on a first-name basis. My fellow passengers ranged in age from early 40s to a vibrant 94 and covered a variety of professions, which made for frequently lively conversation. Most were seasoned travelers and a substantial number were repeat passengers, attesting to the quality of service and itineraries offered. The crew was mostly under 30, many of them recent college graduates who were fascinating to talk to.

An Alaska Sightseeing/Cruise West voyage is not inexpensive, nor is it fancy. There is no casino or glitzy entertainment. The crew is the entertainment, often hilariously, whether involving us in their version of "To Tell The Truth" or modeling "fashions" (hats, sweatshirts, T-shirts and a stuffed bear!) from the gift shop.

The awesome natural beauty enveloping you is the hook here. I found it hard to pull myself away and go inside. But when I did I found the Glacier View Lounge, the main public area, comfortable, with windows on three sides for excellent viewing. However, my one quibble would be that this room could be somewhat crowded if the ship were full and the weather turned bad. All in all, there was a smooth flow in and out throughout the day. There is a library in the lounge stocked with novels and some very useful books about the places we visited and were put to good use. After dinner there were fierce games of Scrabble and Travel Trivia in the lounge, and although videos were available, no one bothered to watch. Many evenings we just sat and discussed what we'd seen that day.

The Grand Pacific Dining Room is comfortable and utilitarian but the food was a wonderful surprise. And, like a family reunion, each meal became a revolving event where new groups formed to discuss the day's events.

While I expected good, solid cooking, what we got from chef Doug Graybeal was excellent (the beef melted like butter in the mouth). A young woman, Joday Griffis, handled baking chores and each morning the most wonderful aromas wafted up from the galley where she produced delicious muffins, rolls, bread, cakes and cookies. Only one lunch and one dinner fell below par, but the food still rated a 9 on a scale of 10, as did the service and enthusiasm of the crew. They made the quiet laugh, the oldest smile, and in general took it upon themselves to see that even those passengers with limited mobility were able to enjoy as much time ashore as possible, going so far as to wheel one elderly lady down a hill and back up during a tour and take her shopping in another port—she had a wonderful time. The knowledge of the cruise coordinator and his assistant was top notch—what they didn't know they found out, either from the in-depth onboard library or a local tour guide. (This was the first voyage on this itinerary for them.)

The average accommodations are small and spartan but adequate with a reasonable amount of storage space and good viewing window. All cabins have private facilities, but in some cases the sink is located outside the bathroom. Remember, this is a very casual trip and one doesn't need a lot of clothes, nor do you spend much time in the cabin.

The breathtaking scenery is the star of these cruises with wildlife playing a strong second banana. Since these small ships are so maneuverable you can see wonders previously enjoyed only by a select few. In magnificent Princess Louisa Inlet (sometimes referred to as a sea level Yosemite), our excellent captain, Becky Crosby (yes, a woman), took the ship right up to a cliff wall where we could look down into the crystal clear water and see enormous starfish clinging to the rock.

That day was mystical with the tops of the canyon walls shrouded in drifting clouds and mist, at times resembling a Chinese painting. Adding to the mystery and magic of this incredible spot was the bald eagle that soared overhead, escorting us through the 100-foot wide entrance. Through the day we counted seven more eagles sitting in their treetop aeries perusing this intrusion on their domain. In the afternoon Becky took us for a closeup look at Chatterbox Falls, at the top of the inlet. By this time the clouds had broken and sun streamed down, illuminating the falls and surrounding rock walls.

The only other way to see the spectacular beauty of the Pacific Northwest or Southeast Alaska in such an intimate way is on a private boat.

Barring that, this is the way to go. The most important thing you need to bring is a "sense of wonder," to quote Rachel Carson, a desire to enjoy quiet moments like sunset and dawn, good conversation, good food and good camaraderie.

In 1995, the company adds a fifth cruise ship, the 70-passenger Spirit of Columbia, *set to voyage 1000 miles along the Columbia and Snake rivers from the Pacific Ocean to Idaho on seven-night itineraries from April through November. The company also adds a new cruising region, the Sacramento River, which will be sailed by the 82-passenger* Spirit of Alaska *from September through November; the one-week voyages include the wineries of the Napa Valley and the historic gold rush region of central California. Alaska Sightseeing/Cruise West offers five two- to seven-night Alaska itineraries with departures from Seattle, Juneau and Ketchikan, with optional land excursions. In addition to the seven-day Puget Sound/San Juan Island cruises, three- and four-night cruises from Seattle to Victoria and Vancouver are available.*

Discounts are virtually nonexistent since these ships are extremely popular with nature lovers and are solidly booked. Depending on the vessel, itinerary and time of sailing, per person, per diem for a minimum outside cabin is $192 to $342, depending on the vessel, itinerary and time of travel.

⚓⚓⚓⚓⚓

STAR CLIPPER/STAR FLYER

Star Clippers; Luxembourg flag; European officers and international crew; constructed in Belgium and in launched in 1991 and 1992; four-masted sailing ships; 3025 tons; 226 feet to top of main mast; 50 feet at beam; 170 passengers; crew of 70; 4 passenger decks.

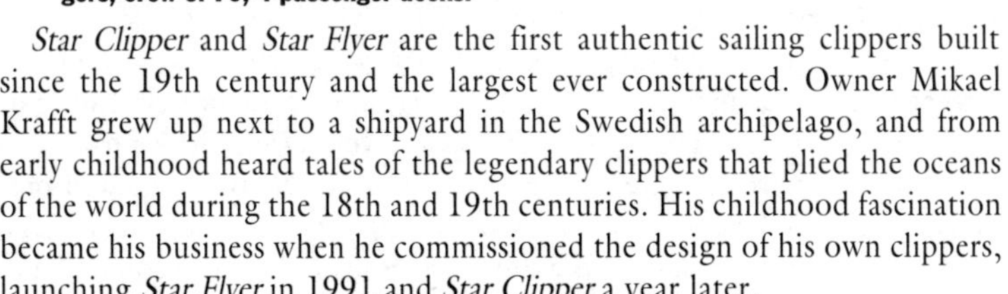

Star Clipper and *Star Flyer* are the first authentic sailing clippers built since the 19th century and the largest ever constructed. Owner Mikael Krafft grew up next to a shipyard in the Swedish archipelago, and from early childhood heard tales of the legendary clippers that plied the oceans of the world during the 18th and 19th centuries. His childhood fascination became his business when he commissioned the design of his own clippers, launching *Star Flyer* in 1991 and *Star Clipper* a year later.

While they are also the fastest clippers ever built—once clocking a speed of 17 knots—these ships are designed for passenger comfort and safety. Anti-rolling tanks and a controlled sailing speed, which rarely exceeds ten or 11 knots on Caribbean and Mediterranean sailings, ensure there is nary a ripple in one's rum punch. And, while a nurse is aboard who can dispense medicine for seasickness, it is rarely necessary—my Caribbean voyage had the gentle movement of being under sail, and no complaints of queasiness, even from first-time cruisers.

While one assumes a sailboat carrying 170 passengers will naturally be large, it is breathtaking to see the mast of *Star Clipper* towering over other ships in port. The 360-foot identical sister ships are roughly one-third the length of the *QE 2*, soaring 226 feet to the tip of the main mast, the same ilk as the grand and graceful tall ship found in a Hudson River regatta.

Following a warm greeting by Captain Gerhard Lickfett upon boarding, I was escorted to the elegant wood-paneled library for check-in. Leaving port at midnight, the excitement and mystique of voyaging aboard a clipper began when the sails were slowly raised. The white canvas billowed in the full moon like silvery clouds, and passengers hushed at the spectacle, a few echoing my thoughts—"can this be real?." Throughout our one-week cruise to the Windward Islands, none missed the grandeur of raising sails while departing port at sunset, always delighted to be once again at sea. In 1995, *Star Clipper* adds a full day at sea to the itineraries of both ships since most passengers, whether first time sailors or experienced yachtsmen, find this the real thrill of the voyage.

Since these are authentic sailing ships (unlike the motorized sailboats of Windstar and Club Med), it is delightful to find a nautical decor that is not overly opulent. Everyone's favorite gathering place was the covered outdoor bar, where Captain Loretto, *Star Clipper's* parrot, squawked orders. It was the gathering place for animated conversation or evening entertainment such as crab races, a crew fashion show and dancing. The piano bar, with white leather banquettes, nautical prints, blue and gold fabrics, brass bar and walled sconces, was popular for drinks and canapes and the late night sing-alongs as the cruise director banged out popular tunes on the grand piano, accompanied by the guitar-strumming maitre d'. The Library, with Belle Epoque marble fireplace, mahogany paneling and original maritime paintings, was rarely used in the Caribbean. Its atmosphere was similar to an English country manor and not consistent with the open, airy feeling of other public spaces.

The dining room, with open single seating, is reached by a wide brass staircase. Its rich burgundy and rose fabrics, warm lighting and nautical paintings are so pleasant that passengers lingered for hours over dinner at leather banquettes and tables for eight. Star Clippers doesn't claim its cuisine is haute cuisine, but meals were always wonderful. Since produce is loaded during port stops, vegetables, fruit and fish were fresh and well-prepared. The pastry chef, who has been perfecting his craft for some 15 years, created some of the best deserts and baked goods I've ever encountered at sea. The chefs and five cooks prepare 14 different menus, so those on a two-week voyage will never find the same fare twice; breakfast and lunch were buffets and dinner alternated between buffets and menu service. Waiter service was adequate, but not overly efficient and lacked a degree of warmth found aboard many traditional cruise ships; an excellent new maitre 'd, recently with Windstar, was aboard to shore up this glitch.

As one accustomed to cruise ships, there were a few surprises. Before turning in the first night, I noticed the room steward had placed a plastic cover over my porthole and removed it. The next morning I woke expecting to find bright Caribbean sunlight streaming in and instead let out a shriek—since we were under sail my cabin was partially beneath the water line, and the effect was like being inside a washing machine. My cabin, #116, a standard outside on the bottom Commodore Deck, seemed more spacious than its 120 square feet. White paneling with wood trim, nautical prints, subdued lighting and mirrored closets and vanity created a roomy effect. Amenities include a television with closed circuit movies, direct dial telephone, more than ample closet space and a small banquette.

The small tiled bathroom is superbly designed, with excellent vanity space, a medicine cabinet, hair dryer and hand-held shower. Water is regulated in both the shower and faucet (you have to push a button for more than 30 seconds or so to maintain a flow)—this is a sailboat, and water is not unlimited! Bathroom lighting was not bright enough and cabins were over air-conditioned for my taste. Room stewards kept everything immaculate throughout. Due to the classic lines of the ship, there are wide variations in cabin size and layout. Moreover, a sleeping passenger can be disturbed by engine vibration if located too far aft, or the noise of the anchor dropping if too far forward.

The best cabins are 108-116 midships on Commodore Deck and 302-308 on Clipper Deck, all with twin beds that may be converted to queen. Deluxe staterooms with tubs and jacuzzi are situated on the main deck and are therefore subject to the sound of crew members working in the early morning.

Inside cabins with upper and lower beds were much too claustrophobic for my taste. In order to maintain the classic lines of a true clipper, these ships lack a laundry room, a handicap for those on a two-week cruise; crew members will do personal laundry for a small extra tip if asked.

The real drama is found on the massive top deck—at 11,400 square feet, it probably has the highest ratio of open deck per passenger.

A hundred comfy chaise lounges and two small pools are sybaritic delights while being under sail; one cannot imagine a more romantic experience than lounging topside at night under a canopy of stars, the gentle lull of the ship and billowing sails the only sound. Adventuresome passengers climb out on the hammock-like netting beneath the bowsprit for the thrill of an up close experience of the ocean beneath and the sails above. A very close second to the experience of this great ship was the wonderful camaraderie fostered among and between passengers and crew.

Passengers covered a broad range of ages (20s to 70s) and nationalities; they included yachtsmen enthralled by the experience of being aboard a real clipper, those who had never cruised before and well-heeled world travelers who had sailed aboard some of the toniest cruise ships (several proclaimed they were converted to sail forever more!). The mixture of singles, couples and families works well on this ship—several romances took flight and the relaxed social atmosphere promoted many new friendships. We constantly socialized with officers and crew, who delighted in explaining the ship's workings. My best day ashore was in St. Vincent, when Ashley, who washed pots in the kitchen, gave me and a friend a personal tour of his home island.

Everyone adored Captain Lickfett, his ironic humor, morning "story time" (a preview of the day's events) and evening constellation lessons. The 50-member crew is comprised of all nationalities, including several Russians who have trained on their country's well-respected clippers. While passengers may help raise the sails, only a handful joined in each day for a few minutes before hoisting their glass and letting the crew tackle this strenuous task.

Those who love watersports will be hard pressed to find better vessels. All but scuba is free, and passengers are given snorkeling equipment to keep in their cabins throughout the cruise. Star Clippers carries watersports instructors on each ship who advise on the best reefs for diving and snorkeling; everyone's favorite activity was the "banana boat," a long inflated tube holding four people who hang on for dear life while being pulled by high-speed Zodiac. On every itinerary there are stops at deserted islands for picnic barbecues and we visited deserted beaches on each island for sunning under fringed palms.

Star Clipper *and* Star Flyer *visit the most lush islands in the Caribbean. On my Windward Island itinerary (St. Vincent, St. Lucia, the Grenadines, Martinique, Iles des Saintes and Dominica) we hiked through rain forests, trekked to spectacular waterfalls, drove past towering peaks to volcanoes and found secluded beaches with nary another ship in sight—the Caribbean of the brochures few ever discover. In 1995,* Star Clipper *will home port in Barbados; the alternating weekly itinerary to the Leeward Islands includes visits to Nevis/Montserrat, Anguilla, St. Barts, St. Maarten, Saba and St. Kitts.*

Star Flyer *cruises the Caribbean from St. Maarten from November through April. The one-week "Treasure Island" itinerary includes Anguilla, St. Thomas/St.Croix, Tortola, Norman Island, Virgin Gorda and St. Barts. The alternating schedule features port calls in Saba, St. Barts, St. Maarten, St. Kitts, Antigua, Iles des Saints and Nevis/Montserrat. From May through September,* Star Flyer *sails the Mediterranean from Cannes on the weekly "Tyrrhenian Route" (Corsica, Bonifacio, Costa Smeralda, Elba, Portofino and St. Tropez) and the "Ligurian Route" (Corsica, Sardinia, the Island of Giglio, Portoverene and Monte Carlo). The ultimate voyage is* Star Flyer's *transatlantic crossing between Cannes and St. Maartin, scheduled each October and April.*

In my opinion, these ships are ideal for singles of all ages seeking a more sophisticated seagoing vacation. The camaraderie of passengers, abundance of activities and the company's guaranteed single rate ranging from $1495 to $1895 make this a real find. This is also my vote for most romantic seagoing experience—you'll never know when kismet is in your stars.

Star Clipper and *Star Flyer* offer a one-of-a-kind cruise experience at a very reasonable price: per person, per diem is around $200. They are perfect for those seeking warm camaraderie of fellow passengers, visits to pristine islands and the thrill of a voyage reminiscent of the romantic era when clippers roamed the world.

N/R
STAR ODYSSEY

Royal Cruise Line; Bahamian registry; Greek officers and crew; built in 1972 as the *Royal Viking Star* A.G. Weser Shipyard, Germany; refurbishment and entered service as *Star Odyssey* in 1994; 28,000 tons; 674 feet long; 83 feet at beam; 750 passengers; 410 crew; cruising speed 21 knots; 9 passenger decks.

The newest addition to Royal Cruise Line's fleet, the 750-passenger *Star Odyssey*, is evocative of the "early" days of cruising (i.e., the 1970s), when passengers rarely engaged in activities more strenuous than bridge or shuffleboard, and one's favorite bartender mixed the perfect pre-dinner martini. Entering Royal's fleet in May, 1994, *Star Odyssey* has been completely refurbished to resemble her earliest incarnation as Royal Viking Line's prestigious *Royal Viking Star*. Built in 1972, she is one of the few vessels in service today with civilized single seating dining and the timeless, classical decor absent in ships constructed during the past decade.

I cruised aboard *Star Odyssey* during her inaugural sailing. During the ship's two-year stint as Norwegian Cruise Line's mass market *Westward* the ship suffered much wear and tear; Royal's crew was still repairing the damage and some refurbishment was still underway. But even with hitches, one can glimmer a ship that, while not everyone's cup of tea, will become a favorite for passengers seeking a low-key shipboard experience with all the pluses only a small ship can deliver.

Those who normally frequent new ships that dominate the industry may notice what is absent—the frenetic pace and bustle of nonstop activities, the sparkle of reflective surfaces and the ambience of a modern hotel. *Star Odyssey's* nautical decor and gracious lines are evocative of a vessel from another era with a warm and casual ambience that is further enhanced by Royal's outgoing Greek staff and crew. The bountiful public rooms and lounges are more conducive to ballroom dancing and afternoon tea than to the constant activity of the larger ships.

Star Odyssey's small size enables visits to outstanding ports in the Mediterranean during the summer months. It also fosters a greater intermingling of passengers and a real sense of being at sea—the wide promenade decks with are closer to the ocean for those who care to lounge on a deck chair and be hypnotically lulled by the ocean. While the new fabrics and furnishings of public rooms and cabins cannot be described as luxurious, there is a warm, unpretentious atmosphere. The Four Seasons Restaurant is one of the most attractive and spacious afloat, where all 750 passengers can dine in a single seating (at assigned tables). The restaurant is actually two separate rooms—one adorned in mint green and peach, the other with cool mauve and beige—with wide panoramic windows making it bright and airy during day; at night the rooms are soothing and conducive to lingering over dinner.

The Seven Seas Lounge, with wide bar and teak dance floor, has navy, white and gold stripped sofas and white canvas director's chairs.

Cocktails before and after dinner drew many to Dionysi's Bar, with soft peach colors and a small marble bar located next to the multipurpose Odyssey Show Lounge, where evening floor shows were staged. The Panorama Lounge on Penthouse deck has 180 degrees of floor-to-ceiling windows and a bar of premium wines, an evening gathering place for relaxing around the grand piano. The adjacent Penthouse Lounge, adorned with warm earth colors and rattan furniture is popular for afternoon tea and late night dancing to a live combo. The casino is large for a ship this size, but enclosed so the sound of slots doesn't disturb.

I found the flow of public rooms left plenty to be desired. Public rooms are located over four decks, and one must constantly climb stairs or take elevators to move from one social area to another. Moreover, this is not a ship for the fitness addict—while a small gym has sufficient equipment for passenger capacity and separate aerobics area, jogging is not permitted on the ship's promenade deck. Additional sports facilities include paddle tennis court and golf driving range. A luncheon buffet is served deck-side, but the absence of a lido deck is a handicap; insufficient tables for the number of passengers on deck by the buffet line and you must climb higher laden with a tray. Additional facilities include a large theater with first-run movies, small library and shopping arcade and beauty salon.

Royal Cruise Line readily admits it has a high repeat clientele (50-88%) due to the friendly, informal Greek crew. Don't expect Swiss efficiency at all times, but staff who seem genuinely interested in your well-being and happiness. Bartenders, cabin attendants and waiters are outgoing, flirty and charming; of all nationalities, the Greeks seem to enjoy passengers more than most. On Royal's ships you'll find captains who are on the dance floor twirling passengers, bartenders who warmly welcome you each day and know your preferences and room stewards who frequently go well beyond their specified duties of just keeping the room clean. And, Fernando de Oliveira is probably one of the world's best cruise directors; he gives the impression that each passenger's enjoyment is of primary importance to him personally (some Royal repeaters book only those sailings he will be aboard). Staff and crew are the main draw for many passengers—several repeaters said they sail because of "Yannis" or "Dimitri" or "Nico," bartenders, waiters and stewards with whom they became personal friends.

While *Star Odyssey* lacks the private verandas common on newer ships in this per diem range, the ship's cabins are larger than generally available on other vessels. Prices increase by location and many good-sized staterooms can be found in less expensive categories. My main gripe is some of the best cabins are found on promenade deck, where there is a steady stream of fast walkers in the morning and strollers at night who liked to peek in (outside reflective glass had not been added during by voyage, but I'm told this is part of the renovation). And, in some cases you may have to change categories if set on a double/queen bed configuration since many twins are bolted to the floor. Deluxe Outside Staterooms on Marina Deck (200 sq. feet), categories J and L, have tubs and are an excellent buy for those who don't want to spend top dollar while avoiding promenade deck. Superior

Deluxe Suites on Promenade and Marino Deck, (categories C and D., at 335 and 260 sq. ft. respectively), are more spacious, but boast little more in amenities aside from small sofa. Penthouse Deck, with butler service, has the largest cabins with verandas, at 550 and 440 square feet. Standard amenities include hair dryers and small televisions.

During 1995, Star Odyssey *cruises some of the most enticing itineraries available. Following a series of 11-day Amazon sailings, she sails the Mayan Caribbean and Panama Canal, then moves to Europe and the Mediterranean for 12-day voyages. Following an Athens to Mombasa voyage in November, she sails the coast of East Africa to Capetown returning to Mombasa, calling in Zanzibar, Madagascar, Ile de la Reunion and Durban, among other ports.*

Wonderful special interest cruises are planned throughout 1995; consult Fielding's Theme Cruise Calendar in "Choosing Your Cruise." I personally love the passenger-friendly size and throwback to the early days of cruising characteristic of *Star Odyssey.* Those who favor the larger modern ships with nonstop activities and extensive facilities may not enjoy the leisurely pace and low-key style of cruising that was popular in the 1970s, once again resurrected with this ship. It is perfect for 60+ cruisers who want languid days at sea followed by evening conversation over cocktails in a quiet lounge, to be charmed by an outgoing crew and Royal's popular gentlemen hosts. It would be unfair to give a star rating to a ship based on an inaugural sailing before the refinement of hitches and levels of service and food are established. But I anticipate this ship will quickly find a loyal following among those seeing a classical shipboard experience and Royal's outstanding itineraries. Average per person, per diem ranges from $150 to $620.

★★★★+

STAR PRINCESS

Princess Cruises; Liberian registry; Italian officers and European crew; built in Chantiers de l Atlantique at St. Nazaire, France, for March 1989 service; 63,500 tons; 804 feet long; 105 feet at beam; 1494 passengers; crew of 563; cruising speed of 19.5 knots; 13 passenger decks.

Launched in 1989 and christened by Audrey Hepburn, the 1470-passenger *Star Princess* is geared toward today's more active passenger who relishes a sparkling, contemporary environment while cruising the waters of the Caribbean or Alaska. This ship is bustling with constant activity from early morning joggers through a hard partying disco crowd in the wee hours of the morn. Demonstrations classes, lecturers, nonstop fitness activity and evening entertainment offer the widest choices possible.

A million dollar plus art collection represents some of the best modern artists of our time. A towering three-story "Plaza" is always an active place: a huge lobby filled with comfortable chairs and low tables, a sweeping staircase leading to a two-story shopping arcade with boutiques filled with duty free merchandise of all kinds. The adjacent La Patisserie is popular for people watching while sipping "designer" coffees and teas, wine and pastries.

One floor above is the Vineyard Bar, for those whose taste runs to vintage wines and caviar. Here, $165 will get you a bottle of Dom Perignon and two orders of Beluga caviar. For those with less esoteric tastes, $60 buys a bottle of Moet and Chandon and two orders of Sevruga caviar.

The Fountain Court Dining Room is lined with picture windows along the port and starboard sides. Tables near the windows have views of the sea and passing ships; inside tables are built on raised platforms to allow sea views as well. There are alcoves with four or five tables, and etched glass panels separate areas of the room and give a hint of intimacy. The room is bright with mirrors, brass, warm peach linens and subtle, effective lighting. Over all, a pleasant but planned and predictable room. Waiters and wine stewardesses are friendly and attentive. Cuisine aboard *Star Princess* is well above average for the most part, fresh, varied and nicely presented. There is a consistency here that is sometimes lacking in other Princess ships.

High up on the forward Sun Deck is Windows to the World, with wrap around glass walls and a spectacular view just short of 360 degrees. This stunning space holds a small stage with a four-piece combo at tea time and for evening dancing. The circular room is furnished with low arm chairs, (designed, it would seem, for slender passengers; others, more amply built will probably be more comfortable seated on the small couches that line the room). Lots of chrome and brass and reflective panels, plants and rich colors make this one of the ship's most popular lounges. The Entre Nous Lounge amidships, is popular for pre-dinner cocktails when the dinner line is long, as is often the case. The art deco decor with black and tan leather upholstery make a comfortable and relaxing room. The Casino is the full width of the ship, with reflective chrome and the general glitz. There are plenty of chances to lose your money: 161 slots, eight black jack tables, a craps table and two Caribbean Stud Poker tables. Here is the only place where housekeeping fell off—the room was often a mess, filled with dirty ashtrays and torn papers.

Cafe Cornucopia offers tea, coffee and juices 24 hours a day in a casual environment; it is convenient for sun seekers, chairs seem impervious to wet suits and towels. The ample deck boasts four hot tubs and two ample pools separated by the Splash Bar. Children from three to teens have a supervised play area, and a program tailor-made for them. Older children also have their own club, called "Off Limits," with games, music and sports activities.

Star Princess' passengers are very active, and one of the ship's most popular areas is the "Fitness at Sea" spa. They will design a personal program for you with aerobics, exercise, personal training, diet and more. Fitness classes are held throughout the day and the exercise room is open into the evening.

Cabins are brightly decorated, spacious and well-equipped. The majority are outside doubles, all with picture windows, twin beds that convert to queen size, TV, refrigerator and bathroom with shower. Suites and mini-suites with verandas have tub and shower.

Princess ships have, in my experience, well-run shore excursion operations and this ship is no exception. There is a user friendly system of booking tours, with some 15 staff members on hand to answer questions and assist in booking (no one waits longer than ten minutes). One wall of the room shows continuous video of all the tours, and the whole process is fun and efficient.

There is a throbbing, pulsating motion to this ship that to this passengers was most annoying. It happens often (even in calm seas), frequently at night and off and on during the day; it was at times difficult to write post cards, use binoculars, even, in some cases, read. And noise control was a problem, especially between cabin walls, the hallways and the dining room.

When all is said and done, a top flight cruise ship must stand out in food and service. This ship's staff is superb, well trained and always ready to help.

There were a large number of wheel chair bound passengers on my cruise, and I was most impressed with the care and concern shown them by staff and crew.

Star Princess *joins the Princess fleet of six vessels in Alaska during the summer season sailing from Vancouver on 7-day voyages. She is one of the line's four superships in the Caribbean all winter on 7-day cruises from San Juan, calling in Barbados, Princess Bay, Martinique, St. Maarten and St. Thomas. Average per person, per diem is $225, including airfare.*

AUTHOR TIP

There is no regulation of cruise rates and in some cases, five travel agents will quote you five different rates for the same ship, date and cabin. Travel agents who specialize in cruises have the best deals, have more pull with certain cruise lines and usually know what's a good deal and what isn't. If you are dead certain that the ship you've picked is the right one for you, call three or four agents, give them date and cabin category and inform each that whoever comes up with the best price gets your business.

★★★

STARWARD

Norwegian Cruise Line; Bahamian registry and Norwegian officers, international crew; built and launched in 1968; refurbished in 1985; 16,100 tons; 525 feet long; 75 feet at beam; 758 passengers; crew of 315; cruising speed of 19 knots; 7 passenger decks.

The *Starward* is a proud vessel, with the completion of extensive refurbishing that not only included cabin furnishings but a redesign of the public areas as well. The former Galaxy Deck is now called the Cabaret Deck, with a glamorous new Windows on the Sea Restaurant aft. Decorated in shades of violet, blue, pink and mauve, with art nouveau glass panels and woven murals of seascapes, the restaurant is a most pleasant space with panoramic views from large picture windows on three sides. Midships on Cabaret Deck are the Monte Carlo Casino and Reflections Lounge. Forward is the Starlight Cabaret, which explains the name of this deck, with padded leather lounge chairs and soft color tones. The cabaret was expanded with new decking at the bow, and now boasts a sophisticated audiovisual setup for the shows.

Above on Boat Deck is Signals Cafe, where buffet breakfast and lunch are served daily overlooking the swimming pool. The table and bar area is now an indoor/outdoor concept, with a signal flag decor and spiral staircase up to the Sun Deck pool. Above on Compass Deck is the Topsiders Bar/hideaway, a good place for private parties and quiet conversation.

Although most of the refurbishment was cosmetic, the Starward *also received a 400-square-foot, 50-ton ducktailed stern to provide smoother sailing in turbulent seas. The new stern also makes the vessel more fuel efficient, by at least 10 percent. The* Starward *sails every Sunday from Los Angeles to Cabo San Lucas, Mazatlan and Puerto Vallarta. Dive-In, pre- and post-cruise tours and air-sea packages are all available.*

★★★★★

STATENDAM/MAASDAM

Holland America Line; Netherlands Antilles registry; Dutch officers and Indonesian-Filipino crew; built Fincantieri Shipyard, Mafalcone, Italy; launched January, 1993 (*Statendam*) and November,1993 (*Maasdam*); 55,000 tons; 720 feet; 101 feet at beam; 1266 passengers; crew of 618; cruising speed of 20s knots; 9 passenger decks.

These brand new sister ships, the *Statendam* is fifth to bear her name in Holland America Line's 120-year history, are the most opulent and exquisitely designed in the fleet. The stately *Statendam* and *Maasdam* artfully capture the era of the great liners with a bold, contemporary flair and it's reassuring to know ships can be built with such spaciousness and attention to detail. Touches like polished wood deck chairs with comfy cushions and refined materials—Italian marble, polished brass and wood, walls padded with leather and suede and leaded glass table lamps—assure one of a well-appointed vessel.

Holland America invested $2 million in art for each vessel. On the *Statendam*, this ranges from 19th century European paintings and nautical antiques to modern stained glass panels. My favorites are the 1740 replica of the warship *Sampson* and the 18th-century Japanese porcelain in the ship's art gallery. However, while HAL considers the three-story high bronze Fountain of the Sirens dominating the *Statendam's* atrium the *piéce de resistance*, I thought it much too imposing for the space.

Both vessels are designed for lengthy voyages, including the *Statendam's* 98-day world cruise and 39-day Mediterranean sailing; the *Maasdam* will sail on a 62-day Grand Australia and New Zealand voyage in the fall. Lido pool area, with a retractable glass ceiling, has Jacuzzis, freshwater pools, comfortable chaise lounges and bars with rattan chairs. The adjacent Lido Dining Room, which most passengers frequent for informal breakfast and lunch, has food stations for each course, including an ice cream parlor, spread out to eliminate long lines.

The bars and lounges all have distinct ambience. Most dramatic is the Crow's Nest on Sports Deck, with its 320 degree view, floor to ceiling windows and marble bar, wonderful for watching arrival in port. Other lounges include the clubby Piano Bar with its lovely Venetian glass; the coral and pink Explorer's Lounge, where cognac and cigars are an after-dinner tradition and the crowded Ocean Bar, its versatile quartet always performing to a packed house.

HAL has carried its art theme throughout the ships: on the Statendam, for example, aqua and marine blue Van Gogh Nightclub, where the artist's Starry Night is reproduced in wall mosaics and a $35,000 sequined curtain. The room's two-tier design adds a feeling of intimacy, its decor plush, with crushed-velvet chairs around marble tables and leaded-glass table lamps.

The Dining Room on Promenade Deck is one of the best designed afloat, with floor to ceiling windows and two tiers (upper level for smokers) and orchestra balcony. Tables are spaced far apart and artistic touches are dramatic on both ships. On the *Statendam*, six enormous gilded Venetian lanterns (reproductions of 15th century pieces) overlook the center section, two beautiful modern stained glass panels, crafted by Californian Helen Weber, grace the walls, and Murano morning glory ceiling fixtures are lighted with fiber optics. The large fake palm trees, however, should definitely go. The room comfortably holds 700 in two seatings at dinner (breakfast and lunch are one seating). There are the usual large selections in each course—seven appetizers, three soups, three salads and five entrees.

Holland America's Passport to Fitness program, offered on all vessels, features a selection of heart-healthy fare from the Perfect Balance in all categories of cuisine.

The *Statendam* and *Maasdam's* recreational facilities are extensive: a large gym and spa, with all the equipment an exercise fanatic could want, separate aerobics room and juice bar; 250-seat theater with three movies each day; shopping arcade and video library with 500 selections. The mahogany-paneled reference library with art/history books, modern titles and current periodicals is one of the most elegant afloat. On the Sports Deck, there is a saltwater pool and jogging track around the length of the deck (15 laps equals a mile). Overall, there is less outdoor deck space for daytime lounging than is found on most vessels this size.

Both vessels 633 staterooms are decorated in warm earth tones and roomy enough for long voyages. Standard outside staterooms are 190 square feet; deluxe outside rooms are 284 square feet (including veranda) and deluxe suites measure 563 square feet with veranda. All cabins have sitting areas, beds that convert to queen size, hair dryers, designer toiletries, color television with VCRs and safes for valuables. Closets are fine for a cruise of standard duration, but fitting clothes for a month or more at sea will test the packing skills of the most inveterate travelers. Outside cabins (80 percent) have tubs and large picture windows and the ship's 120 mini-suites, 28 deluxe suites and one penthouse suite have large ocean front balconies with chaise lounges, a table and chairs. Outside cabins do not face lifeboats, but passengers on Navigation Deck will find views facing a deck, although with reflective glass that does not permit those outside to peek in (it is not used by joggers). HAL's Indonesian and Filipino cabin stewards are friendly, eager to please and very popular with the line's large number of repeat passengers. The company's no tipping required policy ensures one doesn't feel pressured, although passengers normally give something for courteous service.

In 1995, Statendam *cruises from January through April on 10-day voyages round-trip from Ft. Lauderdale to St. Maarten, St. Lucia, Barbados, Dominica, St. Thomas and Nassau before commencing a summer season of one-week Alaska cruises. In October, she returns to the 10 Caribbean schedule. From January through April,* Maasdam *sails on one-week Caribbean itineraries from Ft. Lauderdale to Nassau, San Juan, St. John and St. Thomas, with three glorious days at sea. She summers in the Baltic and Mediterranean on 12-day cruises before returning in November to the Caribbean. Both vessels have average per person, per diem rates of $356 in the Caribbean; in Alaska and Europe, the average is $434. Advance purchase discounts offer savings of up to 45% off these rates.*

AUTHOR TIP

Many enticing vacations are aboard small, little-known vessels that appeal to nature-lovers and cerebral types or explore exotic tribes and locales but don't normally discount. Why not consider a sleek sailing ship, a lazy river boat, barge or self-drive house boat? Those willing to forgo casinos and bingo can have the adventure of a lifetime for a price often comparable to a traditional cruise.

★★★+

STELLA MARIS

Sun Line; Greek registry and crew; originally built in 1960; rebuilt in 1966; 3500 tons; 300 feet long; 45 feet at beam; 180 passengers; crew of 110; cruising speed of 16 knots; 4 passenger decks.

Affectionately referred to as the "baby" of the Sun Line fleet, the small, 180-passenger ship really is yacht-like in size. She is especially recommended for passengers who eschew the larger ships when visiting delightful Greek Isle/Turkish ports. She cruises between Piraeus (port of Athens) and Monte Carlo from May through August, making exotic stops such as Volos, Ephesus, Capri and Portofino, and a passage of the Corinth Canal.

The Athenian Lounge and the Belvedere Room on Sun Deck open onto each other and can hold all passengers who gather here for lectures, movies, cocktails, dancing and buffet lunches. Decorated in peach and ivory velvet, there is live music here in the evening and dancing. The chairs are deep and comfortable, and there is a long bar on one side of the room. Adjacent to the Belvedere Room is a small swimming pool, surrounded by chairs and tables, some shaded with umbrellas. Another small deck space on Lido deck is a quite places to escape. There is no elevator on the ship.

There are 80 outside cabins and 10 inside, all with private facilities. The 16 deluxe cabins are done in patterned fabric wall covering with matching bedspreads. Closet space is ample and there are two chairs and a mirrored dressing table and chest between the beds.

Cuisine is generally up to Sun Line's standards, with excellent soups and salads every day. There is one seating in the Poseidon Dining Room and a lunch buffet each day on Sun Deck.

Sun Line's "baby" is no longer young and it shows. While she is still to be recommended for her warmth and intimacy, she appears due for a major overhaul. The dining room's drapes, upholstery and carpeting are tired and there are a list of cabin complaints, including faulty drains, badly hung doors that disturb passengers at night and a musty clothes closet. And, service has slipped in the dining room, with orders mixed-up from time to time and tables left uncleared.

While *Stella Maris* is far from a luxury vessel today, she still sails steady and has less cabin-to-cabin and deck-to-deck noise than most small ships, while housekeeping remains excellent. Despite her wear and tear, loyal passengers return again and again for her warmth, intimate size and outstanding itineraries. Per person, per diem rates range from $172 to $325.

★★★★ STELLA OCEANIS

Sun Line; Greek registry and crew; originally built in 1965 and rebuilt in 1967 and relaunched; 5500 tons; 350 feet long; 53 feet at beam; 300 passengers; crew of 140; cruising speed of 17 knots; 6 passenger decks.

Those with time for a brief visit to the Greek Islands may want to investigate the *Stella Oceanis.* The four-day Athens-to-Athens itinerary includes visits to five islands plus Ephesus, Turkey, which has some of the most impressive ruins in the ancient world. Carrying just 300 passengers, *Stella Oceanis* is in the middle size of Sun Line's fleet and upholds the company's reputation for superb food and service. This old ship is comfortable, well maintained and has a wonderful flow of public rooms.

This is not a deluxe or glitzy modern ship. She has no vast reception/lobby area characteristic of modern ships and no flashy stage shows. There are no TV's in cabins and the evening entertainment is likely to be Greek dancing and singing, carried off by the all Greek crew with panache and exuberance (and passengers love it!). Unless the ship is in port, there is some sort of entertainment each night, including dancing to live music. The Plaka Tavern, a cozy and pub-like club with its long bar and nautical decor, starts up at midnight for the late crowd and closes "whenever," while serving as a movie theater by day.

The Minos Lounge, with a cinnamon, green and gold decor, has large windows on three sides, a stage and ample dance floor. Murals of Minos the Bull make a nice background, and this room seats the ship's entire passenger complement who gather for lectures and port talks. The Club on Oceanis deck houses a quiet hideaway for reading and writing.

The Aphrodite Restaurant has ocean views on three sides and is a pleasant room whose decor and lighting are now a bit tired-looking. There are two seatings at dinner. Excellent food, beautifully served is a hallmark of Sun Line and on a recent cruise, the veal, and the pasta salads were outstanding; I feasted on fresh, crisp salads with lots of feta cheese and briny olives.

Lido Deck cabins and suites are roomier than one might expect for a small ship. Even the smaller cabins are well-planned. All staterooms have private facilities (categories 1, 2 and 3 have bath and shower); all staterooms are immaculately cared for and there is 24-hour room service. However, bathroom lighting and bedroom reading light is inadequate and there should be better sound proofing between decks. Packing for this cruise is easy—there are no formal nights and only one evening when gentlemen are asked to wear coat and tie (but pack something white and blue for popular "Greek Night"). This ship is an excellent choice for a quick and total immersion into the Greek Islands, with an added bonus stop in Turkey. Sun Line's shore excursions are excellent and the cruise is wonderfully priced (per person, per diem ranges from $150 to $265).

AUTHOR TIP

You won't a pay nickel more for those ships offering theme cruises, so whether it's square dancing and photography with Holland America in Alaska, solving a murder mystery on the *QE 2,* hanging out with Cordon Bleu chefs aboard Royal Viking ships or swinging to the music of many eras aboard dozens of vessels this year, consider one that gives you more than the standard shipboard experience. You'll find a full roster inside this issue.

★★★★+

STELLA SOLARIS

Sun Line; Greek registry and crew; originally built in 1953 and formerly named the *Camboge*; rebuilt in 1973 and launched as the *Stella Solaris*; 18,000 tons; 550 feet long; 72 feet at beam; 620 passengers; crew of 310; cruising speed of 20 knots; 8 passenger decks.

The *Stella Solaris*, flagship of the Sun Line fleet, is a fine vessel, and she is aging gracefully. Launched in 1973, she offers superb food and service plus interesting and imaginative itineraries. Carrying 620 passengers and an all-Greek crew of 310, this is no glitzy vessel with state-of-the-art amenities.

She is homey and comfortable, beautifully laid out, offering busy and enriching land excursions or the option of total relaxation and refreshment. She has an unusually high percentage of "repeaters," always a good indication of a well-run and well-loved ship.

The ship's public rooms are very well laid out, located on one deck (Solaris). They flow nicely into each other, running the whole length and width of the deck. Starting in the stern is the Solaris Piano Bar, port to starboard backed by a huge window, popular with those who like cocktails while watching the sunset or leaving port. Mid ship is the large Solaris Lounge where there is some form of entertainment every evening, intimate with shades of cinnamon, olive and beige. The light and airy reception area with boutique flows into the two-seating dining room with some of the best food afloat.

Nicely prepared and presented, the food is fresh and varied, with staples such as feta cheese and Greek olives, fresh breads and rolls. Few bypass the waffles, fresh every morning at the Lido breakfast buffet. Lunches are served sit-down in the Dining Room or with buffet in the Lido, poolside.

Lunches always have a choice of several appetizers, soups, pasta dishes and fish, three entrees plus a cold dish, salads, cheese and desserts. Dinner menus are similar but more elaborate.

Particularly festive is "Greek night," when the dining room is decorated and everyone dons blue and white native costumes. I toured the kitchens, and they are spotless, a fragrant soup always on the stove. In deck bars, fresh daily-made potato chips are the nemesis of all the passengers—but well worth every nasty calorie.

The *Stella Solaris* has a total of 329 cabins (250 outside) and 218 have showers and tubs. Of the 66 deluxe staterooms, 28 on Boat Deck can accommodate a third person on the sofa bed. These suites are spacious and nicely furnished.

Inside cabins on this ship are larger than any I've seen and can sleep four (the price is a steal, and if you are not claustrophobic and don't spend a lot of time in the cabin, can be a great family bargain). All cabins have TV, plenty of closet space and spacious bathrooms.

Additional public rooms include the Monte Carlo bar; a club-like place with dark wood tables and deep leather chairs. A bright card room has plenty of tables for "bridge," and desks for writing. The Library is a most pleasant room, with a raft of paperbacks, and an abysmal lack of any kind of reference books. The 275-seat cinema shows a movie twice daily. On Golden Deck, a bright exercise room has three Lifecycles, two step machines, weights and stretch bars. Each day there is a steady stream of joggers on the wraparound promenade deck and an aerobic and dancercize class.

If itinerary is important, Stella Solaris *is hard to beat. In the Aegean, she sails on Mondays from Piraeus on two alternating one-week itineraries. The Greek islands and Turkey cruise visits Dikili, Istanbul, Kusadasi, Rhodes, Heraklion, Santorini, Mykonos and Patmos. The "antiquities" itinerary includes many of the above as well as Egypt and Israel. The cruises are offered from late April through October, and may be combined for a wonderful 2-week sailing. This ship's January Amazon River cruises are superb, and the annual "Maya Equinox" voyage draws those eager to witness the magic of the vernal equinox at the ruins of Chichen Itza, plus other famous ruins in Guatemala and Honduras. There are also several Panama Canal transits and the 21/24-day "Primavera Cruise" from Galveston to Piraeus scheduled in April. Worth special mention are the lecturers Sun Line brings onboard to make it all very meaningful. On a recent Mediterranean, Aegean and Black Seas itinerary, there were two Pulitzer prize winners who discussed archaeology, anthropology and astronomy; in the Amazon, Sun Line's speakers include Captain Loren McIntyre, who discovered the river's source. The ship's per person, per diem rates range from $195 to $400.*

AUTHOR'S AWARD

One of the best deals around is the Stella Solaris' *twice yearly 23-day positioning voyages between Caribbean and Piraeus, Greece. With advance purchase savings program, per person, per diem begins at $130, including airfare—and some spectacular Greek Island/Western Mediterranean ports.*

★★★+

SUN VIKING

Royal Caribbean Cruise Line; Norwegian registry and officers, international crew; built in Wartsila shipyard, Helsinki and launched in 1972; 18,559 tons; 563 feet long; 80 feet at beam; 726 passengers; crew of 320; cruising speed of 16 knots; 8 passenger decks.

The *Sun Viking* is the last of the Royal Caribbean vessels of her original size and configuration. Last to be launched in the cruise market, the *Sun Viking* was never stretched because the *Song of America* was ordered, so she now looks small compared with her companions, especially if you are standing in the main entrance hall and looking fore and aft along Karl Johans Gate (where Information, cruise director's office and gift shops are located). Like her sisters, the *Sun Viking's* public areas are named after Broadway hit musicals.

Located on Restaurant Deck are the HMS Pinafore Dining Room, the Merry Widow Lounge, and the Annie Get Your Gun Lounge (with its Sitting Bull Bar over to the side). But my favorite place on this and other Royal Caribbean ships is the circular, cantilevered Viking Crown Lounge ten stories above the sea and reachable only by outside staircase. This lounge is intimate, for it holds just 60 persons, whether for a pre-dinner cocktail or quiet, romantic evening drink. The second most attractive lounge on the vessel is the nightclub/disco, Lounge of the Northern Lights, which features on-the-wall entertainment. There is no cinema/theater on board, so feature films are shown in the Annie Get Your Gun Lounge when convenient. (This lounge was refurbished during a recent wet-docking of the vessel.) Live, late night entertainment can be found in the Lounge of the Northern Lights, after which disco music continues until about 3 a.m. The *Sun Viking* tends to attract a livelier clientele than most cruise ships in the area. These passengers also enjoy the ShipShape program, especially the reward of a free T-shirt if they work hard enough.

The *Sun Viking* has 266 outside and 114 inside cabins, all with private facilities. They are not the most spacious afloat, but are beautifully serviced. The vessel features the same food service and entertainment features as the *Song of Norway*, plus a sauna/massage center adjacent to the topside midships swimming pool.

Royal Caribbean expanded its horizons by announcing the Sun Viking *will sail year-round in Southeast Asia, China and Japan beginning in late December of 1995, the company's first vessel to visit this area of the world. In the meantime,* Sun Viking *cruises on 10- and 11-day alternating Caribbean itineraries between Miami and San Juan.*

AUTHOR TIP

With a good cruise counselor expect to get the third degree about your personal likes and dislikes—preferred ages of passengers, formal or laid-back environment, active or low-key activities you love plus budget and desired cruising region.

★★★

SUNWARD

Norwegian Cruise Line; Bahamian registry and Norwegian officers, international crew; originally built in 1971 and formerly named the *Cunard Adventurer*; rebuilt and relaunched in 1977 as the *Sunward II*; refurbished 1985; 28,000 tons; 674 feet long; 83 feet at beam; 846 passengers; crew of 370; cruising speed of 16 knots; 7 passenger decks.

The *Sunward* is yet another Norwegian Cruise Line success story. This vessel was the former ailing *Cunard Adventurer* that some travelers said was on her last legs and no longer seaworthy (even though not even five years old). But NCL bought the vessel and transformed her into a fun-filled and sunny ship for 3- and 4-day cruises to the Bahamas. NCL scheduled the usual ports of Nassau and Freeport, but added an Out Island just for sunning, snorkeling and swimming. It has worked so well that many passengers choose this cruise just for the beautiful Bahamarana beach party at NCL's Pleasure Island. The ship has about 50 Sunfish, rental equipment for snorkeling and five instructors on board for the beach call. Cabanas have been built past the sand dunes, and the ship's band plays on while you play and party (food and drink are brought ashore). The Dive-in program is Number One here.

A very elegant retired gentleman we know won a cruise aboard the *Sunward.* He upgraded himself to a suite, took along a lady friend, and had a wonderful time. He said he was impressed by the number of incentive groups on board and the good mix of ages. It was not a rah-rah crowd as one might think, but a nice complement of business executives, young couples and families.

The accommodations are standard but well-designed, and there are plenty of suites and larger-than-average outside staterooms. This vessel was refurbished with a few days of good fun in mind, and that is the feeling projected throughout the public areas: the split-level Sunburst Dining Room, the Bahamarana Lounge on Boat Deck where the onboard Las Vegas-style revues are staged, the Crow's Nest Nightclub, the Buccaneer Bar with outdoor stage, and the Lido Cafe/ Disco. In addition, there is an enlarged casino with bar, as well as enclosed cinema on Bridge Deck, and a large swimming pool area with sauna and massage rooms aft on Bahamas Deck. There are a few shops on Atlantic Deck and a beauty salon down on Caribbean Deck.

Every Friday the Sunward *departs Miami for Nassau and one of the Bahamas most beautiful atolls in the Berry Islands. The vessel returns to Miami on Monday morning. Every Monday afternoon the* Sunward II *sails for Nassau, NCL's Pleasure Island and Freeport. The vessel returns to Miami on Friday morning.*

★★★

TROPICALE

Carnival Cruise Lines; Liberian registry; Italian officers and international crew; built in Aalborg, Denmark, especially for Carnival Cruise Lines; commissioned in January 1982; refurbished in 1989; 36,674 tons; 660 feet long; 85 feet at beam; 1022 passengers; crew of 550; cruising speed of 22 knots; 10 passenger decks.

The $100-million *Tropicale* made her debut in January 1982, and Carnival Cruise Lines called its new vessel the eighth largest cruise ship afloat (at the time). Certainly, she was the first of several new ships scheduled to make waves during the decade of the 80s. The 1200-passenger *Tropicale* has a distinctive outward appearance, with a winglike funnel that was originally planned for aesthetic's sake but has proved to be effective in moving the smoke outward. Other innovative features include a below-water bulbous bow for fuel efficiency (makes the vessel appear to be on water skis), and computerized engine room and bridge. A satellite reception dish brings TV signals into the cabins, but does not seem too successful when more than several miles from shore. The vessel is energy-efficient and even recycles about 80 tons of nonpotable water each day for maintenance functions. A squared-off stern was apparently designed for economy in building the accommodations section.

The 511 passenger cabins were installed fabricated; even the lavatories were constructed as entire units. Cabin size is unusually spacious for a modern-day vessel, and the majority have large sea-view windows, as well as twin beds that can be converted to king-size configuration. Wardrobe and storage spaces are both plentiful (beds are built high enough for suitcases to slide easily under them), and all cabins are card-coded, which means you can never forget your number. Closed circuit televisions overhead bring feature films several times daily and 24-hour room service is also available. Keep it simple on the room service order, and expect plastic dishes which is far better than the paper plates that arrived on the inaugural sailing! If plastic in the cabin is offensive, take the stairs to the Boiler Room where your scrambled eggs will be still hot and eaten on deck on plastic plates.

The Boiler Room, aft on Lido Deck, is also the scene of hot dogs and hamburgers at lunchtime and afternoon tea with cakes. There is plenty of deck space on the *Tropicale*, although even three (albeit small) swimming pools are inadequate for the size of the passenger complement. Popular on tropical evenings is the Patio Bar, which remains open until an unorthodox 6 a.m., where a calypso band plays for dancing and fountains take over in the main pool. The Grand Midnight Buffet is also served here. Otherwise, passengers flock to the Tropicana Lounge where extravaganzas are offered nightly after dinner, or to the Islands in the Sun Lounge on deck above, which appears to be a bit more cozy (but is actually huge)! The late night set frequents the Extra-Z Disco or the casino, both of which close only when the last group goes.

The 658-capacity Palm Restaurant, surprisingly, is located down on Riviera Deck (the current trend is to enjoy sea views). Meal presentation is fine and the dinner menus quite a departure from the usual Carnival fare. Special theme nights break the monotony. All beef dishes are excellent and obvious care is used in the selection of top-grade meat. A special wine list selected by Vice-President Bob Dickinson is for those willing to pay a little more.

The *Tropicale* boasts 12 suites up on Veranda Deck, with their own sea-view balconies, bars and bathtubs plus separate conversation areas. The suites are pleasant, although the sitting areas seem less bright and cheerful than the average cabin. The Tropicale was refurbished in late 1989 under the direction of Carnival's in-house architect Joe Farkis, who designed the vessel. The main showroom, Tropicana Lounge, was redone with new stage and banquettes.

Other public rooms with new interiors are Islands in the Sun Lounge, Paradise Club Casino and Chopsticks Piano Bar, converted from the card and video room. The dual promenades and cabins also received attention.

Tropicale *sails from Tampa and New Orleans on Western Caribbean itineraries in 1994.*

★★★

UNIVERSE

World Explorer Cruises; Liberian registry; Chinese and international crew; originally built in U.S. in 1953 and formerly called the *Badger Mariner, Atlantic,* and *Universe Campus*; rebuilt in 1957 and refurbished in 1990; 18,100 tons; 564 feet long; 76 feet at beam; 550 passengers; crew of 220; cruising speed of 15 knots; 6 passenger decks.

The 550-passenger *Universe* provides a different type of cruise experience. The atmosphere on board is casual and friendly and the accommodations all have private facilities, but they have a dormitory feel. Cruise emphasis here is on learning, and the *Universe* makes two around-the-world cruises each year (September and January). This Semester at Sea program can accommodate about 500 students, who do their research and field trips in worldwide ports of call.

From mid-May through August, the learning process is open to the general public as the *Universe* makes 14-day cruises from Vancouver to Wrangell, Juneau, Skagway, Glacier Bay, Columbia Glacier/Valdez, Anchorage (Whittier), Sitka, Ketchikan and Victoria. The vessel offers culture without glitz seminars on arts, customs, history and geology of the ports visited in both slide presentations and lectures. For further research, there is an 12,000-volume library on board.

Lecturers include political scientists, naturalists, historians, anthropologists and geologists, many of them college professors. The cruise manager, Ron Valentine, who teaches advanced law and history when not on board, coordinates the ship's classical entertainment program. Past sailings have featured chamber ensembles, string quartets and light opera.

Black tie and fancy dress are to be left behind on this cruise as there is neither glitz nor glitter of the Las Vegas-type of entertainment on this vessel. Instead, there is plenty of good conversation and even some gentlemen hosts for ladies' companionship while dining, dancing and all ship and shore activities. This is a cruise on which real friends are found and kept, according to so many previous passengers.

There are a few better cabins on Boat Deck, but most are standard and can accommodate third and fourth persons. A few single cabins are available and not overly priced. There are four lounges (the Commodore, Mandarin, Denali and Alyeska, the Aleut word for Alaska), the North Star Nightclub, a full theater, youth center, meeting room, exercise room, full laundry, swimming pool, gift shop and glass-enclosed promenade (one side is nonsmoking). The dining room is located on Main Deck.

World Explorer Cruises has instituted a convenient onboard credit system, so passengers can sign and settle at the end just like the more glamorous ships. Rates are extremely reasonable for such a fascinating experience, and pre- or post-cruise stays are available in Vancouver or Seattle.

★★★

VIKING SERENADE

Royal Caribbean Cruise Line; Bahamian registry; Scandinavian officers; international crew; built in France in 1982 as *Scandinavia*; refurbished in 1985 as *Star Dancer*; refurbished in 1989 and renamed *Viking Serenade*; 27,000 tons; 608 feet long; 87 feet at beam; 976 passengers; crew of 480; cruising speed of 21 knots; 7 passenger decks.

For such a young vessel, *Viking Serenade* seems to have already enjoyed a very full life. Designed to carry vehicles (cars and RVs), as well as passengers, she first sailed from New York to the Bahamas, but not with great success. Most recently sailing as *Star Dancer* for Admiral Cruises, she was brought into the Royal Caribbean fleet in January 1990 to inaugurate the company's presence in Alaska and Mexico, but not before the distinctive Crown and Anchor logo appeared on her stack and the traditional royal blue stripe around her white hull.

Other decorative changes consistent with RCCL style include artwork from Mayan images to Alaskan landscapes in the public rooms, a lobby embellished with brass and bronze and tasteful color schemes in cabins and lounges. The updated Starlight Lounge now features Las Vegas-style revues and cruise staff shows in the evening. Other onboard amenities are Stanley's Pub, casino, disco, library/card room, Sundown Lounge, Lido Bar/ grill, health club/spa, outdoor swimming pool and Windows of the World Dining Room, although I expect Royal Caribbean to change the names to suit its Broadway musical theme.

There are 284 outside cabins with large picture windows and 200 inside cabins, all with two lower beds (some of which are convertible). Some cabins can accommodate third and fourth persons, and some can be combined into suites. There is one handicap-equipped cabin on board.

Viking Serenade *sails from Los Angeles on 3- and 4-day cruises to Catalina and Ensenada.*

★★★★+
VISTAFJORD

Cunard Line; Bahamian registry and northern European crew; launched in 1973; last refurbished in 1994; 24,500 tons; 628 feet long; 82 at beam; 736 passengers; crew of 379; cruising speed of 20 knots; 8 passenger decks.

When we visited *Vistafjord* this summer she was in sorry shape and Cunard plans a much-needed $15 million refurbishment of this once-great vessel in November, 1994. Cunard has retained the services of the Swedish marine architectural firm Tillberg Design AB, to undertake the refurbishment.

New features are planned in the design scheme of *Vistafjord*: the addition of ll new suites, including two duplex penthouses; a business center and an ice cream parlour. A new 40-seat French restaurant is also planned and the Lido Cafe will be enlarged. A roof will be installed over the Sports Deck, allowing for expanded sports activities. The *Vistafjord's* 386 staterooms will be refurbished, with new bathrooms; public areas scheduled for overhaul include the dining room, ballroom, Garden Lounge, Club Viking, Theater, Casino, North Cape Bar, Norse Lounge; Library, Beauty Parlor, and the Purser's Square.

In 1995, Vistafjord *begins the year with South America itineraries, followed by a March through April schedule of Caribbean cruises. From May through November, she is sails in the Mediterranean and Baltic, followed by a return to the Caribbean in December. Per person, per diem rate range from $250 to $500.*

★★★★★

WESTERDAM

Holland America Line; Bahamian registry; Dutch officers; Indonesian/Filipino crew; built 1986 in Papenburg, West Germany, for Home Lines; stretched in 1989 by HAL; 52,000 tons; 798 feet long; 95 feet at beam; 1476 passengers; crew of 700; cruising speed of 21 knots; 8 passenger decks.

The *Westerdam*, originally constructed as the *Homeric* for Home Lines and delivered in 1986, became a member of the Holland America family in November 1988. A year later the vessel was returned to the West German yard for a $65-million refit featuring the placement of a 130-foot section midships. This section, which was part of the original design, added 10,000 gross tons, 247 new cabins, several attractive public rooms and an expansion of outdoor facilities. The 1476-passenger *Westerdam* is now the largest vessel in the Holland America fleet.

Among the cabin additions are four especially equipped for the handicapped (002 and 021 on Navigation Deck; 068 and 087 on Upper Promenade Deck).

Highlight of the refit is the two-level, 800-seat Admiral's (show) Lounge, converted from two lounges on separate decks. Adjacent to the show lounge is a series of new spaces—the Bookchest (library), Explorers Lounge (afternoon tea is served here), Ocean Bar (where all the action begins about 11 a.m.), some meeting and card rooms and boutiques. Aft of the new area is the Big Apple Teen Club, Peartree Saloon and Disco and Casino.

The restaurants aboard *Westerdam* received great attention. The Amsterdam Dining Room increased from 520 to 875 seats, and the Lido Buffet a Holland America trademark was expanded. A second buffet, the Veranda Restaurant, adjacent to the glass-domed Veranda Pool on Sun Deck is also new, as well as additional seating and two whirlpools. More seating and a tennis court were also added to what is now known as Sports Deck.

With the $1 million of 17th- and 18th-century Dutch artifacts (including a cannon brought from the deep by a French fisherman) around the ship, the *Westerdam* has truly become a Holland America family member. She has become a megaship, however, and the length of her corridors can seem endless. Plan extra time for finding the Amsterdam dining room!

In 1995, the Westerdam *sails year-round in the Caribbean from Ft. Lauderdale visiting St. Maarten, St John/St. Thomas and Nassau. Average per person, per diem rates are $282.*

AUTHOR TIP

Whenever possible, select a *pre-cruise hotel stay* in the city of embarkation. A good night's sleep after a tortuous flight and leisurely ride to the pier after a good night's sleep will add an extra day of relaxation to the voyage.

⚓⚓⚓⚓⚓+

WIND STAR/WIND SONG/WIND SPIRIT

Windstar Cruises; Bahamian registry; European officers and service crew; built in Le Havre and launched 1986, 1987, 1988; sail cruisers; 5350 tons; 440 feet long; 52 feet at beam; 4 masts with 6 computer-controlled sails; 150 passengers; crew of 84; 4 passenger decks.

You and your significant other will feel like Katherine Hepburn and Cary Grant aboard these three identical motorized sail vessels, as "yar" as the "True Love" in *The Philadelphia Story.* With white sails billowing from four masts, gracefully curved smokestacks and proud clean lines, they feel as romantic as a private yacht—yet offer most of the services and activities of a small conventional cruise ship. At the end of a week's cruise in the Caribbean, Mediterranean or South Pacific, people look younger, healthier and happy.

But with a staff of 91 catering to some 150 people, everyone gets plenty of pampering. Most voyages have a strong component of repeaters and it's not hard to fathom why. Give *Wind Star, Wind Song* and *Wind Spirit* a relaxation and romance quotient of two to one.

Some debate whether Windstar's ships rank as true sailing vessels, powered as they are by diesel electric motors driving a variable pitch propeller at 200 rpms. But in the Caribbean, *Wind Spirit* averages at least one third of the voyage under sail. Any of the spiffy British officers will happily explain to you that the ship can go faster under sail—or 14 knots as opposed to 12 knots under motor. With a vigilant eye to fuel economy, staff usually combine sail and motor, and when sea conditions are right will shut off the motors, especially during the full day at sea on the Caribbean Leeward Island itinerary I experienced. Let the purists quibble. When these computer-driven sails go up in a spirit-lifting wind and the ship cuts silently through the sapphire-blue sea, "I felt like a Monaco Royal."

Billed as "casually elegant," the onboard atmosphere fulfills its promise. People dress up more or less for the single-seating dinner—women more than men, who throw a nice shirt and slacks after male bonding in the Jacuzzi around sunset. The air-conditioned cabins, all outside and nearly identical on deck two, are beautifully appointed with television, VCR/CD players (the library is very well stocked with complimentary selections), safe and direct dial telephone. Cleverly designed, the 185-square foot cabins afford plenty of storage space plus foldout deck and minibar. The piece de resistance is the cloverleaf-shaped bathroom in subdued gray, with fabulous water pressure I wish I had in my apartment, not to mention two shower heads, one equipped for massage. Thick towels, terry robes and Swiss toiletries leave you feeling like the princess without the pea. All is kept spic-'n-span by a crew of Filipino cabin stewards, who replenish your fresh flowers, fruit basket and ice bucket daily, and a leave you a couple of chocolate mints at turndown time.

They do everything but tuck you in; 24-hour room service is also available and is always prompt.

These are ships for independent spirits, with onboard diversions, great waters sports and well-organized shore excursions. Windstar's clientele ranges from the 20s to the 80s, and this is truly a couples' experience —it's haute romance, and all but the most independent singles may feel left out (bringing along children under 12 is also discouraged). There's a small casino, lovely with comfy bucket leather seats decorated in sand/earth tones, although most prefer hanging out at the pool bar on deck. A library offers hardbound and paper back books, games and the latest videos and some 400 compact discs in all music categories (grab a handful of both the moment you board to get first choice). A small gym boasts two Stairmasters, two stationary bikes, weights, bench and mats. Snazzy Windstar-logoed casual clothing is available in the Signature shops.

Dining is single, open seating in the lovely blue dining room, with tables for two, four, six and eight. The food aboard *Wind Spirit* was sumptuous.

Chef Christian Hoffman has a light touch with sauces, respects the integrity of fresh fruits and vegetables and has a deft hand with rare beef tenderloins and succulent lobster and seafood dishes. Desserts will tempt even the most disciplined and breakfast is equally enjoyable, served at the Veranda restaurant, either in the air-conditioned interior or on deck beneath umbrellas. One can choose hearty American fare such as eggs, sausage, ham and bacon, continental breads and pastries, or healthy cereals and fruit, including Swiss birchermuseli. Windstar is famous for its Bread Pudding—it's utterly addictive!.

Windstar Bread Pudding With Vanilla Cream Sauce (serves 6-8)

4 slices bread

1tbsp. butter or margarine

1 to 2 eggs, slightly beaten

6 tbsp. sugar

1-1/2 c. milk

1/2 c. coconut milk

1-1/2 oz shredded coconut

1/2 tsp. vanilla

1pinch salt

Butter bread lightly and cut in 1/2-inch pieces. Place in baking dish with shredded coconut. Mix eggs, sugar, coconut milk, salt, milk and vanilla. Pour mixture over bread, set in pan of hot water and bake at 350 degrees for about 40 minutes until firm.

Vanilla Cream Sauce
1 quart milk
9 oz sugar
5 egg yolks
1-1/2 oz cornstarch
2 vanilla beans

Cook two split vanilla beans or the marrow of two vanilla beans with the skin in the sauce mixture. Heat milk gradually a little amount at a time, stirring steadily while adding the cool milk. Add egg yolks, sugar, vanilla and cornstarch while still stirring. Bring to a boil, then keep warm. Pour sauce over bread pudding.

It's hard to imagine that Windstar can improve on its cuisine, but the company is introducing the "180 Degrees From Ordinary" collection of recipes from renowned chef/restaurateur Joachim Spilchal of Patina Restaurant in Los Angeles and Pinot Bistro in Studio City. Spilchal was cited as "best California chef" by James Beard Society, and will create some 180 recipes especially for Windstar ships. In 1995, you'll find refined touch in recipes such as towers of marinated salmon with chive creme fraiche, corn risotto with wild mushrooms and basil and naturally, desserts such as lemon sandwich with strawberry salad.

Evening entertainment is casual and fun. One day men were urged to purchase the most outrageous Caribbean shirts ashore for that evening's tropical clothing contest; we danced to combo music and feasted on a tropical barbecue deckside the last evening while a blackjack tourney was spirited in the casino. Everyone enjoys tours of the engine room and galley. On clear nights an officer conducts a tour of constellations—and they are proud to welcome you onto the bridge to learn about the sophisticated radar and navigation equipment. On the last day at sea under sail, guests manned the helm on the flying bridge for photo opportunities with the captain—keeping a 5000 ton sailing ship on course is no easy task, as attested by the squiggly wakes of amateur helmsmen.

While *Wind Spirit* offered the usual catamaran/snorkeling tours and island sightseeing, its "America's Cup Regatta" near St. Maarten was exclusive to Windstar, and a highlight of the voyage. Participants experience the thrill of racing on two classic 70-foot yachts built for the 1987 America's Cup race in Australia, rounding buoys and learning race tactics and strategies from an America's Cup captain. After the race, a special camaraderie prevails among both winners and losers, who also treasure the large color photos bought from a photographer snapping away in a nearby Zodiac. Watersports include swimming from the sports platform at the ship's stern, snorkeling and scuba, waterskiing, kayaking, banana boat rides, wind surfing, sailing and deep sea fishing (the latter during a day at sea). If you don't care to join a shore excursion but prefer to explore ports of call on your own, tenders ferry guests between ship and shore every half hour.

On the last day at sea, I reclined in a lounge chair on forward deck, white clouds low on the horizon lining the sky's blue dome like trim on an overturned Wedgewood teacup. Black dolphins leaped off the starboard bow, seeming to race to keep up with the ship. The sails flapped, the rigging creaked and Elaine de Kooning's motto came to mind: "Never stint on luxuries; the necessities will take care of themselves."

Wind Song *celebrates its eighth year in the South Pacific. Sailing year-round from Tahiti, seven-day itineraries visit Huahine, Raiatea, Bora Bora and Moorea. Both* Wind Star *and* Wind Spirit *operate in the Caribbean and Mediterranean. During winter,* Wind Star *cruises from Barbados on two seven-day alternating itineraries to the Windward and Leeward Islands. Southbound sailings call at Tobago Cays, Bequia, Martinique, Iles des Saintes, St. Lucia and Carriacou. Northbound cruises from Barbados visit St. Lucia, Dominica, St. Martin, St. Barts and St. Kitts.* Wind Star *voyages to the Mediterranean, and from homeport Monte Carlo commences seven-day cruises to the Italian Riviera (Corsica, Portegerraio, Portovenere and Portofino).* Wind Spirit *winters in the Caribbean, sailing from St. Thomas on seven-day cruises to St. Croix, St. John and St. Barts before a season in the Mediterranean. Seven-day cruises from Athens to Istanbul include port calls in Mykonos, Santorini and Rhodes, Greece plus Bodrum, Kusadasi and Istanbul.*

With discounts factored in, Windstar's per person, per diem is $324 in the South Pacific; $305 in the Caribbean and $410 in the Mediterranean. A very enticing 10-day Caribbean package, offered January through March 25, 1995 on *Wind Star*, includes a seven-day cruise, round-trip airfare from Miami, three pre-cruise nights at the deluxe Royal Pavilion Hotel and transfers, priced from $3195 per person, double occupancy; low-cost air add-ons are available between major U.S. gateways and Miami.

WINDWARD

(see Dreamward)

AUTHOR TIP

If on a tight vacation budget, avoid overspending on cruise attire. Despite what is depicted in brochures, everyone dresses in shorts, polo or t-shirts and sneakers or sandals during the daytime. Unless you're aboard the ritziest vessel, evening attire for women does not have to be sequins or gowns they'll never wear again. For women's formal attire (usually two per one-week cruise) one long black skirt or evening trousers and several dressy blouses with jewelry will suffice. Most men don't wear tuxedos these days but stick to the optional dark suit. If you reside outside a climate that is sunny year-round, don't wait until the dead of winter to buy incidentals—bathing suits and sandals are nearly impossible to find and outrageously priced in December on the east coast. Prices on board and in port also tend to be very high.

★

WORLD RENAISSANCE

Epirotiki Lines; Greek registry and crew; originally built in 1966 and named *Renaissance*; 12,000 tons; 492 feet long; 69 feet at beam; 450 passengers; crew of 235; cruising speed of 18.5 knots; 8 passenger decks.

This vessel was the flagship and pride of Paquet French Cruises, but was sold in an economy measure to Epirotiki Lines in 1977. Epirotiki changed her registry and crew to Greek and renamed her *World Renaissance.*

The *World Renaissance* has 173 outside cabins and 40 inside. Decks and public rooms have been renamed to reflect Greek ownership. The El Greco Grand Salon is one of the most pleasant small lounges afloat, and the Lido swimming pool area is perfect for those itsy-bitsy bikinis that Europeans love. In fact, there are two heated pools on board, the other by the Xenia Discotheque/bar.

The Pelagos Dining Room seats 400 and the lounge/grill another 60, so if there is not a crowd, everyone can dine at the same time. The vessel also boasts a gymnasium/sauna and a small theater. The cardroom is perfect for small cocktail parties and there is a small casino. A nice little cruise ship that needs a refurbishment.

During the official Aegean/Mediterranean season World Renaissance *offers cruises either on a 7- or 14-day schedule. Her 1-week sailings may be the Golden Fleece (Greek Islands and Turkey) or the exciting Seven Seas. During the winter months* World Renaissance *represents Epirotiki in the Caribbean or South America.*

YORKTOWN CLIPPER

(see Nantucket Clipper)

AUTHOR TIP

Never take a cruise specifically to find the great love of your life—you stand a better chance of it happening when you least expect it. While tales of dashing officers wedding passengers are legion, don't count on it. You stand a much better chance of simply being a replacement for a woman who tearfully waved good-bye as you boarded the ship.

★★★★★

ZENITH

Celebrity Cruises; Liberian registry; Greek officers; international crew; built in Papenburg, Germany; christened April, 1992; 47,500 tons; 682 feet; 95 feet at beam; 1374 passengers; crew of 657; cruising speed of 21.5 knots; 9 passenger decks.

The caveat "If you get it right the first time, don't mess with it" must be engraved on a bronze plaque in Celebrity Cruises headquarters. While it is difficult to distinguish the company's three new vessels *Horizon*, *Meridian* and *Zenith* having been aboard them all, I find rating them as wonderful is no problem at all.

From the moment you step into the soaring, cantilevered lobby, your eyes, as well as your spirits, go up. And with the superb ambience and services on board *Zenith* you are likely to stay on cloud nine until forced off the ship. Like her sister ship, the *Horizon*, this beautiful new vessel has a wonderful combination of laid-back informality for daytime living and fun in the sun, and a classy, glittering and sophisticated change of pace for the evening hours. Refusing to cave in to the trend for megasize ships, her passenger capacity of 1370 allows for roomy cabins and the feeling of a bustling and busy vessel, but the public space is so well planned that nooks and crannies of coziness and privacy, which we all seek on a cruise, can easily be discovered.

The public rooms are beautifully decorated with richly colored fabrics and carpets, abundant uses of mirrors and etched-glass panels and doors. Every advantage is taken to allow the maximum of sea views. The *Zenith* offers passengers an expanded Olympic Health Club, an especially roomy area with the full roster of state-of-the-art equipment and large mirrored aerobics area. Sybaritic spa experiences include herbal wraps.

I loved the wide wraparound decks, wonderful for jogging in the early a.m. There are two pools (one saltwater) and the whirlpools on deck are always active (it's been my experience that more relationships, acquaintances, friendships or whatever are spawned at whirlpools than at any other location on board ship for obvious reasons). Buffet breakfasts and lunches are available on deck and in the large indoor/outdoor Windsurf Cafe (lunch was the only time I experienced waiting in line).

Lounges are plentiful, so that one always has a choice in ambience. *Zenith's* Fleet Bar, top deck and starboard, is large and sun-drenched by day, chic after dark and the best locale for watching sunsets, and Harry's Tavern is a lovely piano bar perfect for an after-dinner aperitif. The Celebrity Show Lounge is glitzy, brassy and spectacular. Comfortable armchair seats with built-in small trays to hold drinks and snacks insure that you need never be hungry or thirsty, even during the lively floor show. The Mayfair Casino is restrained and clubby. You either enjoy gambling on board ship or you don't; if you do, this is a spiffy place to chance a few bucks.

When it comes to dining, Celebrity ships outshine nearly all vessels in their price range: cuisine really is gourmet, which is rare on a vessel of this size. Under the watchful eye of Michel Roux, Celebrity's culinary consultant, dining is a truly memorable experience: meats are succulent, tender and beautifully sauced. Vegetables and salads tasted garden fresh and desserts are gorgeously sinful, enough so for the most decadent of tastes.

Service throughout is excellent: from the white-glove greeting at embarkation to the inquiry of passenger's satisfaction made during the cruise when each cabin is personally visited by a member of the hotel staff.

The 687 cabins (541 outside; 146 inside) aboard the *Zenith* and *Horizon* are especially well planned and spacious (standard size is 172 square feet), with soft colors and superior fabrics. There is a comfortable sitting area, beds can be converted to queen-size, closets are ample, bathrooms stocked with amenities and hair dryers, television and three-channel radio.

The Zenith *sails year-round on alternating one-week Caribbean itineraries from Ft. Lauderdale. The Eastern Caribbean schedule includes San Juan, St. Thomas and St. Maarten; Western ports are Montego Bay (Jamaica); Grand Cayman, Cozumel and Key West. Average per person, per diem is $275.*

PORTS OF CALL

The Bahamas and Bermuda

THE BAHAMA ISLANDS

Christopher Columbus was the first tourist to this lovely archipelago that begins just fifty miles off the coast of Florida and stretches in a great southeasterly arc to within fifty miles of eastern Cuba and Haiti. Columbus arrived in 1492 on an island he named San Salvador. However, the Spanish never quite got around to settling these islands (seven hundred strong) that are scattered across some 100,000 square miles of the Atlantic Ocean. The British arrived in 1629 and ruled for about three hundred years, leaving behind a legacy in language, architecture, law and some lovely manners. The Bahamas became self-governing in 1964 and independent in 1973, although they still belong to the Commonwealth and Queen Elizabeth continues as head of state.

Ever since Columbus' visit, tourism has played an important role in the growth of these islands. Ponce de Leon came looking for his Fountain of Youth, and when George Washington stopped by in the 18th century he called them Isles of Perpetual June. For cruise vessels, the center of tourism is **Nassau**, the main port and capital city on the island of New Providence. Nassau has retained some charming colonial overtones, although its Bay Street area looks like any mid-American town with all the fast-food chains. Strolling along,

there are shops with prices for British goods not duty free but possibly better than you would find back home. The street is fronted by the British Colonial Hotel and one of the prettiest and most historic places in The Bahamas. But it's an easy town to explore from your vessel docked at Prince George Wharf. The government buildings are all around Rawson Square, which has a high-priced straw market in the middle. Try not to miss the statue of Queen Victoria and the 1797 octagonal structure that was once a prison but is now a public library. You might also want to have a look at Christopher Columbus, who stands in front of government house. If you like forts, three are within easy reach: 1790 Fort Charlotte, named after the wife of King George III; 1741 Fort Montagu, built to guard the eastern entrance of the harbor, and Fort Fincastle. Nearby is the so-called Queen's Staircase, a 102-foot-high set of limestone steps that number the sixty-five years of Victoria's reign. If you take a city tour you will also visit the Ardastra Gardens to see trained flamingos and the Seafloor Aquarium to see dolphins perform. Or, you can take a three-hour catamaran cruise around the harbor, have a rum punch and swim off one of the island's lovely beaches.

PARADISE ISLAND

Just a hop, a skip and a few dollars taxi ride from Prince George Wharf is Paradise Island, an exquisite crescent-shaped beach famous for bathing beauties, nightclub entertainment and gambling. Here are also some beautiful gardens and a 14th-century cloister, but no doubt you will want to take Lady Luck straight into the casino at the Britannia Beach Hotel and then enjoy the Las Vegas style review in Le Cabaret.

In the past few years, Cable Beach has grown into the place to visit. Carnival pushes the Cable Beach Casino and Supper Club, where Les Fantastiques offer Las Vegas type revues. Just remember that the money you lose goes into someone's pocket!

Gambling is also the most interesting distraction in **Freeport**, on Grand Bahama Island, the second most popular cruise call in the archipelago. Here, El Casino is reputed to be the largest gambling den on this side of the Atlantic, and it certainly is the most frequented, especially by those on the 4-day cruises from Miami. When you've had enough of the chips, browse around the International Bazaar for one of those famous T-shirts (my favorite is the one in French), that says, "It's Better in The Bahamas."

The Bahama Out Islands should not be overlooked either. More and more cruise vessels are calling among these little pieces of paradise.

AUTHOR'S OBSERVATION

Those especially enticed by a stop at a private island will find Royal Caribbean's Coco Cay (Little Shrimp Cay) is superb. While many cruise lines share an island with other vessels, this is exclusive for RCCL passengers. In addition to every watersport imaginable, RCCL schedules a full roster of activities through the day ranging from a luncheon barbecue to volleyball, limbo and walk-a-thons. And, there's plenty of space to escape on your own and just gaze at the sea.

BERMUDA

Britain's oldest colony sits out in the Atlantic Ocean some 600 miles due east of Savannah, Georgia, and approximately 775 miles (40 hours) southeast of New York, from where you will most likely sail. Since the late 1st century this tiny coral island with pastel-colored houses and quaint British customs has been a popular watering hole for cruise passengers. Mild winters used to attract the wealthy, who arrived with steamer trunks and servants for a long stay.

Bermuda is booming as a cruise destination lately because it is a clean, safe haven where the natives are friendly. Local prices for accommodations and food tend to be outrageous, so cruises make sense for pleasure-seekers and their pocketbooks! The traditional Saturday to Saturday sailings from New York prevail, with three lovely days in Bermuda and enough time enroute to enjoy all the ship has to offer leisurely.

AUTHOR'S OBSERVATION

Family travel has mushroomed on this itinerary and all vessels have facilities and supervised activities for kids. Celebrity's Meridian and Horizon are the top vessels sailing from New York, and their children's programs are the best.

The "Song of America" in Bermuda

Most cruise vessels dock at the pier on Front Street in downtown **Hamilton**, Bermuda's only city and its capital. Other ships dock in St. George's and spend a day or two at the other end of the island. Hamilton, a nice, clean place, has interesting shops where, despite a few good buys, most British goods now unfortunately sell for exorbitant prices. If you're interested in pullovers and other woolens, check prices at home before you leave to see how they compare with Hamilton stores. My favorite shop is Bluck's, at the corner of Front Street and Bermudiana Road, where the beautiful and expensive china, crystal, silver and antiques will knock your eyes out.

If you don't take the shore excursions (and they are really unnecessary on this tiny island when you have three days to explore) and feel confident on the road, rent a moped the minute you disembark, priced around $30 per day.

It's the best way to get around as no rental cars are allowed and buses are poky. Remember to follow the rules of the road—drive on the left and always wear your helmet.

Exploring this 21-square-mile piece of land that geologists say lies on top of a submerged mountain is loads of fun, especially if you opt to do it with a friend instead of a crowd. Since your ship will stay three full nights in port, if you're on the 7-day cruise, you'll have time to see everything. The Visitors Bureau (on the left as you leave the pier) has terrific maps and pamphlets and will answer any questions. When you go on your jaunts, be sure to take a swimsuit, because you will be tempted by many beautiful beaches.

AUTHOR'S OBSERVATION

The best beaches are the public beaches along the South Shore, especially Jobson Cove or Warwick Long Bay, where you can spend the whole day among cliffs, rocks, and sparkling sand. But when exploring by moped you'll discover the secluded coves of the brochures where there's nary a soul in sight.

At the large supermarket along the way (if you're coming from Hamilton, it's just past St. Paul's Lane on the left) you can stock up on cold drinks and snacks. Don't be shocked by the prices —food is very expensive on this island. For inexpensive lunches, grab sandwiches at Pink's Front Street Delicatessen near the harbor on Front Street.

Try not to miss the Blue Grotto Dolphin Show in Harrington Sound (just before the causeway), the Crystal or Leamington caves, where stalagmites and stalactites form a forestlike maze, and Gibbs Hill Lighthouse. This is the oldest cast-iron lighthouse in the world. Built in the 1850s, the view of the entire island from the top of its 185 steps is fantastic. Gibbs Hill Lighthouse is off the South Shore Road, just behind the fanciful high-rise Southampton Princess Hotel. It's open from 9 a.m. to 4:30 p.m. daily and admission is about fifty cents. What a bargain! Save an entire day for **St. George's**, the island's original capital and in 1609 the landing spot for the 150 passengers of the shipwrecked *Sea Venture*.

Even if you don't like churches, you'll enjoy St. Peter's, which dates from 1713. The headstones in the graveyard read like *Who's Who*. (Some Americans lie there.) Across the street is the Confederate Museum and King's Square, where you can be photographed in the pillory and stocks. The Print Shop houses a working model of a 17th-century press, and the hostess at President Henry Tucker house will entice you with some interesting history and gossip about the days of the American Revolution. Catty-corner to this house is the Carriage Museum, chock full of the custom-built carriages that were used until the advent of automobiles on the island in 1945. The St. George's restoration project at Somers Wharf is wonderful, and you can dine in old warehouses and shop in the less crowded branches of the well-known Hamilton stores. There are plenty of nice beaches in the St. George's area, as well as restaurants (Tom Moore's Tavern).

The Caribbean

"The company consisted of Spaniards, Germans, Frenchmen, Russians, and English, captains of ships. Most of the guests had the air of desperadoes and adventurers and it is no uncommon thing to see joints of meat and glasses flying across the table, and violent quarrels ending in the blows."

Universal Traveler, 1848

BARBADOS

One of the most British of all the Caribbean islands, Barbados lived under the Union Jack from 1625 to 1966. The island took its name from the Portuguese who arrived in 1536 and thought the hanging roots of the banyan trees looked like beards, hence barbados. The capital and main port of the island is **Bridgetown**, the harbor police of which still wear the uniforms of Nelson's sailors. A statue of Lord Nelson stands in the town's Trafalgar Square and is said to be some seventeen years older than its counterpart in London.

Exploring Bridgetown is easily done on foot at a leisurely pace. Begin with the activity-filled Careenage, or Inner Harbor, and the Pelican Village craft center, then head to Trafalgar Square for a look at old Nelson. St. Michael's Cathedral was first built in 1665, but the present structure dates from 1831. Too bad, because if George Washington really came to Barbados (along with his half-brother Lawrence) for a health cure, he worshiped on the site but not in this building. A house on Upper Bay Street is where he may have lived for a while, and one story says he even caught smallpox. Wander through other interesting lanes for local color before you take a taxi to the Barbados Museum at **Garrison**, about a mile out of town. If you've opted for an organized tour, you will most likely stop at another Great House, Villa Nova, the former home of British diplomat Sir Anthony Eden. Beautifully renovated and furnished with Barbadian antiques of local mahogany, it once dominated a large sugar cane plantation.

Barbados has some lovely beaches, especially those adjoining elegant resort hotels. If you are discreet, no one minds if you find a little hideaway from your cruise ship for the day. Taxis are abundant at Deep Water pier, but barter a little before you hop in, as most of the drivers are minor bandits. I have always enjoyed the beach at Sandy Lane, but others have opted for the long ride out to Sam Lord's Castle, which caters to the American palate. Have a peek in the

19th-century mansion built by the legendary Sam Lord, still one of the more famous sites in the Caribbean.

Barbados is the most stable of all Caribbean islands. The Queen of the United Kingdom is also the Queen of Barbados, which may explain why she knighted the island's number one all-rounder for his contribution to the game of cricket—the Bajan national sport. Cricket is a wonderful game to watch when visiting the islands, and Barbados is no exception; in fact, you will find the best cricket here in the whole West Indies. Another local pastime is the Bajan delicacy, flying fish, which is so popular it has become a national symbol of what to eat when on the island. Flying fish are small fish that skim across the top of the water as if flying. They can be found all day long in boats and stalls along the Careenage, as well as in dishes from beachside sandwiches to gourmet concoctions. The Bajan say you have not been to Barbados until you have enjoyed a flying fish sandwich. If you love golf, British civility and sophisticated resorts, Barbados is a terrific port of call.

BRITISH LEEWARD ISLANDS

Lying north of Barbados, between Anegada and Guadeloupe passages, the Leewards consist of Antigua, Barbuda, Montserrat, St. Kitts, and Nevis. Of the group, Antigua is the most popular for cruise ship calls, although St. Kitts and Nevis are coming into their own.

ANTIGUA

This 108-square-mile island was discovered in 1493 by Columbus, who named it after Santa Maria la Antigua of Seville. The British colonized the island around 1623. Its capital and main port is St. John's, where you can see rum made and buy a barbecue pot, but the real attraction of the island is Lord Nelson's Dockyard in **English Harbour**. The romance and history of the harbor recall the days when the 25-year-old Horatio Nelson was senior captain of the Leeward Islands Squadron in 1784. He rose to commander-in-chief and was married on nearby Nevis in 1787 with the future King William IV as his best man. A residence built for the king when he was still the Duke of Clarence can be visited when the present governor is not using it. Nelson House, now a museum of Nelson and naval memorabilia, as well as the Master Shipwright's House, Sew Pit Shed, Mast House, Joiner's Loft and Sail Loft are all part of this fascinating area. And don't forget the charming Admiral's Inn, where you can enjoy a rum punch before the drive back to the capital via

Swetes Village and Fig Tree Hill. Or, you can skip all the sightseeing and take a tour of Buccaneer Cove for lunch and swimming. If you still want to be cruising, try the fantastic West Coast and a stop in Emerald Bay for swimming. Some shore excursions feature the island of Montserrat fifteen minutes away by air for a tour of the capital, Plymouth and the smoking crater, Soufriere, as well as a bit of the Irish who colonized this emerald isle in 1632.

AUTHOR'S OBSERVATION

English Harbour is the be-all and end-well for visiting Antigua and if you are in a group, you may wish to head straight there in a taxi (rates are standardized and published) and forget a shore excursion. Shopping ranges from Gucci to Body Shop and a few local shops with batik clothing. Check local art galleries in English Harbour and have your picture framed while lunching at one of the inns in the complex.

ST. KITTS

Nearby St. Kitts was also discovered by Columbus in 1493. He named it after his patron saint, St. Christopher, who had carried him safely on a voyage to the New World. Often called the Mother Colony of the British West Indies, St. Kitts was first settled in 1623. From here, people set out to colonize the other islands. The English fought over St. Kitts with the French for many years. In 1783 the Treaty of Versailles ceded it to the British at last. The island became an associated state of the British Commonwealth in 1967, but French influences are still intact in names like **Basseterre**, the capital and main harbor.

Basseterre means low land, and the harbor it describes has an Old World charm, with lovely colonial structures like Government House and the Old Court House. If you have four hours, you can drive around all of St. Kitts and stop at the 1694 Brimstone Hill Fortress at Sandy Point for a view of the nearby island of St. Eustatius.

NEVIS

Then carry on to the 35-square-mile **Nevis**, just two miles south. Surrounded by coral reefs, Nevis has at its center three high peaks that usually have halos of white clouds. Columbus thought this was similar to the snow-covered Pyrenees, so named the place Las Nievas. Shore excursions here stop at Fig Tree Church, where Admiral Nelson was married to the wealthy young widow, 22-year-old Fanny Nisbet. Other sites include the house in Charlestown where Alexander Hamilton was born in 1757, the 200-year-old thermal baths, and St. Thomas Church and its ancient tombstones.

BRITISH WINDWARD ISLANDS

St. Lucia, St. Vincent, Dominica, the Grenadines and Grenada are the most beautiful stops in the British Windwards, and most resemble the Caribbean of the brochures. Star Clipper sails year-round to these islands, and this 330-foot authentic clipper ship delivers secluded beaches, watersports and and a laid-back but sophisticated atmosphere. Renaissance is a great bet for those who seek a small but conventional cruise ship. These are the best isles in the Caribbean for nature-lovers, with a laid-back atmosphere, little to do except water sports and exploring waterfalls, lush volcanic peaks and remote coves.

ST. LUCIA

The second largest island in this chain, St. Lucia features Mt. Soufriere, the only drive-in active volcano in the world. You can drive up to the lip of the crater, cook an egg in the steam and visit the sulfur baths. St. Lucia is believed to have been discovered by Columbus on St. Lucia's Day, June 15, 1502, although some scholars claim the Spanish arrived later. Early settlers had to contend with the Caribs, who were determined to keep the white man away. In the mid-17th century the French arrived, and from then until the turn of the 19th century they fought with the British over possession of this island. Although the British finally won in 1802, everyone involved suffered a split personality. The French-sounding **Castries** is the island's capital and main harbor. Unfortunately, nothing colonial or interesting remains. A fire in 1948 completely destroyed the old town. Apart from the volcano excursion, you can also take a tour across the causeway to Pigeon Island, now a national park, where British Admiral Rodney once kept pigeons. If you wish to bypass the Soufriere shore excursion (it's not worth the time and energy necessary), grab a local cab and pop over to one of the lovely resorts.

AUTHOR'S OBSERVATION

Unfortunately, in Castries locals have a very unfriendly attitude towards tourists, which can make the place rather unnerving. You may do better with a shore excursion through the scenic countryside to the Pitons, since roads are bumpy, driving distances long and I wouldn't trust local drivers to deliver me back to the ship on time.

ST. VINCENT

This island, eighteen miles by eleven miles, was named by Columbus when he arrived on St. Vincent's Day in 1498. Another piece of property that the Caribs hung on to for as long as possible, St. Vincent was declared neutral during the fighting between the French and the English in 1748, but it went to the British in the latter part of the 18th century. After the British Captain Bligh brought breadfruit here from Tahiti, it was nicknamed Breadfruit Island, and breadfruit is still a major product. This is another split-personality island with French names and British overtones. And it has its own volcano called Mt. Soufriere, but this one is semi-dormant. You can climb to its 4000-foot rim for a view of the crater lake below. Capital and main port of the island is **Kingstown**, which has some attractive 19th-century dwellings, as well as a 200-year-old botanical garden. The Mesopotamia Valley has twenty-eight miles of rural beauty. If boat tours are offered to any of the Grenadines, hop aboard, especially if you like to snorkel in crystal-clear waters or swim at sparkling beaches.

AUTHOR'S OBSERVATION

This island is spectacularly beautiful. One of my best experiences in the Caribbean was hiring a local taxi for the day and exploring stunning botanical gardens and volcanic peaks with a jolly driver who stopped for bananas and coconuts enroute. Locals are warm and friendly throughout, crime is neglible and there is virtually no hustling.

GRENADA

Originally named Concepción by Columbus, who first saw it on August 15, 1498, this island is nicknamed the Spice Island. Again, the Caribs kept their 133 square miles of volcanic mountains, green valleys and beautiful beaches as long as they were able. The British and the French fought over this small piece of real estate, but the British assumed possession in 1783. Grenada became a crown colony in 1877 and was granted its independence in 1974. Its capital and main port, **St. George**, is one of the most picturesque harbors in the Caribbean. Situated on a protected harbor and blue inner lagoon, the town has pastel warehouses and gabled dwellings. A good walking tour takes about two hours, and you can enjoy such sights as Old Fort George, which has French origins, the Market Place and Maryshow House. There are plenty of local arts-and-crafts exhibits, and you can fill your pockets with cinnamon, nutmeg, ginger, vanilla, bay leaf (laurel) and clove. Organized excursions feature a bus tour or a catamaran cruise to Grand Anse Beach for sunning and snorkeling. The bus goes through the Mt. Parnassus Valley by the famous nutmeg trees, stops for a panoramic view of the harbor from Richmond Hill and drives on to Morne Jalous and the charming fishing village of Woburn. You meet your fellow passengers from the catamaran at Grand Anse Beach.

AUTHOR'S OBSERVATION

The inland shore excursions of Grenada are tortuous because, although the island is lush and beautiful, the roads are up-down and very, very bumpy. Add to this vans that may have no springs or cushions and you will appreciate why it is more fun to remain in the St. George's harbor/Grand Anse Beach area. Both offer a colorful lifestyle and plenty of entertainment, as well as food and drink. And never are you very far from aggressive ladies offering fragrant spices, or young men with guitar and song. You can have a custom-made hat for a few dollars, a potent rum punch, or refreshing local beer from vendors who seem to appear from everywhere!

CAYMAN ISLANDS

Ashore at a turtle farm on Grand Cayman

These are known by locals as the Alligator Islands, because reptiles were once plentiful. Before that, our friend Columbus, who discovered them in 1503 on his fourth voyage, called them Las Tortugas for the many turtles. The islands are also famous for their ring of coral, which has been the nemesis of more than three hundred ships whose hulls and buried treasures keep the intrigue level high. Life on

Grand Cayman, twenty-two miles long and eight miles wide, is slow and casual, with the emphasis for cruise passengers on relaxation and beach parties. The small capital and main port of **George Town** is quiet, and its tax-haven status interests many visitors (Grand Cayman may yet become the Monaco of the Caribbean). There is freeport shopping, and you can purchase a gift package of frozen green-turtle steaks.

There are two primary reasons for stopping by Grand Cayman. The British arrive to stay in their legal (sort of) residences and visit their money (since off-shore banking is the island's number-one business). The Americans fall off cruise ships and head straight for Seven Mile (also known as West Bay) Beach, along which many a high-rise resort has been built where aficionados can rent diving equipment and other water sports paraphernalia. On the other hand, these beach-front resorts are good for coming in from the heat and enjoying a libation at the low-rise bars. Aside from beaches, shopping and fantastic scuba, Grand Cayman can be a bore for those seeking natural beauty or excitement.

DOMINICAN REPUBLIC

After Columbus discovered this island, he installed his brother Bartolome as governor. Bartolome founded Santo Domingo, the oldest European devleoped city in the New World, which drew the influential and adventurous in the first half of the 16th century. The independent Dominican Republic was established in 1844. Its capital and chief port is **Santo Domingo**, which boasts the oldest cathedral in the Americas, dating from 1514. Other sights are the Alcazar of Diego Columbus (built in 1510 and restored in 1957), the 16th-century Casa del Cordon, the National Museum and the Palace of Fine Arts. Also here are a national theater, a national library and the Museo del Hombre Dominicano on the Plaza de la Cultura.

Santo Domingo, on the south coast, has a few historic sites, but one is harrased by begging locals continually in town. Port facilities have been improved and the pier is close to the sights of the old city, but be sure to take an organized shore excursion as English is not spoken here with the fluency one finds on other Spanish-heritage islands.

Puerto Plata is situated on the north, or so-called Amber Coast, of the Dominican Republic, and a more frequent cruise call than Santo Domingo, although the port is not all that attractive. Frankly, neither is the town and there is not much to see. So either take the bus tour and be bored until you end up at the beach for a quick swim, or hop into a taxi with some friends and head straight for one of the familiar hotels at Playa Dorado.

DUTCH WINDWARD ISLANDS

Of these three small dots Sint Maarten, Saba and Sint Eustatius (also known as Statia), Sint Maarten is the most popular for cruise calls.

SINT MAARTEN/ST. MARTIN

Columbus was here, too, on St. Martin's Day, apparently in 1493, but records say that he never went ashore. The island is divided, and only the Dutch side is called Sint Maarten. The larger French section is called St. Martin and is a member of the French West Indies. On the Dutch side, the capital and chief port, **Philipsburg**, has little to offer but a few narrow streets. St. Martin, the French section of the island, is where the shops carry Parisian imports and the restaurants serve up a bit of la belle France in the Caribbean. Some vessels now dock at Marigot, the port for St. Martin, as this section of the island is becoming more and more popular as a cruise call despite the obvious problems that accompany an increased influx of tourists. Other than the 17th-century Fort Amsterdam, now very crumbly, the island has few historical sites.

Beautiful scenery and interesting people are the main attractions. You can take a catamaran cruise aboard the *Maison Maru* to some spectacular beaches (bring your bathing suit) and caves that are not accessible from the road.

AUTHOR'S OBSERVATION

For a day of tranquil beach-going, head for La Belie Creole in French St. Martin, one of the Caribbean's most spectacular resorts, and splurge for lunch at their clift-top restaurant.

FRENCH WEST INDIES

Largest and northernmost of the French West Indies is Martinique, called the Pearl of the Antilles. Cruise ships also dock at Guadeloupe, and occasionally at Iles des Saintes and St. Barthelemy (or St. Barts, which used to be one of the best-kept secrets in the Caribbean).

MARTINIQUE

The capital and main seaport of Martinique is **Fort-de-France**, a city 100,000 strong that will remind you of New Orleans with its iron grillwork-studded buildings. Although Columbus is said to have landed on the western coast of this twenty-by-fifty-mile island, he did not stay long enough to think of a name. So the naming was left to the French, who arrived in 1635 and used the Carib name, Island of Flowers. In 1848, the islanders were granted full French citizenship, and in 1946, Martinique became a *departement* of France, governed by a prefect appointed through the French Minister of the Interior.

Organized shore excursions take you north to **St. Pierre**, once considered a little Paris but destroyed in 1902 by Mt. Pelee, the 4500-foot volcano. You can visit the museum that chronicles the terrible eruption. Then your drive goes almost to the base of the volcano and through forests of giant fern to Balata for a visit to the church that looks like a small replica of Sacre Coeur in Paris. Martinique is the birthplace of Napoleon's wife, Josephine, and a museum in the village of Trois Ilets tells of the local beauty who became Empress of France. Other jaunts might include Absalon, a thermal resort, and Carbet, said to be where Columbus landed, or the restored 18th-century De Leyritz Plantation. A Kon Tiki tour in a catamaran features a calypso steel band and complimentary rum punch. But you may just prefer to explore the bustling port of Fort-de-France on your own to see graceful women in colorful native dress, side streets redolent of Creole cookery, a library, a cathedral, Fort St. Louis overhanging the bay and a statue of Josephine looking out toward her native village.

AUTHOR'S OBSERVATION

In my opinion, Martinique can easily be skipped. This polluted, chaotic city is loaded with over-priced stores selling "duty-free" goods that are rarely a bargain and imported European merchandise priced less in the U.S. Locals are far from friendly and act as if one is doing them a favor by even entering their establishment. Take a shore excursion or hire your own cab with a few friends and head for St. Pierre and the lush mountains.

GUADELOUPE

This island is in two parts, like a butterfly with spread wings. Columbus discovered it in 1493 and named it in honor of Our Lady of Guadeloupe of Estremadura. The French settled here in 1635, but the English interfered for almost two centuries. The Treaty of Paris in 1815 finally made the island French, and in 1946, it was made a *departement* with the same status as Martinique. Guadeloupe consists of Grande-Terre and Basse-Terre, divided by the Riviere Salee. Capital is **Pointe-à-Pitre**, a busy seaport that was a pirate haven in the 18th century (pirate spirits are said to still hover over the city) and that has quaint streets and European-style buildings.

Tours from Pointe-à-Pitre will take you across the bridge of the Riviere Salee to Guadeloupe's verdant rain forest and Parc Naturel, a botanist's paradise. A stop is made at Fort Fleur d Epée, with interesting underground passages and dungeons. This was the keystone of French defense during the long battle against the British, and the view of the sea and other islands from here is spectacular. Other historic sites include Sainte-Marie, where Columbus is said to have landed, and Trois-Rivieres, where relics and rocks bear inscriptions by the Carib Indians. Guadeloupe also has a La Soufriere volcano, which is only sleeping, with extraordinary views from the top (but watch out for the hot-lava bogs).

ILES DES SAINTES

This cluster of eight islands off the southern coast of Guadeloupe includes **Terre-de-Haut**, an occasional cruise call. Here, you can explore the peaceful and charming harbor of Bourg and enjoy some of the best snorkeling that exists anywhere.

You may also climb up to Fort Napoleon, which dates from the 18th century and is noted for its fine walls. Here, you can visit a small museum of island history and hear that the free French were encased within this compound during World War II because the Vichy government took over the town below. Afterward, you can walk through the island and enjoy some great body surfing on the opposite beach (but watch out for the stiff undertow).

ST. BARTHELEMY

Dependent upon Guadeloupe but 140 miles north, St. Barts is considered by a loyal following to be the most chic island in the Caribbean. Its 2500 inhabitants are mostly of Norman-French and Swedish background. Its capital is **Gustavia**, known for fabulous French food and charming atmosphere, but don't let on where you heard this. Some of the smaller cruise vessels now stop in the harbor. Zut alors!

JAMAICA

Another mountainous island, Jamaica has four peaks surpassing six thousand feet. Discovered by Columbus in 1494 and colonized by his son, Diego, this lovely isle of streams and forests (Xamayca, the Arawaks called it) was under Spanish domain only until the mid-17th century. The British seized it in 1655 and allowed it to become a pirate base. One of the greatest pirates of all, Henry Morgan, later became lieutenant governor of Jamaica. The island, independent for almost two decades, depends heavily upon tourism. Cruise vessels concentrate on the northern shore. Port Antonio, one of the cruise calls, is a beautiful little harbor with the majestic Blue Mountains (where that wonderful coffee comes from) as a backdrop. With little of interest to passengers, the port's biggest attraction is river rafting on the Rio Grande.

The bamboo rafts are about thirty feet long and can accommodate three people, two is more comfortable, plus a raftsman. It's a relaxing three-hour journey down the river, with time out for a rest in the shade or a dip in the cool, clear, fresh waters. Bathing suits are a must for this one.

The beach resort of **Ocho Rios** has been built around a pleasant, natural harbor. If your cruise vessel arrives in the late afternoon, don't miss the performance of local dances on the beach, complete with stars overhead and torchlights all around you. By day you can visit Dunn's River Falls, where the sparkling water rushes straight from the mountain to the beach below.

It's fun to explore these beautiful falls, and you can even climb them if you are properly dressed—bathing suit and sneakers will do the trick. If you wish to get away from the water, an interesting plantation tour takes you to the 1200-acre Prospect Estate, where spices and cattle are big business.

Montego Bay, or Mo Bay as everyone calls it, is the largest of these three Jamaican ports. Once the favorite of the international set, Mo Bay's glitter is now long gone. I leave Montego Bay quickly —locals are frequently hostile and there have been reports of crime against tourists. Nearby, restored Rose Hall, once among the grandest of 18th-century plantation homes in the West Indies, attracts many visitors. The house, which has had two novels written about it, has enjoyed a notorious past. Its second mistress allegedly murdered three spouses and a lover and then was mysteriously done in herself. For a different kind of intrigue à la James Bond (his creator had a house here) catch a glimpse of the crocodiles and alligators in nearby swamplands.

Some of these beasts, kept by a fearless young man, will do tricks for you as they did in the James Bond film *Live and Let Die*. Being an avid Noel Coward fan, my personal favorite on this island is Firefly, his beloved home and final resting place. High on a hill, overlooking the sea on all sides, a simple marble slab reads "Sir Noel Coward;" from his simple home comes piped music, gently playing "Always," and other great songs. He would have approved.

AUTHOR'S OBSERVATION

Jamaica, certainly not the friendliest of places, is an island on which cruise passengers should take the suggested tours or travel in groups and not walk the back streets of Montego Bay or Kingston alone. There is crime and there are drugs (I estimate your chances of being offered dope is around 99%). If traveling by taxi, it is best to do some homework before you set out as distances can be quite long and you will want to be home again before dark.

NETHERLAND ANTILLES

Aruba, Bonaire and Curacao (The ABC islands) are popular pieces of Holland not only for their Dutch manner but also for their business acumen. These islands have long offered substantial tax credits to companies incorporated here, and one of the world's largest oil refineries is on Curacao. So, while you explore the delights of Dutch treats in the sunshine, your cruise vessel may be refueling at an economical price. Lying off the Venezuelan coast, all three of these islands were settled by the Spanish.

CURACAO

Willemstad, the capital, might just be the most photographed port in the whole Caribbean; its narrow, 18th-century gabled houses are painted in every color.

The island, discovered by the Spanish explorer Alonzo de Ojeda in 1499, greeted the first Spanish settlers three decades later. They didn't have long to get comfortable, however, because the Dutch arrived, established a colony and named Peter Stuyvesant governor not long after in 1643. It was here that Stuyvesant supposedly lost his right leg in an excursion against Sint Maarten.

As you wander around this charming port, notice the many Dutch-ingrained influences in the little canals, the colorful floating market and the old-style dwellings. Take a walk across the famous

Queen Emma Pontoon Bridge, which swings open to let ships pass in and out of the harbor. Also interesting are Fort Amsterdam (now a seat of government), the 1769 Old Dutch Reformed Church and the 1732 Mikve Israel-Emmanuel Synagogue, which claims to be the oldest in the Western Hemisphere (but then, so do several others). If you fancy refineries, you'll love the one operated by Shell. Another local product, Curacao orange-flavored liqueur, offers a free sip at the Chobolobo Mansion (you can also buy some to take home in pretty Delft jugs).

ARUBA

Alonzo de Ojeda claimed Aruba for Spain in 1499, at the same time he discovered Curacao, but the Dutch moved in here, also, in 1634. Aruba, much smaller and less prosperous than Curacao (although it has a huge oil refinery), is only fifteen miles from the Venezuelan coastline and twelve degrees from the equator. Its capital and main port, **Oranjestad**, is another delightfully Dutch harbor with old-style houses whose red-tiled roofs sparkle in the sunshine. Take a walk over to the schooner harbor and open market, then on to Wilhelmina Park and the nearby street lined with typical early Aruban buildings.

There is virtually no reason to take a shore excursion on this flat island. Those who love beaches and gambling will find it a paradise, but there is little sightseeing aside from Frenchmen's Pass (where Indians allegedly fought the French), the natural bridge and the rock formation garden of Casibari. In the tiny village of Noord, an interesting church, St. Anna's, has an oak altar handcarved in Holland in 1850 by well-known Dutch artist Van Geld. Some rather interesting caves and grottos with hieroglyphics show evidence of Arawak Indian habitation. Aruba also has its own Palm Beach, complete with fancy resort hotels and gambling facilities, if you like that sort of thing.

BONAIRE

Noted for flamingos and excellent scuba diving, Bonaire was discovered by a band of men under Amerigo Vespucci in 1496. Second largest of this ABC group, it seems small and very quiet in contrast to its two sisters. The main port, **Kralendijk**, is storybook pretty, with its tiny harbor and pink fish market. Take a wonderful drive out to the Washington National Park, a game preserve and the first of its kind in this area. And if you aren't watching the lovely flamingos, you will want to be underwater watching the myriad colors of the world below. Visibility supposedly reaches to 65 feet below the surface, and all kinds of equipment can be rented.

PUERTO RICO

On any Saturday during the winter season as many as nine cruise ships may be making turn arounds in **San Juan**, the most popular port for seven-day cruises in the lower Caribbean. From early morning to late afternoon and early evening, these ships will be resting gently in their berths waiting to take on passengers for sailings to La Guaira, Barbados, St. Lucia and the like. But San Juan holds her own as a port of call and is well worth an extra day or two to explore, either before or after your cruise.

It's not hard to see why Ponce de Leon exclaimed puerto rico! (rich port) when he arrived in the harbor in 1508 to establish a European settlement. Columbus discovered the island on November 19, 1493, during his second voyage to the New World, and the Indian inhabitants received him cordially.

When Ponce de Leon arrived fifteen years later to colonize the island for Spain, the chief of the Taino Indians greeted him and, following Indian custom for friendship, the two men exchanged names. Ponce de Leon became the first governor of Puerto Rico and moved the early settlement to the present site of Old San Juan in 1521. A 24-foot-square frame house was built for him here as a reward for his services, but he never lived to occupy it. However, the Ponce de Leon descendants inhabited the house, Casa Blanca, for 250 years. It is now a museum that illustrates Puerto Rican life of the 16th and 17th centuries. The former Spanish colony was ceded to the United States in 1898 as a result of the Spanish-American War, and Puerto Ricans have been U.S. citizens since the Jones Act of 1917. Spanish is still the primary language, although English is the tourist tongue. Old San Juan, which includes the seven-block-square quarter once enclosed by a city wall and the forts El Morro and San Cristobal, celebrated its 465th birthday in 1986, no small feat.

This old section has tremendous charm, and the colonial architecture and ambience are being conserved. Lovely wrought-iron balconies and heavy, carved wooden doors and shutters decorate the whitewashed houses. Inside, the ceilings are supported by beams in such a way that each room is a work of art.

Except for the Caribe Hilton, all beaches in San Juan are public, and sunbathers are constantly bombarded by locals selling everything from soda to jewelry. Head for the Caribe Hilton (a short taxi ride from Old San Juan and the pier) for a more tranquil time and a cool pina colada, which allegedly was invented there.

AUTHOR'S OBSERVATION

Walking is the only way to get around Old San Juan and a shore excursion completely unnecessary, unless you want to visit El Yunque. You can easily design your own tour with a copy of "Que Pasa," the free tourism publication, in hand. (Get a copy at the Visitors Center in the square near Pier Number One.) If planning an excursion outside Old San Juan, however, head there first from the pier and tour San Juan last as it's impossible to get a taxi in town.

El Morro, the 16th- to 18th-century fort built 140 feet above the sea, is the perfect place to begin. Stop next at the Plaza de San Jose, dominated by the statue of Juan Ponce de Leon that was made from a British cannon after an unsuccessful attempt on the city in 1797. This large square also houses San Jose Church, a former Dominican convent that is now the Institute of Puerto Rican Culture, and several renovated buildings that are now museums. On the right side of the square are a small Museum of Santos (small, wooden, religious statues that are a great part of the island's history and folklore) and the Pablo Casals Museum, which has the Maestro's cello. Calle Cristo, Old San Juan's most famous street, runs from the Plaza de San Jose to the harbor wall and is paved with bluish-tint bricks, *adoquines*, which were used for ballast in Spanish ships. Cristo Street runs down past the Cathedral of San Juan and El Convento Hotel (a tranquil oasis to rest and have a quiet drink in the lovely courtyard of this 17th-century former convent) and dead ends at Cristo Chapel, built to honor a miracle that occurred on the spot in 1753. Adjacent is Pigeon Park, which overlooks the harbor and La Princesa Jail. Backtrack a bit and pay a visit to La Fortaleza, the governor's mansion, which is the longest continually occupied executive house in this hemisphere. (Museum times in San Juan are a trial, to say the least. If the guidebook says they're open at certain times and they're not try to convince the attendants. *Mañana* is the common word here.)

Shopping in Old San Juan is fun, especially if you're not in the mood for anything too grand. Some very expensive-looking jewelry stores may tempt you, but for straw items, hammocks and inexpensive beachwear, the place is great. Take advantage of the factory shirt outlet that sells Hathaway and the Ralph Lauren outlet store next door. (Prices are still outrageous even at discount!) I generally stay away from places such as Barrachina that send advertisements to the ships to entice you the day before your flight leaves.

Compare prices before you buy anything, even a quart of rum. Remember, there's always an angle when you are offered something for nothing. If you feel like a visit to the Bacardi factory, bypass the expensive shore excursions offered aboard ship and head for the local ferry from Pier 2 to the Bacardi distillery (round-trip is a few dollars). The tour is free and the booze is cheap. Gambling is a hot activity in Puerto Rico (although high rollers have reported the odds are not great) and the El San Juan is the place for gaming in elegant surroundings. This hotel, the best in San Juan, boasts a stunning mahogany-paneled lobby with top-drawer wine bar and some of the best restaurants on the islands. Located next to the airport in Isla Verde, the cab ride from Old San Juan costs around $8.00 and is worth every nickel if you want a fun night out. It's fun just to hang out and watch dressed-up locals strut their stuff!

AUTHOR'S OBSERVATION

Puerto Rico is a wonderful place to take a pre- or post-cruise hotel stay (the best hotels are the Caribe Hilton and El San Juan). Rent a car and head out on the island for lovely scenery and languid villages (car-napping, however, is now a big problem on the island). The interior of Puerto Rico is undiscovered and lush, roads are excellent and have "scenic" route markings.

ST. VINCENT AND THE GRENADINES

In a search for new and untapped island calls, many of the smaller vessels are now concentrating on the Grenadines, a string of islands between St. Vincent and Grenada that (including St. Vincent) have been independent from Great Britain since 1979. Including Mayreau, Bequia, Mustique, Palm Island and Tobago Cays, they are among the most beautiful and least discovered islands of the Caribbean, as they are accessible only by water (or very small seaplane). Windstar, Star Clippers, Renaissance and Club Med frequent these tiny islands.

Snorkeling and other water sports are perfect on **Bequia**, where your small cruise vessel or private yacht lolls in Port Elizabeth harbor. The beaches boast sand like confectioner's sugar, but you if are aboard *Sea Goddess I* or *WindStar*, you can water ski, snorkel and swim from the mechanized sports platform aft.

Tiny **Mayreau** is so peaceful and picture perfect, it is even a shame to mention it in public! However, if your small ship calls here consider yourselves gone to heaven, if only for the day. **Mustique**, on the other hand, has become just too too, as it is privately owned by a British lord, as well as home and hideaway to such loyal subjects as Princess Margaret and rock stars Mick Jagger and David Bowie (not an unlikely combination as neighbors). There is one fabulous resort on the island, called the Cotton House, or you can have a peek at Les Jolie Eaux (the house of Margaret) and even make plans to rent it when she is not in residence.

The 110-acre **Palm Island** is also privately owned and a delightful stop on many cruise itineraries for a beach and rum punch party/barbecue complete with steel band. The island is not spectacular, like the others, but quiet and attractive and you can walk all around it, swim or eat to your heart's content before sailing into the sunset aboard your comfortable cruise vessel.

AUTHOR'S OBSERVATION.

This is heaven for beach and water-sports lovers and those who eschew the chaotic mass-market islands. There's not much to do but relax and swim from beaches where there's nary another soul in sight. If you like shopping, gambling, golf and sightseeing, The Grenedines can be an utter bore.

TRINIDAD AND TOBAGO

Most southerly of the West Indian groups, Trinidad is the island on which government and commerce are located, while Tobago is the weekend resort and getaway spot. Columbus discovered Trinidad in 1498 on his third voyage to the New World and named it La Trinidad for the three hills around the bay where he anchored. The Spanish settled here a century later, but many battles with the British followed. The island was finally ceded to Britain by the Treaty of Amiens in 1802. The island nation ended its link with the monarchy in 1976 and became a republic.

TRINIDAD

From the capital and main port, **Port of Spain**, calypso and steel bands originated and spread throughout the Caribbean. For people-watching and a walk through the sights and sounds of this exciting place, begin at Queen's Wharf and walk north to Independence Square, Frederick Street, Queen Street and the Red House (seat of government). You may also want to pay a visit to the Angostura Bitters factory and then continue to the 200-acre Queen's Park Savannah area, with its racecourse, cricket fields and diverse architecture.

The park's lovely Botanical Gardens, laid out in 1820 on a 63-acre plot, provide licensed guides who will show you around and be happy to explain the flora. Built on a peak over 1000 feet above Port of Spain is the 1803 Fort George, which offers the most wonderful view all around, including the mountains of Venezuela.The people of Trinidad are well educated and prosperous and it is a delight to visit their lovely island. Take a taxi or tour to the Atlantic side's spectacular beaches. You may want to pack a towel and swimsuit if you feel comfortable with an ominous-looking undertow.

TOBAGO

From Trinidad to Tobago, which some claim was Robinson Crusoe's island, the flight takes fifteen minutes. Tobago is completely unspoiled, and the weather is often better than on Trinidad. Here you'll find some exotic bird life and the main town of Scarborough has a colorful market.

Cruise ships anchor off Pigeon Point and tender their passengers onto the palm-fringed beaches for an afternoon of sunbathing and water sports complemented by calypso music and rum punches. You don't need a shore excursion, unless it's a glass-bottom boat ride to Buccoo Reef. Hire a taxi for a drive around the island which fellow travelers aboard *Ocean Islander* said was the best ever! Tobago is the antithesis of Trinidad's kinetic energy and a good place to enjoy the beaches and relax.

U.S. VIRGIN ISLANDS

Lying forty miles due east of Puerto Rico, the USVI were discovered by Columbus in 1493 during his second voyage to the New World. He christened them Las Virgenes, in honor of St. Ursula's legendary 11,000 martyred virgins. On the island he called Santa Cruz (now St. Croix) he searched for fresh water but was chased off by the Carib Indians and sailed away. The Caribs kept the islands off-limits for seafarers until 1555, when Spain claimed the territory. Throughout most of the century, however, the islands were contested by England, France, Holland and Denmark. The Danish won and kept the islands until 1916 when they sold them to the United States for $25 million. This probably makes the U.S. the only governing power in the Caribbean that ever paid for anything! The package included St. Thomas, St. Croix and St. John, as well as several lesser land masses in the area.

ST. THOMAS

Charlotte Amalie, capital of St. Thomas, is the popular cruise ship stop in the Caribbean, and on any day there may be up to ten vessels and 10,000 people in port. Muggings and violent crime against tourists made the papers across the country (the U.S. Navy even cancelled port calls because of this problem), and local officials are hard at work trying to rectify the problem.

In this little town with cobblestone streets and endless shops displaying gold watches and cases of liquor, Americans can purchase and bring back duty-free twice the amount allowed elsewhere. But the famous bargains are generally a thing of the past, and if you fancy completing your china pattern or purchasing perfume, liquor and crystal, be sure to bring local prices with you. I'm told by professional photographers, however, that cameras are the best buy in the world in some shops (call 47th Photo in New York and request their catalogue of discount equipment to take for purposes of comparison).

If you don't wish (God forbid) to shop, you won't be bored. Hire a local taxi for a flat fee and tour this lovely 30-square-mile island, passing famous landmarks, such as Bluebeard's Castle and lookout tower where the pirate could spot unsuspecting galleons. Continue your drive up Mafolie Hill and have a look at Louisenhoj Castle before catching the view from Drake's Seat of Magens Bay Beach, reportedly one of the ten most splendid beaches in the world. St. Thomas also has a magnificent underwater observatory, and a visit here is not soon forgotten. Called the Coral World Underwater Observation Tower, and located on a lush tropical peninsula on the northeastern shore of the island, the observatory/tower's three stories rise from the sea some 100 feet from shore. On the lowest level hundreds of tropical fish, coral formations and beautiful deep-water flowers are visible. On the second level you will be surrounded by sharks, stingrays, barracudas and huge sea turtles. The top level of the tower is an extraordinary geodesic dome with a spectacular view of St. John's and the British Virgin Islands.

ST. JOHN'S

Another highlight is the excursion to St. John's, a 10-minute ride by motor launch from Charlotte Amalie. (Don't sit at the rail unless you are prepared to be drenched.) At Cruz Bay, you board a motorized surrey complete with the fringe on the top for the short but spectacular ride to Trunk Bay, which is often mentioned as one of the world's most beautiful beaches. Trunk Bay has pristine white sands and coral green seas and is wonderful for snorkeling. A short underwater trail leads to the best look at colorful tropical fish and coral. Don't touch the coral because it's sharp, and don't take souvenirs because that's against the law. You may also go to Coki Point under the auspices of the Virgin Islands Diving Schools, which will teach you how to approach this underwater world and then give you a diploma testifying to your accomplishments. For enjoying the coral reefs with much less effort, join the Kon Tiki raft party, which includes rum punches, a steel band and swimming on the beaches of Honeymoon Bay.

ST. CROIX

As the largest and most southerly of the main islands in the U.S. Virgin Islands group, St. Croix was bypassed by cruise ships following an outbreak of violence against tourists a number of years ago. Today, a number make port calls in **Christiansted** on the northern coast (the capital and largest town) or Frederiksted on the western coast. Both have Danish overtones in architecture and place names, as well as left-hand traffic.

Right on the harbor in Christiansted is Fort Christiansvaern, built of bricks brought from Denmark as ballast in the sailing vessels. It was completed in 1774 and held troops until 1878. The Old Danish Customs House is situated to the west of the fort. Now an art gallery, it dates from the early 19th century. Goods were weighed and checked at the only slightly younger Scale House. The oldest section of Government House on King Street dates from 1747. Nearby is the colorful Outdoor Market, the former Warehouse of the Dutch West Indies Company, and Steeple Building, originally built as a Lutheran church in 1753.

Buck Island, a short boat trip from Christiansted, is now a national park with a reef nature trail for underwater sports enthusiasts. It is a strictly controlled nature reserve, so nothing can be collected of what you may discover along the reef.

Frederiksted has a population of about 4000 and generally livens up a bit when cruise ships come to call. Just north of the pier is the former Fort Frederick, which dates from 1755 and where the abolition of slavery in Danish possessions was proclaimed in 1848. It is now a small museum. Other points of interest in town are the Old Danish School (c. 1830) and Market Square (1751).

Along Strand Street from the pier are the old Customs House and Victoria House. Most of the old Danish buildings in Frederiksted were destroyed by fire in 1848. Outside the town are some former plantation houses, a botanical garden and a good golf course.

BRITISH VIRGIN ISLANDS

Columbus stopped by the British Virgin Islands in 1493, and they remained in Spanish hands until the arrival of Sir Francis Drake in 1595. Drake sailed through the channel south of Tortola, which now bears his name. Britain annexed Tortola in 1672, but many of the neighboring islands were pirate haunts that inspired Robert Louis Stevenson to write *Treasure Island.* Today, the more than 50 islands and inlets, as well as 12,000 people, are subjects of the Crown and Queen Elizabeth is represented by a local governor and other officials. Vehicles travel on the left side of the road, but the local currency is the U.S. dollar! As the largest of the British Virgin Islands, **Tortola** is 25 square miles and has a population of about 9000. Its capital and main port is Road Town, which has an excellent deep-water harbor. The Sir Francis Drake Channel separates Tortola from the smaller BVIs **Norman**, **Peter**, **Salt**, **Cooper** and **Ginger**. Sailing, fishing, scuba diving and snorkeling are the main pastimes here. The beaches are beautiful and the land is lush with tropical fruits and breezes.

Mount Sage National Park is in the southwest of the island and Frenchman's Cays lies offshore. To the northwest of Tortola are the even more spectacular beaches of **Jost van Dyke**, an island originally settled by Quakers.

Although smaller than Tortola, the eight-square-mile **Virgin Gorda** is the principal island for vacationers in the BVI group. Spanish Town is the center of its 1000 population, sheltered as it is by a barrier reef. Virgin Gorda boasts the renowned Little Dix Bay Hotel, as well as some beautiful beaches on North Sound.

The British Virgin Islands are a haven for yachtsmen and you'll only reach them aboard sailing vessels or small cruise ships. Those who love a low-key atmosphere, natural beauty and water sports will adore the BVI.

Central and North America

COSTA RICA

Tiny Costa Rica is about the size of West Virginia, sandwiched between Nicaragua to the north and Panama to the south, not the most peaceful neighbors in the world. However, Costa Rica refuses to join the Central American struggles; it even abolished the military and boasts a true democracy and the highest literacy rate in the area. With coastlines on both the Atlantic and Pacific oceans, it is a natural for cruise calls. Most cruise ships crossing the Panama Canal stop in Puerto Caldera. However, since the antique jungle train was destroyed by an earthquake, there are no options but a seven-hour shore excursion over narrow, bumpy roads to San Jose. While you'll see high mountains, don't expect the jungle or wildlife on this trip.

This tiny country is a paradise for naturalists because 8 percent of the land has been designated to the national park system. The tropical forests are home to one-tenth of the world's known bird species and up to 2000 different varieties of orchids are estimated to grow wild throughout the land. As it is the national flower, collecting the orchid is forbidden except by government permit.

The capital, **San Jose**, has a National Theater, built between 1890 and 1897 with money raised by coffee growers, a national museum located in the former army barracks; enroute back to the ship, shore excursions visit Sarachi, a local crafts community, where hand-carved wood is a popular buy and pounds and pounds of flavorful coffee are sold for a song.

MEXICO

"A traveller who goes from the coast must take with him his household goods and must carry beds, provisions and means for defence...no intelligent wayfarer expects either neatness or comfort."

Universal Traveler, 1848

Our neighbors south of the border extend their arms in welcome to norteamericano cruise passengers who come for a taste of the continual feast of colors, sights and beautiful beaches. Mexico's western coastline is one of the most popular of all cruise destinations, especially for ships originating from southern California. The so-called Mexican Riviera stretches from Mazatlan to Acapulco and includes Puerto Vallarta and Zihuatanejo. If you don't delude yourself into expecting Puerto Vallarta to have the crazy chic of St. Tropez, or Acapulco to be as sophisticated and glamorous as Monte Carlo, then you will enjoy what this Riviera has to offer.

Sailing directly south from San Pedro, California, the port for Los Angeles, many cruise vessels call first at **Ensenada**, a peaceful little community just sixty-seven miles south of the California border, in Baja California (the lower peninsula that belongs to Mexico). Juan Rodriguez Cabrillo founded Ensenada in 1542. However, neither he nor Fra Junipero Serra (who founded San Diego) stayed because they couldn't find fresh water in this beautiful, natural harbor. Today fresh water is found in underground wells, but this is still a frontier town with spectacular beaches and not much else—a pleasant but uninspiring cruise stop.

At the tip of Baja California are San Jose del Cabo and **Cabo San Lucas**, the latter more famous because the waters of the Sea of Cortes and the Pacific Ocean meet here. Sea lions frolic under nearby Los Arcos, natural rock arcades that are best viewed from small boats. Small cruise vessels simply sail by Cabo San Lucas and consider it seen, but others stop for a few hours for the small boat excursion to Los Arcos and a drink on the terrace of the Hyatt Hotel, which overlooks the Bay of Chileno. If you care to return someday, the fishing is considered some of the best in the world.

AUTHOR'S OBSERVATION

Mazatlan, one of the best harbors on Mexico's Pacific coastline, is noted for its shrimp industry, which feeds much of the U.S. market. Fishing here is also good and marlin can be caught year-round. The fishing and the continual sunshine make Mazatlan a popular tourist town.

Local sightseeing includes the Olas Atlas section to the cathedral, Indian market and outdoor cafes. You can watch high cliff-divers at Glorieta's Rocky Promontory, but it's more rewarding to shop for Indian handcrafts and Mexican silver. Or you can find your way to Las Gaviotas Beach and pay a visit to the new hotels that have grown up alongside this lovely stretch of the city. This is the perfect place for swimming and sunning.

Some people I know bought houses in a sleepy, slightly seedy little fishing village named **Puerto Vallarta** before it became fashionable; or shall I say popular, since it's debatable whether or not this town has ever been fashionable. Nonetheless, cruise brochures love to call it an exquisite, picturesque seaside village. Don't expect too much, for aside from a few beaches and an area now known as Gringo

Gulch, Puerto Vallarta does not have a great deal to offer the quick visitor. There are some nice beaches in Puerto Vallarta, so plan to spend your time browsing, people-watching (both the swells and the indigents congregate in this town) and sunning. I thought the city tour was not worth my while or money, so don't feel guilty about passing it up. This is one of the many port calls you can do on your own and be the better for it.

While **Manzanillo** and its beautiful beaches are often the next port of call, **Zihuatanejo** is more interesting for its beaches and its similarity (although smaller) to Acapulco. As a town, it doesn't have much to offer except its five splendid beaches and a few nice restaurants. Shore excursions will take you to Ixtapa's 16-mile beach. The Mexican government has invested heavily in Ixtapa's future as a tourist attraction. The Palma Real Golf Club and some new hotels welcome you and help you relax in resort style. Other than that, what can one say but, enjoy the scenery.

At last, **Acapulco**. A true resort. A port worthy of your time and a city with real bite to it. Acapulco is where even jetsetters take their honeymoons, not to mention brief getaway weekends. It has eternal sunshine, bikinis, no ties, siestas, nonlunches on the beach whatever you like any time of the year.

Although the official season runs from mid-December to the end of April, even Frank Sinatra has visited in the summer. And both the J.F. Kennedys and the Henry Kissingers spent their honeymoons here (albeit in private villas). If there is any real Riviera on the Mexican Pacific coast, this is it. One can play high or low here, either walking casually along hotel row or taking a tour to La Quebrada to watch divers plunge from a cliff 136 feet high into the sinister, swirling waters below. Acapulco is an exciting place with too many high-rise hotels, too-crowded beaches, too-expensive shops, and never a moment to spare for anyone.

If you go on an organized shore excursion, you will see the city and, perhaps, the only historic monument around, Fort San Diego, which was originally built in 1616 and rebuilt in the late 18th century after it was destroyed by an earthquake in 1776. Also here are a beautiful yacht club (where some 1968 Olympic events took place), a cathedral built in the 1930s, the west or older section of town that should become fashionable some day, a new convention/cultural center and a public market. One sight not to miss is Las Brisas, overlooking Acapulco Bay, one of the world's most imaginative hotels. (You will most likely see the hotel jeeps, complete with fringed tops, buzzing all over town.) Some shore tours take you way out of town to the Acapulco Princess/Pierre Marques Hotel complex for lunch and swimming on the beach. This has become *the* place in town, and when you see the others you will understand why.

AUTHOR'S OBSERVATION

The Princess/Pierre Marques has several restaurants and is full of action. It is very near the airport, so if you are planning your last few hours in Acapulco, remember this! Acapulco by night is exciting, as are most resort towns, but in my experience the taxi drivers here are experts in the art of bandido.

If your cruise ship spends two full days at port in Acapulco, you may be offered the opportunity to visit **Taxco**, the city of silver. Taxco is 145 miles straight up from Acapulco, along a narrow highway that might make you exceedingly nervous (it does everyone), but your attention will be diverted from time to time by the children along the side selling iguanas. It's all worth it, though, for Taxco is charming. Reportedly explored by Cortes (who noted the silvermining potential), this cobblestoned, colonial town sits atop some rich silver mines, although more than 200 shops furnish the town with approximately 90 percent of its income. Take a look at the Church of Santa Prisca and Casa Figueroa, the local art gallery and museum. There are also some interesting and vast caves in the area, Las Grutas de Cachuamilpa. Be certain to pack extra sweaters for the excursion to the caves; Taxco is 5700 feet above sea level, and the average temperature ranges only from 66 to 76 degrees.

The **Yucatan Peninsula** on the Atlantic coast of Mexico is a major tourist haven, for both its abundance of comfortable tourist facilities and its historical interest. This is the land of Mayan splendors. The best known and most remarkable ruin is **Chichen Itza**. For cruise passengers it's a three-hour drive from the port of Cancun. Chichen Itza is the chosen city of Kukulcan, the Plumed Serpent, the incarnation of God who founded Mayapan as the civil center of the peninsula (while Chichen Itza remained the religious center). Hundreds of structures here dot the more than six-square-mile complex that straddles the highway, the earliest buildings dating from the 5th century, and additional ruins (some not yet excavated) extend deep into the surrounding jungle. Most impressive is **El Castillo**, or the Pyramid of Kukulcan, which the Spanish used as a fortress. One of the many fascinations of this pyramid is the solar phenomenon that occurs during the vernal and autumnal equinoxes—the sun creates a shadowy serpent up its northeast side. Other points of interest in Chichen Itza include the ball court, the Temple of the Warriors and the Well of Sacrifices. A tour to this ancient site makes for a long day (about eleven hours), but it is worth the effort.

If you prefer to visit an ancient Mayan city closer to the seashore, you will want to see Tulum, a short drive from Cancun. This walled fortress by the sea was first viewed in 1518 and rediscovered only in the mid-19th century.

Tulum is one of the most ancient cities in Mexico, but all that remains now is the tower (or Castillo) of Tulum, a pyramidal structure sitting atop a 40-foot bluff. Down below lies the crystal-blue Caribbean. You may just wish to enjoy the beautiful sea from one of the empty, sweeping beaches of Cancun, a resort that some say is the best in Mexico. Both the flora and fauna are lovely here, and the water is so shallow that you can walk out forever before you reach any noticeable undertow. The Caribbean's newest spa, Cancun means pot of gold in one of the many Mayan dialects. So true.

Two other Mexican calls in the Caribbean are **Cozumel** and **Playa del Carmen**, both popular for their fine beaches, excellent underwater diving opportunities, and resort atmosphere, not to mention terrific beach parties.

THE PANAMA CANAL

AUTHOR'S OBSERVATION

If you want a bird's eye view from deck, stake your claim early (forward, below or above the bridge is the best vantage point). Passengers will be lined up ten deep as you pass through the locks. Most ships have an observation lounge, and it's usually more comfortable to sit in a soft chair sipping a cool drink away from the hot sun and humidity of the Canal Zone

The approximately eight-hour transit of the Panama Canal is a cruise highlight for passengers sailing between Pacific and Atlantic ports. In addition to lush tropical scenery and exciting historical commentary by a shipboard lecturer, the passage of this fifty-mile big ditch will take you through one of the largest man-made bodies of water in the world, the island-studded 166-square- mile Gatun Lake. The Panama Canal was opened to commercial ship traffic in 1914, just ten years after the United States began serious construction of the canal, and almost four centuries after King Charles V of Spain ordered a survey (in 1524) to determine a possible canal route. The 51.2-mile waterway is a commercial enterprise although it was not structured to actually turn a profit, just break even. Tolls are based on vessel size and cargo, and revenues are sensitive to the world economy. For the past few years, the running of the canal has been somewhat of a mess and many cruise lines have stayed away, but the prognosis for Panama's political future has improved and so has the popularity of canal transits. One result of the ordeal with Noriega is that few (if any) cruise vessels still fly the Panamanian flag. The Bahamas has become the country of registry most preferred.

Building the canal was a great human achievement that involved more than just American engineering genius and administrative skill. The problems with sanitation brought about the solution to some monumental public health problems stemming from foul water and causing the rapid spread of malaria. If your vessel passes from the Atlantic or Caribbean side into the Pacific, you will enter the channel at **Limon Bay** at Cristobal breakwater, just before the Gatun locks and lake. One of the most interesting portions of the trip is **Gaillard Cut**, an eight-mile channel through solid rock that got its present name from the engineer in charge. It is often said that Gaillard Cut, more than any other section of the canal, gives the impression of an enormous man-made ditch. Which is just what it is. At the south end of Gaillard Cut are the Miguel and Miraflores locks, the Canal Zone city of **Balboa**, and the Pacific Ocean. Of course, if your ship is traveling from north to south, you will have to read this article backward, but either way, passage of the Panama Canal is an exciting experience. It is possible to experience the transit of the Panama Canal in less than a two-week cruise. And a partial transit is just as exciting, according to the success of *Regent Star* from Montego Bay. The vessels enter Gatun Lock in the morning while on-board lecturers describe the history of the canal. Following a cruise around Gatun Lake, the ships transit through the lock again and return to the Atlantic side.

ALASKA AND THE INSIDE PASSAGE

The Sea Bird *arrives in Glacier Bay, Alaska.*

AUTHOR'S OBSERVATION

While Alaska is most commonly visited by conventional cruise ships, those seeking a close-up peek at Mother Nature and the educational experience of an expedition vessel should check out Alaska Sightseeing/Cruise West, Clipper Cruise Line, Special Expeditions and World Explorer Cruises.

The 1000-mile-long sea corridor that skirts the west coast of British Columbia and Alaska, known as the **Inside Passage**, is a busy waterway from May to September. During this popular season, as many as a dozen cruise vessels sail through what one might call the Last Frontier, our rugged 49th state. The scenery compares favorably with the Norwegian fjords, both with sheer-rock cliffs, massive glaciers and snowcapped mountains. Nature's more somber colors prevail in this spectacular setting. Be forewarned; the weather can be tricky—the locals say it's a good day when it's only drizzling! Hence, choose such cruises carefully—forget sunbathing and shopping and concentrate on shore excursions and equal time for absorbing the majestic scenery.

The longer cruises through the Inside Passage depart from San Francisco, while the shorter, 7- to 11-day sailings originate in **Vancouver**. This delightful seaport is considered Canada's gem of the Pacific for its fine weather, prosperity, rich cultural life and interesting sights. Modern high rises of steel and glass sit beside Victorian structures in a beautiful setting between mountains and sea. The city, founded in the 1860s, has a wonderful historic section, Gastown, which is a renovated gaslight district. Two other areas of interest are Chinatown, second in size only to San Francisco's in North America, and Robsonstrasse with chic European shops and restaurants.

Vancouver built a fabulous new cruise pier for its International Expo several years ago, which is a city in itself with convention facilities, shops, restaurants and hotels. It is well worth exploring, especially to appreciate what can be done when local government gets its act together.

You can head straight for 1000-acre Stanley Park on the northern edge of Vancouver, where you can swim in pools or at the beach, visit a zoo and aquarium, see century-old totem poles, or just stroll among the more than 100,000 trees. (By the way, hockey's Stanley Cup and this park were both named after the same man, Lord Stanley, Governor General of Canada in 1889.) If there is time, drive over the Lions Gate Bridge to see the lovely homes and the symbol of Vancouver, two mountain peaks known as the Lions.

AUTHOR'S OBSERVATION

Vancouver is one of the loveliest cities in North America, and easily worth a two-day stay. The city has charming bed and breakfast hotels, wonderful restaurants and one of the most picturesque harbors in the world. If time permits, take the ferry to the island of Victoria (see below).

Some fortunate cruise passengers aboard ships on the Alaska run will call at the charming city of **Victoria**, capital of British Columbia, on Vancouver Island. Named after Britain's favorite (non-living) queen, Victoria has a milder climate than Vancouver, a delightful colonial atmosphere, as well as a beautiful natural setting. A favorite attraction is Butchart Gardens, a good half-day excursion.

Midtown has horse and buggies, Parliament Square full of Victorian structures, a fabulous museum combining anthropology with natural history, and the landmark Canadian Pacific Empress Hotel, where one can enjoy proper tea in the lobby and the accommodations are certainly a reminder of the past. It's fun to stay here as I once did and listen to the plumbing fixtures conversing all night long! On board and underway, it's time to wrap yourself in a warm blanket, settle into a deck chair and watch the view as the sunshine (you hope) warms the crisp air. Your first sight will undoubtedly be Lynn Canal, where fjords, fishing villages and foothills will keep your camera busy. This is the beginning of the famous 1000-mile Inside Passage. It's beautiful and rugged and somber, and it's easy to relax up here and slip into a slower pace. First port of call for many ships is **Ketchikan**, a city of some ten thousand or so that claims to be both the salmon capital of the world and totemland. Hence a tour of the city includes a salmon hatchery and Totem Park, where these hand-carved poles portray legendary chiefs, mythical birds, and even Abraham Lincoln. Totem Bight State Park, a 15-minute drive north of Ketchikan, which has plenty more of these tall poles as well as a handcarved Ceremonial House, is the center of early Alaskan Indian culture.

Juneau, capital of Alaska, is a product of the 1880 gold rush. For the 49th state, Juneau is considered sophisticated, and suburbanites live in modern, low-slung houses with beautiful views of mountains, glaciers and the sea. One of the most impressive of several tours features Mendenhall Glacier, which is about one and a half miles wide by one mile long. It has been retreating at the rate of approximately 50 feet per year (you stand where the glacier ended around 1940). If you prefer to save your glaciers for later, don't miss the good performances of Tlingit and Haida tribal dances and snacks of fresh, fire-baked Alaskan salmon. For a more adventurous (and costly—about $80 per person) salmon bake, catch one of the seaplanes parked along the waterfront for the half-hour ride to Taku Lodge. This forest-surrounded, log-cabin lodge offers a hearty lunch of salmon, homemade biscuits, beer chilled by glacial ice, baked beans, potato salad, coffee and cookies and there is time to walk it off before the flight back to Juneau.

Highlight of every Inside Passage cruise is **Glacier Bay National Monument**, about 40 miles northwest of Juneau, accessible only by plane or boat. The scenery here is some of Alaska's most spectacular, and park rangers will board your vessel in the morning to comment on the history and habits of glaciers as you cruise along. The better part of a day is spent cruising slowly through Glacier Bay while you relax on board watching the ice floes pass by, occasionally hearing a glacier calve, or crack off, and learning about the rare wildlife that inhabit the area. Perhaps the sun will be brilliant this day, and your stewards will serve a wonderful buffet luncheon on deck.

Final port of call on most seven-day round-trip Inside Passage routes is the former Russian settlement of **Sitka**, a town that lives in the past for the sake of its many tourists. On the site of an ancient Tlingit village, Sitka was founded by Aleksandr Baranof when he transferred the headquarters of the Russian-American Company here. On October 18, the 1867 ceremony in which the American flag replaced the Imperial Russian one is reenacted. Sites to visit in the area include the 54-acre Sitka Historical National Park, where Tlingit tribes made their last stand against the Russians and where Indian craftsmen now demonstrate their carving techniques. (The carvings for sale in town are rather pricey, I feel.) You can tour the onion-domed Russian church. It was rebuilt in 1966 after a disastrous fire, but the icons are original. The Alaska Pioneers Home, the Russian cemetery and a fine museum of local history and artifacts that span two centuries are also interesting. During the summer months, a group of Sitka women perform typical Russian folk dances.

Even more popular these days are Inside Passage cruises that either begin or end in Whittier or Anchorage, with transportation via vintage glass-domed railcars the other way. These itineraries offer a more in-depth view of this spectacular scenery, including Hubbard Glacier, through Valdez Arm into Columbia Glacier (Alaska's most active). Also featured sights on this route are a cruise through Prince William Sound and an arrival in College Fjord, where as many as a bakers dozen of glaciers, with such awe-inspiring names as Harvard, Yale, Radcliffe, and Smith, cascade down the mountain at once. The route also includes Kings Bay, Port Nellie Juan, and Seward gateway to Kenai Fjords National Monument. Whether or not all of the above can be enjoyed on your cruise, the "in" way to go these days is by sea one way and rail the other or a one-week cruise with additional days amidst the beauty of our 49th state.

AUTHOR'S OBSERVATION

Most cruise passengers extend their Alaska cruise vacation by taking land tours offered by most cruise lines. Holland America and Princess offer the most extensive programs inland, including visits to the Russian Far East, glass dome rail excursions and stays at wonderful mountainous resorts.

INTRA-COASTAL WATERWAYS

The* Nantucket Clipper *explores the scenic waterways of the South.

Exploring the beauty and history of our own southeast coastline is gaining in popularity for yachtlike vessels, especially those operated by American Canadian Caribbean Line (ACCL) of Rhode Island and Clipper Cruise Line of St. Louis. The Intracoastal Waterway (ICW) joins random rivers, bays and sounds for some 1085 miles between Norfolk, Virginia and Miami, Florida and provides vessels of all sizes a sheltered passage along this route. The idea dates from the time of the Revolution, but wasn't completed until the turn of this century. The waterway was actually meant for commercial vessels, but whoever dreamed that container ships would be constructed as big as several city blocks? So, today this protected 1000-plus-mile coast is full of pleasure boats and their passengers, who revel in sailing leisurely from one historic town to another. In many of the small ports, shore excursions are led by the local inhabitants in their own vehicles, and the whole experience offers the epitome of American-style hospitality!

AUTHOR'S OBSERVATION

Those who love golf should explore Clipper Cruise Line's golf cruises, which visit some of the best courses in the U.S. The company also devotes at least one cruise each year to civil war sites, with noted lecturers onboard.

The major cruising area along this waterway is between Baltimore, Maryland and Savannah, Georgia either on full two-week sailings between the two ports or as one-week round-trip sailings from each port. **Baltimore**, gateway to the Chesapeake Bay area, has long lived in the shadow of our nation's capital as a rather poor and unsightly cousin. However, an impressive revitalization of the city's Inner Harbor with the renovation of old warehouses and a year-round marketplace, in addition to such tourist attractions as the National Aquarium, has made this the place to be. The restoration has also brought new cultural and leisure activities to the area. In short, Baltimore is definitely worth a visit and a linger before or after the cruise.

Sailing from Baltimore harbor, where American lawyer Francis Scott Key wrote "The Star Spangled Banner" from the deck of a battleship, your vessel enters famed Chesapeake Bay, known not only for its scenic beauty but also for the succulent seafood found in its waters. First call is most likely **Oxford**, on the eastern shore of Maryland and a port of entry since 1694. Oxford has retained much of its early charm, when the town prospered on the exportation of tobacco and the importation of rope and other ships' supplies. Passengers are encouraged to take their own walking tours through the residential and shopping areas, or catch a ride on Tred Avon Ferry, which is said to be the oldest continuously operating car ferry in the country. St. Michaels, Cambridge, Salisbury and Crisfield are other old port towns on Maryland's eastern shore that might be visited.

Yorktown, Virginia is located at the mouth of the York River, and not much changed since its heyday in the 18th century, when the exportation of tobacco made it rich and famous. Today, the port is noted for the Battle of Yorktown in 1781, which is credited with ending the American Revolution. You may explore the silent battlefields on foot, and perhaps feel the ghost of General Cornwallis, who surrendered to the commander of the Continental Army George Washington. Yorktown is just a short distance from colonial **Williamsburg**, located on a peninsula between the James and York rivers and home of our nation's second oldest university (William and Mary, founded 1693). Williamsburg needs no introduction as a tourist attraction, and the 173-acre historic area contains more than 100 gardens and greens and the largest restoration of 18th century public buildings and houses in the world.

Leaving Yorktown and entering Chesapeake Bay once again, passengers will be able to spot Mile Marker No. 1, which marks the beginning of the Intracoastal Waterway south. If your cruise calls at

Norfolk, home of the U.S. naval fleets patrolling the Atlantic and Mediterranean, you can tour some interesting monuments. The port was founded by decree of King Charles II in 1682, but most of the colonial structures remaining date from the 18th century. However, you should not miss the General Douglas MacArthur Memorial or the Chrysler Museum. St. Paul's Church, built in 1739, still has a cannonball imbedded in one wall courtesy of a British bombardment in 1776.

Cruising along the Cape Fear River and Myrtle Grove Sound, your vessel arrives at the port of **Wrightsville Beach**, which is just a hop from the Atlantic Ocean. Wrightsville Beach is a short drive from the lovely town of **Wilmington**, North Carolina, itself a leading port since the 18th century and full of restored antebellum homes. After a half day on the beach, your vessel will sail for Morehead City, N.C. for a tour of **Beaufort** located across the Newport River. This historic town was founded in 1709 and boasts some 25 homes dating from the Revolutionary War period, as well as more than 100 from the Civil War era. In Beaufort, passengers are treated to an escorted tour by members of the local historical society. Of special interest are Bell House (1876), the Third Courthouse and Apothecary (1796) and the Cemetery (1714).

Along the coast of South Carolina, your cruise may call first at **Bucksport** on the Waccamaw River. The town was founded by a Captain Henry Buck, a shipbuilder from Bucksport, Maine. The stretch from here through the Cape Romain National Wildlife Refuge is considered one of the most beautiful of the Intracoastal Waterway. Note, especially, the live oak trees covered in mistletoe along the Waccamaw River.

An entire day in elegant **Charleston** features a three-hour tour of the 780-acre historic district and includes visits to the 1809 Nathaniel Russell House, Rainbow Row, the oldest theater in America (so they say), and the East and South batteries along the waterfront. Charleston was settled by the English in 1670 and named in honor of Charles II. Before the Revolution, it was the largest and wealthiest port south of Philadelphia, but its magnificent public buildings and homes suffered greatly during the Civil War. Today, however, it is again the most famous and visited city in the south and proud of the 18th- and 19th-century structures that have been so lovingly restored by their owners. There are many, many beautiful homes open year-round to visitors, even more during the Festival of Houses in the spring (mid-March to mid- April), and the annual House and Garden tours held for three weeks in October.

South Carolina also has its **Beaufort**, first settled around 1562 by French Huguenots, but not officially founded until 1710. Beaufort is located at the end of a day's cruise along the Stono and Edisto rivers, St. Helena Sound, and through the Coosaw and Ashepoo rivers. Picturesque and beautifully preserved, the entire downtown area of Beaufort is listed on the National Historic Register and has been designated a National Historic Landmark. A three-hour tour of the area is available, highlighting the town's history and the fortunes made here in rice and indigo and the production of Sea Island cotton from the early 18th to mid-19th centuries.

Leaving Beaufort via Port Royal Sound and Skull Creek, your vessel will dock at Hilton Head Plantation on **Hilton Head Island**, off the South Carolina coast. Here, you can explore one of the country's most famous resorts, home of the Heritage Golf Classic at the Harbor Town Golf Course. Check out the posh boutiques in Harbor Town Village, or catch a nearby taxi for a tour of the entire island.

From Hilton Head, your vessel will cruise across Caliboque Sound and up the Savannah River to historic **Savannah**, Georgia's oldest and most sophisticated city. Founded in 1733 on a high bluff overlooking the river, Savannah profited from astute urban planning as early as the 18th century. In the Central Historic District, more than 1000 structures have been restored in the past 25 years, including fine Georgian, Federal, Greek Revival and Gothic Revival buildings. A Victorian Historic District, primarily residential, is now receiving the same care and attention. Self-guided tours of both areas are suggested by the local Visitors Center, and the Historic Savannah Foundation offers other tours featuring sights on the outskirts of the town. If your cruise begins or ends in Savannah, you will no doubt find yourself at the Rousakis Riverfront Plaza, but be sure to save some time for this lovely city.

Following the Georgian coastline south, cruise passengers cannot miss the port of **Brunswick** and two of the so-called Golden Isles—Jekyll Island and St. Simons Island. Brunswick was a rival of Savannah during the 19th century, but has matured to just a quiet place with Victorian architecture, the gateway city to the two Golden Isles. **Jekyll Island** is famous for its Millionaires Village, located between Riverview Drive and Old Village Boulevard. This was a chic colony of some of America's industrialist rich during the late 19th century. Most of those who bought land here for their private retreats are well known in history books: the Rockefellers, McCormicks, Goodyears, Pulitzers, etc. The spacious homes were closed during World War II and later bought by the state of Georgia as a tourist attraction. The cottages can be seen on guided tours and are interesting for their social history, but hardly for their architectural style. **St. Simon's Island** was a strategic spot during colonial times, as Fort Frederica protected English settlers along the Georgia coast. It is now a national monument and open to visitors. St. Simons Lighthouse and keeper's building are also interesting, as the latter now houses a Museum of Coastal History.

Fernandina Beach, on Amelia Island off Florida's Atlantic coast, is one of the first calls in the state of Florida, and a favorite for its colorful history. The beach is strategically located at the entrance to St. Mary's River and Cumberland Sound, and the flags of eight nations have flown here since the 18th century. During the Civil War, the beach was under Union control, and it flourished afterward. Many of the fine Queen Anne and Italianate residences in the historic district date from this period. Fernandina is just north of **Jacksonville**, one of the state's largest and most industrious cities. Located on the St. Johns River, the town was first called Cowford under British rule, but was renamed for Andrew Jackson when it became a U.S. possession. Jacksonville has Fort Caroline National Memorial, which dates from 1564–5, and an excellent Museum of Arts and Sciences.

Everyone loves **St. Augustine**, the oldest continuously occupied city in the United States. A permanent settlement was founded here in 1565 by Don Pedro Menendez de Aviles, on instructions from King Philip II. It existed under Spanish domination until 1821. Much of the center city is an historic district and a National Historic Landmark. At the end of the 19th century, St. Augustine became a winter resort, thanks to the labors of industrialist Henry Flagler, who built two large hostelries here and then bought a railroad to transport his guests to and from winter climes. Both luxury properties have been reborn: the former Hotel Ponce de Leon (1888) as Flagler College and the former Alcazar Hotel (1889) as the Lightner Museum. Don't miss St. Augustine Cathedral (1797), the Castillo de San Marcos National Monument (1672–96) and the city's oldest house.

Port Canaveral is famous for its proximity to the Kennedy Space Center, Disney World, and Epcot Center. A two-day layover here certainly does the area justice. You can be a kid again or step into the 21st century and watch man against the moon all in the same breath.

From Stuart, you will cruise across the **Okeechobee Waterway** to Ft. Meyers on the Gulf of Mexico. Through this inland passage from the Atlantic Ocean, you will have an intimate view of south-central

Florida and the people who work the cattle ranches, the citrus groves, and the sugar-cane plantations. You'll pass through a number of quiet little towns, as well as the St. Lucie Lock and Canal, across Lake Okeechobee (Seminole Indian for plenty big water) and into the Caloosahatchee River at Moore Haven. At least, this is the route that American Cruise Lines offers. Once in **Ft. Meyers**, you can visit the Thomas A. Edison Museum, Sanibel and Captiva islands (South Seas Plantation), and the Darling Wildlife Sanctuary. Whether Ft. Meyers is the beginning or the end of your cruise, linger a while and enjoy some of its fine attractions.

THE MISSISSIPPI RIVER

Ole Man River is one of our nation's most moving folk tunes. Tom Sawyer and Huck Finn of Hannibal are a part of every child's vocabulary early on.

And many of us stumbled over the stinger Mississippi at some school spelling bee and then learned how to say it fast backward. The river flows south some 2470 miles from northern Minnesota to the Gulf of Mexico, offering a historic venue for cruises and an unparalleled view for passengers of a way of life that has endured along its banks—sleepy river towns that are slightly behind the times, plantations that show us what wealth there was in the land, and cities that have become industrial centers but still retain the charm of yesteryear.

Thanks to the Delta Queen Steamboat Company, Mississippi River cruises are now available year round on your choice of the only two overnight paddlewheel steamboats left in America. You can choose the venerable old lady named *Delta Queen*, who is listed in the Register of Historic Places, or her baby sister, the *Mississippi Queen*, launched in 1975 but already a legend. Most of the cruises originate from **New Orleans**, that romantic, much-fought-over city founded by the French in 1718 on the first high ground above the Mississippi Passes, about 95 miles upriver from the Gulf. New Orleans was poverty stricken and sparsely populated in 1811 when the first steamboat, named the *City of New Orleans*, was built in Pittsburgh and launched on her first trip downriver.

By 1840, some 100,000 people lived in New Orleans, and it was the second largest port in America. Just before the Civil War, the number of steamboats at her miles-long terminus numbered at least 100. Today the city is still a busy and colorful port, famous for Mardi Gras, Bourbon Street jazz, the French Quarter, Garden District and the new Superdome. Time is well spent here either before or after your steamboat cruise. Other major ports of embarkation on the Mississippi are Memphis, St. Louis and St. Paul.

Cruising upriver on the lower half of the Mississippi, your first steamboat landing is **Nottoway Plantation**, built in 1859 by John Hampton Randolph. Renowned as the largest plantation home in the South, Nottoway has 64 rooms and boasts 22 enormous columns enhancing its Greek Revival and Italianate architecture! Steamboat passengers may tour the grounds and mansion from the docking at water's edge, enjoying views of the river and century-old live oak trees from the largest of Nottoway's 200 windows.

At the river's 153-mile mark is **Oak Alley Plantation**, first settled in the early 1700s by a Frenchman who had the foresight to plant two rows of oak trees from the house to the river. When the steamboat ties up at the water's edge, you walk to the Greek Revival mansion, built in 1837, beneath an alley of 250-year-old oaks with Spanish moss dripping from their solid boughs. It's a truly wonderful experience, and if you close your eyes and breathe deeply, you can easily imagine hoop-skirted Southern belles with velvet ribbons around their necks stepping daintily down to greet you.

Another restored, antebellum-style plantation complex open to visitors is **Houmas House**, which is also approached from the river. (Perhaps you will recognize this house, for it has been in many television films and was the setting for *Hush, Hush, Sweet Charlotte.*) Named after an Indian tribe that once inhabited this spot, Houmas House commands a river view of several miles in both directions. The Greek Revival mansion dates from 1840, and from that year until the Civil War this 20,000-acre plantation was the foremost sugar producer in America. Houmas was spared the ravages of famine and fighting during the war because its Irish owner declared British immunity—a ploy that worked! Under new ownership and management in the 1880s, the plantation flourished again, reaching a record production of 20 million tons of sugar in one year. But success was short-lived. By the end of the century, the land was parceled off and the house stood in disrepair. It was purchased by a New Orleans doctor in 1940, who devoted the last 25 years of his life to planting formal gardens and to restoring the house and furnishing it with museum-quality early Louisiana craftsmanship. A tour of this house and grounds is a real treat.

Baton Rouge, capital of Louisiana, is situated at the 230-mile mark of the lower Mississippi and named for the red post that once divided two Indian nations here. Founded in 1719, the city was the site of a Revolutionary War battle that did not even involve a colonist—it was strictly between the British and the Spanish (who had possession of this territory). Today this gracious Southern metropolis has wide avenues lined with former plantation homes, like the 1791 Magnolia Mound, now a museum of Federal period furniture. Baton Rouge is also known for Louisiana State University, with the Rural Life Museum, a reconstructed plantation settlement, and the Old State Capitol that overlooks the river from a bluff. The original 1849 Gothic structure that stood here was burned by Union troops during the Civil War (accidentally, they say) and reconstructed in 1882.

The next call for the Delta Queen Steamboat Company is the sleepy river town of **St. Francisville**, Louisiana, which boasted half the millionaires in America during the cotton boom of the 1850s. Today, the luxury and splendor this region knew is recalled only in the restoration of once-thriving plantations, foremost of which are Rosedown and The Myrtles. Rosedown Home and Gardens were built in 1835 by a wealthy cotton planter and his wife, who spared neither money nor means to create a magnificent setting in the style of 17th-century France. The Myrtles was built in the early 1830s, and locals believe that the ghost of a former resident still roams the house. In the restoration, special care was given to the iron grillwork that surrounds a 100-foot veranda. Both these plantations are near Audubon State Park and on the steamboat tour.

Natchez, Mississippi, lies at the 363-mile mark in the heart of the fertile Mississippi River delta. The antebellum homes here also reflect the wealth of early cotton planters who often used European architects and craftsmen. Many of the fine places here can still be visited because General Ulysses S. Grant spared Natchez Over The Hill (as it was called then) in his thrust south during the Civil War. Semiannual events in this gracious river town, founded in 1716, are the spring and fall Natchez Pilgrimage Cruises that bring passengers to view some of the more than 200 antebellum properties in the best seasons. Some of the highlights of these tours are Stanton Hall, occupying an entire block and patterned after an Irish ancestral home; Connelly's Tavern where the first American flag in Mississippi was raised in 1797; a lovely Georgian home named Rosalie; Longwood, looking just as the workers left it when war broke out; and D Evereux, where the most elaborate balls in Natchez were said to have taken place.

Just 73 miles upriver is **Vicksburg**, site of the siege of 1863. To this day the citizens of Vicksburg refuse to celebrate the fourth of July, for on that day their ancestors surrendered to the Union Army that had surrounded the city for three solid months. This peaceful town has many memories, war memorials and cemeteries. The Old Court House Museum, former headquarters of the Confederates, has touching memorabilia from the period—receipts from the sale of slaves, Confederate money and clothing, and photographs of Mississippi River steamboats.

AUTHOR'S OBSERVATION

A few of the local homes that survived are also worth visiting, especially Cedar Grove with a cannonball still lodged in the parlor wall. For a change of pace, your tour may take you to a scale model of the entire Mississippi River system at the Waterways Experiment Station (operated by the U.S. Army Corps of Engineers).

Memphis, Tennessee, at the 736-mile mark on the lower Mississippi, was planned in 1818 and named after the ancient city on the Nile. Hernando DeSoto supposedly came through here in 1541, stopping only long enough to build some barges to cross the river. Memphis became an important port and agricultural center in the 1800s, and the world's largest cotton market was established here in 1873. Located on Cotton Row, the Memphis Cotton Exchange is still active and handles more than four million bales each year. Tours in Memphis include a visit to the Exchange and, when weather permits, to a cotton field and working cotton gin. It's also fun to visit the old Beale Street haunts of famous blues musician W. C. Handy, Elvis Presley's mansion Graceland, Schwab's famous Five and Dime, and the Chucalissa Indian Village and Museum.

At the mouth of the upper Mississippi is the quiet town of **Cairo**, Illinois, whose prosperity was tied to the steamboat trade. Cairo's dreams of a future more exciting than Chicago's were dashed by the southern extension of the Illinois Central Railroad in 1855. However, memories of a glorious past linger, with landmarks like the restored Magnolia Manor and Holiday Park to give us an indication of once-abundant wealth.

St. Louis, Missouri, at the 180-mile mark on the upper Mississippi (from Memphis), was second only to New Orleans in the days of steamboat packets; and as the historic Gateway to the West, St. Louis played host to thousands of famous and infamous settlers, traders and trappers. Wagon trains bound for the west crowded the riverfront as pioneers formed some unusual alliances in their battle against the elements of the new frontier. Among enterprising Americans who made their home in St. Louis, at least for a while, were Abraham Lincoln and Charles Lindbergh, who christened his plane "The Spirit of St. Louis" in honor of the city whose business leaders believed in him. St. Louis has interesting buildings in all styles, from the much-photographed Gateway Arch on the riverfront to WPA projects and historic structures. The Old Courthouse was the scene of the notorious Dred Scott case, and the Anheuser-Busch Brewery is the largest in the world. The Jefferson Memorial has original documents relating to the Louisiana Purchase, as well as some of Lindbergh's trophies commemorating his New York to Paris flight.

Everyone's favorite river town is still **Hannibal** (at the 308-mile mark on the upper Mississippi) where Tom Sawyer, Huck Finn and Becky Thatcher played their pranks. The author of these escapades (Samuel Clemens) was born in nearby Florida, Missouri, but grew up in Hannibal where the arrival of the steamboat was about the only event to raise the dust (or a few waves) on a somnolent summer's day. While still in his teens Clemens boarded a paddlewheeler en route to New Orleans and a combined career of river pilot/writer and Mark Twain was born. Shortly after he left, the railroad came to save Hannibal from extinction when riverboat traffic diminished after the Civil War. Any visit to Hannibal is strictly a do-it-yourself tour about the town, wandering along the street with the whitewashed fence, the Pilaster House with law office and drugstore and the birthplace of Margaret Tobin (also known as the Unsinkable Molly Brown).

Nauvoo, Illinois, at the 375-mile mark on the upper Mississippi, was founded in 1839 by Joseph Smith and followers of the Church of the Latter Day Saints (Mormons). But Smith and his disciples fled for their lives seven years later over a series of disputes with the non-Mormon community. However, they left behind some interesting Mormon-style buildings that have been restored by descendants of the original pilgrims. Nauvoo is also known for its fruit harvests, especially the vineyards that produce abundant native wine. And to enjoy with the wine, try some domestic blue cheese.

As the Mississippi continues and your riverboat cruises upstream, **Dubuque**, Iowa, lies at the 579-mile mark, a commercial city in America's heartland. An air-conditioned motorcoach from the docking site takes passengers to visit the quiet backwater of **Galena**, known for its quaint atmosphere and its 19th-century architecture. The tour features a walk through the town's antique and specialty shops and the former home of Ulysses S. Grant, our 18th president.

Prairie Du Chien, Wisconsin, is near the meeting of the Mississippi and Wisconsin rivers where Indians are believed to have lived for some 10,000 years. The many tribes included the Woodland, Fox, Sauk and Winnebago, and the Hopewell culture built huge burial mounds about 2000 years ago. The settlers built a fort on top of one of the mounds in 1812. It was burned and replaced by Fort Crawford in 1816, which still remains. Prairie du Chien was a thriving frontier settlement in 1826 when Hercules Dousman arrived as a confidential agent for John Jacob Astor, the American Fur Company millionaire. The Dousman family became rich from fur trading and built an enormous mansion named Villa Louis on one of the Indian burial mounds. This restored villa is a showplace of Victorian architecture and furnishings. You can also visit the original Astor Fur Warehouse and restored Fort Crawford, complete with hospital.

At one time, **La Crosse**, Wisconsin, claimed the largest transportation organization on the upper Mississippi with two hundred steamboats landing a month. Three rivers meet here: the Mississippi, the Black and the La Crosse. A stop at Grandad Bluff, 675 feet above the city, offers a view of three states: Wisconsin, Minnesota and Iowa.

At **Wabasha**, Minnesota, in unspoiled wilderness, the two *Queens* dock at Read's Landing. Steamboats brought supplies up to this logging and fur-trading center in the early 1800s and took log rafts back down the Mississippi. The Wabasha Country Museum chronicles the regional history of steamboats and rafts, and if you're interested in a view of Sitting Bull's peace pipe, pay a visit to the Suilman Antique Museum. Visitors can enjoy a tour of the Anderson House Hotel as well, which opened in 1856 (and to this day warms guests beds with hot bricks). Wabasha is also the home of the Nelson Cheese Factory where sampling is part of the tour.

Minneapolis/St. Paul, the twin cities on the upper Mississippi, mark the 839th mile and the final point of navigation on the river and the end of your steamboat cruise. In the old days, ox carts provided transit from this point northward, with as many as 500 wagons per caravan shuttling between the steamboat landing and Fort Garry, which is now Winnipeg, Manitoba. The city of St. Paul grew up around the landing while Minneapolis blossomed next door.

Twin City attractions include the Guthrie Theatre; a 36-foot-high onyx Indian statue; Fort Snelling, established in 1825 by the U.S. Cavalry; the home of the Betty Crocker testing kitchens; the Walker Art Center; and Minnehaha Falls.

THE OHIO RIVER

The Ohio River flows almost one thousand miles from its source in Pittsburgh, Pennsylvania, to its confluence with the Mississippi River at Cairo, Illinois.

Like the Mississippi, the Ohio River was discovered and explored by the French, and many of its early settlers came from the not-so-distant east. The Ohio has played its role in the story of America: the last battle of the Revolutionary War was fought on its banks in Wheeling, West Virginia, and Ulysses S. Grant, general and president, was born near the shore in Point Pleasant, Ohio. The first steamboat, built in 1811 in Pittsburgh and named the City of New Orleans, paddled the entire length of the Ohio River.

Evansville and **New Harmony**, Indiana, are located near the 795-mile mark on the Ohio River. Evansville was established in 1812 when Hugh McCarey crossed the river so his wife could visit her family. The landing grew into a large shipping center for coal, oil and lumber. In the late 1800s this area became known as Lincoln Land, and a Lincoln Heritage Trail winds through Kentucky, Indiana, and Illinois, tracing the life of our sixteenth president. Nearby New Harmony was settled in 1814 by a group of dissident Lutherans hoping to build a perfectly planned community. Your tour will take you to some restored communal Harmony houses as well as the Labyrinth, an elaborate shrubbery maze that leads to a small temple symbolizing harmony.

The home of beautiful women, bluegrass, the Kentucky Derby, and the best bourbon in the south, **Louisville**, Kentucky is at the 603-mile mark on the Ohio River. The city is at its best during Derby Week, the first part of May, when the southern belles come out and Churchill Downs is filled with spectators watching the famous Run for the Roses. A special cruise is offered the first week in May, but if you miss it, some of the excitement and atmosphere can be found in the Churchill Downs Museum. Other sights include the Thomas Jefferson-style Manor House, built around 1810, which stands as the only example of his design west of the Alleghenies, and Bakery Square where an inner-city restoration now holds thirty shops.

Madison, Indiana, is considered the finest example of a typical American town. The town was laid out in 1810 and by the middle 1800s was the largest city in Indiana. Jenny Lind performed in the local pork house (which apparently surprised her). The town today is interesting: the many restored buildings reflect the Federal era, the

Regency period, the classic Revival style and the Americanized Italian villa. Many of the restored and furnished homes are open to the public for a do-it-yourself tour.

Located on the 470-mile mark of the Ohio River, **Cincinnati**, Ohio, is home to the Delta Queen Steamboat Company and a major industrial center of the Midwest. Located here are steel mills, machine tool plants and the bases of many leading consumer products, as well as the Taft Museum, a well-known zoo and the Cincinnati Reds. The first suspension bridge to span the Ohio River, completed in 1867, connects Cincinnati with Covington, Kentucky.

Ripley, Ohio, was a major station on the Underground Railroad for four decades prior to the Civil War, although it was considered primarily a quiet river town noted for the breeding of fine draft horses. Ripley citizens now breed Arabian horses for distinguished sportsmen. Visitors to Rankin House learn that the Reverend John Rankin sheltered more than two thousand escaped slaves and helped them find routes north. You will follow in the footsteps of Harriet Beecher Stowe who visited Rankin in 1851. Upon hearing the story of Eliza Hariss' midnight river crossing on ice floes, Stowe wrote the book that inflamed the nation, *Uncle Tom's Cabin.*

Gallipolis, Ohio, is located at the 270-mile mark on the Ohio River. The town was settled by a group of Frenchmen, almost five hundred strong, who crossed the Atlantic in 1789 for this very purpose. Much of the town's French heritage remains. The Gallipolis City Park houses the first log cabins built here. Ouc House Tavern, now restored, was the center of village social life and boasted a visit by the Marquis de Lafayette in 1825. Crafts passed down by the French settlers are still taught in the schools, and your city tour includes a visit to Bob Evans Farm, which covers over one thousand acres near Rio Grande and offers outdoor recreation activities.

Pittsburgh, Pennsylvania, is located at the junction of the Monongahela, Allegheny and Ohio rivers and became important as early as 1758 as a strategic spot for exploration of the West. Fort Pitt was built by the British in 1764 and named for William Pitt, then prime minister. Pittsburgh flourished and steamboats were familiar sights here for transporting wheat, rye, barley, flour and whiskey to other river ports as far south as New Orleans.

AUTHOR'S OBSERVATION

Today's Pittsburgh is no longer the smoky, polluted city it was, due to an ambitious urban renewal program during the past three decades. Visitors will enjoy touring the Fort Pitt Blockhouse, the Fort Pitt Museum, the Carnegie Museum, the Duquesne Incline and many arts events.

NORTHEAST PASSAGE

AUTHOR'S OBSERVATION

While fall foliage cruises are offered aboard dozens of ships, the Regent Sun *is the only cruise ship with one-week sailings between New York and Montreal from June through October. Regency's special facilities and services for children make this an excellent family cruise vacation.*

From New York to Montreal, summer cruises are popular along the northeast coastline and through the passage of the St. Lawrence and Saguenay rivers. This is the so-called Northeast Passage, through which you will enjoy a wealth of historical sights. A special charm penetrates cruises in this section of North America—the beauty of the scenery and the flavor of these seafaring people.

Along the way, you will sail by centuries of our maritime heritage, from New York's South Street Seaport to Mystic, Connecticut, where America's last wooden whaleship, the Charles W. Morgan, lies in state. You may also see old sea captain's houses in Stonington, Connecticut, and the Bath Marine Museum, built along the broad waters of the Kennebec River of Maine.

One of the first islands to view after leaving New York is **Martha's Vineyard**, Massachusetts, which was settled in 1642 by Thomas Mayhew (who bought it for 40 pounds). Edgartown, the Vineyard's first port and a major whaling center in the 18th and 19th centuries, still boasts many fine old mansions built by wealthy sea captains and ship owners. Whaling was also important to the development of nearby **Nantucket**, called affectionately by locals the Little Gray Lady. Nantucketers caught their first whale in 1672, and the Whaling Museum on Broad Street declares this island was once the center of the world's whaling industry. Few cruise vessels stop here, so it is a treat if you can explore the town's cobblestone streets and old dwellings that remain much as they were 150 years ago. The island is a testimonial to historic preservation and many of the finely restored buildings are open to the public. Herman Melville's whaling novel,

Moby Dick, devotes an entire chapter to the island and its inhabitants.

Newport, Rhode Island, renowned as the playground of the ostentatious rich in the late 19th century, was once the most prosperous seaport on the eastern coastline. Now it is the yachting capital of the Atlantic, with some of the most prestigious races either starting or ending there, including the Newport to Bermuda (even years) and the Annapolis to Newport (odd years). It was also home of the famous America's Cup until Dennis Connor recaptured the trophy from Australia, Connor apparently will have nothing to do with Newport since he is a member of the San diego Yacht Club and feels the Eastern Establishment snubbed him. Aside from the glittering mansions and the beautiful boats, Newport is noted for some fine 18th-century public buildings and its more than 100 colonial homes that have been refurbished and made available for rental. Cruise passengers should not miss the superb 1726 Trinity Church (called a matchless reminder of Colonial America), and the 1763 Touro Synagogue (the country's first), commissioned by Sephardic Jews from Portugal and designed in Georgian style by local architect Peter Harrison. The glamorous mansions of the formerly filthy rich along Bellevue Avenue are now open to the public and worth a visit, as is the distinctive Newport Casino, which houses the Tennis Hall of Fame. If you are lucky, you may be able to catch a tennis or croquet tournament on its lovely grass courts.

Bar Harbor lies on the east coast of Mount Desert Island, off the rockbound coast of Maine. During the mid-19th century, Bar Harbor was an enclave of the very wealthy, and despite a devastating fire after World War II, some of the elegant summer cottages still exist. One prime example, the former wood and stone mansion of the late Nelson Rockefeller, was sold a few years ago for about one million dollars to a member of the Ford Motor Company family.

However, Bar Harbor is no Newport; today the island is known more for Acadia National Park, with views from Cadillac Mountain. The island's succulent lobsters and clams often find their way into local bakes.

AUTHOR'S OBSERVATION

During June, September and October expect chilly weather, especially during days at sea, and take a poncho or umbrella for inclement weather.

Halifax is Nova Scotia's capital and the largest city in the Maritime Provinces. Lord Cornwallis founded the city in 1749 and built the Citadel to guard against the French on Cape Breton Island at Louisburg. Once the mightiest fortress in British North America, the Citadel still dominates the capital but is now a park with military, marine and provincial museums. The only shots fired from the Citadel these days are from the cannon at noontime, a well-preserved tradition. Halifax has a spectacular harbor and water tours aboard the *Bluenose II* are available (but the best overall view is still from the fortress). A large redevelopment plan to save the city's lovely 18th- and 19th-century structures from destruction began in the early 1960s. Even the 18-acre Public Gardens on Spring Garden Road (originally laid out in 1753) have been preserved. Another interesting park is Point Pleasant, the only spot in North America where Scottish heather grows wild. Apparently the seeds were spread when British sailors shook their mattresses out long ago.

Off the coasts of Nova Scotia and New Brunswick, in the Gulf of the St. Lawrence, is **Prince Edward Island**, a garden province that explorer Jacques Cartier in 1534 called "the fairest land tis possible to see." Its capital, a popular cruise call, is **Charlottetown**, named after the consort of England's King George III. Charlottetown has great charm and an atmosphere reminiscent of Victoria, a city on Canada's western coast. In fact, Victoria Park overlooks Charlottetown's harbor and is the site of Fort Edward, with a six-gun battery that protects the harbor's entrance. Province House sheltered the Fathers of Confederation when they met in 1864 to plan the union of British North America and Canada. Visit the more contemporary home of Green Gables in Cavendish (on the island's north shore), which was the setting for the novel *Anne of Green Gables*, and stop at the post office nearby, the most popular on Prince Edward Island.

Gaspé Peninsula reaches out into the Gulf of the St. Lawrence at the southeast extremity of the Province of Quebec. When Champlain landed here, it was called Gachepe or Land's End by the local Indian tribe, the Micmacs. Gaspé is a rugged peninsula, with centuries-old, 12-foot fir trees and streams filled with Atlantic salmon that have been spawning here for thousands of years.

Take an excursion to nearby **Perce**, known for its incredible natural beauty, and for Perce Rock where explorer Cartier anchored his three small ships in 1534. A small boat will take you out two miles to Bonaventure Island, a wildlife sanctuary where you can tour bird colonies with a naturalist and see thousands of gannets, gulls, puffins and kittiwakes nestling in the cliffs.

The piéce de resistance, the Saguenay River, sinuous arm of the St. Lawrence, flows 450 miles from Lake Saint John and boasts sheer granite gorges that rise to 1500 feet. This is one of the most spectacular waterways in the world.

You won't forget the sight of whales feeding here, where the Saguenay and St. Lawrence rivers come together. From May through November, they surge upon this spot and often stay on the surface long enough for good photographs. A sail along the fjordlike Saguenay River will give you some feeling for what fur traders, explorers and missionaries experienced centuries before.

Quebec City, perched high above the majestic St. Lawrence, is often called the Gibraltar of North America; its place in history was forged by its natural assets. The city, founded in 1608 by Samuel de Champlain, is situated along an 8-mile plateau atop solid rock. The highest point, some 360 feet above the river, is Cap Diamant, site of the famed Citadel. The only walled city in North America, Quebec has never lost its French heritage and lifestyle. It is a popular tourist center that is best explored on foot or by caläches, colorful horse-drawn carriages. Romance and drama come to life in this delightful old town whose 17th- and 18th-century buildings have been lovingly restored. Take a look at Place d' Armes, where settlers and Indian traders used to meet. And don't miss Le Chateau Frontenac facing the square—a beautiful old hotel where Roosevelt, Churchill, and MacKenzie King met to discuss strategy during World War II. Off Place d' Armes are streets lined with historic houses, and the sites of the first girls' school in North America and the first Anglican cathedral constructed outside the British Isles. You can also see the Continent's oldest house of worship Notre Dame des Victoires, built in 1688. Recapture even more history from Dufferin Terrace, two hundred feet above the waterway, where Champlain built his fort in 1620; the views are spectacular on a clear day.

Quebec is divided into an upper and lower town. Dufferin Terrace is part of the upper town, the historic center for administration and defense. The old town, along the waterfront, functioned primarily as a post for fur trading and other commercial enterprises. Quebec's heart is crowded with so many restored historic dwellings, museums, shops and fine restaurants that even experienced travelers are surprised and delighted.

Montreal, Canada's chief port and richest cultural center, is located around an island at the junction of three bodies of water. This was such a natural point of interchange that when Cartier came upon it in 1535 he found a community of some 3500 Indians living there. These Indians were soon scattered by French settlers, explorers and missionaries who were determined to make this site their Gateway to the West. Doubtless they would be very pleased to know that they founded the second largest French-speaking city in the world.

Montreal's oldest landmark, Place Royale, is said to have been named by Champlain. The foundations of the city laid here in 1642 were given the name Ville Marie. The old section also boasts a Place d' Armes, rich with history and memories and with beautiful old streets leading away from it. In the eastern part of the old city are lovely homes, open squares, and an 1834 hotel where Charles Dickens once stayed. Many of these 18th-century dwellings have had French, English and American occupants during the city's varied history.

Modern Montreal is just as much fun to explore. The heart of the city, Centre Town, has shopping streets, business districts, cafes and restaurants and fine hotels. Montreal's underground system, a city in itself, is also worthy of attention. Fascinating tours around the island take you to the former Olympic village and along the banks of the St. Lawrence. Of special note is a view of St. Lambert Lock of the St. Lawrence Seaway, a 9,500-mile network of navigable waters extending into the body of this continent.

AUTHOR'S OBSERVATION

When sailing between New York and Montreal, you'll find a wealth of ports that are best explored by foot. The only places where shore excursions are recommended are Newport (the mansions) and Halifax (Louisburg fort).

The Far East

"Chinese of all ranks are passionately fond of gaming and every street is occupied by gamblers who sometimes carry their infatuation to such height as to stake their wives and children upon a throw of dice."

Universal Traveler, 1848

CHINA

That the world's most populous and intriguing country has been a favored destination for cruise vessels and their passengers is not difficult to understand. The first cruise passengers to visit China in recent times were aboard the *France* in 1974, but the ship docked in Hong Kong harbor, and passengers took the train from Kowloon to Canton for a three-day visit. Two years later, groups from both the *Rotterdam* and *Queen Elizabeth 2* followed the same route.

In February 1977, the Greek vessel *Danae* made cruise ship history by sailing up the Pearl River in the dead of night to dock in Whampoa, the port of **Guangzhou** (Canton). The *Danae* was the first Western passenger ship in twenty-seven years to dock at a People's Republic of China port. Today, in addition to frequent cruise calls, there is twice-daily hydrofoil service from Hong Kong to the port of Whampoa, about a forty-five-minute dusty but fascinating ride from Guangzhou.

At first glance, Guangzhou, with its 3 million inhabitants, looked like a drab, gray version of neighboring Hong Kong. As my initial reaction faded, a sense of the city's character began to appear. This old city, dating from about the third century B.C., has been a center for foreign commerce for more than 2000 years. The Portuguese, the first foreigners to appear in this area, arrived in 1514. By 1557, they had received permission to settle Macau, a province they still occupy (although the Chinese have managed the politics for some years). By the 1860s, foreign traders controlled Guangzhou from the Shamian island on the Pearl River in the heart of the city and remained there until 1949. You will pass by this rather forlorn-looking island many times in your travels about the city. Its once-bulging warehouses and churches have been converted to factories.

Tours of Guangzhou are rather standard and under the control of Luxingshe (China International Travel Service or C.I.T.S.). Visits will be made to the zoo, the largest in China, to see the giant pandas and the aviary, and to Yuexia Park with its artificial lakes and Zhenhai Tower. The tower, constructed in 1380, has a fine view of the city and houses a pottery museum. It is also a good spot to observe the local residents. You will also visit a factory or two, sip tea with the approved spokesperson, and be expected to ask questions about production, birth control and life in China. Lastly, you will be allowed to peer through the iron gate at the Dr. Sun Yat-sen Memorial, dedicated to the father of the Chinese revolution in 1911. He was born in Guangzhou and founded the Kuomintang or Nationalist Party there in 1923.

If you are spending a few days in Guangzhou, you will most likely be accommodated at one of the glamorous new hotels, no longer at the Tung Fang (Dongfang) Hotel, which has huge, old-fashioned rooms, broad red-carpeted stairways and lumpy beds that have mosquito-netting drawn about them each evening. The Tung Fang also has a cavernous dining room where Welcoming Banquets are often held. The Tung Fang is across from a theater, where Chinese opera and acrobatics are performed, and the Canton Trade Fair exhibition halls. If your visit coincides with one of the semiannual fairs (mid-April to mid-May and mid-October to mid-November), by all means request permission of your guides to visit. The fair is China's impressive display to the world of her more than 40,000 products—rooms and rooms of bicycles with the brand name Flying Cloud, sewing machines, sneakers lining four walls, machinery, natural resources, synthetics and silks. Unfortunately, as a tourist, you cannot buy at the fair. Your shopping must be done either at the local Friendship Store or department store. Guangzhou also has a nice antique shop, but the guides again must be persuaded to let you stop here. While many of the items are what I would call antiqued rather than antique, the shop has some charming mementos.

The most famous restaurant for tourists in Guangzhou is the **Ban Xi** (also spelled Pan Hsi), a series of old tea houses connected by zigzagging bridges around and across an ornamental lake. Ban Xi is known for its dim sum, or little dumplings, and seems to serve an endless variety. One guide told me gleefully of a Japanese who dined there every day for a week and still did not exhaust the menu. If you think China is a classless society, your thoughts will fly away at the Ban Xi. The pavilions cater to different clientele workers in one area, party members in another, while foreigners are served in a new, two-story pavilion overlooking a lake. As in all Chinese banquets, a sweet and a fiery wine for toasts, beer and orange soda are the refreshments, followed by tea. But the desserts here are the best, especially the little cakes filled with chestnut puree and dusted with sesame seeds. A take-out service is just to the side of the entry hall.

Everything that has ever been written about **Shanghai** must be true, for this is one of the world's most fascinating cities. While today's Shanghai is a far cry from the notorious, bad old days of the 1930s and 1940s when sailors were shanghaied, China's largest city and port has lost none of her excitement.

Her eleven million or so inhabitants (who own and ride some two million bicycles) spread themselves out along the Huangpu, or Yellow River, while the mighty Yangtze is just twelve miles upstream. Shanghai is still the center of China's trade and industry a role that began with the Treaty of Nanking, which granted the British certain territorial trading rights in 1840. From then until the 1940s, the foreign communities lived in large mansions encircled and protected by their concessions (Shanghai International Settlement). So it is not surprising that the Chinese Communist party was founded in Shanghai in 1921 by, among others, a young student named Mao Tse-tung.

Because Shanghai has seen ships come from all over the world with goods and people, it has always been China's most cosmopolitan city. Shops are full of pretty things. Young girls wear colored ribbons in their hair and flowered blouses . Couples hold hands in public and smile as you pass by. Your cruise vessel docks within sight of the Bund, that wide boulevard along the water's edge with handsome European-style buildings. From the deck of your ship you will recognize the former Palace Hotel (now called Peace) with its bronze-green roof and pointed tower. Once the most palatial hotel in the East (and owned by a prominent British family), it carries on as a survivor of the past, with old-fashioned rooms and atmosphere. Pay this place a visit if only to look at the sign that says Ping Pong Room (next to the Barber Shop). The coffee shop serves real coffee and cakes plus some fantastic-looking and intriguingly named cocktails that I did not try. The eighth-floor dining room has a great view of the harbor. Peek in next door at the banquet rooms, where high-level meetings are held.

Other buildings along the Bund once housed foreign banks and trading companies. The Bank of China now has the large building next to the Peace Hotel, and farther down is the Customs House, with a 100-foot clock tower that chimes East is Red at least every hour.

AUTHOR'S OBSERVATION

Behind the Bund is the real Shanghai, with narrow, winding alleys lined with low houses, tile roofs curving up at the corners, built around mysterious looking courtyards. This is the Shanghai to explore, and you're perfectly safe to do so at all hours (although the city locks up early in the evening).

Your ship is so convenient to the city that you can walk up to the Bund in a few minutes or call a taxi from the guard house (if you know where you are going and can speak a little Chinese). Walk along the Bund in the early morning when thousands gather to do their tai-chi exercises. In the evening, musical instruments and singing can be heard floating over the river. My favorite memories of Shanghai are of just standing along the Bund embankment, surrounded by curious but friendly Chinese, watching the parade of boats in the harbor.

Your organized tour of Shanghai will include a factory or two, a school or Children's Palace and the Yu Yuan (Mandarin's Garden), which was built from 1559 to 1577 for Pan Yuntuan, an official of the Ming Dynasty. Although always very crowded, the garden is worth your time and is a preview of the wonderful imperial gardens you will probably visit in Suzhou (Soochow). At the restored Temple of the Jade Buddha, or Yu Fo Si, you will encounter large groups of devout Overseas Chinese (Chinese who do not live in mainland China). Shopping in Shanghai is, to me, the most fun of any city in China not only because of the variety of tempting and inexpensive gifts but also because the clerks are so friendly and helpful. The best place to shop is the Number One Department Store, the largest in the country, just around the corner from the Guoji or International Hotel. This store has floors and floors of jade, jewelry, bamboo flutes, sandalwood fans and other Oriental treasures. On the ground floor, among household items of the cheapest quality, I found some wonderful, cream-filled vanilla cookies for a few cents a pound. At a store next to the Friendship Hotel, a dozen hand-embroidered linen handkerchiefs cost but a few dollars. A friend bought some lovely chopsticks, but we had to draw pictures of rice bowls and the like to get our point across. And down on the Bund where the British Embassy used to be is the state-managed Friendship Store with glorious items from expensive rugs to T-shirts with the simple character that says Shanghai.

AUTHOR'S OBSERVATION

In 1995, you'll find two new companies–Victoria Cruises and Regal Cruises–with a total of nine new European-style river boats sailing Yangtze River.

The upstream voyage begins in Shanghai, along the Huangpu River to **Wusong**, where the **Yangtze River** begins. The first night and following day are spent at **Zhenjiang** in Jiangsu Province, where ancient temples are located on islands in the river or up on hills overlooking them. Opposite Zhenjiang on the north bank is the delightful city of **Yangzhou**, full of gardens and temples, as well as some of China's most famous handicraft and art workshops.

A full day of sightseeing is scheduled for the city of **Nanjing**, famous for its Dr. Sun Yat-sen Mausoleum, the Nanjing Museum and the Yangtze River Bridge. Nearby, you can visit Ming Tombs whose sacred ways are lined with huge stone statues of animals.

An entire day is spent cruising through Anhui Province, enjoying the peace and quiet of the vessel and the passing scenery of small towns and bustling markets. A late afternoon arrival at **Jiujiang** allows time for a stroll. The following morning means a drive to Guling at the top of **Mt. Lushan**, one of China's most renowned resort areas. Here, you can visit the Lushan Botanical Garden, the Immortal's Grotto and the Floral Path, and generally absorb the mountain scenery.

Wuhan, one of China's most important shipping hubs, lies at the confluence of the Yangtze and its largest tributary, the Han River. Sightseeing tours are scheduled for each of the city's three sectors: Wuchang, Hanyang and Hankou. In contrast, **Yueyang** is celebrated for its lovely Dongting Lake, which has been the subject of numerous Chinese poems and paintings. Following a day visiting **Shashi** and **Jingzhou**, your vessel arrives early the next morning at **Yichang**. Here, you will see the mammoth Gezhouba hydroelectric power dam and ancient sites around the city, before the piéce de résistance of the Yangtze River. This is the spectacular cruise through Three Gorges, one of the most memorable stretches of river scenery in the world.

After a short tour of **Wanxi** in Szechuan Province the next morning, the vessel sails for **Shibao Block** and another highlight of the cruise. This tiny rural town has narrow streets and very friendly folk. You can visit the nine-story pavilion in the center before climbing up to the ancient temple at the top of a sheer cliff for a view of the Yangtze and surrounding region.

Chongqing is located on a rocky promontory at the confluence of the Yangtze and Jialing rivers. With its traditional atmosphere of a Chinese city, it is a fitting finale to this wonderful cruise up the Yangtze River. (Note: the one-week sailings transport you between Wuhan and Chongqing, considered the most scenic stretch.) Guilin (formerly Kweilin) is located in the southwestern section of China, and many travelers consider it one of the most beautiful spots in the world. A bit off the beaten track, it is situated in a valley on the Li River and reachable from the major gateways by air, although misty weather often means delayed flights. However, if you have time for a two-day stopover, it may be the highlight of your China tour as the scenery is spectacular. It is rather like a gentle cruise through an ancient Chinese painting.

Xian has become another side trip worthy of effort, for it is here that a vast imperial tomb was discovered in 1974 to contain a veritable army of terra cotta soldiers and horses that had lain buried for at least 2000 years. It is known as the longest graveyard in the world, although only about 6000 of the estimated 65,000 figures have been unearthed to date. Picture taking is forbidden, alas, but there are plenty of publications on the subject available back home.

Tianjin (Tientsin) is China's third largest city after Peking and Shanghai and like them is under direct control of the central government. The city possesses a fine harbor, built during the Japanese occupation of 1937 to 1945, which is often the getaway for cruise passengers to the North China Plain.

An important industrial center, the city is home of the famous Tientsin carpet, said to have originated in 200 B.C. Some eight major factories produce about 150,000 square yards of carpet each per year, and no foreign visitor departs this city without a tour of the Number One Carpet factory, employing more than 1400 people. This is the most interesting factory tour in China, for it allows you to follow the production of a carpet from beginning to end and justifies the price all the more. (If you plan to buy a carpet here, advise your guide. You may be able to purchase one at the factory, or you may be directed to a Friendship Store.) Tianjin also has a fine zoo, an antique shop (highly overpriced), several new and very comfortable western-style hotels. The seventy-four-mile trip to Peking takes about one and a half hours on the train. The trip is a great adventure, especially if you are required to set your alarm for 4 a.m. and 5 a.m., as I was, to make the connections.

The center of **Beijing** (Peking) is Tien An Men Square, now well known for the students' protest, an area that covers almost one hundred acres and accommodates as many as a million people for the May Day festivities. Chances are your first view of Beijing will be from this square, which has the Monument to the People's Heroes in the center. Standing in this vast area, one senses the continuity of China through all her warring periods and revolution. Bounding the northern end of the square is Tien An Men, or the Gate of Heavenly Peace, which contains five passages leading across five marble bridges to five gateways and the Imperial or Old Forbidden City. On the western side is the Great Hall of the People, where the National People's Congress meets and visiting dignitaries are honored in the 5000-seat banqueting hall. On the east end is a large building housing the Museum of the Revolution (in the left wing) and the Museum of Chinese Hichay (in the right wing). But the most impressive structure is the Chairman Mao Tse-tung Memorial Hall, completed in November 1977 after only ten months construction time. If you are in luck, the Memorial Hall may be open and the Chairman able to receive visitors. Leave all belongings on the tour bus and file silently by.

All touring in Beijing is, of course, under the direction of the C.I.T.S., which has taken Chinese interests into consideration when planning your activities.

Fortunately, excursions are confined to exciting historical monuments and you are free from the obligations of visiting hospitals, schools, factories and the like. A half-day is set aside for touring the Temple of Heaven (Tien Tan) and the Forbidden City, where you can easily get lost for several hours. Another half-day will be spent driving to the Summer Palace, about forty-five minutes from the center of Beijing. Since the 12th century, the Imperial Court transported itself to this area during the summer to avoid the city heat, and the Summer Palace (Yiheyuan) grew into a sumptuous playground for the aristocracy. The 650-acre area has an enormous man-made lake for boating, pavilions with such names as Orderly Clouds, Joy and Longevity, Virtue and Harmony, and the famous Marble Boat that the Empress Dowager Tzu Hsi commissioned in 1890 with funds intended to expand the Chinese navy.

The highlight of any visit to China is a climb on the **Great Wall**, Wan Li Chang Chen, or the Long Wall of Ten Thousand Li (about

3000 miles). A comfortable tourist train or motorcoach whisks you from Beijing Station to Badaling, just over two hours away, with tea going and lunch returning. The scenery is spectacular as the train winds up into the Yian Mountain chain, and soon you see sections of the ancient wall undulating along the crests, between flowering trees in the foreground and snow-capped peaks in the distance. Just before Badaling the train stops (for quick leg stretches and photographs) and then backs into the station. After a brisk twenty-minute walk from the station to the reconstructed section of the wall, the stiff climb begins, in the company of thousands of others from all over China and the world. The right-hand section (as you face the wall) is less steep and therefore more popular with first-time visitors. And when you arrive at the top tower you'll know it, for a sign tells you (in Russian, Chinese and English) not to go any further. Indeed, the unreconstructed part of the wall is exceedingly dangerous. (The wall is slippery, so flat shoes with a tread are recommended. It can also be very windy, so hats, scarves and windbreakers should be worn and taken off as you warm up. Layers of clothing are very important here.)

Some tours combine the **Ming Tombs** with the Great Wall. This makes for a long and arduous day, but it's better than to miss something. The Ming Tombs are in the foothills of Beijing, where the wind and water (Feng Shui) were considered favorable to enjoying the hereafter. This beautiful and peaceful area adjoins a huge reservoir that Chairman Mao is said to have helped build (as he also supervised the restoration of the Forbidden City, Summer Palace and parts of the Great Wall). Entrance to the tombs is through the Avenue of the Animals, perhaps the most photographed stone carvings in China. The tomb generally visited is Ting Ling, or Tomb of Emperor Wan Li (1573-1620). The tomb itself is rather a disappointment, but the setting, especially the large square red tower and landscaping, is impressive. And do not miss the two small museums flanking the tower, which portray a chronology of the excavations of the tomb, as well as some of the treasures found—delicately beaten gold objects, silk brocades and money.

No one leaves Beijing without a visit to the three-tiered Friendship Store and a sumptuous meal of the renowned Peking Duck. The Friendship Store on Chang An Jie caters to foreigners and thus has silk pajamas, dresses and T-shirts in all sizes. It also sells such items as Happy Brain Pills, Flying Pigeon bicycles, handpainted silk fans (for twenty-five cents apiece), rugs, furniture, food and liquor. Not far from the Beijing Hotel, on Wangfujing, is a good handcrafts store, a fur shop and a bookstore with revolutionary posters. Good antique shops line Liu Li Chang, or Glazed Tile Works Street, but again, be sure you differentiate between what is antique and what has been antiqued.

Beijing can also boast a bevy of new hotels, including The Great Wall Hotel, Fragrant Hill (designed by Chinese-American architect I. M. Pei) and others that will remind you of Hyatt, Sheraton and Hilton, for good reasons. Accommodations will never be as comfortable or homelike as the ship on which you are cruising, but you will have an adventure, which is what travel is all about! If you wish, you may even attempt the new Maxim's de Paris in Beijing and the growing list of discos that seem to be sprouting like crazy!

The most popular Peking Duck restaurant (and the one you will most likely visit) is known as the Big Duck by locals as opposed to another called the Sick Duck, because it is near a hospital. The feast here seems to go on forever, even before one comes to the platters of crisp, sliced duck served with green onions, brown sauce, sesame buns, or pancakes. For dessert come platters of sizzling apple fritters and bowls of cold water. To consume the delicacy, dip the hot fritter into the cold water and then immediately pop it into your mouth. It's perfectly wonderful!

It is easy to get around Beijing on your own, provided your guide is obliging and you have the time to explore or to visit friends. There are tourist buses at Beijing Station, a subway system, taxis for hire at the large hotels and your own reliable feet or you can do as the local inhabitants (both Chinese and foreign) do and hire a bicycle. But it's best to discuss any personal plans with your guide. The Chinese are easily offended by our abrupt Western ways and prefer to lead a harmonious group in which everyone does and sees the same thing.

The appropriate clothing for a China tour is just the opposite of what you would wear on board ship. You may need two wardrobes. As there are no formal evenings, long dresses and jewelry should be left on board. Casual, washable slacks, skirts and sweaters, or jackets and blouses are best for daytime wear, with something a bit nicer for evening. If you're staying in hotels in China, the laundry facilities are good for men but I wouldn't use them for most ladies' wear. As you will be walking a great deal, as well as climbing on and off buses and trains, daytime shoes should be low-heeled and comfortable again with something a tiny bit fancier for the evening. And then there's the climate. Beijing is bitter cold in the winter, rainy and cold in the spring, and hot as Hades in the summer. Autumn is pleasant. At any time, dress in layers that can be increased or decreased as the temperatures change.

China is a photographer's paradise. If you intend to take many pictures, discuss your trip with a good camera shop. Because of frequent indoor shooting and many fascinating subjects seen from moving buses and trains, you may have best results with high-speed film (400 ASA) for both prints and slides. If you want to draw a crowd quickly, take along a Polaroid-type camera. It's the best device yet for making fast friends anywhere in the world!

HONG KONG

It is an adventure to sail into **Hong Kong**, Jewel of the Orient, that 403-square-mile British Crown Colony sitting on the southern coast of China. Hong Kong is a dazzling collage of modern skyscrapers lining the waterfront and winding their way up the Peak in Victoria; typhoon shelters where untold thousands live out their whole existence on small boats; and nonstop harbor traffic from all over the world. A bustling, dirty city on the sea, it is home to more than five million (no one knows the exact count) people. The majority are Chinese (including more than a million refugees), but just about every nationality is represented here.

Hong Kong has been the brightest jewel in the British crown since 1841; but relations with China, which completely surrounds it, have not always been good. During the years of the Bamboo Curtain, China used the colony as a money exchange (the Bank of China, with its two enormous lion statues, is a landmark). When times were tense, China could have cut off Hong Kong's supply of fresh water and pork. Relations now are friendly, as former British Prime Minister Margaret Thatcher settled the great question that haunted both the Crown and the Colony for a century—who will get Hong Kong at the expiration of the lease in 1997? Well, China won the draw and, after the initial shock, life is still quite the same in Hong Kong, as there has been plenty of time to organize an orderly succession of government and social strata.

Passenger ships dock at the Ocean Terminal complex in the Tsimshatsui section of Kowloon. The clean, well-kept terminal houses a grand bazaar of shops, restaurants, banks, tourist facilities, the Harbour Village with traditional Chinese products and whatever else one desires. One need never leave this three-story building that spills onto the Hong Kong Hotel, but there is much, much more outside. Hong Kong is a walking city, so put on your comfortable shoes the minute you arrive. Five minutes on foot from your cruise ship is Nathan Road, once a famous shopping street, flanked by the fabulous Peninsula Hotel and the Sheraton, the New World Centre and the elegant Regent Hotel. When your feet are tired, God forbid, have a cup of tea in the lobby of the Peninsula where, as the saying goes, you'll see the world pass by and probably everyone you know if you sit long enough.

Two minutes from the terminal in Kowloon is the Star Ferry Building, easily found by its clock tower, where a cross-harbor ferry to Hong Kong Island leaves every few minutes. (Be sure to buy a first-class or upper-deck ticket so you can enjoy the scenery it costs only pennies.) Victoria is the capital of Hong Kong Island, and Central District is its busiest section with deluxe hotels, office buildings and elegant shops. Just behind the Hilton Hotel, another longtime landmark, is the Peak Tram station. The ride up this funny, wooden cog railway is a must because of the lovely residences along the way and the view from the top. Since the 1880s, foreigners and wealthy Chinese have made this former mountain wilderness the place to live, even though it's often fogged in and thoroughly uncomfortable.

At the fishing port of Aberdeen you can eat fresh fish aboard a floating restaurant; or you can take a ferry from Central District (a few minutes walk from the Star terminal) to other islands like Lan Tao or Cheung Chau. Another popular tour is to the New Territories, Hong Kong's only rural countryside (held under that 99-year lease from China that expires in 1997). Most of the land out there is rocky, hilly, or swampy, but you can get a view of the mainland from a lookout point called Lok Ma Chau.

Although Hong Kong is often called the world's number one shopper's paradise, dining out is also continually exciting. Numerous continental restaurants exist, of course, but for Chinese cuisine Hong Kong is the closest thing to heaven. In my opinion, the dishes here are more interesting and tastier than in China because the ingredients are more suited to the Western palate. One of the best restaurants, right near Ocean Terminal, is the Jade Garden in Star House, which seats several hundred hungry customers in a series of rooms. It's especially popular on Sunday afternoons, when whole families eat merrily around tables set up for ten or more. In Hong Kong, you can pick any Cantonese, Hunan, Szechuan and other types of Chinese restaurants by just letting your nose lead the way. If your taste buds shout for Continental food, my choices always include Gaddi's at the Peninsula, Plume at the Hong Kong Regent (nouvelle cuisine and best view in town), Pierrot at the Mandarin (complete with Picasso prints) and Lalique with champagne bar at the Royal Garden. If you're in the mood for a view of the whole colony, go to the top of one of the luxury hotels, all of which have nice cocktail lounges and restaurants (especially the Eagle's Nest at the Hong Kong Hilton).

AUTHOR'S OBSERVATION

As many cruises embark or disembark in Hong Kong, it is definitely worth your while to spend a few days here especially if the ship-line package is reasonable and offers a good hotel. Hong Kong has been building hotels like crazy, but it is still almost impossible to book acccommodation as clothing manufacturers, trade groups, journalists and financiers fly in and out of the colony with regularity.

THE INDONESIAN ARCHIPELAGO

AUTHOR'S OBSERVATION

While cruise ships regularly include major ports in this region on Far East itineraries, those who seek a first hand experience with little-known cultures from a comfortable expedition ship should check out P&O Spice Island Cruises. The company's tiny boats explore remote islands that are inaccessible to conventional cruise ships.

Bali is that paradisiacal island off the eastern tip of Java that you've always wanted to visit and once you have visited, you can't wait to return. It's been called the Morning of the World, but it's not even of this world—it's too peaceful, too perfect. To be on Bali is to be content. Local women walk barebreasted in the street, temple bells tinkle in the breezes and everyday is a Hindu holiday. Life in Bali means a simple sarong, a motorbike and some fruit. It hasn't always been so idyllic. Bali is a Hindu island in a Moslem archipelago, the 13,662 lesser islands and six large ones that make up Indonesia. Ruled by Dutch colonists for 300 years and occupied by the Japanese during World War II, Indonesia announced her independence in 1945. Twenty years of flirtation with Communism under Sukarno ended with one of the worst bloodbaths in modern history—some 300,000 Indonesian communists were killed and whole villages (including some on Bali) were burned to the ground.

The capital of Bali's three million inhabitants is **Denpasar**, a scruffy, touristy town that has no relation to the rest of the island. It does have an art museum and a large market, and large resort hotels are centered on Sanur Beach, a few minutes from town. Despite the influx of Western comforts and customs, the Balinese are adamant about preserving their beautiful island—no building can be higher than a palm tree!

Ubud, about fifteen miles from Denpasar, has long been an artist's colony for both native and foreign craftsmen. Here you can visit the studios of painters who will be delighted that you came to call. The nearby village of **Mas** is famous for the finest woodcarvers in Indonesia. Their sophisticated and stylized figures of polished teak and dark ebony are quite different from the mass productions found in Denpasar. Balinese artisans also make wonderful hand puppets of buffalo parchment for a popular form of entertainment shadow plays, where mythical princes and princesses come to life on a screen while the storyteller chants dialogue from familiar tales.

Entertainment in Bali comes from the temples, so intertwined are religion and theater. Dancing is everywhere and taught by imitation. Although the dances you see are staged for tourists, the impact is not lessened. Two of the most popular are the classical, feminine Legong, the dance of three divine nymphs, and the Ketjak, which features a male chorus of 150 who chant in place of the ever-present gamelon (an Indonesian musical instrument), and who become an army of chattering monkeys at the finale. You will not witness either of these two dances without feeling something of that special spirit that hovers tightly about this island.

Bali is also beautiful mountains and terraced rice fields and Pura Besakih, the sacred temple on the slopes of **Mt. Agung**. The Balinese consider this mountain the navel of the world. It's an active volcano that frets and fumes and last erupted in 1963 (killing several thousand people who were told the gods would take care of them). But wherever you go on Bali, you must leave your cares behind. As a young Balinese once said to me, as he was planning the next day's adventure, "Now leave your sensitive American stomach behind, and we'll have a good time!"

Butung is a small island across the strait from Sulawesi, which once had a reputation for piracy. In fact, the old pirate haunt of Wasuemba can still be seen along the south coast. The inhabitants of Butung are mainly Muslim, who do interesting weavings and copperwork. The capital, **Bau Bau**, is known mainly for the Sultan's residence, built in 1942, which contains some artifacts of the area (skulls, weaponry, china pieces). A nearby mosque was the first built on the island, and it offers a fine view of the sea. Cruise passengers are also treated to some local dances here, and are forewarned that the mode of transportation may be rather primitive. All available vehicles are used, including *bemos* (trucks with benches), antiquated cars and minibuses.

The 200-mile-long mountainous island of **Flores** is inhabited by a population of Malay, Papuan and Portuguese, who have developed their own distinctive cultures. Some two-thirds practice Catholicism, but animism is deeply entrenched, and head-hunting was legal until recently. Villagers dance to celebrate plantings and harvests, weddings and burials. They also make scarecrows to keep away evil spirits. Passengers wishing to enter a village must endure first a welcome ceremony, including a speech and some sort of food and drink. When concluded, visitors may wander around traditional village dwellings.

Larantuka is the administrative center of the eastern end of Flores and a port city in the Portuguese tradition. Here, you will find stone and stucco houses that need a good paint job and a colorful market. Behind the town is Ile Mandiri, a semi-active volcano that boasts the proud village of Lewoleba on its shoulder. You can buy wonderful hand-woven materials here, with designs indigenous to the various clans. Finished products are for sale following weaving demonstrations (and bargaining is certainly expected). Note: Cruise passengers may have to walk up to 50 minutes to the village, if the narrow road is wet and impassable by vehicles.

Komodo is possibly the only island in the world where dragons are said to outnumber people! Indeed, the tiny wildlife island of Komodo is actually a national park and sanctuary for its 3000-strong dragon population. It sounds like an overwhelming number, but their very existence is threatened because only about 300 of the 1500 adult animals are female and they don't mate very often. The Komoda dragon is thought to be a survivor of the prehistoric dinosaurs that once ruled the earth. Up to twelve feet long and 350 pounds in weight, the Komodo is carnivorous, sharp-eyed and keen-nosed. A good hunter, the beast can devour an entire water buffalo without chewing (honest!), and eat its own weight in just seventeen minutes.

In order to view this giant lizard, the creature must be lured from the coziness of its cave by placing a goat (killed the night before) on a stake in a clearing. Before too long (and hopefully as cruise passengers arrive), the Komodo will appear for a snack at the appointed dragon-watching site. However, passengers should be warned that not only is there a wet landing (into the shore from small boats with shoes and camera equipment held overhead), but there is about a

45-minute walk to the viewing area. Hence, passengers should protect themselves from tropical sun or a sudden rain shower and be sure their expensive equipment is covered in plastic during these times. Well, how often do you get to see a real dragon? And even if one does not deign to appear, Komodo itself has a dramatic landscape with 2000-foot mountain peaks and golden green lontor palms. So, the discomfort of visiting the island is not a total loss.

The island of **Java** is the fifth largest in the Indonesian archipelago (after Kalimantan, Sumatra, Irian Jaya and Sulawesi), yet has always been the most dynamic force in the Republic in terms of commerce and culture. About 80 million people live on Java, some 5 million of them in the capital city of **Jakarta**. They consist primarily of Javanese, but a good number of Sudanese live in the western part and some Madurese in the eastern section. Jakarta, once called Batavia by the Dutch traders who arrived in 1619 and stayed around for almost 325 years, is the seamy capital and usually only graced with a half-day tour by most cruise passengers. You will pass by the Bridge of Sighs in the restored port section (Taman Fatahilla), as well as the remains of the Kasteel or fortress. A must visit is made to the Wayang Museum, housed in an old Dutch house, and perhaps there will be a demonstration of the kulit (shadow play) or golek (puppets in the round) show in the courtyard. A drive through the Medan Medeka area, with Sukarno's self-styled tributes, and to the Istiqlal Mosque complete the city tour. The mosque, one of the largest in Southeast Asia, has a celestial white dome and most unusual minaret.

If you plan to stay in Jakarta, the two top hotels are the Hilton and Mandarin, and there are some excellent restaurants around the city. Shopping is also terrific here, especially at the showroom of Iwan Tirta and at the handicraft center. Pasar Baru has fabrics at a song and Pasar Barung is famous for birdcages. Watch out for antiques, as many may only be antiqued while the authentic may not be exported.

Some cruise vessels stop in the port of **Semarang** for a two-day optional excursion to the cultural capital of Java, as well as two of its most famous religious monuments. **Yogyakarta** is a small city of approximately 400,000 that lies at the foot of an active volcano. Some Javanese believe that it lies in the realm of the dead because of its location. Yogyakarta is famous for its handicrafts, especially batik, and many artisans have congregated here to work and live together. They have truly elevated the making of batik to a national art, and you can find not only lovely saronglike fabrics but one-of-akind batik paintings. These are meant to be framed in wood and lit from behind; obviously, they make a wonderful gift or souvenir.

However, the cultural and political life of Jogja (as knowledgeables pronounce it) is the palace of the Sultan. Begun in 1797, it is a maze of courtyards and apartments that now feature handicraft workshops, schools for dance, two museums and a population of about 25,000 people. Visitors are welcome to see the Golden Pavilion, finished in 1792, with its solid teak pillars, and the Glass Pavilion, with its Hindu motifs and Buddhist lotus flowers and writings from the Koran. The Glass Pavilion is furnished European-style, but also houses a collection of royal palanquins, sedan chairs and antique gamelan instruments.

Jogja is definitely the home of Wayang Kulit puppets, which are used to tell tales from the Ramayana. A dalang, or puppeteer, sits behind a lighted screen and the shadowy puppets move across to carry along the tale. *Wayang* means shadow, and the origins of these puppets is traced to animistic beliefs that shadows are the manifestations of ancestral spirits.

The Hindu temple of **Prambanan** stands in a village just outside Jogja. It was completed around A.D. 900 in classic Indian architectural style, but was deserted about 100 years later and collapsed in ruins around 1600. Restoration of the central temple, the masterpiece dedicated to Siva (known as the slender virgin), began in 1918 and was completed in 1953. In addition to having a glorious symmetry and grace, Prambanan is known for its wealth of sculptural detail especially on the base of the main terrace. Here, a menagerie of charming creatures, groups of singers and dancers and Ramayana episodes all enchant the onlooker.

One of the world's great Buddhist monuments and the largest ancient structure in Southeast Asia is **Borobudur**, about a forty-five minute drive from Yogyakarta. Borobudur was begun at the beginning of the 8th century A.D., under the direction of a ruler of the Sailendra dynasty. Completed about a century later, the monument took the labor of 10,000 men and an estimated 2 million cubic feet of stone; the building was supervised by priests of the Vajrayana sect to which the shrine is a testament. Indeed, every aspect of the structure is full of religious symbolism. Forgotten for nearly 1000 years, it was found by a local prince at the turn of the 19th century. In 1815, Sir Thomas Stamford Raffles inspected the site, had it cleared of the jungle and properly surveyed. Proper restoration began only in 1973, partly under the auspices of UNESCO, but more importantly, with aid from business concerns around the world. IBM, among them, offered computers on which each stone was programmed for replacement in exactly the correct spot.

Surabaya is Java's second port/city and is often called The City of Heroes, for its role in the Indonesian struggle for independence. Otherwise, the city is known for some traditional arts and as a port of entry for shore excursions to Yogyakarta or the island of Madura. Just across the strait, **Madura** is the home of the *kerapan sapi*, or bull races. These unusual events can be attended throughout the months of August and September in Pamekasan (the capital of the island) and nearby Sampang by those that like that sort of thing.

Pare Pare is a seaport and the second largest town on the island of **Sulawesi**, and a cruise port for overnight shore excursions to the village of Tana Toradja. About 100 bumpy miles north of the port, **Tana Toradja** rises to some 5000 feet above sea level in one of the most beautiful landscapes in all of Indonesia. The village is inhabited by descendents of an ancient race of Proto Malayan stock, who believe they are all children of the king of gods and one huge family. (Tana Toradja means Land of Heavenly Kings.)

The Toradjas are a study in primitive culture, and their ways have long fascinated travelers. Despite the narrow, treacherous mountain route to the village, you will not leave disappointed unless you run out of film. The dwellings lend much to photography, for they look like richly ornamented ships afloat on seas of ripening rice. They are great arklike structures with geometrical designs, and there is a life-size wood carving of a buffalo (symbol of fertility) at every door. They are built facing north and in such a way that they can be moved in one piece from place to place. Always built on stilts (the cool underneath area is for animals). Only wood, rattan and bamboo materials may be used.

These villagers also believe in eternal life and they make much of funerals or festivals of joy, as they call them. Funerals are postponed until sufficiently opulent ceremonies can be staged, with several buffalo slaughtered. Final burial takes place in caves or hanging graves chiseled from the volcanic cliffs. Life-size wooden effigies are placed at the graves, which make for an eerie sight. About half the Toradjas adhere to the ancestral Aluk Todolo animist religion, while the others are either Christians or Muslims. All in all, this is an overnight excursion that only the most adventurous would appreciate!

Sumatra is Indonesia's largest island and stretches more than one thousand miles from the Andaman Sea to the Sunda Strait. In the northern end of the island, the main port of entry is Belawan, just off the Strait of Malacca. This port is easily accessible to **Medan**, the capital city, which has very little to offer the tourist. Rather, most visitors head straight for **Lake Toba** for an overnight in Parapat. Attractions around this beautiful lake in the highlands include Samosir Island and the Batak Toba villages. If your cruise vessel sails around to **Padang**, the main port for West Sumatra, you will have a lovely drive down and some interesting views of the Indonesian Ocean perhaps even a swim on the beach.

JAPAN

Your cruise ship will come alongside Osambashi, or South Pier, in **Yokohama**; if it's a clear day (and you're very lucky), you may be able to see Mt. Fuji, Japan's highest and most sacred mountain in the distance. Fuji-san, as the Japanese call it, is considered one of the two most beautiful conical volcanoes in the world (the other is Mt. Cotopaxi in Ecuador). But the volcano has not been active for more than 200 years, and Mt. Fuji has served as the favorite subject matter of poets and artists throughout Japan.

As a gateway for visitors to Tokyo and northern Honshu, Yokohama is a cosmopolitan port, although only opened to foreign trade since 1859. Twice devastated in this century (the 1923 earthquake and the 1945 air raids), it is now a city of three million inhabitants, including a large foreign community who add character from their homes up on The Bluff, their boutiques on Motomachi and their bargain shops in Isezaki-cho. This is the shopping center of Yokohama, where the prices are less and the stores even more swinging than on Tokyo's Ginza.

A short cruise call, alas, cannot do justice to this Land of the Rising Sun. You will, though, enjoy a small but delectable taste of what is meant when inhabitants say We Japanese. This nation flowered as early as the 6th century, when Prince Shotoku made his Constitution of Seventeen Articles and encouraged culture and education. Chronicles of the 7th and 8th centuries are still around, as well as the Manyoshu, a collection of some 4500 poems. Todaiji, a temple in Nara, has a repository holding some 9000 art treasures made by Japanese craftsmen or brought from around the world. Each subsequent century, in this floating world that was Old Japan, was more fruitful than the last. During the late 16th century, or Momoyama Period, Japanese arts flourished as never before, and these are the very arts you see and buy today. The tea ceremony, or chanoyu, was raised to the dignity of a national art. Kabuki, Noh, Bunraku and other theater forms developed. Flower arranging became a national pastime and paintings on scrolls and screens reached new grandeur. Today, Japan is industrialized and computerized but, with all the changes, traditional arts are just as important to everyday life as they became during the Momoyama Period.

Tokyo has been the administrative capital of Japan since 1603, when it was known as Edo. But because of natural and man-made disasters, the only thing remaining from this time is in the center of Nihonbashi, an iron post that was used as a highway measure up until World War II. This sprawling, bustling metropolis has a daytime population of about 20 million. (Avoid train and subway stations during the morning and evening rush hours. Pushers on the train platforms pack the cars with commuters, and it's not very comfortable, to say the least. And never try to walk against the flow of traffic in a train station, or you'll be knocked flat.) Many visitors to Tokyo are a little afraid of the city and find it cold and impersonal. But, aside from the gray older buildings like the Imperial Diet and Library, Tokyo is just a series of small towns linked together. Many areas have not changed much in character since the turn of the century.

One of my favorite monuments in Japan is Meiji Shrine, a place of pilgrimage for the Japanese because it honors Emperor Meiji (and his empress), who opened Japan to the rest of the world in 1869 and encouraged Western ideas and social and land reforms. This Shinto shrine, destroyed in World War II but rebuilt in the 1950s, has beautiful gardens where you can enjoy every type of Japanese tree and flower. In the spring, the *sakura* (cherry blossoms) are overwhelming; in summer, a large iris garden boasts a hundred different varieties; and autumn brings pots and pots of *kiku* (chrysanthemums) along the paths. Even in winter the Meiji Shrine is not a bad place, for the days are sunny and bright and all the trees have been wrapped in burlap against the cold. You'll see many young couples spending the day at the shrine. You will also find couples and families enjoying Ueno Park, once the estate of a Daimyo and now a huge complex of museums, gardens, temples, a zoo, a pond and even a pagoda. Nearby is the popular Asakusa Kannon Temple, founded in the 7th century by three fishermen, and now surrounded by one of Tokyo's many entertainment areas the path to the temple is lined with souvenir shops.

Save some energy and money for the crowded Ginza, the famous silver street, lined with shops (where sweet-faced girls with white gloves bow and welcome you to each floor) and billboards. Stop in at the Sony Building and see what the latest invention is. If you're interested in Kabuki, the Kabukiza is just off the Ginza, and you may wander in for an hour or so and then leave. Everyone does, especially in the afternoon. The best actors play in the evening. Don't miss the Imperial Palace plaza where swans float in the moats. You cannot visit the Imperial Palace because the emperor and empress live there, but the grounds are open to the public on January 2 (New Year's) and April 29 (the emperor's birthday and a national holiday). You may enjoy day trips to Nikko, a national park in the mountains north of Tokyo that is famous for Toshogu Shrine, and to Hakone in the west, another national park with hot springs, where the views of Mt. Fuji are the best.

Gateway to the western part of Japan and situated on the edge of the beautiful Inland Sea, **Kobe** has been an important port since Chinese and Korean cultural emissaries arrived in the 4th century. Kobe is a delight, has a sister-city relationship with Marseilles and Seattle and is famous for Kobe beef and the choice Nada sake (Japanese rice wine). Kobe is the starting point for luxury steamers that ply the Inland Sea, carrying sightseers to such interesting places as Beppu (a famous hot spring), Takamatsu, Shikoku, Shodo and Awaji islands. The area is dominated by Mt. Rokko, which you can ascend by cable car for a lovely view of the bay and sea.

But Kobe is also known as a cruise port for the new breed of two-week China/Korea sailings that embark or disembark here. Not far by train or car are the historic sites of Nara and Kyoto. **Nara**, capital of Japan from 710 to 784, is noted for beautiful temples and shrines. The most famous is Kofukuji, or Happiness-Producing Temple, which boasted 175 buildings at the height of its prosperity. All that remains is the reconstructed Kondo, or Main Hall, with a wooden image of Sakyamuni, now registered as an Important Cultural Property. The Five-Story Pagoda is another National Treasure (first built in 730 and rebuilt in 1426). My favorite spot is Kasuga Shrine, built in 768 by a member of the Fujiwara family, the most powerful in Japan (because, among other things, they supplied wives for the emperors), it consists of four small shrines painted in vermilion and built in the Kasuga style of architecture in a serene wooded setting. Don't leave Nara without feeding the deer that roam under the Japanese cedar, oak and wisteria. And walk over to nearby Sarusawa Pond, where the Five-Story Pagoda is often reflected in the still water. Japan's oldest existing temple is Horyuji, built in 607 just outside Nara.

Horyuji, regarded as the fountainhead of Japanese art and culture, is headquarters for the Shotoku sect of Buddhism, named in honor of the progressive Prince Shotoku (574-622). Horyuji consists of several large buildings: Nandaimon (Great South Gate), Kondo (Main Hall), Shoryoin (Sacred Spirit Hall), Yumedono (Hall of Dreams) and a Five-Story Pagoda considered one of the oldest buildings in the world.

Temples and more will entice you to **Kyoto**, where the spirit of old Japan prevails. From Kyoto (cultural capital since 794), the country's arts flowed for more than ten centuries. Although it is Japan's fifth largest city and an important industrial center, Kyoto still exudes so much charm that visitors consider the city the culmination of their entire Japanese experience. Birthplace of most Japanese arts and crafts, it is also the center of the silk industry, and its Gion, or Pleasure Quarter, has worldwide fame. The Gion section, near the Kamo River, where dyed silks were once a common sight drying on the banks, is enchanting by day and night. The quarter is lined with wonderful restaurants offering traditional Japanese dishes, as well as many different noodle shops. Gion is also the home of the Geisha, or Art Lady, who has trained since childhood in the subtle and refined ways of entertainment. The Geisha house is a very respectable place to be seen, although the cost of being so well taken care of for a few hours is almost prohibitive (and always was so, even in ancient Japan). If you are lucky enough to attend a Geisha party (Western women are welcome), it's a delightful experience. During the presentation of the meal, the Geisha and her Maiko (young assistant) will attend to your every wish, filling your tiny cup of sake over and over, even helping you manage the *o hashi* (chopsticks). All the while, you may admire her elegant kimono, powdered neck and face, sparkling white *tabi* (socks with one toe) and symbolic, ornamented wig. When the meal is finished, the Geisha and her assistant will sing, play the *koto* and dance. The real fun begins as they entice guests to join in dances both nice and naughty. There is the Tanko-bushi (coal miner's dance), the Bon dance, the very naughty Ykuyuken (wading dance) and the Japanese baseball dance. It's all orchestrated to break the ice, so to speak, rather like charades or word games at a formal dinner. When the party is over, the Geisha will bow you gracefully from the room and return to her private quarters to await the next assignment or perhaps have a private visit with her patron.

Kyoto was laid out in checkerboard fashion, a plan taken from the Chinese and originally called Heian-kyo (peaceful, tranquil capital), but the name was appropriately changed to Kyoto (capital city) because there was constant infighting in ancient Japan between church (the many Buddhist sects) and state (the imperial court). None of the temples was destroyed during World War II because the Allied forces agreed to save the irreplaceable culture from the ravages of war. Kiyomizudera, or waterfall temple, is everyone's favorite and most closely spans the history of the city itself. It was never aligned with any one sect and survived by managing to remain on friendly terms with all. Approached by a long series of shop-lined steps, the temple has a superb view of the city from the top. For centuries the Japanese have made pilgrimages here and even bathed in the falling waters (brrrh). If you are a gardener, Kyoto will enchant you with wonderful gardens, each evoking its own particular mood, within which are endless variations according to the weather, the season and the number of visitors treading its path. If you linger long enough, a garden will change its mood as a bird flies in to perch, a pine needle falls, or a few raindrops alter the pattern raked in sand and bounce on the lily-strewn pond.

The gardens in Kyoto are often more memorable than the temples they adjoin.

The garden at Ryoanji is famous for its rock symbolizing mountains, islands and fierce animals. The garden of Ginkakuji (silver pavilion temple) epitomizes the spirit of Zen. The garden at Nijo Castle was designed without trees, so the shogun would not be saddened by the sight of passing seasons. Nijo, in the center of Kyoto, on part of the site of the original Imperial Palace, was built in the 16th century (so it is not even old by Japanese standards) for the Tokugawa shoguns, and its wooden pavilions have exceptionally beautiful carvings and paintings of the period. What I like best are the squeaky floors, intended to warn the shogun of anyone approaching.

Kyoto is memorable any time of the year spring means cherry blossoms at the Heian Shrine; summer, willow trees at Uji Bridge; fall, chrysanthemums; and winter snowflakes dusting the swans on Shinsen-en pond.

MALAYSIA

Penang is a relaxing, charming resort city with beautiful beaches and the blend of four cultures Malay, Indian, Chinese and Thai with British overtones in its white, colonial architecture and civic monuments. It's an island-city where life hasn't moved along that fast since the turn of the century. Once you disembark, there is no need to rush about because the tourist attractions are few. Hire a trishaw (a rickshaw that is peddled) and drive along Campbell and Carnarvon streets, where you can find goods from all over Asia. This is a so-called Free Port, which means the prices should be low, but compare before you buy. Above all, enjoy the local color of street hawkers, beautiful women in saris with their children, and old men falling asleep on the curbside. Indeed, one wonders how anything ever gets done in Penang since half the population seems to be having a snooze.

Fort Cornwallis is a pleasant spot in town and great for photographs, along with another colonial landmark, the Eastern and Oriental Hotel, where you can have a cool drink in the palm-fringed lobby or out on the lawn overlooking the harbor. For a view of the colonial side of Penang, take a drive through the old residential area where lovely large homes were built long ago for the British military and civil servants.

Penang has many Chinese temples (including a Snake Temple), Buddhist statues and other religious monuments. My favorite outing is the funicular up Penang Hill for the lush view and a cool drink on the lawn of the restaurant/hotel. Penang Hill is one of the mountain retreats founded by the British in Malaysia and frequented during the oppressive summer heat. If you prefer beautiful beaches, tell the taxi driver to take you to Batu Ferringhi (Foreigner Mile), about 20 minutes out of town. Here you'll find lovely white sand, swaying palms, and casual, family-style hotels where Americans seek solace from the oil fields of Indonesia.

Port Klang is the point of entry off the Strait of Malacca for Malaysia's beautiful capital city, **Kuala Lumpur**. The Klang River connects the two, but no doubt your ship will rest in port while you drive into K.L., as everyone calls it. This is one of the greenest and most charming cities in all of Southeast Asia, and may God please keep the developers away! Here you can view local tigers in the National Zoo, the Selangor Turf Club with its fabulous race course, the National Mosque, the Moorish-style railway station and other structures built under British rule in the late 19th century, and the Padang in front of the Selangor Club. Many sections of K.L. still have a colonial ambience, but there are enough Rolls Royces on the roads to bring you back to modern times. (The country is rather oil rich.) A day spent in K.L. is pure pleasure!

PHILIPPINES

The Philippines stretch some 1100 miles with a staggering 7107 islands, although 94 percentage of the land area and population occupy only 11 islands. This nation of great natural resources and as yet unrealized industrial potential has too much disparity between rich and poor, understandable social unrest and a potboiler political situation. Nonetheless, **Manila** is a romantic and historic capital edging a beautiful bay, an exotic mix of Malay, Spanish and American influences. The Philippines were discovered, more or less, by Magellan in 1521 and, after colonization by the Spanish in 1571, were named for Philip II. For more than 300 years, Spanish rule influenced culture, architecture and religion. Then, following the Spanish-American War, the islands were ceded to the United States in 1898. After Japanese occupation during World War II, the Republic of the Philippines was proclaimed on July 4, 1946. Americans added a legacy of English to Spanish and Tagalog (the local dialect) and the idea of democracy as a way of life.

Port calls to the Philippines will increase as the political situation stabilizes. It's a wonderful country and its people are warm and friendly. They deserve a new lease on life, and, one hopes, the new regime will allow them that.

The Filipinos have given us two lifetime joys—terrific dance bands and the *barong Tagalog*, a loose-fitting, long-sleeved shirt that Filipinos wear from morning to night to keep cool in this hot climate. The more elegant variety is perfectly acceptable in place of coat and tie at the best restaurants and nightclubs. Leave your heavies behind on the ship when you dock in Manila, and head for the nearest shop—the styles have been modified to include pants suits and shirtwaist dresses for women, too.

Your first view of Manila will probably be from the Rizal Monument in the Luneta, a large park along the water. Rizal, a national hero and pride of the Malay people, was executed here in 1896, becoming the first Asian martyr to have opposed Western colonization. The Luneta faces Roxas Boulevard, the city's most famous street, and to the south you will see the pride of former first lady Imelda Marcos, a new complex built on reclaimed land featuring cultural, design, theater and convention centers. To the north is the renovated Manila Hotel, built at the turn of the century and once home to General MacArthur. (It's possible to book the suite of rooms he occupied, but the price is about US $2000 a night!)

Unfortunately, most of the fine old Spanish structures in Manila, including the 17-century Manila Cathedral, were destroyed during World War II. However, St. Augustine Church, second oldest in the country, survived and is the most important landmark. Founder of the city, Miguel Lopez de Legazpe, is buried here; the British left some fine woodcarvings during an invasion from 1762-64; and the Spanish surrender of the Philippines to the Americans occurred here in 1898. St. Augustine's is located inside the former Walled City, or Intramuros Section, whose broad and impregnable walls were built by the Spanish in the 16th century to discourage potential invaders, as well as to control a large Chinese community that lived outside.

AUTHOR'S OBSERVATION

Excursions from Manila include a hydrofoil ride to Corregidor, the island at the entrance of Manila Bay, where Americans and Filipinos fought so hard in 1942, and a trip to Bataan Peninsula. Far more refreshing to the spirit is the drive south one hour to Tagaytay Ridge, where the air is cool at 2000 feet, and you can see a volcano within a volcano at Taal Lake. Farther south by one more hour is the most exciting excursion of all–shooting the rapids in a banca (canoe) at Pagsanjan Falls. The scenery is spectacular and the thrill is something to talk about for years!

SINGAPORE

About the only thing exotic about Singapore these days is the name, Singapura, which means Lion City in Malay. Billed as Instant Asia, this city-island-state at the tip of Malaysia is renowned as a multiracial melting pot. Living and working together in more or less perfect harmony are more than two million citizens who enjoy the highest standard of living in Southeast Asia. The majority are Chinese, of course, but they are joined by Malays, Indians, Pakistanis, Ceylonese, Indonesians, Europeans and Eurasians.

Two men whose names are synonymous with Singapore are Stamford Raffles, an Englishman who founded a trading post of the East India Company here in 1819 because he predicted the island would become a crossroads of the East, and Prime Minister Lee Kuan Yew, a Cambridge-educated Chinese who decided in the 1950s that his people should not be the pawn and plaything of foreign powers and set about putting the British back in their place. Some call his 16-year rule ruthless (he threatened to close down all British clubs that did not accept Chinese members), but his vision and vigor have made modern Singapore successful. What you see is what it is: clean streets (there is a stiff fine for discarding cigarettes); an uncorrupted police force; plenty of parks and housing projects; nonstop automobiles driven by affluent, hardworking people; and high-rises everywhere. You also see the old (buildings) coming down with a fury, and the new going up. Singapore is in a constant leap forward, but some of us yearn for a little familiarity, for a little dirt and intrigue to remain as well! Sailing into Singapore harbor is impressive. The busiest port in Southeast Asia and the third largest in the world, it harbors some 300 vessels unloading raw materials or loading up with rubber, tin and Made in Singapore products. The city itself is small and easy to explore on your own from your landing at Clifford Pier on Colliers Quay. While the downtown business district is becoming a monument to modern architecture, like the multimillion dollar projects designed by I.M. Pei and John Portman for Raffles City and Marina Centre, there are still some purely Asian sights.

My first and most important stop is always Raffles Hotel. I sit under one of the whirling overhead fans in this charming bastion of colonialism, sip a cool drink, and dream of the romantic Far East of long ago. Somerset Maugham, Noel Coward and Rudyard Kipling all wrote about Raffles, which began life as a tiffin house (an Anglo-Indian expression for lunch place) in the 1800s and was the birthplace of the Singapore (Gin) Sling in the 1920s. The hotel's colorful history parallels that of Singapore itself, and there is an encouraging sense of continuity under these fans.

I also love the Botanical Gardens, one of the best and most beautiful in the world, with exotic plants, as well as a well-planned oasis of lily ponds, happy swans, orchard pavilions, and herbarium on 80 lush acres. If you like garish art, stop at the Tiger Balm Gardens, a place I have fortunately resisted on every visit. Save some time for shopping. The prices are on a par with Hong Kong, with almost the same variety in merchandise. At night, Singapore is a different city. Although the government has moved much of the street life to a more sanitized location behind the Singapore Tourist Promotion Board (STPB), there are still some wonderful festivities to enjoy behind the main thoroughfares. Don't look for Bugis Street, however, because the government never approved of transvestites and closed down their parade ground. What the government has done is build gigantic hotel/office cities within the city. Raffles City and Marina Centre are the two most recent and, alas, the real Singapore of today.

SOUTH KOREA

The Republic of South Korea's principal port and historical gateway from Japan and the Western world is **Pusan**. This city of two-million-plus inhabitants once sequestered another million or so refugees, as the only major area never to fall into Communist hands during the Korean Conflict. Situated on the southern tip of the peninsula and becoming a popular port of call for cruise vessels on the China circuit between Hong Kong and Kobe, its name Pusan derives from the Koryo Dynasty period (936 to 1392). Pusan refers to the mountain peaks that rise 2500 feet behind the port and make the city around the harbor resemble something of a cauldron, or steaming pot.

The occupying Japanese opened the port of Pusan to outside trade in 1876 and began construction of a railway northward in 1904. Although always considered a commercial and industrial center, the city is also now enjoyed as the main tourist center in the South. It boasts a splendid beach, a milder climate than most other places in both summer and winter, and some not-so-bad attractions. Optional shore excursions of the city offered by Pearl Cruises feature the Fish Market, the famous United Nations Cemetery and a panoramic view from the 387-foot Pusan Observation Tower. In proper weather, Haeundae Beach and neighboring resort hotel are both perfect for a few hours relaxation.

Less than one hour along the excellent Pusan-Seoul Expressway is one of the country's largest and most interesting temples. This is the 35-structures-plus Tongdo-sa, built in 647 (during the reign of Queen Sondok) by the Priest Chajang. This priest, who studied in China and was considered a *taeguksa* or Great National Priest, founded many temples around the land, but this one is considered to be his most prestigious legacy. The Zen-sect Tongdo-sa means To Save the World by Mastering the Truth, and its uniquely different main hall (Taeung-jon) has been designated as National Treasure No. 144. Up in the hills around the temple are a dozen or so small hermitages where the resident priests retreat for enlightenment.

Another hour along the super-highway is Korea's piéce de resistance—the museum without walls that dates from the great Silla Dynasty (57 B.C. to A.D. 935). This is **Kyongju**, which still boasts royal tombs, temple sites, Buddhist reliefs and fortress ruins in impressive states of preservation. It is a full-day (seven and a half hours) tour to this cradle of Korea's ancient culture and worth every moment. Here you will see many recent findings in the National Museum, visit several recently excavated Silla tombs, marvel at the beaten gold crowns and girdles, see the oldest observatory in the world and wonder at other ancient sites.

Kyongju offers inspiration to all of us, and the Korean government is paying considerable attention to the area as one of the country's most impressive tourist attractions. A special Korean luncheon at one of the new resort hotels on Bodrum Lake is also included in the tour.

If your vessel calls at **Inchon**, a booming harbor and Korea's fourth largest city, you are fortunate in being a short distance from **Seoul** South Korea's capital and center of commerce and culture. En route to Seoul, most likely, you will hear the story of dawn on September 15, 1950, when Gen. Douglas MacArthur directed a brilliant amphibious landing of U.S. forces that turned the bitter Korean struggle in favor of the south and its allies.

Seoul is one of the world's most fascinating metropolises and is, indeed, the pulse of this country. Life never seems to rest here, and the ancient world of the capital coexists quite peacefully with some of the most modern buildings and facilities in all of Asia.

NamSan (South Mountain) is the focal point of the city, and two of the original nine gates that surrounded Seoul still exist—Namdaemun (Great South Gate) and Tongdaemun (Great East Gate)—as subtle reminders of a 10-mile-around ancient wall of stone erected some 500 years ago. There are many historic monuments to visit in Seoul, in between shopping forays and rest stops at sophisticated new hotels. Kyongbok (Shining Happiness) Palace is a good place to begin as its grounds also include the National Museum and National Folk Museum. Changdok (Illustrious Virtue) Palace dates from the year 1405 and still has members of the former royal family living in it; however, its secret garden (Piwon) is now a public park. On the grounds of Toksu (Virtuous Longevity) Palace are a statue of the great 15th-century King Sejong, who commissioned scholars to develop a distinctive Korean writing system, and the National Museum of Modern Art. As most of the sights of Seoul mean a great deal of walking out of doors, be sure to pray for good weather!

In addition to the above, Seoul now boasts a number of new structures built for the 1988 Summer Olympiad that, no doubt, guides will insist upon showing all visitors. Tell them to hurry through because *kimchee* and *bulgogki*, the national dishes of pickled cucumbers and grilled garlic/sesame-coated beef chunks, are awaiting!

SRI LANKA

Sri Lanka means Resplendent Land. It also means curry and rice, swimming in the Indian Ocean, graceful women in saris, men in dhotis and serene monks. A favorite memory is of a monk walking down a road, barefoot and alone, oblivious to a sudden summer rain. Sri Lanka is both the ancient and contemporary name of this beautiful island that has been called Ceylon; it lies just 31 miles from the southern tip of India, and 550 miles north of the equator.

Sri Lanka's first inhabitants came from northern India in the 6th century B.C. and their descendents were converted to Buddhism in the 3rd century B.C. Indeed, we are told the religion was brought to Sri Lanka by a missionary son of India's famous Emperor Ashoka. The island seems to have been on an important trading route, for the Arabs appeared in the 12th century. When the Portuguese occupied the coastal areas in the 16th century, they called the island Celaio (Ceylon), a name that stuck for 450 years. The Dutch took over from 1658 to 1795, when they deferred to the British. In 1802, Ceylon became a British Crown Colony (except for the kingdom of Kandy, which did not submit until 1815). She gained her independence from Britain in 1948 and reassumed the name Sri Lanka in 1972.

The best way to approach **Colombo** is by sea, the way the early visitors came, because the capital has a superb harbor (made even better by the British). The city is a hodgepodge of British colonial architecture, Oriental bazaars and industrial suburbs. Your ship will dock in front of the Fort, the scene of many a battle but today a commercial hub with large banks, shipping offices, jewelry shops and kiosks. The western fringes of the Fort dissolve into the *pettah* (outer fort), which gives the appearance of an Oriental bazaar—a rabbit warren of streets and nonstop haggling for just about anything in the world. Among other items, Sri Lanka is renowned for gems—rubies, amethysts, emeralds, aquamarines, garnets, topazes and moonstones. South of the Fort is another complex, in the Galle Face section of the 72-mile Galle Road.

You'll want to see Victoria Park, now called Vihara Maha Devi, the Colombo Museum with its throne of the last king of Kandy, the performing elephants at Dehiwela Zoo, the President's Palace and Clocktower and the sun setting over the Indian Ocean from the Mount Lavinia Hotel. Or you can cross the Victoria Bridge for a visit to Kelaniya and the 2000-year-old sacred shrine where Buddha is said to have bathed in the river. The temple is called Raja Maha Vihare and is one of the three most sacred places in Sri Lanka.

During a recent visit to Sri Lanka, my charming guide, Constance Perera, told me that some cruise ships now call at **Trincomalee**, a major east-coast city whose harbor is considered to be one of the best sheltered in the world. Trinco, as aficionados call it, was home base for the Allied fleet during World War II and a major Royal Navy base thereafter. Today it is known mainly for some of the most unspoiled beaches in the world and for whale-watching off its shores. If your vessel calls at Trinco and then Colombo, you will have the best of all worlds including a three-day overland journey to **Ratnapura**, city of gems, **Kandy** and the verdant hill country where tea and spices grow in abundance plus a peek at the cultural triangle. This latter area features the ancient cities of **Anuradhapura**, the ruins at **Polonnaruwa** and the citadel at **Sigiriya**. Accommodations are excellent throughout Sri Lanka to compensate for the lousy roads.

THAILAND

Bangkok is the most exhilarating and exasperating city in all of Southeast Asia. To say it is a city of contrasts is putting it mildly. It's hot and humid all the time, noisy, dirty from traffic fumes and dotted with tawdry bars and shops (left over from the Vietnam War, when this was a favorite R & R). Yet the city has the most charming people on earth, beautiful traditions and exquisite temples and houses. A curious melange of the old and new with four million inhabitants, Bangkok has been the capital of Thailand only since 1780, when a General Chao P ya Chakri became King Rama I and moved his court from Thon Buri across the Chao Phya River. Today's Thailand (the former Kingdom of Siam) is still a monarchy, albeit modified, and the present King Bhumibol Adulyadej (Rama IX) and his lovely Queen Sirikit (he calls her his smile) live in the Royal Palace in the center of town. They are much loved by their people, although it is no secret that some stern generals behind the throne really control things.

This is the city of *klongs* (canals) and *wat* (temples). Between the two, you'll be well-occupied. Some say there are more than 300 wat in Bangkok which isn't too difficult to believe. These religious structures are a mixture of Indian, Chinese and Khmer (Cambodian) influences, with the addition of Thai, fancy in their colorful, multitiered roofs and curved gables. Adding even more local color is the endless stream of barefoot monks who wander about, their rice bowls extended for contributions while their saffron robes sway gently in the warm breezes.

The best place to begin a tour of Bangkok is the Royal Palace complex, a fascinating mixture of European and Thai architectural styles.

In the royal compound is the most famous wat in the country, the Chapel of the Emerald Buddha (Wat Phrakaeo), a 31-inch statue sitting on a high altar. (Men are requested to wear coat and tie and ladies a skirt and appropriate shoes on the Royal Palace tour. And Thais remove their shoes when entering temples.) The Temple of the Reclining Buddha (Wat Po), close to the Royal Palace, houses a 160-foot statue of the Reclining Buddha, symbolizing the passing of Lord Buddha into Nirvana. In the courtyard of this temple is a bodhi tree, said to have sprung from a branch of the very tree under which the Buddha once rested. Another impressive temple is Wat Trimitr, the Temple of the Golden Buddha, with its five-and-one-half-ton seated Buddha of gold. My favorite landmark in Bangkok is Wat Arun, or Temple of the Dawn, on the banks of the Chao Phya River. Near it is the collection of the king's barges, ornately carved and gilded for ceremonial occasions. When you have had enough of wat, it's time for the klongs, where you will see another side of life. On these canals that wind through Bangkok are long, narrow boats loaded with fruits, flowers, vegetables and handmade wooden products. See them early in the morning (6:30 a.m.) when the floating markets are in full force, and you will also observe the many families living along the banks as they rise for the day. (A guided tour is best for this excursion, but you can also bargain for your own boat.)

Thailand's National Museum is one of the most interesting in Southeast Asia. For a view of more personal treasures, visit Jim Thompson's House (open weekday mornings) or the charming Suan Pakkard Palace, former home of the Queen Mother. Both are good examples of typical Thai houses, which are actually exquisitely carved teak pavilions pieced together. Don't forget to look for the spirit house on the grounds. This interesting birdhouselike object on a pole is kept filled with fresh flowers, food, and incense to appease the spirits who first inhabited the land.

If you can make it through the smog and traffic and the noise of the three-wheeled cycles that act as cheap taxis, see the beautiful Thai dances on the lawn of the Oriental Hotel. Here, in the somewhat cooler breezes of the Chao Phya River, you will be treated to tales of the Ramayana, the Monkey King, and such, danced by local beauties wearing rich Thai silk costumes. It's worth the effort to get across town. If you take taxis on your own, be sure you know how much to pay. The Thais haggle over everything, taxis included. You must set a price with the driver and then disregard what the meter says as it ticks merrily on all the time. And remember, traffic jams are endemic in Bangkok, so leave for appointments early and be patient.

If your vessel calls at the beach resort of **Pattaya** on the Eastern Gulf, you may opt for an air-conditioned bus tour of Bangkok or just taxi a few minutes into town to see what all the shouting is about. Pattaya was a sleepy little fishing village until the early 1960s, when American servicemen arrived in force and turned the place into a boomtown. Since then, the natives have never looked back. Pattaya is Atlantic City, Miami Beach and Waikiki with Thai overtones. Good times is the name of the game here, and there is plenty of sun and surf to make anything happen. There are some good hotels and good seafood restaurants, but take care not to overpay. The place lives on tourists, most of whom are one-time visitors. Pattaya is not a place for serious sightseeing or shopping; it is strictly for relaxing (R & R, the soldiers call it) and people-watching.

VIETNAM

Those who remember the evening news footage of the late 1960s and early 1970s may find it incredible that Vietnam is so popular that "household names" like Cunard, Princess and Holland America are just a few of the cruise companies scheduling port calls in this country. My cruise line sources inform me that ex-soldiers are well represented among passengers, intrigued to revisit old haunts as well as the country's spectacular natural beauty, colorful pagodas and bustling cities under more relaxing conditions. Now that the embargo has been lifted, Americans are racing to catch up with Asians who have been investing in Vietnam for years; neon Sony and Toshiba signs light up downtown Ho Chi Minh City. If you want to beat McDonalds and Hilton to this country, it's best not to wait.

AUTHORS OBSERVATION

The majority of cruise ships visit Saigon for a day or two at most. Those seeking an in-depth exploration of Vietnam are advised to check Pearl Cruises' 17-day cruise/tours, which focus exclusively on Vietnam and carry experienced lecturers and tour guides. Also, see Fielding's Vietnam *for an in depth listing of in-country tours available.*

The Vietnamese are indeed resilient people. Prior to U.S. military involvement from 1965 to 1973, the 329,556-square-mile country had been besieged by foreign occupation and civil war since its people first appear in history.

Around 100 B.C., Viet Lang (as it was then named) was overrun by Chinese, who ruled for 10 centuries until expelled by rebel forces. Over the next six centuries, uneasy independence fraught with civil war and internal strife prevailed until the Nguyen dynasty came to power with French assistance. In 1857, Napoleon III ordered an attack on Vietnam and the forming of several provinces under French rule; some 30 years later Laos and Cambodia completed the French-dominated Union of Indochina. The revolutionary hero Ho Chi Minh spearheaded a revolt against the French who continued to administer the country despite Japanese occupation during World War II. In 1954, independence from the French and division of the country into the communist North and the non-communist South resulted in on-going guerrilla insurgency directed from Hanoi. With the South Vietnamese regime on the verge of collapse and Communist reunification imminent, U.S. forces entered the fray in 1965 in what was to become one of America's most turbulent periods. North and South Vietnam were formally united in 1976 when Communist forces from Hanoi overran weak southern resistence; two years later a treaty was signed with the Soviet Union. With Vietnam's fragile economy on the verge of collapse following the cutoff of aid following the dissolution of the USSR, humanitarian aid arrived from old enemies, the United States and France. A new constitution adopted in 1992 by premier Vo Van Kiet formalized free-market reforms and the election of a president from within the legislature. U.S. tourism began with a trickle in December, 1991, when the U.S. treasury department legalized the sales of air tickets and hotels by American travel agents and tour operators.

In 1995, six cruise vessels (*Song of Flower*, *Ocean Pearl*, *Aurora I*, *Seabourn Pride*, *Marco Polo* and *Sea Goddess II*) will call in Vietnam. Moreover, we're welcome now by locals and officials who know it is only a matter of time (since the U.S. lifted its embargo) before American dollars pour into a tourism infrastructure still in its infancy. Those who want to capture the real flavor of this remarkable country before the ubiquitous Hiltons and McDonalds spring up had better journey soon!

What you'll find is one of the world's most naturally beautiful locales, thick mountains, jungle with peaks reaching 10,000 feet where water buffalo and elephants are found, verdant deltas and a shoreline dotted with craggy rocks. Cruise ships calling in Ho Chi Minh City enter Ha Long (Descending Dragon) Bay, lined with jagged mountains of grey rocks, to be met by locals on fishing sampans. This city of some three million is still the teeming, bustling metropolis bursting with fragrant cooking smells and colorful temples U.S. servicemen recall. While a few modern taxis may be spotted, bicycle rickshaws, ox-drawn carts and motorcycles chaotically ply boulevards and narrow side streets.

Downtown Saigon's neoclassical buildings recall the era of French occupation and house many of the sightseeing attractions. Reunification Hall, constructed as the French Governor's residence in 1868 also served as the presidential palace and today stands as a museum. The **National History Museum** contains archeological finds from the Bronze Age throughout Vietnam's quixotic history. The former U.S. Embassy, designed by Edward Durrell Stone in 1967, is presently headquarters of the State Petroleum Authority. Sightseeing attractions also include **Cholon**, the city's Chinatown, and **Xa Loi Pagoda**, an ornate Buddhist pagoda.

However, the most fascinating sites for visiting Americans are remnants of the period when we were directly involved in the country's history. There are surprisingly few around, however. A repainted U.S. army jeep stands before Notre Dame Cathedral and the War Crimes Museum, housed in the former headquarters of the U.S. Information Agency, has gruesome photos and displays of atrocities committed by American soldiers against the Vietnamese—not for those with weak stomachs. Moreover, the most astonishing remains are in the underground city of Cu Chi, located a short drive from Saigon near the Cambodian boarder. The Vietcong constructed more than 125 miles of 20-foot deep underground tunnels with command post and living quarters directly under a former U.S. military base.

AUTHOR'S OBSERVATION

The dilapidated waterfront Majestic Hotel is still a haunt for ex-patriots and a funky place to visit for colonial-era French atmosphere and a drink on the roof top bar.

The Mediterranean

EGYPT AND THE NILE RIVER

AUTHOR'S OBSERVATION

At press time, terrorist activities against tourists in Cairo and its environs continue and make this a country to watch closely. While a few cruise ships have port calls in Egypt scheduled in 1995, it is advisable to check the U.S. State Department for travel advisories regarding safety.

While many cruise vessels call at Port Said, then pack their passengers onto a bus for the three-hour ride through the desert to Cairo, the real gateway to Egypt and the Valley of the Kings is **Alexandria**, the country's second largest city. Founded by Alexander the Great almost by chance, he was enroute elsewhere but liked the fine harbor. Alexandria was an important trading and commercial center for the ancient world. Its lighthouse on the Isle of Pharos shone for centuries and was considered one of the seven wonders of the ancient world. Culturally, the city was also prominent, and its library had only one close rival, Ephesus. Politically, Alexandria was the base for Egypt's rulers Ptolemy I and his son Ptolemy II, as well as Cleopatra, who lived here with her lovers Julius Caesar and later Mark Antony.

Poets have always loved Alexandria for its romance and color; Lawrence Durrell even dedicated his *Alexandria Quartet* to the place. However, in the present metropolis you will have to look around corners and through shabby exteriors to imagine the glories of yesteryear. Pay a visit to the Greco-Roman Museum with its busts of Alexander and various Roman emperors to realize that this was, indeed, a classical town; the Roman amphitheater; the catacombs used when Christianity tried to take hold; and the many mosques established after the Muslims conquered the land in the seventh century. A pillar once attributed to Pompey is now thought to be a victory column dedicated to the Roman Emperor Diocletian by his troops.

Outside of Alexandria only ten miles is a former residence of the royal family known as Montaza Palace. Here King Farouk abdicated on July 26, 1952 (a calendar with the date still hangs on the wall). The palace is as gaudy and overdecorated as Farouk and his family left it, but the lovely grounds have landscaped gardens and a small beach where you can swim. About an hour from Alexandria is the town of Rashid, where the Rosetta stone was discovered in 1799, which is worth a visit for those with time to spare.

But all roads lead to **Cairo**, the capital of Egypt and a city of mansions and squalor, peace initiatives (Americans are now treated well) and hostile looks (Muslims are sometimes insulted by the way we dress, so leave your skin back on the ship, please), and baksheesh (tips) every time you turn around! If your time is limited, and it is for most cruise passengers, the best deal in town is the Egyptian Museum, one of those rare museums that even those who usually don't like museums seem to agree is beyond description. But there are other museums of interest: the Islamic; the Coptic; the Center for Art and Life; the Papyrus Institute; and the Cotton Museum. Within Cairo you can also tour the early Christian churches in the Old City, an abundance of mosques, and a shop for every kind of souvenir possible—even have a caftan made while you wait. If you are adventurous, try an outrageously priced camel ride or an economical and thoroughly enjoyable sail on the Nile in the age-old, much-photographed, high-masted boat called a *felucca*.

But, no doubt, the Sphinx and pyramids are what you came to see, and your tour will take you to nearby Giza, actually considered a suburb of Cairo. Of the nine pyramids in the Giza complex, the Great Pyramid of Cheops is the most impressive and well known, and you may wish to visit only this one.

Long ranked among the wonders of the ancient world, it was constructed about 2500 B.C. to ensure the Pharaoh Cheops a trouble-free afterlife. (The Egyptians prepared themselves richly for what happened with death, while the Greeks were in love with being alive.) The pyramid took twenty years to build, and several thousand slaves moved more than two million blocks of stone. (Herodotus, the Greek historian, claimed that it took 100,000 men per year to do the job, but later historians say this is a slight exaggeration!) If this is the only pyramid that you desire to tour, you will find it the best example of what these luxurious resting places were all about. You may go inside all three of the Great Pyramids, but if you are tempted to climb them be forewarned that the stones have weathered over thousands of years and are very crumbly (and I certainly wouldn't want to lose you at this point). Alas, more than one tourist has fallen to his demise.

Six smaller pyramids and many lesser tombs are in this area, as well as the Solar Boat (which may not be open to the public) used to ferry the body of the pharaoh from his palace in Memphis to this final resting place. Below the valley of the pyramids sits the majestic Sphinx, with the head of the Pharaoh Chephren (owner of the second pyramid) and the body of a lion. It measures some 240 feet long by 66 feet high but seems much smaller than you had imagined. Between its paws is an inscription that tells of a young prince who rested in its shadow, and was promised the double crown of Egypt if he would remove the sand from its paws. Of course he did, and that prince became the Pharaoh Tuthmose IV (whose reign lasted from about 1425 to 1417 B.C.), who had the inscription carved.

AUTHOR'S OBSERVATION

One-day tours will not include Memphis and Saqqara. If you have the time, though, go to this ancient city and its necropolis on the west bank of the Nile not more than a dozen miles south of Cairo.

Memphis, capital of ancient Egypt during the Old Kingdom and part of the Middle Kingdom periods (from approximately 2700 to 1800 B.C.), was reputed to have matched the splendor of Babylon. Not much is left to see of all this past glory but a few statues and a lovely site covered by palm trees! Out in the desert lies the necropolis of **Saqqara**, the city of the dead. Here you will see a large complex of pyramids and tombs of the important personages of Memphis (try to visit in the early morning, afternoon heat can be intense). The most famous is the step pyramid of Zoser, the first pharaoh in whose name a pyramid was constructed. As he lived a very long time, what began as an elaborate tomb became a continually expanded stepped pyramid.

Sailing slowly on the **Nile River** in a small, air-conditioned ship is one of the highlights of worldwide cruising for here are all the names of ancient monuments you have read about and always wanted to see. You pass by six thousand years of civilization, magnificent scenery and ancient, unspoiled villages. A view of life on any river, and especially the Nile, is an unparalleled experience. In the company of your fellow passengers and guides you will understand why Herodotus wrote some 2500 years ago, Egypt is the gift of the Nile.

The cruise ships vary from small, almost private yachts that carry not more than twenty passengers to larger, more luxurious vessels that hold about eighty passengers and come with swimming pools and on-board boutiques. You have a choice from three days with stops at just the most popular sites to two full weeks on some six hundred miles of the river. Most of the vessels feature their own hand-picked Egyptologists who ensure that your mind is busy and not too muddled by all the dynasties, kingdoms, and gods and goddesses of ancient Egypt. (If you are especially keen on Egypt, choose one of the longer Nile cruises operated by Swan Hellenic of London or Abercrombie and Kent of Chicago. They are more expensive but worth every penny for the excellent lecturers and tours.)

A few of the more famous monuments that you will visit on your Nile cruise are the temples and tombs at Abydos, among the most ancient in all Egypt; the temple of Hathor (the cow-headed goddess) at Dendera; the temples of Karnak and Luxor commemorating the victories that made Egypt a great power in the ancient world; Thebes and the Valley of the Kings (as well as the Valley of the Queens); Aswan with Elephantine Island; and the great temple of Rameses II at Abu Simbel. In addition, you will see something of rural Egypt and the forty million people who live along the banks of the Nile in the very footsteps of their ancestors. All this adds to the appreciation of how vital this river was to the ancient world, and why the Egyptians believed that even their gods traveled upon these waters. Who knows? Perhaps they did.

FRANCE

AUTHOR'S OBSERVATION

One of France's little-known jewels are the riverboats, luxury hotel barges and self-drive house boats that transport you to the loveliest regions. Check out the offerings of Abercrombie & Kent, KD River Cruises, Premiere Selections, Le Boat, Cruise Company of Greenwich and The Barge Lady to discover the myriad ways of uncovering the hidden jewels of France.

One of my most favorite cruise discoveries is **Bordeaux**, that wine capital that lies on a graceful curve of the Garonne River in the southwest corner of France. Bordeaux, sixty miles upriver from the Atlantic Ocean, is one of France's major ports and most historic areas. The city is famous for the great quantities of wine produced in the surrounding area and shipped down the Gironde to England and northern Europe. Indeed, according to the late Alexis Lichine in his excellent *Guide to the Wines and Vineyards of France*, the equivalent of 1 million of today's cases was recorded shipped in the year 1350! Considering the adult population of Europe at the time, that 1 million figure is even more astounding.

My first view of the Bordeaux area was from the deck of the *Vistafjord*, as we sailed slowly up the Gironde and then Garonne rivers to dock right in the center of the town's medieval structures. It was early September, just a few weeks before harvest, and the perfect time to see the famous chateaux with last year's wine lying peacefully in barrels in the cool *chais* (Bordelaise for caves), and the plump grapes on the rows and rows of vines just waiting for that special moment of picking. The Bordeaux countryside is varied and two days in port do not do it justice, but it certainly beats just sailing by!

Shore excursions in the Bordeaux region feature wine tours and tastings at the various chateaux as well as some superb meals. If you are very lucky, you may visit Chateau Lafite-Rothschild and Chateau Mouton Rothschild with its fine wine museum (the two properties are side by side but the proprietors do not speak unless absolutely necessary). You may also see Chateau de Beychevelle, the very elegant Chateau Palmer (where a set lunch is often served) as well as the famed Chateau Margaux, and neighboring Chateau Prieure Lichine (owned and operated by the son of the late wine connoisseur Alexis Lichine). If there is time, the valley of the Garonne features Entre-deux-Mers (which means between two rivers) and Sauternes. Our guide, Gilles Le Paire, took us up to the exquisite medieval village of St. Emilion; we tasted the wines of Chateau Ausone and Chateau Cheval Blanc, and bought some sparkling Bordeaux (yes, there is such a thing) in the ancient cloister of Cordeliers. Only the French would sell wine in a cloister!

If tasting the previous harvest is not your thing, there is plenty to do in Bordeaux itself. From the ship's berth just across from the Place de la Bourse (stock exchange), it is just a hop into the old section of town. Here, the narrow back streets are lined with wonderful old buildings and open on to delightful squares filled with cafes and tables in the sunshine. The city has some fine museums, including the Musee des Beaux Arts and the Musee D'Aquitaine, as well as an impressive Grand Theatre, considered one of the most beautiful in France. It is said that the double stairway inside was copied by the architect Garnier when he designed the Paris Opera House. There are some very pleasant restaurants lining the street beside the theater. I can't remember the name of the one we chose for that evening, but it had pink tablecloths and excellent local seafood.

AUTHOR'S OBSERVATION

If you are interested in a wine cruise to Bordeaux, be certain the ship calls in September as tout le monde goes on holiday during the month of August and the chateaux are closed to visitors.

From Marseille to Menton, the **French Riviera** unfolds a spectacular coastline onto a blue-green sea. The Cote d'Azur, as an obscure nineteenth-century poet named it, has almost eternal sunshine, sparkling waters and flowered hills. It's not surprising that painters, poets and other artists continue to find their muse here.

Queen of the Cote d'Azur is **Nice**, a year-round vacation spot and the cultural center of the Riviera. The city was founded in 350 B.C. by Greeks from Marseille, who called it Nike (victory), and has always been a popular watering hole for royalty, especially when they were out of favor at home. Napoleon visited in 1794 (when he lived at 6 Rue Bonaparte, three blocks behind the port) and in 1796 (when, anguished by parting from Josephine, he wrote her a famous letter from here). The British discovered Nice in the eighteenth century, as an alternative to their own dreadful winter weather. In 1820, the British colony paid for the magnificent boardwalk spanning the length of the Baie des Anges and appropriately named Promenade des Anglais. For more than 160 years this promenade has been the meeting place for summer and winter visitors, with its one side facing the sea and the other lined with impressive facades of elegant hotels and mansions, public buildings and casinos. Athough the beach in this area is not sand but rather large pebbles, this deters no one. It's body to bronze body from May to September! East of the Quai des Etats Unis is the Castle, and behind the port is the Old Town, where narrow, winding streets are lined with medieval houses, wonderful food shops, a few interesting museums and the famous casinos. Less swinging and more sophisticated is the Cimiez district, up in the hills, which boasts Roman ruins, the former residence of Queen Victoria and her retinue, and the Matisse and Chagall museums. (Both Henri Matisse and Raoul Dufy are buried there.)

If your time in Nice can be extended (I am not suggesting you jump ship, but some cruises do embark and disembark here), you can take exciting excursions in all directions. From Nice to Menton, you have a choice of three different routes, or corniches, as the French say. The Corniche Inferieure (lower road) takes you through Villefranche (which also gets its share of cruise calls), Cap Ferrat, Beaulieu, Monaco, and Cape Martin. The Moyenne Corniche (middle road) offers good coastal views and access to the medieval mountain town of Eze.

But the high road will thrill you most. The Grand Corniche, built by Napoleon along the remains of the ancient Aurelian Way, is definitely not for the tender-hearted! It's a continual grade that's straight up and then down, but a chance encounter halfway through is worth wearing the lining of the car's brakes. This is the small village of **La Turbie** (population: 1800), which overlooks Monte Carlo 1400 feet below and offers splendid panoramas of the coastline. In the center of La Turbie sits the famed Alpine Trophy, commissioned by the Roman Senate in 6 B.C. to commemorate Augustus's victory over forty-four previously unconquered tribes (uniting Italy with Gaul and Germania); erected with the aid of slaves and elephants on the spot where the principal roads crossing the Alps met, it's an astounding sight to come upon way up here. Even the poet Dante was so impressed he dedicated some verse to La Turbie. You can read it on the plaque of a nearby house.

All three routes terminate in **Menton**, the easternmost town of the Cote d'Azur. Smack at the Italian border, this resort has the warmest climate of all, influences from both countries, and was another favorite of the British. Artist Jean Cocteau decorated the Salles des Mariages in the Town Hall and left enough memorabilia behind for a museum in his honor, in a seventeenth-century fort near the harbor.

Modern French artists so loved the Riviera that they left memorials. Marc Chagall and his wife donated some 450 works of art to the country he embraced when he left his native Russia, and the French government built a museum in Nice, not far from the Matisse Museum. Between Nice and Antibes, in the little town of Cagnes-sur-Mer, is Les Collettes, where Pierre Auguste Renoir lived from 1908 to 1919, now a museum. Four miles from Antibes is Diot, where Fernand Leger lived. After he died in 1955, his widow dedicated a museum with the largest collection of his artworks ever assembled. In Antibes itself is the Picasso Museum, another great collection personally donated by the artist (actually, it's on a permanent loan). I personally treasure the Matisse Chapel in Venice. In 1947, the seventy-seven-year old artist created this small chapel for Dominican nuns and then called it his masterpiece...the culmination of a whole life dedicated to the search for truth.

AUTHOR'S OBSERVATION

Just outside the medieval town of St. Paul de Vence is the Maeght Foundation, a gallery occupying a magnificent site overlooking the Mediterranean to the south and the snowcapped Alps to the north. In a series of open and enclosed courts, surrounded by pine trees, rosemary and lavender, are works by Braque, Chagall, Miro, Giacometti, Calder, Chillida, Ubac and many, many more. Within the town is La Colombe d'Or (the Golden Dove), one of the region's most celebrated restaurants. Being lucky is sitting on the terrace and watching the doves turn golden in the sun!

If your cruise ship calls at **Cannes**, you may wish to remain on the western edge of the Cote d'Azur where the bikinis are said to be the briefest. Cannes has been fashionable since the mid-19th century, and since then the Promenade de la Croisette has been sauntered along by everyone who's anyone. The harbor is packed with yachts during the season, and in the elegant shops and casino are tanned beauties of all sexes. Things are even livelier at bad-girl **St. Tropez**, the carnival town that Brigitte Bardot made famous a few decades ago. You will notice varying types of chicness along the Riviera, and St. Tropez is one extreme.

Traveling westward toward the Spanish border, your cruise ship may depart fromToulon, which has a beautiful, natural harbor and is the home of the French naval forces. During Roman times the port was famous for the purple dye it produced. It was also the site of Napoleon's first important victory against the British in 1793. During World War II this harbor was under German occupation. The National Memorial to the Provencal Landing is up in the peaceful hills, on the Corniche road to Mount Faron. The summit of this mountain has superb views. Stop also at the square featuring the craft workshops and studios potter, weaver, ceramist and wrought-iron smith.

Marseille is the most famous name in this part of France, for it is the country's largest port and oldest city (founded in 600 B.C. by Greeks from Asia Minor). This city is credited with France's national anthem, although the song was actually written in Strasbourg as the war song of the Army of the Rhine. During the French Revolution, however, Marseille's 500 volunteers heard the song and sang it along the way to Paris. By the time they arrived in Paris the tune was well known and identified with them, and so it was renamed the **Marseillaise** and adopted as the nation's anthem. In Marseille, museums might easily be bypassed, but people-watching is a must. Find a sidewalk cafe, have a coffee or a glass of local wine and enjoy the variety of people that parade in this busy harbor.

Known as the Island of Beauty, **Corsica** has a rich and varied landscape that features beaches of honey-colored sand, secret coves, rocky crags, and rolling hills of pine, chestnut, oak, olive and cork trees. Between the sea and the forests are scented herbs and bushes that perfume the air. I'd know it if only from its fragrance, said Napoleon of the island on which he was born.

The main port of call for cruise ships to Corsica is **Ajaccio**, with a splendid harbor and a French-Italianate atmosphere. This is where old women walk slowly, slightly bent over and always dressed in black, cats dart about the narrow streets, and children play among donkey carts. You can visit the birthplace of Napoleon in town as well as the Napoleon room in the Hotel de Ville, or city hall, where you will find that nothing much has changed since the eighteenth century. Visit the Fesch Museum of Italian Primitives, and you'll understand a little more of this island that France has owned for just over two hundred years.

GIBRALTAR

This 2.28-square-mile British Crown Colony, sitting strategically on a peninsula at the mouth of the Mediterranean, was ceded to Great Britain by Spain in the Treaty of Utrecht of 1713. Spain has been attempting to recover it ever since.

Relations between the two countries were so tense in the 1960s and 1970s that Spain closed its border with Gibraltar. Today the border has reopened as talks on control continue and a few thousand Spaniards enter the Rock daily to shop for duty-free British woolens and other luxury items. There are no natural resources here, other than a 1400 foot-high rock, a natural fortress that holds some of Britain's most sophisticated defense equipment. The commander of the fortress is also the Governor of Gibraltar and appointed by the Crown. About 30,000 people live in Gib or The Rock, mainly of Genoese, Portuguese and Maltese descent. The two official languages are Spanish and English. With little to see or do, it's a perfect cruise stop for just a few hours. You can visit St. Michael's Cave, with its huge stalagmite and stalactite formations and a natural amphitheater that was the setting for a beauty pageant the day I visited. You can also go up the Rock by cable car for a spectacular view of the Spanish mainland and the African coastline. Don't forget a brief stop to see the wild Barbary apes but hang on to the handbag. These apes are famous for being impolite!

GREECE

AUTHOR'S OBSERVATION

The best months to explore Greece are May, September and October. July and August are frequently unbearably hot, with temperatures often reaching more than 100 degrees.

Piraeus is the proper name for Greece's first port, one of the largest in the entire Mediterranean. Gateway to Homer's wine-dark sea, the Aegean, as well as to all of Greece and the monuments of the Golden Age of Western Civilization, it dates from the third millennium B.C. and reached its peak in the fifth century B.C. In 493 B.C., Themistocles started the Long Walls that joined the port with Athens, seven miles away. Only sections remain, the rest having been destroyed by the Spartans at the end of the Peloponnesian War in 404 B.C.

Athens, thirty minutes away by taxi, tour bus, or electric train, is home to more than one-third of Greece's 9 million people, and it's difficult to do it justice in just one day. If you have extra time to spend abroad, spend it here. Syntagma, or Constitution Square, with the Parliament Building and Tomb of the Unknown Soldier, open-air cafes that seat 3000 people for hours on end, banks and travel offices, is the center of city life. The Plaka area teems in daylight with shoppers, and at night revelers at the tavernas enjoy tantalizing food, a fine variety of reasonably priced wines, and entertainment.

(Some tavernas have rooftop gardens where you can dine under the spell of the Acropolis.) The Acropolis dominates Athens from rosy-fingered dawn to sunset, and if your visit coincides with a full moon you are lucky indeed. Air pollution, however, is speeding the city's disintegration more than all the centuries of war, and you are no longer allowed to wander through the Parthenon or to view the caryatids in their rightful place on the portico of the Erechtheum. (They, poor dears, are now captive in the Acropolis Museum.) Just below the Acropolis is the Agora, or ancient marketplace, where excavations for the past half-century have been under the direction of the University of Cincinnati and the American School of Classical Studies in Athens. This is a wonderful place to roam, and the Theseum, a temple dedicated to Theseus, perches on a grassy knoll overlooking it all.

When you have visited Hadrian's Arch and the Temple of Jupiter, the National Archaeological Museum, and the smaller Benaki and Byzantine museums, taken the tram up Mt. Lycabettus, and wandered the many back streets, it's time to see the rest of Greece. The local CHAT tours (4 Stadiou Street) have comfortable day trips to Sounion (where the Temple of Poseidon overlooks the sea and the cape), to Delphi on Mt. Parnassus, and to the classical sites of Corinth, Mycenae and Argos, Nauplia and Epidaurus. Local buses are plentiful and a more adventurous way to get about. A trip to the Plains of Marathon, for example, is about one hour from Athens each way (unless, of course, you plan to run back).

AUTHOR'S OBSERVATION

Athens has terrible air pollution so sufferers of asthma and other bronchial conditions may want to bypass this city.

If the lure of the sea remains strong, excellent day trips from Palaion Phalero (between Athens and the airport) go to three nearby islands on a choice of cruise ships. (The cost for the day is about $40 including a lunch tray at sea, and the companies will pick you up and deliver you back to your hotel.) First call is usually at the island of **Aegina**, where a donkey ride through vineyards and pistachio fields will take you up to the Doric-style Temple of Aphaea or, if you prefer, you can have a swim in the bay of Aghia Marina. The next call is **Hydra**, an artists' colony with quaint, brightly colored houses along the waterfront. It's a wonderful place to stroll, shop, or sip ouzo. In the afternoon your ship visits the charming, unspoiled island of Poros, an important religious center in antiquity and home of the marble that was used, among other things, to build the Temple of Solomon. **Poros**, a weekend retreat of many Athenians who catch the hydrofoil on Friday evenings from Piraeus, has a beautiful harbor, windmills, fruit orchards and olive groves.

And then it's a two-hour sail back to Palaion Phaleron in the late afternoon, while you have a cool drink in the lounge and learn Greek dancing from the crew.

If you dock at **Itea** on the Gulf of Corinth and take the half-hour bus ride through Parnassus Country to **Delphi**, your route is through a sea of olives, probably the finest groves in all of Greece. First stop on your tour should be the Delphi Museum, with more than ten thousand items found in the excavations begun by French archaeologists in 1892. Most impressive of the artworks is the bronze charioteer, dating from 478 B.C., a barefoot, life-size figure. Other works include stone friezes, toga-clad statesmen, a sixth-century B.C. sphinx presented by the island of Naxos to the oracle, and pottery fragments dating from the Mycenean period (1600 to 1100 B.C.).

Renowned throughout the ancient world, the Oracle at Delphi was often consulted for political reasons and thus thought to have changed the course of history many times. The woman who spoke was called a Pythia, and she had to fast three days and then bathe in the nearby Castalian Spring before she spoke. The upper precinct at Delphi includes the remains of the sanctuary, the Sacred Way leading to the Temple of Apollo, a fourth century B.C. theater, and a stadium where seven thousand spectators would watch the Pythian games every four years (it's a tough climb up to this one, but worth it.) The lower ruins feature a large gymnasium, the Temple of Athena, a lovely *tholos*, or round temple, whose purpose is unknown. The mystery makes it the most interesting structure of the lot.

During the Panhellenic games held in **Olympia** every four years, a truce of God was proclaimed. Rivalries were abolished so all of Greece could come to Olympia in safety for the spirit of the competitions and social functions that followed. The greatest honor and achievement was to be an Olympic victor and to wear a crown of wild olives. The winner would be feted, paraded, and even immortalized in poetry and sculpture. The status of winners was great; even important generals would defer to a winner. The first Olympic games were probably held in 776 B.C. and were continued every fourth year until 394 A.D., when they were abolished by the Roman Emperor Theodosius II on the grounds they were a pagan ritual. The games were held in midsummer under a full moon, and male athletes competed in the nude. Women were barred from the premises (and the events), but male spectators were encouraged to come from all over Greece and, indeed, the ancient world. The games were held on a site adjoining the Sanctuary of Zeus in Olympia, in the northwest area of the Peloponnese. This is where the Olympic torch is still lit today (with a magnifying glass and the rays of the sun) and then carried by runners to the location of the games, a tradition that began in 1936. As you walk among the ruins today, you pass through the fifth-century Temple of Zeus, the gymnasium, what is thought to be the oldest hotel in the world (to house spectators), the workshop of the sculptor Phidias (whose gold and ivory statue of Zeus here was one of the seven wonders of the ancient world), the house of Roman Emperor Nero (who introduced contests like singing into the games), and the fabulous stadium. (Perhaps one day the Olympic games will again be held here, where they belong.) The Olympia Museum displays artifacts found on the site (first excavated by French archaeologists in 1829 and continued by Hitler during World War II) and a scale model of the entire area. The Olympic Games Museum has a collection of memorabilia dating from 1896, when the games were revived in Athens.

Six of the islands in the Ionian chain Corfu, Paxos, Lefkas, Ithaki, Kefallinia, and Zakinthos lie off the western coast of Greece. The seventh is near the southeastern Peloponnese this is Kithira where, according to Greek mythology, Aphrodite made her first appearance.

Of the Ionian group, **Corfu** is an international tourist spot and popular cruise stop. It has an interesting history and provides a much-needed respite on sailings between Venice and Piraeus. All other Greek islands envy Corfu for its year-round greenness due to cypress groves and millions of olive trees. Of all the islands, Corfu is also the most un-Greek. Italian was spoken here for more than five hundred years, and the island was under the protection of the Venetian Empire from the fourteenth until the eighteenth century. Venetian occupation was followed by Russian, French, and British, the latter leaving a definite mark. The entire chain was ceded to Greece in 1864, and Corfu soon became a summer residence of the Greek royal family. Sailing into the port of Corfu you see the charming town nestled between two Venetian forts. The newer fortress (mid-sixteenth century) overlooks the port, while the older fort has a view of the Esplanade, or main square. The old Venetian-style town is fun to explore and good for shopping. Once in a while you'll happen upon a British legacy like the Royal Palace, the cricket field and many of the statues in the Esplanade. Be sure to pay a visit to Saint Spiridon, the church dedicated to the patron saint, who is believed to have saved the island from plague in the seventeenth century and an invasion by the Turks in the eighteenth century. After you have wandered about the town, you may want to head for one of the beautiful beaches to sun on Corfu's famous golden sands. If your ship stays long enough, don't miss the Sound and Light performance (in English) in the Venetian Palace four nights a week.

Two out-of-town shore excursions of Corfu are known for fine views (and not much else). The first stop is Kanoni, a landscaped area named after the French cannon that was once placed here. From this precipice you can photograph the so-called islet monasteries the white convent of Vlachernae and the chapel on Mouse Island. When your eyes have absorbed the beauty of this setting, your tour will go on to the Achilleion, the former palace of Empress Elizabeth of Austria, which is now a casino/hotel near the village of Gastouri.

The 200-year-old structure is rather hideous, due to the questionable taste of the empress as well as of Kaiser Wilhelm II (who owned it subsequently), but the proprietors and their guests certainly had lovely views from the terrace.

Shopping in Corfu town is always a pleasure, but remember that shopkeepers close from about lunchtime to 4 or 5 p.m. There is a very good branch of Lalaounis here, one of the famous Greek jewelers, as well as several other shops selling gold and silver at (almost) giveaway prices. Corfu also claims to make the best and the lightest olive oil in the world and I paid about $8 recently for a two and a half gallon can. Getting it home was worth the agony!

Focus of the Cycladic Islands is the deserted island of **Delos**, whose only inhabitants these days are some caretakers of its ruins and a few archaeologists. According to Greek legend, Delos arose from the sea just in time for Leto, Zeus's paramour, to give birth to Artemis and her twin brother, the sun god Apollo. This has always been a sacred island, and when the cult of Apollo was prominently practiced it became wealthy as offerings to the Temple of Apollo filled its coffers. It was the banking center for the Eastern Mediterranean, with money loaned out to other islands at an outrageous rate, and its inhabitants also did a brisk business in the slave trade. Then, in 88 B.C., Delos was caught in a dispute between Athens and Rome. To make his point for the Athenian side Mithridates, King of Pontus, completely devastated the island, carrying off all the valuables. Delos never recovered, and its commercial role was usurped by Rhodes.

Walking tours of ancient monuments in Delos take about two hours and give you ample evidence of the island's glorious past. The most impressive memorial is the Terrace of the Lions, where five archaic beasts (seventh century B.C.) still hold vigil, crouching on their hind legs. You will also see the remains of the Temple of Apollo, the Sacred Lake (now dry), and ruins of elegant villas with their delicate mosaic floors in the Roman quarter. Especially beautiful houses are the Dolphin, the Trident and the Masks. If you have time, climb the steps up Mount Kynthos for a splendid view of the other Cyclades—Syros, Naxos, Paros, Tenos and Mykonos.

If I had a genie I would wish to be transported from time to time to the relaxing nearby island of **Mykonos**. Mykonos has some much photographed windmills, a church (they say) for every day of the year, and a whitewashed maze of narrow and charming back streets that were designed to confuse raiding pirates. Refresh your soul by sitting in a sidewalk cafe by the seawalls and letting the sparkling sun take over. Because of the pleasant atmosphere and cordial natives, Mykonos has drawn artisans from all over the world who paint, make sandals, weave, sculpt, design jewelry, knit, crochet, and who can even make you a dress in two hours. One wonders why the sign on the pier—"Help Keep Our Island Clean"—is necessary. I like best the sign in front of the statue in the town square, "Please do not park backpacks here."

AUTHOR'S OBSERVATION

While days may be spent on the beach, evenings are always spent in town, watching people parade and then finding a superb little taverna for a leisurely meal (my favorite is Antonini's on the square).

Santorini, sometimes called **Thira**, is the southernmost island in the Cyclades, and its eerie place in history is due to theories it may be the lost island of Atlantis. Recent excavations at Akrotiri reveal that a cosmic event in 1520 B.C. destroyed a flourishing civilization. As your cruise ship sails into the Bay of Santorini, note that this island, known as Strongyle or the round one, in ancient times, is in five sections, of which Thira is the largest. Soaring 900 feet above the sea and plunging 1200 feet into the submerged core of its volcanic crater, which seems fathomless, the island has a feeling of bareness, with rugged black lava cliffs topped by whitewashed houses and chapels that have a frenzied, surreal look about them.

From your cruise ship to shore is undoubtedly by tender; from the shore up to the tiny, terraced town of Thira, you can either walk the winding and slippery eight hundred steps or pay a ripoff fee to ride a donkey. (While the ride is not one of my favorite travel memories, it is an experience you might want to try once! You may even buy a photograph of yourself to prove that you did it.) Once upstairs in the little town, you can shop around, have a coffee or explore part of the island. If you have at least two hours before the tender leaves again, hire a taxi to visit the excavated site of Akrotiri, which is believed to have been contemporary with the Minoan civilization and then destroyed by the same holocaust of volcanic eruptions and tidal waves in 1300 B.C. If the site is closed, as it tends to be now on Sundays, you can take a twenty-minute taxi ride to the little town of **Iea** at the other end of the island, where it's fun to walk among the whitewashed houses built into the cliffs and look out at the sea below.

(Your cruise ship will look very, very far away from up here.) Our taxi driver on this excursion stopped along the way to show us a charming little chapel dedicated to St. George. If you happen to miss Akrotiri, findings from the excavations are in a special series of exhibit rooms on the second floor of the National Archaeological Museum in Athens and include wall paintings, pottery and a small person's bed.

The most important city in Macedonia was named after the stepsister of Alexander the Great, Thessaloniki. Founded in 315 B.C. by one of Alexander's generals, **Thessaloniki** (also called **Salonika**) has had a stormy history, primarily due to its situation at the crossroads of the main routes between East and West, Asia and Europe. As a proud and cultured city, it is layered with the legacy of the Romans, Saracens, Normans, Venetians, Turks, Germans, Balkans, and more Turks, peoples who passed through and often conquered.

Despite the frequent destructive fires and wars the city endured, you'll find early Greek or Macedonian treasures, Roman monuments, Venetian ramparts, Byzantine churches, and occasional vestiges of the Moslem culture imposed by the Ottoman Empire (although when the Greeks recaptured the city in 1912, they destroyed all the mosques and minarets within reach). Ironically, Thessaloniki, which boasts the tomb of Philip II of Macedon, father of Alexander the Great, is also the birthplace of Kemal Ataturk, who became the father of modern Turkey. A landmark of the city is the fifteenth-century White Tower, constructed by the Venetians at the boundary of the no-longer-standing city walls. Nearby is the Archaeological Museum, with findings from Hellenistic tombs and a rich collection of gold from Macedonia and neighboring Thrace. A road from the White Tower leads to the university named after the philosopher Aristotle, who came from Macedonia.

Either before or after your cruise from Thessaloniki, take a tour around the old town to see the prominent Rotunda, an ancient Roman structure intended as a mausoleum but turned into a Christian church in the fifth century (and dedicated to St. George by Theodosius the Great, who commissioned some fine mosaics). In the sixteenth century the Turks made it into a mosque and added a minaret (which is still there). A few minutes walk from the Rotunda is the house where Kemal Ataturk was born in 1881, preserved by the Turkish government and open to the public.

The Arch of Galerius is another Roman monument, built by the Emperor Galerius in A.D. 303 to commemorate his victory over the

Persians. It's surrounded by wonderful old houses and tiny Byzantine churches, and straight up behind are the ancient city walls, with a fourth-century atmosphere and a fine view of the harbor. Cruise passengers are also offered an excursion to Pella, the capital of Macedonia from the fifth century B.C. to 168 B.C. and the birthplace of Alexander in 356 B.C., with fascinating ruins as well as beautifully preserved pebble mosaics, streets and sewer systems.

A one-week cruise itinerary from Thessaloniki, in cooperation with the Greek government (which likes to see the tourist dollar spread around), calls at the islands of Skopelos, Skiathos, Lesbos, Lemnos, and Thasos as well as the port of Kavalla. No longer on most cruise schedules is the all-male enclave of Mount Athos, where women have not been allowed for more than nine hundred years (cruise ships with women aboard may not even sail within 500 yards of the main port). Mount Athos, a holy mountain harboring ancient monasteries of the Eastern church, once welcomed male visitors for a meal and overnight. Today, however, men must apply at the Ministry of Foreign Affairs and prove they have serious religious or scientific interests that warrant a visit to the community.

Kavalla, at the Thracian border in eastern Macedonia, is the port for shore excursions to Philippi, another ancient city at the crossroads of history. On the plains of Philippi important battles took place and legendary figures met their fates. St. Paul preached here and sowed the seeds of Christianity before he was detained in prison and finally forced to flee. Brutus is said to have seen Caesar's ghost on the Philippian plains, just before he and Cassius were defeated by Octavian and Mark Antony in the famous 42 B.C. battle. Ruins here include a large agora, or marketplace, a Roman forum, some baths, the prison in which St. Paul languished for a spell and some early churches.

Skiathos and Skopelos are members of the Sporades, or scattered islands. Beautiful **Skiathos** is known for wild strawberry bushes and olive trees as well as for lovely bays and beaches that invite lounging in the sun. Shore excursions here are relaxing—a short tour of the village and then a quick transfer to one of the beaches. Less than two hours by sea is **Skopelos** ("rock"), green as well as rocky, where charming, whitewashed houses have colorful shutters and doors. The island is noted for its plentiful fruit, especially the plums that you can taste fresh or in various stages of being cured for export.

Lesbos, the third largest island in the Aegean (after Crete and Rhodes), is close to Asia Minor and convenient for excursions by small boat to Dikili, the Turkish port near the archaeological site of Pergamum. Lesbos has played an important role in Greek literature since the eighth-century-B.C. school of poetry was founded here. Native sons and daughters have included Aesop, the great storyteller, and Sappho, who wrote erotic lyrics to other women and was said to have practiced what she preached. Her poems were allegedly burned by the church in the eleventh century. Nonetheless, she left a legacy to the world in the word lesbian. Legendary figures associated with this island include the lovers Daphnis and Chloe.

Lesbos has a large population (about 150,000), many olive trees (approximately 11 million), and multitudes of sheep and goats. From the capital city of Mytilini you have wonderful views of Asia Minor plus relics of the long Turkish occupation. The countryside is especially beautiful, and shore tours visit the fishing village of Petra up the coast, the pottery town of Agiasos, and the quaint harbor of Molivos (swimming is available nearby). Because Lesbos is so close to Turkey, you will see many Greek soldiers on guard around the island, but don't be put off—it's a way of life that is unfortunately thousands of years old.

The last two islands visited on this special itinerary from Thessaloniki are Lemnos (or Limnos) and Thasos in the Thracian Sea. **Lemnos** is the larger and has the better beaches (your shore excursion will probably take you to Santa Barbara). Rich in legend, this island was home of Hephaestos, blacksmith to the gods. Greek mythology says the Argonauts stayed two years on Lemnos (fathering a generation of children) during their search for the Golden Fleece.

A Greek warrior, Philoctetes, was marooned here during the Trojan War. The capital of Lemnos is Mirina (Kastron), a small town dominated by its Genoese castle built in the Middle Ages. The town has a cool, dry climate as well as an inspiring view of Mount Athos especially at sunset. **Thasos**, in contrast, is hot and humid. Once a prosperous island-state, it was known in the ancient world for gold, marble and wine exports. The main town of Limin (also called Thasos) is built around the ruins of an agora, a theater and city walls. The local museum is interesting, but the best finds, alas, were reportedly carted off to the Louvre.

As a member of the baker's dozen Dodecanese islands in the Eastern Aegean, **Kos** lies close to Asia Minor and is best known as the birthplace of Hippocrates, the father of medicine. The main port, founded in the fourth century B.C., has relics of former glories of the Hellenistic, Roman and Byzantine periods. A twelfth-century

Venetian castle lies in ruins to one side of the harbor, its walls lined with the shields of the Knights of St. John, who stopped here in the fourteenth century on their way home from the Crusades. (Of all the sites on Kos, the castle is the least interesting, especially if your cruise is calling at Rhodes.)

AUTHOR'S OBSERVATION

Just a few minutes walk from the harbor you will find the ancient Greek agora as well as the temples of Apollo and Venus. For a splendid view from the top, climb up the tier of seats in the well-preserved theater. The museum on Liberty Square is also worth a visit. It has a 400 B.C. statue of Hippocrates, which was found under the theater, as well as a splendid Roman mosaic floor.

Two miles out of town on a beautiful hillside with pine forests, natural springs, and a view of the sea and Asia Minor, the Greeks built the Aesclepion of Hippocrates. One's imagination can run wild up here. Even historians admit they do not know what went on here in ancient times. You will find the Temple of Asclepios, the god of medicine and healing, several curative rooms, plus a swimming pool and a stadium for physical therapy. Some believe that the Greeks performed surgery here, but the Romans built their baths on top of the operating rooms. In town, natives will show you a plane tree that Hippocrates is said to have planted and lectured under, but botanists today doubt this.

Northernmost island of the Dodecanese, **Patmos** is considered to be the loveliest of all, with beautiful bays and capes and spectacular views at every turn. Although barren like most of Greece (especially in summer), Patmos has on its southern side that sparkling-white architecture found also in the Cyclades islands. Patmos is a place of pilgrimage, for here St. John the Divine received the revelations and wrote the book of Apocalypse (which he actually dictated to a disciple), in a cave that is now enshrined by the Church of the Apocalypse. Nearby, the pretty village of Hora has an eleventh-century monastery founded by St. Christodoulos, a former hermit, as a School of Virtue and Holy Purpose. (For those whose purpose was considered unholy, burning oil was ready for pouring from atop the gate.) A tour of this monastery is a must, although the lovely pebble beaches on the island also beckon. In the monastery compound is a treasury of costly icons and liturgical costumes and a library lined with glass cases containing over nine hundred handwritten books as well as some ninth-century illuminated manuscripts. You can also tour where the two dozen monks live, eat and study. On the return to the port of Skala, stop in at the seventeenth-century house (if you can find it), a rich trove of folk art, furniture and greenery.

Just over a mile from the shores of Turkey, **Samos** is another Greece in Asia island, known for its wine, its Temple of Hera (one of the wonders of the ancient world), and engineering marvels that still exist. Samos is characterized by mountainous terrain on which olives, dates, palms, poplars and vineyards flourish. In the sixth century B.C., Samos was Queen of the Seas, due to its tyrant leader Polycrates, who used slaves from Lesbos to build the Temple of Hera, a harbor mole and the mile-long tunnel that brought fresh water through the hills. Parts of the harbor mole and the tunnel are still around, but all that remains of the temple is a single, standing column a few miles west of Pythagorion (birthplace of the man who discovered that proportion forms the structural principle of the universe). Other sights on this lovely isle are two monasteries, the seaside village of Kokari, and many little mountain towns in sweet-smelling pine forests. If you are in the mood to taste a little of the local industry, visit the winery in Samos for a sampling of the new, young nectar of the gods. Some visitors also use Samos as the jumping-off point for a tour of the classical site of Ephesus (near Kusadasi in Turkey), while others head for the magnificent, uncrowded beaches.

When I asked Captain Michael Benas, now retired master of Sun Line's flagship, the *Stella Solaris*, which island in the Aegean was his favorite, he beamed and gave me a predictable answer, "Why, Rhodes, of course!" As we were sailing toward Rhodes at that very moment, I couldn't have been more delighted, for this island has long captured my fancy as one of the most enjoyable places in the entire world. **Rhodes** is the largest of the Dodecanese.

Greek mythology tells us that the island rose from the sea and that Apollo took it as his domain, although he had to uproot some lesser gods who had already established squatter's rights. The island flourished as early as the eleventh century B.C. and reached its commercial and cultural prime in the fifth century B.C. Two centuries later, the Colossus of Rhodes was known as one of the seven wonders of the ancient world.

This 100-foot bronze statue representing the sun god straddled the harbor of the ancient port of Rhodes. It was erected in 290 B.C. by a local sculptor to commemorate the steadfastness of the Rhodians and as a warning against invasion. It seems that after an Alexandrian military man withdrew his troops in frustration when his one-year siege failed to intimidate the Rhodians, they simply melted down his machinery and made their colossus. Unfortunately the Colossus toppled over in an earthquake about fifty years later, and its site is now marked by two pillars topped with bronze deer, the symbol of present-day Rhodes.

Rhodes, about six hundred square miles in area, has three separate layers of history to explore the ancient, the medieval and the modern. The most splendid of the three ancient cities of Rhodes is **Lindos**, about a forty-five-minute drive from port to the western end of the island. Lindians worshiped the goddess Athena, who is said to have rained gold down upon their city. Her fourth-century-B.C. temple on the acropolis of Lindos is one of the oldest sites in all of Greece. The acropolis, a steep climb up from the small town below, has wonderful views of the Bay of St. John and the harbor where St. Paul is reported to have landed in A.D. 51.

Your cruise ship will dock within sight of the old town of Rhodes, which lies within the reconstructed medieval walls built by the Knights of St. John in the thirteenth century. (Some of the larger passenger vessels must anchor out and tender passengers in, however.) In the northern section of the old town are the Palace of the Grand Master and the former inns of the crusaders that still line the Street of Knights. A fifteenth-century Hospital of the Knights houses the Rhodes Archaeological Museum, which has fine exhibits, including the lovely Aphrodite Thalassia found in the waters nearby and dating from the first century B.C. The medieval ramparts and buildings were all reconstructed during the Italian occupation, which lasted from 1912 to 1943 (all the good roads were built then too), and Rhodian guides will tell you that Mussolini had his eye on the 300-room palace as a summer residence (it's an impressive place, but I wouldn't want to live there). But Il Duce never got to fulfill this dream. An excellent Sound and Light show is aimed at the palace during the summer, and many ships stay in port for it. The English version begins about 9 p.m. And, if you prefer more sight-seeing to shopping (the main area is Sokrates Street, the former Turkish bazaar), take a taxi to the mile-long Valley of the Butterflies about twelve miles from the port of Rhodes along the western coastal road to commune with millions of red and black butterflies that flutter through the trees.

Rhodes has thousands of foreign visitors (it's dubbed Scandinavian Haven) who fly in, come by overnight car ferries from Piraeus, or sail into the harbor on private yachts and sailboats from as far away as

Australia. I love to walk along the breakwater, look at the boats, listen to the many languages spoken, and then sit in a waterfront cafe to watch the spectacle. This beats even the butterflies!

Crete is Greece's most southern island in the Aegean Sea and its largest (second in size only to Cyprus in the entire Mediterranean area). It is the legendary birthplace of Zeus, whose mother (Rhea) hid him in a cave lest his father (Cronos) swallow the baby whole as he had all preceding brothers and sisters. (Cronos did not want any competition.) Crete is also the birthplace of Domenico Theotokopoulos (El Greco), in 1545, and Nikos Kazantzakis in, 1883, (whose popular novel *Zorba the Greek* is set here).

Heraklion (or Iraklion) is the most popular cruise port on the island, because it's closest to the Palace of Knossos and the fine Archaeological Museum. Although Heraklion has about 70,000 inhabitants, only a few Venetian relics (a castle, a lion, a fountain and a loggia) are of interest here. But it is the gateway to a view of the magnificent Minoan civilization, which flourished here from 2000 to 1450 B.C., and the wonderful tales of King Minos, the bull, Daedalus, the Minotaur,Theseus and Ariadne. No visit to the island is complete without a tour of Knossos. Excavations were undertaken by Sir Arthur Evans in 1900 to uncover and reconstruct the palace, which was the center of a large town that Evans felt had a population of around 100,000 at its peak. The palace, which had 1200 to 1400 rooms, is built on a plan so complex that archaeologists believe it is the origin of stories about the Minoan labyrinth.

The complex was not even fortified, which meant that the king (both a divinity and a monarch) was as confident as he was powerful. Evans's restoration features large red wooden columns made broader at the top than at the base, wall reproductions, the throne room, the queen's bathroom (she supposedly took milk baths) and the sophisticated sanitary system. You can see charred remains from the fatal fire of 1450 B.C. that makes it seem people lived here only yesterday. You can also walk down the oldest street in the world, once lined with homes of aristocrats, and peek into the huge garbage receptacle where broken pottery was thrown.

At the Archaeological Museum in Heraklion, guides shout at the top of their lungs in every language possible. By all means avoid the frustrating tour here. Get away from your fellow passengers as quickly as possible, head upstairs for the frescoes, and then visit the 1:50 scale model of the Palace of Knossos and the cases downstairs. The museum is unique, in that it contains all the findings at Knossos and other sites in Crete. Not one object was carried off to European museums as happened so often at these classical sites.

If there is sufficient time before your ship sails, wander about the town a bit. The fruit market is spectacular, and you'll find interesting shops for souvenirs as well as tempting handwoven rugs in colorful Cretan designs.

ISRAEL

Whether your tour of the Holy Land begins in the well-equipped harbor of **Ashdod**, one of Israel's planned cities and perched on sand dunes, or in the three-tiered port of **Haifa**, populated since biblical times, you will find yourself on a journey like none other you have experienced before.

AUTHOR'S OBSERVATION

Your cruise vessel may not be in port long enough for you to visit everything you would like, and you may have to choose between Jerusalem and Bethlehem, or the Nazareth/Tiberias/Sea of Galilee route.

If you are lucky enough to sail into Haifa, from the deep-blue sea to the top of God's vineyards, Mount Carmel, you will enjoy panoramic views at every level: from the harbor with its broad bay, the Hadar or midsection business area; and the Carmel residential level of homes and parks and fine hotels. From Haifa, the heart of the Holy Land, Nazareth, Tiberias and the Sea of Galilee are easily accessible. Before you depart on your full-day tour give courtesy to Haifa itself, especially Elijah's Cave, where the prophet is said to have hidden from the wrath of King Ahab and his wife Jezebel, and where the Holy Family was sheltered on the return from Egypt.

The drive to Nazareth takes about an hour through Israel's largest and most fertile valley, an impressive array of fruit trees, vineyards, and green fields that were carefully nurtured from swampland. From the valley, your bus will maneuver hairpin turns through the King George V Forest and into Nazareth. Here is the Basilica of the Annunciation (built over the site of earlier structures), where the angel Gabriel is said to have announced to Mary that she would bear the Son of God. Nearby is a church where Joseph's workshop is thought to have been, and the synagogue Jesus attended. Two other historic sites are: Mary's Well, where you will see women carrying jugs of water on their heads just as they did in Jesus's time; and a Franciscan church, on the site where Jesus is believed to have dined with his disciples after the Resurrection.

The road leads directly from Nazareth to the Sea of Galilee, a tranquil freshwater lake thirteen miles long and some seven hundred feet below sea level. En route you will pass by Cana, where Jesus is said to have turned water into wine, and you will glimpse Mount Tabor, site of Jesus's transfiguration. The ancient town of Tiberias, built by Herod in honor of the Roman Emperor Tiberius, was a major center of Jewish life in the Holy Land (the learned men of Tiberias introduced grammar and punctuation into the Hebrew language). This resort is still noted for curative hot springs, famed for more than 3000 years. From Tiberias, you go on to the Church of the Multiplication of Loaves and Fishes and to the town of Capernaum, the center of Jesus's activities in the Galilee. On the return to Tiberias you will see the Mount of the Beatitudes, where the Sermon on the Mount was delivered and where Jesus is said to have chosen his twelve apostles.

Jerusalem, continually inhabited for more than four thousand years, is not only a great historical center but the cornerstone of the world's three great religions. Jews, Christians and Moslems pay homage to their respective shrines. Jerusalem's inhabitants are thought to be members of the greatest melting pot mankind has ever known. The Old City, or walled section, of East Jerusalem is a living testament to that. Here you can visit the Wailing Wall, now referred to as the Western Wall (remnant of a wall that once supported the Temple on the Mount). Nearby is the gleaming Dome of the Rock, or Mosque of Omar, a Moslem sanctuary built over the spot where Abraham was prepared to sacrifice the life of his son and where Moslems believe that Mohammed ascended to heaven. On the Via Dolorosa, the route to Calvary passes fourteen Stations of the Cross marked for prayer. Pay a visit to the Church of the Holy Sepulchre, believed to be the site of the crucifixion. Also in the Old City are the Church of St. Anne, the Pool of Bethesda and the Arch of Ecce Homo. From the Mount of Olives, you will catch your breath at the spectacular view of old and new Jerusalem before visiting the Church of all Nations, the Tomb of the Prophets and the Garden of Gethsemane. From Mount Scopus, the panorama includes the Judean desert and the distant Dead Sea. As your drive takes you through West Jerusalem, you will see the memorial to the six million Jews of the holocaust, Hadassah Hospital (largest medical center in the Middle East), and the Kennedy Memorial and Peace Forest where you can plant a tree for a small fee.

Bethlehem is seven miles south of Jerusalem from the Damascus Gate (it is traditional for pilgrims to walk it on Christmas). En route you will pass the Tomb of Rachel, wife of Jacob and mother of Joseph, and revered by Moslems, Jews and Christians. At Bethlehem the Church of the Nativity on Manger Square is the principal shrine. The church is the oldest in the country, and the manger is believed to be in the crypt underneath the altar. Another historic site is the Milk Grotto, where Mary's milk is said to have turned the stones chalky white. And by all means, pay a visit to the bazaar where local merchants make a good living selling artifacts to the pilgrims.

ITALY

The Song of Flower *arrives in lovely Portofino.*

AUTHOR'S OBSERVATION

Few countries in the world warrant the purchase of a pre- or post-cruise hotel stay than Italy. Many cruises begin or end in Rome and Venice, and your travel agent can arrange additional nights if the cruise line offers only a one-night add-on. If making independent flight arrangements, TWA has two non-stops per day between JFK and Rome/Milan and if holding sufficient frequent flyer miles, it's a cinch to upgrade to business class (the eight-hour flight can be torture). However, if traveling independently, ask your travel agent to inquire about purchasing transfers to the ship.

Italy's largest seaport, **Genoa**, is a spacious and attractive city that has some fifteen miles of quays receiving ships from all the seas of the world. A popular embarkation point for cruise ships sailing under the

Italian flag, Genoa is an exciting port for the start of any adventure. The city is built up the side of a mountain and boasts many, many fine Renaissance palaces of the sixteenth and seventeenth centuries that overlook the bay (drive along Via Garibaldi and Via Balbi in the Porto Vecchio section). Genoa is midway on the Italian Riviera, which encircles the Ligurian Sea. The western end, or Riviera di Ponente, runs 101 miles to Ventimiglia and features such resorts as San Remo, capital of the flower section of this area and known also for its race course and casino. The eastern end, or Riviera di Levante, runs only seventy miles to La Spezia, a trading port and excursion center.

The rugged, rocky Portofino Peninsula is becoming a popular cruise call. **Portofino** is a small fishing village loved by artists. Except for the summer crowds and traffic, it's a rather sleepy, picturesque scene. My favorite walk is out to the lighthouse at sunset, to gaze out on the Gulf of Rapallo and along the coast to La Spezia harbor.

South of La Spezia is **Livorno** (Leghorn), an ancient trading port that one of the Medici princes linked by canal to Pisa in the sixteenth century. Pisa was a large commercial port in the eleventh century, rivaling Genoa and Venice, but her power declined after the fourteenth century, about the time the Leaning Tower was completed (it was built between 1174 and 1350). Since it began to lean, the tower has become Pisa's most renowned monument, and even native son Galileo used it in the seventeenth century to work out his theory of gravity. The tower leans almost fourteen feet now, due to a fault in the design of the foundation as well as to the poor subsoil on which it was built. It serves as the campanile, or bell tower, to the adjacent twelfth-century Romanesque cathedral and fourteenth-century baptistry.

Some cruise lines use Livorno for the port of entry to Pisa at the mouth of the Arno River, as well as for excursions to **Florence** (approximately one hour's drive from port), where the purest Italian is spoken (Dante was a native son) and some of mankind's most magnificent masterpieces were made. The artistic capital of Italy from the fourteenth to seventeenth centuries, Florence has always been pleasing to the eye to great patrons—the Pitti, Strozzi, Pazzi, and Medicis, whose names still linger on palaces, public buildings and in dedications. Florence remains an art center and its modern craftsmen do beautiful work in leather, silver, wood, gold, and fashions. The term Florentine reflects a special style, just as it was during the Renaissance when talents included Botticelli, Leonardo da Vinci, Raphael, Michelangelo Buonarroti, Brunelleschi, Donatello and Cellini. A visit to Florence is a delightful minicourse in the history of art—no musty classrooms, just beautiful buildings still in use, and paintings and statues everywhere. It's difficult to know where to begin, but the most practical place would be the Ponte Vecchio, that old bridge where the city began and which is now lined with shops.

If you have just one day to spend in Florence on a shore excursion, you will only get a taste of the beauty here. You won't want to miss the bronze doors of the Baptistry, or the Piazza della Signoria, the former center of political life and now the perfect spot to watch the action from a cafe or on the steps of the Loggia del Lanzi. The Pitti and Uffizi are two of the world's finest museums; but my favorite in Florence is the Bargello because it's small, is in a charming former palace, and has a lovely courtyard. It also has some interesting pieces by Michelangelo, Donatello and Della Robbia. Save some time to walk around, have a *gelati* (ice cream) from a sidewalk vendor and read the plaques on old buildings. The last time I was in Florence, I discovered Casa Guidi, at 8 Piazza San Felice, the former home of Elizabeth Barrett and Robert Browning.

On television I saw an old movie with the Bay of Naples in the background and an ocean liner anchored in the harbor; the hero had to choose between his wife on board the ship and a woman whose villa overlooked the bay. Well, the hero chose the woman with the villa, because of the magical quality of the bay. **Naples** is the prime port for passenger traffic in Italy. It is also the birthplace of spaghetti and pizza (the real thing, not what we find in America) and the capital of bel canto. A fascinating, frustrating, and continually surprising city, it is a world apart from the rest of the country. Neopolitans are known for being independent, crafty, tenacious and wary of strangers. Families here are the brotherhood of man once a member . . . never out of mind.

Naples began as the Greek colony Neapolis, and although conquered in the fourth century B.C. by the Romans, never gave up Greek language or customs until the end of the Roman Empire. Since then, seven royal families have reigned over but never really ruled Naples. From ancient times the city has been a popular winter retreat, and the bay has a deserved reputation for providing interesting environs, including mountains, lovely capes and islands. Today, Naples is the jetty for cruises to Capri, Ischia and Sorrento.

Naples is also the principal port for excursions to **Pompeii**, that ancient town smothered in molten ash in the year A.D. 79 from the eruptions of Mt. Vesuvius. The population of Pompeii, about 25,000 at the time, many of them wealthy aristocrats from Rome, had little warning. The entire area was quickly covered in hot lava and cinders, and was rediscovered in the seventeenth century. Excavations have been going since 1748, and today two-thirds of the city can be toured. It's an unforgettable feeling to wander among the uncovered ruins, to walk the stone streets still marked from chariot wheels, enter what were once luxurious villas full of exquisite frescoes and mosaics, and visit the Stabian Baths where both men and women exercised. It's as though the people of Pompeii have never left, their spirits still linger.

On the return to your ship you may want to visit Naples' old quarter (Quartiere Vecchio), the new castle (Castel Nuovo) built in 1282, and the National Museum located in a sixteenth-century palace, full of treasures uncovered at Pompeii as well as at Herculaneum. **Herculaneum** was a nearby town buried in the same eruptions of Mt. Vesuvius but not excavated until the beginning of the nineteenth century. Historians have discovered that this town was for workers and the poorer folk, since instead of luxury villas they have uncovered what appear to be blocks of tenements.

Capri, Song of Flower

If time allows, an excursion to the isle of **Capri**, a long-time haven for the international set, might be on your agenda. This island of dreams is four miles long and two miles wide, yet has some lovely wild and lonely spots, Blue Grotto sea cave, and 951-foot Monte Solaro (a chair hoist takes you up for a spectacular view). Or take a funny old convertible taxi up the Corniche Road to Anacapri, past the lovely villas owned by movie stars to the Piazza della Vittoria where you can sit in the sun, try the local wine and drink in the atmosphere.

Since the reign of Emperor Trajan (A.D. 53–117), Civitavecchia (old city) has been the port for **Rome**, capital of Italy and cradle of Christianity. Called the Eternal City, Rome is thought by historians, poets and artists to have no equal in all the world. A brief, one-day cruise call can never do justice to Rome, but it can give you a feeling for the many great monuments that have existed here for centuries. Unlike many other historic cities, Rome is alive, vibrant, and full of action, which makes its many ruins more appealing, its piazzas more exciting, and its many churches more interesting. Legend says the city was founded by twins Romulus and Remus, the offspring of Mars and Venus, who were abandoned in the Tiber River and brought up by a she-wolf. Ancient Rome was first a republic, then capital of an empire whose influence reached to England and Asia, and later divided into the Western Empire (Rome) and the Eastern Empire (Constantinople). Under the reign of Constantine (324–337), Christianity became the state religion and the era of the pagans versus the Christians began. And when there were no more emperors in the political forum, the popes wielded power and often assumed absolute authority.

AUTHOR'S OBSERVATION

Any tour of this metropolis actually encompasses three separate cities ancient Rome, Christian Rome and the Rome of the people. This last is the Rome you can't miss even on a quick visit–tourists sitting on the steps of Piazza di Spagna, policemen in white gloves, cars and buses going in circles, and the new next to the old and the ancient.

Ancient Rome consists of the Forum, the Palatine Hill, the Coliseum (where gladiator contests took place and early Christians were confronted with lions), the Arch of Constantine, the Imperial Forums and the Baths. Also visit the Pantheon, the most perfectly preserved ancient building in the world, and the beginning of the Appian Way (Via Appia Antica), which was built in 312 B.C. and runs all the way down to the port of Brindisi.

Christian Rome centers on Vatican City, which (with 109 acres) is the smallest independent state in the world. By tradition, its Swiss guards wear uniforms designed by Michelangelo and all come from the same town of Valais, in Switzerland. Walking through Piazza San Pietro is an overwhelming experience. This square is an extension of the basilica itself, site of papal funerals and the enthronement of new popes. The Emperor Constantine built the first St. Peter's on this site in the fourth century; the present basilica dates from the sixteenth century and is the combined work of Bramante, Sangallo, Raphael and Michelangelo who designed the dome. After St. Peter's, you may wonder if it's worth visiting other churches in Rome. Yes, but only at a very, very, leisurely pace. Dominating the Tiber River, and a personal joy, is Castel Sant Angelo, built by the Emperor Hadrian in A.D. 135 as a mausoleum and turned into a fortress in the Middle Ages. It's connected to the Vatican by a tunnel handy for several popes during difficult times. The interior is a museum of ancient weapons and some works of art. You can also see the prison cells and apartments of the popes (some combination!). From the top, the view of Rome is wonderful. I also like the seven hills of Rome, the white-marble Victor Emmanuel monument, Mussolini's balcony and the Via Condotti where Gucci, Ginori, Valentino and Bulgari display their wares. But the fountains of Rome will beckon, and if you do not stop to throw two coins over your shoulder into the Trevi Fountain (one to ensure your return to Rome, the other to fulfill a wish), then you have not really been to the Eternal City.

AUTHOR'S OBSERVATION

The Grand and Excelsior are Rome's best hotels and if seeking a "Lifestyles of the Rich and Famous" experience, check out three-night hotel packages for decadently opulent experience.

Ever-changing **Venice**, one of the most romantic cities in the world, was used by Shakespeare as the setting for *Othello* and *The Merchant of Venice*; Thomas Mann wrote *Death in Venice*; and in Ernest Hemingway's *Across the River and Through the Trees* the last line is, "Take me to the Gritti" [hotel]! Of Venice's many painters, my favorite is the 18th-century Venetian who so frequently recorded the play of light on canals that he was called Canaletto. In this romantic city you'll fall under the spell of gondolas, narrow canals, bridges, the sun setting on St. Mark's Square, funny houses in back alleys with their balconies and flower pots, palaces of the rich and noble, and the sound of water lapping as you walk along the quiet streets. Once under this spell, you're under forever.

The best way to approach Venice is by water, for the city is wed to the Adriatic Sea. Alas, the waters rise more each year and the city sinks. Although pessimists predicted the city would not be standing by the end of this century, the Italian government finally began a preservation project to give Venice a long and happy life.

Founded in the 9th century, Venice was made a republic with a Doge (leader), and soon enjoyed such great prosperity via the Crusades (which were much more an economic than a religious endeavor) that an empire evolved. The Venetian Empire, whose influence reached as far as Asia Minor, was at its height in the first half of the 15th century and began to decline after mid-century, just as the arts began to flourish. The 16th century gave us the painter Titian, as well as a special style of architecture that became synonymous with grand palaces and civic buildings.

The best way to see Venice is on foot, following no specific route (but with a good map in hand). I like to begin and finish each day in St. Mark's Square, home of thousands of pigeons, unending aperitifs, old-worn charm and elegant shops. The square changes person ality by the hour. On the square is St. Mark's Basilica, a jumble of styles put together through the centuries, which has played host to innumerable historic events and figures. The interior decoration is dazzling, but pay special attention to the bronze horses over the doorway, brought back from Constantinople in 1204 by one of the Doges. Unfortunately, what you see today are copies of the original works because the priceless bronzes were deteriorating from air pollution. Take a ride up the bell tower (this is a real campanile) for an overview of all Venice, and then tour the Doge's Palace for a taste of how the city's famous leaders lived and treated their enemies to the famous Bridge of Sighs.

Venice consists of 117 islands, 150 canals, and some 400 bridges! A ride on the Grand Canal is mandatory either by gondola in the moonlight or water taxi during the day for the 2-mile stretch of the largest concentration of 12th- to 18th-century palaces in the world. Stop, if you can, at the Rialto Bridge (with the famous hump) and visit the shops and galleries overlooking the canal. This is the business section of Venice and a good place to browse.

Across the canal from St. Mark's Square is the Island of San Giorgio, a few minutes away by water taxi. Here, in a peaceful and serene atmosphere, the church of San Giorgio Maggiore is in stark contrast to the Basilica across the way. Sit for a spell on the quay, waiting for the vaporetto to return, to view the hustle and bustle going on across the water! For a lighter diversion, the Lido is a fashionable resort about a half-hour's ride by water from St. Mark's Square. It's known for its lovely beach, beautiful people and casino. Another popular excursion is the island of Murano, a glass works since 1292. You can visit the main canal-street, lined with Renaissance houses, and the glass works and museum, but shop prices are high here.

AUTHOR'S OBSERVATION

I'd hock the family farm to spend a few nights in the Gritti Palace in Venice (built in 1500 and a former residence of the Doge)–you'll think you've died and gone to heaven if your windows open on the Grand Canal. If your cruise begins or ends in this city, check out CIGA's three-night hotel package for the Gritti.

Italy's islands Elba, the Lipari, Sardinia and Sicily are especially popular as cruise calls, for they offer a varied landscape and history. **Elba**, the largest in the Tuscan archipelago, is often called the Island of Sea Horses, but it is best known as the home of exiled Napoleon Bonaparte from 1814 to 1815. Here Napoleon reigned for less than a year following his abdication in Paris, and brooded over the view of his native Corsica. Cruise ships dock at Portoferraio, the sleepy capital of the island, guarded by two ancient forts. A walk along the waterfront and up the steps into the old section of town will take you to the Villa dei Mullini, where Napoleon often stayed and where he left mementos. A short ride from town is the Villa Napoleone at San Martino. Set in the beautiful hills, with terraced gardens overlooking the bay, this was the former emperor's summer residence, a mini-version of Versailles (but hardly so well kept in fact, it's a very poor relative). Though the setting is lovely, I get a feeling of sadness.

The Lipari are an archipelago of seven small volcanic islands known for stark beauty and brilliant sunshine. Also known as the Aeolian Islands, because the ancients believed that Aeolus, the God of the Wind, lived here, the islands are Lipari, Vulcano, Alicudi, Salina, Filicudi, Panarea, and Stromboli. **Stromboli**, featured on the cruise circuit, has a smoking crater, vineyard-covered hills and Moorish-style houses. The crater has minor eruptions of lava, and the spectacle of fiery stones falling into the sea is especially dramatic when seen from your ship at night.

Sardinia is a large island in the Tyrrhenian Sea, second in size only to Sicily, its southeastern neighbor. The island is said to have been colonized by the Cretans, which puts its first civilization around 2000 B.C., but a number of different peoples occupied it in rapid succession before the Spanish took over in the early 18th century. As a result, Sardinians have a keen sense of hospitality (they have no choice, one might say), honor and are tough men and women of agriculture.

Cagliari, Sardinia's capital, once a flourishing Carthaginian city, is now a busy seaport. It boasts a fine Roman amphitheater and a national museum of antiquities. St. Saturninus Basilica dates from the 5th century and is thought to be one of the oldest Christian churches in the Mediterranean area. Cagliari's bustle is quite a contrast to the peaceful and rugged countryside, where native women wear long, pleated skirts and lace mantillas (left over from the Spanish days, no doubt) and shy away from the approach of strangers. Menfolk wear funny horned hats and are never far away from their dwarf-like donkeys.

Sardinia was put on the map of the international set a few years ago when the Aga Khan organized the development of the Costa Smeralda area on the northeast coastline. Here, where the scenery is spectacular and the sea an emerald green, he poured millions of dollars into luxury hotels, seasonal apartments and yacht basins for his friends and their friends. He used good taste—the buildings blend beautifully with the terrain and local Sardinian architecture. Those who do not come off yachts can fly into nearby Olbia for a visit to the eighty sun-filled beaches, or they can disembark for the day from cruise ships that dock during the season in the port of Olbia.

Sicily, the largest and most mysterious of the Mediterranean islands, is home to some five million people noted for dark complexions, despite a few vestiges of the old Norman days in the occasional blond, blue-eyed baby. Sicilians are also reputed to have sinister characters, a sweeping and unfair appraisal drawn from movies about organized crime in the United States. The truth is, most Sicilians simply cultivate their vines, almond trees, fruits, and vegetables and have little to do with the outside world. Sicily is called the archaeological museum of Europe for its Greek temples and theaters, Roman bridges and aqueducts, Saracen mosques, Norman churches and castles. It houses so many interesting relics of European power struggles during the past 2000 years that it has many ports in which cruise ships call: **Agrigento**, with its Greco-Roman quarter and Valley of the Temples; **Catania**, which has been destroyed several times by eruptions from Mt. Etna; Messina; **Palermo**, the capital and chief seaport and the crossroads of civilizations for centuries; **Syracuse**, once the rival of Athens, with its beautiful bay and fine ruins of a former Greek city; and **Taormina**, a beautiful resort overlooking the sea and facing Mt. Etna.

Mt. Etna dominates Sicily in one way or another. It is the largest active volcano in Europe. In ancient times 135 eruptions were recorded, but the worst was in 1669, when the lava almost totally destroyed Catania. Already in this century, Etna has erupted 11 times; another could occur at any moment. Nonetheless, visitors adore the ascent of the volcano to the huge black cone with fruit trees flourishing on its slopes. From Catania to the summit is about 20 miles, plus 20 minutes by cable car, and just under one hour on foot (high heels should not be worn on this climb). If you like to see the earth smoke and sputter, you will enjoy this excursion, provided you are dressed warmly enough. Otherwise, you may prefer a peaceful terrace in town and a glass of local wine. Later, stroll in the Bellini Gardens for a fine panorama of the city and Mt. Etna.

MALTA

Your cruise ship will sail into **Valletta**, the capital that dominates the grand harbor of the Maltese Islands of Malta, Gozo and Comino. These islands have had their share of shipwrecks. Ulysses supposedly spent some time in the arms of Calypso on the island of Gozo; and Apostle Paul is said to have drifted to shore in about 60 A.D. and lived three months in a cave between Rabat and Mdina while converting the island of Malta to Christianity. These islands, strategically located in the middle of the Mediterranean, have been the center of a struggle between maritime powers for centuries.

The Maltese Islands are thought to have been affiliated with Sicily as well as North Africa. The first known inhabitants were Sicilian Neolithic farmers of about 4000 B.C. The Phoenicians arrived later (700 B.C.) and used the fine harbors for their trading activities. They left the basis of a language that is still in use today. But Malta's most interesting period dates from 1530 to 1798 when the Knights of St. John made their home here and built fortifications, palaces, inns and churches. Shortly after the knights arrived, in 1565, an attack by the Turks was repulsed and brought great fame to Malta. (This military prowess was repeated from 1940 to 1943 when Malta resisted the Axis powers.)

Valletta, founded in the mid-16th century, reflects the island's rich heritage. For a tour of beautiful places in the capital, begin at St. John's Cathedral and move on to the Palace of the Grand Masters and Armory. A fine national museum of archaeology is housed in the Auberge de Provence, one of the inns of the Knights of St. John of Jerusalem (who founded Malta). Later than these mid-16th-century structures, but considered one of the oldest theaters in Europe, is the Manoel Theatre built in 1731 by one of the Grand Masters, Manoel de Vilhena. Outside of Valletta you can tour some unique sites, including the megalithic monuments of 2500 B.C., the Ghar Dalam Cave with fossils of animals that roamed some 170,000 years ago, a Blue Grotto that rivals the one in Capri, and the cave in which St.

Paul is believed to have lived during his 3-month stay in A.D. 60. (An account of his shipwreck can be found in Acts XXVII and XXVIII.)

The Maltese Islands also mean beautiful bays, beaches and brightly colored boats called *dghajjes*, which you can take for touring the grottos and caves, as well as for visiting the islands of Gozo and Comino. And when you're in the mood for shopping, the local crafts feature handmade tiles, plates, and glassware and that wonderful Maltese cross!

MOROCCO

AUTHOR'S OBSERVATION

In Morocco you'll be harassed unmercifully by throngs trying to sell you stuff—especially "antique" rugs. Real antique carpets are rare in Morocco today, but merchants bury them in lime for a few days to give them that appearance. A colleague was chased down the street with a carpet-toting fellow trying to get $200 (original price was $3000). To avoid harrassment in the bazaar, it's better to hire a "guide" who will fend off the locals, while still trying to steer you to places where he gets a commission.

The Kingdom of Morocco, at the westernmost point of North Africa, is the land of the Casbah, couscous, caftans and Casablanca. Once part of the Carthaginian empire, and later a part of the province of Mauritania under the Romans, Morocco was conquered by the Arabs, the Portuguese, the Spanish and finally the French. It first became an independent Arab kingdom in 788 but broke up by the 10th century. Independence from France was finally gained in 1956. Couscous (made of semolina, meat and vegetables) is the national dish and caftans are the native dress. The famous Casbah, though, is in Tangier, which is a less frequent cruise call than Casablanca. You can prepare yourself by catching the movie classic *Casablanca*, with Humphrey Bogart and Ingrid Bergman. Actually, the bustling city you sail into has no relation to the Casablanca of the 1940s; it is a thoroughly modern, 20th-century city the gateway to North Africa.

Casablanca has one of the largest harbors in Africa, and three gateways connect the old medina with the port. It's called Casa by those who live here and the Great White City by visitors. More new than old, Casablanca is also more Moroccan than French. It has both an old and new *medina* (the latter built by the French in 1921), a royal palace where the king stays when in town, United Nations Square and Arab League Park. The most beautiful part of the city is the seaside residential area with lovely homes and romantic views. You may have heard of one quarter, Anfa, because Churchill, Roosevelt and De Gaulle met here during World War II for the Casablanca Conference.

Just 57 miles northeast along the Atlantic coastline is **Rabat**, capital of Morocco and home of King Hassan II. The drive is worthwhile. Only Moslems are allowed to enter religious monuments in Morocco, but you can visit the Quadias Casbah and Museum of Oudaia for a stroll through the gardens and the overwhelming displays of native arts and crafts. You may also climb the Tower of Hassan for a view of the city of Sale across the Bou Regreg. Take a walk through the medina, whose walls date from the12th and 17th centuries. Here you can peek at souk after souk, visit the old wool market, and pass by the *mellah* or Jewish quarter. And if an item grabs your fancy, bargain. The experts become serious only after your third offer.

The *pièce de résistance* in Morocco is the all-day tour to **Marrakesh**. This imperial, red-ochre city founded by the Almoravids in the 11th century is the jewel of the Islamic world. Marrakesh, 150 hot miles from Casablanca, is an oasis at the edge of the scorching Sahara Desert. The temperatures during the summer months average more than 100 degrees (F), which is why the city was once a winter playground for the rich and famous. Winston Churchill used to stay at the famed La Mamounia Hotel, the gardens of which came straight from the Arabian Nights. Add a stroll through this magnificent hotel to your sightseeing list. The landscape of Marrakesh is dominated by the pink sandstone Koutoubia, or Mosque of the Scribes, which has a minaret 222 feet high. This great monument of Moorish architecture and decoration was built in the 12th century. Below the mosque is the Djemma El Fna, the country's largest marketplace and greatest free entertainment center, where you can buy anything in the world from just about everyone. This is the most famous square in all North Africa; and if you survive it, you're on your way to becoming a native. It is a sight to behold—the sea of water-sellers, story-tellers, acrobats, soothsayers, dancers and snake-charmers creating a incredible biblical atmosphere (in the epitome of a Moorish town). Other sights to tantalize the senses include the *medina* and *mellah*, the 16th-century monument of Medersa Ibn Yussef, the royal tombs, Bahia palace and gardens (provided no guests-of-state are in residence), Dar Si Said (arts and handcrafts museum) and the many imperial gardens. Marrakesh is famous for its beautifully planned gardens replete with olive groves, especially the Aguedal and Menara

as well as the Mamounia (attached to the deluxe hotel of the same name). These gardens are all the more impressive and inviting when you remember that the mysterious desert is but a step away.

THE SUEZ CANAL AND THE RED SEA

The opening of the Suez Canal in 1869 was honored by the presence of royalty, including such personages as the Empress Eugenie of Austria, for whom a palace was built at the foot of the Great Pyramids (now the Mena House Oberoi Hotel where you may have lunch). Italian composer Giuseppe Verdi wrote his spectacular opera Aida (with live elephants on stage) just for this occasion, and the royal guests reportedly received it with a tumultuous welcome at the newly constructed Cairo Opera House. What an inaugural for the 100.76-mile canal that joins the Mediterranean with the Red Sea!

It took a full decade to build the Suez Canal, and years of study and indecision passed before a shovel even touched the earth. The Suez is probably not the first canal on this site. Scholars believe that a passageway of some sort existed between the two seas as early as the 6th century B.C. but was closed through neglect. From 1869 to 1980, the Suez closed only twice—the last time from the 1967 war to June 5, 1975, when it was reopened by Egyptian president Anwar Sadat. The western gateway to the canal is **Port Said**, a town that boomed during the late 19th century and is now known as a free port. You'll find little to do or see here, and most cruise ships call only as a courtesy and to offer full-day tours to Cairo, which comes into view at the end of a 3-hour bus ride through the desert. (You can amuse yourself during the ride by counting the numerous checkpoints, rusted tanks left over from the recent battles and the villages full of tents topped by television antennae.) From Port Said the transit through the canal to Suez takes about 18 hours and passes by many little canal towns, of which the prettiest is Ismailia. The city of **Suez**, the southernmost port of the canal, is a wonderful spot to view what you have just passed through (or if you are sailing in the opposite direction, what you are about to experience). Suez also sparks little interest for me, but it is another good embarkation point for visits to Cairo, since it's a reasonable two-hour drive from here.

Having transited the Suez Canal, your cruise vessel continues down the Gulf of Suez, between the Sinai Peninsula and Egypt's eastern desert. The first noticeable settlement of any size on this rocky, undeveloped Red Sea coastline is Hurghada, approximately 250 land miles south of Suez. From Hurghada you can see Mt. Sinai (Gebel Moussa) on a clear day. Just below the city lies the port of

Safaga, from where all-day tours to Thebes, Karnak and Luxor on the Nile River are arranged. The tours, although lengthy (12 to 14 hours), are wonderful, for you will visit the Valley of the Kings (tombs of Tutankhamen and Ramses VI) as well as the Temple of Queen Hatshepsut, eat an enjoyable lunch, and then ride by horse-drawn carriage to the Temple of Karnak.

Following a visit to the Temple of Luxor, you may have time for a sunset sail on the Nile in a felucca before returning to your ship in Safaga for a late supper on board (according to the fine itinerary planned by Raymond & Whitcomb of New York). If your ship schedules another day in Safaga, try to fly down to the temple complex of Abu Simbel, about 160 miles south of Aswan (at a cost of about $150 per person). Here you can explore the Great Temple of Ramses II and the smaller temple dedicated to his consort and queen, Nefertari. These two monuments were rescued from the floodwaters of the Aswan Dam in 1969, in a scheme that involved moving the temples, piece by piece, to a new site that was seven hundred feet away but two hundred feet higher. The project took four and a half years and cost millions of dollars, and one engineer reportedly said that Abu Simbel qualifies as a wonder of both the ancient and modern world.

From Safaga your cruise vessel sails northeast to **Aqaba** in Jordan, a port town at the tip of the gulf that separates the Sinai and Arabian peninsulas. Aqaba is a biblical town, said to date from as early as the 10th century B.C. Known for its trading because of its location on the gulf, at one time it was a part of Egypt. Little of this past history remains, and the area now emphasizes splendid scuba diving on its beautiful coral reefs equal to any throughout the world. As a result, Aqaba is becoming a fashionable Middle East resort. Even King Hussein finds the 30-minute flight from Amman (capital of Jordan) short enough to make him a frequent visitor to his villa on the beach.

Two unforgettable shore excursions, to Wadi Rumm and Petra, leave from Aqaba. **Wadi Rumm** is a great desert valley, about an hour's drive from the port, through which the famous T. E. Lawrence passed in his pursuit of the Turks during World War I. The route that Lawrence and his Desert Legion followed is fascinating, and your journey, either by car or camel train, will eventually end at the fort of the Wadi Rumm Desert Patrol, which is also the home of several Bedouin tribes. Huge, red-stone cliff scenery; an almost perfect cloudless sky; and colorful Bedouin costumes combine to create an impression that boggles the mind. You may even be invited to a traditional Bedouin feast, although I understand that sheep's eyes are no longer served to foreign guests!

The rose-colored city of **Petra**, also known by the biblical name of Sela, lies in the desert near the Dead Sea and can be entered only through a narrow passageway that is just comfortable for humans and horses. Petra means rock, as does sela, and this narrow passage (or siq) is lined with towering cliffs of rosy-hued stone. Petra, one of the world's most unusual ancient sites, could date from as early as 2000 B.C. Through the centuries it was home to several different nomadic tribes, but the city reached its height under the Romans, who carved magnificent monuments out of the distinctive rock (the Treasury is the most perfectly preserved example). Later it became part of the Byzantine Empire, fell to the Arabs, and then was forgotten for centuries until it was rediscovered by a Swiss explorer in the early 19th century. What he found and what you see is a dazzling array of classical monuments, historic sites such as the Tomb of Aaron (the brother of Moses), and splendid views of the surrounding ancient lands.

PORTUGAL

Portugal's capital on the Tagus River, **Lisbon**, is a low-key city that may seem drab in comparison to other European capitals, but visitors soon appreciate its special character. Legend says that Ulysses founded the town, but the credit to the Phoenicians in 1200 B.C. is more believable. Historically, Lisbon has gained many honors, for the great discoverers Vasco da Gama (the Indies) and Pedro Alvares Cabral (Brazil) set out from here in the late 15th century when Portugal reigned as a major maritime power.

Medieval Lisbon, the city's most fascinating section, begins with St. George's Castle overlooking the sea, then winds down into the Santa Cruz quarter of narrow streets and old houses. Between the Tagus and the castle is the Alfama, or former Moorish section, with stair-streets, tiny squares and blind alleys lined with 16th- to 18th-century houses. Walking is the best way indeed, the only way to get around. From the castle, you can walk all the way down to the Praca do Comercio (Commerce Square) on the water. Here, where the Stock Exchange has replaced the former Royal Palace, the Portuguese king would walk down to greet every returning ship to collect incoming gold and riches.

Manueline Lisbon is up the Tagus in a suburb called **Belem**. A 16th-century monastery lies along the harbor here, its cloister a masterpiece of rich sculptured stone. On the riverside is a Monument to the Discoveries, erected in 1960 to honor the 500th anniversary of Prince Henry the Navigator. Nearby are the museums of popular art, ancient art, and the Coach Museum. The latter is installed in the former riding school of Belem Palace and holds some of the most ornate royal coaches from the 16th to 19th centuries. Most of them appear well-used, while others served merely as small gifts of appreciation between monarchs. All look extremely uncomfortable! Another museum worthy of a visit, the Gulbenkian, shows the extensive collection of an Armenian who willed his entire cache of artworks to his adopted country, Portugal, at his death in 1955.

Europe's longest suspension bridge spans the Tagus River. Originally called the Salazar Bridge after Portugal's hardy dictator, its name was changed after the 1974 revolution to the April 25th Bridge. Across the bridge are some interesting towns, especially those on the Atlantic coast—the quaint fishing village of Sesimbra; Setubal, with its sardine boats and 12th-century castle; and Arrabida, where the scenery from mountain to sea is spectacular. Estoril, that fashionable gambling resort where deposed monarchs live out their twilight days in splendor, is only about fifteen miles south of Lisbon, and a few minutes more is charming Cascais, where former royalty also resides. But the most beautiful destination for a day trip from the capital is Sintra, nestled high in the Sierra de Sintra range; Lord Byron once called it a glorious Eden.

AUTHOR'S OBSERVATION

Philip Sousa, an astute colleague, recently tried a new cruise along the Douro River and proclaims it an outstanding way to visit lovely villages and hamlets where locals turned out to dance with passengers, while crossing Europe's largest lock and tasting the local vintages. EuroCruises offers one-week sailings aboard the Lady Ivy May, round-trip from Oporto.

At the end of the day in Lisbon, you must do what the Portuguese do: have a glass of red wine and listen to a little fado, haunting songs of fate sung to the accompaniment of romantic guitars. Early tradition held that only women sang these sad songs, but recently males have also sung them.

The 35-mile long island of **Madeira**, 560 miles southwest of Lisbon and on the same latitude as Casablanca, is often called the Pearl of the Atlantic because of its mild climate year-round, its lush subtropical vegetation and its vast panoramas of volcanic landscapes. The

Portuguese refer to Madeira proudly as the floating garden because the floral splendor includes bougainvillea, jacaranda trees, hibiscus, frangipani, poinsettia, Bird of Paradise and all varieties of orchids. Madeira arose from the sea floor as the result of a volcanic eruption in the Tertiary Period.

Thus, its rocky shoreline abuts right Petra's beautiful tombs and temples, and cliffs that change character with the rays of the sun, almost require you to set out with plenty of film and good hiking shoes.

Inland, Madeira's mountains are so steep that farmers must not only dig out narrow terraces on which to plant, but also build *palheiros*—small thatched sheds in which to keep their cows (lest the cows miss their step and fall over the cliff).

Funchal, capital and chief port of Madeira, was named for the sweet smell of fennel. When Portuguese explorer Joao Gonclaves Zarco discovered the island in 1419, called it Madeira (wooded isle), and claimed it in the name of Prince Henry the Navigator, he also named Funchal. The English relate a more romantic tale: they say the island was first found by the English adventurer Robert Machim, who was shipwrecked here (with his mistress) in 1346. Perhaps because of this story, but more likely because of the comfortably mild climate, the English love Madeira.

Cruise ships dock in Funchal, which lies at the end of a beautiful bay. Most of the city's 98,000-plus inhabitants live in charming white houses perched on terraces in the surrounding hills. At night the twinkling city lights give off a fantasy-land feeling. And if you're an early riser, just a few steps from the cruise ship pier you can find the small flower market where local women in traditional costumes are as colorful as their merchandise. If you wish to have some Madeira, m'dear, this is the right place. The Madeira Wine Association on Avenida Arriaga has a tasting lodge (as do all the local firms) where you can sample as much as you like, from the sweetest Malmsey (Duke of Clarence is the most popular brand) to the driest Sercial. Whatever you wish to purchase will probably be packed in a locally made wicker basket. Wicker and exquisite embroidery are two of the island's best known cottage industries; both products are worth the entire visit.

Your sightseeing excursions should include a visit to Quinta das Cruzes, a villa (built by Zarco) that is now a museum surrounded by a beautiful orchid garden; Camara de Lobos, the fishing village Sir Winston Churchill painted on his visits to the island; further along the coast, Cabo Girao, the world's second highest sea cliff (at 1900 feet), with a proper railing so you can look without falling off. And if you like a thrill now and then, take a toboggan ride down to Funchal from Monte, four miles away. Two straw-hatted professionals who wear rubber-tire shoes will guide your toboggan, a wicker basket on wooden runners, as you slip and slide down the smooth pebble path. Each toboggan holds two people, so you can cling together during the fast turns.

AUTHOR'S OBSERVATION

The area around Funchal has many good restaurants and smart hotels. My favorite is the famous old Reid's Hotel (again, where Churchill loved to stay) where the terrace view of the harbor is lovely. Reid's also has a wonderful garden, and if you're confused about the name of a particular plant or flower, the manager might just get out his book and look it up for you. Closer to town is the ultramodern Casino Park Hotel, designed by the renowned Brazilian architect Oscar Niemeyer, in a complex that includes the Casino of Madeira (so if you like roulette, blackjack, French bank and slot machines, drop in between 4 p.m. and 3 a.m.). If you hunger for real country food, take a taxi up into the hills where the restaurant A Seta serves hot, crusty bread, ***espetada*** *(beef on a spit); pitchers of local wine; and Madeira honey cake for a bargain price.*

SPAIN

As your cruise ship sails into the harbor of **Barcelona**, your senses will tell you that full enjoyment lies ahead. For Spain's second largest city and principal port has character, beauty and charm. The people who live here call themselves Catalans and speak their own language, which they insist is not a combination of French and Castilian Spanish. But they, and the city in which they live, are certainly influenced by the proximity to neighboring France as well as to the varied cultures that have come through this port since the 3rd century B.C.

Barcelona has wide boulevards lined with sidewalk cafes and elegant shops; flowers everywhere and palm trees (which tell you about the climate); a gothic quarter with narrow streets and 13th- to 15th-century buildings (visit the Palacio Real where Columbus paid a visit following his return from the New World); Montjuich Park and Tibidabo Mountain; the Ramblas section; and the historic port section with a statue of Columbus, a replica of the Santa Maria and an interesting Maritime Museum. While touring the city, every visitor must stop to pay respects to two favorite sons: Pablo Picasso and Antonio Gaudi, the latter a surrealist architect who died in 1926 (run over by a tram). Gaudi left behind some crazy concoctions, the most famous of which is the church of the Sagrada Familia (Holy Family), begun in 1884 and still unfinished because he left no plans (and so far, no one has been able to interpret his motives).

Other examples of gaudy works are Guell Lodge and Park and some luxury flats on the Paseo de Gracia. By contrast, the Picasso Museum will seem like an old friend. Located in the 14th-century Aguilar Palace at 15 Calle Montcada (the street is lined with medieval Catalan architecture, so be sure to walk the entire length), the museum contains some 2500 works donated by Picasso. The artist lived here as a young man, in Bohemian style down near the port. Some of his wonderful early sketches of Barcelona show us what the city was like around the turn of the century.

Malaga is the undisputed capital of the Costa del Sol, Spain's sun coast and a year-round tourist spot. It is also the most important town on the Mediterranean side of Andalusia. The Moors, who occupied this part of Spain for eight centuries, gave it the name Andalusia, and the Arab influences are still very much felt in Malagan houses, folklore and colorful native costumes. Some say the best flamenco, the soul of Andalusia, can be seen here—a good complement to *gazpacho*, the region's gastronomic specialty. Malaga, prosperous and lively, is protected by mountains in the north and the sea to the south. Not far from the harbor and the lovely, park-lined Paseo de Cintura del Puerto are two fortresses that made Malaga one of the major strongholds of Andalusia. The higher one, Gibralfaro, commands a spectacular view from its 14th-century ramparts. The lower, Alcazaba, was built over a Roman amphitheater and has lovely Moorish gardens, art and atmosphere. Walk back to the seafront via the 16th-century cathedral and the fascinating shops along Larios Street. Stop at a local cafe for a glass of wine, some crusty bread and a bowl of iced *gazpacho*.

Only one small town in Sicily gets as much sunshine as Malaga, I've heard, so when you're ready for the beach, take a tour to **Torremolinos** where the white, sandy beach is five miles long. It's no longer a quaint little village supported by the sugar cane industry. Now it's row upon row of modern, high-rise hotels and apartment houses. When you've had enough of this impersonal air, you can always return to the Old World atmosphere of Malaga, the Arab-Spanish-gypsy town that gave birth to Pablo Picasso at 15 Plaza de la Merced.

The port of **Vigo**, on Spain's Atlantic coast just north of the Portuguese border, has been an important natural harbor since Roman times. Primarily, it is the point of entry for **Santiago de Compostela**, Spain's holiest of cities. Since the Middle Ages, pilgrims from all over the world have made their way to Santiago where, it is believed, the remains of the Apostle St. James the Greater were buried. The relics were discovered early in the 9th century, and by the 11th century a pilgrimage to St. James shrine in Santiago de Compostela ranked equally with a visit to Jerusalem or Rome. The Apostle became Patron Saint of Spain during the Reconquest. For the half to two million pilgrims a year, a Pilgrim Guide existed, written in the late 12th century by Cluny monks. It described the best routes to take and what sights to enjoy along the way (this may have been the first guidebook ever written).

Santiago de Compostela has changed little since medieval times. One can still wander the winding, stone streets that lead to the plaza and cathedral, just as devoted Christians have done for centuries. The present cathedral, believed to be on the very site where the Apostle's tomb was found, dates from the 11th through 13th centuries. Its huge edifice is always welcoming the faithful and curious who come to pay their respects to the 13th-century statue of St. James and to his relics. If you happen to visit the cathedral on a holy day, as I did a few years ago, you may be able to observe the ceremony of the incense, when a huge, smoking pot is thrown from side to side in front of the altar. I was lucky; in the crowd that day was Spain's handsome King Juan Carlos who had come to pay his respects, and he personally greeted everyone within sight, including a friend and me! In 1982, Santiago de Compostela celebrated a Holy Year Jubilee, a year-long fete that occurs only when July 25, the Day of St. James the Apostle, falls on a Sunday. The jubilee officially begins on December 31 of the previous year, and the Holy Doors on the east face of the cathedral are opened at this time. Like the Holy Doors at St. Peter's Basilica, these doors are allowed to be opened only during a jubilee year.

A tour to Santiago is not complete without a visit to the Hotel de Los Reyes Catolicos on the cathedral square. This remarkable parador (government-run inn) was founded by Ferdinand of Aragon and Isabella of Castile in the late 15th century as a pilgrim inn and hospital. Most of the original carved columns and grillwork are still intact; enjoy them as you walk through the four beautiful patios, large dining room and lovely, antique-filled guestrooms. On the same Plaza de Espana (the cathedral square) are the 12th-century Bishop's Palace, the 18th-century Raxoy Palace (now the Town Hall) and the 17th-century San Jeronimo College. Take your camera. All are worth several thousand words!

BALEARIC ISLANDS

One of Spain's forty-nine provinces is the Balearic archipelago, which consists of Mallorca, Minorca, Ibiza and the small Formentera. Capital of the group and most popular tourist center is **Palma de Mallorca**, a port city spread around the back of a beautiful, wide bay. Palma has a mild climate year-round, lovely old mansions of the 15th and 16th centuries and an interesting harbor. It claims to receive more visitors (by air and sea) than any other place in Spain. The island has been a part of Spain for most of its discovered life (with the exception of three hundred years during Moorish occupation) and boasts its own school of painting (from the 14th to 15th centuries) and at least one well-known native son, Junipero Serra (1713–1784). Born in Petra (a town near the center of the island), Serra became a Franciscan, went to the New World to work with Indians in Mexico and California, and founded several missions and the cities of San Diego, Monterey and San Francisco. Not bad work for a local boy.

Along the waterfront you can see the cathedral, which took from the 13th century to the year 1601 to complete; the Bishops Palace; Almudaina, former residence of the Moorish kings; and Lonja, a 15th-century commercial exchange. But save some energy for a stroll through the Old Quarter with its many beautiful old mansions, public buildings and Moorish Baths left behind from the days of Palma's caliphate. A long climb westward (about two miles) brings you to the site of the 14th-century Bellver Castle, summer residence of Mallorcan kings and later a prison. If you still have the energy to climb the winding steps of the tower, you will enjoy a panoramic view of Palma Bay. And if you are in the mood for shopping, you will find good quality leatherwork here. For a view of the countryside take a tour to Valledemosa, an old Mallorcan village and Carthusian monastery that harbored two famous visitors during the winter of 1838—composer Frederick Chopin and French author George Sand.

The second largest of the Balearic Islands is the cavernous **Minorca** where the remains of a Bronze Age people have been found in the form of *talayots.* These great stones, used to cover funeral chambers, perhaps also formed the bases of primitive houses. The thirty-mile island is dotted with them. Other interesting finds include Stone Age monuments called *navetas*, or upturned boats, that may have been tombs. Check the Archaeological Museum at Conquista Square in Mahon, the capital, for more complete information on and examples of the findings. Minorca is quite a different island from Mallorca, and suffers from its second-best rating. Tourism is less developed here, and the atmosphere is more peaceful and subdued. A certain 18th-century British influence flourishes, attributable to a British occupation of the island. Admiral (Lord) Nelson is said to have visited briefly and even put the finishing touches on a book here during the fall of 1799. And the fishing is reputed to be superb around Minorca. The locals even claim to have invented mayonnaise to serve with their catch of the day.

Tourism is growing on **Ibiza**, the third largest of the Balearic Islands, often called the White Island because of its many whitewashed, limestone buildings with terraced roofs designed to catch rainwater. This mountainous island, with a population of only 35,000 on its twenty-five miles, has been important to Mediterranean trade routes since the 10th century B.C. when the Phoenicians stopped here en route from Spain to Africa. They left behind a splendid graveyard, a necropolis, overlooking the main harbor, with some 2000 tombs.

La Ciudad the city is the primary port town, with about 20,000 inhabitants, busy streets lined with shops, and open-air cafes along the waterfront. In the fishermen's quarter the cubic, whitewashed houses are built one atop the other, leaving space for nothing in between. The pine forests, which fringe the island, explain why the Greeks called this place Pitiousa, or Pine Island.

But there are other trees: almonds, olives, figs, and palms. Just three and one-half nautical miles south of Ibiza lies the Wheat Island, the eight-mile long Formentera. Fourth in size of the Balearics, Formentera has little to attract tourists, but your cruise vessel will probably sail by closely enough so you can see the small harbor of Cala Sabina.

CANARY ISLANDS

Another island-province of Spain, the Canaries lie just 72 miles northwest of Africa and 650 miles south of Europe. The island group consists of Furteventura, Grand Canary, Lanzarote and Tenerife. Cruises often call at the popular ports of Las Palmas and Santa Cruz de Tenerife. **Las Palmas**, capital and main seaport of Grand Canary, is a scallop-shaped island with steep cliffs on the north and south coasts. Founded in a palm grove in 1478, Las Palmas was visited by Christopher Columbus at the commencement of each of his discovery voyages to the New World. Where he actually stayed in 1502 became the palace of the island's first governors and is now a museum of fine arts with a collection of 15th-century maps, charts and navigational equipment used at the time of these voyages.

Like the whole chain, volcanic **Grand Canary** offers some spectacular views from the mountainous areas of black sand beaches over lush fruit trees and tropical flowers. Wonderful excursions begin at Las Palmas, the most interesting of which is to Cruz de Tejeda where, at 4750 feet, you can see a petrified forest. Actually, it's the village of Tejada that stands in a huge volcanic basin. If you climb even higher, to 6496 feet, you can see the island's meterological station as well as a panoramic view of the countryside, the coastline and the sea.

Tenerife, largest of the Canary Islands, possesses the highest summit on Spanish territory, the snowcapped volcanic peak named Mount Teide, on the Las Canadas plateau. For one of the most breathtaking views in the world, visit the cone. You can do so from Santa Cruz, the island's capital and main port. The drive from Santa Cruz passes through La Laguna, the oldest town on Tenerife (founded in 1496) and its first capital. Travel on to the floral paradise of Orotava where the ascent begins. The road up to Teide is twenty-four miles long, past the Aguamansa woods, by the Dornajito and Monteverde springs, and then to the Altavista Resthouse where the funicular will whisk you up to the cone. From here, it's a forty-five-minute climb to the edge, where at 11,664 feet, you'll get one of the thrills of your lifetime. If you prefer to stay in town, Santa Cruz, a free port since 1852, has some charming old houses with wooden balconies that are typical of the island.

TUNISIA

Tunisia's leading seaport is **La Goulette** (Halq al-Wadi), famous for its 16th-century fort (built by Charles V of Spain to safeguard his many conquests in the Mediterranean) and its fish restaurants, which draw people from the nearby capital city of Tunis to the sidewalk tables. La Goulette is but a short distance from the capital the Romans once called Africa Vetus, and from the ruins of the ancient Mediterranean power of Carthage.

Approximately one million people live in greater **Tunis**, a typical North African metropolis that blends the old with the new, and the Oriental with the Occidental in a dizzying fashion. For here was a culture in which the conquering sword of Islam smote the early

Christianity of Byzantium and brought about a vigorous flowering of new art forms. In the 11th century, Tunisia entered another aesthetic era as influences shifted from the eastern Mediterranean to the Moslem West of Andalusia (southern Spain). The art of this period, delicate and refined, appears in illuminated manuscripts, copperwork, carved wood and stucco lacework. In the 16th century Tunisia became part of the Ottoman Empire, and Turkish art introduced a new dimension that became increasingly baroque. In 1881, the country became a French protectorate. It received its independence in 1956 and today is a nation poised (as they say) on the brink of change.

Nonetheless, as you drive through Tunis you will see the city's layers of history evident on every street corner. The medina, or inner city of shops and old houses, is considered one of the most beautiful in the Islamic world. There is the great mosque Djamaa Ez-Zitouna, with 184 columns that were pilfered from the Roman temples of Carthage. The National Library of Tunis, which the Turks used as a barracks, has a remarkable collection of illuminated Koran manuscripts, and the beautiful Palace of Dar Ben Abdullah is one of the Tunisian great houses. Outside the Medina, boulevards and buildings with whitewashed fronts and light-blue shutters to filter the bright Mediterranean sun give the air of a French provincial town. (French is still the second language here, after Arabic.)

Just a short drive from this richness are the Carthaginian ruins of Punic and Roman Tunisia. The Phoenicians founded **Carthage** in 814 B.C., and the city became a Mediterranean power by the 6th century B.C., influencing civilizations as far as southern Spain and the Balearic Islands. As the ancient Romans grew stronger and conquered lower Italy, they disliked the Carthaginians more and more and referred to them as Punics, which applied not only to the language they spoke (a dialect of Phoenician) but also to the fact that they were considered treacherous and perfidious. A series of wars broke out, known as the Punic Wars; during the second Punic War (218 to 201 B.C.), a Carthaginian general named Hannibal crossed the Alps with the aid of elephants and invaded Italy, much to the disgrace of the Roman armies. Carthage was then totally destroyed, condemned to death by the Roman Senate in 146 B.C. The city, resurrected by Emperor Augustus, became a Roman province. The baths, built in the 2nd century A.D. under Antoninus Pius, were among the largest in the empire. Built on the seashore near the site where the first Phoenician ships anchored, this magnificent structure measured seven hundred feet in length. Its sumptuous decorations were second to none. Other relics of these two Carthages that were nine centuries apart are: the Necropolis; the city gate; a theater; the Tophet (where Carthaginians first offered human sacrifices, then substituted animals) and some interesting, beautifully decorated private houses.

Some shore tours also stop at **Sidi bou Said**, a Moorish village along the coast from Carthage, and a photographer's paradise with its whitewashed houses untouched by the modern world. Here you can wander the steeply winding streets, past tiny shops, cafes and benches crowded with village elders having a smoke. Where else, you may wonder, is the sky so blue, the cypress so green and the bougainvillea so scarlet? Look across the Bay of Tunis to Bou Cornine, the twin-peaked mountain, and you will understand why this charming oasis is so popular with artists and lovers alike.

TURKEY

The little fishing village of **Dikili** on the edge of Asia Minor is a relatively new call for ships cruising the Aegean. A thrilling stop, Dikili is just a 35-minute bus ride away from the classical ruins of **Pergamum**, the ancient city that flourished for some four centuries (from the 2nd century B.C. to the 2nd century A.D.). During the height of her power, Pergamum was a city of some 160,000 inhabitants and governed most of western and central Asia Minor. Bergama (the modern name) lies on a plain with the ancient Acropolis to the north and the Asklepeion to the southwest.

The Acropolis was the site of various kings palaces, temples, a theater and the second largest library in the ancient world (after Alexandria). The library is said to have contained approximately 200,000 papyrus scrolls; when the Egyptians stopped exporting papyrus (they were becoming slightly jealous of the competition), the people of Pergamum simply invented parchment and continued writing books. The Egyptians, however, had the last word, for Mark Anthony carried away most of the library's contents in 41 B.C. as a present for his beloved Cleopatra. The beautifully restored theater, on the side of the Acropolis, features a white marble stage that hosts the annual Pergamum festival. Next to the theater sits a small temple dedicated to Dionysus, the god of wine. Archaeologists believe that this temple was placed on the first dead-end street in the world, for a covered walk led from here all the way down the hill to the Asklepeion, about a mile distant. The Asklepeion, a complex dedicated to the god of medicine and reputed to be the second largest hospital in the ancient world (after Epidaunus), specialized in psychotherapy. It was so popular that the coffers of Pergamum swelled from the many patients who came for treatments. The cure featured lolling in mud baths, getting lots of sleep, watching comedies (never tragedies) in the 3500-seat open theater and running naked through the halls. Perhaps because of this last exercise, the treatment center had a central heating system.

A short 25-minute drive from the small port town of **Kusadasi** brings you to the archaeological site of one of the most extraordinary cities of the ancient world, **Ephesus**. In just a few hours tour it is impossible to absorb this great and vast metropolis whose life spanned two thousand years, especially when one realizes that less than 20 percent of the city has been uncovered and excavations have been going on for more than a century! Late Mycenean pottery from 1300 B.C. has been found in the area, but historians say the city was first settled around 2000 B.C. on a sheltered harbor around a sanctuary dedicated to the goddess Cybele (later held equal to Artemis). As the harbor silted in, the city was twice relocated in 1000 B.C. (Ephesus II) and in 334 B.C. (Ephesus III). Today the sea has receded all the way back to Kusadasi and left a valley fertile for the growing of tobacco, fruit and olives.

The Temple of Artemis at Ephesus was one of the Seven Wonders of the Ancient World; at least one historian, Pausanias, considered it the most beautiful work created by humankind. Artemis symbolized nature, virginity and fertility and protected naval voyagers and wild creatures. The temple was destroyed several times but always rebuilt. Now, however, practically nothing remains so we can only speculate on its former beauty.

The classical tour of Ephesus covers the remains of the third city, or Hellenistic period, as well as some monuments left from the following Roman era. (I had been told by the cruise director of the *Stella Solaris* that Ephesus would be the highlight of my Aegean cruise, and this was true.) The marble-paved streets lined with statues of important personages of 2000 years ago inspired me. Curetes Street, with its many shops and porticos, leads to the Library of Celsus and the junction with what is now known as Marble Road. On the right-hand side of this corner is every tour guide's favorite structure the brothel! Scholars say it was constructed between A.D. 98 and 117 and featured baths, a public lavatory and a series of small rooms on the second story. Mosaics depicting the four seasons and the usual pastimes of life inside a brothel have been found. Across the street from this building is an advertisement in the sidewalk—the head of a woman, a heart and a foot pointing toward the brothel.

Arcadian Avenue leads from the huge amphitheater of Ephesus to what must have been the edge of the harbor in ancient times. The theater was renowned for its seating capacity of 24,000 and for its perfect acoustics. Now restored, it probably looks much like it did when St. Paul came to Ephesus in A.D. 54 to preach. If you have time and energy left after your tour of Ephesus, you can hire a taxi outside the gate at the end of Harbor Street and continue on to the Archaeological Museum, or drive up to the House of the Virgin Mary on Mount Solmisos (where it is believed she spent her final days) before you return to Kusadasi for some light shopping and the comfort of your cruise vessel. (By the way, tax-free liquor is sold on the pier here during the late afternoon.)

The approach to **Istanbul**, the city that spans two continents, begins about 13 hours prior to reaching the port. Your ship must enter the Dardanelles, the narrow strait that separates Europe from Asia and the Aegean from the Sea of Marmara. This is the gateway to a strategic area that has been both the bridge and battleground between the exotic East and the Western world for more than two thousand years. Istanbul has been known by many names in its many-layered history. Founded about the 5th century B.C., it was first called Byzantium after the mythical figure, Byzas. As a crossroad between the East and the West, the city fell to the Persians and then to the Greeks. In the 1st century A.D., the Romans added Byzantium to their empire, and it remained in their interest for the next several centuries.

In A.D. 330, the Emperor Constantine I renamed the city after himself and pronounced it the capital of the East Roman Empire. Although these later Romans built some fine monuments in Constantinople, few of the structures remain, because the city was on the Crusade route and thus went through several severe sackings. In the 13th century, Constantinople again fell to the Greeks and then finally landed with the Turks in 1453. The Turks built mosques for the devout, palaces and other places of intrigue for the sultans and beautiful fountains for everyone. They also changed the name to Istanbul, meaning city of Islams, and made it capital of the Ottoman Empire. When the empire fell, Kemal Mustafa (also known as Ataturk) formed the modern Turkish Republic and moved the capital to the more central location of Ankara in 1922.

Istanbul today is home to about two million people and more than four hundred mosques, the domes and minarets of which make striking silhouettes on the busy skyline. It is truly a city of two continents, separated only by the 18–1/2-mile long Bosporus, the narrow strait that joins the Sea of Marmara with the Black Sea. Your cruise ship will dock in front of the old Customs House, or Yolgu Salonu, and you can see the newer section of the European side rising up before you. Across the Golden Horn, that inlet to the north, are the older quarters Galata and Beyoglu. If you do an about face you'll be looking at the Asian side of Istanbul, which can be reached by numerous ferries as well as the only suspension bridge linking Europe with Asia. It's thrilling to sail into Istanbul (the only way I would ever want to approach this city), because you and your ship are immediately in the center of all the activity, the vibrancy and the color that makes this area so fascinating. Churning, dirty and busy, Istanbul catches you in this crazy collage of colors, sounds and smells as soon as you disembark from your cruise vessel.

One of your first stops should be the Blue Mosque, built by the Sultan Ahmed between 1609 and 1616, and covered on the inside with over 21,000 blue porcelain tiles that give it its popular name. One Turkish author writes that the exterior of the mosque, with its six slender minarets, caresses the eyes like a beautiful flower. The interior is equally impressive because of the brilliant blue tiles overhead and the multipatterned Turkish rugs covering the stone floor. (You must remove your shoes when you visit a mosque, so carry a pair of heavy socks to counteract the dampness and chilliness of the stone floors.) Nearby sits another magnificent monument, Haghia Sophia, built by the Emperor Justinian between 532 and 537 with the aid of at least 10,000 slaves.

The cost is said to have been some $7.5 million at the time, an amount that exhausted Justinian's treasury and forced him to impose new taxes. The ornamentation throughout was renowned, but little remains from the Fourth Crusaders final looting in 1204. In 1453, Sultan Ahmed converted this ancient sanctuary into a mosque and covered many of the beautiful mosaics with Arabic script and sayings from the Koran. Then Ataturk made Santa Sophia a museum in 1935, so that all could enjoy the beauty of the building. He encouraged the restoration of the mosaics. On a recent visit, I was told that plans have been made to uncover the mosaics in the central dome, which are believed to be especially fine, but the procedure will be complicated because the Arabic script covering cannot be destroyed in the process.

Any tour of Istanbul must also include the Mosque of Suleiman the Magnificent, possibly the most beautiful Islamic structure in the city. It was constructed between 1550 and 1557, by the order of the Sultan whose 46-year reign of the Ottoman Empire was considered the

Golden Age of literature, science, arts, technology, geography, and military tactics. The interior of this mosque is light and airy, despite the tremendous size of the structure. The echo heard in certain parts is one of its most distinctive features. If you have time to go about on your own, take a taxi to a small, jewel-like mosque (now museum) known as the Khora (Kariye in Turkish). Built around the 7th century, it houses priceless treasures in Giotto-style mosaics of the 12th to 13th centuries.

Topkapi Palace, former home to the sultans and their 6000 or so retainers, is one of the most famous museums in the world. You may have even seen it in the movies. The palace contains the largest Chinese porcelain collection in the world, gathered by the sultans who believed that poisoned food served on this porcelain would change color and warn them. The palace has four rooms of ornaments made by the palace jewelers, some of which hold precious stones the size of your fist. Upstairs in another wing are the harem rooms, but they are only open at certain times and not to large groups, so it's best to consult your guide if you wish to stay later to visit them. A separate room, open more often, gives an indication of the private lives of the sultans; and just outside, you can catch a glimpse of your ship in the distance. Before you leave Topkapi, follow the sign to the restaurant, stop at the first level, and take in a lovely view of Istanbul.

No visit to this city is complete without a tour to the largest oriental bazaar, or souk, in the world. Thousands of little shops comprise this covered bazaar, and untold numbers of peddlers try to entice you to patronize their stores (suede is a good buy). Most of the hawkers are downright annoying, but a few can be amusing, such as the man who promised he could find me a very nice flying carpet!

AUTHOR'S OBSERVATION

Several cruise directors have advised that when purchasing a carpet in Istanbul, plan on carrying it home if you want to see it again. All too frequently shipped carpets never reach the U.S.

Frankly, I prefer the smaller Spice (or Egyptian) Bazaar, which is quieter and redolent of the wonderful smells of local teas, pastries and oriental spices. (If you're overcome by the aromas, you can take refuge in a very good restaurant here called Pandelis.) Another favored excursion in Istanbul requires you to hire a taxi and drive through the newer section of the European side past the deluxe hotels and over the Bosporus Bridge to the Asian side. Two continents in one day is no small feat.

The Black Sea

BULGARIA

Varna is Bulgaria's largest seaport and the jumping-off point for visiting nearby resorts, such as Zlatni Pyassutsi (or Golden Sands) some eleven miles up the coast, renowned for the silky beaches that stretch some five hundred feet into the sea. Midway between the two towns is the coastal resort of Drouzhba, with its 18th-century monastery. South of Varna lies Bulgaria's largest and most popular resort, Slunchev Bryag, or Sunny Beach. A few miles inland, the 6th-century Aladja Monastery is built right into the rocks. You can find traces of Bulgarian history all along the coast. Life here began in the 7th century when Finno-Tartar tribes mingled with Slavic settlers and held their own against the Greek and Byzantine empires in the south.

ROMANIA

The seaside resort of **Constanta** was built on the ruins of an old Greek colony called Tomis, where the poet Ovid is said to have spent his last years. The country actually was founded by the Roman emperor, Trajan, who conquered Dacia in A.D. 106 and called it Romania. Constanta (also spelled Constanza) today is a modern city with narrow streets and mosques left over from the days of the Ottoman Empire. Nearby resort towns along the coast are famous yearround health spas for the treatment of nervous disorders and skin diseases. Pay special attention to the Romanians enjoying their beaches, for they are among the most independent and interesting of all the Eastern European peoples. Some even say that their Latin heritage has never been stronger nor more apparent than now. The tourist shops offer romantic, richly embroidered scarves and blouses, peasant skirts, rugs, ceramics and charming handcrafts. Shore excursions in Constanta are lively and the local scenery is very interesting. Following a visit to the local museum, a drive to the countryside through farmland and vineyards features a visit to a winery where tastings are in order, as well as ample samplings of grainy breads and full-bodied cheeses. The wines are light and refreshing and glasses stamped with the winery seal are presented to all visitors. Guides are friendly and a good time is enjoyed by all!

UKRAINE

Yalta, the most famous of all Black Sea resorts, was a favorite with 19th-century Russian princes, who built many beautiful palaces along its shores. Originally a Greek colony, Yalta passed through the hands of Romans, Genoese and Turks before becoming Russian at the end of the 18th century. Fifty years later, Yalta was a major battleground in the Crimean War. Today this large seaport and spa backs up on Livadia, where the 1945 Yalta Conference took place. Livadia Palace, the White Palace, where the conference was held, was built in 1911 for Tsar Nicholas II in Italian Renaissance style. Every window looks out on a different view. Opposite the entrance is a marble column, which was a gift from the Shah of Persia to the tsar. This palace, like so many others in the area, is now a sanatorium. Yalta is the most interesting of all Black Sea resorts, especially for Americans. Franklin D. Roosevelt Street, one of Yalta's oldest avenues, leads straight into town, linking with Lenin Promenade. Monuments are everywhere to Lenin, to Gorky, and to playwright Chekhov, who lived on Kirov Street from 1898 until his death in 1904 (his house is now a museum). The Alexander Nevsky Cathedral, built in the old Russian style in 1902, is open to visitors daily, but other churches are generally closed or have been turned into museums. In Alupka, the farthest town on the Yalta coastline, is a palace built by Count Vorontsov, a confirmed Anglophile and a favorite of both Alexandra and Nicholas. Vorontsov's palace (built between 1828 and 1846) was designed by an English architect who used Indian styles. An Arabic inscription repeated tenfold says, "There is no happiness but that which comes from Allah." This palace is now a museum of European and Russian paintings, with a bust of Vorontsov himself and a bust of British statesman William Pitt the Younger in the winter garden. The area has many other lovely palaces, plus beautiful but crowded beaches.

Odessa, the third largest city in the Ukraine, is home port of the Black Sea Shipping Company, whose cruise ships sail all over the world but not from North America. One would hardly call Odessa the jewel of the Russian Riviera, as one ship brochure does, but it is certainly a city of note and history. A fascinating period was 1803 to 1814, when the Duke Richelieu was mayor and the city prospered from all the customs duties he collected. By the end of the 19th century, Odessa was Russia's largest port and third most important city, after Moscow and St. Petersburg. Today Odessa is an industrial, educational and tourist center that claims to have inspired poets and prides itself on its revolutionary past. Among many fine monuments cruise passengers can visit is another palace built by Prince Vorontsov in 1826, this time in the classical Russian style. The lighthouse in port also bears his name.

A few of the famous old churches are open for services and tours, including the five-domed Uspensky Cathedral. An archaeological museum has a large collection of artifacts from ancient Greek settlements along the Black Sea coasts. But the most striking monument of all is to the Russian poet Pushkin from the citizens of Odessa, a tribute to the four years (1820 to 1824) the writer was forced to live here in exile.

Western Europe

Seabourn Spirit *arrives in London via the Thames.*

BRITISH ISLES AND IRELAND

Every harbor in this varied island world called the United Kingdom is loaded with history, pride and tradition. Each has an individuality molded by adaptation to landscapes ranging from the isolation of the Shetland Islands to the subtropical Channel Islands to the highlands of Scotland and the gentle lands of Ireland. Language has often kept these peoples together, while religion, politics and plain stubbornness have set them apart. All share a fierce love for a rich past, however, and will proudly point out relics of the Stone Age, leftovers from Julius Caesar and four centuries of Roman rule, Saxon influences and evidence that Saint Patrick really was here. Don't forget to appreciate the Norman towers, the country gardens, heather on the hillsides and a misty climate that is thought to be good for your skin (since it is obviously not good for anything else). A cruise from the Atlantic Ocean to the Irish and North seas is one of the most worthwhile itineraries available.

The traditional gateway to England for seafarers, at least in modern times, is **Southampton**. Now the country's number one passenger port, Southampton dates from Saxon times. Both a local dwelling and a nearby abbey/monastery date from the 12th century. One site not to overlook is the memorial tower to the Pilgrim fathers who set out for the New World on August 15, 1620, in a vessel called the Mayflower. Southampton is in Hampshire, the most interesting city of which is Winchester, a historic center linked to the legends of King Arthur, with a cathedral dating from 1079.

The controversial **Channel Islands** are closer in culture and climate to France than to England. The two largest are Guernsey and Jersey, of which Guernsey is the more popular as a holiday (and tax) haven. The main harbor is St. Peter Port, a small town with not much more than its gentle hills and Victor Hugo's house. The French writer, exiled here from 1855 until 1870, lived in a small house overlooking the harbor, and his mistress lived nearby. He is said to have written some of his masterpieces here, including *Les Miserables.* If you cannot find the house (the way is tricky), you can at least communicate with a fine statue of him in Candide Gardens, which also have a lovely view of the harbor.

The white cliffs of **Dover** have been famous ever since Caesar is said to have sailed past them. Some interesting Roman remains here, discovered in the 1970s, include a fort, bath building and painted house. The port also has one of England's oldest and best-known castles, built by Henry II in the 12th century and used again during World War II. In Queen Victoria's time Dover was a seaside resort, but today it is better known as the closest car-ferry port to France.

Hull is the port for one of England's most delightful towns, historic **York**, which is still encircled by 13th- and 14th-century walls. York was also known as a Roman town and, in fact, became a bishopric during the reign of Emperor Constantine (around A.D. 315). Today York is most famous for its minster, a cathedral surpassed only by rival Canterbury. Called the Church of St. Peter, the cathedral was built on the site of a Roman fortress and is the largest medieval cathedral in England. Also of interest are the York Castle Museum, a collection of everyday objects displayed in a former prison; the Treasurer's House, dating from the 11th century and built over some Roman ruins; and the Shambles, the best-preserved medieval street in the country.

The port of **Leith** is the gateway to **Edinburgh**, the cultural capital of Scotland. Edinburgh Castle dominates the city; its origins as a fortress are thought to have begun as early as the Bronze Age. The castle building dates from somewhere in the 12th century. Edinburgh comprises the medieval old section and the Georgian new districts. After paying a visit to the castle, walk along the Royal Mile to the Palace of Holyrood at the opposite end. Along the way you will see St. Giles Cathedral, John Knox's House (the 15th-century dwelling of the founder of the Scottish Presbyterian Church) and plenty of

17th-century timbered buildings with attractive overhangs. At the end is Holyrood Palace and Abbey, begun in the 12th century, where Mary Queen of Scots lived between 1561 and 1567. (You can visit if the present Queen is not in residence.) Most interesting in the new towns is 7 Charlotte Square, a restored structure known simply as the Georgian House and headquarters of the National Trust of Scotland. This dwelling, an excellent example of 18th-century architecture, contains period furniture and decorative items. Also of great beauty is Hopetown House, the residence of the Marquess of Linlithgow. This huge country home (a mini-palace) is on the Firth of Forth, a pleasant drive away from Edinburgh. Don't leave the city without paying your respects to the monument of Sir Walter Scott, the favorite native son, which is in the East Princes Street gardens. (Some of Scott's characters are part of the statue's design.) You may also find a theatrical performance or an evening of colorful and energetic Scottish dancers while your ship is in port.

Just off the tip of Scotland lie the **Orkney Islands**, 67 small islands that the Romans described in writings from the 1st century A.D., although megalith monuments date from about 4000 B.C. The islands were settled by Norsemen, who built some exciting monuments that have been restored—St. Magnus Cathedral, Earls Palace, and Bishop's Palace in Kirkwall (which means Church Bay). Kirkwall, capital of the Orkneys, is the focal point of their culture. The cathedral has enjoyed more than 800 years of worship, and an annual music festival is held every June here (alas, too early for most cruise calls). You may also visit the Neolithic chambered tomb called Maeshowe (built sometime before 2700 B.C.) and the Neolithic settlement of Skara Brae on the western coast. This complex of seven stone houses connected by covered alleys was inhabited probably between 3100 and 2450 B.C.

Some cruises sail up to the Shetland Islands, but these are a bit distant for most casual tourists. Closer to the mainland of Scotland and a bit warmer are the **Hebrides**, which consist of Inner and Outer groupings. Largest of the Outer Hebrides is the island of Lewis and Harris, whose only town and port is called Stornoway. Apart from its Neolithic and Norse history, the island's biggest claim to fame is Harris Tweed, which has become Stornoway's best industry. It's not real Harris Tweed unless it's woven on this island. The lovely Island of Skye is a popular port of call in the Inner Hebrides. The scenery is magnificent and so is Dunvegan Castle, seat of the MacLeod clan since 1200. Open to the public, Dunvegan is said to be the oldest inhabited castle in all the British Isles.

Sailing southward between Britain and Ireland, some cruise vessels disembark passengers just below Conway Castle on the Welsh town of **Conway**, then reboard them in **Holyhead** on the island of Holyhead. This all-day tour of northwest Wales features a castle built by Edward I in 1284 and the surrounding town he laid out. The town is considered one of the most perfectly walled examples in Europe. Four miles south of Conway are Bodnant. They overlook the lovely mountains of Snowdonia, through which you will drive on your way to Carnarvon Castle. Built by Edward I and finished in 1322, this well-preserved castle dominates the town's skyline. From the castle, your tour will proceed across the Menai Strait and the island of Anglesey, to the port of Holyhead.

Eire, or the Republic of Ireland, is a delightful country to call upon, especially by the sea. Many charming port towns offer easy access to the heart of the land. **Waterford**, originally settled by the Danes but granted its first charter by King John in 1205, is famous for beautiful hand-blown crystal. At nearby **Cashel**, the Rock of Cashel is said to have been visited by Saint Patrick in A.D. 450. The 13th-century Cathedral of Saint Patrick shares the rock with the Round Tower and Cormac's Chapel. In the southwest section of the country, **Bantry Bay** lies at the head of Glengarriff and the gateway to the great lake district of Killarney. If you do not visit **Killarney**, you have not seen Ireland! The three lakes, surrounded by lovely scenery and some interesting historical sites, are worth the drive from Bantry Bay. Also within the lake district is an 11,000-acre national park presented to the Irish people in 1932 by its American owners, who also restored the property's famous mansion. Known as Muckross House, it was built in the mid-19th century and received many important figures of the day. The house is now a fascinating museum that details local Irish life of the last century. For another view of Ireland some cruise vessels call in **Galway Bay**, gateway to the strongest of Gaelic traditions. People here are among the most individualistic, and the living can be rugged. The sea breaks against the rocks with such force that the spray is constant. In the bay are the Aran Islands, populated first in prehistoric times and much later by Christian hermits. County Galway boasts a fine monastery, the Ross Errily Franciscan Friary, founded in the mid-14th century, although most of its buildings date from the late-15th century. Your tour may also take in **Connemara**, known for its beautiful scenery and fine ponies of the same name.

THE NORTH CAPE

"The amusements of the Norwegians include Halling, which resembles tumbling more than dancing...Polsk, in which male dancers exhibit a number of lascivious attitudes...and skating upon snow."

Universal Traveler, 1848

From Stavanger to Spitsbergen, along Norway's western boundary, the cruise passenger is treated to an unending spectacle of some of the world's most exciting scenery. This is the land of fjords, and nothing equals it. Mighty fingers of snow and ice reach out as you sail by, while white-capped mountaintops glisten in the brilliant sun. The views are the same whether you choose to cruise along in a luxury vessel or in a cozy mail boat laden with locals. Chances are you won't be tempted much by sleep, for this is also the Land of the Midnight Sun. From mid-May to the end of July, as you sail farther and farther north, the sun stays longer and longer within sight, until you can't get away from it at all. When you reach the island of Mageroy, the most northerly point of Europe, the entire disc of the sun is visible 24 hours a day.

If your journey northward to the Cape begins in **Stavanger**, you will find a romantic seaport full of historic wooden buildings and a modern boomtown full of North Sea oil-riggers. The cathedral here was dedicated in 1125, and the marketplace has been the center of life since the 9th century. The oldest wooden house, built in 1704 and known as the Consul Fred Hansen House, is now a shop (so you can visit it). Stavanger is a good starting point for explorations to the southern arms of the fjords, Lyse and Ryfylke, as well as Gardens, 70 acres of plants and trees most suited to the wet climate of Wales.

A few hours north by sea is **Bergen**, the country's second largest city after Oslo, founded in 1070 by the Viking, King Olav Kyrre. During the Middle Ages, Bergen became Scandinavia's primary port for trading. Many buildings from this period still exist, despite the ravages of nature and man. Don't miss the medieval fortress of Bergenhus, built in 1262, the coronation site of King Haakon. Bergen, a cosmopolitan city proud of its university and music, was the early capital of Norway. Just outside the city is the former summer home of composer Edvard Grieg where he composed many of his famous works. Amid all this culture and history you can find easy excursions to some of the most beautiful natural attractions in all of Norway—Sorfjord, Samnangerfjord, Tokagjel Gorge and Steindalsfjoss Waterfall. Hardangerfjord and surrounding countryside is a visitor's

haven from spring to fall, for the area is rich in flowers, especially orchids. You may also see Granvinfjord, with its crystal-clear lake; the Hamlagro mountain plateau and the fertile Bergsdalen Valley. This is the classic discovery route and a splendid introduction to the natural resources that makes this country so special.

Eidfjord is the eastern extremity of the larger Hardangerfjord, and the village at the head of this fjord arm has served as a junction of eastern and western Norway for centuries. A shore excursion from the village takes cruise passengers along the banks of the river Eie (known for its abundance of trout and salmon) and into the majestic Mabodal Canyon. The bus ascends through the massive rocks and crags decorated with pines and wild flowers to the observation platform at the top, where you overlook the mighty Voringfoss Waterfall, one of the highest and most impressive in northern Europe plunging 600 feet to the floor of the canyon below.

The village of **Flam** lies by the end of Aurlandsfjord, which is at the tip of Sognefjord. Flam is famous for its 12-mile electric railway that climbs 2845 feet to Myrdal through some dramatic panoramas. The train follows a serpentine path in and out of tunnels, but halts now and again so you can photograph some of the more spectacular waterfalls. From Myrdal station your journey will take you on to **Voss**, on the shores of Lake Vangsvatn. This village, known for its wealth of folklore, has a 13th-century Gothic church with a timbered tower, and a wonderful folk museum that traces the early farm life of the area. From Voss it's an easy drive along lovely Oppheimsvann Lake to Stalheim, where you can see Stalheimskleiv gorge and waterfalls. From here, travel down to the village of **Gudvangen** and return to your ship.

Geirangerfjord is one of Norway's most celebrated fjords; and what a sight it is to cruise by, passing the cascading Seven Sisters Falls. Nestled at the head of this waterway is the charming hamlet of the same name, **Geiranger**, one of the most popular resorts in the country. From here you may drive 5000 feet up to Mount Dalsnibba for a panoramic view of glaciers, waterfalls, lakes and more mountains. You may even see your ship below like a tiny toy at anchor. If you begin your overland trip from **Hellesylt**, you will enjoy the same beautiful panorama of snowcapped peaks, glaciers and the Geirangerfjord.

Molde's sheltered location and gentle climate warmed by the Gulf Stream make it the center of the country's rose industry, which gives it the nickname of City of Roses. Many of the buildings in Molde are recent because bombs and fire destroyed two-thirds of the town in 1940. Molde Church is the largest postwar church to be built in Norway. Its modern style is a great attraction in this tourist center, and over the baptismal font is a charred reminder of the bombed ruins. On the outskirts of town is the Romsdal Museum, an open-air complex of more than two dozen wooden houses dating from the Viking period to the 15th century. During the cruise season, local children in regional costumes perform Norwegian folk dances and provide a colorful scene for photographers. Following the performance, take time out for the fabulous view of the eighty-seven peaks of the Romsdal Alps and the island-studded fjord below. Both can be seen from the deck of the Vardestua Restaurant some 1300 feet high.

From Molde you can travel overland to **Andalsnes**. Take a ferry across Romsdalsfjord to Vestnes, and then go by bus along Storfjord and Norddalfjord to the town of Valldal, noted for its mountain scenery and its abundant strawberries. From here the drive will take you along one of Norway's serpentine roads among the King, Queen and Bishop mountains and by the 500-foot Stigfoss Waterfall, then down through the valley to the small village of Andalsnes on the banks of the Rauma River. (Or if you've had enough of fjords and high drives at this point, and it's the first week in August, check in Molde for the International Jazz Festival, fast becoming Europe's best.)

Trondheim is Norway's third largest city (after Oslo and Bergen) and one of its most interesting. It lies on the south bay of the Trondheimfjord, some 425 miles north of Bergen, and was founded by the Viking king Olav Tryggvasson in the10th century. Trondheim was both the medieval capital of the country until the 13th century and the most important religious center in all of Scandinavia. Nidaros Cathedral, dating from the 11th century, drew many a medieval pilgrim who came to worship at the shrine of the canonized King Olav. Ten Norwegian kings are buried here, and this was also the coronation site of King Haakon VII in 1906. Other attractions in Trondheim are the folk museum complex, with old timbered houses and a gold-colored stave church, and the Museum of Musical History at Rinvge Manor. The mansion, birthplace of a Norwegian sea hero, is often considered the highlight of the Trondheim tour, for it contains a collection of approximately 2000 musical instruments from all over the world. During the summer season, daily tours in English are offered in the morning. Your guide will play a selection of the instruments, demonstrating their position in musical history.

If you're looking for the Midnight Sun, you'll find it in **Narvik**, a town situated 250 miles north of the Arctic Circle on the Ofotfjord. This industrial town that dates from 1903 has continuous sunshine from late May to mid-July, although August is known for having its share of mysterious lighting. Tours from Narvik may include a train trip to Riksgrensen in Lapland or to Gratangen for the thrilling panorama of fjords and mountains. **Tromso** is another town about 250 miles north of the Arctic Circle. Tromso, a boomtown, is very expensive now because of the North Sea oil projects. Skip it if you like, unless you're interested in visiting the world's northernmost university, which dates from 1972.

Hammerfest, the most northerly major town in the world, was founded in 1787 and then totally destroyed during World War II. Now very much rebuilt, it is a lively, ice-free port where fish and furs are loaded onto ships. It is also a shopping center for Lapps and you may see reindeer in town, so keep your cameras in focus. Here, too, the sun does not set from mid-May to the end of July; to offset this feat, it doesn't rise from late November to late January. The world's northernmost village and gateway to the North Cape is **Honningsvag**, on the southern side of Mageroy Island. Also situated on this island is **Skarsvag**, considered the most northerly point in Europe. Skarsvag offers a wonderful view of the Arctic Ocean from its 1000-foot elevation.

NORTHERN CAPITALS

Naturalist in Norway, "Special Expeditions"

AUTHOR'S OBSERVATION

If seeking a more in-depth experience of the Baltic and North Cape than port-a-day schedule of conventional cruise ships, check the offerings of EuroCruises. The company represents visa-free river cruises from Finland to St. Petersburg, river boats that ply the interior of Russia, a quaint paddle wheel steamer through Sweden's Gota canal, expedition vessels to the Arctic circle and over-night passenger ferry service throughout the Baltic sea.

Hamburg is one of those cities that belongs to the Venice of the society. In this instance, it is called the Venice of the North because of its many canals and its traditional coexistence with the sea. With nearly 2 million inhabitants, Hamburg is Germany's largest port, welcoming ships and sailors from every flag imaginable. It is the perfect starting point for the itinerary known as the Northern Capitals. A harbor cruise is a sensible way to begin a tour of this city, followed by a drive through the St. Pauli district to City Hall, the 12th-century St. Petri church and the Altmannbrucke commercial center. Continue around the shores of Aussenalster, a lovely sheet of water in the center of the city, to millionaires' row and then to Poseldorf for some shopping and browsing.

AUTHOR'S OBSERVATION

Despite what the cruise lines tell you, shore excursions are unnecessary in Copenhagen, Helsinki and Stockholm. They are best explored on foot, and require only a street map (tourist offices are located ports).

The capital of tiny Denmark, **Copenhagen**, is as friendly and lively a city as one can find in the Baltic area. Here beautiful palaces and parks, great museums and shops share top billing with the world's greatest amusement park, Tivoli. Copenhagen, a charming port touched by the magical spirit of Hans Christian Andersen, is home to the Little Mermaid who sits in the harbor, a patient subject for your photographs. But where should you go first? There is so much to see—the dazzling display of the Danish crown jewels at Rosenborg Castle; Amalienborg Palace, where Queen Margrethe II lives; Gefion Fountain, named in honor of the Danish goddess who, in a single night, ploughed the island of Sealand out of Sweden, and the many fine art museums.

But the best views come from the countryside of North Zealand and tours of the castles Frederiksborg, built by King Christian IV in 1620 and now the National Historic Museum; Fredensborg Palace built in 1723 and still a summer residence of the royal family; and Kronborg in Elsinore. Renowned as the dramatic setting for Shakespeare's Hamlet, Kronborg was built by Frederick II between 1574 and 1585. Or, if you prefer a more rural atmosphere, visit the open-air museum of Frilandsmuseet, covering some 40 acres. Here the Danish farmlife of yesteryear flourishes, with windmills, country houses and period pieces and utensils.

A drive back to Copenhagen will take you through even more countryside to Frederiksdal, one of the most beautiful areas in all Denmark.

After dark, Tivoli offers diversions for all ages—a pantomime theater, a concert hall, ballet, clowns, acrobats and aerialists in a fantasy world of merry-go-rounds, swans and boats on the tiny lake, games of chance, a Ferris wheel and plenty of places to dine. If this isn't enough, visit a brewery. It's free and you can drink all you want at either the Carlsberg or Tuborg breweries, where guided tours are available two or three times each weekday.

Oslo, at the mouth of the island-studded 60-mile-long Oslofjord, is Norway's capital and largest city. It is, however, neither its most interesting nor cosmopolitan city (those honors go to Bergen). Oslo, founded by a Viking king in the 11th century, was made capital of the country around 1300 by King Haakon V. In square miles, Oslo is one of the largest cities in the world but has a population of less than half a million who live amid great natural beauty. In fact, many of the city's great attractions are out-of-doors, including the 75-acre Frogner Park where the city financed 175 sculptures by Norway's A. Gustav Vigeland, a monumental project that took some 30 years to finish. The 35-acre grounds of the Norwegian Folk Museum on Bygdoy Peninsula exhibit other fine examples of local craft. The museum comprises 170 old buildings transported from all over the country, representing all facets of Norwegian life; it even includes the reassembled study of playwright Henrik Ibsen just as it was left at his death in 1906.

Also on the Bygdoy Peninsula are three of the famous Viking longboats, 8th- and 9th-century relics excavated at Gokstad and Oseberg, and the balsa-wood raft, *Kon Tiki*, that in 1947 Norwegian scientist Thor Heyerdahl and five colleagues sailed from Peru to Polynesia. The raft is housed in its own museum along with exhibits pertaining to Heyerdahl's projects, including his visit to Easter Island. You can also drive out to see Holmenkollen ski jump, one of the best known in the world and the highlight of the annual winter ski festival. A ski museum at the base of the jump houses many interesting exhibits. Your drive should also take you past City Hall (noted for both its modernity and ugliness) and Akershus Castle, built in 1300 and used as a fortress and royal residence for several centuries. Last but not least, save a little time for the Edvard Munch Museum, with its vast collection of works by Scandinavia's leading painter, who is most known for his melancholy and morbid depictions.

> *"To Sweden, I give the travelling premium over every other country. The traveler is in no danger of being imposed upon and will find clean inns and civil people. Horse-stealing is utterly unknown."*

Universal Traveler, 1848

Stockholm, capital of Sweden, is a city built on 14 islands. The water in every direction provides a good excuse to tour this beautiful archipelago by launch. After traveling the canals and waterways, under bridges of every shape and size and past all the important and historic buildings, you may wish to visit some of the more imposing structures such as the 18th-century baroque-style Royal Palace or the 13th-century Riddarholm Church, the second oldest in Stockholm. The royal flagship Wasa is a Scandinavian vessel of renown that also has its own museum. The Wasa was raised from Stockholm harbor just 20 years ago, after she lay at the bottom for three centuries after the ignominious sinking on her maiden voyage in 1628.

High on my list of "must-sees" is the 75-acre open-air Skansen museum, where 150 18th & 19th-century dwellings have been reassembled. The museum offers continual exhibits of the country's crafts through many historical stages.

For more modern artworks, visit the sculpture garden by-the-sea of Carl Milles, Sweden's foremost sculptor and friend of Rodin (who is also represented here). The garden, on the residential island of Lidingo, provides a lovely setting as giant ships pass by on their way out to the Baltic.

On another island, in Lake Malaren, sits the 18th-century palace and theater known as Drottningholm. The palace is still visited by the royal family, and the theater still uses the original stage machinery and scenery. The delightful performances here complement the entire compound, one of the most charming attractions in all of Scandinavia. Before you return to your cruise vessel, make a walking tour of Gamla Sta n or Old Town, which has wonderful antique shops, narrow cobblestone streets, and a historic marketplace.

Although the island of **Gotland** is not a capital, it is a popular call on Baltic cruises, for the walled city of **Visby** is considered one of the medieval jewels of Europe. The short-lived seat of the Hanseatic merchants from the late 12th to early 13th century, the commercial Queen of the Baltic was sacked in 1316 by the Danes, and the island drifted into obscurity not emerging as a tourist center until recent times, when its medieval ruins became known as the best in northern Europe. A tour will take you to the old Hanseatic harbor, past the town's oldest building (Kruttornet), and by two of the more famous towers in the old walls, Maiden's Tower, where a peasant girl was buried alive for helping a Danish nobleman, and Powder Tower, the most ancient fortification in Visby. Then you will drive by Gallow Hill, a medieval hanging station used until the mid-19th century, and explore the ruins of the 13th-century monastery of St. Nicholas, where operas are staged for the Visby summer festival. Finally, a fine historical museum and the Botanical Gardens give Visby its title, the City of Ruins and Roses.

AUTHOR'S OBSERVATION

One of Sweden's little-known treasures are three- and six-day Gota Canal cruises aboard historic paddle-wheel steamers. Represented here by EuroCruises, these tiny 65-passenger ships navigate countless locks as you cruise by scenic countryside and visit quaint on villages.

Helsinki, the white city of the North, is one of Europe's most underrated capitals. Although founded in 1550 by King Gustavus Vasa of Sweden, most of the city belongs to the 20th century and is a tribute to modern Finnish design. Helsinki, built on a peninsula, is skirted by islands that dot the harbor. The marketplace at the water's edge, the most active and colorful square in town (especially in the early morning), is a good place to begin a walking tour. From here, you can take a ferry to Suomenlinna Fortress, known as the Gibraltar of the North, which has guarded the entrance to the harbor for two centuries. Another island to visit, Seurasaari, has its own open-air museum, which offers a view of Old Finland with 17th- and 18th-century structures, including an original sauna. In the summer, folk dancing delights many museum visitors.

Pride of the Finns, though, is Tapiola, a self-contained city-within-a-city, a look at the world of tomorrow. Perfectly planned, this striking area six miles west of the capital has parks, fountains, well-designed homes and apartment buildings, playgrounds, shopping centers, schools and churches. If you're hungry, you can eat at a self-service restaurant that sits atop a large office building. Another area worth visiting is Hvittrask, a center for Finnish art and handcraft. Built in 1902 by three of Finland's noted architects, Saarinen, Lindgren and Gesellius, for their residences and studios, the site features buildings made of natural stone and logs, which blend into the surrounding forest, lake and majestic cliffs. Saarinen's house is open to the public, and the grounds outside contain many sculptures by all three artists. For a look at other artisans, pay a visit to the Finnish Design Center, which has a permanent exhibition and shop, and the Arabia ceramic house, which exports both utility pieces and artworks. A first-rate restaurant, sauna, beach and natural park enhance the experience.

Many cruise vessels also call at the western seaport of **Turku**, just 102 miles from Helsinki. Turku is Finland's oldest city and considered the cradle of Finnish civilization, because it was an ecclesiastical center in the 13th century and the capital until the early 19th century. Among the sights here are Turku Cathedral, dating from the 13th century and one of the most important medieval monuments in the country; the equally old castle at the mouth of the Aura River, now the Turku Museum; and the open-air handcraft museum, perfectly preserved from the 18th century, in the only part of the city that survived the great fire of 1827. The houses of this compound, original, not reassembled, dwellings are now the homes of craftsmen.

AUTHOR'S OBSERVATION

St. Petersburg is rampant with muggings, so leave camera and jewelry aboard ship and definitely dress down. Those lovely lacquer boxes are frequently fakes–use the lens of a camera as a magnifying glass and if you see dot matrix, it's not the real thing.

St. Petersburg, the second largest city in Russia, was the capital of the Russian empire until 1918. It was founded in 1703 by Peter the Great, who named St. Petersburg after himself. In 1914 it became Petrograd. Ten years later, the name changed again to honor Lenin after his death. By any name, this city is also called the Venice of the North for its many canals that connect some 100 islands. The city boasts more than 1000 architectural and historical monuments and houses great cultural riches in more than 50 museums and 2000 libraries. St. Petersburg was the city of the Czars, great art collectors who also admired fine buildings and churches. The finest of all the buildings, the baroque Winter Palace now known as the Hermitage

Museum, has more than 1000 rooms and reception halls, almost 2000 windows and more than 100 staircases. Many of the rooms have been decorated in semiprecious stones malachite, jasper and agate. A ton of malachite was used just for the columns in what is known as Malachite Hall. Amid all this splendor are more than 8000 paintings, a collection of artistic treasures almost unparalleled anywhere in the world. If you pay attention to nothing else in St. Petersburg, a visit to the Hermitage will make your trip worthwhile. Here are two dozen Rembrandts, a whole room of Rubens, numerous works representing five centuries of French painters and masterpieces from the ancient world. Even the Impressionists are well represented (if you can make it to the top floor), with early works by Gauguin and Van Gogh that few people have ever seen. Truly one of the world's greatest museums.

AUTHOR'S OBSERVATION

While nearly everyone is rushed through the Hermitage on shore excursion tours, the experience is richer solo. The line for individual entry is horrendous, but purchasing group tickets at the door is only a few dollars–the poor Russians waiting in line will be thrilled if you distribute the extras.

Driving through St. Petersburg will acquaint you with the Admiralty built by Peter the Great, St. Isaac's Cathedral and Square, the Blue Bridge (which was once a serf market), St. Nicholas Cathedral, and the Kirov State Theater. But a more popular excursion takes you 14 miles south to the town of Pushkin (named in honor of the poet), where Catherine the Great built a palace and fine parks. Go four miles more and arrive at Pavlovsk, the site of another 18th-century palace and English-style park. Visits are allowed into the park only, which has interesting sculptures, artificial ponds and wet jokes (if you happen to step under the wrong arbor, you will be drenched).

The Pacific

HAWAII

AUTHOR'S OBSERVATION

While many cruise ships visit Hawaii, American Hawaii Cruises sails here year-round and offers a superb experience of the islands. AHC's Independence undergoes a major refurbishment in late 1994—a grand old liner restored and spruced up at last.

The glorious islands that make up our fiftieth state were formed from volcanic eruptions on the sea floor thousands of years ago. Inhabiting this landscape of red-hot volcanos, verdant mountains, paradisiacal valleys with daily rain showers, plus some of the most spectacular, unspoiled beaches in the world, is a potpourri of the earth's people: Polynesians, Orientals, Americans, Europeans, Africans and the most exquisite combinations of all the above.

What a pleasure to visit these islands, this land of aloha where everyone is gracious and friendly, the weather so sublime and the sights so refreshing.

Most visitors to Hawaii arrive, alas, by air and thus miss the fun. Nothing is quite so thrilling as sailing to or from Aloha Tower in Honolulu, past Waikiki Beach and Diamond Head (an extinct volcano that was the legendary home of Pele, the fire goddess), to be greeted by the Royal Hawaiian band, complete with floral leis (if you throw your lei into the sea and it returns to shore, islanders say, you will return to this land). At this writing, American Hawaii Cruises offers regular weekly sailings from the famous Aloha Tower to four ports of call on three other islands.

OAHU

If you arrive at Honolulu International Airport beat, you will not be alone. It's a long flight from the mainland, as Hawaiians call the continental U.S., and a five-hour time change if you began your journey on the east coast. Have a good rest at your hotel along Waikiki (American Hawaii Cruises utilizes the Hawaiian Regent and it's an excellent choice), then a swim in the seductive Pacific Ocean and the world will look good again! As state capital, **Honolulu** is a thriving metropolis with more to its credit than that two-and-ahalf-mile coastline called Waikiki, which lies in the shadow of Diamond Head. If you are planning to spend some time on Oahu, at either end of the cruise, rent a car or take the bus for some spectacular touring. The Bishop Museum, Liliuokalani Gardens, Queen Emma Summer Palace, the National Memorial Cemetery of the Pacific (where 21,000 servicemen from two world wars, Korea, and Vietnam lie buried), the Royal Mausoleum (with the bodies of five Hawaiian kings and one Queen) and the East-West Center at the University of Hawaii. This center is a federally-funded institute to promote mutual understanding among the peoples of Asia, the Pacific and the United States.

If you have only a few hours in the Honolulu area, the most important and sobering monument is the **Arizona Memorial** in Pearl Harbor. This monument was built over the sunken battleship where so many Americans lost their lives on December 7, 1941. If you take the 2-1/2 hour cruise aboard the *Pearl Kai*, you will also see the famous Battleship Row and memorial of the USS *Utah*.

There is also a 3-hour cruise aboard the *Adventure*. Both cost under $10 per adult. At the submarine base, there is a museum of some interest (Wednesday through Sunday) but you need a pass and instructions from the guard at Nimitz Gate (located off the highway of the same name). And, if tall ships are your thing, save some time for the *Falls of Clyde*, berthed at Pier 7 adjacent to Aloha Tower. The world's only full-rigged, 4-masted ship is open to the public. For about $3, you may tour the *Clyde*, view the double-hulled Polynesian canoe Hokule'a and see the maritime museum in Aloha Tower.

HAWAII

The big island of Hawaii celebrated its silver jubilee of statehood with the eruption of two of its five volcanos, **Mauna Loa** and **Kilauea**, among the world's most active. The **Kilauea Caldera** is the legendary home of the Hawaiian goddess of fire, Pele, and famous for the many rituals that have taken place here for centuries. From **Hilo**, the Big Island's major seaport and only city, visitors can travel along Chain of Craters Road up through the volcano country to the National Park Visitor Center. You can walk on lava along the way, and then dine at Volcano House, a hotel perched on the edge of Kilauea Crater.

The Big Island also claims some 22,000 different varieties of orchids, the 224,000-acre Parker Ranch (largest ranch under single ownership in the United States), which produces between 10 and 11 million head of beef annually, and an abundance of macadamia nuts. Halfway between Hilo and Kona is the town of **Honokaa**, known as the Macadamia Nut Capital of the World. There are factories and outlets all over the islands, but don't expect any bargains for this rare delicacy acclaimed as the perfect nut, or in the more than 200 gift items related to it!

On the other side of the Big Island is the town of Kailua-Kona, known as **Kona**, famous for the wonderful coffee grown in the area. Along the beautiful Kona coastline is Kealakekua Bay, a sacred place known as pathway of the god, where Captain Cook arrived on January 17, 1779. Cook, the most famous navigator-explorer of his time, had discovered what he named the **Sandwich Islands** in 1778 at Waimea, Kauai. However, his return to these islands and this particular harbor was not fortuitous, and the dear fellow was murdered and dismembered by the natives less than a month after his arrival. He was just 50 years old. A 27-foot white pillar monument on the far shoreline of Kealakekua Bay was erected in his memory in 1874, and can be seen on both bus and cruise tours.

The most interesting part of the Kona coastline is the oasis-like village of **Pu'uhonua O Honaunau** or City of Refuge. It is now a National Historical Park; but during ancient times, Hawaiians pardoned sinners of *kapu* (strict social laws) and other crimes who were able to reach sanctuary here. It was not easy to arrive here, because this area was owned by royalty and it was against kapu for any commoner to set foot upon royal ground. Nonetheless, enough swam ashore to make the place famous. The park provides a very nice map for your own walking tours as well as a short lecture by one of the guides. What is left of the sanctuary is worth visiting.

On the other hand, the village of Kona is tacky, tacky, with overpriced and overtouristed shops. Even Kona coffee seems to be less expensive on the mainland, and the selection of island wear (aloha shirts and muumuus) is better on Maui or Oahu. There is good snorkeling here, however, and a lovely private beach for the use of passengers. Those with real adventure in their souls will enjoy the deep-sea fishing aboard charter boats with a professional crew.

MAUI

Many visitors agree with Mauians, who say Maui No Kai Oi or Maui is the best ever! Maui is the second largest island in the group, and **Kahului** is its principal seaport although Lahaina (23 miles away) is its historic heart and the first capital of the islands. This was the center of the whaling industry (1840-1865) and humpback whales from the Arctic still come to these Hawaiian breeding grounds during the winter months. But Maui is best loved for its magnificent scenery, especially the stunning white-sand beaches on the western shore, the lush Iao Valley that cuts through the island and Haleakala

National Park. It is said that Haleakala's enormous crater, with a circumference of 21 miles, could swallow all of Manhattan. It is called the House of the Sun, because Polynesian legend says that the demigod Maui captured the sun and held it captive to give his people more daylight hours.

Maui is definitely everyone's favorite island, if you only visit beautiful **Kaanapali Beach** with its fabulous resorts, great surf and snorkeling trails (be sure to take a little bread along for the fish). During the 7 a.m. to 6 p.m. call at Maui, passengers could even play golf or tennis at the Sheraton Hotel on Kaanapali Beach. In addition to being an old whaling town, **Lahaina** is great for shopping and there are many charming boutiques to peruse. As the pineapple island, it is best to order a box of the succulent fruit for delivery to your flight in Honolulu. The prices at Take Home Maui are less than anywhere around, and the fruit was dutifully awaiting our check-in at the Honolulu airport. (Cash only, in case you are interested.) Other shore excursions on Maui include the west coast and Launiupoko Canyon, Olowalu Valley and tallest cliffs in Hawaii tour by helicopter. Another expensive but unforgettable helicopter tour is of west Maui and the north shore of Molokai. This one features sea cliffs, cascading waterfalls, hidden valleys and a rest stop on one of Molokai's inaccessible beaches.

KAUAI

Just 95 miles northwest of Honolulu, Kauai is known as the Garden Island because an abundant rainfall makes for a wide variety of native flora as well as for large taro, pineapple and sugar plantations. Kauai claims to have the wettest spot on earth, the 5170-foot Mount Waialeale, with 486 inches of rainfall annually. It also has the only navigable rivers in Hawaii. The Wailua River, where the first Polynesians landed in the archipelago some one thousand years ago, has a motor-launch cruise impressive for lush vegetation and unique tropical varietals. Nearby is the beautiful cave called Fern Grotto, its entrance framed by huge fishtail ferns. And a short distance by road is Wailua Falls where, if you survive the steep trail, you can swim in the natural pool surrounded by hala trees.

Lihue is Kauai's commercial center, but large vessels must dock south of it in the deepwater port of **Nawiliwili**, beside freighters loading sugar. More historic is **Waimea** where Captain Cook landed in 1778. No doubt Cook explored the island's biggest tourist attraction, Waimea Canyon, a miniature version of the Grand Canyon best seen from Puu Ka Pele mountain and the lookout at Kaana Ridge.

There are many popular shore excursions here, including the beach where South Pacific and other movies have been filmed. There is also a typical Hawaiian luau one evening that offers a flavor of the feast that some Hawaiians used to enjoy. The food is excellent and everyone loves the hula show afterward! Another popular excursion on Kauai is the 1-hour flight by helicopter over the 5000-foot rim of the Waialeale Crater into the wettest spot on earth, down Waimea Canyon and along the Na Pali coastline with 3000-foot mountain walls. Hanalei Bay with its adjoining beaches is considered one of the most beautiful sights in the world, especially by air. All this for about $100, and those who took the ride said it was worth every penny! But only the brave should apply, as the ride is rather bumpy at times.

AUSTRALIA AND NEW ZEALAND

AUSTRALIA

"Nearly all the natives have a peculiar talent for mimicry; the singularities of the colonists are represented with great correctness; they are proficient in the vulgar language of the convicts."

Universal Traveler, 1948

If I had to pick a good point to begin a South Pacific quest, it would have to be **Sydney**, capital of New South Wales and the oldest, largest (3 million people) and liveliest city in Australia. This bustling metropolis is home to more than 20 percent of the country's population, and its beautiful harbor is both a welcome and familiar sight to every sailor. Imagine yourself coming into this port aboard a luxury cruise vessel, past the sparkling new high-rises and the famous Opera House complex, with a design so evocative of billowing sails.

Sydney is often called the Cradle of the Country; it is the oldest civilized settlement in the southwestern Pacific (although one might question the criteria for being civilized). Nonetheless, history says that Captain Cook visited this harbor in 1770 and called it Port Jackson after a secretary of the British Admiralty. Actually Cook was only at the head of the harbor; and Captain Philip founded Sydney Cove on January 26, 1788, the anniversary of which is now celebrated as Australia Day. The best way to see Sydney is to emulate these founders; take a launch around the harbor to appreciate Harbor Bridge, the Opera House and the skyline of the business district. Sydney has a smalltown mentality and a rather happy-go-lucky atmosphere people seem to work only when they must, and the magnificent beaches north and south of the city are the most popular places to relax (the sun shines approximately 342 days of the year).

For a view of the city from 50 stories up, try the revolving restaurant at the top of the Australia Tower (actually on the 49th floor), which takes two hours for a full 360-degree, effortless turn. Wander by Sydney's oldest building (the 1815 Cadman's Cottage near the passenger terminal) and the Argyle Arts Center where local craftsmen sell their wares. The latter is a large convict-built brick building that dates from the 1820s when convicts were once housed in the cellars. A stroll around Circular Quay brings you to the Opera House.

Tours are conducted daily (except Saturday), and you can sit on the open-air terrace and watch ships sail by in the harbor. Other sites of interest include the Australian Museum (for a fine collection of aboriginal and South Sea art and the zoo). You are now in the land of kangaroos and koalas, and Taronga Zoo is one of the best in the world. For an even closer look, take a bus to Koala Park in Pennant Hills where you can cavort with koalas, kangaroos and emus.

Sailing northward along the eastern coastline of Australia, your ship will enter the region of the **Great Barrier Reef**, a stretch of coral some 1242 miles long extending from Gladstone to Cape York. The reef teems with marine and bird life; they are among the world's most beautiful natural attractions. In this area totaling more than 80,000 square miles with over 600 islands live several hundred kinds of coral, at least 900 different species of fish, and birds that migrate from as far away as Japan and Siberia. Other birds that are nearing extinction elsewhere survive well here. Cruising the Great Barrier Reef is intriguing, and some of the larger islands have resort facilities, many of which are great for watersports. Your cruise vessel may also call at **Cairns**, one of the most northerly cities in Queensland, a tropical resort that serves as the base for excursions into the outer reef areas.

NEW ZEALAND

"The charge of cannibalism has been alleged against the New Zealanders, and although by some denied, it is now certain that the charge is true."

Universal Traveler, 1848

A certain amount of rivalry exists between Australia and her neighbor, New Zealand, and not all of it is simply on the surface. For example, New Zealanders are quick to point out that their country was not settled by convicts. Australians counter that they are not 50 years behind the times. Striking differences do exist between these two lands and cultures, which makes it a must to visit both. New Zealand is small compared to the vast continent next door. It consists of North, South and Stewart islands which, all told, about equal the size of the state of Colorado. Called the land of the Long White Cloud by Polynesians some six centuries ago, New Zealand lies halfway between the Equator and the South Pole and has some of the most spectacular scenery in the world. Sheep outnumber people by 80 to 1 at last count, and there are about 5-1/4 million acres of national parks. The largest and most famous is South Island's Fjordland National Park that comprises some 3 million acres of bays and fjords, of which Milford Sound is the most popular for local cruises.

New Zealanders refer to themselves as Kiwis (turkey-like birds) and say that they live upon God's Own Country, which was discovered by a Dutchman in 1642 (who named it Nieuw Zeeland). The islands were pretty much ignored until Captain Cook arrived aboard the *Endeavour* in 1769. The first English settled in 1840 near Wellington. These new Westerners had to contend with a large native population who clung to their own considerable culture. These aborigines, the Maori, still number 8 percent of the population and contribute a great deal to life in this land.

Windy **Wellington**, a port city that will remind you of San Francisco, is the capital of New Zealand and named in honor of the Duke of Wellington's victory over the French in the Battle of Waterloo. The city is built upon a series of steep hills at the southwest tip of North Island. To best understand the layout, climb to the summit of Mount Victoria (558 feet) where you can see the entire harbor and, sometimes, the tip of South Island just twenty miles across Cook Strait. A bust of Wellington rests on this summit, as well as a memorial to the American explorer, Rear Admiral Richard Byrd, who used New Zealand as a base for his Antarctic expeditions. Wellington is a pleasant, clean and very British capital of about 350,000 with some pleasant but not overly exciting sights to see. It is a government town, and one of the largest wooden buildings left in the world houses the government headquarters.

Auckland, often thought of as the largest Polynesian city in the world, is a much more exciting metropolis of about 800,000 people. Situated at the separation of two seas, the Pacific and Tasman, and two harbors, the Waitemata and Manukau, the city has been built on top of seven extinct volcanos in addition, the volcano called Rangitoto Island sits in Waitemata Harbor. A former Maori fortified village, Mount Eden is a 643-foot cone of an extinct volcano from which you can see the Pacific on one side and the Tasman Sea on the other. One Tree Hill, another former Maori site, has one tree and a memorial to the Father of Auckland. The city offers a 300-acre park (where sheep graze close to the streets), a zoo where you can see the indigenous kiwi, a museum of transport and technology and some lovely harbor cruises. Or you can take an excursion some 126 miles from the city to the Waitomo Caves to visit the Glowworm Grotto, eerie underground caverns illuminated by their many glowworms.

AUTHOR'S OBSERVATION

Far more interesting from a cultural point of view is **Rotorua**, *one of the country's prime attractions. Known as Sulphur City, this area about 150 miles south of Auckland is one of the traditional homes of the Maori people. From here, take an excursion to the thermal baths of Whaka, the Maori Arts and Crafts Institute, and the Ohinemutu Maori Village with its church and meeting house rich in local carvings. You can also attend a Maori concert and a typical Maori feast, which is cooked in the ground.*

Sailing northward from Auckland, some cruise vessels call in the **Bay of Islands** for a brief visit to Russell and Waitangi. The latter is known as the birthplace of New Zealand history, for it was here that the Treaty of Waitangi was signed whereby, in 1840, the Maoris accepted the sovereignty of the British Crown in return for ownership of their traditional lands. Russell, across the bay from Waitangi, was the short-lived capital of this new colony; it still retains its Old World charm.

THE SOUTH PACIFIC

The arrival of Wind Song *in Tahiti"*

Following in the wake of Magellan were adventurers of the western world—Captain Cook, Captain Bligh and the crew of the Bounty, Robert Louis Stevenson, Paul Gauguin and Somerset Maugham—who discovered the paradisiacal islands in the South Seas that today are the last bit of exotica extant. Many who came to the far-flung Polynesian kingdom stayed. For where else is the sky so blessed with sun and blue, are the beaches so shining and sensuous, the waters so clear and the flowers so brilliant? Among all this perfection live people who are friendly and relatively untouched by the world outside.

FIJI

Fiji is an archipelago of more than 300 islands, which are the most populous and economically advanced of the South Sea group. A tropical paradise 1100 miles south of the equator, Fiji is the center of communication for the area. An independent sovereign state, it holds a population of more than half a million. Its capital is **Suva** and its prime minister is an Oxford-educated hereditary tribal chief. Suva is a thriving commercial port with duty-free shops, Government House, a museum containing local artifacts dating from 2000 years ago and the University of the South Pacific. Everything goes here, and the mode of dress ranges from the sulu of the local population to the sari of the large Indian community to the many varieties of European dress. One short excursion from Suva takes you to Orchid Island, where the flowers grow wild beside vanilla, coffee and tea. You can also see mongooses, iguanas and monkeys.

Fiji is also known for its kava and fire-walking. The former is a beverage made from the root of a pepper plant; the latter is practiced by both the native-born Fijians and the Indians who were imported by the British for labor and who now make up more than half the population. The fire-walkers are followers of Maha Devi. Visitors may be invited to the ritual now and then, for a small fee, of course!

THE SAMOAS

The Samoas (American and Western) are considered the Heartland of Polynesia, and the same language and customs prevail on both sets of islands. Western Samoa is an independent Polynesian nation whose capital is **Apia**. American Samoa is an unincorporated territory whose native inhabitants are U.S. nationals but not citizens. Its capital is **Pago Pago** (pronounced Pango), made famous by author Somerset Maugham in a short story called "Rain." Anthropologist Margaret Mead also spent some time in American Samoa, which resulted in her book *Coming of Age in Samoa*; and Robert Louis

Stevenson lived the last four years of his life in a large villa overlooking the port of Apia. While American Samoa is well subsidized by the U.S. and therefore rather rich, Western Samoa is poor. But the people on both groups of islands are simple and friendly, still ruled by the chieftain system and witchcraft. In fact, traditionalism caused both governments to issue a behavior code for tourists, which discourages revealing dress, requests no disturbances at prayer time and advises how to eat and sit Samoan style (cruise passengers will probably not be bothered with the latter). Other than a few admonitions, Samoans just want you to enjoy the surrounding grace and beauty (and stay away from fiery kava and the local transvestites).

TONGA

Last of the Polynesian kingdoms and the only set of islands in the South Seas that has never been colonized, Tonga was a British protectorate and is now an independent nation within the Commonwealth. This group of 150 coral and volcanic islands, with a population of under 100,000, is one of the world's smallest nations. The name of its capital, **Nuku'alofa** (Land of Love), was chosen because Captain Cook supposedly referred to this archipelago as the Friendly Islands. Unfortunately, Tonga is very poor and rather feudal, and its present monarch (King Taufa Ahau Tupou IV) has had to rely on outside sources for funds (Russia, Libya and Japan); but he and his nobles hope that tourism will fill the coffers. Interesting sights around Nuku alofa include the Royal Palace (which can be viewed over low walls but not visited), the Royal Tombs and Ha amonga Trilithon. The Trilithon is a stone calendar, erected about A.D. 1200 that predicts the summer and winter solstices. Not far from the capital in a village called Kolovai, flying foxes hang upside-down all day. They look like fruit and are considered sacred—only members of the royal family may touch them. For more natural phenomena, go see the blowholes where water shoots up sixty feet at high tide and visit the caves dripping with stalactites and stalagmites near the village of Haveluliku.

FRENCH POLYNESIA

French Polynesia consists of some 130 islands, of which **Tahiti** is the most familiar. The island was first sighted in 1767 by Westerners by the captain and crew of the English vessel *Dolphin*. A year later, French explorer de Bougainville claimed it for his country and left his name on the brilliant wild-flowers found everywhere here, the bougainvillea. Captain Cook arrived the next year aboard the *Endeavour* to set up a scientific observation post at Point Venus. Cook is also credited with giving Tahiti its name (from what he understood the natives called it), before he sailed away to discover the Society Islands, Australia and New Zealand. He returned to Tahiti three more times; a monument to his memory stands at Point Venus. Another well-known captain to visit Tahiti, the infamous Bligh, was master of the HMS *Bounty*. In October 1788, the captain and his crew began a 5-month stay on the island. Just after the vessel sailed again, the mutiny occurred, and Bligh was left in a boat along with 18 of his men and some provisions. The group survived and landed in Indonesia. (The true story is even better than the movie!)

Papeete, Tahiti, a bustling and noisy capital and port town, must rebuff complaints that it has lost its paradisiacal charm as high-rises replace interesting old buildings and powerboats replace outrigger canoes in the lagoon. But do not despair, just get out of town! Pay a visit to Point Venus, tracing the steps of the explorers and their men. Stop by the Museum of Discovery, with wax figures of captains Wallis and Cook and Frenchman de Bougainville as well as Tahitian chieftains and dancers. Some artifacts and engravings at the museum tell of the white man's arrival. **Papeari**, 30 miles southwest of Papeete, offers another museum of interest, the Gauguin Museum, which contains three original paintings as well as some drawings and doodlings made by the artist during his years on the island (it is said that he left some of his talent in one or two of the local population). And one thing is certain you will eat very well (but not cheaply) on Tahiti.

If you are lucky enough to be aboard *Wind-Song* while sailing among these beautiful islands, your cruise will take you to Huahine, Tahaa and Raiatea, Bora Bora and Moorea, but not necessarily in the order above.

Moorea, called the older sister of Tahiti, is actually twice the age of the better-known island and is separated by eight mountain ridges. The ship anchors in Pao Pao, or Cook's Bay, and even the well-known sea captain was said to have been overwhelmed by the island's natural beauties, which include Mou'a'-roa the needle-shaped mountain known today as Bali Ha'i. Moorea is famous for its agricultural experimental park (full of vanilla, pineapple and coconut plantations as well as farm animals, wheat and corn) seen via air-conditioned Land Rovers, and Le Belvedere for spectacular views of both Cook's and Opunohu bays. Those preferring to be alone together on the island will find some lovely resorts and beaches (including one called Bali H'ai) as well as plentiful snack shops.

Bora Bora is the best known of the Society Island chain and the epitome of a South Pacific paradise. Our friend Captain Cook claimed the 6-mile long island for England in 1777, but a more friendly invasion occurred during World War II, when some 5000 Americans were stationed here and rebuilt both port and land facilities. It is fun to rent a car in Bora Bora for a few hours and drive the 17-mile road around the lagoon, past many colorful villages and fabulous resorts including Hotel Bora Bora, one of the most expensive in the South Pacific. Bora Bora is surrounded by charming motu or small islands where beach barbecues are often held.

AUTHOR'S OBSERVATION

Another popular spot is Bloody Mary's Seafood Restaurant, a short drive from the pier by Le Truck bus. For those who enjoy seafood still squiggling, an outrigger canoe excursion features feeding the sharks (!) that congregate near a reef surrounding the island. Swimsuit, mask and snorkel are necessary for this exercise.

Tahaa and **Raiatea** are also sister islands, now separated by a 2-3-mile-wide strait, though both geological and mythological evidence says they were once connected. Shaped like the flower of an hibiscus, Tahaa is reachable only by sea and surrounded by dozens of motu. Vanilla is grown here and its distinctive fragrance fills the air.

Raiatea is considered the center of ancient Maori culture, from whence derived Tahitians, Tongans and Samoans, as well as the original Maori who paddled all the way to New Zealand. When Captain Cook anchored *Endeavor* in Opoa Bay in July, 1769, he claimed Raiatea and all islands in sight for England, naming them the Society Islands (including Huahine, Tahaa, Bora Bora and Maupiti). Known today as the leeward Society Islands, they were annexed to France in 1888.

As the largest of this group, Raiatea is also the most interesting and industrious, and its main town Uturoa is the administrative center for the islands. Raiatea boasts the group's only navigable fresh waterway the Faaroa River, which is thought to be the ancient launching pad for those Maoris later found in New Zealand and Hawaii. Raiatea is full of legends and was once considered sacred in Polynesian history. Indeed, many Polynesians still feel that their soul will return to this spiritual homeland, known as Havai'i. An excursion up the Faaroa River is a lovely way to spend a morning. The energetic may enjoy a 3-hour walking tour to Mount Tapioi Point lookout, but there is no backup transportation available.

Huahine-Nui and **Huahine-Iti** (big and little) are another set of islands thought to have been united once as they still share a common barrier reef. Quiet and calm, the islands boast coffee, vanilla and mango plantations, a main village called Fare and an open-air museum of restored religious sites known as marae. However, a Heritage Tour here is not worth the time and money. Most visitors can make use of the local beaches and nautical activities.

Shopping in Tahiti and the Society Islands is mind-bogglingly expensive. Even postcards cost around $1.25, and that doesn't include the airmail stamp! The black South Sea pearls are beautiful and an excellent investment, but my jeweler can get them cheaper in New York. Food and drink on the islands is very costly (a Coke is about $5) and most of the souvenirs are imported. In short, save your money; indulge in the beauty of the water, the sky, the beaches and the lush mountainsides, especially if your ship is cruising at sunset.

South America

South America! That magnificent land mass that bulges east to west below the equator, and then slims down to a graceful point at Tierra del Fuego, is often misunderstood and rarely visited by its friendly northern neighbors who also call themselves Americans. Hardly a continent to ignore, it covers some 12 percent of the earth's surface, has a population of well beyond the 200 million mark, and is growing rapidly. Its 6,866,000 square miles of land are bordered by the Caribbean as well as the Atlantic and Pacific oceans. South America claims the world's largest river, the Amazon (3915 miles); the world's three highest volcanos; Guallatiri (19,882 feet) and Lascar (19,652 feet) in Chile, and Cotopaxi (19,347 feet) in Ecuador and the world's driest spot in Chile's Atacama Desert where the rainfall is barely discernible.

Culturally, this continent was influenced from the 12th to 16th centuries by the fabulous Inca Empire that embraced some 25 million people and covered a territory that now includes Bolivia, Peru, Ecuador, northern Chile and part of Argentina. Christianity was imposed upon the native population in the 16th century when the Spanish conquistadors and the Portuguese navigators began to colonize their discoveries, building churches and palaces lined with the newly found gold. The largest Spanish- and Portuguese-speaking population resides within the borders of South America; and races blend here unlike on any other continent. Called the ultimate in contrasts, South America boasts too much activity in all directions for any superlative to take hold. Here you can visit Machu Picchu (the mysterious legacy left by the Incas) and Brasilia (the ultramodern capital that symbolizes today's South America) in the same breath and believe in both!

ARGENTINA

> *"The enthusiasm with which the Spaniards regard the female sex has been exaggerated; their attention is founded on real respect...Smoking cigars is a general practice with men, women and children."*
>
> **Universal Traveler, 1848**

Buenos Aires, capital and port of Argentina, is considered the Paris of Latin America for its broad boulevards, sophisticated shops, art galleries, theaters, nightclubs, opera and fine public buildings. It is also the city of Evita, where inflation can run extraordinarily high and where foreign business executives often hire 24-hour bodyguards as a deterrent to local terrorist groups. Despite the political and economic undercurrents, Buenos Aires still prides itself on its more than 150 beautiful parks and the best beef in the world. So, enjoy the romance and excitement of this city from the convenience of your cruise ship. Touring should include a visit to the Grecian-style Colon Opera House; Palermo Park on Avenida Libertador General San Martin (named after the national hero); the Plaza de Mayo and the pink Government House (known as Casa Rosada); the cathedral, which is one of the country's oldest buildings and where General Jose de San Martin is buried and the Museum of Fine Arts. For a more charming and colorful view of life in Buenos Aires, you can visit La Boca, where local artist Benito Quinquela Martin helped change the scenery from slums to a picturesque fishing port. Don't miss the area museum stocked with his waterfront paintings. Some delightful restaurants are here, too, where gourmet food is served with pride.

AUTHOR'S OBSERVATION

Buenos Aires has some of the world's finest shopping, the descendents of Italians still devoted to quality. Try Rua Sui Pacha for great buys on custom-fitted leather clothes and shoes, buttery cashmere and dyed, stamped nutria jackets and coats.

For a different look at this land of the gauchos, you can travel out of the city to a nearby estancia (ranch) for some congenial Argentinian hospitality that may include a sumptuous barbecue that would put even Texas to shame! Or you can take a 2-hour cruise aboard a 160-passenger catamaran that allows a view of the Parana delta area and a peek at the Lujan, Sariento, Capitan, San Antonio and Urion rivers.

Argentina stretches south some 2150 miles to Cape Horn at the lower tip of the continent. The bottom portion, called Patagonia (or Land of the People with Long Feet), boasts such fascinating place names as Tierra del Fuego and Ushuaia (the most southern town in the world). North of Cape Horn is the Strait of Magellan.

BRAZIL

RIO DE JANEIRO

AUTHOR'S OBSERVATION.

Never, never try Rio on your own. Muggings are commonplace in broad daylight on the crowded streets of Copacabana and Ipanema. Leave cameras and all jewelry in the hotel safe and carry a moneybelt.

If I had to choose just one South American city to see, it would have to be **Rio de Janeiro**. Some say that this city has the most beautiful natural setting in the world. Truly, it competes with Hong Kong and San Francisco, and Rio is definitely a fun capital, a city where the action rarely ceases from dawn to the following dawn. Brazilians love excitement, music and the sun, and Rio has plenty of all three. Approximately 16 beaches are within this beautiful 15-mile long bay. The most popular (and chic) is Copacabana, followed closely by Ipanema. If you want to beach it like a pro, go early in the day (8 a.m. to about noon) and wear as skimpy a suit as possible (remember, the string was invented here!). Leave everything you do not want to lose on the ship. Thievery is a real problem here, and some young natives are adept at stealing everything, whether one is wearing it or carrying it.

First among the city's attractions is the cable car ride to the top of Sugar Loaf; then in the late afternoon, take a taxi or the cogwheel train up to the Corcovado Christ for a sunset view. The famed statue that symbolizes Rio in many photographs was designed by a French artist. Standing 120 feet high and weighing about 700 tons, the statue was inaugurated in 1931 and paid for by contributions from the citizenry of Rio. Impressive from any angle, the statue gives way to an especially thrilling panorama of this seaside city as the sun sets and dusk signals the illumination of lights below.

Rio is a city of great wealth and great poverty (next to luxurious hotels stand favelas, enormous communities of tin and cardboard shacks). You may notice considerable French overtones. Its largest park was laid out by a French architect, and the Municipal Theater is an exact copy of the Paris Opera House. The many elegant and expensive shops feature the latest fashion ideas from Paris, either originals or quickly turned-out copies. Many women of Rio spend a lot of time shopping and dressing and adorning themselves. Rio is also the hometown of Hans Stern, the world-renowned jeweler who combines much gold with Brazil's fabulous array of semiprecious stones. On your walking tours, you may come upon some magnificent baroque churches with gold-covered interiors, the worthwhile Museum of Fine Arts, and many exciting restaurants featuring freshly caught seafood and the local specialty feijoada (traditionally served at Saturday lunch so you can rest after eating such a large meal). If your time allows for sightseeing outside of Rio, drive to Tijuca Forest, once a private estate; and to Petropolis where, in 1845, the Emperor Dom Pedro II built a summer palace that is now the Imperial Museum. Displaying items used by the Imperial family during this period, the museum is open daily (except Monday). The Emperor and his wife, Dona Teresa Christina, are buried in the cathedral nearby.

SÃO PAULO

Just as I think Rio is an exciting tourist city, **São Paolo** is not. This metropolis of 10 million is the industrial center of Brazil—sprawling, congested and stacked with new skyscrapers. The Paulistas love it, but a friend who lives there laments: "When visitors come, there's no place to take them, little of interest to see!" Well, there are lots of new buildings, including the largest snake farm in Latin America as well as Edificio Italia, the highest structure in South America. São Paulo also boasts one of the world's largest parks, Ibirapuera Park, and three art museums. The city's port, Santos, claims the biggest dock area on the continent in addition to its lovely tropical climate and beautiful beaches. Given the choice, I would venture no farther than the beaches.

THE AMAZON

The mighty **Amazon River** descends some 3000 miles from its source high in Peru down to the Atlantic Ocean. Early Spaniards explored the river around 1592, according to legend, and were so taken with its vastness that they called it Rio Mar or the River Sea. Legend also says that they came upon a race of women warriors they named the Amazones from Greek mythology and soon the whole region was called Amazon. In South America, distances are often larger than can reasonably be conceived, and the Amazon region covers some 3 million square miles including 3900 miles of waterway from Atlantic to Pacific oceans and more than 10,000 tributaries along the way. Its width varies from a meager 1-inch at the source (so they say) to more than 200 miles at the mouth at Belém. Large commercial vessels may navigate all the way to Iquitos, approximately 2700 miles upriver.

Although little of the Amazon region has been thoroughly explored, it totals some 25 percent of the world's fresh water and some of its most colorful jungle. Botanists say that there are about 18,000 different plant species in the Amazon Basin, and ichthyographers claim some 1600 species of fish. Plus the fact that the region is exceedingly rich in gold, diamonds, lumber, rubber, oil and jute, and has a population of less than 2 million people. Quite frankly, however, the only sensible way to explore the Amazon basin is by boat, particularly a comfortable cruise vessel that has air-conditioning, hot water, a bar, a laundry service and all those other wonderful things we can not possibly live without!

The port city of **Belém** is gateway to the mighty Amazon River, and located about 90 miles from the Atlantic Ocean. Although set in the midst of tropical foliage, it is a city of white buildings and wide boulevards. Tourist attractions include the Praáa da Republica, the Goeldi Museum and Zoo, the Jungle Park public garden and the Agricultural Institute. The port of Belém can be explored by motor launch, and the suggested best time for photographers is between 5 and 10 a.m. The really adventurous may also want to fly out to the Island of Marajo, a larger land mass than the country of Denmark, noted for its cattle production and lumber industry.

Santarem is located approximately 500 miles upriver, just halfway between Belém and Manaus. It is a city of about 150,000 inhabitants, which was settled by American Confederates from South Carolina and Tennessee in 1865. Indeed, the Confederate flag still hangs from some of the local watering-holes and some of the most common surnames in town are Higgins, O Malley and McDonald. Santarem is something of a boomtown these days because gold has been discovered and the local citizenry are busy supplying prospectors. It is also a loading point for crude rubber out of the jungle. Away from the docks, you can see another world of primitive transportation and habitation.

If Santarem happens to be closed down because of a holiday (we visited on January 1st), bypass the city and head straight for the Tropicale Hotel, where there is a wonderful pool, lovely sunset views, a small zoo for the children and nice cold drinks. Sun Line's evening excursion to a barbecue on the terrace is wonderful. The food and presentation are excellent.

The magnificent city of **Manaus** lies at the 1000-plus-mile mark of the Amazon and the confluence of the Rio Negro rivers, surrounded by dense jungle. The city became rich from the rubber boom of the late 1800s and nothing was too advanced for its inhabitants. It was the first city in South America to have streetcars and, it is said, many folk sent their laundry all the way to London! Its famous Opera House was completed in 1910, just as the rubber boom burst but never mind, Jenny Lind once sang here. Never used for traditional opera, it is the town's number one tourist attraction and worthy of a visit. Following two years of scaffolding and $8 million, the Teatro Amazonas reopened in March 1990 with a Brazilian-composed opera, and the following weekend Placido Domingo (among others) flew into town to sing Carmen. Manaus entrepreneurs hope that this La Scala copy will once again attract well-known names, whom they plan to fly in from Miami, as the newly refurbished structure is gleaming and its red-velvet chairs are free from the termites that used to live under the covers!

Other sights to behold at this anomaly in the jungle are the Custom House and Lighthouse, which arrived dismantled from London, the Salesian Mission Museum, Taruma Falls, several churches, a rubber plantation or two and the City Market Building. You can also take a boat trip on the Rio Negro into dense jungle, filled with tropical birds and wild monkeys. Since Manaus is a free port, its shops are stocked with goods from all over the world that have made the upriver journey, but most of the shops are selling electronic equipment. In fact, several blocks look like Little Tokyo. Beware also of the kids on the street selling fake perfume. The House of the Hummingbird is an interesting shop selling handicrafts, and the new Tropicale Hotel (far out near the airport) is fun for lunch and a swim. A branch of H. Stern is in the shopping arcade. Be sure you get taxis with meters and it won't take a fortune to go out and back.

CHILE AND EASTER ISLAND

Chile has to be the longest, narrowest country on earth, for it measures 2625 miles from north to south and only 312 miles at its widest point. Ships sailing through the Strait of Magellan often stop at its southernmost city, Punta Arenas. More interesting, though, is the seaport of **Puerto Montt**, gateway to Chile's lake district. Beautiful Lake Llanquihue is surrounded by magnificent volcanos, including the eternally snowcapped Osorno. Puerto Montt has a zone of glacial channels that offer fantastic views wherever you look, and is noted for fine seafood.

Valparaiso, Chile's main port, is colorful and enchanting. Founded in 1536, the old town and commercial section is built on reclaimed land along a low terrace, while the residential area clings to the

slopes of the many hills surrounding the port. In between the two are narrow, twisting streets that delight tourists and photographers. Culturally, Valpo (as the locals say) has produced poets and writers, and its historical spots are many. For the best view in town, try the Miradero O'Higgins (named after the first ruler of the republic) located in the Alto del Puerto. Have a look also at the naval school, the Beaux Arts Museum and the universities located here.

Just 10 minutes along the coast from Valpo is the resort town of Viña del Mar, with beautiful beaches, lovely gardens and flowers, friendly atmosphere and a large casino one of the main attractions. But **Santiago**, on a 1706-foot plateau with the snowcapped Andes as an impressive backdrop, is the capital and center of Chilean life. Nature has endowed this setting with much favor; the city is built around beautiful hills. The most familiar is Santa Lucia, which has two fortresses, a lovely park and superb view. Santiago also abounds with man-made beauty, exemplified by its many churches (the cathedral dates from 1558) and more than a dozen museums. If you disembark in Valparaiso, look into the many excursions possible in Santiago Province.

One excursion, albeit far out and remote, takes visitors to the mysterious **Easter Island**, the most eastern member of Polynesia, 2300 miles west of the Chilean coastline. Easter Island is considered an open-air museum, not to mention an archaeological question mark overflowing with evidence that a sophisticated and complex culture once flourished on this remote piece of land in the Pacific Ocean. Easter Island draws many eager cruise passengers to its isolated 7-by-14-mile shores to see the intriguing masonry-lined caves, the gigantic statues, the engineering and astronomical accomplishments and the petroglyphs, as well as the attractive beaches and the hospitable Polynesian people (who call their island Rapa Nui). If you can't make the journey out this time, console yourself with the excellent introduction to these artifacts in Santiago's National Museum.

COLOMBIA

Cartagena is a popular call on cruises to the lower Caribbean, for it offers a taste of South America, a mere whiff of what lies below the equator. Colombia's 1200-mile coastline borders the Caribbean, and Cartagena de Indias (the proper name) is the most important gateway. Founded in 1533, the city never allows visitors to forget its early history, and ancient fortifications still protect the harbor, reminders of 17th- and 18th-century attacks by the French and British. The old city is appealing, with Iberian architecture, narrow streets made crooked to deceive pirates, and baroque monuments to Christianity. Don't miss the spectacular view from La Popa, a restored 17th-century monastery, and the colorful local market surrounded on three sides by the bay. If you prefer a more relaxed day, taxi to the splendid Hilton Hotel for a fresh tuna, a swim and some lovely local shops.

Sailing in and out of Cartagena is also quite spectacular, so find yourself a good vantage point on deck with camera ready. Although this beautiful and historic port has much to offer and is known for emeralds and other semi-precious stones, do not wander off on your own. Stick to the organized tour, which will offer every opportunity (including shopping). Cartagena is a drug haven and the U.S. government is cracking down on the cartels in town. Avoid doing business on the street and never, never accept a package for someone else.

ECUADOR

If your cruise vessel happens to call at **Guayaquil**, Ecuador's main port and largest city, my advice is to get out as quickly as possible. This metropolis of a million-plus people is a hot, dirty, sprawling flat area sprung from the Guayas River, about 35 miles from the Gulf of Guayaquil. That this city grew too big too fast is evident. Don't try to mail anything from its one post office. It also has only one cemetery, which may be its most interesting feature. As one of my Quito friends said, typifying the rivalry between Ecuador's two major cities, "People are so brave to live in Guayaquil that they are given nice burials."

The best way to leave Guayaquil and see something of the countryside is by the autoferro to Quito, a 12-hour journey of just under 300 miles. The autoferro is a single bus on rails, with a driver (motorista), a conductor (ayudante), reserved seats, a toilet in the back and no food. It means planning ahead, spending the night in Guayaquil (where hotel rates are exorbitant), packing a lunch and getting to Duran railroad station by 6 a.m. The train leaves approximately on time (at least by South American custom), and all seats not reserved by tourists are quickly occupied by locals traveling from one small village to another. In many of these villages, the autoferro is the only reliable source of communication, so the motorista and his ayudante deliver packages, messages, produce and livestock along the route and pick up letters for the post office in Quito. Often, they will grab pieces of paper and envelopes from outstretched hands

without even stopping. It's a unique performance, so try to get seats up front and watch.

If you're still sleepy the first few hours out of Guayaquil, don't worry, for the scenery is flat, tropical and rather uninteresting. The spectacular views begin around 10 a.m. when the autoferro climbs one thousand feet up the Nariz del Diablo (Devil's Nose), a series of switchbacks and zigzags along a sheer gorge. From here it's a climb of 10,000 feet into the Andean highlands with breathtaking views of the snowcapped Mt. Chimborazo in the distance. If you're exceptionally brave, you are welcome to ride atop the autoferro, along with the chickens and the onions! The first and only rest stop comes around noon at Riobamba, capital of Chimborazo Province, a town known for its healthful, rarefied air at 9000 feet.

From Riobamba the line climbs to Urbina Pass, the highest point at 11,841 feet, and then skirts the base of Mt. Chimborazo to Ambato, an important Indian market town. From Ambato to Latacunga the line skirts Mt. Cotopaxi, which is not only the highest volcano in the world (19,200 feet) but also one of the most perfect cones. Then you coast into Quito, arriving between 5 and 6 p.m. It's a long but fascinating day, and there's no better way to see the country in between.

Quito, capital of Ecuador, is a charming city spread out on an Andean plain some 9,375 feet above sea level. Because of this height, sightseeing should be taken slowly, otherwise you may feel tired and weak. Quito lies on the equator (the marker is about a 20-minute ride from town), yet has a splendid climate of sunny days in the seventies and brisk, cool nights. The colonial section of Quito, founded in 1534 by Sebastian de Benalcazar, was declared a site of world cultural heritage by UNESCO in 1979 and is now being carefully restored. Among the many fine projects in progress is the courtyard and cloister of the Monastery of St. Augustine, dating from 1573. The inner city is marked by churches and palaces with interiors shining with gold culled by the Spaniards from their newly conquered land.

Among the gold leaf that impresses is in La Compania, one of Quito's most spectacular churches; visit also La Catedral, which has noteworthy artwork and the tomb of Antonio de Sucre, the liberator of Ecuador. Near the Plaza de Independencia are structures of great splendor the Placio Nacional, the Palace of the Archbishop, and Arco de Santo Domingo a classic arch dating from colonial Quito. A wonderful view of the city, including the historic district, can be enjoyed from Panecillo Hill, where it is said that Incans worshipped the sun.

AUTHOR'S OBSERVATION

While local Indians sell their wares on every street corner, there is a famous Saturday market at Otavalo that has handcrafts for everyone no doubt sold by the cousins of the Quito merchants! Quito is a lovely city and there are many interesting things to do as long as you are aware of the altitude and acclimate yourself accordingly.

GALAPAGOS ISLANDS

AUTHOR'S OBSERVATION

The Ecuadorian government has banned cruise ships from these islands in the hopes of protecting wildlife from tourism. Small local excursion boats, such as Galapagos Cruises, are permitted to bring visitors to the islands.

If you have never swum with a sea lion nor scratched the neck of a giant tortoise, one might say that you have not yet lived. Certainly, you have not yet visited the Galapagos Islands where these antics are commonplace and part of a thrilling cruise experience. The Galapagos form an archipelago of six minor and 13 major islands covering some 3000 square miles across the equator in the Pacific Ocean. Discovered by Spaniard Fra Tomas de Berlaya in 1535, they were claimed 300 years later by Ecuador, its coastline approximately 600 miles due east. Shortly thereafter, Charles Darwin, the 26-year-old British naturalist, visited while aboard the HMS *Beagle*; the rest is history. Here Darwin observed the relationships of land-, sea-, and air-life; these observations guided him as he wrote his controversial theories concerning the origin of species. Scientists and naturalists still use the Galapagos archipelago to study behavioral patterns of animals and plants. The Darwin Research Station on Santa Cruz (or Indefatigable) Island is especially well known.

Some visitors refer to these islands as the world's zaniest zoo, for here a multitude of animals coexist in their natural habitat: sea lions, fur seals, land iguanas, sea iguanas, lava lizards, Galapagos tortoises, penguins, cormorants, frigate birds, blue-footed boobies, lightfoot crabs and at least 13 different varieties of Darwin's finches as well as many other birds. The wildlife is safe, since the Galapagos were declared a national park in 1959 and tourism is tightly controlled. Cruises of 3-, 4-, and 7-day spans are available on government-ap-

proved Ecuadorian vessels only, and passengers are accompanied on each island by guides trained at the Darwin Research Station.

Ecuador's National Park Service, which manages the islands, requests that visitors leave nothing more than footprints and take nothing but photographs. Other more stringent rules advise visitors what cautions should be employed when observing the flora and fauna on the islands, and that introducing certain foreign objects can destroy the delicate ecological balance.

Within this archipelago approximately 50 different inlets and areas are accessible, but the guides generally stick to the carefully marked paths on the less treacherous volcanic rock. Most landing parties use small boats, or pangas, that resemble lifeboats. Disembarking onto the islands for your twice daily (morning and afternoon) hike is often tricky and not recommended for the timid. Often to get ashore you must either jump feet first into the water (with pant legs rolled up and shoes in hand overhead) or jump onto slippery rocks. When a dock (or semblance thereof) is available, it seems an unaccustomed luxury. As your cruise within the Galapagos progresses, you will pick up a new language in addition to all the names of plant and animal life—wet landings and dry landings. The islands generally visited are Santa Cruz (for the Research Station and giant tortoises), Santiago or James (for flamingos and fur seals), South Plaza (for land iguanas, sea lions and swallow-tailed gulls), Hood or Espanola (for blue-footed and masked boobies, albatross from April to December, marine iguanas and lava lizards), Floreana or Santa Maria (for flamingo), Tower or Genovesa (for frigate birds, red-footed and masked boobies, fur seals, petrels and lava gulls), Isabela or Albermarle (for flamingos, Galapagos tortoises, flightless cormorants), or Fernandina or Narborough (for flightless cormorants, penguins and marine iguanas) and Seymour (for frigate birds and blue-footed boobies).

Hood or Espanola (most of the islands have both an English and Spanish name) seems to be just about everyone's favorite. Here the hike lasts from three to four hours. You may become very fond of the blue-footed boobies, beautiful birds with blue feet and a rather dumb gaze that makes them appear like a dumbbell, or booby. They are charming when caring for their young or squawking that you mustn't get too close to the nest. In the proper seasons, you can also watch an albatross mating dance, rather like a fencing match with beaks, or even observe the new mothers feeding their young with an oil secreted from their body. And Hood has the Blowhole, where the surf pounds upon the lava-lined shore and then blows straight up through a huge natural hole in the porous rock, a big hit with children, who adore the Galapagos. As one brother/sister pair said to me one summer, "This is much better than Disneyland!" The Galapagos Islands are definitely for the young in mind and body. In addition to the strenuous shore excursions with wet landings and extensive hiking in the hot equatorial sun, entertainment is limited to evolution, ecology and the forces of nature. The islands did not strike me as being particularly beautiful. One might even say that they are ugly volcanic, spare and arid. Although it's possible to swim almost every day, I only saw one beautiful beach Espumilla where I had a lovely sunbath and an exquisite swim. When friends snorkeling off the end of the beach sighted some baby sharks, I swam closer to the shore; but there was no danger. As the equatorial sun is direct and strong, burning is a hazard, so beachtime should be used sparingly if you are susceptible. I also recommend that you wear a large-brimmed hat at all times to prevent sunstroke.

Among the regulars with Ecuadorean flag is the *Santa Cruz*, a ninety-passenger vessel built in Spain in 1979 just for these islands. The *Santa Cruz* has a charming captain named Carlos, an excellent crew and good facilities. Her guides conduct tours in four languages (English, French, German, Spanish), give fine briefings before each shore excursion and are ready to answer questions. For most tours the passengers are divided into four groups (Albatross, Booby, Cormorant, Dolphin) to alternate embarkation of pangas for shore. The cruises are highly structured, so passengers see the most in the shortest time. Wake-up call is 6:15 a.m., breakfast at 6:45 and departures to the islands begin at 7:30. Return to the ship about 11:30 a.m.; lunch starts at 12:30 p.m. while the ship sails to another location; afternoon excursions are scheduled between 3 and 6 p.m.; and dinner follows at 7 p.m., succeeded by a briefing of the next day's activities. Bed down early!

AUTHOR'S OBSERVATION

To get the most out of your Galapagos experience, spend a full week cruising the islands and fly to and from your vessel from either Guayaquil or Quito.

These charter flights aboard Ecuadorean Navy planes are very safe. The best time of year to travel here is probably June through September, when the weather is coolest, although the seas can be a bit rocky. Since the *Santa Cruz* sails between 2 a.m. and 8 a.m. most mornings, the tossings can be a detriment to sleep. Metropolitan Touring's twelve-passenger *Isabella* is also popular, although rather less elegant. Its size, however, does allow calls at some smaller islands.

PERU

Peru's main port, **Callao**, lies a convenient eight miles from **Lima**, capital of this nation that was once home to the spectacular Inca civilization and the subsequent center of Spanish power in the New World. Lima was laid out along the left bank of the Rimac River in 1535 by Francisco Pizzaro, who named it Ciudad de los Reyes (City of Kings). Pizzaro, slain six years later by his own men, is famed as the conqueror of the Inca Empire as well as the founder of the Spanish Empire in South America. The city is centered around the Plaza de Armas, just as Pizzaro planned, but many of the fine colonial structures were destroyed by an earthquake in 1746 and have been replaced by modern buildings. Still, some survivors of the quake remain, and the churches lined with gold and intricate artwork are relics of a sumptuous 17th century. Lima claims the oldest university in the Americas, San Marcos, founded in 1551.

Within the Museum of Art, located in the 1868 Exposition Palace, lies 5000 years of Peruvian culture. The Museum of Anthropology and Archaeology displays more than 80,000 objects discovered throughout the country, in addition to a constantly changing exhibition of exciting new finds. Historical monuments mingle comfortably with modern life, for Lima lives very much in the present and its commercial activity is indicative of a prosperous future. Limenos relish a beautiful city in which to enjoy life. If you are offered a sip of Pisco Sour, a local cocktail, expect a kick.

AUTHOR'S OBSERVATION

For those interested in pre-Inca ruins, the nearest site is 20 miles south of Lima in the Lurin Valley. Known as Pachacamac, the 4-square-mile area is believed to have been a sacred city from A.D. 600 to about 900. The Temple to the Creator God here has 400-foot terraces, frescoed walls and doors inlaid with semiprecious stones. Irrigation and reservoir remains are also evident.

Peru's leading tourist attraction and piéce de resistance, however, are **Cuzco**, ancient capital of the Incas, and the mysterious fortress of **Machu Picchu** just 77 miles away (most cruise ships schedule overnight shore excursions to this famous ruin). Both take some doing to explore (Cuzco is 11,400 feet up in the Andes and Machu Picchu is another 1,000 feet higher), so plan ahead for full enjoyment of one of the most exciting excursions of your travels.

STRAIT OF MAGELLAN

This passage between the Atlantic and Pacific oceans that many have called the greatest natural wonder on earth is just north of Cape Horn. The spectacular 340-mile Strait slices off a small portion of Argentina and Chile, and its navigation is the highlight of any South American cruise itinerary.

The Strait was discovered in 1520 by the global circumnavigator Ferdinand Magellan as he explored the Rio de la Plata and Patagonia regions of Argentina. Passage through the Strait takes most ships about 36 hours, but this depends upon the seas, which can be rough. Although much of the sailing takes place at night under the Southern Cross, you will want to be out on deck as much as possible; the majestic views equal or surpass Norway's fjordland and Alaska's Inside Passage. Often during the passage, Chile's Institute of Patagonia enlists passengers to spot whales and record data for a whale population study. A major portion of the world's whale population has been migrating to the peaceful environment of Patagonia and Tierra del Fuego.

Passengers participating in the whale-spotting program are given full-color whale charts with illustrations and descriptions of the different species of whales, plus special forms providing space for information on type of whale spotted, time of day, latitude and longitude. When you've navigated from the Atlantic Ocean to the Pacific (or vice versa, as some ships sail), it's time to celebrate. After all, one does not do this sort of thing every day.

VENEZUELA

La Guaira is the bustling gateway to Venezuela's capital **Caracas**, which spreads along a valley some 12 miles from the sea via a winding mountain road. The city, founded in 1567 and christened Santiago de Leon de Caracas (after its patron saint), has lost most of its colonial character and is a major financial and commercial center with a *nouveau riche* atmosphere. An acquaintance who resides in Caracas said, "The already aggressive population has become even more so, because of all this new oil wealth." Nonetheless, the city is a major attraction in South America, especially noted as the birthplace of the continent's liberator and hero, Simon Bolivar. His family home, now called Casa Natal, is a national monument. Next door is the Bolivarian Museum, which details the Conquest, Colonial and Independence eras of South America. Also on the heroic tour is Cuadra Bolivar, another restored home of the Bolivar family (Simon was born of noble and wealthy parents in 1783) that has a tamarind tree in the garden that is said to have been taken from the Santa Maria hacienda near Cartagena, where Bolivar died an impoverished and forgotten man in 1830.

Visit the Colonial Art Museum, a beautifully restored mansion filled with art and objects from the Spanish-influenced colonial era; the Plaza Bolivar and cathedral (the latter dates from 1595); Quinta Caracas, where local artists can be found at their easels on the colonial-style patio; and the 400-acre University City, a former sugar plantation. Designed by local architect Villanueva in free-flowing concrete, University City gives me a jolting, futuristic feeling. Adjacent to the university, where 50,000 students fill the campus each day, is the 175-acre Botanical Gardens where you can refresh your spirit among elegant and abundant orchids and other tropical plants.

THE ORINOCO RIVER

Listed as the eighth largest river in the world, the mighty Orinoco extends some 1700 miles from its headwaters in the Parima Sierra (near the Brazilian border) to the Atlantic Ocean, where its enormous delta spreads some hundreds of square miles over tropical jungle. It is one of South America's major river systems and, with all its tributaries, provides over 10,000 miles of navigable waterway. The Orinoco is a mysterious river whose real source was only discovered in 1951 by an official expedition of the Venezuelan government. However, its vastness was not missed by Christopher Columbus, who is said to have remarked, "Never have I read nor heard of so much sweet water within a salt ocean." And his son Ferdinand wrote of the impact of the mid-rainy season outflow of the Orinoco on the Equatorial current flowing westward across the Atlantic from Africa, "The noise of the waves made it seem as though the very waters were fighting..." (The above was printed in Ocean Islander's program, December 23, 1986, as the vessel entered the Delta Amacuro at noon that day.)

Ciudad Guayana was created in 1961 as a major port, but was actually founded in 1595 by Don Antonio de Berrio. Now a prime industrial center of Venezuela, the area boasts the famous Cerro Bolivar open cast-iron mine as well as one of the world's largest hydroelectric plants. **Ciudad Bolivar** is capital of the state of Bolivar and gateway to the Guayana Highlands, which lie just below the Andes.

Ciudad Bolivar was originally named Angostura, and was the first home of the famous bitters.

Angel Falls is a great adventure for cruise passengers who fly over the giant cataract that is 15 times higher than Niagara Falls and has a cascade of water of more than 3000 feet. The falls were first sighted by a Jimmy Angel, who crash-landed his plane on the rugged top of Devil Mountain in 1935, and they bear his name. A special Avensa-chartered Boeing 727 leaves Ciudad Guyana airport around 8 a.m. for the 35-minute flight. If the weather is good, the pilot can fly as low as possible over the falls and try to give both sides of the plane a peek. However, the windows are very small and most of them filthy, so don't expect breathtaking views. Following the falls, the plane drops in on Camp Canaima for a few hours. Here, passengers are offered a rum punch, a canoe ride, a swim in the lagoon and a walk around the grounds. There are a few souvenir shops in the area. The enthusiastic may also take a smaller plane ride over the falls or a jeep ride into the savannah for an extra fee, of course!

PORTS OF EMBARKATION

The QE2 *departing New York Harbor*

In all the excitement of sailing, the port where you board or leave the ship sometimes gets lost in the shuffle. Many cruise lines offer pre- and post-cruise vacation packages, but even if you have only a few hours while waiting for the ship to leave or the flight home after the cruise, there may be time to get a feel for the place to enjoy the local color, sample traditional foods, even do some shopping. In many ports of embarkation, the most interesting sights, tastes and bargains are virtually dockside.

AUTHOR'S OBSERVATION

Those traveling on an air/sea package will be transferred from the airport directly to the pier. If you have purchased air separately, however, and are responsible for getting to the ship on your own, ask your cruise counselor about approximate costs of taxis or other recommended means of transportation.

The Caribbean and Bahamas

BRIDGETOWN, BARBADOS

The capital of an island noted for its beaches and resorts rather than spectacular sightseeing or shopping bargains. The port, often filled with the British Navy, is a warm, ten-minute walk or quick cab ride from the center of town ($10–15). Agree on the fare in advance.

Trafalgar Square is the center of political life. **St. Michael's Cathedral** was visited by George Washington...the **Barbados Museum** contains maritime, local and Indian artifacts and memorabilia...**Andromeda Gardens** is a refreshing taste of Caribbean flora...**Farley Hill National Park** overlooks the island's Scotland District, and Queen's Park combines plant life with historical buildings. The best way to get around is by taxi, and the beaches and resorts along Barbados **Platinum Coast** are only minutes away from town.

Pelican Village and Temple Yard, both only minutes on foot from the dock, are good places to buy arts and crafts, and most duty-free shopping is located on Broad Street. Local menu favorites include flying fish, lobster, curries and spicy, thick soups. Restaurants are plentiful in all price ranges...hotel buffets are a good way to sample the best of island cuisine...don't forget the famous Barbados Mount Gay rum.

FORT-DE-FRANCE, MARTINIQUE

A delightful blend of the tropics and Paris as it was maybe 30 years ago. The port is within walking distance of shops selling the latest in French perfumes and clothing, as well as outdoor cafes, restaurants and markets. The airport is only five miles from town and taxi fares are government-controlled.

Musée Departemental de la Martinique features Caribbean Indian and colonial historical objects. **Musée de la Pagerie** contains memorabilia of Napoleon's Empress Josephine, who was born here... **Gaugin**, the painter, spent time here as well and there is a museum in his honor...and a collection of rum-making equipment and tools at the **Musée du Rhum**.

Rue Victor Hugo, Rue Schoelcher and the narrow streets around them comprise the main shopping district where French goods, particularly luxury items, clothing, shoes and perfumes, can be a bargain. The many sidewalk cafes and snack trucks at La Savane, the main square, are two ways of sampling the local refreshments...crayfish, langouste, blood sausage and hot, creole dishes are among the best...French wines are plentiful, as is the local concoction, a white rum with lime punch.

MONTEGO BAY, JAMAICA

One of the island's major resort areas; the port is easily accessible to beaches, as well as sightseeing attractions. The airport is less than five miles from the port area and most taxis charge flat fees between points.

One of the island's 200 beaches is **Doctor's Cave Beach**, a good spot to see Jamaica in action; others tend to be more secluded...**Rose Hall Great House** is a fine example of 18th-century Caribbean architecture. **Greenwood** was home to Elizabeth Barrett Browning...the **Governor's Coach** tour, by diesel rail car, provides a quick glimpse of plantations, coffee groves and villages outside the city...Jamaica's famous **rafting** is available nearby on the Martha Brae River.

Fabrics, embroidery, resort wear, artwork and rum are among the local products worth investigating. Duty-free imports include watches, porcelain, jewelry, cameras and recording equipment. The **Jamaican Crafts Market** is a good place for local handiwork. Pepperpot soup is just one of many local favorites that have made Jamaican cooking popular with visitors. Rice and peas, curried goat, saltfish, pastries (meat and spice-filled pastries) and local fruit-flavored ice creams are not to be missed either.

PHILIPSBURG, ST. MAARTEN

The Dutch end of an island whose flip side is French. Philipsburg is noted for shopping bargains, while many of the best beaches are near Marigot, the French capital, and only a few minutes away by taxi or local bus. The airport is halfway between the towns, and all but the very smallest cruise ships anchor off Philipsburg.

There is very little in the way of historical landmarks or museums; people come here to shop and sun...the entire island can be circled in less than four hours and, for the very brave, mopeds are available for hire...**beaches** are beautiful, often topless on the French side and within walking distance of the pier in Philipsburg.

St. Maarten has the reputation of being *one of the Caribbean's best shopping areas for bargains on imported goods of all kinds*, including gold jewelry, and Philipsburg is little more than a hectic collection of dozens of shops along the town harbor. Between shopping sprees or a plunge in the ocean, try one of the numerous seaside, open-air restaurants along the harbor.

ST. JOHNS, ANTIGUA

St. Johns, Antigua, is a sleepy little town on an island noted for very glamorous resorts. The port itself is isolated from everything except a small crafts market and a few shops selling local products. Taxis are available at the pier for trips to town or other attractions.

St. Johns itself is not why people come to Antigua, although the botanical gardens, the museum in the Old Court House, **St. John the Divine** cathedral and many of the restored colonial buildings have an understated appeal...**English Harbour**, with its handsomely restored Nelson's Dockyard and once home to Horatio Nelson's British fleet in the late 1700s, is well worth a visit...and there are **365 beaches** to choose from.

Local products include printed fabrics and clothing, pottery, straw work and Antigua rum...duty-free goods include liquor, perfume and jewelry...**Redcliffe Quay** and **St. Mary's Street** are the main shopping areas in St. Johns. Fresh fish, lobster and native pineapple are among the local favorites...English Harbour is a particularly pleasant place for an outdoor lunch.

SAN JUAN, PUERTO RICO

One of the biggest cities in the Caribbean offers a variety of attractions and amusements found nowhere else in the region. Allowing for chaotic driving, a taxi ride from the airport ten miles away takes approximately 30 minutes. The port in Old San Juan is within walking distance of the historic landmarks, shopping and restaurants of a beautifully restored old city.

Old San Juan is a six-block-square area of narrow streets, squares, monuments and museums...**El Morro Castle**, at one end, protected the city for 500 years...San Juan Cathedral, **La Fortaleza** (the oldest governor's mansion in the New World) and a number of **museums** dedicated to such things as books, glass, the Puerto Rican family, Indians and Pablo Casals are other attractions within walking distance...seaside resorts with casinos and floor shows to rival Las Vegas are found in the Condado area close to the airport...across the bay from the cruise terminal is the **Bacardi Rum factory**.

The streets of Old San Juan are filled with **shops** of every description...jewelry, crafts and fashion boutiques are good buys, as well as cigars, rum, religious carvings and musical instruments. The old city also has plenty of breezy cafes, bars and restaurants, many of them on the second floor to catch the sea air...One is across the street from the cruise terminal.

ST. THOMAS AND ST. CROIX

St. Thomas and St. Croix are the major ports of the U.S. Virgin Islands. The piers, depending on where your ship is anchored, are within minutes of shops and eating places; some may be dockside. Major shopping areas and beaches are easily accessible by taxi from the pier in both ports.

AUTHOR'S OBSERVATION

No one goes to St. Thomas for sightseeing; they go to shop and, although prices are not what they used to be, there is certainly a larger selection here than anywhere else in the Caribbean.

There are also beautiful beaches on St. Thomas, and **Magen's Bay**, about 30 minutes away from the ship, is the best...**Coral World Marine Park** provides safe underwater viewing. The nearby island of St. John, home to **Caneel Bay resort** and the **Virgin Islands National Park**, is a must if you have a day to spare. On St. Croix, Buck Island Reef is the only U.S. **underwater national monument**...**Whim Greathouse**, built in the 1700s, and Fort Christianvaern, a remnant of the islands' Danish heritage, are also worth visiting.

Items of every description are available in small shops and huge, frenzied warehouses...Most large stores will deliver to the ship...but does it really make sense to save a dollar or two on a bottle of whiskey if you have to schlep it all the way home?

Europe

BARCELONA

Barcelona, Spain's second largest city, is cosmopolitan, gracious and busy. The port is in the heart of the city, close to museums, historic neighborhoods and dozens of seafood restaurants.

In the port area are the **Picasso Museum**, Plaza Puerto de la Paz with a bronze statue of **Columbus**, a replica of Columbus's flagship **Santa Maria** and a Maritime Museum...Barcelona's Gothic **cathedral** up from the port is a must...the **Ramblas** is a lively promenade lined with shops, markets and cafes...the **Gothic Quarter** dates back to the 14th century...**Ciudadela Park**, near the Picasso Museum, contains a zoo and the museums of modern art and natural history...**Montjuich Park**, with its castle overlooking much of the city, contains a cluster of museums, including the Museum of Catalan Art and Ceramics, the Archaeology Museum and the Joan Miró Foundation.

The best area for shopping is **Paseo de Gracia** and **Rambla Catuna**, although the best for antiques is around the cathedral...El Encants are Barcelona's lively flea markets. Plaza Real is ideal for outdoor cafes, nearby Calle Escudellers is filled with bars and some of the city's oldest restaurants...the otherwise seamy Barcelona neighborhood near the port is a favorite spot for inexpensive seafood restaurants...in addition to seafood, snails and pasta dishes are favorites among local residents.

COPENHAGEN

The capital of Denmark, Copenhagen is one of the most enjoyable cities in Europe. The port itself is about ten minutes from the city's center and roughly ten miles.

Tivoli, the city's non-stop amusement center (during the summer and fall months), is the most famous attraction, featuring classical and jazz concerts, an amusement park, gardens, firework displays and theater...among the **museums** are the Ny Carlsberg Glyptotek (ancient to 19th-century art), Kastellet (a 300-year-old fortress), Dunstindustrimuseet (decorative, European and Oriental art) and the Kobenhavns Bymuseum (the 800-year history of Copenhagen)...**City Hall Square** and **Stroget**, a pedestrian mall, are good places to get a taste of city life.

Quality, design and, of course, price are the main ingredients of shopping here, although visitors can take advantage of tax-free shopping...silver, clothing, toys, glassware are worth considering.

DUBROVNIK

In what was once Yugoslavia, Dubrovnik is now heavily damaged by war, but is still a medieval masterpiece guarded by walls 1000 years old and built around an ancient harbor.

AUTHOR'S OBSERVATION

We do not recommend selecting the Dalmation coast for a destination until the current civil war is resolved and order restored.

GENOA

Genoa is huge, noisy, steamy and exciting, the biggest Italian port. Fortunately for visitors, the docks are located within easy access to the city's center. The maritime terminal is roughly three miles from the airport.

One of the best ways of seeing Genoa is by **boat tour** (an hour's trip) on the harbor...**Via Garibaldi** is a street lined with historic palaces, many of which contain rare works of art, and small museums ...The **Royal Palace** on Via Balbi contains works by Van Dyck...**San Lorenzo Cathedral** reflects several hundred years of architecture and art, and **Piazza San Matteo** is noted for its houses originally belonging to the Andrea Doria family...**Piazza de Ferrari** is modern Genoa's busy center. For a quick and tasty bite to eat, try a **tavola calde** or coffee bar, where you can stand at the counter with the locals.

HAMBURG

Almost completely destroyed in World War II, Hamburg is a modern, fast-moving city, Germany's second largest. The port, 70 miles from the North Sea on the Elbe River, is busy and huge, but the city itself can be seen quickly and easily. Cruise-ship berths are roughly 20 miles from the airport, with a travel time of one hour.

Most of Hamburg's attractions can be seen on foot from the city center...the famous **opera house** is ultramodern, near the botanical gardens, originally laid out in 1821...the **St. Pauli** district is noted for its shady evening activities...**museums** include the Kunsthalle (the city's primary art museum), the Hamburg Historical Museum and a museum for decorative arts and crafts...at the harbor itself is the Oevelgonne Museumshafen (the harbor museum).

For quality luxury goods try the stores on Jungfernstieg, Neuer Wall and Dammtorstrasse...there are also a number of arcades and less expensive department stores. Eel soup, pea soup, pig's feet and herring are favorite dishes among the locals.

LISBON

Capital of Portugal, Lisbon is a place for strolling and lingering on boulevards and in cafes. The airport is about seven miles from the docks; allow 30 minutes. The city center is 15 minutes from the port.

Praça do Rossio is the center of action in the city...**St. George's Castle** has guarded the city since the Middle Ages, and just as old is Largo da Se, the cathedral...the section called **Alfama** is the oldest part of Lisbon, one that reflects the city's strong Moorish influences...the Gulbenkian Foundation Museum and the Gulbenkian Modern Art Center feature works by many of the great impressionists...the **Tower of Belem** honors some of the country's most famous explorers, and along the river are museums, a planetarium and a monastery.

Leather goods, embroidery, clothing and pottery are among the bargains in Lisbon, to be found in small shops in the downtown section (Chiado and Baixa).

AUTHOR'S OBSERVATION

Lisbon is famous for its tiles, and you can have your own patterns done if you wish. Essential to any visit to Lisbon is a stop at one of the hundreds of cafes where the population gathers to watch the world go by.

MALAGA

Malaga is the heart of Spain's Costa del Sol, not as attractive as smaller resort areas along the coast but vibrant and growing.

The city's **cathedral** dates back to the 16th century and contains an interesting art collection...a series of parks and gardens lead to the Moorish **Alcazaba**, site of the city's Archaeological Museum...the resorts of Torremolinos and Marbella are nearby...prehistoric **caves** can be found on an excursion to Nerja. Try the seafood restaurants along the beach road; the catch is right off the boat.

MONTE CARLO

Monte Carlo hardly needs an introduction. Tiny, elegant, a center for arts and entertainment, as well as good living, it is the jewel of the Riviera. The airport at Nice is 12 miles away. By helicopter it's ten minutes; by taxi allow 45 minutes. Once at the port you are within walking distance of the entire city, and taxis are also available.

Much of the **royal palace** is open to visitors, as is the **Palace Museum**, the **Waxworks Museum** and the **Oceanographic Museum and Aquarium**...the cathedral, the **ramparts** of the city, the **Misericorde Chapel** and the **Gardens of Saint Martin** are also worth a visit...and there is the famous **casino** and **opera house**. Tours of Monte Carlo are available by helicopter and motorcoach.

Don't look for cut-rate bargains here, but if it's luxury items, such as art, designer clothing or jewelry you're shopping for, this may be the place.

NAPLES

Naples is a teeming, chaotic Italian city whose reason for existence is shipping, notably passenger shipping. The port is conveniently located within walking distance of much of the best of the city.

For most tourists Naples is, unfortunately, a passing-through place while on the way to **Capri**, the **Amalfi Drive**, **Pompeii** or **Sorrento**, but it has a charm worth sampling...near the port is **Piazza del Plebiscito**, the center of social life, and the galleria at **Piazza Trento e Trieste**, which houses cafes and shops under four wrought-iron arcades...the impressive **Castel Nuovo**, built in the 13th century, the **Royal Palace** and the **National Archaeological Museum** (containing one of the world's best collections of Greco-Roman antiquities) are well worth a visit...the tiny port of Santa Lucia has a song named after it...at the **Capodimonte Palace**, the **National Galleries** contain works by some of Italy's best-known painters...if you have time, excursions on your own or by motorcoach are possible to Pompeii, Herculaneum, Vesuvius, and, of course, the glamorous island of Capri.

Via Roma and **Via Chiaia** are popular shopping areas among local residents, and tourists will find higher-priced items around Piazza dei Martiri. Try the cafes up from the port in the arcades at Piazza Trento e Trieste...for seafood, Santa Lucia offers tiny restaurants built on the edge of the harbor.

NICE

Nice lies at the heart of the French Riviera, a bustling city, as well as a seaside resort. The airport, 4 miles away, is approximately 15 minutes from the port area. The port area is only minutes from the center of city life, which is the beach.

The great French artists Chagall, Matisse and Renoir are well represented here in **museums**, but the major attraction, of course, is the **waterfront** with its bikinis, cafes and **restaurants** specializing in the zesty Mediterranean school of cooking, with an emphasis on fish, fresh produce and Italian influences.

PIRAEUS

Piraeus is the not-terribly-attractive port for Athens. A huge center for international shipping it is, thankfully, only about five miles from more appealing attractions, such as the Acropolis. The port is about 30 minutes from the Athens airport and about the same from the pier to the city center. Be sure to agree on the price before setting out.

In addition to the spectacular **Acropolis**, which perches above the city, there are dozens of archaeological landmarks and museums in the city, all dedicated to 4000 years of Greek history...on a more modern note, the **Museum of Greek Popular Art** contains examples of folk art and culture, and the **National Picture Gallery** is dominated by the 19th century...the **National Gardens** and the **Zapio Gardens** provide a green contrast to a city that is overwhelmingly concrete- gray...the **Maritime Museum** is in Piraeus itself.

Two primary shopping areas are located near the famous **Syntagma**, the hub of modern Athens. **Stadiou** and **Upper Venizelou** are for luxury items; **Ermou** and **Monastiraki** for less expensive goods, where bargaining is still a way of life in the big city...antiquities are not cheap and come under strict government control. For local color try any of the hundreds of tavernas or cafes. The **Plaka** is a good spot for the former, which serve relatively inexpensive Greek food; **Syntagma** and **Kolonaki** are best for people-watching and thick Greek coffee...there are also inexpensive, non-touristy seafood restaurants on the waterfront of Piraeus.

SOUTHAMPTON

Southampton is one of two ports commonly used for cruises embarking in England, the other being Tilbury. Southampton is usually reached by train from London, a 1-1/2-hour trip arranged through Britrail or your cruise line.

Although it dates back prior to the Norman Conquest in 1066, much of Southampton was destroyed in World War II and most of what is worth visiting lies outside the city...the **New Forest** is 9000 acres of unspoiled countryside and forest, originally the private preserve of William the Conqueror...nearby **Beaulieu Abbey** is a remarkable country home that was once a Cistercian abbey and today includes one of the most comprehensive automobile museums in the world...the Isle of Wight, long a favorite with yachtsmen and writers, is a short ferry ride away. For lunch, try one of two or three remaining historic pubs, which date back to the 14th century.

TILBURY

Tilbury is on the outskirts of Greater London, 40 miles from both Heathrow and Gatwick airports and 25 miles from the city's East End. There is really no reason to spend time in Tilbury with London so close, and the one-hour trip to the city can be made by train or motorcoach.

VENICE

Without a doubt, Venice is the strangest and sometimes most beautiful city in Europe. Be prepared to sightsee by water or on foot because all other forms of private transportation are forbidden. And everything is expensive. Depending on which pier your ship is assigned, the trip from Marco Polo International Airport (nine miles) takes roughly 40 minutes by private water taxi. There are also water buses available between the airport and the Lido or St. Mark's Square. Count on a 15-minute water taxi ride from the docks to St. Mark's Square.

Piazza San Marco (St. Mark's), the **Rialto Bridge** and the **Grand Canal** are some of the famous sights to walk through...along the way are numerous **palazzos**, often containing impressive art collections and dozens of churches...St. Mark's, in addition to wonderful cafes, offers St. Mark's Basilica, museums and the **Doges' Palace** for sightseeing...the **Academy of Fine Arts** contains a record of Venetian painting since the 14th century...the **Lido** is the playground of Venice, with one of the few casinos in Italy. The secret to eating well in Italy is to sample what's in season...**trattorias** are the best bet for sampling typically Venetian dishes at moderate prices...local favorites include seafood, such as squid and prawns, and wines from neighboring regions, including Valpolicella and Soave.

Far East/Pacific

AUCKLAND

Auckland is New Zealand's largest city, which is not very large but very enjoyable. The port is about 15 miles from the airport and right in the downtown shopping district.

Among the attractions are the **Auckland War Memorial**, which has beautiful examples of Maori art, and the Museum of Transport and Technology, providing a glimpse of curious tools and machines of the past...**Victoria Park Market** is a bustling flea market/arts and crafts show/marketplace...**One Tree Hill** includes one tree, an observatory and a towering obelisk...**Mt. Eden** provides a view of most of New Zealand, at least it seems that way...the **Kelly Tarlton Underwater World** takes the visitor beneath the sea for a look at local fish and sea-life...**Parnell Rose Garden and Village** is a shopping complex in a colonial setting.

Shoppers should visit the greenstone factories around town. The type of jade is a traditional stone used by the Maoris for jewelry...and because there are more sheep than people in New Zealand, wool products are definitely worth investigating...as is the pottery turned out by some 5000 craftsmen in the country. Fish and chips is a popular snack in Auckland, but try some of the local fruits, cheeses and fresh seafood as well. Lamb, of course, is ever present on menus, and tearooms are plentiful...if you can find a Maori **hangi**, or feast, don't miss it.

BALI

Bali is considered by many travelers to be among the world's most beautiful places. Part of Indonesia, it is 90 miles long and rich in religious traditions.

Among the attractions of Bali is the **Denpasar Museum and market**, which includes a museum of Balinese culture...the **Bat Cave** is creepy but interesting...visit the **Batur temple** and volcanic lake with more than 300 shrines...the **Celuk gold and silver works** are in a small village near Denpasar...the **Gunung Kawi** is a Hindu Balinese sanctuary...**Kuta Beach** is a popular resort, and the **Sangeh Monkey Forest** is home for the island's sacred monkeys...**Pedjeng** is considered the center of ancient Balinese dynasties...**Ubud**, with its painters, galleries and studios, is essential to any visit.

Food is very important to the Balinese and is used in religious ceremonies and festivities that are held virtually year-round...among the local favorites worth trying are suckling pig, sea turtle, rijsttafel, duck, fish and the ever popular Dutch Rijstaffel.

BANGKOK

Capital of Thailand, Bangkok is huge, sprawling, chaotic, and a city of astounding contrasts ranging from the unbelievably serene to sordid. The main port is some distance from the city (150 miles approximately; a four-hour trip), but smaller vessels can maneuver the Chao Phraya River. The airport is 30 minutes from downtown Bangkok.

This is a city of wonderfully gentle, lovely people, more than 400 magnificent **temples**, chaotic **shopping** bazaars and pockets of **sex clubs** and bars that seem to be terribly exploitative of the Thai people...from the Chao Phraya River you can take in the **Grand Palace** complex and the temple of the **Emerald Buddha**...other temples (you can take half-day and full-day tours of temples only) include those honoring the Reclining Buddha and the Golden Buddha...the **National Museum** is one of the biggest in Asia and represents 6000 years of Thai culture...outside Bangkok is the **Ancient City**, worth a visit if you have the time...as is the **Crocodile Farm** with its 10,000 inhabitants ...the best way to see the city if it's your first time is by an organized tour, which can be arranged at any of the major hotels.

Thai silk, emeralds and semi-precious stones are the real shopping bargains, but some of the shopping bazaars are a must, even if you don't buy. There are entire streets filled with shops selling nothing but paraphernalia for temples and temple worship, and another section of the city in which shops sell nothing but chains of gold...Thai food is very good, very spicy and can be very, very hot, so be careful...the seasonings are heavy on garlic, basil, coconut and lemongrass...Thai buffets at some of the hotels are a good way to sample.

HONG KONG

Hong Kong, with its non-stop activity, millions of people and boats of every description, may be the world's most exciting harbor. Be sure to take the Star Ferry at some point in your visit. The short trip between Kowloon and Hong Kong Island is a unique way to see the city and costs almost nothing.

Tiger Balm Gardens and **Sung Dynasty Village**, a reconstruction of a complete Chinese town dating back to the Middle Ages, are musts...**Statue Square** and **Victoria Park** are popular social and recreation areas...the **Fung Ping Shan Museum** contains a collection of porcelain...other museums include the **Hong Kong Museum of Art** and the **Jade Museum at Tiger Balm Gardens**.

Hong Kong is best known for two things—**shopping** and **food**. Be prepared to bargain for jade, designer clothing and accessories (some are counterfeit), porcelain, ivory, fabrics, antiques, and electronics, but be sure you're getting a good deal; U.S. prices for much of what is now sold in Hong Kong can be competitive...Li Yuen Street, Hollywood Road and Kansu Street are favorite shopping areas, and the **Poor Man's Nightclub** near the Macau Ferry, with its massive piles of merchandise and food stalls, is a unique experience any time of day...Cantonese cooking is the predominant cuisine in Hong Kong, but the variety within it is astounding and everything else is possible, from nouvelle cuisine to Indian...dim sum is a chaotic but delicious way to sample a wide variety of dishes.

HONOLULU

On the Hawaiian island of Oahu,Honolulu is known for two things, Waikiki and Pearl Harbor, but there are other reasons for spending some time there. The port is in the downtown section, halfway between the airport and Waikiki (15-20 minutes).

Waikiki is a stretch of beach, resort hotels, shopping centers and a multitude of restaurants that often surprises first-time visitors by its small size. It's a good introduction to Hawaii, but there are more spectacular beaches...Oahu can be circled by public bus or by car, and that's a good way to get a taste of the island...the **USS Arizona Memorial** at **Pearl Harbor** is a moving tribute to the sailors who died there...the **Bishop Museum** is a fine collection of Hawaiian art and cultural artifacts, and the Honolulu Academy of Arts, built in the Spanish style around courtyards, has dozens of galleries.

For the hungry, Waikiki restaurants range from fast food to elegant dining, and **Restaurant Row** is a new area downtown.

KOBE

Kobe, Japan, is best known in America for its beef, but there are other attractions as well. The port is 20 miles from the Osaka airport (40 minutes by taxi) and only five minutes from the city center. It is also possible to reach Kobe by bullet train from Tokyo or Osaka, the latter trip costing about $15.

If you're lucky enough to be in Kobe during the spring, **cherry trees** will be in bloom...**Mt. Rokko** provides a view of the surrounding region...the **Ikuta** and **Minatogawa shrines** reflect traditional

Japanese life, and the **Hakutsuru Art Museum** contains a good collection of bronzes, pottery and ancient art from Japan...the **Municipal Art Museum** reflects the influence of the West on Japan's history...there is an **underground shopping arcade** at Sannomiya. Most of the shopping is in the downtown business area, but the **Kobe International House** is another option.

Kobe beef, pampered and massaged before it reaches the table, is about the best in the world, and the city is also known for the quality of its sake...you might also consider local favorites, such as blowfish or fugu soup.

PAPEETE

Papeete is the hub for the enchanted islands of French Polynesia, which we tend to lump together as Tahiti. Tahiti is, in fact, the largest of several islands, and Papeete is the capital city. This is a part of the world fantastically rich in legend and myth created by some of the best writers and painters of western civilization. Melville, Robert L. Stevenson, Jack London and Paul Gaugin are just a few. Captain Cook was not the first to bring these islands to the attention of Europe, but has received most of the attention. The port is in the town center, close to the airport.

Among the sights worth visiting are the **Paul Gaugin Museum** at the opposite end of the island from Papeete, the **Captain Cook Monument** outside the town and numerous **waterfalls** along the coastal road...the major attraction, of course, is the **natural beauty** of the island itself, particularly the dazzling beaches...in Papeete, itself, there is a cathedral, a cultural center and **Bougainville Park**, named after a French explorer.

SINGAPORE

Singapore may be the easiest, and certainly the most curious, city in the Far East to visit. It's a city of gleaming skyscrapers where everything works and efficiency is prized. In the midst of this 21st-century atmosphere, centuries of tradition of at least four cultures are reflected in unexpected places. The port is roughly 30 minutes from the airport and five minutes from the downtown area.

In Singapore, it's a choice of towering shopping centers in which hundreds of tiny shops are connected by escalators, or pockets of history...**Orchard Road** is lined with hotels and shopping centers...tiny **Chinatown** has survived the onslaught of skyscrapers...Serangoon Road is known as **Little India**...the colonial past is reflected in such buildings as Parliament House, the Victoria Theater and City

Hall...**Raffles Hotel**, a wonderful vestige of Singapore's British past, is, perhaps, the single most interesting experience in the city.

Shopping and eating in Singapore are remarkable adventures and, unlike many other Asian cities, relatively safe and carefree. It would be useless to list the shopping bargains because virtually anything can be bought here. Electronics can be especially good buys...in a city of wonderful Chinese food that little resembles the American equivalents, as well as surprisingly excellent hotel restaurants. One of the taste treats in Singapore is the street food that is, thanks to strict government supervision, quite safe and delicious.(The Singapore government is strict about everything and consequently everything works, even if it sometimes seems slightly oppressive). So don't be afraid to try whatever looks good or strange.

SYDNEY

Sydney must rank among the top five port cities in the world. Friendly, sunny and entertaining, its spirit is invigorating and contagious. The ports, depending on where your ship puts in, are about ten miles from the airport and you can be literally in the historic district or just minutes away by taxi.

Sydney is a city of villages, neighborhoods and coves surrounded by water...just up from the cruise piers is the **Rocks**, a restored area originally settled by convicts transported from Britain. It is now a collection of shops, restaurants and bars, a favorite social spot for residents and tourists alike...dominating the harbor is the world-famous Sydney **Opera House**. Tours are conducted throughout the day...one of the best ways to see the city is by **ferry**. It doesn't really matter where you go, but **Manly**, a seaside resort that is a delightful throwback to a simpler age, is wonderful, and the views of the city from the **zoo** across the bay are spectacular...among the museums are the **Australian Museum**, for a look at the continent's natural history, the **Art Gallery of New South Wales**, and an interesting **Geological and Mining Museum**...there are **beaches** everywhere and they're all worth visiting.

Shoppers can find anything and everything, but many look for Australian opals...**Double Bay** is a trendy shopping area, and **Paddington** is a wonderful neighborhood of small, less expensive shops and art galleries, as well as restaurants...eating is a breeze in Sydney, ranging from coffee and tea shops to the most elegant nouvelle cuisine at the glamorous hotels, such as the **Regent of Sydney**. The Rocks is convenient for eating if time is limited...Try the local seafood such as John Dory, prawns and bugs...and don't overlook the Australian wines; they may put you off California wines for good.

TOKYO

Tokyo is an expensive city to visit on your own. A taxi from Narita Airport to the port is about $200. From the pier, however, you can get to the downtown area for about $30-45. It is also possible to take a bus from Narita to the downtown air terminal. To get around the city itself, consider the subways.

One of the newest museums in Tokyo is the **Fukagawa Edo Shiryokan**, which includes reconstructions of 19th-century Tokyo, then called Edo...the **Meiji Shrine**, and its spectacular grounds, is one of the required items on any city tour...the **Asakusa district** is a good example of old Tokyo, and **Shibuya** is an example of the new...**Kiyosumi Garden** is worth a visit, and all roads seem to lead to the **Imperial Palace**...**Ginza** is one of best-known shopping streets in the world ...among the dozens of museums are the **Japan Folk Crafts Museum**, the **National Museum of Modern Art**, the **Japanese Sword Museum** and the **Tokyo National Museum**, which is the largest in Japan.

AUTHOR'S OBSERVATION

Beware of shopping in Tokyo: Prices may be very high due to the currency exchange, and many items made in Japan, especially electronics, cameras, etc., can be purchased for less money in the United States...Silk kimonos can be found for good prices...the International Arcade is a good place to look...local handicrafts, such as lacquerware and pottery, are also bargains.

North America

ANCHORAGE

Anchorage is Alaska's "big" city and gateway for the ports of Seward and Whittier as well. The airport is about seven miles from downtown. Passengers are generally transported by train or bus to the port areas.

Among the historic sights in Anchorage are the **Anderson House**, one of the earliest homes, which is located in Elderberry Park...in Crawford Park is the first schoolhouse built in the city...the **Anchorage Museum of History and Art** has a good collection of Indian and Eskimo artifacts...**Earthquake Park** and the **Anchorage Zoo** are two of the nature-related activities in town.

Shoppers should look for **Native American** crafts, including jewelry, totem poles and baskets...Anchorage also is noted for its furs...the **Alaska Native Arts and Crafts Cooperative** is a good place to watch artisans at work and purchase their products.

BALTIMORE

Baltimore, for a rather small city, is a huge port. Allow 30 minutes from the airport by taxi, and from the Dundalk Marine Terminal to downtown about 20 minutes ($10). There is parking available at the pier.

Harborplace is Baltimore's pride and joy, a gleaming complex of restaurants and shops at the city's inner harbor...the **National Aquarium** features a 17-story shark tank...from the World Trade Center, the **Top of the World** provides a view of the entire city and then some. Other attractions include the frigate U.S.S. *Constellation*, the **Maryland Science Center** and the **Davis Planetarium**...two **museums** worth visiting are the Baltimore Museum of Art and the Walters Art Gallery, downtown.

The **Chesapeake Bay** provides some of the city's best meals...be sure to try soft-shelled crabs if in season, or the spicy, hard-shelled variety if they're not...oysters and clams are also indigenous, and **Harborplace** has several restaurants where you'll find them.

BOSTON

The gateway to New England, Boston is a relatively small city with a huge, meandering harbor. The Black Falcon Cruise Terminal is about 15 minutes from Logan Airport by cab or ten minutes from downtown. Parking is available across the street.

Boston is a pleasing combination of old and new...the **Freedom Trail** takes you past and through many of the most famous sites of the Revolutionary War, as well as through the city's lively North End...**Quincy Market/Faneuil Hall**, near the harbor, has been restored and turned into dozens of restaurants and shops...the **Boston Aquarium** across the street is one of the best in the world...Beacon Hill and Back Bay are good for wandering through narrow streets, past elegant homes and interesting shops...across the Charles River, **Cambridge** and **Harvard University** are worth a visit...museums include the **Museum of Fine Arts**, one of America's best, the **Gardner** and the **Fogg**. Kids will love the **Children's Museum**, very close to the harbor area.

Shoppers should head for **Filene's Basement**, a local tradition for bargains, or **Copley Place**, one of the newest giant shopping complexes in the downtown area. Newbury Street is also a choice spot for small, elegant shops...food is good everywhere, but the Quincy Market area offers an amazing variety of snacks and quick meals, as well as some of the city's oldest and best-known restaurants. Italian North End is a great place for coffee.

FORT MYERS

At one end of Florida's intercoastal waterway, Fort Myers is on the relatively undeveloped Gulf Coast (compared with Miami, at least). The airport is about 30 minutes from the downtown area.

The primary attraction in the Ft. Myers area is the **Gulf of Mexico** and its resort areas...**Sanibel** and **Captiva** islands are definitely worth a visit (the beaches are noted for their huge variety of shells)...the **Jimmy Connors Tennis Center** is nearby...**Ding Darling** is the name of a fascinating wildlife refuge where alligators sometimes hold up traffic...the **Edison Winter Home and Museum** is a charming combination of history and tropical gardens.

Try the local **seafood** at smaller restaurants, but if you're looking for a fancy meal, a number of resorts on Sanibel and Captiva can provide it, often with spectacular Gulf views.

JACKSONVILLE

Close to the Georgia border on Florida's northeast coast, Jacksonville is worth a visit with a car because its attractions tend to be widespread. The airport is roughly 20 miles from the port.

Riverwalk, on the banks of St. John's River, is a complex of shops, restaurants and entertainment venues...**Saint Augustine**, the oldest town in America, is about 30 minutes away, and Anheuser-Busch has a **brewery** outside of town where visitors can take tours and sample the merchandise...the **Jacksonville Zoo** has 60 acres, including an African veldt display...**Kathryn Abbey Hanna Park** has 450 acres on the ocean for picnics, camping and swimming...**museums** include the Jacksonville Art Museum with a fine collection of Oriental porcelain, and the Museum of Arts and Sciences...Riverwalk is a convenient place for a bite to eat.

KETCHIKAN

Ketchikan is a popular port of call for many cruise ships, and also is a port of embarkation for some of the smaller vessels. The airport is a ten-minute ferry ride from downtown.

Ketchikan is one of Alaska's centers for Native American cultures...**Saxman Totem Park** has more than 20 **totem poles** on display, and the **Tongass Historical Society** is on Dock Street near the port...the **Totem Heritage Cultural Center** has more than 30 poles and other artifacts of Indian life...the **Creek Street Historic District**, a winding collection of wooden houses on pilings was, at one time, Ketchikan's rowdy nightlife area; there is even a brothel museum called **Dolly's House**...Ketchikan is a good place to buy crafts and the works of local artists.

LOS ANGELES

Los Angeles is a great city with a depressing port 25 miles away from almost everything. There is no parking at the pier, although areas can be found within a mile or two. So do your sightseeing in glitzy L.A. instead.

Disneyland is only one of many **amusement parks**; Universal Studios and Knotts Berry Farm are others...the **La Brea tarpits** have their own museum next door to the gorgeous Los Angeles County Museum of Art...other **museums** of note include the J. Paul Getty Museum and the newish Museum of Contemporary Art...the **El Pueblo de Los Angeles State Historical Park** is the oldest part of the city.

Shoppers will find whatever they can imagine in the L.A. area...Beverly Hills' Rodeo Drive is a must, even if you can only afford to window shop, and Melrose Avenue has things Californian...Century City has an enormous shopping mall of chic department stores and boutiques...whatever you want to eat is here. There's **Little Tokyo** for Japanese, Mexican is all over town (Melrose is good for Mexican and Italian), there are the "in" spots with big names and prices, and the drive-ins. Public transportation is not Los Angeles' strength; if you're planning extensive sightseeing it would be better to rent a car.

MIAMI

Miami has had an exciting rebirth, complete with a new, glittering skyline, a renaissance of hotels and restaurants and a new appreciation for its heritage. The port facilities, among the best in the world, are about 20 minutes from the airport and minutes from Miami Beach and the downtown area. Parking is available at the pier.

With a few hours to spare in Miami there are several options...**Miami Beach**, with its restored art deco sections, glamorous seaside hotels and chic shopping, is only 15 minutes away...**Key Biscayne**, a quieter stretch of beach resorts, is no farther...cultural attractions include the **Dade County Art Museum**, the **Museum of Science**, the **Space Transit Planetarium**, Coral Gables and the Biltmore Hotel is a must for architecture buffs....Kids will enjoy **Planet Ocean**, **Seaquarium** and **Metrozoo**.

Shoppers are in luck because of the close proximity of the port to the downtown shopping districts...Miami Beach is another prime location...and very close to the piers is a new shopping complex on the waterfront that combines attractive small stores with an entire floor of eateries, offering a taste of everything.

MONTREAL

Montreal is a wonderful combination of old and new. The port, on the St. Lawrence River and within walking distance of the city's center, is 40 minutes from Dorval International Airport.

Old Montreal and **Notre Dame Cathedral** lie at the heart of the city and should not be missed...Mont Royal overlooks the area, and the **Botanical Gardens** are the third largest in the world...Benjamin Franklin slept in **Chateau Ramezay** near **Place Royale**, the city's oldest landmark...museums include the **McCord**, for **Native American** artifacts, the **Montreal Museum of Fine Arts** and the **Saidye Bronfman Centre**, noted for its avant-garde exhibits.

Shoppers will be amazed by the city's vast underground (remember the winters are cold) of shops, but Saint Catherine Street is another prime location for spending money...food is taken seriously here, and the accent is on Quebecois cooking, which tends to be hearty and flavorful. Saint Denis, de la Montagne and Crescent are lined with restaurants and nightspots.

NEW ORLEANS

With its French and Cajun heritage and its traditions of jazz and nightlife, New Orleans is like no other city in the United States. The cruise piers are minutes from the center of everything, including the French Quarter, and about 40 minutes from the airport. Parking is available close by.

Two good ways to explore New Orleans are by the CBD shuttle bus or the Charles Avenue Streetcar, a 152-year-old historic treasure...the **French Quarter** is the center of social life and jazz life, while the quieter residential **Garden District** is lined with 19th-century mansions...Audubon Park boasts a highly respected **zoo**, and the old **Pontchartrain Hotel** is worth a walk through just to soak up the atmosphere.

Shoppers flock to Canal Place and its swishy shops and **Riverwalk**, a spectacular complex of 200 stores and restaurants in what were originally river warehouses...the **New Orleans Center**, another shopping complex, just opened in 1988. Even if your taste doesn't run to blackened redfish, there's bound to be some Cajun cooking to suit your palate or something else to be found at Riverwalk or the **Jackson Brewery**, a rapidly expanding renovation of an old brewery that now holds shops and eating places...and for something really weird, New Orleans has a restaurant that originally perched halfway up the Eiffel Tower in Paris.

NEW YORK

The Big Apple, has one of the world's most exciting approaches by water and, despite its size, is remarkably easy to visit for a few hours or a few days. The port is located on the Hudson River at midtown Manhattan, an hour from JFK airport and several long blocks from Rockefeller Center. There is parking at the pier.

A visitor could easily spend weeks in New York, but with only a few hours there are certain musts...the top of the **Empire State Building** or the **World Trade Center**...a stroll down **Fifth Avenue**...the Metropolitan, Modern, Guggenheim or Whitney **art museums**...Greenwich Village and Little Italy, Chinatown or Soho...a tour of Rockefeller Center or Radio City Music Hall...if you're overnighting, a **Broadway**, off-Broadway or off-off-Broadway show or an opera, ballet, or symphony performance at **Lincoln Center**.

Shoppers have an entire city to choose from...the giant department stores such as Saks, Lord & Taylor and Bloomie's, the bargains on Orchard Street...the posh shops of Madison Avenue and Columbus Avenue...the bargain cameras and electronics in midtown...the art galleries and boutiques of Soho and the Village...and for the hungry there's Chinatown, Little Italy, Little India, Hell's Kitchen (closest to the piers), the trendy restaurants of the Upper West Side or the Eastern European eateries on the Lower East Side...pasta places are fashionable and affordable, but there are world-famous spots, too...and don't ignore New York's street food—just about every nationality and type of snack food is represented.

PHILADELPHIA

Philadelphia is an old city that is relatively new to cruising. The port at Penn's Landing is adjacent to some of the city's most historic areas and has its own maritime museum. The trip from the airport will take roughly 30 minutes unless it's rush hour.

Although history has always been Philadelphia's strong point, in recent years it has had a renaissance of hotels and restaurants and its museums, theater and music can hold their own with most American cities...Independence National Historical Park includes **Independence Hall** and some 40 buildings dating prior to the 1800s...the **Liberty Bell** is also here...Society Hill is famous for its architecture, gardens and courtyards...**museums** include the excellent Philadelphia Museum of Art, the Pennsylvania Academy of Fine Arts (the oldest museum in America) and the Academy of Natural Sciences Museum...the **Franklin Institute of Science** is a favorite with kids of all ages...one way to see the city is by **horse-drawn carriages**, which leave from Walnut Street.

Shoppers can choose department stores, including the well-known **John Wanamaker**, or chic boutiques on Walnut Street...if you're hungry, try the **Reading Terminal Market**, where the food stalls and small restaurants mingle with butchers and grocers and where you can get Philadelphia cheese steak...there are also great Italian restaurants near the Italian market, including **Victor's**, where you can sing opera along with your meal. If Mario Lanza, who grew up in the neighborhood could, so can you.

PORT CANAVERAL

Port Canaveral is about an hour from the Orlando International Airport and 90 minutes from Walt Disney World. There is parking at the pier.

There's little reason to spend much time there except to visit three of America's biggest attractions: **Disney World**, **Epcot Center**, and **Cape Canaveral**, launch site for NASA's space program. The John F. Kennedy Space Center is just north of the port, and taxis are available. Disney World and Epcot each require at least half a day's visit, and that's rushing.

PORT EVERGLADES

The port for Fort Lauderdale, which is only minutes away, is rapidly giving Miami a run for its money as busiest cruise port in Florida. The port is only two miles from the airport and three miles from the center of town. Miami is some 60 miles south.

Fort Lauderdale has been called the Venice of America, but its major claim to fame is its welcoming attitude toward millions of college kids who cover its beaches each spring...despite efforts to upgrade its image, the Strip, which runs along the ocean, has a rather appealing seediness, with its inexpensive hotels, restaurants and bars...a more classy impression is created along Las Olas Boulevard, where renovation has resulted in **trendy shops** and eating places...**Stranahan House**, the oldest building in Fort Lauderdale is now a museum, and there is also a **Museum of the Arts**...If you're traveling by car, **Flamingo Gardens** and the **Everglades Holiday Park** are good for a visit...**Ocean World** is right next to the port.

SAN DIEGO

San Diego in sunny southern California, is just the right size for quick exploration, and many of the attractions are very close to the pier. The port is roughly 5 miles from the airport.

The emphasis in San Diego is on rest and relaxation...the **San Diego Zoo** is world famous...**Sea World** has re-created Antarctica for hundreds of penguins...The **San Diego Wild Animal Park** is outside the city in the San Pasqual Valley...There are 75 **golf courses** in the area. Cultural and athletic pursuits can be followed in **Balboa Park**'s 1000 acres of museums, theaters and sports facilities...Among the **museums** are the San Diego Museum of Art, the Timken Art Gallery and the Aerospace Museum...The **Gaslamp Quarter** and **Seaport**

Village provide shops and dining in re-created historical settings...and **Tijuana**, Mexico, is less than 20 miles away.

SAN FRANCISCO

San Francisco collects visitors' hearts for good reason: The vistas are breathtaking, the attractions and amusements rewarding and there's something about the climate that is invigorating. The port is roughly 20 miles (30 minutes) from San Francisco International Airport and 15 minutes from the center of the city. There is also a quick bus service from the airport that delivers to Fisherman's Wharf and the major hotels. There is parking convenient to the port.

Take your walking shoes and climbing sticks or money for cab or cablecar fare; San Francisco is all hills...**Golden Gate Park**, probably the most beautiful park in the U.S., is a must...**Chinatown** is the closest thing to being in China you'll find in North America...**Nob Hill** is luxurious and lovely...**Fisherman's Wharf** and the surrounding arcade/piers are crowded and lively...The ferry to Sausalito or a tour by boat of San Francisco Bay is a delight (you can even visit **Alcatraz**)...**museums** include the notable DeYoung in Golden Gate Park and, for the kids, the **Exploratorium**, a touchy-feely place at the Palace of Fine Arts.

Shoppers should head for Union Square, where all the ritzy department stores are located, but nearby Chinatown has more bargains. And the only problem with eating in San Francisco is deciding where and what: North Beach for Italian, Chinatown for obvious reasons, and seafood at cafes and restaurants all over...there's good Mexican food in the less affluent Mission district near the convention center and wonderful, informal restaurants on Geary and Haight.

SAVANNAH

Savannah is Georgia's historic capital on the banks of the Savannah River. The port is about 10 miles, or 15 minutes, from the airport .

Savannah's official Historic District encompasses most of its visitor attractions...These include **Davenport House**, **Owens-Thomas House**, and the **King-Tisdell Cottage**, which contains a museum dedicated to black history and the cultures of the **Sea Islands**...The **Juliette Gordon Lowe Scout National Center** is where the Girl Scouts were started, and **Old Fort Jackson**, Fort Pulaski and Fort Screven commemorate Savannah's role in three wars—the War of 1812, the Civil War and the Indian Wars.

ST. LOUIS

St. Louis, in the heart of the American Midwest, has been a cruise port since Mark Twain's riverboat days. The modern port is some 15 miles, or 20 minutes, from Lambert St. Louis International Airport.

Gateway Arch is the most spectacular sight in St. Louis, and it contains the Museum of Westward Expansion, which is what the arch celebrates...The **Anheuser-Busch Brewery**, in art deco buildings, is a National Historic Landmark...The **National Museum of Transport** focuses, naturally enough, on train travel, and provides hands-on activities...other attractions include the **Missouri Botanical Gardens**, and **Grant's Farm** and **Six Flags Over Mid-America**, two amusement areas of particular interest to kids...Art enthusiasts will enjoy the **Laumeier Sculpture Park**, with its 96 acres of gardens and sculptures, and the **St. Louis Art Museum**.

Shoppers have a choice of several retail complexes: **St. Louis Center**, **West Port Plaza**, **Plaza Frontenac** and **St. Louis Union Station**. And if you're hungry, don't forget this is beefsteak country, but the city's restaurants also reflect its varied cultural heritage and most ethnic varieties are available.

SEATTLE

Gateway to Alaska, Seattle has a wonderful combination of adventurousness and sophistication. Sea-Tac Airport is about 30 minutes from downtown, where the port is located. Parking is available. From the piers, much of Seattle's best is within walking distance or a short cab ride.

For a bird's eye view of the city, journey up the **Space Needle**, originally built for the 1962 World's Fair...the waterfront has enough to keep you busy all day, including restaurants and warehouses full of shops. There is also a fascinating aquarium depicting local sea-life.

Pike Place is a bustling market in a historic setting where most of Seattle seems to gather...there are also dozens of shops, restaurants and cafes high above the harbor...the **Pioneer District** has preserved what was the seamy side of town during Gold Rush days...the southern end of the **Klondike Gold Rush National Historical Park** is here, the rest being in Alaska. Next door is the city's colorful Chinatown... Seattle Center, built for the World's Fair, continues to attract visitors to its theaters, exhibitions and amusements...museums include the **Museum of History and Industry**, which details the history of the Northwest, the **Seattle Art Museum** and the **Charles and Emma Frye Art Museum**.

The waterfront, Pike Place, downtown and the **University of Washington** area are the best for shopping, and seafood, especially salmon, oysters and other local catches, are essential ingredients for a good meal.

TAMPA / ST. PETERSBURG

Tampa, St. Petersburg is the center of Florida's popular Sun Coast. Depending on where your ship is sailing from, the airport is roughly 20 minutes from the Tampa port area; 35 minutes from St. Petersburg's port.

Being vacationland, much of Tampa/St. Pete's interests are outdoors...**Florida Downs** is a major race track...**Busch Gardens'** Dark Continent is just outside of Tampa...Ybor city is the former Cuban neighborhood...In St. Pete are the **HMS *Bounty*** and **Historical Museum**, the **Sunken Gardens**, the **Salvador Dali Museum** and the **Museum of Fine Arts**...Along the Gulf coast is the **Suncoast Seabird Sanctuary** and the **Tiki Gardens**.

VANCOUVER

Vancouver is the most northern of the great cities of the Pacific Northwest, a blend of pioneer spirit, cosmopolitan flair and British tradition. The port is smack-dab in the middle of the city, within walking distance of downtown attractions. The airport is 45 minutes away.

The best thing about Vancouver is just being there, but there are attractions as well...**Robson Square**, basically a business area, deserves a look for its architecture...the Seawall Promenade at **Stanley Park** provides magnificent views of land and water, and the park itself contains a zoo, the well-known Vancouver Aquarium, a miniature railway and other amusements...in **Vanier Park** are the MacMillan Planetarium, the Maritime Museum and the Vancouver Museum...the **Museum of Anthropology** includes what may be the world's best collection of Indian relics...the **Sun Yat Sen Garden** contains a full-size Chinese garden.

Granville Island is a lively collection of shops, markets and waterfront restaurants...other shopping can be done in department stores, such as **Eaton** and **Hudson's Bay Company** or in Gastown, where turn- of-the-century buildings have been converted into shops and restaurants...other shopping/dining areas of interest are Chinatown and Robson Street...and for a view, you might consider one of the city's three cloud-high revolving restaurants.

South and Central America

ACAPULCO

Acapulco may be Mexico's oldest seaside playground, but it still has a lot of appeal. The port is about 15 miles from the airport and within walking distance of the city center.

The best thing to do in Acapulco is soak up the sun and the local lifestyle...begin at any of many **beaches**, including Condesa, Icacos and El Morro...the oldest part of the city is Caleta Beach...for cliff divers, go to the Quebrada Cliffs in the early afternoon...El Fuerte San Diego, which used to guard the city, now is a museum...kids will like **CICI**, a combination amusement park and dolphin show, and **Parque Papagayo**, the zoo...there's also a small archaeology museum in town.

You don't have to leave the beach areas for anything in Acapulco. Vendors sell food and merchandise, and the waterfront streets are lined with shops. From **Condesa to El Morro** is a particularly good area for shopping, and Puerto Marques is packed with food stalls. There are, of course, high-priced restaurants scattered on the hills of the city, and many of the resorts are a good choice for an informal lunch at the beach. **Shoppers** should look for clothing rather than crafts.

BUENOS AIRES

The capital of Argentina and the largest city in the southern hemisphere, Buenos Aires has been called the Paris of South America because of its European ambience and beauty. The port is almost 50 miles from the airport and only 15 minutes from the city's center.

In a city the size of Buenos Aires, it is difficult to see everything in a few hours...consider the **Fine Arts Museum**, the largest in Argentina or the pedestrian mall called Florida...historical monuments include the **Old Monastery of Recollect Friars** and the **Cathedral** and **Mausoleum of the Liberator General**...the **La Boca** area is noted for its color, charm and artists' studios.

Shopping is particularly good for leather products and antiques...the antiques bazaar at **Plaza Dorrego** is open on Sundays...stores along the pedestrian mall are popular with visitors. For taste treats, remember that Argentinians consume more beef than any other nationality in the world...informal steak grills called **parril-**

ladas are plentiful and have a cheerful, unpretentious atmosphere...and be sure to take advantage of the cafes along the boulevards.

MANAUS

Hundreds of miles up the mighty Amazon River, Manaus is a quaint outpost complete with spectacular 19th-century **opera house** *and orchids growing like dandelions. It's a tiny place, easily explored, and usually at the end or the beginning of an Amazon/Caribbean cruise.*

PUERTO MONTT, PUERTO WILLIAMS AND PUNTA ARENAS

Puerto Montt, Puerto Williams, and Punta Arenas are all jumping-off points for Antarctica or South Pacific cruises after long flights from Miami or New York. They are tiny outposts of civilization where the weather is rugged and the rugged people isolated. Fishing is a major industry; the mountains, lakes and rivers are spectacular.

RIO DE JANEIRO

Rio de Janeiro may be the world's largest tropical playground. The port is about 30 minutes from the airport and 20 minutes from the central beach hotel district.

Beaches, mountain peaks and more beaches comprise most of what Rio has to offer...Copacabana and Ipanema are the best-known beaches to visitors, and they are also the most crowded...**Barra da Tijuca** tends to be deserted by comparison. The beach is central to the lives of those who live here, so be sure to take in the local color...**Corcovado**, with its famous statue of Christ, overlooks the city and can be reached by train...**Sugarloaf**, not as tall but equally stunning, is reached by cable car...museums in Rio include the national **Museum of Fine Arts**, with a good collection of Brazilian works, and the **Museu Chacara do Ceu**, which includes works by modern European masters...the **Botanic Garden**, with thousands of species of tropical plants, is near **Rio Jockey Club**, one of South America's great race tracks.

Shopping, as well as eating, is good in Ipanema...seafood and beef are local favorites, and much of the dining is done outdoors, in bistros, adegas and bars...*churrascarias* are the noisy, crowded and friendly places where beef is the specialty, often all you can eat.

INDEX

A

B

C

D

L

M

P

Q

T

U

V

W

Y

Z

PHOTO CREDITS

Caption	Credits
Graceful Sculpture	Holland America Line`
Taking the Plunge Snorkeling	Princess Cruises
Leisurely View Mediterranean	Swan Hellenic
Staff/Celeb Cruises	Celebrity Cruises
Princess Ship Pizzaria	Princess Cruises
Using A Sextant	Worldwide Travel & Cruises Assoc.
Keeping fit aboard Norway	Norwegian Cruise Line
Lady Luck	Royal Caribbean Cruise Line
Greek dancers in Crete	Royal Cruise Line
Shopping	Norwegian Cruise Line
Song of America	Royal Caribbean Cruise Line
Grand Cayman-Turtle Farm	Princess Cruises
Glacier Bay, Alaska	Special Expeditions
Nantucket Clipper	Clipper Cruise Line
Portofino, Italy	Seven Seas Cruise Line
Tahiti	Windstar Cruises
The Thames, London	Seabourn Cruise Line
Naturalist in Norway	Special Expeditions
Crystal Harmony in Venice	Crystal Cruises
Star Princess, Caribbean	Princess Cruises
Royal Viking Queen, San Francisco	Royal Viking Cruise Line
Watersports on the Seabourn	Seabourn Cruise Line
Antarctic Residents	Abercrombie & Kent
Arriving in Cologne	K.D. River Cruises of Europe
Wind Spirit, South Pacific	Windstar Cruises
Crown Odyssey, Greek Islands	Royal Cruise Line

All photos in "Ships and their Ratings" courtesy of respective cruise lines.

FIELDING'S WORLDWIDE CRUISES

Favorite People, Places & Experiences

ADDRESS:	NOTES:

Name

Address

Telephone

Name

Address

Telephone

Name

Address

Telephone

Name

Address

Telephone

Name

Address

Telephone

Name

Address

Telephone

Name

Address

Telephone

Favorite People, Places & Experiences

ADDRESS:	NOTES:

Name

Address

Telephone

Name

Address

Telephone

Name

Address

Telephone

Name

Address

Telephone

Name

Address

Telephone

Name

Address

Telephone

Name

Address

Telephone

Favorite People, Places & Experiences

ADDRESS:	NOTES:
Name Address Telephone	
Name Address Telephone	
Name Address Telephone	
Name Address Telephone	
Name Address Telephone	
Name Address Telephone	
Name Address Telephone	